W9-CFB-760

DATE DUE

DEMCO 128-8155

CHRISTIANITY

෩෩෩෩෩

THE FIRST TWO
THOUSAND YEARS

David L. Edwards

ORBIS BOOKS
Maryknoll, New York 10545

Published in Great Britain by Cassell

Published in North America by Orbis Books, P.O. Box 308, Maryknoll, New York 10545-0308, USA

© David L. Edwards 1997

Queries regarding rights and permissions should be addressed to: Orbis Books, P.O. Box 308, Maryknoll, New York 10545-0308

First published 1997

Library of Congress Cataloging-in-Publication Data
Edwards, David Lawrence.
   Christianity : the first two thousand years / David L. Edwards.
      p.   cm.
   Includes bibliographical references and index.
   ISBN 1-57075-160-9 (cloth)
   1. Christianity—History.   I. Title.
BR145.2.E26   1998
270—dc 21   97-24093
                                                 CIP

Typeset by Ensystems, Cambridge
Printed and bound in Great Britain by
Bookcraft (Bath) Ltd., Midsomer Norton, Somerset

eseseses

Contents

	Preface	vi
1	*Beginnings*	1
2	*Early Christians*	38
3	*Byzantine Orthodoxy*	81
4	*Orthodoxy after Byzantium*	129
5	*Medieval Catholicism*	153
6	*Reformations*	281
7	*In the Modern Age*	350
8	*The Americas*	479
9	*Global Christianity*	530
10	*In the Postmodern Age*	589
	For further reading	631
	Index	645

What's past is prologue.
WILLIAM SHAKESPEARE
The Tempest

To Sybil

ↄ৻ↄ৻ↄ৻ↄ৻ↄ৻

Preface

MANY people think that they ought to understand more about the history of Christianity. It is not controversial to say that here is one of the most important movements in human history, with developments since the days in Galilee or Jerusalem which are astonishing. Near AD 2000 there may be about 1,700 millions alive who are in one sense or another Christians, according to the estimate in the *Encyclopædia Britannica*. Their numbers have approximately trebled during the twentieth Christian century. The committed Christians have an obvious motive for wishing to learn more about the spiritual family to which they belong, even if it means seeing more fully that the family's history contains much that is disgraceful and a bewildering variety of hearts and minds. Many of those 'Christian' millions are not deeply committed to Christ or at least not to a historic church's doctrines about him—yet they go on asking questions, often with an interest which is keen. Many others, who respect Jesus more than Christianity, also ask. So, amid all this diversity, complexity and uncertainty, is it at all possible to begin to decide what in the past was good or evil, true or false, essential or local and temporary? Christianity seems to be in its infancy but its history has already been substantial enough to be thought-provoking. What lessons do these beginnings of the influence of Jesus of Nazareth hold for the future? Christianity's future may cover two thousand million years if humanity is allowed the survival which now seems possible before this planet is expected to become unfit for habitation.

These are not questions which are easy to answer, the difficulty is increased if due attention is paid to the social and psychological as well as to the intellectual and mystical elements, and a further problem is that we do not have enough time to study the past worthily, for the present sets its own tasks. A few sentences about an Englishman's unimportant life may show that I appreciate this. More than forty years ago I was excited to be elected to a Fellowship in All Souls College, Oxford, and about a dozen years later I had another much valued academic opportunity through appointments as Dean of King's College, Cambridge, and as a university lecturer in church history. But wisely or unwisely I have felt a stronger call to be involved in the religious life of the present, particularly in London, and most of my working years were spent as the editor of a theological publishing house (the SCM Press) and in a share of responsibility for the busy life of three great churches, Westminster Abbey, Norwich Cathedral and Southwark Cathedral. Colleagues allowed me time for study and travel and I managed to write, but it was not a life spent in libraries. Only when I had retired from such duties could I devote some years to this book, thanks to the unfailing support of my wife Sybil and to the resources of the Cambridge University Library. I hope that this non-academic experience has enlarged my sympathies.

It is, I admit, a book which covers ground largely well trodden. In my own unsatisfactory way I have written three volumes on the history of what I called *Christian England* (to 1914), a book about the worldwide situation in the 1960s (*Religion and Change*), another about the prospects in the 1980s (*The Futures of Christianity*) and another about the outcomes of theological debate (*Tradition and Truth*), in addition to paperbacks. But in the 1990s there still seems to be room for one man's fresh overview of this vast field. Certainly I have enjoyed reconsiderng some territory previously surveyed and educating myself about other subjects and new developments in research and reflection; and I have learned a lot by thinking out the unities between the details and trying to share what seem to be the most significant truths with others who have limited time.

It may help the potential reader if I say that I do not assume in you either previous knowledge or a closed mind, and if I offer a few words (I hope not too impertinently) about some recent histories which are different from this one. In comparison with the essays in the *Oxford History of Christianity* edited by John McManners this book has the disadvantage of less distinguished authorship, but a continuous narrative may offer some advantages. There are no pictures in this book, as there are in the *History of Christianity* where the text is a long essay by the king of English church historians, Owen Chadwick, but no pictures means more text. There is less about the author's theology here than in Hans Küng's magisterial *Christianity: Its Essence and History*, and one of the reasons is that my position is less worthy of attention than his. No doubt my own viewpoint is often evident, for like all other historians and commentators I cannot jump out of my skin, and I submit some of my own reflections, but mainly I offer down-to-earth history with the ambition to be fair to everyone. There is less about Europe here than in Kurt Aland's *History* but I felt that I had to make room for the Americas and Africa, Asia and the Pacific, the regions where live about three-quarters of the Christians now alive. Obviously I have left out far more than I have put in, but for that very reason this book, with all its defects and limitations, may be a readable alternative to the histories in many volumes which often seem to be left to gather dust on library shelves. Paul Johnson's *History of Christianity* (1976) is a warning to me that even the most vigorous writing does not excuse errors and Vivian Green's *New History of Christianity* (1996) repeats that warning and adds the lesson that honesty in recounting faults and failures does not entirely compensate for aloofness from the life of some regions and past generations and for unreasonable gloom about the present position. Of course this book must contain errors of fact and judgement despite my best efforts and learned advice, and these I deeply regret. For comments on parts of the book before its final revision I am happily indebted to Henry Chadwick, John McManners and Kallistos Ware in Oxford and to scholars in the USA assembled by my American publisher, Robert Ellsberg: Randall Balmer, Bill McCarthy, Sam Moffett and Lamin Sanneh. I am also deeply grateful to Gillian Patterson and other editors in Cassells for their encouragement of a project liable to seem over-ambitious.

I am an Englishman but this book is not centred on England. I am a priest of the Church of England but this is not an advertisement for Anglicanism; for example, in accordance with common usage where I have written 'Catholic' I have usually meant 'Roman Catholic', remembering that most Christians in the world are Roman Catholics. I share the attitude of many other Anglicans that our own heritage is imperfect. I have echoed some frequently made modern or postmodern criticisms of mighty traditions and giant thinkers and teachers, but that does not mean that I think that the past ought to be despised or that there ought to be no hope that the future, having learned from the past, will be better because more truly Christian. I have tried to be accurate but not pedantic; for example, I have called people by the names thought to be most quickly recognized in the English language. I have relied on the labours of real scholars and I hope that my list of suggestions for further reading in English shows what a wealth of good research and good writing has become available in recent years, to some extent outdating earlier general histories. Technical terms are listed in the index.

DAVID L. EDWARDS

Winchester,
Easter 1997

I

ⲉⲋⲉⲋⲉⲋⲉⲋ

Beginnings

Jesus of Nazareth

CHRISTIANITY began when Jesus of Nazareth began to live, about two thousand years ago and almost certainly within the period conventionally described as 'before Christ'. After thirty years or so in great obscurity he worked in public for a short time, not much more than one year (including only one Passover festival) according to three of the four gospels in the New Testament.

His followers remembered much about that brief period and facts about him can be recovered by a close study of those three gospels and of the historical background. But as a strong movement in the history of the world Christianity took off only after his death and then it had to survive great hostility. A Roman aristocrat, the historian Tacitus, writing in about AD 100, dismissed it as a 'deadly superstition' marked by a 'hatred of humanity' and named after a criminal executed under Pontius Pilate. He recorded that in Rome a 'great crowd' of *Christiani*, accused of starting a fire which had destroyed a large part of the city in the summer of AD 64, had been crucified, or sewn up in the skins of animals and then thrown to wild dogs, or used as living torches to illuminate an evening party in the emperor's gardens. They had aroused some pity as the victims of the cruelty of a tyrant, Nero, of whom Tacitus also disapproved. But the main point for this very superior historian was that this 'criminal' group deserved to be 'hated for their abominations' and to receive 'extreme and exemplary punishment'. It was even more objectionable than the Jewish religion out of which it had come like poison.

Many Jews were also hostile to the Christians. Another Roman historian, Suetonius, who was contemporary with Tacitus, attributed the fire in Rome to Nero himself but recorded that during the reign of Claudius who had died in AD 54 the Jews had been expelled from Rome because of 'continuous

I

disturbances at the instigation of Chrestus'. This probably refers to disputes about Jesus and elsewhere Suetonius mentioned Christianity as a 'new and very evil superstition'. But at approximately the same time as that action was taken against troublemakers in Rome one of the Christians, Paul, was reminding the group in Corinth of what he had taught. He had told them that after his death Jesus had 'appeared' to a list of named disciples and to 'more than five hundred of the brethren at the same time', some of whom were still alive. And then he had 'appeared' to him.

Very strange events convinced these people that Jesus was truly and gloriously alive despite his terrible death. Many thought then, and have continued to think, that what the Christians believed was an illusion, but if that was the case it may still be reckoned the most influential of all the experiences which rightly or wrongly have persuaded people that human existence is after all not ultimately pointless or merely tragic. And if it was an illusion, it was not comfortable. It brought a command which was personal to each one of them and it was a summons to courage amid suffering. A Christian writer, John, who lived in the same period as Tacitus and Suetonius was not a historian like them; they also had their motives in writing, but John the evangelist had a motive which overwhelmed any interest in recording detailed facts accurately. He wanted to say what was the meaning of the facts. We can see this in the stories which he told about the appearances of Jesus after his death: each was also a story about the continuing fascination and power of 'the Lord'. In the garden outside the tomb, 'early in the morning while it was still dark', the heartbroken Mary of Magdala thinks he is the gardener until she hears the familiar greeting 'Mary!' As dawn breaks over the sea of Galilee a figure is seen in the mist on the beach and a disciple suddenly knows who it is: 'It is the Lord!' And to meet this Lord is to be commanded. Mary of Magdala is told: 'Do not cling to me but go to my brothers.' When these 'brothers', the disciples, meet him, the double message is: 'Peace be with you! As the Father sent me, so I send you.' When Peter has leaped into the sea in order to talk with this Lord, the last words which he hears are 'Follow me!'

At the top of Syria, in Antioch, the followers of Jesus were called *Christianoi* because they were so often talking about *Christos* ('the Anointed'). The name points to the difficulties in any talk about him. It was odd to discuss him in Greek and in the third city of the Roman empire. He had been a thoroughly Jewish villager speaking Aramaic, the popular dialect of Hebrew, and Sepphoris, a Greek-looking town four miles from Nazareth, is not mentioned in the gospels. As carpenters probably he and his father Joseph had found employment there, but he seems to have felt no call to preach to Gentiles: he was 'sent' to the Jews. It was also odd to apply to him the Greek version of a Jewish title, Englished as 'Messiah', which usually

2

indicated that a successor of King David would lead his people to victory, freedom and prosperity. Among his followers there was a tradition that somehow he was descended from David, but non-Christian Jews have always protested with good reason that he had not inaugurated the dramatically improved Messianic kingdom. The title was also inadequate to cover developed Christian beliefs about him, for to call a man 'Messiah' said nothing about his own divinity, only that he was God's special agent in establishing that kingdom. But the first Christians felt that they had to talk using words which came to hand, for their hearts burned within them as they met him on the roads of the world. Luke told the story of the disciples who took some time to recognize who was walking with them to Emmaus but eventually did so as 'he vanished from their sight'. Since then the puzzled talk has never ceased.

Who was he?

He was a Jew, as Jewish as his forerunner John the Baptist. He and his followers worshipped the God of their fathers. Reports about them indicate that they prayed in private, attended synagogues every Sabbath, paid the annual tax to support the temple in Jerusalem, went to that temple for festivals, seldom had any contact with Gentiles and were never accused of eating unclean food. Much of what Jesus taught about God or the neighbour expressed what could be found in the Hebrew Bible and in other Jewish teaching although his simplified emphases, his vivid expressions and the intensity of his demand for a complete trust in God were unusual. His central message was partly old and partly new. He proclaimed that the new age, the 'kingdom of God', would arrive through God's action. Many Jews then hoped for that kingdom, for the fulfilment of the promises in their Bible, but with somewhat different understandings of what was meant. Probably for most the hope was for political independence and a dramatic improvement in their everyday conditions. For some what was meant was more spiritual; for some it was the end of the world. Jesus had his own interpretation, summed up in his prayer that the Father's reign would be as complete 'on earth as in heaven'.

He told very short stories, each making a point about that kingdom; stories not about Israel's past but about daily life around him. He had a sense of humour, often basing these 'parables' on ridiculous situations, but the joke was a weapon. He uttered armour-piercing sayings, each indicating (rather than legislating) how life was to be lived as this reign of God dawned, transforming all life. All that he said and did was a commentary on that message. He shared the urgency of John the Baptist, by whom he had been baptized: the End was imminent, the Crisis was near. He shared John's death, execution by alarmed authorities. But he did not share John's puritanism or his concentration on warnings of doom. He did utter warnings but he often spoke about a banquet to come, to which all were invited, including the down-trodden and disreputable. In anticipation of it he and his followers did not fast; instead they had meals with 'sinners'. Even on the Sabbath when all work except the essential stopped he healed sick people, for the kingdom brought health, and in accordance with the beliefs of his time this was the expulsion of demons using the 'finger of God'. A layman, he combined admiration or compassion for 'the people of the land' (as they were called perhaps contemptuously by others) with a challenge. He urged his hearers to be loving far beyond the ordinary, imitating God's love which was about to be triumphant, living in the faith that the triumph was already beginning. Thus he sided with the more liberal rabbis in extending the usual permission to attend to human needs on the Sabbath, but not when they defended the current frequency of divorce which degraded women. He befriended and taught women with a freedom which was not considered respectable behaviour for a rabbi. He valued specially their capacity for grateful love. A small group of men followed him with some women.

One of them betrayed him to the police and he was not so popular as many Christians have liked to think. He would not have got into so much trouble if he had merely blessed babies and talked about the Father and love in general terms, but although he was not a political agitator he believed in a completely new government of the world with himself as God's prime minister, and people remembered his laments over the small towns and villages in Galilee which had rejected that message. For months a wanderer, he was more homeless than the foxes or the birds. Ardent with the hope of the kingdom which God would establish, he issued his final challenge by going up to a Jerusalem which was crowded and tense during the Passover festival, probably in AD 30. He allowed his supporters to stage a small demonstration with patriotic cries and he himself demonstrated against the commercialism of a grandiose temple built by an objectionable king and controlled by four rich families of priests collaborating with the Romans. In the new age there would be a pure temple, a house of prayer for all, and it seems that he expected the new age to begin at this Passover.

These disturbances caused the high priest, Joseph Caiaphas, to secure a quiet arrest, to interrogate him in front of advisers and, when he refused to clear himself by a promise to respect the authorities, to send him to the Roman colonial governor with the recommendation that he should be dealt with as a dangerous troublemaker. Pontius Pilate was interested only because of the prisoner's talk about a kingdom not Rome's. His previous behaviour had shown that Pilate's attitude to the Jewish religion was one of contempt and boredom: on his arrival in Palestine as 'prefect' he had ordered his troops to demonstrate Rome's supremacy by bringing images of the emperor into Jerusalem but had cancelled the order after peaceful Jewish protests, not feeling that the matter was worth a riot. But this talk about a kingdom seemed to be more than religious fanaticism. There had been Jewish risings, large or small, since the conquest by Pompey in the year which was to be called 63 BC. In AD 6 Rome had got rid of Herod the Great's son as the puppet ruler of Judaea and had imposed direct rule with a census for taxation, producing a rebellion led by Judas of Galilee and many crucifixions in punishment. Now, at a time when Jerusalem might explode into a riot during a festival which celebrated the Jews' liberation from Egypt long ago, Pilate's duty seemed obvious. This man who was accused by the leaders of his own people and who did not explain himself satisfactorily was flogged and crucified along with two bandits. If the year was 30, the day was 7 April. Crucifixion was a public, slow and fatal torture which turned a naked man into a lump of meat attractive only to the flies. When used by the Carthaginians it had shocked the Romans by its cruelty but now it was used to punish rebels, particularly rebellious slaves—in this case, to make sure that the prisoner would never become 'King of the Jews'. Rome prided itself on its toleration of many religious beliefs, with or without respect, but where it faced rebellion or a hint of it Rome was ferocious.

Pilate was later dismissed for brutality excessive even by Rome's normal standards and in the same year (AD 36) Caiaphas was removed from the high priesthood. As those two disappear from history we should note that many leaders of discontented Jews also disappeared after defeat and death. Those who were crucified were usually left on their crosses to be eaten by birds or to rot and their bodies or bones were buried obscurely in their utter disgrace; only one broken skeleton of a crucified man has ever been discovered in a Palestinian tomb (in 1968). But Jesus continued to arouse excitement and controversy.

His movement was at first led by twelve *apostoloi* (envoys) representing the twelve tribes of Israel; their number is one of the indications of the hope that the coming kingdom of God would include the restoration of the glory of Israel, but evidently the Romans did not bother to execute them. The movement then developed a centre in Jerusalem under the leadership of his brother James, a man devout by both Jewish and Christian standards, and it is understandable that it hoped to survive and even flourish within Judaism despite the opposition. When the New Testament was written such hopes had been dashed and there were passages in its gospels which obscured the fact that Jesus had been a faithful Jew; Mark, for example, claimed that he had 'declared all foods clean'. Yet the New Testament included in its stories distinguished Jewish sympathizers such as Joseph of Arimathea who provided a tomb for Jesus and two leading Pharisees, Nicodemus who provided costly spices and Gamaliel who tried to protect his followers. And it told of many conversions among Jews not long after his death.

This was a time when the whole of Judaism was going through an identity crisis. Because of the way in which the crisis was resolved, we too easily concentrate on those who advocated and practised violence against the Romans—and against each other, for the rebels did not unite—and on those who preserved Jewish purity amid paganism by maintaining a very strict obedience to detailed religious laws. But the evidence suggests that many Jews wanted a happier age without self-defeating violence against the Romans or against each other: that had been the message of Jesus. Many were classified as 'sinners' because they were unable or unwilling to keep the whole of the scriptural 'Law of Moses' (plus additions) in every detail. The orthodox doctrine was that they could be forgiven if they repented and when this was possible offered a sacrifice in the temple, but Jesus had reached them by his stories to the effect that the Father longed, and was already working, to show his love to them—and by his direct assurances that as they turned to the Father they were forgiven, without sacrificing. Many did not share the overwhelming emphasis of the official religion on the temple in Jerusalem, perhaps because they lived at a distance from it (five times more Jews lived outside the Holy Land than in it), perhaps because they did not respect its present management. Jesus, a layman from Galilee, had represented them. Many Jews wanted a fresh, simple and strong interpretation of the collection of the histories, laws, prophecies and poems which constituted their bulky Scriptures. Jesus seemed to be a prophet who could teach with authority. In Alexandria, then a great centre of Jewish life, Philo interpreted the Hebrew Bible as other scholars interpreted Homer's tales of gods and warriors, by presenting the stories as allegories symbolizing deeper, timeless truths. But Philo's conclusions were intelligible only to those who shared his background of cosmopolitan education. Jesus could be understood by people whose worries were about weeds in their fields or coins lost in their dark cottages. Like some of the professional rabbis he taught by telling stories, but his were not intended merely to illustrate the application of a religious law: in Jewish terms they were not only *haggadah* ('telling') to explain what was required in *halachah* ('walking'). They were challenges to walk in a new direction, to enter a new kingdom without delay. In Qumran by the Dead Sea a group of Essenes lived as monks, preserving their own purity and dreaming of the day when God would do battle to rescue the 'children of light'. Jesus addressed people who lived nowhere near a monastery; he pictured the intervention by the Father as a banquet not a battle; he urged everyone to accept the invitation to that feast, to the 'music and dancing' in welcome to the prodigal son.

Most Jews did not accept the Jesus movement's answer to these hopes and prayers for a new Jewish identity. But some did and they formed the movement's launching pad: without them its mission to the world could not have got started. Moreover, Judaism was rebuilt accepting Roman rule, without a temple and without sacrifices. There was now less sense that religious laws oppressed ordinary folk: some laws were interpreted with more sensitivity to human problems, as in the *Mishnah* compiled in Galilee about 170 years after the death of Jesus, while others were accepted more readily as defiant badges of Jewish identity now that the violent assertion of that identity had led to disaster. Thus many of the criticisms which Jesus had made of the religion around him ceased to apply as the practice of Judaism was transformed by overwhelming events. And there was a radical reinterpretation of the Scriptures. It became Jewish orthodoxy to believe that the arrival of the Messianic age would be speeded by the devoted study and keeping of *Torah*, the religious and moral law with its 613 commandments. There arose a belief in what was almost a new covenant between the God and the people of Israel: it was now held that Israel's God (Yahweh) would liberate his people not by a mighty act overthrowing all their enemies but by using their suffering and obedience in purposes which could not yet be fathomed. In other words, the new exodus of the Jewish people, their entry into the promised glory, would come through their acceptance of a suffering not totally unlike a crucifixion. So the first Christians' hopes of influencing their fellow Jews were not completely foolish, for parts of their gospel did appeal to many Jews and did coincide with ideas which renewed Judaism.

It was a further fact that the movement started by Jesus the Jew ended by taking to the ends of the earth those elements in his ancestral religion which had the widest appeal to people who were not Jews. While he had had only a few dealings with Gentiles in Galilee, by this time many Gentiles there and elsewhere had become associated with Judaism as 'God-fearers'. In the gospels friendly centurions represent them, as do the 'Greeks' who in John's gospel wish to 'see Jesus'. Gentiles knew that the Jews regarded them as dogs, not as the children of God; a tradition was preserved that a Gentile woman had accepted this from Jesus but had delighted him by turning it into a joke, 'the dogs eat the scraps that fall from the children's table'. Certainly not many Gentiles were willing to tackle the whole menu of Judaism. Another story told of a Gentile who asked the great rabbi Hillel to sum up the whole of *Torah* while he himself stood on one foot. (He got the reply 'Don't do to others what you hate: the rest is commentary'.) Men were not willing to be circumcised: the operation was painful and it seemed a barbaric custom deforming a man's body, celebrated by many nude statues. Nor were they willing to eat only the food which the fussy Jews considered clean. Many other things about the Jews seemed admirable and attractive, however: their strong faith in one, holy God, their assurance that he had revealed himself, their sense that human life had a clear purpose and must be disciplined and clean, their prophetic vision of justice and peace in all the earth, their strong family life. It could seem that the Christians had not lost these Jewish characteristics while they had dropped the more objectionable parts of Judaism. So in a sense Jesus of Nazareth became a Jewish missionary and a uniquely successful one, walking through many doors and across wide seas.

Jewish Christianity

The New Testament supplies some evidence about the early stages of the Christians' development out of the apparently total tragedy of their Lord's crucifixion. It shows that the first shape of the Jesus movement was as thoroughly Jewish as his own life had been. When Luke wrote the Acts of the Apostles he pictured the intense life of a small community in Jerusalem: 'They met constantly to hear the apostles teach, to share the common life, to break bread and to pray.' The message was for Jews: 'The God of our fathers raised up Jesus . . . as leader and saviour, to grant Israel repentance and the forgiveness of sins.' They were often in or around the temple. It makes a picture of harmony. But other evidence shows the tensions.

In the Letter of James a 'servant of God and the Lord Jesus Christ' addresses fellow Jews ('the twelve tribes dispersed throughout the world') with a moral sermon almost every word of which could have been preached by a rabbi. He mentions that 'you believe in our Lord Jesus Christ who reigns in glory' but does not draw any lesson from that distinctive belief. Instead he hastens to teach that poor people should not be humiliated or exploited, and that the tongue should not be used in angry or boastful speech, warning that 'faith divorced from action is dead'. When he recommends patience and prayer, he cites the examples of Job and Elijah. He leaves the impression that belief in Jesus as the Messiah has the effect of reinforcing a morality already known and accepted by good Jews.

In the Acts of the Apostles we hear echoes of a faith which was much harder for Jews to accept, although not impossible. Luke recounts that the group in Jerusalem with Peter as its spokesman believed that Jesus, although condemned by all the authorities, had been 'a man approved by God'; that he had been raised from the dead and declared to be the Messiah by God. Moreover, he would soon return as the Judge sent by God: already the last days had begun with that resurrection and with the almost equally dramatic outpouring of the 'Holy Spirit' during the festival of Pentecost. All this was far less conventional than the Letter of James and we are told in Acts that the original group was joined by Greek-speaking (Hellenist) Jews who completely rejected the temple in Jerusalem; they had seven leaders with Greek names. Their spokesman was Stephen, who was stoned to death as a

8

law-breaker. It was the beginning of what was to become an enormous phenomenon, Christian diversity, for the Greek-speaking Jews associated with Stephen's attack on the temple, when expelled from Jerusalem, promptly began a wider mission which according to Acts reached the countryside of Judaea and Samaria and even led to evangelism on the desert road to Egypt. But other chapters of Acts depict followers of Jesus who still regularly worshipped in the temple, kept the Law of Moses and needed to be persuaded that Gentiles could be admitted to baptism and table-fellowship without being initiated as Jews by circumcision and without keeping the laws about food. Jewish orthodoxy held that Gentiles would be given a share in the life of the 'age to come', but this influx implied that the glorious age had already begun. It took time to decide what it all meant: the Letter of James or the Pentecostal excitement, the attack on the temple or the adherence to all the devout customs, the Jesus movement as a Jewish sect or the Christian Church open to all.

In the Acts of the Apostles these tensions lie beneath the surface but Paul's letter to the Galatians brings them into the open. He was angry. He was angry with those who were still trying to make Gentile Christians believe that they needed to be circumcised—furiously angry. He was angry to remember that he had still had to hide himself from 'Christ's congregations in Judaea' when he had made contact with Peter and with 'James the Lord's brother' three years after his conversion. He was angry that fourteen years later he had still felt compelled to argue with the leaders of the church in Jerusalem—'men of no importance' to him—before they would acknowledge his right to be a missionary to Gentiles who need not keep the whole Jewish religious law. He was angry that he had still been obliged to argue with Peter, who took meals with Gentile Christians in Antioch but changed his mind and kept himself aloof when rebuked by envoys from James in Jerusalem. 'I opposed him to his face, because he was clearly in the wrong' and his attack on Peter was 'before the whole congregation'.

Nevertheless, Paul knew that he had to put his case in Jerusalem. He was a Jew no less than his critics and it was a daring idea that Christianity should no longer be a Jewish sect. When he went on to remind the Galatians that 'we know that no one is ever justified by doing what the law requires, but only through faith in Christ Jesus' he first said: 'We ourselves are Jews by birth, not Gentile sinners.' His letters, although always Christocentric, were almost always couched in Jewish terms. No one unfamiliar with the Hebrew Bible would have understood much of what this Jew taught about Jesus, his fellow Jew. His letter to Rome showed the intensity of his conviction that 'God has not rejected the people which he acknowledged of old as his own ... God's choice stands', so that in the end 'the whole of Israel will be saved'. And about AD 59 he paid a great tribute to the Jerusalem church, and all that it stood for, by doing the work and taking the risks needed to bring it a collection of money. He put his life where his theology was and it is not surprising to be told in the Acts of the Apostles that this dangerous journey led to a riot when he arrived in Jerusalem and to his imprisonment by the Roman authorities. He could explode with impatience about Christian leaders who were 'reputed to be pillars of the community' but who spread 'a different gospel': he did so when writing to the Christians in Galatia, cursing those who had sent 'agitators' to try to persuade these converts that they must be circumcised. They were trying to 'distort the gospel of Christ' and could go and 'castrate themselves' for all he cared. But when writing to the Christians in Rome as he prepared for that last journey into danger, he put into equally passionate words his conviction that his whole life as an apostle to the Gentiles had the supreme purpose of 'provoking' his own people, the Jews, into the acceptance of Jesus as the long-awaited Messiah. He never attacked 'Jewish legalism', or demanded that Christian Jews should no longer keep the law, as later Christians were to do. In his own experience the strict observance of the Jewish religious law had not brought peace or joy but he knew that Jews could observe the Law of Moses as thanksgiving to God, as part of a covenant with their gracious God. As James Dunn has put it, 'What he aimed his arguments against was the law understood and practised in such a way as to limit the grace of God, to prevent Gentiles enjoying it in full measure'. And despite his boast to the Galatians, even he probably felt a touch of awe when in the presence of James, the Lord's brother who preserved as much as he could of the religion which had been taught to the family in Nazareth.

James was given the highest honour in this 'sect of the Nazarenes' (as it is called in Acts 24:5). He seems to have presided over the church in Jerusalem for about a quarter of a century before his execution in or about AD 62. A Jewish historian, Josephus, recorded that the 'very insolent' high priest who illegally ordered his death was deposed by the Romans after protests by other Jews. The real reason for this Jewish execution of a respected Jew against Roman wishes may well have been that he had criticized the gathering spirit of rebellion, which at this stage the leading priests of the temple were inclined to support. The 'gospel of Thomas' (to be discussed later) was to claim that Jesus had said that heaven and earth had been created for the sake of James. A more reliable tradition says that he was called 'the Just' and that his knees were worn by prayer like a camel's. He was not to be remembered with any greater clarity in the Christian tradition, but it is significant that he was followed in the leadership by a cousin, Simon, according to the careful church historian Eusebius. This Jewish sect honoured Jesus by honouring his family. John's gospel says that his mother was cared for by 'the disciple whom he loved'. Although Mark's gospel preserved an awkward tradition that at one stage the family of Jesus had thought him out of his mind and had set out to take charge of him (getting the reply that the disciples were 'my mother and my brothers'), the Acts of the Apostles related that when the Church consisted of about 120 people soon after the resurrection, these included 'Mary the mother of Jesus and his brothers'. Paul reminded the Christians in Corinth that the risen Lord had 'appeared' to James but no record was kept of any appearance to the rest of the family.

In AD 66 the Palestinian Jews rebelled, massacring the Roman garrison in Jerusalem. Four years later the temple was burned down along with most of the rest of the city as the Roman army imposed order with larger massacres. Other revolts in Egypt and elsewhere caused the Romans more trouble and increased their dislike of the Jews. When circumcision was forbidden by the emperor Hadrian another large-scale rebellion broke out, only to be crushed (132–135). Any remaining Jewish inhabitants were banished from Jerusalem and the city was rebuilt, renamed and made thoroughly pagan. Temples to Jupiter and Venus, the divinities of power and sex, were placed in the sites of the death and burial of Jesus, although a small Christian congregation of Gentiles was, it seems, allowed to lie low in a house on Mount Zion. Some Jewish Christians survived elsewhere, in Palestine and outside it, but like all other Jews they must have wanted to weep. In Luke's gospel Jesus predicts this time on his way to his own death: 'Then they will start saying to the mountains "Fall on us" and to the hills "Cover us".'

The report seems reliable that the Jewish Christians had left Jerusalem as a body before or during the siege in the 60s. Such 'treachery' was a major factor in the mounting Jewish hostility towards them, for the defeated were understandably very bitter. Many Jews of the Diaspora (in other countries) were also bitter, for Christian missionary work coincided with the Jews' own rebellions in spoiling the opportunity for Judaism to become the answer to the search of many educated people in the Roman world for a clearer revelation of the one God who was real behind the names of all the gods, old and new. Matthew's gospel says that the Pharisees 'cross land and sea' to win a single convert, but partly because of Christian competition this Jewish sense of an urgent mission to the world declined. And many Jews outside Palestine were now anxious to remind the authorities that they were loyal to the empire. Theirs was an acceptance of Roman rule which the surviving ex-rebels also made in the end.

Jews in these various categories wanted to separate themselves sharply from the Christians, a group not only disloyal and heretical, even blasphemous, in the Jewish context but also rumoured in the empire to be superstitious and antisocial, atheist and anarchist. Josephus, a Jewish priest who went over to the Romans from the rebels in the 60s and became a pensioned historian explaining his people to the conquerors, was not isolated in wishing to demonstrate that the Jews were essentially respectable, with an ancient faith in God and a strong morality. Their rebellions had been caused by a mixture of Roman misgovernment with the agitation of an extremist minority. They had been hot-headed and had deserved God's punishment, but their past disputes between themselves about religion had been like the disagreements between philosophers. (Unfortunately the main reference to Jesus by Josephus in surviving copies of a book written early in the 90s has been edited by Christians, but it seems probable that he thought Jesus a 'wise man'—a compliment possible for him, to which the editor has clumsily added 'if indeed one ought to call him a man'.) And the policy of collaboration advocated by Josephus paid. Despite bitter memories of the rebellions, despite local tensions and even riots, good relations slowly became normal between the Roman authorities and the Jews, who were subject to a special tax but excused from many civic duties involving the need to sacrifice to the pagan gods. Taxpaying and prayers for the emperor in their synagogues were now regarded as sufficient proof of their political loyalty. The imperial government upheld the authority of the patriarch of the Jews until that post was abolished by a Christian emperor in 425. The contrast with the treatment of the Christians is striking.

Nothing has survived which can be proved to be a substantial Jewish commentary on Christianity made during its first century but the references which do survive, of uncertain date, are contemptuous and about AD 90 some Jews (how many is not clear) began to add some curses when they used the traditional 'benedictions' during worship in their synagogues: 'May there be no hope for the traitors and may the kingdom of wickedness be rooted out soon in our days! May the Nazarenes and the heretics perish quickly and may their names be erased from the Book of Life!' These curses were roughly contemporary and parallel with the Christian attacks in the Revelation of John against 'those who claim to be Jews' but are the 'Synagogue of Satan'. In the gospel of John (a different John) it is claimed that already in the lifetime of Jesus anyone who acknowledged him as Messiah had been 'banned from the synagogue'. John also claimed that from an early stage 'the Jews' had looked for a chance to kill Jesus and that Jews who had ceased to be his disciples had been warned by him that 'you will die in your sins' because 'your father is the Devil'. Such was the atmosphere when John wrote. He wrote with power about love, but it was love between Christians: 'the Jews' are enemies.

The other three gospels included some harsh denunciations of 'scribes and Pharisees' which seem to have been influenced by the situation in which they were written. It is of course probable that some of the religious teachers of Palestinian Jewry were 'hypocrites' (actors) to some extent; that is true about some religious leaders in all places and at all times. It is also unsurprising that Jesus was reported to be far more indignant about the pride of the complacently good and the comfortably privileged than he was about the struggles of 'sinners' who were often poor; that is true about all prophets who burn with the sense that God alone is fully holy and fully merciful. But the histories of Josephus are among the evidence that suggests that Jesus lived among people who, whether or not they obeyed it in detail, accepted the Law of Moses as the spiritual identity of their proud race—and who, whether or not they admired it entirely, paid the customary tax to support the temple. Every community of Jews had its synagogue and almost every synagogue had its school like the one in Nazareth which educated Jesus. Jews then often disagreed about what *Torah* meant: the Pharisees, the Sadducees and the Essenes had different ways of being strict; the Zealots were eager to fight for freedom and the 'people of the land' had more modest ambitions; the Jews in Judaea or Galilee, in Alexandria or a little town in the scattered Diaspora, were all different. But Jews did not very often excommunicate each other, and most of the evidence in the gospels suggests that Jesus the Jew argued with other teachers while remaining within this tradition. The passages which suggest otherwise seem to have been shaped by a later situation, as when Matthew had a crowd of Jews shouting before the Roman punishment of crucifixion: 'His blood be on our heads and on our children's!'

Interpreting Jesus

Many Christians cursed by Jewish orthodoxy must have felt a great unease. They could no longer take part in the worship in which Jesus and his first followers had all shared—and they were no longer protected by the recognition in Roman law that the beliefs and customs of politically loyal Jews, however eccentric, constituted a licensed religion. The Christians were on their own now, and their anxiety must have increased as their first generation died without seeing the coming of the kingdom of God. Would the kingdom whose arrival had been the central message of Jesus ever come? Paul's earliest surviving letter, to the little church in Thessalonica, warned against stopping everyday work in the belief that the kingdom was sure to come soon. 'The day of the Lord', he told them, 'will come like a thief in the night.' But later he told the Christians in Rome that 'salvation' was nearer than when they had 'first believed', and the Christians in Philippi that the Lord was 'at hand' so they should 'rejoice'. And after Paul's death another letter (2 Peter) still had to answer a question which put the reliability of the Lord himself into doubt: 'Where now is the promise of his coming?'

The question did not destroy the faith of the Christians. Amid all the ardent hopes there was a tradition that Jesus had said that he did not know the 'hour' of the End—a tradition which was probably accurate, since the Christians would have been reluctant to think their Lord ignorant. There was also a tradition that as he prayed in the olive grove of Gethsemane during the night before his crucifixion he was terrified in a very human way—another story which the Christians were unlikely to invent. But he had not made his escape while it was still possible and that decision had been part of his prayer that the Father's will, not his, should be done; that the Father's kingdom should come as the Father would decide. This was the prayer which preserved the hope of God's kingdom when the End did not come as quickly as was expected. Christians could tell themselves and others that like their Lord they did not know the 'hour'; that if they were to do the Father's will they like their Lord would have to endure disappointment and agony as the End was delayed; but that the Father could be trusted and that already, in what Jesus had said and done, the Father's kingdom had been inaugurated.

What, then, had Jesus said and done? The Christians collected, pondered and preached many traditions somewhat different from each other: they were different because the preachers were different and the communities in which they were passed on were different. Eventually the process of collection, editing and communication resulted in the writing down of 'gospels'. The author of one of the earliest to have survived, Luke, introduced his gospel by saying that already many existed. He went on to claim that he had taken care to gather reliable facts about events and certainly it is remarkable how much of the situation of Jesus of Nazareth was preserved by Luke (as by Mark and Matthew) although that situation was now remote. To some extent the writers of the gospels were historians in the modern sense. But a Christian writing in the second century of the Church, Justin, was mistaken to call these gospels the 'reminiscences of the apostles'. The men who wrote them have been called more accurately 'evangelists': they were men with messages and the events they recounted had been filtered through other men's sermons and through their own devout meditations and imaginations. Having announced that he was going to give his reader 'accurate knowledge' Luke did not hesitate to introduce an angel into his narrative a few hundred words later, signalling that this story was to cover holy ground.

So far as was remembered, Jesus had left nothing in writing behind him. Even in speech he had never fully explained who he thought he was. He had, indeed, said little about himself—although he had certainly thought that he was God's chief agent in the inauguration of the new kingdom, and therefore had not hesitated to say that people's reaction to him was spiritually decisive. Mark came nearest to outlining what was thought to have been the self-estimate of this mysterious 'Son of God' when he said that Jesus had replied 'I am' to the question put by the high priest: 'Are you the Messiah?' But many others, from kings downwards, could be called sons of God and the functions of the hoped-for Messiah were human. (The Essenes of Qumran expected two Messiahs, one a general, the other a priest.) According to Mark Jesus had repeatedly told people not to call him 'Messiah': only when very solemnly challenged by the high priest did he say 'I am'. Even then, he went on to speak about the 'Son of Man'—which could refer to the highly exalted figure in the Book of Daniel representing the saints of Israel, although the phrase could mean less than that, as it does in the Book of Ezekiel. And although both Luke and Matthew used Mark's gospel, neither reported that 'I am' about Messiahship.

Matthew included very high praise for Peter's recognition that Jesus was 'the Messiah, the Son of the living God'—but also a terrible rebuke for Peter's failure to understand what was implied: 'Get behind me, Satan!' The impression left by these three gospels is that Jesus lived a life and left the interpretation of it to others. 'Who do you say that I am?' he asked—and never said that any reply was adequate.

The Christians who wrote these gospels had remarkably limited space: it has been suggested that each gospel had to fit the size of one scroll if it was to be convenient for reading before the development of the book-like *codex*. They also had limited knowledge. It seems that none of them had experienced any of the events—with one possible exception. In the next century two bishops, Papias and Irenaeus, believed that the author of the earliest surviving gospel (in a scroll which seems to have lost its beginning and end through much use) was John Mark, a Jew brought up in Jerusalem who had become first Paul's and then Peter's assistant. But Marcus was a very common name in the Roman empire and the author of this gospel, whoever he was, wrote in a place where customs of the Jews such as washing the hands before meals had to be explained to readers. Also, he had no intention of being romantic either about the life of Jesus or about the response of the apostles to it.

In this gospel Jesus manages to unite his own family and the leaders of all the Jewish parties against him: it is a remarkable coalition. He performs miracles which overpower demons but he is not without human weakness: thus he is able to cure a woman but feels that power has gone out of him, and to still a storm but has been in exhausted sleep during it. 'Why do you call me good?' he asks. 'No one is good except God.' As he dies he utters one terrible cry: 'My God, my God, why have you forsaken me?' His few followers are fools who constantly misunderstand him and despite their ridiculous ambitions they are cowards. Yet it is understandable that they are frightened as in their bewilderment they follow him to his arrest and to his mysteriously empty tomb, for he warns that every follower of his must 'take up' his cross. At least in the earliest copies of this gospel which have survived, no resurrection appearances are narrated. But some disciples do follow, barely glimpsing the glory. The only person who literally carries the cross of Jesus in this gospel is Simon of Cyrene, who was conscripted by the soldiers to do so, but presumably he became a Christian as a result of what he saw, for he is known to Mark's first readers as 'the father of Alexander and Rufus'. According to Mark, Jesus the 'son of God' and the chief of martyrs ransoms many by dying, as slaves are ransomed; and so this gospel is a gospel for Christians such as Alexander and Rufus who may be martyred or may see a new age with a blood-red dawn. Its tense atmosphere seems to belong to the 60s. In Rome in 64 Christians were crucified or otherwise killed with great cruelty, as we have noted. Probably Peter and Paul were executed then. Two years later the Palestinian rebellion revived predictions that the institutions of Judaism were to be replaced amid great suffering, heralding the kingdom of God. Written in rough Greek, Mark's gospel seems to be breathless with fear and excitement.

Very different is the vision in Luke's gospel, probably written in the 70s, also for a Gentile readership but more elegant in style, more confident about the attractiveness of Jesus, more happy to celebrate the 'acts of the apostles' (the title which was later given to the second volume). Luke is generous towards Jewish Christianity but his chief interest lies in the mission to Greek speakers in the Roman world, a mission which only begins in Jerusalem. Mark had reported Jesus as saying that even he did not know when the End would come; now Luke saw the delay before the End as 'the days of the Gentiles', the delay being needed as an opportunity to bring the good news to a representative sample of non-Jewish humanity. Jesus is full of 'the power of the Spirit' as he announces the news for the poor, for women, for foreigners, for all. This gospel tells the stories of the prodigal son and the good Samaritan: God's forgiving love for all sinners must be reflected in the treatment of all as neighbours. And Luke hopes that people will respond to such a message. Even Pilate in this gospel and the Roman officials in Acts contribute, however unintentionally, to the progress of the invincible mission. Both of Luke's volumes are dedicated to a 'Most Excellent' (and therefore high-ranking) enquirer called Theophilus ('Lover of God'). We do not know who he was, but it is evident that Luke expected him to be impressed by a beautiful story told in beautiful words, a story which continues the song of the Christmas angels about 'peace on earth'. The passages in Acts which refer to 'we' indicate that Luke joined Paul at a late stage but he did not go along with the controversial elements in Pauline theology. He was mentioned in Paul's letter to Philemon but almost certainly wrote Acts without reading Paul's other letters. His smoothly diplomatic account of the 'council of Jerusalem' which reached agreement about the status of the

Gentile Christians is hard, if not impossible, to reconcile with Paul's earlier account given to the Galatians.

Different, too, is the gospel of Matthew, who wrote probably in the 70s or 80s and probably in Antioch. His own material presents a Jesus who fulfils the predictions of the Hebrew Bible and is the new Moses, not laying down the law but lifting up the eyes to a vision of the God-like life. The Sermon on the Mount sums up the new morality: 'I say to you . . .' Those who enter the new kingdom must avoid hatred and contempt, not merely murder; lustful thoughts, not merely adultery; showy religion, not merely immorality; anxiety about material needs, not merely theft; and they are to be recognized by their lives, not merely by their words. The precise relationship between this new morality and the Law of Moses is left unclear; both conservative and radical passages can be quoted from this gospel. But the Church (the *ekklesia*, the Greek word for an assembly of a city's full citizens) is told that its leaders are not to be like the rabbis who lecture others. There is only one Teacher, to whom has been given 'all authority in heaven and on earth'. And the humble people who hear this Teacher's message and act on it are the truly happy. They carry not 'the yoke of the law' (the rabbinical phrase) but a yoke made in Nazareth which fits easily on a back which already has had many burdens. They are to be perfectly good because perfectly merciful, like God the Father of all. Although both Paul's first letter to Corinth and the Acts of the Apostles show that the earliest form of Christian baptism was 'into the name of the Lord Jesus', here baptism is 'in the name of the Father and the Son and the Holy Spirit' for the power to live at this level comes from these three sources. The alternative can be very grim: Christianity's traditional pictures of hell came from Matthew's gospel.

These three gospels, for all their differences, may be seen together: that is what is meant by calling them 'synoptic'. Luke and Matthew incorporated much of Mark, although with subtle changes. Mark preserved the early Christians' bewildered and frightened fascination with their Lord; Luke told the stories which were to shape the Church's year, the Church's confidence and the Church's imagination; Matthew gave the moral teachings which were to be read out when the Church assembled in humility but now knowing the power of God in three ways. However, for the deepest thoughts about the new Lord we have to turn to a gospel which does not rely on those three—to John's gospel, embodying a tradition which is claimed to go back to an anonymous 'beloved disciple' who was placed next to Jesus at his last supper. In the epilogue this origin is vouched for by a group called 'we' and the gospel has certainly been fed by a distinctive community's spirituality, probably in the 80s or 90s: a fragment has survived of a copy made not later than AD 130. Tradition said that it was written in Ephesus by one of the Twelve, John the son of Zebedee, but the close examination of this very strange document which has been made by many modern scholars has seldom suggested to them that here is an accurate account by that eye-witness. At any rate this is a book from the frontier between Jew and Greek. It is also a book from the frontier between time and eternity. Luke and Matthew included in their gospels different versions of the family tree of Joseph although both stressed that Joseph was not the physical father of Jesus: Luke went back to Adam, Matthew to Abraham. John's gospel began long before Adam and it did not mention anything strange about the birth of Jesus except this: eternity was born into time.

The gospel contains some historical material which may well be accurate: for example, Jesus recruits his first disciples from men who, like him, have already been given a life-changing experience through the work of John the Baptist. But much of the material seems symbolic rather than factual: for example, Jesus cleanses the temple soon after his baptism and not as the final challenge to the authorities. The crucifixion takes place on 14 Nisan in the Jewish calendar, when the Passover lambs are being ritually slaughtered in the temple, instead of on 15 Nisan as in the other gospels, which suggest that the last supper on the previous evening was a Passover supper (although this is uncertain since they do not mention a lamb). The pace of this gospel is somewhat more leisurely, including three Passovers, and much of it consists of long speeches in a style very different from the synoptic gospels. The kingdom of God is barely mentioned. In the middle of the long prayer on the last evening comes a sentence which is the key to this fourth gospel's meaning: 'This is eternal life, to know you, the only true God, and Jesus Christ whom you have sent.' The 'last day' is still expected, but eternal life already 'is', here and now. Miraculous signs where Jesus is always in control manifest his glory which brings wine to replace water, life through new words, freedom from paralysis, bread for the hungry, light for the blind, resurrection for the dead, a cross which draws all. As early as 1:41 Peter is told that 'we have found the Messiah'. As early as 4:42 people who are not Jews know that Jesus is 'truly the Saviour of the world'. Speeches by Jesus declare that he is the Son of Man who came down from heaven, the Son of God who is one with the Father, the bread of life, the light of the world, the good shepherd who is willing to die for the sheep. This Lord makes his disciples clean, humble and loving and he assures them with the greatest promises ever made. They are to achieve works greater than his; in all their tribulations they are to be kept in peace and joy, in a union with him like his own union with the Father; they are to be received into his own glory in heaven. That is what Jesus meant to at least some of the Christians towards the end of the first Christian century. And in this gospel are the beginnings of a distinction between Jesus and 'another' whom the Father gives 'to be your Advocate, who will be with you for ever—the Spirit of truth ... who will teach you everything'.

Near the end of this gospel Thomas, previously a despondent doubter, calls the risen Jesus 'my Lord and my God', but in common with the rest of the New Testament John usually distinguishes between 'Jesus' and 'God'. Somehow Jesus lived with the Father before he became a man but the glory of that existence before the coming to earth, or the glory of the return to the Father, is nowhere explained. Nearest to an explanation is the prologue, which uses about Jesus the idea of *Logos*. This is usually translated as 'Word' but it would mean more than that to the mixed audience of Jews and Gentiles whose minds John wished to reach. It would impress them more than a story about a birth to a virgin. It would link Jesus with the whole of history, not merely with a line going back to Adam, and instead of tracing a descent from Abraham it would prepare for what Jesus says in this gospel: 'Before Abraham was, I am.'

Jews would connect the word *Logos* with the mighty word of the Lord which came to the prophets; with the Spirit and the Glory which had descended from time to time; with the personified (and female) Wisdom pictured as God's agent in the creation of a wonderful world and in the inspiration of humanity; and with the religious law believed to express God's wisdom. Within the Hebrew Bible Wisdom was God's 'architect' or 'master workman' (Proverbs 8:22–31) and 'the fashioner of all things' (Wisdom of Solomon 7:22). But educated Gentiles would recognize *Logos* as the rational ordering of the universe. In Stoic philosophy *logoi* (in the plural) were the true essences of beings and the *Logos*, the chief of the essences, took the place of the more popular gods and angels as the means by which the whole universe took its shape. Philo, a Jew living like John in a Gentile environment, used *Logos* to refer to the chief instrument of the Creator (some 1,400 times in his surviving writings). The *Logos* is the 'name' or 'face' of God, but also an *hypostasis*, a distinct entity, on the frontier between the Creator and the creation, 'neither uncreated like God nor created like you'. The *Logos* is the mediator who crosses this frontier, like a messenger appearing in the Bible with the word of the Lord but also like a high priest carrying messages from humanity to God. The *Logos* may even be called the 'Son' or the 'Spirit' of God. But the idea that the name or face of God might become a human being, might be 'flesh', seemed impossible to this philosopher. It was the central belief in what John held to be the truth which was the way to understanding and living the new life.

Perhaps this idea of the *Logos* may be translated for moderns in this paraphrase of John's prologue, often thought to have begun as a hymn separate from the gospel:

> In the beginning was the Plan,
> God's plan, divine!
> Everything took shape through it,
> nothing without it!
> It brought life and light for all,
> shining in the dark, never overcome!
> It entered the world it had planned,
> yet the world refused to know!
> God's own people refused!
> But all who accepted, who trusted,
> could become God's children,
> not born in a woman's blood,
> not conceived by any man,
> but born of God!
> And the Plan became flesh
> in a life among us,
> and we saw his glory,
> the glory of the Father's unique Son,
> full of grace and truth!

However, John saw the *Logos* not as a plan but as a person. Christians who have retained a belief in God as Creator while also accepting the discoveries of modern science have often expressed their faith by saying that God makes and governs (in some sense) a universe which is older and bigger than the human mind can imagine, and that Jesus provides the clue to the riddle of the meaning of it all. But the ancient world did not think in terms of a great plan governing an empire, let alone the inconceivably ancient and vast universe. They thought of the ruler, human or divine, as ruling personally, with equally personal assistants. The world was obviously under control by personal but supernatural power; quite small and quite new, it had been made more or less as they saw it. It should not surprise us that the idea of the *Logos* was expressed in the image of the definitely personal Son, divine or semi-divine. When this Son lived in heaven he was the active agent in the work of creation, shaping a world which had been 'without form' (as it was pictured in Genesis 1:2). Later he 'took' human flesh somewhat as a young man might take working clothes in order to do a dirty job for his father. This Son was pictured as being like a craftsman making the stars, Earth and Adam and Eve. When Christians in their early centuries read in Genesis 1:26 that God had said 'Let us make Man in our own image', it was easy for them to imagine the Father and Son as two people doing the job— they might add, with the Spirit's collaboration and the assistance of the angels. In much the same way the Spirit was pictured as an advocate or a teacher, images more human and therefore more powerful than wind or fire or dove.

Despite this use of images which people could understand because they were images of other people, John's gospel was to be called the 'spiritual' gospel by Clement of Alexandria a hundred years later. It could seem too spiritual and for some time some churches refused to include it in the New Testament. Ordinary Christians, knowing their own families, could prefer to think of Jesus as the Son of the Father. They were moved by the stories of the birth of Jesus in a cave or shed where an inn kept the animals and of the foundation of the Eucharist (so called from *eucharistia*, 'thanksgiving') on the night when he was betrayed to death—stories which John does not tell. They thought they understood at least the human touches in the parables of Jesus, none of which John repeats. They were helped to live and die by remembering the sufferings of Jesus, which John turns into 'glory' as the cross becomes the greatest of the 'signs' lifting up the *Logos*: the pain is forgotten, the whole world is drawn to this light and the manifestation of 'grace and truth' is 'accomplished'. And if Christians looked for the expression of a passionate faith always close to earth and to human blood, they could find it in the letters of Paul. These were written before any of the four gospels.

Paul

Paul, like John, was not concerned to echo the exact words of Jesus, but he was down-to-earth. He told the Galatians (for example) that 'God sent his Son, born of a woman, born under the law, to buy freedom for those who were under the law'. He told the Christians in Rome that his gospel was about Jesus Christ, 'on the human level a descendant of King David but on the level of the Holy Spirit declared Son of God by a mighty act in that he rose from the dead'. He always insisted that he had been appointed an *apostolos* (envoy) by Jesus Christ himself, who 'once took hold of me'. In addition to the sermons about Jesus which he must have often preached, his letters show that he passed on traditions which he had 'received'—about Christ's death 'for our sins' and his later appearances, about his last supper with his disciples, about the extraordinarily intimate prayer to God as 'Father' (using the Aramaic *Abba* as children did to their fathers), about the future return in glory (using the prayer in Aramaic *marana tha*, 'Lord, come!'). Plainly he did not invent the Christian belief that sinners can become friends with God as 'Father' through Jesus as 'Lord', but what he had 'received' was seen in the light which according to the Acts of the Apostles had at first blinded him on the road to Damascus. He had somehow 'seen the Lord': 'God chose to reveal his Son to me and through me.' And he had seen that this Lord was 'the Son of God who loved me and gave himself up for me', so that 'I have been crucified with Christ: the life I now live is not my life, but the life which Christ lives in me'.

Because he saw 'the glory of God' in the face of Christ, he saw also 'God's hidden wisdom, his secret purpose firm from the beginning to bring us to our full glory'. It was now his conviction that God is not merely just (as all Jews believed) but also willing to 'justify' sinners, counting them as righteous and making them so if only they put their trust in Christ, being in a profound sense united with him. 'There is now no condemnation for those who are in Christ Jesus': he wrote that to Rome, where he was to be condemned to death. He told the Christians in Corinth he had known a contact with glory, with 'the Lord of Glory', which could never be put into words—and when he had prayed to that Lord in despair, he had been told that 'my power comes to its full strength in your weakness'. He wrote about the 'harvest of the Spirit' in the life of a Christian and the miracle was that this harvest had grown in his own life since the days when he had been zealously, even fanatically, a Pharisee anxious to keep the Jewish religious law meticulously, and to demand its keeping by all other Jews, yet unable to find peace for himself. 'The good which I want to do, I fail to do; what I do is the wrong which is against my will . . . Who is there to rescue me?' He remembered that misery when writing to Rome but he had found a rescuer and with it, as he wrote to Corinth, 'love, joy, peace, patience, kindness, goodness, fidelity, gentleness and self-control'. And he gave thanks: 'By the grace of God I am what I am.'

His was an experience recognizably human rather than exclusively Jewish: the experience of finding security and fulfilment not in obedience to rules which are most profoundly felt to be impositions, but in the authentic and spontaneous expression of the best part of oneself, the humanity given by God and accepted by God, which then reaches out to the best in other people. Because of it he could communicate by love with Gentiles, particularly with those already drawn to the basic faith of Judaism but unwilling to accept all its laws and traditions. As he reminded the church in Corinth, most of his converts were people without much education, power or prestige in society. Many were slaves; probably most were women. But in a church which Paul founded all could experience a liberation which was like a new birth. He had found that new life as a Jew. If they were not Jews, Christians could experience it as liberation from a paganism which had a bewildering multitude of gods with tales about them which were often without any moral content; from a religion which made a god out of an emperor; from civic religion which was at bottom worship of the city itself; from rural religion which was fear of natural forces; from the coarse sensuality of a sex-sodden world which ended in the unenjoyable night of death; from the control of brief lives by the stars; from the magic which had little power to tame the anger of the gods or the malice of the demons or the capriciousness of fortune. Rival philosophers offered deliverance from this world, its fables and its superstitions, but they were all elitist—the Stoics too aloof from human emotions, the Platonists too high in the realm of pure 'ideas', the Epicureans too sure that if gods existed they cared nothing about the earth, the Cynics too keen to destroy all conventions. And groups which did speak of divine saviours in emotional terms which non-intellectuals could understand spoke through the myths and rituals of the 'mystery' religions, offering initiations into unions with Greek and Egyptian divinities, not offering any agreement with anything said by any philosopher.

Paul knew that confused pagan world from his boyhood, inheriting Roman citizenship because he was born into a well-to-do family in the city of Tarsus and the family had received this honour which was given to very few Jews. But he had reacted against Tarsus with a young fanatic's zeal as a Pharisee. In his maturity, at the peak of his spiritual power, his letter to Rome opened with thunder against that world's immorality caused by idolatry. He had all of the Jewish sense of sin, of human iniquity: 'All have sinned and fallen short of the glory of God.' And he had all the Jewish pride: 'They are Israelites and to them belong the adoption by God, the revelation of his glory, the covenants with him, the giving of the law by him, the worship of him and the promises by him; to them belong the patriarchs and from them, according to the flesh, comes the Messiah.' But he counted everything outside this Christ 'sheer loss', he told the Christians in Philippi, because 'everything is far outweighed by the gain of knowing Christ Jesus my Lord, for whose sake I did in fact lose everything. All I care for is to know Christ . . .' Looking back over his life, he summed it up: 'To me life is Christ and to die is gain.' For this Lord had shown him what life ought to be and could be, without end: life knowing God's love.

As he talked about Christ he put new meanings into words familiar to Gentiles who were seekers in religion—in his case, not *Logos* but mystery, spirit, knowledge and wisdom. The keys to the new life were a purifying initiation and a sacred meal not totally unlike those in the mystery cults although with origins in Jewish baptisms and Jewish fellowship-meals. He used images very different from the parables of Jesus, images drawn from athletics, wrestling or military service. He made 'Christ' almost a surname of Jesus, without identifying the term with Messianic hopes for a new Jewish kingdom, and he presented him as the dying and rising 'lord'—the 'saviour' (a word he used to the Philippians) for whom those attracted by the mystery cults were looking. But always he preached not a myth but the facts of real history in Palestine, Christ 'nailed to the cross' and 'raised from the dead'. He told Christians in Corinth that he himself had 'become everything in turn, to people of every sort, so that in one way or another I may save some', trying to think like a Gentile in order to explain what Christ had done.

What moved him most deeply was the thought that Christ, who 'knew no sin', had in a sense been 'made sin', or had 'become a curse', by consenting to be crucified among accursed sinners. That had been the ultimate sacrifice, made to restore a right relationship with the Father. To the Greeks, as he reminded the Corinthians, it was 'sheer folly'. To Jews, he confessed, this execution of Christ as a criminal was a 'stumbling-block', tripping up anyone who was conventionally pious and moral. But the significance which he found in this death shows how Jewish his mind was: he had to wrestle with the scandal of the cross, to extract a meaning from that horror and degradation, and in the end he concluded that it had been the means of at-one-ment as the sacrifices of animals in the Jerusalem temple had been. And providing this very strange at-one-ment had been the 'foolishness of God' which is also 'the power of God and the wisdom of God'. For 'from first to last this was the work of God'. 'God designed him to be the means of expiating sin by his sacrificial death ... We have now been justified by Christ's sacrificial death ... When we were God's enemies, we were reconciled to him through the death of his Son.' Now true life could begin.

He reminded the Galatians that in the new reality 'there is no such thing as Jew and Greek, slave and free, man and woman, for you are all one person in Christ Jesus'. Christians retained their racial, economic and sexual identities; indeed, to a large extent they kept to their places in the rigid class and sexist systems of the Roman empire; but in their hearts they were not segregated. They had entered a unity far greater than the unity of that empire and even closer than the unity of the Hellenistic culture which had permeated all the cities of the eastern Mediterranean apart from Jerusalem since the conquests of Alexander the Great. Those two unities gave Paul his opportunity for evangelism: the imperial peace enabled him to travel, the use of Greek enabled this Jew to communicate with Christians scattered around the empire. To reach the people he now wished to reach, he used Jewish terms and spoke Greek: he did not actually need to 'become everything'. But his message was potentially for everyone and the unity which it offered went beyond any unity which anyone had known. Wherever they came from, the Christians had joined a 'new creation' through the local church which was 'God's temple' and 'Christ's body'. They were 'in Christ'.

Many people previously told to obey in silence could now exercise the gifts which the Holy Spirit had poured out. The congregation which was assembled was 'all baptized in one Spirit' and the liveliness proved it. In its meetings could be heard ecstatic 'tongues' or babblings, more coherent 'prophecies' or lay sermons, and hymns of triumphant praise. It was, Paul told the church in Corinth, a 'partnership in the Holy Spirit'. The cargoes in ships setting out from Corinth's two ports might be owned by partners; the Holy Spirit, although more precious than any cargo, was a definite reality in which all Christians shared. Meetings included not only 'the Lord's Supper', sharing in the body and blood (in another word, the life) of Christ, but also an ordinary supper.

Paul placed an enormous emphasis on the unity dramatized as they ate together in joy. There must be no divisions into rich and poor, into factions preferring different teachers, into different spiritual levels, or into demands for different food. Contrary to what is reported in the Acts of the Apostles as the decree of the council in Jerusalem, in these mixed congregations Jews must not demand *kosher* meat, slaughtered in accordance with the law which insisted on the draining of the blood. Gentiles who guessed that the animal had probably been sacrificed by pagans to idols in a temple before the meat was sold were allowed to eat without raising questions, but if they were explicitly told about the meat's origin they should abstain in order not to offend the conscience of the stricter 'brother for whom Christ died'. Paul told the Christians in Rome that he was 'absolutely convinced' that no food was unclean but that the charity which was more than courtesy must come first. By letters and visits the little congregation must preserve its unity with Christians in other cities. Christians must be deeply interested in the affairs of other churches; they must collect money to relieve the poverty of the mother-church in Jerusalem. They must live under the gospel and under the guidance of apostles appointed by Jesus—and when the church had been founded by Paul, under his continuing jurisdiction coupled (he told Corinth) with 'anxious concern' every day. Paul's need to rebuke many sins in the congregation at Corinth (a notoriously dissolute city) shows that the human reality was far from ideal; his teaching that 'all things are lawful' in the new life had been taken too enthusiastically. He had to repeat the commonplaces of morality. But his letters list many of the friends (many of them women) with whom he explored the new life 'in Christ', 'in the Spirit', in the Christ-like love which he described to a Corinth more familiar with the lust, greed and ambition called love (in the famous thirteenth chapter of the first letter). On the road to Damascus it had struck him: to persecute Christians was to persecute Jesus, who lived and suffered in them. He took the message of death and new life 'in Christ' along many roads.

In the letters which are certainly his he shows no interest in the kind of theology that has been called metaphysical or speculative. He reminds the Corinthian church that although Christ 'was rich' yet he 'became poor' but he does not explain how the Lord was rich or how he became poor. He puts 'the grace of our Lord Jesus Christ' before 'the love of God' in his written farewell to Corinth. But no more than John does he attempt to explain the relationship between the Father and the Son in eternity. Nor, indeed, does he clearly distinguish between the Son and the Spirit—and the Spirit is for him 'the Spirit of God' as well as 'the Spirit of Christ'. What interests him is the power of the example given by the 'poor' Jesus to inspire Christian generosity in giving to charity, and the power of the grace of the 'rich' Jesus to communicate God's love. 'My God', he assured the Philippians, 'will supply all your wants out of the magnificence of his riches in Christ Jesus.'

It was in order to preach humility, not theology, that he quoted a hymn to the Philippians. The hymn was unlike pagan celebrations of gods who descend from the heavenly heights in order to show their power to mortals, for it celebrated the life of a man humble enough to accept crucifixion. In the background may be the belief, mentioned in Paul's second letter to Corinth, that the humble obedience of Jesus reversed the proud sin of Adam the first man; or this may be an idea closer to the idea of Christ as the *Logos*, the Word of God who was said by John to be 'closest to the Father's heart' before he came to earth from the Father, from glory. What is clear in this hymn, an outpouring of praise sung by Christians under many pressures and quoted by a man awaiting execution, is the faith that the crucified has been crowned:

> He was in the form of God
> but made no claim to be God's equal.
> He made himself nothing,
> taking the form of a slave,
> born as a man.
> And being found in that human form,
> he humbled himself;
> he was obedient even to the point of death,
> death on a cross!
> Therefore God raised him to the heights
> and gave him the name above all names
> that at the name of Jesus every knee shall bend,
> in heaven, on earth, in the depths,
> and every tongue say 'Jesus Christ is Lord'
> to the glory of God the Father!

Early Catholicism

So Paul's gospel was both spiritual and earthy, as his Christ was both the saving Lord and a crucified man, doing divine work but not 'God'. However, even here we have not seen the most influential gospel in the New Testament. That message may be found in half a dozen letters which claim to be written by him but which modern scholars usually conclude were the work of others, perhaps incorporating fragments of Paul's surviving correspondence.

These letters differ at many points of substance and style from the certainly authentic letters and the modern question is 'Forgery?' Early Christians could also ask: they hesitated about the authorship of John's gospel and about the authority of the Revelation of John, and they rejected as forgeries the gospel, Acts and Revelation of Peter together with many other writings. In that world, however, it was thought modest and honourable for disciples to teach in the name of their master, as when Plato taught in the name of Socrates. Few or no questions were asked if it seemed that the tradition had been developed within acceptable limits. The writers of the gospels felt no duty to be accurate when quoting Jesus and the author of the Acts of the Apostles saw no need to reproduce Paul's own theology exactly. A similar freedom to develop Paul's message may be detected in the letters addressed 'to Hebrews' (the least likely to be Pauline), to churches in Colossae and Ephesus (and probably to other churches, since the earliest copies do not mention Ephesus), and to Paul's assistants, Timothy and Titus. They constitute evidence for the development of the Jesus movement through a new firmness in teaching about belief and behaviour, the Church and its leadership. This development after Paul's death has been seen by modern scholars as the early form of 'Catholicism', using a word first found in a letter from Bishop Ignatius of Antioch to the church in Smyrna very early in the second century. Ignatius wrote that 'where Jesus Christ is, there is the Catholic Church'. *Katholikos* means 'universal'.

Christ was now seen as doing divine work in the Church and (by deduction) in the universe. The letter to the Ephesians seems to be quoting an acclamation of praise:

> One God the Father,
> from whom all things exist
> and towards whom we exist;
> and one Lord, Jesus Christ,
> through whom are all things
> and through whom we exist.

And in the letter to the Colossians is a hymn which develops that fairly simple affirmation of dependence on the one God through the one Lord. It is a hymn about the glory of Christ:

> He is the image of the invisible God,
> the first of all created things!

27

In him everything in heaven and on earth was created,
things visible and invisible, sovereignties, rulers, powers—
everything through him and for him!
He exists before everything, everything is held together in him,
and he is the head of his body, the Church!
He is the beginning, the first to be born from the dead,
to be in all things alone supreme,
for in him God's whole being chose to dwell!
Through him God chose to reconcile everything on earth or in heaven,
making peace through his blood shed on the cross!

The passion of this exultant, *katholikos*, faith is unmistakable, but many questions which will interest later generations in the Church are left unanswered. Was Christ fully divine in eternity? Or as the great 'heretic' Arius was to assert, was he created? What did it mean to say that 'everything' had been created in, through and for a Lord who was known as the head of the Church? And how had 'everything' been reconciled to God through that Lord's death on the cross?

Such questions are not answered in the letter 'to Hebrews'. Here Christ is 'the radiance of God's glory'. Through him God created everything and now he 'sustains the universe by the word of his power'. So he is superior to the angels, but the main message for these Jewish Christians is that he is also superior to Moses and is the true high priest, offering his own life as a sacrifice superior to the sacrifices of animals in Jerusalem, where the temple has been 'only a copy and a shadow of the heavenly temple'. And these Christians who have been rejected by their fellow Jews are assured that this Lord did not make this supreme sacrifice without suffering. He made it 'with loud cries and tears' and since he himself 'passed through the test of suffering' he is able to sympathize like a brother with his followers. They are now undergoing the same test and they need faith because the sound does not reach them clearly from the crowd which is encouraging and applauding them in heaven. So this letter is not an essay in theology: no less than Mark's gospel, it is a call to be prepared for martyrdom. The urgency of this call is such that the letter does not make clear who is likely to persecute Christians; it does not even say whether or not the temple in Jerusalem is still standing. What matters is what is shouted in another hymn, preserved in the second letter to Timothy:

If we died with him, we shall live with him;
If we endure, we shall reign with him;
If we disown him, he will disown us;
If we are faithless, he remains faithful—
for he cannot disown himself!

In the same letter we hear the cry: 'I know whom I have trusted!' What these Christians believe about that Lord is summed up in the simple creed quoted in the first letter:

> There is one God,
> and one mediator between God and humanity:
> Christ Jesus, himself human,
> who gave his life as a ransom for all.

That is the creed of people who were previously told about many gods or about the One who is remote from human affairs—and it is the creed of people who know what ransoming from slavery means. It often trembles on the brink of saying that Jesus is divine as well as human and a reference to 'our God and Saviour Jesus Christ' is found in the letter to Titus and in the document called 2 Peter. These were titles which the emperor Domitian insisted should be applied to himself. But in the letter to Titus the original text may have referred merely to 'God our Saviour' as it does in some early copies of this passage and twice elsewhere in this letter. The theology about Jesus has not yet been formulated.

In these letters the background which helps to explain who 'Christ Jesus' is does not come from the metaphysics of the Greek philosophers. It comes from the Greek translation of the Hebrew Bible. This 'Scripture' is said to be 'inspired' (the Greek means 'God-breathed') and 'useful in teaching the truth'. Its usefulness seems to have been increased by collecting from its total contents (which were very bulky) 'testimonies' which were claimed to foretell the coming of Jesus as the Messiah. Prominent in all these Christian documents are denunciations of 'enemies of the truth'. Titus, for example, is warned against 'Jewish myths' outside the Bible. Such unorthodox developments in Judaism are not described clearly, but they seem to have taught reliance on self-mortification (especially fasting and sexual abstinence) in order to obtain access to secrets about the angelic beings who under God's supreme command govern human life behind the scenes. These angels, the Christians are told, exist—but are 'powers' hostile to humanity and are now conquered by Christ. Another late document admitted to the New Testament, the letter of Jude, urges Christians to 'join in the struggle for that faith which God entrusted to his people once for all'. The 'faith' which to Paul was a volcanic explosion rising from the depths of a passionate encounter with Christ is now cooling into an ordered religion, based on Scriptures, on doctrines and on morality. Jude launches a tirade against the moral wickedness of heretics. In these letters standards of everyday morality familiar in the more respectable quarters of the non-Christian world (Jewish or pagan) are firmly endorsed, with brief references to reasons why a Christian should be specially motivated to be recognizably good, an advertisement for a faith which deserves respect.

In this period of Early Catholicism Christians met for worship in the homes of their wealthier sisters and brothers, and most of them had to practise morality in families. So now the emphasis was on the stable household: husband and wife, parent and children, master and slaves, all honouring one another but leaving the control in the hands of the husband, the father and the slave-owner. Women were now told to keep silent in Christian assemblies. Paul's first letter to Corinth said the same in the copies which became current but that passage in chapter 14 may well have been added after his death, for in chapter 11 he has told women to cover their heads modestly when 'prophesying' to the congregation. Elsewhere he acknowledged women as leaders in congregations: his letter to Rome commended Phoebe as both 'deacon' and 'patron' of her congregation and Junia (a woman's name; in some manuscripts the male Junias) as 'outstanding among the apostles', thanked four other women who 'toiled' for the Church, and named Prisca before her husband. The post-Pauline silencing of women was part of a wider movement attempting to make Christianity less exposed to the widespread belief that because it was unconventional it was immoral and criminal. The new situation did not mean that women were despised; the second letter to Timothy makes a point of praising his mother Eunice and his grandmother Lois. But the attitude had become different from Paul's celebration of the active leadership of congregations by women and even more different from the attitude of Jesus. Not only does Luke's gospel frequently emphasize the Lord's unusual sympathy with the personalities and concerns of women: John's very different gospel gives the same picture. The Jesus of John is happy to talk about religion with a Samaritan woman alone by a well (the traditional place for flirtations) and with the spiritually minded Mary while she neglects a woman's traditional duty of humble housework. That Samaritan woman becomes the first Christian missionary and Mary of Magdala is the first person to meet the risen Lord. Although in the ancient world it was inconceivable that a woman should be given the role which seems to have been given to the initial apostles ('the Twelve'), Jesus was, it is clear, remarkably uninhibited. But now Early Catholicism was taking a safer path, developing the more traditional attitude to Eve and other women which Paul (always half a rabbi) sometimes also expressed.

Enthusiasm was reserved for membership of the Church, a body wider and more glorious than the local congregation (and more clearly so than in Paul's own letters). The Church is 'God's household, the pillar and bulwark of the truth'. There is 'a single new humanity' which can grasp what is 'the breadth and length and height and depth of Christ's love'. It comes as no surprise when we read that Christians who belong to 'a chosen race, a royal priesthood, a dedicated nation, a people claimed by God for his own' and called to be 'alive with the life of God' (in 1 Peter) can share in 'the very being of God' (2 Peter 1:4). But it is also no surprise that these Christians are now told that they need leaders in order to fulfil their high vocation. They need the guidance of 'apostles, prophets, evangelists, pastors and teachers' (as in the letter to the Ephesians). In the first letter to Timothy there is a sketch of the character desirable in an *episkopos* (superintendent) who is to be a model to the congregation. Good behaviour is also demanded of the *diakonoi* (assistants). But these jobs are not described in detail. Their titles seem to be derived from those used in the leadership of a *collegium* (club or vountary society) which in the Roman world might have religious purposes.

The Acts of the Apostles told of Paul's farewell speech to the *presbyteroi* (elders) who were the leaders of the Christians in Ephesus. *Presbyteroi* also feature in the first letter to Timothy and their title seems to have come from the older men who led the congregations in the Jewish synagogues and whose responsibilities were very different from the work of priests in temples, who were primarily butchers. The letter to Titus envisaged *presbyteroi* in every congregation in Crete and also mentioned an *episkopos*. It seems that there was as yet no firm distinction between *episkopoi* and *presbyteroi* (in English, between bishops and presbyters). But neither was there complete equality: *presbyteroi* who worked hard as leaders, preachers and teachers could be paid double the normal stipend.

In these letters less was said about the world, but what was said more or less repeated the teaching of Paul. Although the Christians in Ephesus were reminded that the pagan world was 'without God and without hope', Timothy was told that whatever extreme puritans might argue 'everything that God has created is good'. Although the infection of evil was not denied, Titus was reminded that 'the grace of God has dawned upon the world with healing for all'. The infant Church, however small, however preoccupied by its own experiences, was thus potentially world-embracing as Catholicism was to be in its truly world-wide development. Indeed, with a bold exaggeration the letter to Colossae already celebrated the Church's univer-sality, for the 'gospel' (the good news) was 'bearing fruit and growing in the whole world'. And the political authorities were seen as allies, at least potentially. People in high positions deserve prayers because they can ensure 'a quiet and peaceable life in all godliness'. The burning hatred of the Revelation of John for Rome and its evil empire has been dampened by this teaching that the Christian revolution is not to be politically subversive. Paul's own instruction to the Christians in Rome that they must obey the orders of the empire, the emperor Nero being 'God's minister', is to prevail for everyday purposes, although in the ultimate choice Paul's own acceptance of martyrdom under Nero must be the choice of true Christians.

Early Diversity

We are fortunate to have as much evidence as we possess about those first years of Christianity. Almost all of the lives of all of the Christians apart from Paul must be hidden from us but what we can see shows a considerable diversity within what the letter to the Ephesians called 'one body' inspired by 'one Lord, one faith, one baptism, one God and Father of all'.

For many centuries the Revelation of John was to be read as a prediction of events which must come to pass; the only problem was how to decipher it. Gradually the numbers have increased of students who have seen that it is an assembly, not neatly organized, of images adapted from the Hebrew Bible and from Jewish 'apocalyptic' literature claiming to disclose the future. The book was attributed to the John who wrote the gospel (but who was he?). However, quite soon there were readers who saw that its message and style were very different from the gospel's. So who was this John? Presumably as a prisoner, he was 'on the island called Patmos because I had preached God's word. It was on the Lord's day and I was caught up in the Spirit and I saw one like a son of man . . . and I fell at his feet as though dead.' That vision on a day which is very significantly called 'the Lord's' (not Sunday) inspired stern letters to Ephesus and six other churches in cities in the Roman province of Asia. It inaugurated a book full of the shock caused by the martyrdom of Christians in Rome and by the fall of Jerusalem to the Romans amid further scenes of horror. It was therefore also full of a sense that a great crisis was near, with a war to the death between the faithful few and a hostile world, ending as the new Jerusalem comes down from heaven 'like a bride adorned for her husband'. So far as we know from the surviving evidence, although Asia Minor saw some martyrdoms there was no general persecution of the Christians at that time; yet we may guess that this message 'like the sound of a trumpet' awoke many from a more or less relaxed posture.

John saw a more-than-imperial Christ, 'the First and the Last and the Living One', the Lamb 'with the marks of slaughter still upon him' now on the throne of God. He quoted hymns of praise addressed directly to this Christ which seem to be echoes of the worship developing in some churches. He wrote letters to churches which show that some shared his own total commitment to Christ, as in Smyrna and Philadelphia, while others simply hoped to be allowed to get on with their quiet lives. The Laodiceans were in the second category; they lived near water which had cooled since coming from hot springs and they were 'neither hot nor cold' as Christians. In a country town which prospered as the centre of a trade in luxuriously soft black wool, they did not realize their need to 'buy white clothes to hide the shame of their nakedness'. Their neighbours sold a famous powder which was believed to cure eye troubles, but these lukewarm, stupidly complacent Christians did not see that they were blind.

Letters to three cities on the main imperial road mixed warnings with encouragements. The congregation in Pergamum lived in 'the place where Satan has his throne'—which may refer to a very large altar to Zeus the father of the Greek gods on the Acropolis on the hill above the city. The Christian who is victorious in the spiritual war against such pagan idolatry is promised the biblical food manna and a 'white stone' with a 'new name' written on it; it may be relevant that the names of those invited to the festivities connected with the official cults were written on *tesserae*, small pieces of stone which served as tickets of admission. But some Christians had compromised to the extent of eating 'food sacrificed to idols'. Presumably they had bought meat in the market place without asking awkward questions or had joined in supper parties when the main course had been slaughtered in a temple or on the host's domestic altar. The letter to Thyatira attacked a prophetess who had encouraged such laxity: in the coming judgement she would be pinned down on a banqueting couch to watch the 'children' she had misled being killed. And the letter to Sardis could praise only a few who were not thus defiled.

The early history of the church in Ephesus is obscure, although it was a rich city and a centre of communications by sea and land. Paul taught there (in the lecture-hall of Tyrannus, for two years according to Acts) and there were traditions that the apostle John lived there, with the mother of Jesus. The city was the proud and profit-making 'Keeper' of the great temple of the fertility goddess Artemis, also called Diana, and John of the Revelation lamented that the Christians in Ephesus had lost their 'first love' for Christ: 'think from what a height you have fallen!' But we are not told who were the false 'apostles' who had been expelled, any more than we know about the 'angel of the church' to whom John addressed this message of praise and blame. Did the community behind the gospel and letters of the New Testament's other John belong to Ephesus? If so, had the church which the John of Revelation rebuked recovered its first love—or had this community split from it? And what did Ephesus remember about Paul? Did all its Christians acknowledge Bishop Onesimus as their leader, as Bishop Ignatius was to urge? Had this Onesimus been the runaway slave about whom Paul wrote to Philemon? We do not know, but the suggestion has been made that Onesimus kept that letter which had saved his life as a boy and added to it all the other letters by Paul which have survived.

Three other letters in the New Testament are in the style of the gospel of John. They were addressed by 'the elder' to a very closely knit community. Its members are told to love not the world, and not the 'many antichrists' who have deserted this group, but each other. 'We have crossed over from death into life' because now, through this intense love between the disciples, God's own love is known as the supreme reality: 'God is love' and 'he first loved us'. That love, manifest in Jesus, inspires the community's mutual love and guarantees the eternal life into which believers have already entered. But nothing is said clearly about the coming reign of God on earth, and meanwhile the community is said to need only one ultimate teacher, the Spirit. Day-to-day leadership is disputed between Demetrius (the writer's favourite) and Diotrephes. The atmosphere is sectarian although the theology is sublime.

We know nothing about any Christians who met for their worship near the scenes of the life of Jesus in Galilee. A tradition was preserved by the first church historian, Eusebius, that the emperor Domitian interviewed a family of farmers descended from Jude the brother of Jesus and was persuaded that they were 'men of no account' when they showed him their hands hardened by manual labour. It is an unlikely tale but it reflects the obscurity of Galilean Christianity. Even more obscure is whatever history lies behind the hint in John's gospel of evangelism in Samaria. Almost all the surviving evidence suggests that in its first and second centuries Christianity was almost entirely an urban movement, but we know nothing about the arrival of Christianity in the empire's second most important city, Alexandria. Nor is anything known about the first churches in Spain or Gaul which had other cities, or in the lands to the east of the Euphrates where large communities of Jews existed.

The names of the apostles Thomas and Philip came to be honoured in the east and a romantic account of the 'Acts of Thomas' in India may date back to the beginning of the third century. Eusebius believed that Thaddaeus was sent as a missionary to an eastern kingdom when its king (Abgar) had corresponded with Jesus, and also that the apostle Bartholomew took a copy of Matthew's gospel in Hebrew to India. These, too, are improbable tales but at least they suggest early Christian activity in the east. Eusebius seems more reliable when he names Pantaenus, a Christian scholar in Alexandria said to have visited India about 180, for it is known that trade between Egypt and India used the monsoon winds.

Modern scholars tend to agree that Christianity spread with remarkable rapidity, however thinly, in these early years but that almost nothing can be known about any activity by 'the Twelve' apart from Peter. They may have remained in Jerusalem until they died or had to leave it. Luke cherished the thought that they had a mission 'to the ends of the earth' (Acts 1:8) but if he knew the story of that mission he did not write it down in any book which has survived. Another puzzle is why he did not recount the martyrdoms of Peter, Paul and others in Rome, but it seems that it suited his optimism to end with the arrival of the apostle to the Gentiles in the empire's capital.

We have only a glimpse of Christianity in rural Syria through the *Didache* ('teaching'), a short document discovered in 1873. It may have been written in the same period as the Revelation of John or may be as late as 140. In their Eucharist each 'Lord's day' these Christians who have been shaken by the fall of Jerusalem to the Romans pray for the end of the world: 'Let Grace come and this world pass away!' Grace is here a name for Jesus. But in what is recorded about their worship they speak of Jesus as no more than God's *pais* (child or servant) and they do not mention his death. At least the Jewish background (if nothing else) is made clear when it is said that over the cup at the Eucharist thanksgiving should be offered for 'the holy vine of David, your *pais*, which you made known to us through Jesus, your *pais*'.

These Christians do, however, baptize 'in the name of the Father, and of the Son, and of the Holy Spirit' (preferably in running water but if necessary by pouring water three times on the head). The *Didache* is more realistic than the Revelation of John: 'If you can bear the whole yoke of the Lord, you will be perfect—but if you cannot, do what you can.' Bishops and deacons are mentioned, apparently being unpaid but appointed in keeping with developments elsewhere, but up to now the leadership has come from travelling leaders called 'apostles' or 'prophets' (also 'your high priests') and there is no clear direction as to who is to preside at the Eucharist. These Christians are warned that 'not everyone who speaks in the spirit is a prophet', particularly not if a prophet does not practise what he preaches. Apostles and prophets are welcome to teach a church as its guests for up to three days but if they stay any longer they should be told to earn their living like everyone else. In the prayers recommended there is thanksgiving to God for 'your Church' but no vivid sense that its organization ought to be strong and the same everywhere. It is in the kingdom to come that the Church will be gathered, as wheat sown on many hillsides is brought together in the loaf on the cottager's table. Over the bread at the Eucharist this prayer is said (after the prayer over the cup): 'Remember, Lord, your Church, delivering her from all evil, and making her perfect in your love, and gather the sanctified Church from the four winds into the kingdom you have prepared for her.'

There is a contrast between those simple country churches and the developed church in Rome. This is revealed to some extent in a letter probably written in the 90s which does not give the writer's name, or explain his authority, but is traditionally known as *1 Clement*.

It is addressed from Rome to Corinth, where some presbyter-bishops have been removed. No doctrinal dispute is indicated as the cause of this clash but Early Catholic doctrine emerges quite clearly in the Roman church's criticism. The apostles, it is said, appointed some of their first converts 'to be bishops and deacons' and arranged that 'if they should fall asleep other approved men should succeed them in their ministry'. Subsequently other 'eminent men' appointed presbyter-bishops 'with the approval of the whole church' and those appointed have 'ministered blamelessly to the flock of Christ in a humble, peaceable and worthy way'. A faction in the congregation had no right to remove such pastors.

What was meant by the statement that the first presbyter-bishops were chosen by 'apostles' is, however, not clear. Paul's letter to Rome mentions no founder of that church. He himself founded the church in Corinth and his first letter to the Thessalonians mentions Silvanus and Timothy as 'apostles' who could work as missionaries, but his surviving letters to Rome and Corinth do not include any mention of presbyter-bishops. His second letter to Corinth shows that like the *Didache* he expected ordinary Christians to decide whether or not visitors were genuine 'apostles' commissioned by Christ. His first letter shows that when he had to deal with divisions in the Corinthian congregation (with one group looking to him, another to Apollos, another to Peter and another exclusively to Christ) he did not talk about obedience to duly constituted leaders: he talked about the crucifixion of Christ and asked 'was Paul crucified for you?' and 'is Christ divided?' Nor is it clear who were the 'other eminent men' mentioned in this letter from Rome who took the lead when the apostles were dead, or what has happened to them; this letter is addressed by the whole Roman church to the whole congregation in Corinth, not to any leader who is able to put things right. But the general impression left by the letter is clear. These presbyter-bishops have 'offered the gifts', presumably in the Eucharist; their function is honoured highly and is traced back to the early days; and there is no such emphasis on Spirit-filled 'prophets' as in Paul's letters or in the *Didache*, any more than there is an emphasis on the future kingdom. From these beginnings the church order of Catholicism could develop.

This letter to Corinth resembles the letters to Timothy and Titus in some ways but its atmosphere is far from Pauline. The style is much more wordy and pompous. The theology has, it seems, not passed through the crisis of faith in the crucified and risen Lord. Christ's example of humility is not said to be decisive. His resurrection is mentioned (it gave the apostles 'confidence') but so is a legendary bird, the phoenix, which every five hundred years rises from the nest where it has died. The presbyter-bishops make 'offerings' but no details are given about Christian worship because the concentration is on the orderliness of the worship in the temple in Jerusalem. There is also comparison between good order in a congregation and discipline in the Roman army. The church in Rome assumes the right to rebuke another church, but does not explain why. There is pride in being

36

the place where Peter and Paul taught and were martyred, but it is not claimed that Peter speaks through this writer and those apostles' deaths are blamed on 'jealousy', perhaps hinting that some Christians (or Jews) in Rome had betrayed them to the police. It seems that the Roman Christians have been able to afford to send financial gifts to Corinth, which had been rebuilt by Julius Caesar with the intention of making it a Roman colony. That would strengthen their right to send fatherly advice.

No doubt there was even more diversity than is demonstrated by the surviving evidence about these early Christians, but in the material which we possess we may trace the faint marks of the first steps of a baby, the Catholic Church. It hopes to escape too much unpopularity without abandoning its faith. It has other gospels which are more comforting than Mark's. Its morality is higher than any other in that ancient world but more conventional than the message of Luke or Matthew. The Pauline, as well as the Johannine, intensity of the new life 'in' Christ and the Spirit has been reduced to a steady respectability for the sake of good order. Scriptures and short creeds begin to define doctrines and hymns express prayers more emotionally. Presbyter-bishops lead a small, peaceful and still obscure movement which hopes to spread widely with, or even without, the state's tolerance. Even in its infancy this Catholic Church has a character which is to lead to developments which would have astounded Tacitus or Suetonius, Nero or Pontius Pilate. This movement which called Jesus of Nazareth 'Lord', prayed to him and celebrated his 'grace', was to become the strongest source of religious and moral authority in the Roman empire and emperors were to revere his cross. Even within history there was to be what John of the Revelation imagined at the end of time: 'a great multitude which no one could count, from every nation, from all tribes and peoples and languages, standing before the Throne and before the Lamb'.

2

cnencnencn

Early Christians

A Variety of Teachers

LARGER numbers were now to enter the experience which in Clement's letter the Christians of Rome said they shared with the Christians of Corinth: 'life with immortality, splendour with righteousness, faith with assurance, self-control and holiness'. They were to enter it through 'Jesus Christ, the high priest of our worship and the protector of our weakness'.

These larger numbers included few Jews. Although many Jewish beliefs and traditions marked all Christianity permanently and a thoroughly Jewish kind of Christianity survived into the fourth century, the Jewish Christians who had been prominent in the New Testament were reduced to a remnant. One group survived in the east, beyond the Roman empire; another in Syria and Egypt. They had their own 'gospel according to the Hebrews' but of this only five fragments survive, quoted in other documents. In the absence of that authority it is impossible to know what most of them believed: it may have been close to what James the brother of Jesus believed. In the fourth century Eusebius thought that some of them denied the virgin birth of Jesus but others accepted it while denying that he had existed before his conception by the Holy Spirit. Eusebius knew that they were called Ebionites meaning 'poor' and he believed that the term was appropriate because of their 'poor and low opinions of Christ'.

Writing a little earlier than Eusebius, Origen quoted an Ebionite belief that Jesus had said that he had been 'taken by my mother the Holy Spirit by one of the hairs of my head'. Another poetic expression which could be ridiculed was a version of belief about the Trinity where the Son is 'the cup', the Father is 'he who was milked' and the Spirit is 'she who milked him'. That comes from the *Odes of Solomon*, a collection of 42 hymns rediscovered in 1905 which seems to voice the piety of some Jewish

Christians in their second or third century. One hymn says this about Jesus, and it is not merely quaint:

> His love for me brought low his greatness . . .
> He took my nature so that I might understand him,
> My face so that I should not turn away from him.

And the last of these hymns imagines 'the Just One hanged by the roadside' moving from his cross to join the dead and saying:

> They ran towards me, the dead . . .
> And I heard their voices and wrote my name on their heads,
> So they are free and they are mine.
> Alleluia!

Christian teaching became hostile to Judaism, as in the *Letter of Barnabas* which was probably written early in the second century. It was claimed that an evil spirit had inspired the Jews to misunderstand the purposes of God throughout their history. Their rejection of Jesus had been both stupid and wicked since the coming of a Messiah with his character had been predicted clearly in their own Scriptures. The destruction of their temple and nation had been punishment by God and richly deserved. Such arguments became familiar but failed to convince many Jews. Some of the passages in the Hebrew Bible quoted by the Christians depended on the Septuagint, a translation into Greek which was to be replaced by a more accurate version. Other passages were better understood in the context of the history of Israel, which was not entirely sinful: an example was the picture of the Suffering Servant of God in Isaiah 53. Some touches in the gospels (particularly Matthew's) had probably been added in order to claim that prophecies had been fulfilled. Above all, no prophecy had predicted a Messiah who would be crucified as a common criminal and then worshipped as in some sense divine.

Disputes about the meaning of the Hebrew Bible were usually futile since neither Christians nor Jews could enter with any sympathy into the experience of what had become another religion. On both sides anyone who wished to be loyal to both religions was regarded as a traitor. Bishop Ignatius of Antioch warned the Christians in the city of Magnesia: 'It is outrageous to utter the name of Jesus Christ and to live as a Jew.'

Near the beginning of the second century Ignatius did not hesitate to talk about Jesus as 'our God' whatever might be the objections of Jews. Normally he maintained the New Testament's usual distinction between Jesus and God: he did so in this letter to the Magnesians, writing that 'God is one and has revealed himself in his Son Jesus Christ, who is his Word issuing from the silence'. But he said that the zeal of the Christians in Ephesus had been aroused by 'God's blood' and when he begged the Christians in Rome not to try to prevent his own martyrdom he wrote: 'Let me imitate the suffering of my God.' He was not interested in offering any philosophical defence of such expressions, for the main thrust of his letters was a plea for Christians to unite and to stand firm under their leaders. Still less was he interested in finding common ground with Jews or with any others who did not share his faith. He was the first (so far as we know) to use the Greek word which was to be translated as 'Christianity' and he said that its greatness 'lies in its being hated by the world'. What he knew was where he wanted to go. 'I am God's wheat and I am ground by the teeth of wild beasts so that I may become Christ's pure loaf . . . Come fire, cross, a battle with wild beasts, the wrenching of bones, the mangling of limbs, the crushing of my whole body, the cruel tortures of the Devil—only let me get to Jesus Christ!' When he wrote that 'my Love is crucified' he meant not only that Jesus had died in that way but that his own human passions had died with Jesus. Paul had also said that, but Ignatius went beyond the more balanced Paul by saying plainly that he was 'in love with death'.

When more relaxed appeals not inviting 'hatred' were possible in less dramatic circumstances, Christianity's main partners in conversation were now not Jews but pagans, or more often people who were seeking reality in religion and not finding it either in official Judaism or in civic paganism. The great question was: what did such seekers have to believe in order to be Christians? If Christianity was no longer a Jewish sect, how far could it go as it left its Palestinian birthplace? Could it go on to speak about mysteries hitherto left to what Ignatius had called 'the silence'?

Answers were given by groups which spread their messages with claims that what they believed was what Jesus had taught in secret to the inner circle of his disciples. The gospel of Thomas, widely circulated in the second century, was rediscovered in Egypt in 1945. It is the most interesting of 52 religious writings which a camel-driver discovered in a jar buried near the village of Nag Hammadi. It collects 114 sayings, many of which are very different from those used by Mark, Luke and Matthew and different also from the discourses in John's gospel. Here Jesus speaks to individuals, and specially to women, about a life withdrawn from all the concerns of the world and the body, a life of spiritual ecstasy in union with a God more mysterious than the God of Israel. Many of these sayings would be riddles to the uninitiated but the community which was guided by them must have lived at a high level of spiritual intoxication and poetic expression.

A number of such spiritual movements have been grouped together under the name 'Gnostics' ('people in the know'). These were aimed at the select individual's mystical union with God, escaping from the world and the body. They flourished in the same atmosphere as the various 'mystery' cults which offered the experience of salvation to their initiates in private clubs, for it seems that in this period many people in the Roman empire had moved beyond official paganism because they no longer relied on the formal public worship which, mainly through the sacrifice of animals, petitioned divinities who personalized either the forces of nature or the strength of the city or the empire. But as we have noted, many Jews had also moved beyond the limits of their ancestral religion. It seems probable that there were also many people who rebelled against the official religion of the Persian empire. We do not know to what extent such movements which can be called 'Gnostic' were important before the arrival of Christianity. Many teachers had to be rebuked in the documents of Early Catholicism for falsely claiming 'knowledge' (as in 1 Timothy 6:20) but the sources of this river of religious excitement and imagination lie beyond the evidence which is now available. What we do know is that many Gnostics claimed to be Christians—and it was not always easy to say exactly where their teaching went beyond the use made by Paul or John of ideas which were in the air. Indeed, some modern scholars have claimed that Paul and John were themselves Gnostics. Certainly Paul often writes about the Christian's 'knowledge' of God or Christ, and John presents Christ as the Revealer who came from heaven and promised union with him and eternal life, but whether that makes them Gnostics depends on one's definition of that term. Often both Paul and John denied the Gnostic teaching that Christ did not suffer physically: a crucial point.

Some Gnostics were accused of indulging in orgies with the pretext that the body was now morally insignificant, perhaps adding that the soul had to taste every kind of experience before being liberated. However, such accusations were the standard practice in religious controversies in the ancient world and we need not be too troubled about them. What is really troublesome is to know what was essential in the teachings of these varied Christian-Gnostic movements with their orgy of myths and doctrines. Until the finds in Nag Hammadi most of the surviving evidence about these people consisted of attacks on them. But now it is possible to understand with more sympathy at least some of the ideas of these Gnostics who claimed to 'know' but were defeated.

They told stories about spectacular magic performed by Jesus even as a child, but much grander stories were developed in order to say how the world had come to be so unsatisfactory and to indicate the way of escape from its darkness. They began with a serious look at the self: was it entirely material, entirely mortal, entirely corrupted, or was it a stranger in the world? So did various philosophical movements of the time. Gnostics taught that the deep, true self could be freed by knowing its origin and therefore its potential. So did many other spiritual teachers, saying that the soul had been imprisoned in one body and would be imprisoned in another by reincarnation after death unless it could break free. Gnostics, however, imagined the journey of the human soul, descending from its divine origins and returning to them, in a wealth of mythology.

Mostly these myths said little about the ultimate Reality: it could be called Father or Mother but more appropriately Depth or Silence. It seemed more possible to picture the lesser divine realities ('aeons') emanating from that source. For Christians 'the Son' was in this category, but other names could be used: *Logos*, Mind, Wisdom. Somehow formless matter now emerged, to be shaped by a divine craftsman (the Demiurge) or by angels; and somehow souls were inserted into it. The scattered souls were now like lights flickering in a dark world, but more light was brought by an Illuminator or Saviour, whose name to devout Christians was of course Jesus. Some souls were predestined to listen to the message; in one text Jesus revealed to his disciples that they had originally been part of his own 'strength'. In order to be human Jesus had to use a body, but Christian Gnostics explained that this was scarcely physical. They welcomed both the unique birth from a virgin and the unique descent of the Spirit at the baptism but at least some of them believed that the spiritual Christ had left the human body before it was nailed to the cross. With this Illuminator the chosen few could ascend to the realm of light, if necessary passing through many incarnations; but the number of such souls was limited and for the rest there would be perpetual darkness. Many Gnostic myths were told about male and female 'aeons' in fertile couples but it was emphasized that at the end male and female would be one.

Gnostic teachers were attacked by the Catholic Church as depraved heretics, but men such as Basilides in Alexandria or Valentinus and Ptolemy in Italy were more ambitious intellectually than any contemporary Christian later reckoned orthodox. And many Christians were attracted, whether or not all these myths with their mysterious implications were fully understood. For many years most Christians in Alexandria, for example, seem to have been more or less Gnostics. The festival of the Epiphany, which spread widely, originated in Alexandria. It celebrated on the local New Year's Day the baptism when the heavenly Christ had descended into the body of the human Jesus. And as we shall see, when theologians who were orthodox Catholics at least in their own eyes began to teach powerfully in Alexandria their presentation of Christianity was to have Gnostic elements. The gospel of Thomas had claimed that Jesus had said: 'Cleave the wood, raise the stone, there am I.' At least the historian must record that for a time the influence of Gnosticism could be found in many places.

As the impact of the first wave of Gnosticism diminished, from about 250, a new wave was to arrive from Persia, started by a religious genius, Mani, who spread a 'gospel of light' improving on all earlier creeds including

Persia's Zoroastrian religion. Among the Manichees the enlightened 'elders' were extreme puritans and complete vegetarians. 'Hearers' could eat meat and have sexual relations at the cost of needing several more reincarnations before they became pure, but all non-believers were sent to hell. In North Africa Augustine, the greatest Christian theologian before the medieval Thomas Aquinas, was to be a Manichee 'hearer' for nine years. When the Roman empire became Catholic the Manichees were the only heretics considered so dangerous that they were automatically put to death; yet their ideas, so far from being exterminated, surfaced in two large medieval heresies, the Bogomils and the Cathars. In China, too, there were Manichees. However, in the Persian empire Mani was executed with great cruelty in 276 and the Roman emperor Diocletian issued an edict against his followers some twenty years later.

Another movement which was more spiritual and more exciting than Catholicism issued its challenge about AD 150. Montanus and two women companions, Prisca and Maximilla, claimed to be prophets of the Paraclete (the Holy Spirit), inspired to announce in the 'language of the Spirit' that the thousand-year reign of Christ was about to begin as the new Jerusalem descended on two villages in the interior of Asia Minor. Before its arrival great austerity was demanded, martyrdom was welcomed and condemnation by Catholic bishops was met by organizing a new network of churches. Montanism combined some of the heady atmosphere of Gnosticism with a revival of the excited spirit of the Revelation of John. Although its early prophecies were disappointed, it appealed not only to marginalized women and country folk but also to educated men such as Tertullian, North Africa's most influential theologian before Augustine—and not everyone will have been shocked when it was reported that a woman who was a Montanist prophet claimed that 'Christ came to me as a woman clad in a bright dress'. We hear of survivors of this movement being converted to Catholic orthodoxy as late as 867. And we shall meet Spirit-filled excitement of this sort again, for example in the Pentecostal churches of the twentieth century.

Some more conventional second-century Christian teachers looked less impressive than the Gnostics or the Montanists. Papias, for example, although the bishop of Hierapolis in Asia Minor, believed in the coming of a thousand years of Christ's kingdom on earth with a faith as simple as the faith of the untutored Montanist prophets. In a work now surviving only in fragments he recorded traditions (often dubious) about the authorship of the gospels already being read with official blessing—but he dangerously declared that he preferred 'the living voice' to transmit what the apostles had taught, ignoring the reality of many conflicting voices. The scholar-bishop Eusebius was later to reckon Papias 'a man of exceedingly small intelligence'.

In Rome, Hermas was a former slave and a failed businessman. In *The*

Shepherd he wrote down dreams in order to correct the presbyters of his church in whose hearts there was 'poison'. To his fellow laity he conveyed the offer of one last chance to repent. He, too, thought that the End was near: he saw the Church as a tower nearly completed. But meanwhile he and others had to cope with human problems arising out of the expectation that real Christians must live like angels. In one dream he was criticized for what he had been thinking when he had helped his former owner out of the river where she had been bathing. He was instructed to rebuke his wife who was a lying gossip and to live with her as brother and sister. He was reminded that his children were not yet believing Christians. But in a later dream he was kissed and fondled by beautiful virgins who turned out to be angels, unlike him. Remarkably, what he wrote was to be treated as Scripture by theologians of stature: Irenaeus, Tertullian and Origen.

The strongest mind among the Christians of this second century belonged to Justin, a Greek from Palestine who taught in Rome and died about 165. He composed an imaginary conversation with Trypho, a Jew, which displayed an unusual wish to enter into such a dialogue. He also related Christianity to the philosophy of the pagans. His detailed arguments would not have convinced either group. Jews were again told that God had punished them for not understanding the clear predictions of Christ in their Scriptures; in his wrath he had inspired the Romans to destroy Jerusalem. Pagans were told that their religion was the work of demons (a regular Jewish attitude). Any resemblance between it and Christianity was due to the demons' cunning ability to confuse. Plato's philosophy was better but this was because he had studied the books of Moses.

A more original theme in Justin's teaching developed the idea of the *Logos* in the prologue to John's gospel. For him as for John, the *Logos* was divine yet somehow distinct from 'God' and personal yet somehow wider than Jesus the man. Hebrew heroes (whom Justin called 'barbarians') such as Abraham and Elijah had been instructed by this *Logos*. So had Greeks such as Socrates and Plato who had lived 'according to reason': they, too, 'are Christians' and 'whatever things are rightly said among the teachers are the property of us Christians'. It was not that Justin accepted the whole of Platonism as Christian. On the contrary, his own intellectual pilgrimage was from Plato's teaching about the eternity of 'ideas' and 'forms' and the natural immortality of 'souls' to the Bible's teaching that souls and bodies depend for their existence on the Creator. But here was a suggestion that not everything in Greek philosophy was the work of demons: it was indebted not only to Moses but also to the *Logos*. Justin was, however, still not very clear about the status of the *Logos*: 'After God himself we worship and love the *Logos* who comes to us from the unbegotten and ineffable God', yet the

Logos is also 'another God', even 'the begotten God'. Here were seeds of the future in theology.

For the present Justin's ablest pupil was Tatian, an ardent young man who detected and scorned the ambiguities in this developing Catholicism. Justin had accepted much of the civilization of this age of the Antonine emperors, which was to seem the best of all civilizations to Edward Gibbon in the eighteenth century; but what Tatian saw of pagan Rome when not listening to Justin seemed to him sheer evil. Nor did he admire the philosophy derived from Athens. He wrote an angry book to denounce 'the Greeks' and went to live and teach outside the empire, in Mesopotamia. There he wrote an account of the life of Christ which merged the four approved gospels—and he wrote in Syriac, not Greek. According to a shocked Bishop Irenaeus, he also 'proclaimed marriage to be nothing but corruption and fornication'.

In the ultimate test Justin had much in common with Tatian. As a young man he had been a Platonist, until he had ceased to believe that souls could, if they tried hard enough, remember their pure life before birth. He became fascinated and persuaded by the belief of the Christian martyrs that if only they were faithful to the end they would be welcomed into heaven immediately after death. He was martyred himself together with six of his pupils.

Critics and Martyrs

It is easy to gain from Christian traditions the impression that the Roman empire always persecuted the Church on a large scale. In fact, before 250 such executions as took place were due to temporary measures or local demands. Numbers have been exaggerated: in the 240s Origen wrote that the empire's peace had been vitally important in Christianity's spread and that so far martyrs had been 'few'. The converting effects of the martyrdoms have also been exaggerated.

We have to try to understand why the Christians did not receive the toleration which the Romans extended to the Jews and seemed specially dangerous amid all the strange cults which the authorities disliked but did not persecute. People dissatisfied with conventional paganism found such cults exotic and therefore interesting but not too alarming. If they joined a cult they could claim the right to be left alone among the legally recognized *collegia*, clubs which met for religious or social purposes or for mutual help as primitive insurance societies. Why, then, was Christianity denied the status of a *religio licita*? Why did the authorities bother about it and why did the public raise the cry which Tertullian reported, 'Christians to the lion'?

The main factor seems to have been that the Church's refusal to allow its members to offer even token sacrifices to 'our gods' or to 'Caesar' suggested that it thought of itself as a state within the state, with its own king. That was not true of any other religion or philosophy in the empire: even the odd and troublesome Jews were identifiable as a race which had attempted to establish a state outside the empire and had been so completely defeated that they had made peace. In contrast, the Christians could be found almost anywhere. They did not riot but they might well be plotting. Their 'king', Jesus of Nazareth, had been a potential rebel: if he deserved execution, so did his followers. Moreover, the Church's membership, although not large, cut across the divisions into races, classes and sexes and its propaganda was both argumentative and popular: it therefore had a potential for growth which was alarming. At the same time this potentially dangerous conspiracy seemed easy to detect and suppress, for while the members of other cults were willing to offer the normal sacrifices when required, these Christians were told by their religion to refuse. A simple test could be applied and a refusal could justify the sentence of death.

People who did not share the worries of the authorities responsible for law and order had their own feelings which perhaps can be better understood now that many religious 'cults' have appeared in the modern world. In the ancient world this mysterious movement claimed to be morally superior. Christians were not joiners; one could not relax, drink and laugh with them. They seemed to be kill-joys, to criticize everything in the familiar world, to claim a monopoly of the truth while clearly talking nonsense, to think that they alone would enjoy life after death; and they were 'atheists', denying all existence to 'our gods'. They added to the irritation because they attracted some converts. One's friends in the street or at work might turn out to be involved in this strange business. One's own wife and children might be brainwashed by this propaganda and corrupted in their morals, destroying the unity and respectability of the family. Yet this small sect had, it seemed very clear, no right to make its arrogant claims. The reason why it kept strangers out of its meetings, or questioned their motives closely, might well be that it did not want what went on there to become known. The members of this secret society were widely rumoured to behave worse than the notorious devotees of Bacchus the god of wine, who at least were not hypocrites. A writer who defended Christianity, Minucius Felix, quoted a Roman scholar who was for a time tutor to a future emperor (Marcus Aurelius). This responsible scholar had alleged in writing that the Christians drank 'blood' but it was the blood of a murdered baby. They 'loved' each other but it was during drunken orgies, when incest was frequent in the 'shameless dark'. The evidence suggests that ordinary, decent people often approved the decision of the authorities to execute these anti-social, atheistic criminals. They also felt entitled to enjoy the public executions. It was fun to see how a preacher who was believed to have presided over cannibalism and incest met a lion who was truly noble, or to watch a young woman who had scorned the duties of a pagan marriage being tied in a net and gored by a maddened bull. Attractively, the vindication of respectability and piety was accompanied by the pleasures of sadism.

Even people who did not believe the more salacious rumours dear to the public did not waste much sympathy on the Christians. The philosopher Celsus wrote a whole book about them, *The True Doctrine* (about 175). He mocked their cult as a ridiculous superstition. The Christians' invitation was 'let no one educated, no one wise, no one sensible draw near!' Their aim was that children, perhaps allowed or even encouraged by their stupid mothers or by the slaves who were their servants, should escape from fathers and teachers and go to the shop of a cobbler or washerwoman 'that they may learn perfection'. God, said Celsus, exists in his changeless, infinitely superior, perfection and he listens to the prayers of such fools no more than to the croaking of frogs in a pond. Christian assemblies are like worms meeting in mud. Jesus deserved to be executed as a charlatan and the miracles recounted in the Christian scriptures were like the tricks of a magician. The stories that he had been born of a virgin and had risen physically from the dead were 'contrary to reason'. The claim that he was God come down to earth was 'most shameful'. To expect that a criminal would be the Judge was to 'babble'. 'Is it only now, after such a long time', Celsus asked, 'that God has remembered to judge humanity?' In fact Jesus was a bastard, the son of a soldier named Panthera and a country woman whose husband (a respectable carpenter) had thrown her out for adultery. He had learned his tricks while he and his mother had lived among the dregs of society in Egypt. If Christians are as moral as they claim to be, they ought to worship the unknowable God through the familiar gods (it 'makes no difference' which one is named) and they ought to support the empire to which they owe so much. They ought to be sensible and conform to what is customary—as Celsus did.

The medical writer Galen diagnosed a weakness in the mind. He regretted that Christians drew their faith from 'parables and miracles' since they were 'unable to follow any demonstration by argument'. This was a pity since their 'contempt of death and of its sequel' and their willingness to refrain from sex were 'obvious to us every day', so that by a coincidence they sometimes acted 'in the same way as those who practise philosophy'. The clever satirist Lucian knew that the Christians were charitable but presented them as the dupes of rogues, being themselves the dupes of an irrational faith. In the Romano-Greek world, 'faith' was not admired: it was for the stupid, or at least it was inferior to knowledge (as it was for Plato). Nor was 'humility' admired: it was for the weak. Chastity was admired in theory but, it seems, not often practised—at least not by young men. Compassion might be praised, most easily when it was shown by women, but charity was certainly not the best of all the virtues. To well-educated, rationally moral men such as Celsus, Galen or Lucian, proud of living in a civilization which was sophisticated and very powerful, these Christians seemed extremely odd. Perhaps laughter was the best answer but a few executions would help to stop the nonsense.

The records of a number of martyrdoms compiled and distributed by Christians show that officials of the empire could be reluctant to execute people merely because they were unpopular. The earliest account which has survived was an awe-struck document sent to a neighbouring church on behalf of the church of Smyrna, describing the arrest, trial and death of its bishop Polycarp, probably in 156. The circumstances were unusual: a crowd was already assembled and excited after the end of 'games' including the deaths of wild animals (and probably also of gladiators), the man accused was remarkably old and he was brought before the proconsul and the crowd in the arena instead of being challenged to offer a sacrifice. But the proconsul's interrogation, as remembered by the Christians, reveals mainly irritation at the old man's obstinacy in refusing to escape a painful death. He urged Polycarp to 'have respect to your age', to 'swear by the fortune of Caesar', to say 'away with the atheists!'—all in order to prove his innocence as a respectable subject of Rome, as other officials were to try to persuade Christians that offering a pinch of incense to an image of the emperor was a little thing. Even when the proconsul's patience had snapped and he had told Polycarp to 'curse Christ', he 'persisted' in his efforts to avoid an execution after hearing the old man's reply: 'For 86 years I have served him and he never did me any wrong. How can I blaspheme my king who saved me?' And even when it had to be announced to the baying mob that 'Polycarp has confessed to being a Christian', this proconsul refused to bring out a lion to kill him; the games, he said firmly, had been closed. Then Polycarp was burned (which was the legal punishment for magicians) and, when the fire failed to kill him quickly, despatched by a dagger.

About 110 a Roman governor (Pliny) wrote to an emperor (Trajan) asking how he ought to deal with Christians in a province which he had been sent to clean up after misgovernment. He had found that the infection of Christianity, presumably with 'the vices associated with their name', had spread into villages as well as towns. His speciality was finance and he had never been present when Christians were examined in Rome. Several had been brought before him but the torture of women *ministrae* (deacons) had failed to produce evidence of orgies. On the contrary, the members of this strange sect had admitted only to taking part in worship before work began on a

Sunday. They had met 'on a fixed day before sunrise', had heard Scriptures being read, had sung or said a hymn 'to Christ as a god', had taken an oath to do no harm and had dispersed peacefully. They had later reassembled to hold a harmless supper until the government had banned secret meetings. Some of those accused had denied belonging to this group; others had said that they had left it; all of these had sensibly offered incense and a little wine to an image of the emperor. Those who were guilty of 'inflexible obstinacy' had been either executed or, if citizens, sent for trial in Rome. Pliny now asked whether merely being a Christian was a crime. The emperor did not answer that question directly but Pliny's executions of self-confessed Christians were not criticized. What interested Trajan, as being in keeping with the enlightened spirit of 'our time' and the dignity of imperial justice, was ordering that Christians were not to be sought out, that anonymous charges should not be heard and that those who abandoned Christianity should be pardoned for the folly they had renounced.

These responses were recorded and, it seems, regarded as the law for more than a hundred years. So Christians were in theory now free to worship together provided that they did not do so provocatively. On the other hand, at any moment a Christian could be properly accused, arrested and executed if he or she refused to worship 'our gods'. A protest survives from Athenagoras of Athens: since the rumours about the Christians are false and 'names do not deserve hatred', and since they are very far from being atheists, a just emperor should not allow them to be punished. But it may be doubted whether any emperor of this period read any Christian literature. Marcus Aurelius, to whom Athenagoras appealed, made one reference to the Christians in his *Meditations*. While he approved of a dignified suicide in an appropriate situation, he could not praise the Christians' 'theatrical obstinacy'. Although he was a great reader who used to take a book with him when he felt obliged to attend the cruel games which delighted his subjects, it is not likely that he studied the gospel for martyrs written by another man named Mark.

The word 'martyr' comes from the Greek for 'witness'. Their fellow Christians treasured detailed accounts of their courage, defying fear, torture and death in agony, and they celebrated the day of a martyr's death as his or her 'birthday' into the life of heaven. This was the beginning of what was to develop into the Church's great emphasis on the 'communion of saints'— and because these dates added to the celebration of Easter, it was also the beginning of the Church's crowded calendar. If we ask what particularly impressed the Christians, the evidence suggests three answers. The willingness of men and women to suffer every kind of humiliation and torture because of their faith suggested that they were not degenerate and depraved people addicted to the grossest sensuality. The nearness to Christ and to

49

heaven which the martyrs proclaimed amid their sufferings showed that the Christian religion was concerned with nothing less than eternity. And the refusal to compromise when accused was an advertisement for a religious loyalty which was very rare in that world. The custom was to treat a god or goddess as a patron who was honoured in a particular situation but who was by no means the only divinity in the world. Even those involved in the emotionally intense mystery religions were willing to take part in other cults. For the time being an emperor might be honoured as somehow a god but he could quite easily be displaced in one of the frequent civil wars or coups.

The records which the Christians kept of these martyrdoms described hatred, contempt and gloating over pain and death as the usual reactions among the spectators. That was the case when 48 Christians were put to death in the amphitheatres of Vienne and Lyon in southern Gaul, in AD 177 when Marcus Aurelius was emperor. The victims included an aged bishop but also a slave girl, Blandina, who was tortured in public on successive days: flogged, tied to a stake amid wild beasts, chained to an iron chair over a fire and finally gored by a bull. She kept on saying 'I am a Christian and we do nothing wrong'. In 202 five Christians were subjected to similar treatment in Carthage. They included Perpetua, a young mother, and her slave Felicitas. In prison Perpetua kept a diary, the earliest writing by a Christian woman to have survived. She defied her pagan father who begged her to save her life but was encouraged by a dream telling her that her prayers had helped a dead brother: years later, this was to be quoted in defence of the practice of praying for the dead. When a gaoler asked sneeringly how a weak woman expected to cope with the wild beasts in the arena, she replied: 'Another will be in me and will suffer for me and I shall be suffering for him.'

The evidence does not support the idea that many spectators were converted on the spot. But the report about the martyrs in Gaul says that some Christians who had at first denied their faith were shamed by the heroism of the martyrs into sharing their deaths. It also seems significant that the persecution was not prolonged: the scholarly bishop Irenaeus was elected to take the place of the martyred Pothinus in Lyon and had the leisure for theological activity. The story of Perpetua says that her gaoler, a tough soldier, was so impressed by the *virtus*, the true manliness, in her that 'he believed'. There was truth in Tertullian's boast that 'the blood of Christians is seed'.

Catholicism Takes Shape

Neither the argumentative defences offered by the few Christians who were writers, nor the dramatic advertisements provided at such cost by the martyrs, would have been enough to make the Church more truly universal, or even to make sure that it survived as one cult in an empire swirling with cults. But two decisive steps were taken.

One was to reach agreement about the new Scriptures which should be placed alongside the Hebrew Bible and read during worship in the Catholic Church. A document which was included in that category, 2 Peter, already referred to Paul's letters as scriptural (although also as in parts hard to understand). It was probably written early in the second century. The *Didache* began with an exposition of 'the way of life' based on Matthew's gospel (probably also Syrian) and there may be quotations from Matthew, Luke and John in the letters of Ignatius, who clearly refers to the letters of Paul. The famous four gospels and the letters ascribed to Paul apart from Hebrews seem to have been generally accepted by the end of the second century but there was no agreement about other books later included in the New Testament, and some books not so included were authorized in the earliest surviving list, compiled probably in Rome in about 200. This list seems to have been provoked by the demand of a bishop's son and wealthy ship owner, Marcion, who was something of a Gnostic, that the Hebrew Bible should be rejected totally. Approval should be given only to censored versions of Luke's gospel and of ten of Paul's letters. When excommunicated in Rome in 144, Marcion founded churches which spread this version of Bible-based Christianity widely and the decision against him did not halt the manufacture and circulation of other Scriptures elsewhere. Eventually the whole of what became known as the New Testament was agreed, although the earliest surviving list of contents in the form that proved permanent dates from no earlier than 369 and was blessed by a council of bishops in Rome twenty years later. Thus it is in keeping with the historical facts about the emergence of the 'canon' of the New Testament to say that the Christian Bible is the Church's book; in Greek a *canon* is a rule and it was the Catholic Church that gradually made the rule about the New Testament's contents. But it is also true to the facts to say that the Church intended to be ruled by Scripture. The contents were selected not because they were thought to be interesting but because they were believed to be the Word of God.

Catholic bishops now had a Bible with agreed contents to which they could appeal—and, in another vitally important development, those who replied that the Bible still needed interpretation could be told that the bishops themselves were authoritative as spokesmen of churches which had remained loyal to the apostles' teaching.

The leaders who gained the exclusive right to the title of *episkopos* seem to have emerged from the ranks of the presbyters at different paces in different churches. Very little evidence about the process has survived but it seems reasonable to suppose that much depended on local personalities and circumstances. We do know that in the first half of the second Christian century first Ignatius of Antioch and then Polycarp of Smyrna were dominant bishops in their part of the world. Ignatius told the church in Smyrna that 'nothing to do with the church should be done without the bishop's approval'. Polycarp and four other bishops are mentioned in his surviving letters and he could tell the church in Ephesus that similar leaders had been appointed 'all over the world'. But this seems to have been a rhetorical flourish, for he mentioned no bishop in his letter to Rome and as we have noted the letter to Corinth from that church does not suggest that there was a bishop in the Ignatian sense in either place. Hermas speaks of bishops and presbyters as one group and Justin mentions only a 'president' of the presbyters. It seems that the church in Rome was so conservative that it kept this New Testament pattern for its clergy for years after the development of Ignatian-style bishops in Asia Minor, although of course it is probable that at any one time one of the presbyter-bishops (for example Clement) was specially gifted and respected. It also appears from the letters of Ignatius that the insistence on one bishop's right to run a church was a recent development which people had to be urged to accept. It has been suggested that the development occurred in Asia Minor precisely because Christians including Ignatius were being martyred there. A rule about who could make the decisions would have been specially necessary in this emergency, to answer the obvious questions: what compromises with a hostile government and public were legitimate, how should those who made excessive compromises be treated, what should happen when one or more of the presbyters had been executed? But Ignatius did not explain the origins of this office of 'bishop' in his surviving letters. In many ways bishops continued the work of the apostles to be met in the New Testament, but there was as yet no clarification of the claim that they inherited the apostles' authority. Ignatius told the church in Tralles that the bishop represented God and should be obeyed 'as if he were Jesus Christ' but also that 'the presbyters are like God's council, an apostolic band', and that 'the deacons represent Jesus Christ'. Clearly his chief concern was for unity around the clergy in a time of danger: as he wrote to the church in Magnesia, 'You must have one prayer, one petition, one mind, one hope, dominated by love and unsullied joy—and that means that you must have Jesus Christ.' It also meant that they must have one bishop.

It seems that the practice of having Ignatian-style bishops in at least the main Christian centres spread during the second century; there is definite evidence of such a bishop in Rome from the 140s. Lists began to be compiled of these bishops, going back if possible—or even if impossible—to an apostle or a companion of the apostles. Mark, for example, was said to have been the first bishop of Alexandria. But it seems that the third century had come before a bishop could control all the Christians in that city or ordain bishops for other towns in Egypt. It is probable that when Demetrius of Alexandria died in 231 he was the only bishop in Egypt. Later there were so many bishops in Egypt and in other countries around the Mediterranean that it seems clear that often they controlled church life in no more than a small market town and its rural neighbourhood. The big 'diocese' came later, in northern Europe where the social unit was the tribe under its king or chief.

Being able to turn to a bishop for a decision was also useful in conflicts over 'heresy'. This was a worry for Ignatius, who had to deal with the belief that Christ had only appeared to be human and in particular had not really suffered on the cross (Docetism). He hoped to dispose of that idea by asking why, in that case, he himself was about to be killed by the wild beasts for the entertainment of Rome. Later bishops had to produce longer arguments.

In the last two decades of the second Christian century Bishop Irenaeus used almost the whole of the New Testament as he defended the Catholic rule of faith against all heresies, Ebionite as well as Gnostic or Docetic. He rejoiced that the Church was by God's grace the teacher of humanity. 'Where the Church is there is the Spirit of God and where the Spirit of God is there is the Church and all grace.' He also rejoiced that 'the tradition of the apostles, made clear in all the world, can be seen in every church by those who wish to behold the truth'. He celebrated in particular the loyalty of the Roman church to the teaching of Peter and Paul whom he described (wrongly) as its founders; and he listed a dozen of its faithful bishops. He came from Asia Minor and as a boy he had been impressed by Polycarp who used to say that he had been 'taught by apostles' and had 'talked with many who had seen Christ'. Basing himself on that proud tradition, he developed it cautiously. The Son and the Spirit were like the Father's two hands in the work of creation. All humanity was present both in Adam who first sinned and in the fully human Christ who saved from sin. The Hebrew Bible, with its affirmation of the goodness of creation, is to be retained whatever the Gnostics may say. Since the 'image of God' has now been restored in Man it is to be hoped that all will be brought to the final glory. When that comes (but there is no promise that it will come quickly) the glory will include the resurrection of the flesh and a new earth. Thus in the teaching of Irenaeus an ecclesiastical conservatism was combined with cosmic optimism. 'The glory of God', he affirmed, 'is a human being come alive'—and the tradition of the Catholic Church has to be preserved because it alone proclaims the promise of this glory. A bishop can be the reliable spokesman of a church which is faithful to this great tradition.

Bishops now held office for life, an arrangement for which there was no parallel in pagan religion. *The Apostolic Tradition* (about 215) taught that they alone ordained presbyters and deacons (although presbyters joined them in the ordination of a fellow presbyter, to signify their assent) and that new bishops were ordained only by bishops (to signify their unity as Catholics). Once ordained, Catholic bishops did what they could to keep in touch with one another by letters, visits or synods (meetings). A tomb of a bishop in Asia Minor who probably lived in this third century records that he travelled west to Rome and east beyond the Euphrates and 'everywhere' met fellow Christians. The leadership was now firm and could exercise financial control: bishops were entrusted with endowments and were expected to run considerable charities with the assistance of the deacons, but a part of a church's income, as calculated each month, was reserved for the bishops themselves and for the clergy under them. In Rome in 251 the Christians supported more than fifty full-time clergy (assisted by more than a hundred lesser ministers such as exorcists who were unpaid) and more than 1,500 widows and other needy folk. Although the city's total population was about a million, this was an organization with a future.

But on the whole its stronger organization did not make the Catholic Church more narrow-minded. Precisely because they now had a clearer authority, bishops could be generous with absolutions as well as with salaries and gifts. Christians who had yielded to the temptations which had worried Hermas could receive more comfort than he had thought possible. Even Christians who had compromised in order to avoid or postpone martyrdom need not be excluded forever from the Eucharist or from heaven. A Syrian manual of advice to bishops, *Didascalia*, shows that in serious cases the penance imposed was a period of fasting in exclusion from the Eucharist, but it was for the bishop to decide how long this period must be. In Rome a theologian who held a rigorist position, Hippolytus (almost certainly the author of *The Apostolic Tradition*), was not elected bishop. The honour went to a former slave convicted of fraud in his business dealings, Callistus, who promised to be merciful to sinners. Hippolytus set up his own church as history's first antipope, but the Catholic combination of discipline and compassion proved too strong for his attempt to restore the old exclusive puritanism.

During its third century Christianity became more popular in this Catholic shape. From this period there is definite and widespread evidence of the baptism of the children of Christian parents and of courses to educate them (for all attended pagan schools). Adults seeking baptism (preferably by the bishop at Easter) were usually, but not always, required to wait two or three years for instruction. Solemn questions were being asked as candidates finally declared their faith in Father, Son and Spirit, standing naked in the water according to Hippolytus. The questions were being standardized; those now being asked in Rome formed the basis of what was to be called the Apostles' Creed. (That confession of faith is known to us in approximately its present form in a letter written about 340 and was first connected with the apostles in a letter written not much later.) Other ceremonies of baptism included exorcisms driving out devils, anointing as the sign of dignity, clothing in clean robes as signs of a new life, kisses of welcome and the tasting of wine and honey as symbols of the promised land. Christians were expected to attend the Eucharist every Sunday, taking away some of the consecrated bread (presumably for devout consumption on weekdays); to fast on bread and water every Wednesday and Friday; and to pray at least three, and preferably seven, times a day, standing up with arms outstretched like Christ on the cross. Hippolytus urged Christians to pray at midnight and to arise at cock-crow. At least in the better organized churches the clergy met every morning, weekday services made instruction in the Bible and doctrine available, and in the evening, when the lamps were lit ceremonially, prayers gave thanks for the blessings of salvation and of the day; but there was as yet no daily Eucharist. Although the *agape* or 'love feast' was no longer held regularly after the Eucharist, the bishop often presided at hymn-singing suppers for the congregation. Although any involvement of women in church leadership had also lapsed, deaconesses were now appointed to minister to women (particularly when being baptized in the nude) and were recruited from the church-supported elderly widows.

In the middle of their second century Aristeides of Athens wrote an account of the lives of his fellow Christians which does much to explain why increasing numbers wished to join these congregations. It took the form of an *Apology* addressed to the emperor and was rediscovered in a Syriac version in 1889. His theme was that 'truly this people is a new people and there is something divine mingled with it'. He described a group with an intense love between its own members: when one needs food, the others who are almost equally poor will 'fast two or three days' in order to provide it. They live quietly and 'do not proclaim their good deeds in the ears of the multitude', but they 'comfort those who wrong them and make friends of them'. Evidently Aristeides was fully aware of the difficulty in communication between this small and often maligned group and the pagan world around them, so majestic in Athens, but one feature of his description of the attitudes of these Christians surprises almost everyone who reads his *Apology* expecting something very like modern (or postmodern) Christianity. He says that 'when any righteous person of their number passes away from the world they rejoice and give thanks to God, and they follow the body as if the movement were only from one place to another'. When an infant dies, 'they praise God mightily as for one who has passed through the world without sins'. Such were their standards of behaviour because this was their faith: 'They labour to become righteous as those who expect to see their Messiah and to receive with great glory what has been promised to them.'

An anonymous *Letter to Diognetus* survives from about the same period. It was probably also written in Athens and addressed to the philosopher of that name who taught Marcus Aurelius. Unlike Aristeides this writer emphasizes that his fellow Christians 'do not dwell in cities of their own, or use a different language, or practise a peculiar style of life'. Yet he goes on to say that their lifestyle is indeed 'wonderful' because 'their citizenship is in heaven'. 'They obey the established laws and in their own lives they surpass all laws.' 'What the soul is in the body, Christians are in the world . . . The soul dwells in the body but it is not of the body; Christians dwell in the world but are not of the world.' And the writer asks whether it is right that these people who 'love all' should be 'persecuted by all'.

The Christians maintained that their refusal to conform to pagan habits was dictated not by a 'hatred of humanity' as Tacitus and others alleged, but by an exalted view of the dignity of every human life. Thus proper Christians did not use abortion, did not expose unwanted babies (specially girls) to die, or corrupt boys, or smile when men got girls into trouble, or ignore orphans and widows, or ill-treat slaves, or join the crowds watching people or animals die in the arena, or go to the theatres where the entertainments were often pornographic, or waste money needed by families on perfumes, jewels and feasts. Volunteering for military service, or killing during it, was forbidden although some Christians served as conscripts or police. If they were compelled to serve in local government they were expected not to come to church during any period when they had to be present at pagan sacrifices. Although they traded alongside pagans, with perpetual problems of conscience about the inevitable contacts with idolatry, they were expected to be more than averagely honest. Although they mixed with their pagan neighbours (how else could they convert them?), they had problems about eating meat sacrificed in the temples and they embarrassed easy-going neighbours. They were indeed 'a new people'.

Evidence of the quiet joy of these Christians as their second century became their third has survived in the catacombs of Rome. In these underground burial chambers we find none of the gloomy fatalism of many pagan tombs. A few brief inscriptions on the walls refer to the 'peace' and 'refreshment' of the dead and the folk art indicates the victory of Christ. His horrific crucifixion is not shown: he is the good shepherd, the calm teacher, the young hero in images borrowed from pagan art: he is handsome and beardless like the most attractive of the male gods, Apollo. Pagan myths as well as the Old Testament are used to illustrate the triumph of good over evil, of life over death. However, little crosses scratched in the cement indicate the new source of hope. Many pictures allude to baptism and to the Eucharist, which Ignatius as he confronted death had called 'medicine for immortality'.

Christians would sometimes meet for worship underground since there was no need to avoid the bones of the dead who were now 'in light'. But the living Church normally met in ordinary houses, now often being adapted for larger numbers, and some special halls were being built as city churches, although simply and inconspicuously. Christianity was still mainly an urban religion, as it had been in Paul's day. Between the cities was a countryside still pagan or almost entirely so. One reason was that the Church was still mainly Greek-speaking, even in Rome until the middle of the third century. But this religion which had been rejected by most of the Jews, and reckoned criminal by the authorities of the empire, was spreading through personal contacts. It seems that the joy of the Christians, maintained even as they buried their dead, was winning hidden victories despite all the rumours and suspicions.

The Eucharist was, it seems, predominantly still a service of thanksgiving which united these Christians in joyful communion with their Lord, who could say to them as is said in the Revelation of John: 'I was dead and behold I am alive for ever and ever!' In *The Apostolic Tradition* we may notice the absence of emphasis on features which were to dominate the Mass later in Rome: there is nothing which might be seen as a re-enactment of Christ's death, no stress on his sacrifice as the propitiation taking away the Father's wrath against sin (but he 'took away the chains of the devil'), no exclusive formality about the offering of bread and wine (cheese and olives could also be brought up and blessed as symbols of God's good creation), no detailed intercession for the living or the dead, no commemoration of named saints. We cannot be sure how typical was the order of service set out in this *Tradition*, for until the seventh century there was no standard set of words for Catholics in the west (and even then the standardization was not complete), so that possibly other Eucharists were more or less different. But the atmosphere in this simple act of worship is one with the atmosphere in the catacombs, for here is a celebration that Christ is the Conqueror. 'Lift up your hearts!' says the president of the Eucharist and the people are given to drink not only the wine meaning blood but also honey-flavoured milk meaning Paradise. That is remarkable when we reflect that many impressive monuments in Rome commemorated the conquests made by this vast empire where Christianity was illegal, where Christ had been crucified.

Both Hippolytus and the true bishop of Rome, Pontian, died as prisoners set to work in the salt mines of Sardinia. It seems that they were reconciled before they died shortly after Pontian's resignation in 235 and that their bones were brought back to Rome together. It was a kind of triumph.

Progress

Third-century Christianity now expanded to west and east. This was the time when churches spread into Gaul, Spain and North Africa. There were some Christians among the pagans in Germany and by the beginning of the fourth century there were three bishops in remote Britain. Between Jerusalem and Damascus, Bostra was a centre of vigorous church life. In Dura-Europos on the Euphrates (the empire's frontier) the Christians found that the room they had been using was too small and in the 240s two rooms were joined, to hold about sixty. Beyond the empire to the east a king in Edessa, Abgar, at least sympathized with the Church. At his court an eloquent teacher and hymn-writer, Bardaisan, resisted the Gnostic denial of a good Creator. In Edessa something was known about Asia as well as about the empires of Rome and Persia and Bardaisan wrote a little book about the laws and customs of this vast area, while stressing the superiority of 'the law of the Messiah'. That law called for perfection and it was, it seems, in this region that Christian men and women seeking perfection were expected to live together without sex. (But marriage was regarded by most Christians of this time as a contract after consent not needing a wedding service and its normal consequences were usually blessed.) And from the east Christian influences came into the empire. One emperor, Philip the Arab, was rumoured to be a Christian and a predecessor was said to have kept a statue of Jesus with other divine heroes in his private chapel. This emperor (Alexander Severus) had used a Christian scholar, Julius Africanus, to organize a public library. In a history of the world, based on the Bible, this scholar worked out that the Church would have as many as 300 years ahead of it before the Lord returned. They might be good years. The Church's appeal at this time when many were looking for the renewal of religion can be summed up in some words of Hippolytus: 'He who was from the beginning appeared new and was found to be old, and is born young in the hearts of his saints.'

The opportunity for this expansion was provided largely by the confused condition of the empire. Marcus Aurelius, who died on campaign in 180, is commonly regarded by historians as the last of the 'good' emperors. After the assassination of Alexander Severus the years 235–270 were a time of troubles. Barbarians from across the Danube and Persians invaded; there was a recession in trade; inflation soared; the currency was devalued; there were severe epidemics; civil wars were waged between armies demanding payment through heavy taxes. In their distress many people turned to the old gods, but inevitably the prestige of the empire and the prosperity of its cities, including the temples, could not remain at the old levels. It was no coincidence that when Philostratus wrote a biography of a first-century pagan saint, Apollonius of Tyana, he made him look somewhat like Jesus. He related that after a miraculous birth and a visit to India, Apollonius had performed many miracles of healing. He had wandered around accompanied by disciples and had been a stern reformer of a slack religion, stressing morality and refusing to be present at sacrifices of animals. Pagan priests had persecuted him but the saintly hero had escaped from the emperor's court and later from prison, to vanish into a choir of angels escorting him to heaven. It was also significant that this biography was written at the command of Julia Domna, now the wife of a Roman emperor but the daughter of an hereditary prince-priest in the east. She encouraged the spread of eastern cults which marked this troubled period. But no major reformer now renewed traditional paganism.

Another light on this age is shed by what little survives of the attacks on Christianity made by Porphyry, the disciple and biographer of the great Platonic philosopher Plotinus. His master had, it seems, scarcely mentioned Christianity in public: it was beneath a philosopher's notice. But Porphyry thought that the movement had spread so widely that a long refutation was needed. He repeated some points made by Celsus but took the whole subject much more seriously. He reckoned that Jesus was more than a magician. Although not divine (how could a god undergo a human birth?) he was a wise man, 'pre-eminent in piety', on whom the gods had been pleased to bestow immortality. Porphyry had far less respect for the Christians but took care to concentrate his attack not on accusations about their morals but on their claim that their Bible was completely true and from beginning to end a witness to Christ. He criticized in particular their use of the Hebrew Scriptures. And when he criticized their doctrines, he did not ridicule them as Celsus had done. His main point seems to have been that Christians were wrong to claim that theirs was the 'universal' religion, true and apt for everyone. No religion could claim that, although each in its own way pointed to the One about whom (or which) Plotinus had taught. And when Christianity became the empire's official religion, both Celsus and Porphyry received what was in a sense a tribute: their anti-Christian books were ordered to be burned, so that they are now known only through the passages quoted by two great Christian theologians, Origen and Augustine, who replied.

The religious confusion in the empire grew. One religion was the worship of the Persian sun god Mithras, who had slain a bull symbolizing Darkness. From the carcass had sprung a vine and corn and adherents could be initiated into communion with the divine conqueror by being soaked in the blood of a bull slaughtered on top of them. Women could turn not to that exclusively masculine cult but to the worship of the fertile Mother Goddess under one or other of her many names. The emperor Aurelian did what he could to popularize a religion in which everyone could join, the cult of *Sol Invictus*, the Unconquered Sun—although in 275 he did not escape being killed. That was the fate of fifteen emperors (all except three) after the death of Marcus Aurelius. To people who worried about the future of an empire which had been thought eternal, it could seem that faith in the empire's gods was not in good health.

However, the Church's progress was far from smooth. In the early years of its third century there were a number of martyrdoms due to local demands. Then in 249 Decius, who was temporarily the emperor after killing Philip the Arab, ordered the first systematic persecution of those who refused to sacrifice to 'our gods': they were now to be sought out instead of waiting for accusations. His edict did not name the Christians but those who carried it out concentrated on arresting the bishops. When Decius had been killed in battle by the Goths the persecution was continued by his successor and then by Valerian, who for the first time made it a capital offence to attend a Christian meeting. He ended up by being an embalmed corpse exhibited in a Persian temple. Then in 261 his son and heir assured the bishops (who were thus for the first time recognized by the government) that they were safe to resume their leadership of Christian worship and their ownership of cemeteries. Christianity had become a *religio licita*.

The persecution had killed fewer than had been intended. There had not been time to organize the entire empire or to make sure of ruthless efficiency: Dionysius of Alexandria had been arrested but rescued from the soldiers when asleep at night by men, presumably fellow Christians, who had heard of his plight while at a wedding party. Another factor was that thousands including bishops had abandoned Christianity: some certificates (*libelli*) of their willingness to sacrifice to 'our gods' have survived. But some deaths had been very moving. In Rome the bishop (Fabian) and his entire staff of deacons remained faithful unto death. In Smyrna the bishop was among those who lapsed, but a presbyter, Pionius, was given the opportunity to speak up in defence of Christianity: his replies interested people more than usual because they knew he was about to be martyred. The more lasting damage was done by the renewal of the disputes between Christians who did, and those who did not, believe that God and the Church could forgive and reinstate clergy and laity who had betrayed Christ as 'apostates'. Novatian, a Roman presbyter who believed that no mercy should be shown to Christians who had lapsed, set up a church for puritans as Hippolytus had done. In North Africa, where Christianity had made dramatic progress, two remarkable men became involved in the controversies arising from this systematic persecution or from the earlier, more local executions.

Tertullian used a fine education and a trained eloquence to attack many evils in the empire. 'What has Athens to do with Jerusalem, the Academy with the Church?' 'Why do we need curiosity when we have Jesus Christ?' He denounced fashionable dress (young Christian women ought to wear veils out of doors) and fashionable ideas (the newly popular practice of baptizing infants was nonsense). The Christian life must be distinct, redeemed by a sinless Saviour, purified by the Holy Spirit. The Christian faith must be expressed clearly and believed firmly. He used legal terms, although there is no definite evidence that he had been a lawyer. God is Judge; the sins of Adam and his descendants are crimes; the just penalty is death; virtuous actions are needed if justice is to be satisfied; only the Saviour is sufficiently virtuous to pay the appropriate penalty. The first to write theology in Latin, he invented not only the term *trinitas* but also the trinitarian use of Latin words with a great future. Father, Son and Spirit are three *personae* and because they all possess the *substantia* of divinity they are all *Deus*, God without qualification. It may be relevant that in Roman law *substantia* meant property which might be owned by *personae* as a group.

His books give us glimpses of a community where physical actions are the signs of a spiritual union with God the Son. He insists on baptism (of converted adults). 'We are little fishes called after our great fish Jesus Christ' because in Greek *ichthus* (fish) is an acrostic referring to Jesus Christ, God's Son and our Saviour: 'We are born in water and can survive only by staying in water.' 'Is it not a marvel that death is washed away by bathing?' Yes, but baptism is indeed 'the abolition of sins which faith secures when sealed in the Father and the Son and the Holy Spirit'—and the fact that the baptized receive the Spirit is now brought out in a separate service ('confirmation') when the bishop anoints and lays his hand on the head with a prayer. Tertullian mentions the Eucharist of the baptized at 'meetings before dawn', including the reading and preaching of the Bible and among the prayers 'offerings for the dead as birthday celebrations on their anniversaries'. 'We think it wrong', he explains, 'to fast, or kneel in worship, on the Lord's day' or between Easter and Pentecost. He writes: 'At every new movement or action, on entering or leaving the house, getting dressed, putting on shoes, having a bath, beginning a meal, lighting the lamps, going to bed, sitting down—in fact, in all the activities of daily life—we make the sign of the cross on our foreheads.' But we may doubt whether every Christian made this sign quite so often as Tertullian claimed.

Beneath his pride in describing the life of the Christians, and beneath his unfaltering eloquence, may be seen a change of mind as to whether the Church was meant to be Catholic or a pure sect. For long he wrote with the assurance of a Catholic, denouncing heretics, demanding that the Bible should be treated as the Church's book, extolling the authority of the clergy. He could argue that the gospel ought to have a universal appeal: 'the soul is naturally Christian' because almost everyone believes that God exists and if the truth is known about the life of the Christians it ought to be known that God has been revealed. He could believe that the emperor Tiberius had reported the resurrection of Jesus to the senate in Rome, having been informed by Pontius Pilate. And he could boast about the Church's popularity: 'We began only yesterday and we have filled everything you have—cities, tenements, forts, towns, markets, camps, tribes, palace, senate, forum.' But having become a Christian as an adult, he became unsure about the conversions of others. He grew impatient with the laxity of the Catholic bishops and joined the Spirit-filled Montanists who awaited the coming of the new Jerusalem and the perfect Church. He then maintained that 'not to expel sinners from the Church is to agree to expel the Holy Spirit' and he contended that in the absence of the clergy the laity could 'offer' the Eucharist. He could defend doctrines such as the incarnation or the resurrection in a style which gloried in their demonstration of the limits of human reasoning: such super miracles are 'credible because impossible, certain because absurd'. He wrote a book about marriage and dedicated it to his wife, but gave higher praise to the Christians whose moral strength enabled them to remain virgins. He died in his bed and in his sixties (not long after 220) but devoted his richest eloquence to the celebration of the heroism of the martyrs.

In the 250s Cyprian was the senior bishop in North Africa, as bishop of Carthage. He was said to read Tertullian, 'the Master', every day but his own preoccupations were consistently Catholic and disciplinary: he showed no uncertainty.

Before his acceptance of baptism and a bishopric he had seemed destined for high office in the state and his sense of order did not desert him now that he was a Christian leader. 'A person cannot have God as Father', he wrote, 'unless he has the Church as Mother'—and he knew what he meant by 'the Church'. The Church meant Christians under bishops. He fought to save the right of bishops to forgive sinners after due 'penance'. He fought to retain the authority of bishops even when 'confessors' who had remained faithful under trial, but had escaped death, were handing out certificates of forgiveness to the lapsed, arguing that their own courage compensated for the weakness of the fearful. He fought to defend the bishops' united policy: thus he criticized Bishop Stephen of Rome who went so far as to readmit lapsed clergy and to accept the baptisms of Christians previously not in communion with Catholic bishops. To Cyprian the sacraments of heretics were not valid but demonic: 'No heretic or schismatic whatsoever has any power or rights at all.' If a bishop of Rome did not agree he could be reminded that while 'Christ builds the Church upon one man in order to signify unity . . . the rest of the apostles were the same as Peter was, endowed with an equal share of honour and power'. True sacraments were presided over or authorized by the Catholic bishop, called by Cyprian with great emphasis 'the high priest'. True bishops must preach the true faith and administer the agreed discipline—and be ready for a martyr's death, as he was when it came, under the emperor Valerian.

Despite such examples of heroism under persecution, by the 270s the Church in Egypt seemed so worldly that a young farmer, Antony, withdrew into the desert: he had heard a priest read out the command of Jesus that 'if you will be perfect go, sell all you have and give to the poor and come, follow me'. In the desert he could be alone with God, praying and fasting. But he had misjudged many of his fellow Christians, for many went to see him, even to join him; and he taught them when he had emerged purified by years of isolation. Before his death in extreme old age he had become so respectable that a great bishop of Alexandria, Athanasius, wrote a biography which further increased his influence. And he was more than respectable: the prayer that he practised as he grew in holiness was called the 'prayer of fire' and the flame spread to many other 'desert fathers' under the burning sun. Many who went into the desert to pray and to seek perfection through self-discipline were women and it says much about the society they had left behind that many of the stories about them begin with a future spiritual mother (*amma*) being a prostitute. But in the 320s another Egyptian, Pachomius, who had been a soldier, was to offer an alternative to Antony's own life as an illiterate, extremely ascetic, always praying and fasting hermit. By the banks of the Nile he founded monasteries where hundreds of monks were to live together. They had to be able to read, to be sensibly restrained in their self-denial and to be willing to work with their hands. They were strictly organized, high walls were built to keep out unwelcome visitors and obviously women would be safer in such communities. However, in the next century bandits and raiders made the desert so unsafe that many of these hermits, monks and nuns moved north into Palestine and Syria. Those who settled near Alexandria got entangled in ecclesiastical politics, but another sequel to this story is considerably more edifying.

Pilgrims from many places went to learn from these desert fathers; one such, for many years, was John Cassian. A deacon of rare ability, he was then employed by the bishop of what had become the capital of a Christian empire and sent on a mission to Rome. But he went further west, founded monasteries near Marseille and wrote down his memories of the lives and conversations of the desert fathers in order to guide the monks now beginning the great monastic tradition of Gaul (France). About 410 Honoratus was inspired by a reading of the life of Antony to found a monastery confronting the coast of the Riviera on the rocky island of Lérins, which became a centre of training for the missionary leadership of the Church. It also became a centre of theological teaching, producing the famous formula in which one of its monks, Vincent, defined Catholic orthodoxy as 'what has been believed everywhere, always, by everyone'. This missile aimed at the destruction of innovations was directed in part against the disciples of one of the greatest of all theologians, Augustine, who seemed to underestimate the importance of human collaboration with the grace of God. Both John Cassian and Vincent of Lérins resisted all attempts to reduce the significance of the human struggle to reach holiness. In the Egyptian desert or near the beauties of the southern coast of Gaul, men who wanted their human passions to be consumed by the 'prayer of fire' knew that a very tough fight was essential. To them it was a battle against demons who made the Church worldly and could still tempt a hermit in his dreams.

Clement and Origen

While those Christians went into the desert or onto an island in order to pray, others who were in their own ways no less courageous explored the mystery of God in order to think.

A movement arose outside Egypt which has been called Monarchian because it stressed the monarchy of the one God. Its founders became little more than names to later generations, for they were condemned as heretics: Noetus in Smyrna and Sabellius the Libyan suffered this fate. It seems that some differed less than others from the positions which were later to be authorized as orthodox. Some taught that Father, Son and Spirit were three aspects or 'modes' of the one God, and this understanding of the Trinity might be regarded as a balancing corrective to Tertullian's teaching about the three *personae*. Others taught, or were alleged to teach, that what was divine in Jesus was the Father, 'the Son' being merely the human body used by the Father. Tertullian could complain about one of these Monarchians that 'Praxeas crucified the Father and banished the Spirit'. All that is clear is that serious attention was now being paid to the intellectual problems of trinitarianism. 'Praxeas', however, seems to be a dismissive nickname. It means 'Busybody'.

Another movement outside Egypt was to be called Adoptionist. It was brought to the attention of the Roman church when a leather-worker, Theodotus, tried to spread it (about 190), but its centre became Antioch and its leading exponent, Paul of Samosata, was the controversial bishop of that city.

He used a word which was to become the battle-cry of orthodoxy, *homoousios* ('of one being'), but he used it in order to teach a relationship between the Father and the Son which was to be thought heretical. The Son had descended from heaven to dwell in the man Jesus at his baptism, but that descent had not made Jesus himself more than 'a man like us although in every way greater'. Such teaching was criticized for failing to proclaim with John in the New Testament that the *Logos* became flesh, that the eternal Son became Jesus, and it was condemned at a bishops' council in 268. Part of the problem was the personality of Bishop Paul. He was an agent of a Jewish queen who was for a time in control of Antioch; he got women to sing in the choir and to applaud his sermons; two of his assistants were women who were too pretty—and all this at a time when men and women were usually separated in a congregation. When the Roman empire had recaptured Antioch, the emperor (Aurelian) was asked to say whether Paul should remain as bishop. He referred the question to the bishops of Rome and the rest of Italy, who were negative. But merit was seen in Paul's insistence that the Son shared 'being' with the Father. The bishop of Rome wrote to the bishop of Alexandria with a warning against any suggestion that Christians worshipped three gods: the monarchy of one God was, he declared, 'the most sacred teaching of the Church of God'. The reply came that the only reason why *homoousios* was not a word used in Alexandria was that it was not biblical. A reminder of what was at stake was given by the fact that both bishops were called Dionysius, after one of the many pagan gods to whom Christians refused to sacrifice. As the debate began about the Son's eternal relationship with the Father, Christians struggled to affirm both the revealed unity of God and the experienced reality of 'God in Christ'. Inevitably they could be thought to need warnings about the dangers of saying less or more than that this one God was 'in Christ'.

Clumsiness could not be alleged about the great theologians of Alexandria. The first famous teacher there was Clement, who (with more skill than Justin) presented Christianity as the true philosophy, the 'knowledge' which the Gnostics had sought.

He did not hesitate to speak about 'Christian Gnostics'. God is 'the Father and Maker of the universe' (a quotation from Plato). The created world is essentially good, so that what it offers, including riches and marriages, may rightly be enjoyed—but not to buy luxury or sinful pleasures, for we need to be disciplined by holiness before we can be united to God by love. When a rich young man is told by Christ to sell all he has, 'what he is told to banish from his soul is what he believes about his wealth'. Very fortunately, the *Logos* is present in all that is good in the world, teaching or healing anything less than good. The taking of flesh by this *Logos* has enabled humanity to become holy. Any suffering on the way is necessary discipline and the purpose of this discipline is nothing less than human perfection. 'A noble hymn to God', he wrote, 'is Man' (but he was emphatic about the spiritual equality of men and women). He believed that Jesus had spoken two sayings which he loved. 'When you see your neighbour, you see God.' 'He who seeks shall not cease until he finds, and when he finds he shall wonder, and wondering he shall reign, and reigning he shall rest.' He died about 215.

His successor was Origen, less relaxed as a man, even more learned as a scholar, much bolder as a thinker both Christian and Gnostic. Given the use of a substantial secretariat by his patron Ambrose, he dictated so much material that he kept all sides of the controversies of the next century supplied with quotations. The theological tide turned against him about 400 and he was to be condemned as a heretic by bishops' councils between 440 and 553, but to this day students of his work have argued about what he really thought.

He was, he always insisted, a churchman. He lived very austerely and when women joined the 'catechetical school' (a college for all ages) where he taught, he had himself castrated. His father had been martyred; he had tried to join him but his mother had hidden his clothes. Later he wrote in praise of martyrdom and he was tortured in his old age, refusing to abandon Christ but dying of his injuries (about 254). His chief interest was in the study and exposition of the Bible. He learned Hebrew and assembled different manuscripts in order to be more expert than any previous Christian. He was tirelessly laborious in explaining the Bible as a commentator in writing or as preacher, although he complained that some young people chattered during his sermons. He wrote a book about prayer which was also the work of an expert. He advocated a daily discipline of prayer, giving us invaluable knowledge about what was then expected of the average Christian. But his theme was prayer as being educated by God, not asking for material favours. He quoted two sayings which he thought came from Jesus: 'Ask for the great things and the little things will be added to you' and 'Ask for the heavenly things and the earthly things will be added to you'. He replied at length and with great skill to the attacks on Christians and Christianity by Celsus. This reply showed a determination to defend Christians who believed very simply and lived with a simple goodness, but also a confident ability to counter-attack: the stories about the pagan gods which Celsus said were illustrations of the reality of the One were more mythical than anything in the Bible and merely encouraged idolatry and devilry. It was natural that a scholar of such eminence and such sanctity should be trusted by many bishops as the expert to be consulted when one of their own number was accused of heresy. The transcript of his decisive part in one such investigation was discovered accidentally near Cairo in 1941.

But he could be suspected or condemned by fellow Christians. His own bishop in Alexandria refused to ordain him and when another bishop did oblige, this dedicated churchman found himself excommunicated and exiled from the Alexandria which had been so completely his place. He withdrew to Caesarea in Palestine and went on studying, teaching and writing. The reason behind his bishop's action may have been the common understanding that a castrated man was disqualified for the priesthood. It may have been simply that a bishop was jealous of a theologian who was cleverer. But it seems probable that there was a serious charge against Origen, that his theology mixed Platonic and Gnostic ideas with the Bible. As a young man Porphyry, who hated Christianity, met him and judged that he was 'educated in Greek learning' but was unsuccessful in connecting its wisdom with the 'foreign fables' of the Christians' Bible, so that at bottom he was still a 'barbarian'. Conservative Christians could observe the same mixture of ideas and call it heretical. Origen never surrendered to either attack. He knew where his heart lay and quoted an otherwise unknown saying of Jesus: 'He who is near me is near the fire.' But his name was derived from the ancient Egyptian god Horus and his mind was shaped by the Greek culture of Alexandria, where long before him pagan or Jewish scholars had extracted Greek-looking ideas from texts ascribed to Homer or Moses. He would do the same for the Christians' Scriptures. He was willing to become a Christian martyr but unwilling to let his Alexandrian mind die, for he was convinced that God had inspired both the Bible and the Greeks. He was willing to take endless trouble over the text of the Bible: under his supervision the whole of the Old Testament was copied out in six columns, showing the various versions in Hebrew and Greek. But he was also determined to restate the Bible's message in terms which could reach educated Greeks.

When he commented on the Bible, he usually began with the literal meaning of the passage. He was more conservative about authorship and historicity than most modern scholars would have been and he did not have the modern idea that God's revelation was gradual and progressive: he thought that the whole Bible had the same authority. But he spotted historical problems. Noah's ark could not have held all those animals if it had been that size; the family tree of Jesus was different in the gospels of Luke and Matthew; John's gospel differed from the other three. He could not accept the fundamentalism of Athenagoras, who had said that God dictated the Bible like a musician playing on a flute. Indeed, sometimes the literal meaning of a passage in the Old Testament seems to have so worried Origen that he hastened immediately to the spiritual meaning. And always the spiritual meaning seemed the more important. He wrote a commentary on the gracefully erotic poetry of the Song of Songs in the Hebrew Bible and it was to have great influence as suggesting that the book was an allegory: it was really about the love between Christ and the Church.

We cannot be sure exactly what he thought the spiritual meaning of the Bible was. When some of his writings were circulated he complained that he had meant them to be provisional and private. His most important book, *First Principles*, survives only in fragments of the original Greek and in a Latin translation which may well have been censored. But it seems clear that for him God is purely spiritual and perfectly one. In eternity God 'generated' his *Logos* containing the 'seeds' of everything that was to exist. Origen was so convinced about the essential goodness of the creation, and about the need of the God who is love to create, that he wrote passages which can be understood as meaning that the creation itself is eternal. Originally everything was without blemish, including souls sharing God's own immortality. But almost all the souls chose to sin. Some became angels and some became stars, while some fell so far as to become demons and in the middle grade some were placed in human bodies. However, the world was still not entirely evil. The *Logos* was available for the rescue as a 'second God'—in a sense, as Origen was careful to add while using Plato's phrase. The *Logos*, already united with the one soul that had remained absolutely pure, was now united with a human body 'as fire heats iron'. This incarnate *Logos* could then so illuminate the darkness of the world by his teaching and example that in the end all will be saved, even if they need further education after death—education which would be painful but 'in, as one might say, a lecture hall'. And by 'all' Origen meant all, including the demons. In 'spiritual bodies' all will become divine—in a sense. The wills of all are essentially free despite their fall from their own glorious origin. They are free to be educated and so to return to that glory.

This was a scheme indebted to the myths of the Gnostics and not to be found in the plain words of the Bible, and it is not surprising that Origen, the early Church's greatest theologian, was suspect and in the end condemned. But for many years he fascinated spiritually minded intellectuals and now that controversies about him have become remote it may be agreed that some things stand to his credit. He saw that God is great, greater than any thing or any one; he celebrated the whole creation as good; he was not blind to the problem of evil; he believed in Christ as God embodied; believing in God's inexhaustible love and patience, he did not condemn most of humanity to predestined hell. As Peter Brown wrote in his study of the culture of *The World of Late Antiquity* (1971), 'Origen and his successors taught the pagan that to become a Christian was to step, at last, from a confused and undeveloped stage of moral and intellectual growth into the heart of civilization'.

This great optimist contemplated, as a foretaste of God's final and total victory, the possibility that one day the Roman empire might become Christian, but it was a prospect which seemed very unlikely in the civilization which existed. A later Christian scholar, Lactantius, seemed more realistic when he expected the end of history to come before the empire's conversion: Antichrist's reign would come soon as history's finale and would be followed by Christ's. The same opinion was held at this time by the historian Eusebius. Such pessimism about the course of history in this world seemed wise, for in 303 the most systematic and severe persecution which the Church had ever suffered broke out and could easily be understood as the final tribulation before the End, when the martyrs would be rewarded by resurrection. But Lactantius and Eusebius lived to change their minds. For very strangely, the ordeal turned out to be the beginning of the process which led to the Catholic Church's triumph. As Eusebius wrote, 'most marvellously, as in a thick darkness, God caused the light of peace to shine upon us'.

Constantine

In 284 yet another general, Diocletian, seized control of the Roman empire. A man impatient with the old system (his own ancestors had been slaves), he was determined to repel the barbarians and Persians and to end the inefficiency within the empire. He reorganized the army and the government, sharing his power with another 'Augustus' and two 'Caesars' in order that government might be effective. (A statue of these four strong men together survives outside St Mark's in Venice.) He commanded order in every sphere, including a planned economy, heavier taxation and the fixing of prices. Eventually, like the military emperors of the 250s he acted to secure uniformity in religion. His main target was the Church. He wished to eliminate it in each of the twelve 'dioceses' into which the empire was now divided.

In 303–304 the magistrates and police were given orders to destroy Christian Bibles and buildings, to prohibit Christian meetings and to execute without trial any who refused to sacrifice to 'our gods'. The persecution was continued and even intensified when an exhausted Diocletian had abdicated, and the Church suffered many casualties and desertions. But the plan to obliterate Christianity did not work. Many pagans, high or low in society, did not now want it to work: contempt or hatred for a clearly evil cult had changed to a puzzled admiration. Tertullian had reported that pagans said 'See how these Christians love one another!' In the centuries to come that phrase was to be repeated in bitter irony, but at the beginning of the fourth

Christian century it could be meant as simple praise. In Gaul and Britain not much happened by way of persecution. In Italy, Spain and North Africa, and in the east, the cruel deaths were many, as were the examples of heroism by Christian women and men; Bishop Eusebius compiled a fairly detailed account of these 'magnificent martyrs of Christ' who 'furnished a clear proof that the power of our Saviour is truly divine and inexpressible'. But while persecution continued in the east, in the west the dying emperor Galerius conceded toleration to the Christians in 311, asking for prayers 'to their god for our safety'. The bishops were wise enough not to close the door to those who had lapsed and now sought readmission; a return to the Church would take ten years (in theory at any rate) but it was possible.

It was more difficult to think the Christianization of the empire possible. Probably the Church now included almost a tenth of the population, about five amid sixty million. It was stronger in the east than in the west but even there it was a small minority. The astounding change in its fortunes in the next few years was due in large measure to the personality of a brilliant general, politician and propagandist, ambitious, shrewd and ruthless, who was the victor in further civil wars. Constantine equalled Paul in his trans-forming influence on the movement which acknowledged Jesus of Nazareth as Lord, but the evidence suggests that he did not become a Christian as the answer to his spiritual needs. He turned to the Church because Christianity spoke about Christ but it seems that he turned to Christ because he needed help in what really interested him: first the conquest and then the reconstruc-tion of the empire. He was a Christian version of Diocletian.

The son of an Augustus, bitterly disappointed by not being made a Caesar by Diocletian, he withdrew with his father to the army's headquarters in York and on his father's death had himself proclaimed emperor by the troops. Alternately cautious and courageous, he then waited or fought until he had acquired a power greater than Diocletian's. Before the battle which gave him the death of his chief rival and the possession of Rome, fought near the Milvian Bridge across the Tiber in 312, he became convinced that his best ally was the heavenly Christ. He spoke about a dream and years later he said that he had seen something stranger. It is possible that this was a rare but natural phenomenon of light (a parhelion). At any rate he claimed to have seen a cross of light in the autumn sky, adding more improbably that he had read beneath it the caption in Greek, 'conquer by this'. His father had worshipped the Unconquered Sun, and when younger he had himself claimed a vision of the sun god Apollo, but this was better. He got his troops to paint on their shields two Greek letters, *chi* and *rho*: they were now under the protection of Christ. The next year he persuaded his remaining imperial colleague to agree to an edict (the 'edict of Milan') granting perpetual toleration to Christians and to other worshippers of 'whatever heavenly deity exists'. This co-emperor (Licinius) resumed persecution before long, but Constantine disposed of him in 324 and soon signalled his own religious loyalties and hopes. He was in some sense converted.

Taking advantage of a boom in the economy now that there was peace, he used taxes to pay for great churches to be built on the most significant sites. One arose in Bethlehem over the cave reputed since early in the second century to be the birthplace of Jesus; another in Jerusalem over the place whose probable authenticity as the place of his death was not destroyed by the fact that the emperor's eager mother Helen found buried here his 'true' cross which was to supply many relics; another over the tomb of Peter on the Vatican hill, a site which twentieth-century archaeology was to show to be almost certainly authentic since the simple shrine which was uncovered in the 1940s was constructed in 165. To reinforce the message of official favour, each church looked like a *basilica*: such a rectangular, pillared hall would contain a crowd awed by the display of imperial justice in the apse at one end but would also be familiar as a community centre, since when not needed as a court of justice it was used as a market.

Bishops were entrusted with endowments which would enable them to begin charitable work on a larger scale among the public as well as among Christians. In Rome the bishop was given the Lateran palace as a residence. In North Africa the emperor backed the Catholic bishop of Carthage against the Donatists. These tough Christians objected to the softness shown to those who had lapsed in the great persecution—and to the wealth of the Romanized rich who were now beginning to move into the Catholic Church's welcoming embrace. In particular the Donatists complained that this bishop (Caecilian) had been consecrated by another who had surrendered the Church's Scriptures during the persecutions. From the confusion Donatus emerged as a rival bishop of Carthage allied with many other bishops and priests leading the religious and social protest. Constantine announced his determination to settle the dispute: it was, he now claimed, his 'constant practice, after expelling error and destroying rash opinions, to convince everyone to agree to follow the true religion'. He financed a council of western bishops, a grander affair than the regional synods which had met in previous years. When the Donatists refused to accept those bishops' ruling against them he announced that he would impose it personally, before thinking it wiser to leave the issue to God. The defeated party turned to violence, led by thugs called Circumcellions because it was said that they lived around the *cellae* or tombs of the heroic martyrs. Violence was used in the empire's response.

Constantine would perhaps have been wise to stick to that decision to keep out of ecclesiastical disputes, but such a policy was not in his imperious character. He cautiously began the work of converting the empire to Christianity as he understood it. As early as 321 he ordered the law courts and all businesses to close on the day when Christians met for worship, although the day was still named after the sun god and agricultural labour might still continue. To some extent his legislation embodied Christian values: he improved the conditions of slaves, debtors and orphans and his taxation no longer discriminated against the unmarried. At least one of the very large statues which he erected to himself included a cross. An instrument of utterly humiliating torture and execution, which earlier Christians had not liked to picture, increasingly became the public symbol of Christianity, and the development was helped by a decree forbidding crucifixions in the future. If an emperor who dominated the Roman world could carry a cross and if no more men were to die on one, it was no longer so likely to arouse horror or mockery. There is a total contrast between this statue and the earliest surviving picture—or, rather, cartoon—of the crucifixion of Jesus, found on the wall of a second-century house in Rome which seems to have been a residence for young men in training to be smart pages and civil servants in the imperial court. It shows a donkey being crucified with a figure beside it and under this has been scratched 'Alexamenos adores his god'.

Although Constantine ordered or allowed non-Christian symbols to appear on coins or monuments which had to be generally acceptable, he disliked, snubbed and avoided Rome with all its parade of his predecessors' paganism. And he dramatized his revolution by transforming the little town called Byzantion in Greek or Byzantium in Latin into his capital in the east. The city was to be called Constantinople and was to contain many churches including the church of Peace. He summoned the eastern bishops to achieve a unity in doctrine and in the dating of Easter, and in Antioch on Good Friday 325 he addressed many of them with a self-centred philosophy of history. The all-powerful God revealed by the eternal Son of God had frustrated all pagan persecutors and had blessed his own rise to power. Now this God willed that the reunited empire should indeed have a single and strong religious basis as Diocletian had wanted—but the basis was to be Christian, and moreover Catholic. He recalled seeing the ruins of imperial Babylon and of the Pharaohs' Memphis: similarly, the day of the pagan Roman empire was over. So, he hoped, was the time when the Church had been troubled by heresy. It was not long before he had banned meetings of the Gnostics and Manichees and of the lingering followers of Marcion, Montanus, Novatian and Paul of Samosata: the whole history of dissent in early Christianity was to be closed. And he obviously, and correctly, expected that the paganism which he had to tolerate would continue its decline and begin its fall now that the weight of the Roman state had been put behind the Catholic Church.

A Golden Age?

As we pause in the story soon after the beginning of the fourth Christian century we can see that already the movement started by Jesus has survived persecutions and problems to become the Christianity which was to be present, and often prominent, in many situations very far from Nazareth. With this start the Christians were on their way to becoming the controllers of the eastern and western halves of the Roman empire and the makers of Europe. They had set out on a long journey which was to take them into Byzantine and Russian churches of splendour and into the soaring magnificence of Gothic cathedrals; into baronial castles, monasteries and universities; into the making of much of the world's greatest art, music and literature; into the births of modern science and democracy; into many fields and many cities; and into Indian villages, Brazilian slums, Siberian prison camps and Chinese house churches. These were the early days of a movement without which neither North nor Latin America, neither Africa south of the Sahara nor the islands of the South Pacific, can now be understood. This movement, so tiny in its origins, was to break through the barriers which divided Jew and Gentile, the enslaved and the free, the man and the woman, the intellectual and the practical person, the rich and the poor, the white and the coloured. Many millions, believers more or less, have tried to combine what has been remembered and felt about Jesus with their own involvements and experiences.

According to Luke's gospel Jesus said that he had come in order to 'set the world on fire'. The fire did not come in the all-consuming way that was hoped for, but Origen's boast was to be justified by the facts of history: 'Our Jesus has been able to shake the whole human race . . . more than wise men or conquerors or generals in any part of the world.' And the first three hundred years of this conqueror's march were in many ways glorious. In them the Church proved able to survive excommunication by the synagogues and the disappointment of the hope that its Lord would soon return to the earth, establishing the kingdom of God to which he had looked forward so ardently. The New Testament was written with stories and commands which were to prove dynamic in the emotions and consciences of many generations. Its books included the writing of two spiritual and theological figures with the stature of giants, Paul and John. Early Catholicism developed a shape which was to be accepted by Constantine, who was no sentimentalist, as an organization almost as useful as the army, and Christian thinkers from Justin to Origen linked the Church's doctrine with the whole mental world of Greek philosophy. Martyrs in the arena, and hermits and monks in the desert, raised Christian discipleship to heroism. Nowhere else in the ancient world was there this fusion between the spheres of religion and moral philosophy, between thoughts about eternity and skill in organization on earth, between the mystical and the popular. And not least of the glories was the fact that the expansion of Christianity in these centuries was not planned like a military invasion or sales campaign. It depended on people talking with people and speaking most loudly with their lives and deaths.

It is instructive to reflect on the unintended compliment which the emperor Julian paid to this achievement when he was trying to restore the traditional Roman religion in the 360s. He urged his supporters to imitate the Christians. In every province there should be a priest as the religious leader, like a bishop of the Church; sermons were to be preached, hymns were to be sung, charity was to be organized instead of leaving it to the 'impious Galileans' to 'support not only their own poor but ours as well'; non-Christian theology was to be thought out and defended vigorously; in the schools the great classics of pagan literature were to be treated as Scriptures; above all, the old gods were to be believed in with passion and were to inspire lives of active goodness. Thus the Church which he detested was held up as a model by the last of the pagan emperors. These early centuries have often been treated as the golden age in the history of Christianity and later developments have been seen as a decline. And much is true in that verdict. As this story unfolds we shall notice many occasions when attention to the Church of the New Testament, and to a lesser extent to the Church of the next two hundred years, has revived and guided individuals and communities. As Eusebius wrote in his preface to his *Ecclesiastical History*, voices from that time reach us 'from afar and crying from on high, as out of some watch-tower'.

Yet the true picture is not one of Christians merely repeating the words of Jesus and agreeing that nothing more needed to be said. Although many of the sayings of the Lord were remembered, neither Paul nor John thought it necessary to quote many of his actual words as they expressed the significance of what was to be called by later theologians the 'Christ-event'. This was because the new life 'in Christ', the life of the disciple's union with Jesus 'my Lord and my God', depended on events after the death, the events called the resurrection. The spiritual power which was then called 'Jesus Christ' or 'the Holy Spirit' or 'the Spirit of Jesus', and which is referred to in modern theology as 'the Christ of faith', was greater than any impression made by the teacher and healer from Nazareth before he was crucified. This power created Christianity: whatever may be the mystery surrounding its origins after what seemed to be a complete tragedy in Jerusalem, this power entered the kind of history which an historian can record with assurance. Because a tomb was believed to be empty, many hearts and minds were full.

What had power was originally not a system. There have been many attempts to treat the parables and sayings of Jesus more or less as a legal code or a philosophy, with timeless and universal authority. When it has been seen that what is remembered about Jesus does not amount to a system, the reply has often been that he made arrangements for an authoritative interpreter entitled to formulate the code which is needed. But all such beliefs run up against the frequent indications in the surviving evidence that the arrival of the kingdom of God was his central message and that both he and his followers hoped that it would come quickly, so that no system would be needed. This hope has often been revived in a fairly literal manner, predicting the End in the near future, but so far it has always been disappointed. That does not necessarily discredit either Jesus or his followers. Indeed, the only direct evidence which we have about him and his hope was written down as teaching about the 'Son of God' between twenty and seventy years after his death. Paul, Mark, Luke, Matthew and John all knew that the most optimistic expectations had not been fulfilled, yet such writers and their audiences were prepared to live and die in his cause.

This was the case because it was believed to be possible for Christians to find some interpretation of the original hope of the End which would fit and illuminate the realities as known to them. A careful study of the parables makes it clear that at a very early stage Christians were telling and interpreting a story which had offered an urgent promise or warning to hearers in Galilee or Jerusalem in such a way that it was a message to a later generation about a postponed End and about the life to be lived during what might be a long postponement. This seems to illustrate the fact that over the continuing centuries Christianity had to develop: it was not entirely something given once and for all.

The necessary reflection and discussion began in the communities which lay behind the writing of the New Testament. It therefore seems wrong to dismiss completely the provocative opening sentence of Rudolf Bultmann's *New Testament Theology*: 'The message of Jesus is a presupposition for the theology of the New Testament rather than a part of that theology itself.' Bultmann certainly did not mean that the message of Jesus was irrelevant to the Christians who wrote the New Testament or that his character and the outline of his life had been forgotten: he wrote important books about the gospels as evidence of the reporting and interpretation of Jesus at that early stage. But it was a fact that Jesus was not a theologian any more than he was a Gentile. Interpreting his message intellectually, and understanding its significance in new situations, with or without a repetition of his words, was a task for the Christians.

75

They were not daunted. Some knew much, most knew little, about the lifetime of Jesus of Nazareth—about what Bultmann called *Historie*, the facts about what really had happened. It mattered far more to them that they had experienced *Geschichte*, history with a meaning for life, and now they relied on the ever-present 'Holy Spirit' sent by Christ. The Spirit guided them, they believed, to remember what mattered and the Spirit gave them power to live and die in that shining light. However, their understanding of such guidance and power remained human, coloured by their own personalities and shaped by the structures of life and thought in the societies to which they belonged. Even when 'the Spirit of truth' guided Christians to write down memories and to develop theologies about Jesus, the results included their own concerns and convictions. These were mixed with traditions about events already quite distant, although not so difficult to recall as events at a similar distance would be for our own more cluttered minds. There were in the end four 'canonical' gospels, not one, all offering interpretations of a Lord who needed to be interpreted, and as we have seen there were other interpretations by Paul and by the Early Catholics who developed Paul's teaching. Each one of the 27 documents which the Church received as the New Testament reflected the beliefs of the person who wrote it. To use George Tyrrell's famous image, everyone who has ever tried to find what Jesus means for him (or her) is to some extent like a man looking down a well and seeing his own face in the water. And when some image of Jesus had been seen in New Testament times or later, there remained the problem of seeing what Jesus meant in the total scheme of things. Was this crucified man in some sense 'God'? If so, how and why? A. N. Whitehead famously remarked that Christianity has always been 'a religion seeking a metaphysic' because its founder did not provide one (unlike the founder of Buddhism).

As Christians looked down that well hoping to see the face of Jesus, or sought to see how he revealed ultimate reality, of course they did not completely agree. Irenaeus of Lyon stated an ideal, that bishops should be the spokesmen of churches which agreed on a message taught by the holy apostles and recorded in the holy Scriptures, but in practice he added to the Church's heritage in theology. Vincent of Lérins insisted on the conservatism of 'what has been believed everywhere, always, by everyone', but in practice a diversity as great as that which is undeniable in Christianity in the modern age is to be found in the first three centuries. It began with Greek-speaking 'Hellenists' in Jersualem who according to the Acts of the Apostles disagreed with most of the first followers of Jesus by rejecting that great temple. They took the message about Jesus to the Samaritans, a half-breed race with whom pure Jews had no dealings. Not much later, a mixed group of Jews and Gentiles in Antioch became the first people in the world to be called Christians. To call the early Church 'undivided' refers to the obvious fact that the divisions between eastern Orthodoxy and western Catholicism, and between the Roman Catholics and the Protestants, lay in the future. But saying 'undivided' ignores the large numbers of people who claimed to be Christians but who were not recognized as such by the Catholic bishops. This category included everyone in the Jewish Christian tradition and before long it was to include not only all the various groups called Gnostics but also Origen retrospectively, as a collaborator with the Gnostics. It included the Montanists who claimed to be directly inspired by the Holy Spirit and the Donatists who ranked the heroic martyrs and 'confessors' above the morally compromising bishops. The Catholic Church excluded all these. There was significance in a story preserved by Eusebius, that the apostle John, on hearing that the heretic Cerinthus was also using the bath house in Ephesus, immediately left the building, warning others that it might collapse.

Large decisions had to be made by these early Christians. For a time the Jesus movement could try to resume the life which the disciples had lived before the crucifixion, expecting the kingdom of God to come soon and meanwhile sharing what money they had and praying within the Jewish tradition. But the circle of disciples which had followed Jesus had been small. He had called them to leave everything—work, wealth, wives, children, parents—in order to be with him in his urgent mission, but probably for a short period. Now growing numbers meant that an organization must be developed. It had to be developed for the community in Jerusalem which was both Jewish and Christian. It also had to be developed for a church in a city such as Antioch which was largely Gentile. And as the preaching about Jesus continued to spread, Christians had to decide whether their baptized Church was open to Gentiles unwilling to accept Jewish practices. Jesus had not moved among Gentiles, although incidents could be cited showing his good will towards them. The memory of his saying that he had been sent 'to the lost sheep of the house of Israel' seems to have been accurate. Yet gradually, and amid controversies, the Church came to consist almost entirely of Gentiles, and this was accepted by most as being the will of the exalted Christ. And the Church lost the earlier Jewish willingness to let a number of movements dispute—as did Judaism.

Many Christians in later generations, particularly in modern times, have believed that there was loss as well as gain in this development. Jesus had spoken mainly about God as 'Father' and about an urgent invitation to sinners to accept the Father's reign; about his own status he had been far less explicit. Now the Church spoke mainly about the eternal divinity of God the Son and about its own pure holiness and exclusive claims—or so it could seem. The original message of Jesus about the Father's kingdom became strangely subordinated as (in Bultmann's phrase) 'the Proclaimer became the Proclaimed'. In particular the Proclaimer's insistence on the admission of forgiven sinners to the banquet of the kingdom got obscured. In these early centuries Christians who had sinned seriously had to be excommunicated and to undergo severe times of 'penance' (derived from *poena*, Latin for penalty) before they could receive the Church's forgiveness; later on, all sinners had to do penance in time or eternity after that forgiveness had been pronounced. According to the synoptic gospels the disagreements between Jesus and the leaders of orthodox Judaism in his day had arisen not because he totally rejected that religion but chiefly because of his attitude to 'sinners'. His friendliness with them had been unconditional and he had assured them that the Father was waiting to forgive them and to lavish on them the banquet which his love would provide. There was no memory of a story that a prodigal son who had decided to return home faced a prison sentence. Jesus was remembered as saying that prostitutes would enter the kingdom of God before Pharisees; that 'Heaven' rejoiced more over one sinner returning home than over 99 of the righteous thinking that they had never left home. His demonstration within the temple (the incident which brought his disagreements with official Judaism to a head) had been inspired by indignation that it was no longer a house of prayer open to sinners who wished to pray for the Father's mercy without being robbed by priests. But now the Church's emphasis seemed to be on discipline and condemnation. Baptism was therefore often postponed until quite late in life, often until the brink of death as in Constantine's own case, because that was a comparatively painless way of obtaining the forgiveness of sins. The Church could not be called what Jesus of Nazareth had been called, 'the friend of sinners'.

The sins which chiefly attracted attention and punishment were not to be sins of behaviour. They were to be sinful errors in belief, for bishops and theologians were to become increasingly absorbed in disputes about Christ's existence before his human birth and 'before all time', and it was to be believed that the Church had a duty to settle these disputes authoritatively and to rejoice when its decisions were made compulsory for all.

There was not to be the same anxiety about the absence of a firm doctrine about the at-one-ment between God and humanity achieved by the Lord's life and death on earth. There the variety of images in the New Testament continued to offer the possibility of various interpretations. In a society full of anger Christ was an example of patience; in a society full of harsh justice he satisfied the demands of God's own stern laws; in a society full of temples he provided the perfect sacrifice; in a society full of slaves he provided the liberating ransom; in a society full of the fear of demons he conquered them. All these things could still be said and the creeds emerging in the Church made no attempt to choose between the images in order to define Christ's work. But the same diversity of interpretation could not be allowed when the discussion turned to the life of God the Son before his human birth or to the relationship between his two 'natures', divine and human. It was to be an intricate discussion and its fascination could eclipse the warning in the first letter to Timothy to shun the teacher who is 'morbidly keen on mere verbal questions and quibbles, which give rise to jealousy, quarrelling, slander, base suspicions and endless wrangles'. When involved in debates which ended in the exile or persecution of the defeated, Christians could forget the question reported in Luke's gospel: 'Why do you call me "Lord, Lord" and do not do what I tell you?' And they could forget their own earlier sense of priorities, when for the most part they had spread their gospel by how they behaved, the communication of an outline of their theology (the *traditio* or handing-over of their creed) being reserved for the final stages before baptism.

No doubt agreement about really basic doctrines was necessary if Christianity was to say how it differed from Judaism and if it was not to be lost in a jungle of Gnostic myths or drowned in the ocean of religious varieties in the Roman empire. It was necessary to agree what the Catholic Scriptures were and who the Catholic spokesmen were, because it was necessary to proclaim that the one, true and eternal God had embodied his saving love in Jesus. But the extent of the doctrinal agreement which was to be required has often been thought to be open to question. For Irenaeus the consensus needed was a harmony between the bishops as the spokesmen of their churches and it had to be a repetition of what the apostles had taught. Now there was to be a rather different demand: for the acceptance by individuals of an orthodoxy considerably more elaborate than the faith defended by Irenaeus, who had simply compared the Son and the Spirit with the Father's two hands and had never defined how it was that divinity and humanity were united in the Son. He had assured the faithful that they should not be ashamed to leave to God 'mysteries too great for us'. An earlier bishop, Ignatius, compared the Church to a temple built by the Father who used the cross of Christ as a crane and the Holy Spirit as a rope to hoist the stones, but he did not speculate about the origin in 'silence' of the Son as 'our God'. He had something better to do, for there were Christians to encourage and unite and, above all, there was a death to die. Now the Church was to insist that individuals should accept the words agreed by bishops' councils about the Son's origin within that eternal silence.

It is understandable that it was thought necessary to impose this conformity to the bishops' doctrinal decisions and it is also understandable that from the fourth century onwards many Christians were to welcome the willingness or eagerness of emperors to enforce the decrees of the bishops' councils over which they presided, using the weapons of exile or worse. For many years the hostility of the Roman state had seemed to be the Church's chief problem; now by a miracle hostility had turned to a patronage which showered privileges and subsidies while there was little theological thought about the proper relationship between Church and State. But what is understandable is not necessarily admirable. Inevitably theology was to get mixed up with the empire's politics. Inevitably the decisive voice in many disputes was to come from the emperor, who might or might not be qualified to hold and to enforce a theological opinion. Inevitably the Church was to drift some distance from the position of Jesus of Nazareth who had advocated two loyalties, one to Caesar and one to God, and who had suffered under Pontius Pilate. While in the wilderness after his baptism, having to decide what would be the character of his mission, he had rejected as diabolical temptations the ideas that he might join the well fed, display to all what it meant to be 'Son of God' and take over the kingdoms of the world. Now, some three hundred years later, the Church plunged into theological controversies which were concluded by imperial laws. Inevitably some baser elements tarnished the glory of its spiritual tradition as the persecuted became persecutors.

3

cksckscks

Byzantine Orthodoxy

A Spiritual Tradition

EASTERN Orthodoxy is the kind of Catholicism that has been shaped by an experience covering two-thirds of its history: it was the official religion of the eastern half of the old Roman empire. 'Orthodoxy' comes from Greek words meaning 'correct beliefs'. These were the beliefs held to be correct in that empire, whose capital Constantinople had been called by an earlier name, in Latin Byzantium.

The Orthodox Church in the Byzantine empire was a powerful and wealthy institution with very close links with the imperial government and even when it has been a minority in a foreign land, even when it has been persecuted systematically, Orthodoxy has tended to be identified with the traditional culture of an ethnic group, Balkan, Greek or Russian, as during eleven centuries it was identified with Byzantium. But Orthodoxy has also inherited a tradition which originated in Christianity's beginnings and persisted after Constantine—a tradition of prayer amidst poverty, of faithfulness amid suffering, of heroism capable of rising to martyrdom. This tradition survived the fall of the Byzantine empire. Indeed, it spread more widely than that empire, for it spread to Russia, and moreover the spiritual life in the Nestorian and Monophysite churches which were Orthodox in their own eyes defied the empire's decision that they were heretical. These churches are now properly called 'the Church of the East' and 'Oriental Orthodox'. And in the twentieth Christian century this tradition survived all that Communism could throw at it—the bullets of the firing squads, the cold and hunger, the diseases and the exhaustion of the labour camps, the corruption of some of its own bishops and clergy, the anti-God propaganda, the constant, quiet exclusion from opportunities.

But Orthodoxy has become a puzzle to many people including many modern Russians and Greeks. Here are bearded clergy who wear strange robes, chant strange words and disappear behind the saints portrayed on a golden screen, the *ikonostasis*. The 'throne' (altar) is hidden behind the 'royal' (central) doors. Yet the church which may seem very strange indeed even to other Christians is to the Orthodox a spiritual home. The 'icons' (pictures) of Christ, his mother and his saints are reminders about the glory which really surrounds the faithful: they are doors into heaven. These sacred figures are never shown in profile and seldom in action: they are symbols of the worship in heaven, painted in order to be venerated and as aid to the worship which the saints already offer. And here the faithful are not self-conscious as they pray by silent devotion, crossing themselves, lighting candles and kissing icons. By tradition unaccompanied by any musical instrument, they sing hymns many of which have been loved since Byzantine days. They assent to the deacon's litanies (prayers). They do not sit as an audience but stand as the Church, in a tradition older than the custom of kneeling to pray. With justice it has often been said that despite the great authority of the bishops' councils and of the living, local bishop the real guardians of the Orthodox tradition are not the bishops but these faithful, the *laos* or 'people'. The transformation of the bread and wine into Christ's body and blood is thought to be effected not by the priest's words but by the Holy Spirit, poured out on the priest and the people. All are included in the *leitourgia*, a word which originally meant any kind of public work; it could mean, for example, the building of a road. In the Orthodox Eucharist or 'Liturgy' the people do the work as well as the priest and when they communicate physically they receive both the bread and the wine, not the bread alone; usually the consecrated bread is administered on a spoon after dipping it in the wine. It is customary for the Liturgy to be held only on occasions when a congregation will be present and for priests to say that they only 'serve the Liturgy'. After the service blessed bread is distributed to the people including non-communicants. Outside the Liturgy the consecrated bread and wine are reserved for consumption by people who are sick, but not for adoration on the altar in private devotions: prayer through the icons is the substitute for that. The people's worship is traditional but not regimented; despite love for the most famous liturgies and veneration for the historic creeds, among those proudly claiming to be Orthodox nearly a hundred texts are now authorized for use in the Liturgy. In Latin *sacramentum* was originally an oath which was legally binding and in western Catholic history there have been many disputes as to which sacraments are valid according to a law which binds God and Man, but the Orthodox word is *mysterion*. The Liturgy is a mysterious drama, not understood in detail but celebrated together. It is the heart of this undying spiritual tradition because it feeds the people. Where the Liturgy is, there is the Church. As Vladimir

Lossky wrote, 'to be in the tradition is to share the experience of the mysteries revealed to the Church'.

Orthodoxy has not so far found it necesssary to adjust to the forces which have reshaped western Christianity: medieval Catholicism, the Renaissance, the Protestant and Catholic Reformations, the modern Enlightenment, critical history, modern science and democracy. It accepts the authority of 'holy fathers' who in the fourth or fifth Christian century disputed about the relationships within the Trinity before time began. It reveres monks or wandering holy men (even 'fools of Christ' deliberately unconventional) who would be recognizable against an Indian background but now seem exotic or crazed to other societies. It therefore seems out of this world, in a world which is dead. Yet this Liturgy-centred tradition is loved by insiders because to them it seems to have preserved Christianity's early spiritual power with neither too little nor too much doctrine or law. Even Christians who are not Orthodox may also be grateful for the defence of treasures which elsewhere have often been forgotten or obscured: the primacy in Christian life of prayer to the transcendent Creator, the sense of the nearness of the Saviour and his saints, the ability to maintain strength under trials by dependence on the Holy Spirit not on a mass of legislation, an affirmation of the beauty of the created world (brought into the Liturgy) and therefore of art and music, a spiritual life which is lived together with joy rather than by solitary, anxious pilgrims. And it is a life under a mystery. In Orthodoxy there is of course agreement about the doctrines held to be vitally important, but there is also liberty to debate matters not defined dogmatically and even the compulsory doctrines are believed within an 'apophatic' tradition which sees that no human words can pin down the essence of God. 'Anyone who tries to describe the ineffable light in language is truly a liar', said Gregory of Nyssa—and he was a theologian who tried to make himself understood by using images drawn from daily life. The best theologian, he taught, is the one who 'assembles more of Truth's shadow'. In the sixth century a Syrian monk who took the biblical name of Dionysius the Areopagite assembled many shadows in his account of the nine choirs of angels based on the 'sacred pictures' which he found in the Bible, but he also produced a classic statement of the 'apophatic' or negative way in thoughtful theology: since God dwells in 'the brilliant darkness of a hidden silence', preferably he is not to be argued about but is to be contemplated in the 'silence of the heart'. Maximus the Confessor was a strictly orthodox theologian who paid with his life (after torture and mutilation) for his defence of the faith against his emperor, but he insisted that God's being must be 'unknowable, inaccessible and completely inexplicable, beyond both affirmation and negation'. 'The infinite is without doubt something of God', he granted, 'but not God himself, who is infinitely beyond that.' Gregory of Nyssa did as much as anyone to explain how God became flesh, but he also said that it was as marvellous as a flame burning downwards. Essentially Orthodoxy is not speculation, not even the acceptance of authoritatively declared doctrines: it is adoration.

For most of the faithful, what matters most is their kind of participation in the Liturgy. For many centuries that did not usually involve the physical reception of the consecrated bread and wine, since the self-searching confession of sins before a priest was a necessary preparation, and still today communion four times a year may be regarded as normal, but the earlier practice was for the faithful to communicate frequently and this practice is being revived. In the fourth century a great bishop, Basil of Caesarea, defended the custom of taking some of the consecrated bread home so that the faithful might consume it frequently, even daily. When Nicholas Cabasilas (a layman) wrote about *Life in Christ* in the fourteenth century, he presented this life as the heartfelt membership of the eucharistic people producing a union with the heart of Jesus. To this day Christ is not respected as a figure in history but known through the Church, his living body; not imitated as a moral example but joined through the sacraments; not accepted in an introspective conversion but grown into, in a community and in a lifelong love. What characterizes Orthodoxy is neither the sermon nor the private meditation on a story about Christ. It is the Liturgy and, flowing from that, it is 'the prayer of the heart', supremely the 'Jesus prayer' which can be repeated very often: 'Lord Jesus Christ, Son of God, have mercy on me a sinner.'

Much of what the Orthodox believe about sin and salvation has been shared by other Christians, but the Orthodox emphasis is that humanity inherits from the Fall of Adam and Eve not guilt but death. The sacrifice of his life offered by Christ on the cross was made not chiefly to 'purchase redemption' as other Christians, Catholic and Protestant, have said: it was made in order to open the way to eternal life. Gregory of Nazianzus taught: 'Is it not evident that the Father accepts the sacrifice not because he demands it or feels some need for it but in order to carry out his own plan? Humanity had to be brought to life by the humanity of God . . . Let the rest be adored in silence.'

When little more than twenty years old Athanasius expounded 'life in Christ' and he stuck to this interpretation during almost half a century as bishop of Alexandria including five periods of exile: eventually he was vindicated. God the Son, he taught, became human for this staggering reason: 'in order that we might become God'. A little later Basil of Caesarea said that 'the human being is an animal who has received the vocation to become God'. This belief that the destiny of Man is deification, *theosis*, does not imply that Man can be perfect without trouble. On the contrary,

Orthodoxy holds as firmly as does any other kind of Christianity the beliefs that 'fallen' humanity is corrupted, chained and doomed and that the work of the Saviour is needed if there is to be salvation. But the Orthodox celebrate the salvation with a joyful hopefulness which is as least as great as any glad praise to be heard elsewhere. Preaching in Constantinople in 380, Gregory of Nazianzus expressed classically the triumph song of Orthodoxy: Jesus Christ is God the Son, in eternity 'of one being' with God the Father, he is the Word who 'exists in all things that are', in his work on earth he is Wisdom, Power, Truth, Light and Life. The eternal glory which is now possible for Man depends utterly on this divine Saviour, on the 'God-Man' as Athanasius called Jesus.

As expounded by the authoritative teachers of Orthodoxy, *theosis* does not admit creatures into the inner 'essence' of the Godhead. It is entry into the divine 'energy', into the glory of which the Bible speaks. If Christians highly advanced in holiness share this glory before death they are bathed in 'uncreated' (the western word is 'supernatural') light, but God the Son is alone 'Light from Light'. The Christian who sees the creative self-expression (*logos*) of God in all the reality, order and loveliness of a wonderful creation sees this divinity most clearly in the splendour of Christ, and in that light the imperfections of the world can move a Christian to tears. 'What is a charitable heart?' asked Isaac the Syrian. 'It is a heart which burns with charity for the whole of creation—people, birds, beasts, demons, all creatures.' He insisted that such compassion should have practical results but he based it on the contemplation of the Creator's purposes (*theoria*). Orthodoxy clings to the belief that God never intended any evil in anything he made and to the hope that in the end there will be no evil. Gregory of Nyssa said that God gave Adam a palace fit for a king. And although Origen was ultimately condemned for a lack of caution in his doctrine that in the end all imperfections will be healed, the similar hopes to be found in Gregory of Nyssa's writings escaped official censure. 'In any and every case', he wrote, 'evil must be removed from existence.' Orthodoxy has known the power of evil in its own bitter experience but has never lost the vision that when God triumphs all of humanity and all of the rest of the creation will be transfigured into immortal glory, as Christ was. This has often been called the Church of Easter, a festival kept with an excited delight all the more joyful because of the previous fast.

Of course many of the Orthodox laity, like many other Christians, may clutch at their traditions by keeping up half-understood habits or half-sincere appearances. Of course many of the leaders of Orthodoxy have been too comfortable or too fanatical, like other church leaders. But the persistence of Orthodoxy under persecution has testified to the power of a faith carved deep into hearts. Infants naked as on the day of natural birth are baptized by immersions in the water which is the symbol of Christ's life, death and resurrection. They are breathed on, symbolizing the expulsion of devilry; they are anointed with oil consecrated by the bishop and symbolizing the outpouring of the Holy Spirit; they are clothed in pure white; and they are immediately given the consecrated bread and wine, their first taste of the spiritual food which will sustain their whole lives. When this baptism is spoiled by later sins, they can tell a priest who will stand beside them, pray for them and assure them of God's forgiveness. When they are married they will be reminded of the love between Abraham and Sarah in the Old Testament and between Mary and Joseph in the New and they will be crowned. 'When husband and wife cleave to each other in love, there is a remnant of Paradise': so said the far from sentimental John Chrysostom. Because marriage is meant to have this emotional content, Orthodoxy accepts, however reluctantly, that a relationship can die. When there has been adultery or desertion, profound incompatibility or extreme cruelty, after the applicant's penitence for any fault on his or her side the Church may bless a second marriage (and even a third). When sick the faithful can be anointed, with readings about Christ the healer. When they are buried there will be majestic prayers that they may share the reward of the saints. After death they can be purified (rather than punished) unless they should finally reject God's always available love. If only they will co-operate with the divine grace, they will find in the end deathless—in a sense, divine— perfection; and all the way the Church will have gone with them.

This spiritual tradition can be seen most intensively in the conversion of individuals from unbelieving nihilism (as Raskolnikov is converted in Dostoevsky's *Crime and Punishment*), or in prayer when in great danger (as in Tolstoy's account of the devotion of the soldiers before an image of Mary 'the God-bearer' as they prepared for the battle of Borodino), or in the spiritual growth of obstinate believers amid appalling horrors (as in Solzhenitsyn's *Gulag Archipelago*), or in the memory of a vision of glory amid inescapable compromises (as in Pasternak's *Dr Zhivago*). But the spiritual tradition also comes to life, day by day, as hermits, monks and nuns take to heart what Isaac the Syrian said in the seventh century: 'the beginning of the path of life is always to be instructing one's mind in the words of God and to live in poverty.' Since the sixth century Orthodoxy has chosen most of its bishops from among its monks, hoping for such holiness.

In this tradition the abbot John wrote his *Ladder of Paradise* in the seventh century, in the monastery at the foot of the mountain believed to be Mount Sinai, and there are Orthodox churches near Gethsemane where Jesus prayed in agony. And the tradition spread. Mount Athos, jutting into the sea off northern Greece, has been the spectacular home of many monks drawn from many countries since 963. In the fourteenth century the writing of Gregory

Palamas made public the monks' experience of entering 'uncreated' light through the 'prayer of quiet'. This 'hesychasm' aroused suspicion and controversy (it could be parodied as monks making themselves divine through spiritual exercises, even through monkish gymnastics), but at least it may be said to have been the spiritual summit of the Orthodox monastic tradition. This tradition created a thousand Russian monasteries and at its best has been close both to the spiritual heights and to the earth. In the fourteenth century Sergius the head of the Holy Trinity monastery near Moscow, the counsellor of princes, revered as a saint in his own lifetime, dressed like a peasant because he often worked as one in the kitchen garden. Russian monks eventually took Christianity, and following it civilization, into the forests and the wilderness, up to Finland, east to the Ural mountains, across Siberia and into Alaska. Earlier monks who were called 'heretics' but who claimed to be conservatively Orthodox had built their churches from Ethiopia to China.

Orthodoxy has enjoyed the patronage of many rulers. It has been expressed in glorious achievements of theology or art. But its main strength has been in its prayers and its main supporters have been the people of Christ's blessings which are often sung in the Liturgy: the poor, the mourners, the meek, the seekers, the merciful, the pure in heart, the peacemakers. That is a spiritual tradition, rich in many senses, which deserves to be honoured. But those who want a tradition to be strong in the future ought not to be romantic about the past. It has to be asked whether the Byzantine empire, where Orthodoxy assumed most of its present shape, was perfect.

The Byzantine Empire

The Byzantine empire was the first attempt to apply the religion which called Jesus of Nazareth 'Lord' to the government of a whole society. It is of course difficult to discuss in a few words. Even specialist historians are often at a loss because so much of the evidence has disappeared and because there were so many differences between periods, places and personalities. But some features are reasonably clear.

The empire lasted from 330 when Constantine I dedicated Constantinople as his eastern capital to 1453 when Constantine XI was killed as it fell to the artillery of the Ottoman Turks. The first Constantine's empire stretched from the Atlantic to the great rivers of Mesopotamia and from Hadrian's wall defending Roman Britain to the sacred island of Philae more than six hundred miles up the Nile. Before long it was, however, clear that this vast territory could not be governed by a single emperor. Even when the empire had been divided between the sons of Theodosius I in the 390s, neither the western nor the eastern half was impregnable. To the east there was another great empire, Persia's, which was in the end defeated but after great struggles. From the north barbarians poured in as raiders, mercenaries, settlers and conquerors. In the seventh century the Arabs conquered rich Egypt and much else. From the sixth century to the ninth the east as well as the west knew dark ages, when in addition to those great surrenders to invasions the climate was worse, recession and inflation wrecked trade and bubonic plague and other epidemics arrived from Asia. But between the ninth and the eleventh centuries an empire now more definitely eastern and Greek recovered more quickly than did the west. In the eleventh century it shrank again under blows from the Seljuk Turks; in the thirteenth it suffered again, now at the hands of fellow Christians who were 'crusaders' from the prospering west; yet even in the fifteenth, when it had become a very small remnant around a doomed city, some hoped that after so long a survival and so many recoveries there would be a miracle.

About a hundred years after its foundation Constantinople was protected by new walls of great strength. Together with a chain across the large natural habour (the Golden Horn) they were to save the city during a number of fearsome sieges, although this was before the development of artillery. At the same time Theodosius II codified the laws which were to be like walls around his empire. Many of them were against heretics who were 'insane' and deserved to be 'smitten'. Little more than a hundred years later Justinian caused these laws to be revised and extended, gave any remaining pagans three months in which to be baptized and closed down all pagan lecture halls including the Academy where Plato had taught. Because the cathedral had been burned down during a riot against high taxation, this emperor ordered the massacre of many thousands of rioters, increased the taxes and rebuilt the great church which became even more grandly the empire's spiritual centre. It was dedicated to *Hagia Sophia* (Holy Wisdom).

A famous story tells how envoys of Vladimir, the prince of the pagan Russians who was notoriously cruel and lustful, thought that here they might be in heaven and urged their master to embrace the religion which could create such a spectacle. The building was a stunning feat of engineering. The dome seemed to be suspended on little more than a circle of windows and it is not surprising that it had to be rebuilt after an earthquake. Silver lamps hung down and innumerable candles sent light up through the vast space as incense swirled and the clergy chanted: at one time sixty priests and a hundred deacons were on the staff. The sense of the triumph of Christianity was increased by the rows of multi-coloured marble pillars brought from pagan temples and by the shimmering golden mosaic on the walls. Some mosaics have survived censorship by Orthodoxy's own puritans (the icono-clasts) and by the Turks who used the church as a mosque until it became a museum in 1930. In the 1990s some Christians and Muslims still dream of restoring it as a house of prayer.

Emperors were crowned here from the fifth century onwards and many of the empire's political dramas were enacted here. The spheres of both the emperor and the bishop or 'patriarch' came to be called 'ecumenical' because they were claimed to cover the *oikoumene*, the inhabited world, however vaguely. In theory the two men collaborated in acknowledgement of the rule of God, so that the empire was a theocracy, under God's government. 'The beginning, the middle and the end of our legislation', Justinian pronounced, 'is hope in God.'

The empire was also an autocracy, whose one ruler could exercise virtually unlimited power while he possessed that power. His visitors were expected to fall prostrate before him as mechanical toys added their homage: golden birds sang, lions roared and thumped their tails, the throne rose in the air. Justinian included in an edict of 535 this definition of the spheres of the priesthood and the emperor: 'the first serves divine things while the latter directs and administers human affairs.' It was a division between prayer and power. But the concentration of power in the hands of one man (or sometimes one woman) meant that it could be seized by another, usually a general. A surprising number of the Byzantine emperors were either killed or dethroned; the emperor John V was deposed three times. An ex-emperor, if not murdered, was usually blinded, since a physically defective man could not aspire to a recovery of the throne, but anyone with a whole body and with sufficiently powerful support could be ambitious for the top since no constitution altered the practice of the pagan Roman empire: while normally a new emperor would be the son (natural or adopted) of his predecessor the position of *imperator* was essentially military and the road to it could also be military. And even a powerful emperor who kept his throne until a natural death would know, if he was shrewd, that despite all the pomp and sanctification he was surrounded by critical eyes. Procopius, the official and stately historian of the military and architectural feats accomplished during the reign of Justinian, also wrote a *Secret History* (discovered in the Vatican Library in the seventeenth century) in order to express his real mind. About Justinian and his wife he was scurrilous and about the emperor's generals he was scornful. About the emperor's theology he was sceptical, even in his published history of the wars, since 'I consider it a mark of insane folly to investigate the nature of God'.

Inevitably emperors depended on the commanders of the army and on the senior civil servants. Often they were well supported, but a price had to be paid. The senior officers had to be rewarded by the grant of large estates and this was one of the reasons why the peasants lost their earlier degree of freedom. The need for military manpower had to be met not by enlisting peasants who hoped for small grants of land but by paying large numbers of mercenaries through heavy taxation. The civil servants collected these taxes but had less ability to encourage the creation of the wealth which would have made the taxes easier to pay. And in battle the mercenaries were unreliable.

The control exercised in the emperor's name over the economy provided an early example of over-regulation enforcing what was believed to be morality. Cities which had prospered commercially with considerable independence before the Byzantine empire's dark ages were not rebuilt on the same scale, physically or legally. There was a contrast here with the prosperous cities in the vast trading areas which fell under Islam, and also with the cities of post-imperial Italy, of the Baltic and of the region between the Somme and the Rhine; these were the birthplaces of modern capitalism and the modern world. Venice, Genoa and other Italian cities did not arouse much competitive innovation in this tradition-bound Byzantine empire. Instead their traders were granted privileges including lower tariffs and their own self-regulating quarters in Byzantine ports. Too much commerce (like too much culture) was concentrated on Constantinople, where it basked under imperial patronage but grew unenterprising under imperial control. In the end the ruthlessly energetic merchants of Venice, formerly a Byzantine colony, ruled the eastern Mediterranean in rivalry with Islam.

The emperor's control over the Church was oversimplified when some modern scholars called it 'Caesaropapism'. Unlike some pagan Caesars the Byzantine emperor did not claim to be divine. Nor was he a pope. He was meant to rule in harmony (*symphonia*) with the bishops who were responsible for the doctrinal content of Orthodoxy. He was entitled to legislate about the administration of the Church but even in that more worldly sphere he was expected to be guided by the doctrines defined by the bishops and to leave most of the detailed work to them. Such was the theory.

In practice an emperor might insist on his own religious policy, he could browbeat a bishops' council before enforcing its decrees, and it took a courageous bishop to go against his will in any matter. In particular his was the decisive voice in the election of a bishop of Constantinople and ways could be found of declaring invalid the election of a bishop of whom he later disapproved. Thus Gregory of Nazianzus was more successful as a theologian and devotional poet than as the capital's bishop and soon found himself back in Nazianzus. The ninth century witnessed the removal of one bishop (now the 'patriarch') at an emperor's command, the removal of his distinguished successor, Photius, when that emperor had been murdered, and further changes of fortune for Photius, who was again appointed and again deposed.

But courage could be found in bishops. We shall see that some of them opposed emperors' policies over doctrines and over icons. John Chrysostom (the 'Golden-mouthed') was while bishop of Constantinople outspoken in his attacks on the immorality of the city and of the imperial court including the empress. He paid for his courage by exile and by treatment which succeeded in killing him, in 407. In the tenth century successive patriarchs resisted Leo the Wise because he married too often. When in the 1260s an able general, Michael Palaeologus, seized a tottering throne and threw out the Latin 'crusaders' who had occupied Constantinople, thus giving the empire another two hundred years of life, he was excommunicated as a cruel usurper.

Thus the subordination of Altar to Throne, although substantial, was not complete. Indeed, as the power of the emperors declined to zero in the fourteenth and fifteenth centuries the position of the patriarchs in church life was strengthened. The other eastern patriarchs were now under Muslim rule; in Constantinople, as part of Orthodoxy's greater emphasis on a spiritual life defying both Islam and western Catholicism, most of these men were primarily bishops not officials and many of them were monks.

In the fourth century Basil of Caesarea, a bishop who organized men as energetically as he organized theology, gave firm answers to questions put to him by monks. He treated monks as Christians called to 'perfection' but had no wish to cut them off from other Christians: indeed, he urged them to help the poor and to run schools, to welcome people who came seeking spiritual guidance and to share the Liturgy with others. But particularly as revised in the ninth century, his 'rule' gave answers, often austere, to 368 questions while avoiding the extreme self-denial of many of the hermits. Monks were tightly controlled (or punished) by the abbot, whose election was to be controlled by the local bishop. In the earlier centuries the average monastery was a commune in the countryside, employing labourers to do the agricultural work and in its turn owing profits as well as prayers to those who had founded it or to their descendants. Local people valued its prayers and turned to it for charity and guidance. For good or bad it was rooted in the local soil, not in an 'order' (organization) with many houses in many places, not detached from society to the extent which had been advocated by both Antony and Pachomius in Egypt. In later years many monasteries were founded by royal and other patrons in Constantinople and other towns and it became the custom that their considerable possessions should be managed by laymen who often rewarded themselves handsomely, not by the monks themselves as in the west. No 'order' combining, stimulating and supervising monasteries was allowed, however: emperors and bishops still feared the independence of monks. The result has been that the Orthodox monastic tradition, while full of examples of personal holiness and of lay gratitude, has not been so creative, because not so diverse, as the western tradition with its many orders, separate from 'the world' and from each other, all making history. To this observation the Orthodox reply is that it is not the task of the monk to make history. It is to pray, to be humble, to learn the wisdom of the Fathers, to help other humble Christians in private conversations, and thus to 'become God' in a totally thrilling although restricted sense. Diversity in the sense of different 'orders' is not needed although allowance has often been made for individual monks to live according to their own 'rhythms'. A place in history is not relevant: what the monk hopes for is a place in heaven.

Sunday by Sunday, and on the festivals of Christ and his saints, the people were—or were meant to be—involved in the Liturgy. To them, this religious unity was probably more significant than was membership of the empire as taxpayers. When 'heretics' such as the Arians, the Nestorians or the Monophysites defied the imperial version of Orthodoxy, motivated partly by their local loyalties, they maintained that their own version of the faith conserved the truth without any corrupting innovation and they hoped for the emperor's conversion. In Orthodox and 'heretical' churches alike prayer was taken seriously, the Liturgy of the baptized was central, festivals were observed, bishops took the lead, priests were in the villages, monks were valued as intercessors and spiritual guides, the Bible was established as the moral law (and as the final authority for much else), and churches were arranged and adorned in a standard pattern. There were disputes about the right faith but very seldom about the right shape of church life, for it seemed obvious that this was the right shape to correspond with reality as seen in the Byzantine centuries. On earth an emperor would be surrounded by a court; God in heaven was surrounded by angels and saints; so the Church must be orderly everywhere, even where the earthly emperor was rejected. All of Nature was full of proofs that everything had been created wisely and all of Scripture was full of proofs that the ordered perfection intended at the creation was being restored. The celebration of the Liturgy was the great drama of this restoration as bread and wine, building and people, were all transfigured into glory. But clergy, monks and nuns were needed to wage a spiritual war against the demons who remained active even after Christ's triumph—in Gregory of Nyssa's image, as a snake's tail may twitch when the head has been killed.

The privileged clergy lived off endowments given by the faithful and salaries paid out of taxes. The leading bishops controlled large wealth which they could use to support churches, charities, monasteries, their own staffs or their own prestige. Parish churches could be imposing, like the churches of the richer monasteries. Most churches, however, were quite small chapels and their clergy depended on small fees or gifts or on what their own hands could earn as farmers or craftsmen; and the bishops of rural dioceses had to keep an eye on their own fees. There were many churches—too many to be justified in economics, but that did not trouble the Byzantines who lavished money on their beauty. Most have been lost. Byzantine Jerusalem was made a ruin by the Persians in 614. Byzantine Alexandria lies under the sea or the less quiet modern streets. Byzantine Antioch can scarcely be detected under a twentieth-century city rebuilt after disasters including an earthquake. Constantinople has become Istanbul, partly Islamic and partly secular, after the destruction of all its Byzantine archives and of almost all its Byzantine art. Although many mosaics have survived in Thessaloniki its most majestic church, dedicated to its patron saint Demetrius, was destroyed by fire in 1917. But many churches are still suggestive. In Ravenna, once the western centre of Byzantine power, emperor and empress, courtiers and saints, stare down on visitors less sure of themselves. In Venice St Mark's cathedral shows that merchants wanting to build and rebuild a sumptuous, five-dome church copied Constantinople's architecture—and later installed treasures looted from the Byzantine wealth of beauty. Although many Byzantine traces have been obliterated in Asia Minor, the cave churches of Cappadocia still witness to a tough faith able to resist or escape many invaders. In Greece (most notably on Mount Athos or in the mountain-monasteries of the Meteora) and the Balkans monasteries have survived as communities, not merely as buildings, since the days of the empire. In Sicily the splendid mosaics of the twelfth century in Monreale in the hills above Palermo do their best to persuade uplookers that Norman kings did homage to Christ in the style of the Byzantine emperors whom they had ejected.

Byzantine architecture and art lost their prestige in the west but the twentieth century has viewed them with more understanding and admiration. Their symbolism has been appreciated: the church built as a basilica deliberately resembles an imperial court of justice and the cross-shaped church with a dome (a later development) suggests heaven. Turkish whitewash has been cleaned off mosaics and centuries of candle smoke have been removed from icons, restoring strong colours and careful details. The image of Virgin-and-Child, owing something to Isis-and-Horus in ancient Egypt, was as popular here as anywhere else. Christ was usually depicted as the Lamb of God or the Good Shepherd before he became the Judge of the mosaic made around 1100 under the dome in Daphni near Athens. In the course of this development he could be a man, even a man stripped for baptism or crucifixion. Archaeology has unearthed the wide spread of another style in the homes of the rich (and in some churches), a style which kept artists in employment even in the years when a puritan zeal forbade the painting of icons: a style happily Hellenistic, full of animals and birds, plants and fruits, with pleasant landscapes. Under the last Byzantine dynasty a new style of art, more representational, flourished. It was not so revolutionary as what Giotto did to Italian painting as the fourteenth century began, but in mosaics, painting and embroidery artists proved that there had been no decline in their skills. The town of Mistra near Sparta survives impressively from this late period. Selecting from the wealth of this developing tradition, the wonder of the twentieth century has fastened on the painted icon and the carved ivory. These almost always kept within strict conventions but there could be variations, as when musicians perform the work of composers. Here are images of a divine holiness which can be compassionate but never sentimental; of a glorified humanity which remains austere.

Byzantine literature is more difficult to admire. Much of it is tediously repetitive. When they used words about religion the Byzantines who wanted to be safe had less scope for subtle adjustments than in the visual arts. But Byzantine theology will demand our attention because it deeply influenced the later intellectual life of Christianity and we should remember that theologians worked as men who had been educated in the Greek classics: thus for his brother's benefit the patriarch Photius compiled summaries of 279 books including pagan works and the encyclopaedist Psellus conserved much ancient science. The more privileged Byzantines belonged in early manhood to the intoxicating world of Homer's gods and heroes and as adults enjoyed reading Hellenistic novels. Alongside this heritage from antiquity, and with curiously little sense of contradiction, Christian beliefs and behaviour were taught as the way to reach a greater glory. Because of this system of education the empire was served by a large and confident elite able to undertake leadership in Church and State, whether ordained or not. The leading clergy were expected to be equipped, and prominent, in tasks not strictly ecclesiastical. That was also the case in the western Middle Ages, but in the east, as not in the west, the laity included many theologians, from emperors downwards. Thirteen patriarchs of Constantinople in the Byzantine centuries had been laymen for most of their working lives. Theology and church were never left to the professionals.

And they were not left completely to the men. Although the early days of prominence in church life were now distant, the position of women in this Christian empire seems to have been somewhat better than the position in the surrounding societies. Laws about property and divorce were more favourable and several women were accepted as regents or as influential or even reigning empresses. Galla Placidia, the daughter of Theodosius I, ruled the west as regent 423–450 and her niece Pulcheria was empress in the east: both were great patrons of the Church. The most famous imperial woman was Theodora, formerly an actress (and, it was said, worse), who became the highly dignified consort of Justinian and an independent person of strong opinions who fully shared his appetites for government and theology. Gregory of Nyssa wrote a biography of his sister Macrina which with good reason presented her as a wise and creative saint, and his wife Theosevia was highly cultured as well as strongly religious. A developing cult centred on Mary the 'God-bearer' must have done something for the status of her sex: from late in the sixth century the formally recognized festival on 15 August celebrated her 'dormition' or falling-asleep, escaping a normal death. Books which would nowadays be classified as novels told stories about Mary or about the women to whom the apostles preached, most famously Thecla who 'sat at a nearby window and listened night and day' to the gospel being proclaimed by Paul. But the evidence which survives is almost all about aristocrats or saints who were nuns. Women who fell into neither category have almost all disappeared from the history written by men, as was normal.

In practice the position of people who were both female and poor was probably not very different from slavery. What we do know is that slavery was a generally accepted institution in the Byzantine empire. It had been accepted from the early days of Christianity but a big difference was that now the Church owned slaves. Even a preacher such as John Chrysostom, who was not afraid to rebuke the mightiest in the land, could say that the unpleasantness of being a slave was part of God's punishment of sin after the Fall of Adam. Other preachers said—as preachers were to say for many centuries to come—that there was no alternative. But there were many warnings against treating slaves harshly.

It is not difficult to see why the memory of this empire has haunted the minds of the Orthodox. Although the excitement of the fourth-century transformation from pagan to Christian died down and the vast territory became a remnant, this empire still claimed to have inherited and baptized the glory of Rome. Its rulers and many of its inhabitants identified themselves as 'Romans' living in 'Romania'. Or the Byzantines might simply call themselves 'the Christians'. In the sixth century the monk Dionysius Exiguus arranged the chronology of the known or biblical world around what he wrongly thought was the year of Christ's birth. Whether or not they used his method of dating, Byzantine historians put the history of their empire at the centre of the history of a world which, they often believed, had begun some 5,500 years before Christ and was due to end soon. In the 940s a scholarly emperor (Constantine VII) supervised the recording of the empire's customs for the benefit of his assistants and successors. Ceremonies surrounded him and the glamorous routine which he described was now established firmly, but with an equally scrupulous care he analysed the strengths and weaknesses of the many peoples entrusted into his care by God.

Councils under Emperors

The astounding change in the position of the Church owed everything to Constantine I, one of the most powerful of all the iron-willed men who ruled as Romans. When Bishop Eusebius of Caesarea orated about the thirty years of his reign in 336, in his presence, the eulogy might almost have been about the coming of the kingdom of God. The bishop's later biography was no less extravagant in praise. This dictator was officially called 'Equal of the Apostles' and his tomb was surrounded by memorials to them. He was, however, not baptized until death was near, since he relied on that sacrament to wipe away all his sins and at times he may have been aware that his sins were not few. Although his laws introduced some humane novelties he was as ruthless as any pagan emperor in pursuit or defence of power. He had his wife, his eldest son and 'many friends' put to death. That was in the year after his presidency of the Church's first 'ecumenical' council, held in his palace in Nicaea in 325.

We do not know exactly what went on then, but probably Constantine thought *homoousios* ('of one being') a grand word with which to refer to his own divine patron, under whose cross he had hacked his way to the throne of the Roman world. As we have briefly noted, the term had appeared in Christian theology in order to declare the unity of Father and Son but had been suspected because it was not in the Bible. Many churchmen who by temperament were far from heretical saw no need to use it. When Eusebius initially objected to its official endorsement he did so because he was satisfied with a more traditional faith which preserved the monarchy of the Father, who 'begat the Son by an act of will'. He had inherited the great library which Origen had collected: nowhere in it was this word regarded as the key to sound doctrine about Christ. But in Nicaea any hesitations were shouted down.

The bishops took their cue from the emperor. Eusebius, for example, although he hesitated over the word had no difficulty in believing in the full divinity of Christ—and now he was not going to argue against an emperor whose patronage had so dramatically improved the Church's position. When the decision had been taken he wrote a long, nervous letter to the church of which he was bishop. He assured it that the 'most pious emperor' had assured the council of the orthodoxy of Caesarea's familiar creed but had explained convincingly why the new word was needed in addition. Confident that his theological opinions would be received with respect, dressed in purple and gold with scarlet boots, Constantine did not hesitate to hold forth although he was neither a theologian nor a baptized Christian. When the voting was over all but two of the 220 bishops had agreed to *homoousios*. The two were exiled. The persuasive emperor was now host to a splendid banquet in honour of the others. They sat awed and marvelling, remembering the persecutions which had ended only a dozen years previously. Some of them still bore the marks left by their tortures.

The trouble had been caused by Arius, who had already denounced *homoousios*. Tall and gaunt, clever and talkative, this parish priest in Alexandria had learned theology in Antioch and thought he knew better than his bishop, Alexander. He was deposed but not deterred. However, he met his match theologically when he got a new bishop in 328. Physically little but even more combative, Athanasius made *homoousios* his battle cry.

Arius claimed to be loyal both to the New Testament and to Origen's example in thinking philosophically. As we have seen, in that age many people who thought about religion were sure that the One, being eternal, perfect and remote, needed at least one subordinate to do the dirty work of creating a world now experienced as imperfect. But it was by no means clear how divine this subordinate was. Even Plato had been unclear about whether the 'Craftsman' who did the work using the pattern provided by the perfect 'forms' or 'ideas' was identical with the 'Maker and Father of the universe'. Stoic philosophers had not agreed as to whether the *Logos*, the Reason in all things, was also beyond and above all things. So how was the relationship between Father and Son to be clarified, if the Son created everything according to the Father's will and was 'in', but also 'above', everything? Tertullian had compared the 'persons' of the Trinity with a partnership in ownership but he had also called Jesus 'this ray of God'. Origen had said that Father and *Logos* or Son were like sun and sunshine—but also that Christ was like a solid statue of the Father. A previous bishop of Alexandria (Dionysius) had made a series of comparisons for Father and Son: a spring and a river, a root and a plant, the maker and the sailor of a ship. Probably most Christians imagined Father and Son as a family but were even less clear than the theologians about their precise relationship. Inheriting this confusion, Arius chose to say that the Son was the agent of the Father in creation, himself either 'created' or 'begotten' by the Father 'before all ages'. He used both words but his tendency to prefer 'created' became highly alarming when he popularized slogans: 'the Son had a beginning but God is without beginning', at one stage in eternity 'the Son was not', the Son was made 'out of nothing', the Son was 'not equal' to the Father. It was deduced that he did not really believe that the relationship between the Father and the Son was very close. It was alleged that he had reduced the Son to the status of one of the divinities in the myths of the pagans, although his main intention seems to have been to defend the divinity of the Father.

The opponents of Arius also claimed to be interpreting the New Testament, but to be safeguarding its twin proclamations of God's unity and

Christ's divine power. Their way of keeping the two together was to insist that the Son had been 'begotten not made', coming 'out of the Father', from the Father's *ousia*, and not 'out of nothing' as if he had been like all creatures. Athanasius asked: 'Has God ever existed without his Son?' It seemed a simple question although it becomes not so simple once we ponder the difficulty of talking or thinking about the derivation of the eternal Son from the eternal Father. In the end it got the answer which Athanasius advocated because in Greek philosophical language this answer expressed the Christian experience that God's love known in Christ is part of the energy which has created all that exists. And the expression belonged to the Greek world of thought. God's life is eternal and perfect; God's Word or Son belongs to that life, yet has entered human existence and brought salvation. 'As the Lord became human by putting on the body', wrote Athanasius, 'so we who are human are made divine by the Word, by the fact that he has made us his own through the flesh; and from now on we inherit eternal life.' Christ had supplied what had been missing: a bridge within history between eternity and flesh, a bridge built by God.

That reply prevailed but the victory took half a century longer than was expected in 325. Constantine was not as rock-like as Athanasius. Most of the bishops did not stick to their council's decision when they had recovered from their banquet. Eusebius of Caesarea, who had hesitated and then conformed, now hesitated again and became a compromising emperor's favourite theologian. Another Eusebius who more openly regretted the conclusion of Nicaea was at one time in disgrace but was then brought to Constantinople as its bishop. He was eventually summoned to baptize the dying Constantine, who had changed his own attitude to the disputants because all he really wanted was quiet. When Arius became more amenable, agreeing that the Son was 'made of the Father', he was allowed to return to Alexandria before a peaceful death. It was not long before the eloquently unyielding Athanasius found himself deposed, exiled and sought by the police. Although he remained a hero in Egypt, he spent seven years as a refugee in Rome, and bishops who agreed with him were also removed. Hosius, who had been Constantine's ecclesiastical agent before Nicaea, protested that the next emperor, Constantius, had no right to interfere in church life by penalizing those who were loyal to that council. Athanasius more bluntly called the new emperor Antichrist. But when Constantius demanded a compromise very few of the bishops refused. Some 560 of them attended councils held in the east and the west in 359. Abandoning *homoousios*, they agreed that God the Son was 'begotten of God before all ages, like to the Father who begat him, but no one understands his generation except the Father who begat him'. In the next year Cyril the bishop of Jerusalem delivered a comprehensive series of lectures close to the site of

Christ's empty tomb, expounding 'the glory of him who was crucified here'. He did not mention *homoousios*. Valens, who was emperor 364–378, positively disliked the word as a source of trouble.

However, the bishops of the west were never happy with the minimalist formula which emperors such as Constantius and Valens favoured for the sake of peace. They preferred the strong trinitarianism of Tertullian and now produced their own champion of Nicaea, Hilary of Poitiers, 'the Athanasius of the west'. And eastern bishops, more sophisticated than the westerners in theology, were (it seems) relieved when death removed Athanasius of Alexandria from the scene. His combative personality had angered emperors.

The three 'Cappadocian Fathers' now appeared on the scene with a calm theology based on the Church's worship and life. It moved away from the disputations about the relationship of the Father and the Son, rejecting in particular the theology of an Arian bishop, Eunomius, who argued that since the Father is 'Unbegotten Being' and the Son 'Begotten' they cannot share the same being. To him it seemed perfectly clear that the Son was produced by the Father and the Spirit created by the Son. The reply of the Cappadocian Fathers was to say that the Trinity is indeed a mystery but that enough of the truth has been revealed in the Church's experience. For centuries Christians had been baptized 'in the name' of the divine Three—in a single 'name' but not into the name of the Father only. Christians had prayed to the Son as well as to the Father, their prayers had been answered and they had found the Spirit to be as real in their experience as the Creator or the Saviour. The Church had met Three, not One or Two, and all Three were fully divine.

In his youthful book on the Incarnation Athanasius had almost ignored the Spirit, although later, when Arians treated the Spirit as they had treated the Son, he made it clear that he believed in the Spirit's full divinity. Now Basil, the spiritually minded and masterful bishop of Caesarea the capital of Cappodocia, published a carefully considered treatise on the Spirit in 375, replying to an explicit denial of the Spirit's full divinity by another bishop, Eustathius, who in his youth had learned his theology from Arius. Five years later in his lectures as bishop of Constantinople Gregory of Nazianzus dwelt on the definitely threefold glory, beginning: 'When I say God I mean Father, Son and Holy Spirit.' This was not a mere appeal to a trinitarian formula. It did not even depend on the experience of the Church's worship in accordance with the principle which was to be formulated as 'the law of prayer makes the law of belief'. Certainly it was significant that baptisms had been in the threefold 'name', at least from the time when Matthew's gospel was written, and certainly the tradition was strengthened in the Church's worship. But the developed emphasis on the Spirit as one of the Three was due basically to the Christian experience of the Spirit teaching truth and making holiness in a miraculous triumph over all the intellectual and physical forces of the pagan Roman empire. Had it not been for this experience attributed to the power of the Spirit, it seems conceivable that the Church would have worshipped Two not Three. As it was, the emphasis on the Three could be defended at length and in the terms of the current philosophy. Basil's younger brother Gregory was bishop of the little country town of Nyssa and he had the leisure to write eloquently in Basil's defence against Eunomius and Eustathius. Basil and Gregory of Nazianzus had been fellow students in Athens and probably it was from their teachers in that still largely non-Christian university that they had learned the philosophical language which they now used in the interpretation of the Christian experience of the Three.

Each of the divine Three, they taught, is an identifiable *hypostasis*. Originally the word meant 'support', something standing under something else. In the Letter to Hebrews (11:1) faith gives *hypostasis* to our hopes. The Cappodocian Fathers, however, used the word to indicate what is particular in something, to answer the question 'which is it?' rather than 'what is it?' To answer the second question they used another word, *ousia*, whose earlier meaning had been very close to *hypostasis*. It can be translated into English either as 'being' or as 'substance'; in the latter case the English word depends on the Latin *substantia*, which we met in the teaching of Tertullian. The Greek word *prosopon* could be used as an alternative to *hypostasis* in its new meaning as an answer to 'which is it?' Originally that word meant 'face' and it could be used about the various masks worn by the three actors who between them took all the main roles in the tragedies and comedies of ancient Greece. But these three Cappadocian Fathers did not mean that the divine Three have roles which are temporary: as Basil said, the Three are made of eternal divinity as three coins are made of bronze. Least of all did these bishops advocate belief in three gods. They taught that the Three are distinguished from each other as human thought interprets what has been revealed in human experience, but always the unity was stressed by emphasizing the origin of the other Two in the Father. Basil of Caesarea, using the old comparison between the Father and the sun, said that the Father visiting the earth directly would have been like the sun visiting: so the Son was needed to avoid a total devastation. Gregory of Nyssa wrote a book *On Not Three Gods* and taught that 'all action which reaches the creature begins from the Father, is made present through the Son and is perfected in the Holy Spirit'. To grasp the Son, he wrote, is to take hold of him on both sides: 'on the one side he will bring the Father with him, on the other the Spirit.' Although *prosopon* was translated into Latin as *persona* and into English as 'person', the divine Three are not three people in the ordinary sense. They are Three-in-One, 'triune'.

The emperor who was supreme over the east from 379, although not secure in the west before 394, was a Spanish soldier whose understanding of trinitarian theology had been acquired from teachers in the west who stood by Tertullian and Nicaea. All emperors wanted unity in their empire and now Theodosius the Great was determined to achieve religious unity on the basis which he was convinced was correct. A council later reckoned to be, like that of Nicaea, 'ecumenical' (representing the whole world) but actually consisting of eastern bishops only was summoned to Constantinople. It met under the emperor's eye in 381 and a creed emerged out of it. This removed the explicit denunciations of Arius from the creed of Nicaea but otherwise reaffirmed it with important additions. Faith was now declared in the Holy Spirit, 'the Lord, the Giver of Life, who proceeds from the Father, who with the Father and the Son is worshipped and glorified together, who spoke by the prophets'. And to show that the Spirit had not ceased to speak, the council also declared faith in 'one, holy, Catholic and apostolic Church'.

After this agreement by the bishops, step by step Theodosius forbade not only all pagan sacrificial worship but also all assemblies of Christian heretics. Heavy fines and exclusion from the courts of justice were decreed as the penalties which were, however, not systematically enforced. It was not what Athanasius had wanted (while persecuted, he had considered persecution 'a device of the Devil') but this use of the state's power was not irrelevant to the gradual acceptance and use of the creed of 381. Athanasius was the defender of the conviction that in Christ Christians met nothing less than the true God; the Cappadocian Fathers defended the belief that when experiencing the Spirit Christians had experienced God; and now, if anyone doubted or resisted, the power of the government was placed on the side of the bishops' council. Here was a combination which few wished to resist. But that has not stopped modern theologians from raising questions, about the use of Greek philosophical terms as well as about the use of imperial power. One expert scholar, Christopher Stead, has claimed that all the theologians who took part in these debates were 'not trained philosophers' and that 'all the terms they had available at this stage carried a variety of senses which their users only half-understood'. Whether or not all the debaters deserved that low mark for their efforts to do philosophical theology, it is the case that many Christians have been uneasy about the imperial enforcement of the terms chosen.

The fourth-century dispute was called by a fifth-century historian (Socrates) 'a battle in the dark'. In Greek *ousia* is an ambiguous term, which was one of the reasons why most of the bishops were ambiguous in their attitudes to it: they suspected, then welcomed, then abandoned, then accepted it. Paul of Samosata had used *homoousios* precisely in order to defend the divine unity which Arius also wished to defend. To say that the Father and the Son were only 'of similar being' (*homoiousios*) might seem to be heretical—or it might recall the kind of belief which we have observed in the New Testament. To say that the Son was 'begotten' rather than 'created' sounded a more exalted statement, yet at one stage (in 360) a weary Athanasius said that the two words essentially meant the same. To say that the Son was 'begotten' but the Spirit 'proceeds' may also be to use two words with one meaning. To say that there was never a time when the Son 'was not' sounded correct, but many modern Christians have thought that to talk about time in eternity is nonsensical and that it does not make sense to speculate about the life of Christ before he became Mary's son. In Orthodoxy itself the 'apophatic' tradition is one of reserve about speculations.

In that age as in ours, a battle over words could seem an irritating distraction. Many wanted it over without a clear victory for either of those inflexible controversialists, Arius and his bishop. When Constantine first heard of it he sent a stern message to Alexandria: 'It was wrong to propose such questions as these or to reply to them when propounded.' He of all men was in the best position to know how fragile was the Christianization of the empire which he had begun against the wishes of most of his subjects. That revolution might still be reversed and in fact his nephew Julian launched a determined counter-revolution with widespread support when he became emperor in 361. When he announced that he would encourage debates among Christians and pagans alike, it was (a contemporary pagan explained) because Julian knew from the recent controversy that 'there are no wild beasts so hostile to mankind as are many of the Christians to one another'.

It is certain that this controversy diverted the energies of bishops (at least) away from the more urgent tasks of basic evangelism and pastoral instruction in a time of great opportunity. The difficulties of spreading and deepening the empire's 'conversion' were great anyway, but were increased by this felt need to attend to abstruse theology because a wrong decision might result for a bishop or preacher in personal disaster. It seems likely that at least half the population of the empire was not Christian, not even nominally, before the 390s, when in a civil war against Theodosius in the west an army fought with pagan symbols on its shields. It was amazing that the membership of the Church grew from perhaps five to perhaps thirty million during its fourth century but often the evidence suggests that the conversion was only skin deep. Christians used about others the word *pagani*, which was originally used by professional soldiers about their unprofessional assistants who did the lowly jobs in the army. But now in practice there was often no sharp distinction between the Christian and the pagan.

The aristocracy was largely non-Christian; not until 421 was it thought possible to exclude pagans from the empire's management. Even those who had adopted the emperor's faith often retained pagan symbols in their homes and presumably also in their hearts. It may be felt that the Christian gospel could never have appealed to such self-interested materialists whose real religion was money and pleasure and who conformed to official paganism, or to official Christianity, in order to belong to a ruling class owning many slaves and exploiting the peasants. But some of these powerful aristocrats were thoughtful—for example Symmachus the governor of Rome, whose essential criticism of Christianity was that a mystery so great as the being of God could not be approached by a single path. Until it was closed in 529 Athens remained the most prestigious centre of higher education in the empire and what it taught the young was not utterly unlike what Plato or Aristotle had taught long before Christ. As a lonely and bookish teenager the future emperor Julian thought his way out of Christianity into a religion deeply considered and deeply believed. At the age of twenty, after being allowed to study various philosophies and religions, he finally lost the Christian faith in which he had been baptized and brought up. At the age of thirty, in 361, when he became sole ruler of the Roman world, he thought it safe to 'worship the gods openly' along with most of the army. He now used nights to write a book *Against the Galileans*, later burned as the books of Celsus and Porphyry had been but quoted in fragments by Christians trying to reply. He concentrated his attack on the claims made by the contemporary Church (not, he stressed, by the Bible) that Jesus was divine. 'All of us, without being taught, have reached belief in some sort of divinity'—but the real God cannot be crucified. And in answer to the Christian claim that Jesus had been raised from the dead, Julian seems to have proposed to resurrect Judaism by rebuilding the temple in Jerusalem. It was indeed fortunate for the Church that he was killed in battle after reigning for twenty months.

Men such as those were unlikely to be impressed by the bishops' councils and their consequences. Some intellectuals were Christians, but the recorded difficulties of Augustine's spiritual pilgrimage before he was baptized as a Catholic show both that the Catholic faith seemed far from obviously true in educated elites in Carthage, Rome and Milan and that the problems being debated there—problems about the character of God and the character of the creation—were far from identical with the abstruse questions which preoccupied the bishops' councils. Nor did these councils answer the protests which had been made by Celsus and Porphyry about the Christians' naive use of the Bible and their arrogant attitude to non-Christian religion. Nor was there any serious thought about the relationship with Judaism.

Although it is not easy to recover evidence about the lives and thoughts of ordinary folk, it is revealing that 'canons' (laws) agreed at Nicaea had to cope with many ordinations of men who had turned out to be unsatisfactory Christians. At this time many laypeople who wished to be counted as

Christians postponed baptism until near death, as Constantine himself did: they were content to be 'catechumens' with fewer obligations to change their ways. And when they died, pagan as well as Christian symbols were often put on or in their tombs, as excavations have shown. In the towns the old customs in public entertainment still continued, without or with public reference to patronage by the old gods: gladiators fought each other to the death in the arena and many plays were still grossly obscene. Emperors' laws against 'games' involving gladiators do not seem to have been fully effective before the 680s. Although Constantius forbade pagan sacrifices in the 340s the decree proved impossible to enforce everywhere for another half-century, and even where sacrifices stopped many temples remained open for other uses until the fifth century. In Alexandria in 391 riots involving both Christians and pagans ended with the destruction of one of the greatest temples in the pagan world, the Serapeum, with the emperor's approval, but that did not mean that everyone in the city became a devout Christian. In Constantinople the fans of the rival theologians behaved somewhat like the Blues and Greens who were the fans of the charioteers racing in the hippodrome of Constantinople; and those fans could back theologians instead of sportsmen. Bishop Gregory of Nyssa complained that when one asked for change one was given instead an opinion about the origins of God the Son— and, what was worse, it was an Arian opinion. If one wanted a loaf of bread one received the information that the Father was greater than the Son. If one needed a bath one was told that the Son had been created out of nothing.

This good bishop was perhaps not convincing when he compared the moral and spiritual life of a Christian with the excitement of a chariot race, but certainly the care now being taken by bishops for the sick and the unemployed communicated. There were also successful developments of feasts and fasts. In Rome by 336 the birth of Christ was being celebrated on 25 December: it was the day of Saturnalia, the carnival of the sun god as the days began to lengthen. On 29 June the apostles Peter and Paul were celebrated: it was the day of a midsummer carnival in honour of Romulus, the founder of pagan Rome. Such festivals could still be exuberant but in this period the custom of Lent spread. During forty days before Easter Christians were urged to fast and pray: it was a move to preserve something of the Church's austerity. And the drama of baptism must have impressed countless people who were not likely to be immersed in the theological disputes: according to Cyril of Jerusalem, candidates were stripped, buried three times in the water and anointed with holy oil from hair to feet. We may wonder whether it was wise for the Church to place so much emphasis on dry arguments about an event in eternity.

We may also wonder whether it was necessary to persecute Christians who took the wrong side in these battles over words, particularly since we know that some of these dissenters became effective missionaries among the people who conquered most of the western half of the Roman empire.

Wulfila (or Ulphilas) had been a priest in a Constantinople which inclined more to Arius than to Athanasius and he always preferred the creed of 359 to that of 381. He was made a bishop for the Christians among the Goths who had settled in the Balkans and he translated the Bible into their language. Teaching based on this Gothic Bible and accompanied by worship in the same language shaped a form of Christianity that proved remarkably successful. Its appeal was mainly to Germanic peoples who settled within the borders of the old Roman empire and wanted a new religion to go with their new life, but also wanted clergy who would not take orders from Rome or Constantinople. It lasted until the end of the sixth century as the creed of the Visigoths as the ruling class in Spain. The Vandals who occupied much of North Africa adhered to the same creed until the middle of that century, as did the Ostrogoths who occupied much of North Italy; and the Lombards who swept into Italy after those Goths kept this faith until their last strongly Arian king died in 671. Until many abandoned this faith— which in North Africa and Italy was largely a matter of yielding to Byzantine military force—Arians could regard themselves as the true Christians, adhering to the Bible and to the pre-325 Church. This belief was convenient when Visigoths or Vandals enthusiastically sacked Catholic Rome, or when Vandals wished to eliminate the Catholic landowners in North Africa. On their side Catholics thought that they knew that Arians were heretics. This attitude helped to divide kingdoms ruled by Arians but inhabited by many Catholics. In Italy the Ostrogoths, being Arians, found that their kingdom was fatally disunited when attacked by the Byzantines. In Spain, where the Catholicism of the dominant Visigoths was fairly recent, the Catholic people did little to resist the Muslim invasion in 711 and one battle de- livered almost the whole of the country into the hands of these new masters. And it is not entirely clear that this fateful division between Catholics and Arians was inevitable. When we look at the churches built for the two groups in Ravenna, it is obvious that the Arians had less skill than the Catholics. It is not so obvious that they belonged to a different religion, for church life seems to have been much the same under the two creeds and probably few on either side were seriously interested in the theological arguments.

However, just as those who lost in civil wars lost their lives or at least their eyesight, so bishops and other teachers defeated in theological battles should expect no mercy. When they had the opportunity Arians could be as merciless as the Catholics who in the end prevailed. Accordingly the Catholic bishops' council of 381 did what such a council was expected to do: it exerted discipline. It not only condemned the memory of Arius; it also dealt harshly with a theologian who had been the close friend and ally of Athanasius and was then a bishop in his seventies. As he had grown older and eccentric, Apollinaris had begun to interpret the faith of Nicaea with excessive emphasis on Christ's divinity. He had taught that when God the Word became 'flesh' he had no human soul. It was then believed both that the soul came from God through the human father and that Jesus had no such father, but Apollinaris was also motivated by the thought that the possession of a soul might have exposed Jesus to the possibility of sinning. His fellow bishops were unimpressed, agreeing with the doctrine of Gregory of Nazianzus that if Christ had not 'assumed' a soul as well as a body, human nature would not have been 'healed'. And it was made a crime for any preacher to disagree. In the eyes of Church and State Apollinaris became what he had foolishly said Jesus was: a non-person. A number of books which embody his teaching have survived but under the names of other authors, whether or not he wrote them. Books which he certainly did write have been lost, probably deliberately. In collaboration with his father he had written a version of the Bible in classical Greek in order to get its message across to the cultured, and he had defended Christianity at length against two formidable pagans, the philosopher Porphyry and the emperor Julian. He had also written many commentaries on the Bible. But all this work counted as nothing in comparison with his lapses in old age.

He was lucky in comparison with Priscillian, a Spanish bishop who was executed in 385 along with four priests, a widow and a poet. They had been convicted of 'sorcery'. Actually they seem to have been guilty of an eccentric kind of occult mysticism and extreme asceticism, probably a variety of Christian Gnosticism. An equally austere but definitely orthodox bishop, Martin of Tours, was among the Christians who expressed dismay at this turn of events. Less than seventy years had passed since the Roman empire had stopped killing people for being Christians.

The Church of the East

As we have noted, the council of 381, although reckoned 'ecumenical', consisted of eastern bishops only and was summoned by the emperor to meet in his palace in Constantinople. One of its decrees was that 'because it is the new Rome the bishop of Constantinople is to enjoy privileges after the bishop of Rome'. This was rejected in Rome; mockery was to greet the legend that the church in Constantinople had been founded by Peter's brother Andrew. The decision also displeased Alexandria which was no longer to hold the second place. In 403 a bishop of Alexandria secured the removal of John Chrysostom from the bishopric of Constantinople on fabricated charges of heresy: the lesson intended was to teach 'the new Rome' that as the corn which it needed grew in Egypt, so did the theology. A riot in the capital resulted in the brief return of its bishop until the emperor bowed to the will of his wife who had been affronted by John Chrysostom's persistent preaching against immorality. Egypt remained determined to press its claim that Constantinople needed to be instructed in orthodoxy and in 431 a highly energetic bishop of Alexandria, Cyril, found himself in a position to assert his theological superiority when he presided over an ecumenical council of bishops, convened in Ephesus to consider charges against another bishop of Constantinople, Nestorius.

The accused had criticized the popular use of the title *Theotokos*, 'God-bearer', in honour of Mary. The church where the bishops met was dedicated to Mary as *Theotokos* and if any further argument against heresy was needed it could be explained that since Christ was God as well as Man the title was orthodox. (Origen had used it.) In defence Nestorius agreed that Christ was God the Son in eternity and that Mary should be honoured as 'Christ-bearer' since the human nature which the Son 'assumed' obviously needed a mother, but he still objected to the popular title as theologically unsound. However, he was too frightened of physical violence to argue his case in public: no doubt he remembered that only sixteen years previously a mob of monks in Alexandria had murdered a scholarly woman who was the last of the pagan philosophers, Hypatia. His condemnation was inevitable. In vain did he send the assurance that he worshipped Christ: he was denounced as a 'man-worshipper'. Cyril of Alexandria led what seemed to be a simple insistence that Christ was fully divine, in the womb as later. His formula was 'one nature of God the Word incarnate': although he thought it came from Athanasius, modern scholars have shown that Cyril was unintentionally quoting the condemned Apollinaris. Unquestionably the council's decision about Mary was welcome in the Church at large: in Rome it was celebrated by adding mosaics about her life to the great *basilica* of Santa Maria Maggiore, already about eighty years old.

Both Nestorius and Cyril were deposed and imprisoned by an emperor anxious for his empire's unity and contemptuous of this arcane dispute. Cyril bribed his way back into freedom and favour but Nestorius became a monk in the Egyptian desert and continued to protest that he had been misunderstood: he had intended no heresy. Most of his writings were burned but a complicated theological treatise in which he attempted to clear his name survived and was discovered in 1889. At considerable length it demonstrates that he was no 'Nestorian' in the sense later developed, when Nestorianism was to be identified, at least by its enemies, with the simple statement that in Christ there were two 'persons'. Nestorius did defend the idea that there were three 'persons': the divine nature, the human nature and their union. But this defence made it clear that he used the word which was to be translated as 'persons' in a sense very different from 'three people'. The Christians who were to be called 'Nestorian' were to have an official theology which attributed a single *prosopon* to Christ. So he founded no school of thought.

A group of bishops in East Syria who had supported him proved more obstinate. Their tradition had already become distinctive, expressed in Syriac not Greek, fed by the prayer and mysticism of austere monks, meditating on the Bible with a theology more poetic than philosophical. They continued to teach in this tradition and eventually they escaped to Persia, now the centre of an empire under the Sassanian dynasty: they received a welcome because they had dissociated themselves from the Byzantine empire by rejecting its official theology. This was the real beginning of the 'Church of the East' which was inaccurately to be called Nestorian.

In 486 the Persian bishops issued their version of belief about Christ, robustly defying the authority of Constantinople. They also decided that all Christians, including bishops, were entitled to marry, in acknowledgement of the Persian belief that celibate men were insufficently masculine. A centre of biblical and theological study was established in the garrison town of Nisibis, on the Persian side of the frontier with the Byzantines. These Christians were never more than a minority in Persia but they became a protected minority. Before the anti-Byzantine 'Nestorians' arrived the Persian Church had been persecuted: it had been perceived as a nest of traitors. Now the aristocracy was still expected to adhere to the official Zoroastrian religion but people in the lower classes (including many Arabs and slaves captured from the Byzantines) were permitted to be Christians, for the Church's patriotic credentials were accepted. And the Nestorian version of Orthodoxy continued to be tolerated when the Muslim Arabs had conquered the county in the 630s and had prohibited Zoroastrian practices as pagan. These Christians were used by the Arabs as craftsmen, administrators and scholars. The theological centre in Nisibis had a wider use, for translations of Greek books into Syriac conveyed much useful knowledge. With their hands or their brains the Nestorians contributed substantially in the transformation of the Islam of the Arabian desert into a culturally rich civilization.

In an even more surprising development this splinter-church of Orthodoxy spread from Persia along the trade routes to the east. It was taken by the caravans along the Silk Road across the empty steppes of central Asia to China and Mongolia and by the little ships of the spice trade across the Persian Gulf to South India, Sri Lanka and Indonesia. Already the bishops who had assembled for the council of Nicaea had included one who had signed himself 'John the Persian', representing 'the churches of great India'. About a hundred years later a merchant of Alexandria (Cosmas) reported that Christians in India were under 'a bishop appointed from Persia' and that there were 'Persian Christians' in Sri Lanka. Probably these missions to the east and south depended on traders and did not win many converts, but the Nestorians had hundreds of bishops and also a chain of monasteries where prayer was intense and life was austere: they were, it seems, fully a match for the piety of the Byzantine Church and for some centuries their numbers were larger. Isaac the Syrian, whose writings on the spiritual life have been influential throughout Orthodoxy, was a Nestorian monk.

In the seventeenth century an inscription was found in Hsianfu, which for a period was the capital of China. It had survived from the eighth century. Using Chinese idioms, it proclaimed the 'origin of origins' in the world's creation by God, the arrival on earth of the 'shining saviour' and the gift of the Holy Spirit bringing 'the capacity to do good through the true faith'. This saviour's ministers, it said, worship seven times a day and once every seven days offer a 'bloodless sacrifice'. And it proudly recorded that about 150 years previously, in the year 636, 'a man of great virtue called Alopen' had been welcomed by the Chinese emperor and given permission to preach. No mention was made of what Nestorians were alleged to preach heretically, that Christ was 'two persons'.

When in the thirteenth Christian century the Mongols swept out of central Asia to east and west, the Nestorians were needed by the new conquerors. These were horsemen who found it easier to acquire an empire stretching from the Mediterranean to the Pacific than to administer it. So the Mongols, like the Arabs before them, used these Christians who could read and write and were willing to serve. The Nestorians' position under their new rulers seemed so secure that there were hopes that they might help to arrange an alliance between Catholics and Mongols against the Muslims. A Nestorian priest sent to Rome and Paris in the 1280s was received in such a friendly fashion that he thought he was being treated as a fellow believer in the apostles' faith. But in the 1290s the Mongol khans (princes) in Persia decided to move beyond their contemptuous toleration of their subjects' various beliefs into a more advanced religion. Mongols to the east were already turning to Islam and Buddhism. If the khans ever considered the Nestorians might serve as religious instructors, they rejected them as not soldierly and instead embraced Islam. Despite the Muslim tradition they now saw no need to tolerate any religious minority and soon began a brutal persecution. The most savagely successful of the khans, Timur, often massacred fellow Muslims but made a special point of exterminating Christians before his own death in 1405.

In China the Mongols' policy of religious toleration was less contemptuous than it had been in Persia, partly because the great Kublai was more of a diplomat and had a Christian mother and Christian advisers and assistants at his court. A merchant of Venice who stayed in China for many years, Marco Polo, was asked in 1266 to convey Kublai's invitation to the pope to send a mission but when John of Monte Corvino, a Franciscan already experienced in Armenia and Persia, got to the great man at the end of 1293 only a few weeks of Kublai's life were left. His successor was polite rather than interested and John faced trouble from the Nestorians, who regarded him as an intruder. In his turn he viewed them as 'far removed from the Christian religion'. He managed to build churches and to make converts; a delighted pope made him an archbishop and sent other Franciscans to join him before his death in 1330. It seems that the Nestorians remained the chief representatives of Christianity in China, however; Marco Polo had heard reports about their churches in at least a dozen cities although like the Franciscan missionary he did not acknowledge them as fellow Christians, observing merely that 'they are the worst of heretics and heretics make heretics'.

Clearly both Nestorians and Catholics depended on the Mongol emperors' policy of religious toleration in China and their hopes declined as that dynasty's power declined, to end in 1368. No one knows what then happened to the Christians, who may have been mostly Mongols. A cross has been found on a helmet in Japan or in a grave in Manchuria and it may well be a Christian symbol from that century, but from China itself there is silence. What is known is that the next dynasty, the Mings, seized power amid peasants' rebellions against the foreign and oppressive Mongols. They revived their own immense country's prosperity but after 1450 most contacts with the outside world were broken off and Chinese ships were forbidden to leave coastal waters. Confucian traditions were reasserted by the upper class and popular religion received an injection of spirituality from a Chinese-style Buddhism. The Nestorians had always been conscious of Buddhist rivals, whose monasteries were prominent along the Silk Road. They had not won the competition.

In the twentieth century this 'Church of the East' numbers no more than half a million, found mostly in Iran and Iraq and as refugees from Islam in the USA. It had failed in its courageous attempt to expand Christianity across Asia, but that was, it seems, not because of any distinctive theology. It had failed because the distances which had to be covered were so vast and because so many Christians had been killed.

Chalcedon and its Rejection

Theological controversies within the Byzantine empire were now to lead to another large group of Christians, the Monophysites or 'Oriental Orthodox', making their exit from imperial control. This movement was to start from a point in the theological spectrum very different from the 'Church of the East' but it, too, was to convey the Christian message to new peoples. And it was to be established more permanently than the churches called after Arius and Nestorius.

The disputes were still about the 'nature' or 'natures' of Christ. A council of bishops meeting in Ephesus in 449 under the presidency of the bishop of Alexandria agreed, as instructed by him, that Christ had only one nature (Monophysitism). They agreed with such enthusiasm that the bishop of Constantinople, who disagreed, died of his injuries. At the time the emperor supported this decision but two years later another emperor (Marcian) convened another council, more representative, more peaceful and more inclined to reach a settlement—which was what the new emperor, a military man, wanted. More than five hundred bishops met in a suburb of Constantinople, Chalcedon.

The famous 'Chalcedonian definition' on which they agreed leaned some way towards the Monophysitism favoured in Alexandria, but it did so by decreeing not that the incarnate Son had one *physis* (nature) but that he had one *prosopon* (person) or *hypostasis* (existence) in two 'perfect' natures. The union of these two natures was 'without confusion, change, division or separation'. To many modern theologians this has seemed the final defeat of Antioch's insistence on Christ's full humanity, for according to the council there was no human *hypostasis* in Jesus. It has often been asked whether the formula did justice to the simple fact that Jesus was a man, with a human personality. A frequent protest has been that Chalcedon moved too far beyond the New Testament into the over-ambitious subtleties of Greek philosophy. Its 'definition' of Christ was more theoretical than the creed of 381 had been and it managed to describe him without emphasis on his teaching, death or resurrection: by now, these things could be taken for granted. The definition was, indeed, so theoretical that it spoke of 'natures' which cannot be either confused or separated, ignoring the question of how they may be distinguished and discussed: that possibility, too, was taken for granted. Moreover, while being so theoretical it offered no definition of the key terms *physis*, *prosopon* and *hypostasis*, which as we have noted had many possible meanings. But immediately after this council trouble did not come from people who protested that the humanity of Jesus had been over-shadowed by a cloud of undefined metaphysics. It came from people with a very different objection: that the council had fallen for what could be regarded as an innovation, the idea that Jesus had a human 'nature'.

The most important rejection of Chalcedon's decision came from Egyptian bishops who were loyal to the teaching of Cyril of Alexandria that there was only 'one nature of God the Son incarnate'. They were prepared to say that when Jesus was miraculously conceived, this one nature had been made *from* two natures, divine and human, but they absolutely refused to add that after the conception his existence was *in* two natures. In Greek the difference between 'from' and 'in' is the difference between *ek* and *en*, so that the dispute may be dismissed by impatient critics as a theological war about a single letter. But at the time the difference seemed to matter. It mattered so much that it provided the theological justification for a major split in Orthodoxy.

One reason why it mattered was that the bishops responsible for the new definition had not been content to repeat Cyril of Alexandria. With their emperor's encouragement they had adopted some phrases suggested by Leo, bishop of Rome, in a weighty 'tome' or letter. The Egyptian bishops protested that when they got back to their own people they would be killed if it was said that they had abandoned Cyril in favour of a definition which had begun its life in Rome. The offence given to the pride of Egypt was, moreover, increased by a new 'canon' law: the council decreed that 'the most holy throne of the new Rome' should have privileges equal to those given by 'the fathers' to 'the throne of the old Rome'. This development in Constantinople's ecclesiastical position, an advance on 381, was justified on the ground that it was 'the imperial city'. It angered both Rome and Alexandria—and in Alexandria there was an additional reason for rejecting the council. The people of Egypt and Syria spoke Coptic or Syriac, not the Greek of Constantinople—and they objected to paying the heavy taxes which went to the capital. In other words, the empire was disintegrating.

But the dispute was not merely about the prestige of rival bishops, or about language, or about taxes. The decision that Christ had a human nature seemed to go against the whole Egyptian emphasis on Christ as the divine Saviour—more divine than the ancient gods whose temples were still the chief sight of Egypt, more saving than the ancient passwords to the heavenly home of the gods. Egypt was now a land where the most important institutions were the monasteries and where monks were among the Christians ready to demonstrate their fervent faith in the divine Saviour by violence, as they had done when accompanying their patriarch to the previous council (when the terrified representative of the bishop of Rome had been forced to cling to the altar as he shouted his disagreement with Monophysite theology). Alexandria's next bishop, a Chalcedonian imposed on the Monophysites by the Byzantine army, was murdered.

Even when Byzantine rule was reimposed, most of Egypt refused to accept the theology of Chalcedon. So did most of Syria, where the 'Jacobites' were able to evoke memories of the now remote first-century beginnings of Christianity under James (or Jacob) of Jerusalem. And the theological conservatism of these Monophysites led to several novelties in their church life. The creed of 381 was now for the first time recited in the Liturgy: they meant it to show that they were more traditional than the Chalcedonians, although the Chalcedonian churches adopted the custom as an affirmation of their own loyalty to the heritage. Cyril had insisted that 'one of the Trinity' suffered on the cross, so 'who was crucified for us' was now added to the traditional acclamation of Christ as 'holy God'. Cyril had also insisted that Mary was highly exalted as the 'God-bearer'. The earliest belief was that her soul was taken to heaven (which has remained the central theme in Orthodox art) but a story of uncertain origin but known in fourth-century writings spread that at the end her body had been 'assumed' into heavenly glory. Traces have survived of rival stories that her body had been taken to heaven by angels on its way to burial, or had been raised to life after death. All such stories reflected the belief that the body which had once carried God the Son could never be corrupted, but it seems that the Monophysites found it easiest to believe in the assumption of the body before death and it is known that the belief was held in Constantinople in the seventh century. A factor in the growth of devotion to Mary seems to have been delight in the thought that her entry into glory offered hope to women and men. Monophysite teaching about Christ did not deny his humanity but made it less obvious than Mary's, at least for non-theologians.

As positions on both sides hardened, this combination of religious and social protests gradually produced a network of bishops not in communion with Constantinople. They also objected to the local or 'Melkite' hierarchy which accepted Chalcedon and was now regarded as an imperialist intrusion. A bishop in Syria, Jacob Baradai, was more instrumental than anyone else in making the 'Jacobite' schism definite and permanent. In 35 years of travel before he died in 578 he ordained large numbers of bishops or priests to serve inside and outside the empire, which added to the excitement by trying and failing to catch him. Another response by the authorities of Church and State was the increasing use of the title 'patriarch' to refer to the imperially approved bishops of Rome, Constantinople, Alexandria, Antioch and Jerusalem, whose seniority had been affirmed at Chalcedon. Their participation in the making of bishops in their regions was now regarded as essential.

Later another Jacob (of Edessa) arose and worked out a Monophysite theology. And these Monophysites developed an evangelism (although not a theology) similar to the Nestorians'. Going where the emperor had no power, Coptic Christians went further up the Nile, planting churches among the Nubians. Muslims were to conquer and convert much of this area (Sudan) but the effects of this Christian missionary work were still visible in the sixteenth century. Monophysites also strengthened Egypt's religious links with Ethiopia; not until 1959 did their patriarch in Alexandria admit that the large Ethiopian Church was completely self-governing. Jacobite Syrians built up churches in Mesopotamia. And towards the Black Sea, Armenia's ancient church emerged as permanently non-Chalcedonian. Its theology may not have been identical with the theology of the Monophysites in Egypt and Syria, any more than Ethiopian theology was identical, but there was certainly a refusal to receive dictation from Constantinople.

Thanks to the never-forgotten mission of Gregory the Illuminator which converted King Dirtad, Armenia had become an officially Christian kingdom shortly before Constantine's conversion. For a century and a half it remained Orthodox with the normal faith and organization, but it learned to its cost that the empire could not defend it against Persia and it declared its ecclesiastical independence shortly before half of its land was lost to the Persians in the 380s. It then began to use its own language in worship. By the end of the next century most of what was left of the Armenian Church had repudiated the theology of remote Chalcedon as a novelty and later reconciliations with Constantinople did not prove permanent. The Byzantine empire provided no protection when the Arabs came in the 650s and Armenians suffered again when what was left of the country was absorbed into the empire in 1045, for now they were persecuted as heretics. Within twenty years massacres by the invading Turks had begun another kind of suffering. Turkish occupation reached its climax in Turkish genocide between 1893 and 1918 and the suffering continued at a lower level of persecution under Communism. Not until 1991 did Armenia recover its political independence, with its staunchly conservative church once again acknowledged as the church of a martyred people.

After Chalcedon

After the council of Chalcedon emperors tried to reunite the empire by attempting to conciliate the Monophysites without alienating the Chalcedonians. It seemed to be a shrewd policy to reaffirm Chalcedon's decisions but also to praise the theology of Cyril of Alexandria, stressing the unity of Christ's two natures and accepting what had become the Monophysite slogan that 'God died' on the cross. In 482 the emperor Zeno issued an 'edict of union' along these lines but Monophysite bishops who welcomed this peacemaking had to face a rebellion in their own ranks while Orthodox bishops of Constantinople found themselves out of communion with bishops of Rome and the loyally Chalcedonian west. The edict died. In 543 a more determined emperor, Justinian, issued his own theology, condemning the memories of three bishops who had earlier contributed to the tangled discussion; they had been acquitted of heresy at Chalcedon but were obnoxious to the Monophysites because they had criticized Cyril. Ten years later he summoned the second 'ecumenical' council of Constantinople which unsurprisingly endorsed his condemnations.

However, this move, too, failed to win over the Monophysites. What it did was to add a further incident to the story of Constantinople's relationship with Rome. The current bishop, Vigilius, had reluctantly accepted the emperor's theology in 544 and then, after protests by other western bishops, had withdrawn his acceptance. Now after prolonged ill-treatment in Constantinople he withdrew his withdrawal, but he died during his journey back to Rome. Justinian had won and during the last dozen years of his life nothing interested him so much as the enforcement of what he knew to be Orthodoxy. His army's victories broke the power, and subdued the religion, of the Arians in North Africa and Italy. But a Byzantine emperor had dangerously set himself up as the world's most authoritative theologian and had come into open conflict with a bishop of Rome. Rome's bishops remained for many years the empire's subjects, paying taxes, but the future was to show that they would throw off this allegiance when the empire could neither dominate nor defend them.

Many of the military conquests made in Justinian's name melted away but the seventh century brought a very able general to the Byzantine throne: Heraclius, who while unable to reconquer the west did smash the Sassanian empire in Persia. Heraclius also wished to revive Justinian's policy of religious unity within his own empire, again favouring an interpretation of the decisions of Chalcedon which might help to reconcile the Monophysites. In the continuing theological debate the question had been raised whether if Christ had two natures he also had two wills. The emperor persuaded the Orthodox patriarchs to give a useful answer: one will. Perhaps 'one will' would console the Monophysites for 'two natures'? But the monks of the east resisted what seemed to be a betrayal of Chalcedon and the bishops of the west supported them; and under such counter-attacks Heraclius had to admit defeat shortly before his death in 641.

Forty years had to pass, however, before another emperor (Constantine IV) saw that there was no point in trying to reconcile the Monophysites. These years included the brutal treatment of another bishop of Rome: condemned for treason, Martin died of cold and hunger having been exiled to the Crimea. The empire's most distinguished theologian, Maximus the Confessor, also died in exile, having had his tongue cut out and his right hand cut off. The tongue and the hand had been used in resistance to the doctrine of Christ's one will (Monothelitism) which had then enjoyed imperial favour. Now, in 681, the emperor summoned bishops to his palace in Constantinople in order that the doctrine might be condemned as a grave heresy. This ecumenical council also condemned the memory of an unfortunate bishop of Rome (Honorius) who had thought it wise to yield to an earlier emperor's will even if it meant accepting that doctrine.

For the Orthodox this ended the formal disputes between Christians about Jesus in the Byzantine empire—or in what was left of it.

Battles about Pictures

By now the Byzantine empire was very much smaller. The territories over which the eastern patriarchs presided, with the exception of Constantinople, had all been conquered by the Arabs—warriors who instead of disputing about the sense in which Christ was divine placed him second to a man, Muhammad.

Long ago the apostle Paul had lived in Arabia, 'at once' after his conversion to Christ (as he told the Galatians). Perhaps he went there for solitary meditation or perhaps for his first, clumsy, mission. But no Christian evangelist in Arabia since his time had possessed anything like his power. When Muhammad sought an alternative to the paganism of Mecca, he had to wait before revelations began to come during his trances (about 610, when he was aged about forty). He did not have direct access to the Bible: it is said that he could not read and it is known that there was no Bible, not even a New Testament, in Arabic. The inaccurate references to the Hebrew and Christian Scriptures in the Quran seem to reflect conversations with Jews or Christians whom he happened to meet in the course of his business as a dealer in camels. They were probably not very well equipped to pass on biblical knowledge and the Christians were heretics by Byzantine standards. Islam has sometimes been called the greatest of the Christian heresies and in the medieval west there was a legend that Muhammad had been baptized. Actually, the Prophet was given no real opportunity to become any kind of a Christian. Christians were to make great play with mistakes in the Quran suggesting that their Trinity consisted of Father, Mother and Son, and that someone else was crucified as a substitute for Jesus; and they mocked the expansions of stories in the Bible. Actually, these passages show how ineffective Christian evangelism was in the Arabia which the Prophet knew. It seems clear that in his eyes his changing relationship with the Jews were more important: having for some years turned towards Jerusalem when praying, he turned against the Jews and drove a large community of them out of Madina in the 620s. Two Christians tribe became his allies after his control of Mecca in 630, but it mattered little. Nor, in the end, did it matter that one of his wives, named after Mary, was a Christian: she was not going to instruct him. Nor did it matter that their son, named after Abraham, who might have been his successor (*khalifa*), and who might have been influenced by his mother, lived no longer than any of his half-brothers: he died before he was two. Until AD 661 Islam was led by caliphs who belonged to the same Bedouin tribe as the Prophet; and they led a community which was sure that its superiority over the Christians was spiritual as well as military. The caliphs who succeeded them took the same view. The Shi'ites who regarded all these caliphs as usurpers did so because they were convinced that an *imam* descended from the Prophet's son-in-law Ali must be infallible.

When the warriors of Islam erupted from the desert, after the death in 632 of the Prophet who had been a soldier himself, they met opposition as tame in religion as in war. The Byzantine patriarch who was also the governor of Egypt was not as resolute against the Muslims as he had been against the 'heretical' Monophysites. The naval base of Alexandria might have held out but after a half-hearted defence the Byzantines sailed away in 643. All Egypt's Christians were now at the mercy of the Arabs. At first the invaders were often welcomed by the people as fellow-Semites and liberators from the taxes and persecutions inflicted by a 'Greek' empire; and for a time local church life seemed to have a good future. In the early years the Arabs were little more than warriors still more or less nomadic and they promised to treat Christians and Jews as *dhimmi* ('protected'). When the Egyptians ('Copts') and Syrians ('Jacobites') discovered the full disadvantages to them of Arab rule there was no Byzantine connection from which they could draw spiritual strength; they insisted on their growing isolation. Nor was there unity with the Nestorians; there was rivalry or hostility, now as in the days when Monophysites and Nestorians had spread different churches into northern Arabia. Many remained Christians but over the centuries most changed their religion. A conversion to Islam meant the end of taxes and discrimination even heavier than those which had been endured under the old empire; and in many incidents discrimination could amount to violence. It also meant adopting a religion more relaxed about human nature than was the puritanism within Orthodox or Monophysite piety which encouraged the total renunciation of the world. Muslims did not admire feats of holy athleticism such as the performances of the Stylites who stood on the tops of pillars by day and night over competitively long periods. And some Christians were attracted to a brotherhood with no priests and a short creed.

The Copts who were indestructible as Christians in Egypt lived in their own villages or urban ghettos, noted for their craftsmanship, unpopular but indispensable because they staffed the civil service, speaking their own language (a mixture of ancient Egyptian and Greek) until it was overwhelmed by Arabic. They suffered from much local Muslim violence because they collected the normal taxes as well as paying specially high taxes themselves, but their numerical decline was chiefly in the period 1250–1400, when all Christians in the Middle East were hated because associated with the crusades from the west or with the Mongol invaders from the east. The Jacobites of Syria also gradually withdrew into the life of a hereditary underclass. Christian evangelism was everywhere prohibited and any Muslims converting were punishable by death, but in any case arguments would probably have been as futile. Monophysite theologians refused to take the religious claims of Islam seriously and remained engrossed in their arguments against the Chalcedonians. What ordinary Christians did take seriously was the need never to compromise or change in religion. As John Meyendorff has written, 'Islam not only obliged the Christians to live in a tiny enclosed world which concentrated on the liturgical cult; it also made them feel that such existence was a normal one. The old Byzantine instinct for conservatism, which is both the main force and the principal weakness of Eastern Christianity, became the last refuge which could ensure its survival in the face of Islam.'

The surviving part of the Byzantine empire also believed that it had little or nothing to learn from the doctrines of Islam. Its theologians repeated that Muhammad was a vice-ridden impostor with no true knowledge of God and that the effect of his religion was to destroy human dignity. But the military power of Islam was undeniable: the Arabs attacked Constantinople itself over five years in the 670s and besieged it again in 718, and although they had to withdraw from that prize their empire now spread from the Atlantic coast of Africa to the river Indus, the historic frontier of India. A volcanic explosion in the Aegean further damaged Byzantine morale and raised theological questions. Was the God who in the Old Testament had condemned the idols of the heathen now directing his wrath against the pictures treasured, almost worshipped, by the Orthodox, the icons? Was this the reason why Muslim armies were being victorious? And was the true Orthodox tradition also hostile to icons? Origen had replied to the paganism of Celsus with the teaching that Christians did not need man-made images, for they knew the spiritual realities. Eusebius of Caesarea had admitted that icons existed in his time but had rebuked a request for a portrait of Jesus even though it came from Constantine's sister. So had the developing prominence of icons been an innovation, perhaps idolatrous, which real conservatives ought to terminate? The question was asked with sincerity. Moreover, icons were dear to the monks whose influence over the people was resented: they were exempt from military service, they paid no taxes and they undermined the authority of the bishops and the parish priests who were more securely under imperial control. And it irritated soldiers that military successes were attributed to the power of icons such as the image of the living Christ printed on a cloth or a portrait of his mother by St Luke, both treasures of Constantinople.

In reply it was maintained that the icons were essential. From outside the empire the theologian John of Damascus taught that. So, at great personal cost, did the patriarch of Constantinople and Theodore of Studios, the empire's leading monk. They testified to the Orthodox faith in the Son who united divine and human natures. Had the question about icons been pressed in their time, the 'holy fathers' would surely have blessed them—for if Christ could not be pictured, was he truly human? If Mary the *Theotokos* and the saints could not be shown in glory, did the Church truly believe that they had been glorified? If these pictures which had assisted the prayers and the sanctification of many generations of the Orthodox were condemned, would the Church be apologizing for being different from Islam? Before becoming a monk John of Damascus had worked as a senior civil servant under a Muslim caliph, almost certainly with the job of collecting the taxes of his fellow Christians, but now he wrote about icons: 'I see the human face of God and my soul is saved.' He explained: 'I do not venerate matter, but I venerate the Creator of matter who for my sake became matter.'

These arguments between haters and lovers of sacred pictures were not left to be resolved peacefully, any more than arguments about words had been. An 'iconoclastic' (anti-icon) emperor who was a successful soldier (Leo III) launched a campaign in the Church and his successor persuaded a council of bishops to ban these pictures as 'Devil-inspired' in 754. Thousands of beautiful works of religious art were now destroyed and any opposition was suppressed brutally. This campaign was halted by an 'ecumenical' council in 787, convened by the first reigning empress (Irene). Resumed in 815 by another soldier-emperor (Leo the Armenian), it was ended by a council in 843, again under an empress (Theodora). That last event is still celebrated as 'the Triumph of Orthodoxy'. Byzantine art renewed and increased its creativity and Christians (apart from the puritans in later centuries) have been glad to join in the celebration of the triumph of beauty as an aid to prayer— a triumph against persecution. But at the time there was an objection to the use of an ecumenical council to settle this Byzantine dispute.

At the court of Charlemagne (Charles the Great, the 'king of the Franks') the response to this council was an assertion of religious independence. In 794 bishops from the widespread territories under Charlemagne's rule were gathered for a council in Frankfurt. In their churches could be found images of Christ and the saints which had never been removed but more attention was paid to copies of the Bible and to the bones of the saints encased in jewel-studded gold. So these western bishops did not add any new verdict on the use of icons: they saw no need. They loftily rebuked extremism on both sides of the eastern dispute, both renovation and destruction, both superstition and persecution. Why quarrel about pictures? Further, they complained that eastern bishops had repeatedly legislated on matters of little or no concern to the west after little or no consultation with it. More than a hundred 'canons' (church laws) had been decreed in this manner by an eastern council in 691–692. The council of 787 was now dismissed as not truly ecumenical and without saying explicitly that they were retaliating against such unilateralism, these western bishops felt entitled to bless the addition of a word to the creed of 381.

In Latin the word was *Filioque*, asserting that the Holy Spirit proceeded 'from the Son' as well as 'from the Father'. Charlemagne liked the word, which was used in his chapel; no doubt it seemed a compliment to his patron Christ, as *homoousios* had once seemed to Constantine. Bishops who depended on him liked it too and were not alarmed because its use would displease bishops in the east. But we do not know why in Toledo in 589 the Spanish bishops had adopted the creed of 381 with this addition. They had no motive to be unorthodox; on the contrary, they were renouncing Arianism in obedience to their king, Reccared, who had seen the danger of being a heretic. His father, an old Arian, had nearly been dethroned by a son who claimed to be entitled to be a rebel because he was an orthodox Catholic in his religion. Reccared, who knew that his father had had to punish this brother of his by execution, was determined to make his throne secure. He may have made a mistake about the creed which he recommended to his bishops, not knowing that it was a mistake because the emphasis on the fully divine dignity of the Son seemed to be Orthodox rather than Arian.

When *Filioque* had to be defended theologically, a defence was possible because passages supporting it could be gathered from the works of prestigious western theologians such as Tertullian and Ambrose, Hilary of Poitiers and Augustine himself—and, indeed, from the New Testament. Isidore, a great scholar who became bishop of Seville about 600, defended it as he defended other features which distinguished the Spanish Church from the churches of lesser peoples. Isidore so disliked the memory of Justinian (whose army had conquered southern Spain) that he refused to acknowledge that Constantinople had a patriarch: in addition to Jerusalem, Antioch and Alexandria only Rome had that status (not that Isidore was enthusiastic about Rome). But to the eastern bishops, tampering with the Orthodox creed seemed blasphemy against the Holy Spirit who had inspired the council of Constantinople to proclaim it. It would also reduce the worship due to the Father and would even be a danger to the essential faith in the ultimate unity of God, safeguarded by the insistence of the Cappadocian Fathers that all divinity has one source, God the Father. And did not John 15:26 declare that the Spirit 'proceeds from the Father' without adding *Filioque*? One complication in the theological debate was, however, uncertainty about whether the 'procession' being discussed concerned the Spirit in eternity or in history: if in eternity, the Cappadocian Fathers were no doubt correct in their ultimate monotheism, affirming 'from the Father' alone, but if in the history which Christians had experienced, the Spaniards might not have made a mistake after all, for the Spirit could be called in the New Testament 'the Spirit of Christ' or a teacher 'sent' by Christ.

Had there been a strong desire for reconciliation, a formula was available and might well have been adopted by another ecumenical council. It was widely acceptable to say that while the Father was the source of the Spirit in eternity the Spirit proceeded 'through' the Son in the course of history. But there was no such desire. The west was beginning to despise the east, whose battles over pictures seemed like fights between children. The east had no respect for—and almost no knowledge of—western attempts to do theology. When Photius was appointed patriarch of Constantinople in 858 at a new emperor's behest, the pope claimed to be entitled to depose him and to reinstate his predecessor, but in the prolonged dispute Photius, a considerable scholar, was able to defend himself not only by relying on imperial power (which in the end failed him) but also by rebuking the pope for condoning the heresy of *Filioque*.

This rebuke was somewhat unfair, since in Rome the innovation was resisted for some time. When Charlemagne asked Leo III to comply, the pope was diplomatic: he assured the emperor that he agreed with his theology, but he had the unchanged creed engraved on tablets of silver and placed near the tomb of St Peter. Under continuing pressure, however, popes allowed the use of the innovation privately: this use could be private because the custom of using the creed of 381 in public worship had not yet reached Rome. But in 1009 a new pope formally wrote to Constantinople that he accepted *Filioque* and five years later when the emperor Henry II was crowned in Rome with public solemnity the word was used when the creed was recited. The use became permanent and almost a thousand years later the question about *Filioque* continues to divide Catholic and Orthodox. Belief in the 'fellowship of the Holy Spirit' celebrated in the New Testament has not produced a solution to this problem.

The Orthodox have not acknowledged any council meeting since 787 as truly ecumenical. Dogmas taught by councils convened by popes have been deplored as western attempts to impose a uniform faith in areas best left without compulsory beliefs. For example, although Mary the mother of Jesus has been venerated as *Theotokos*, 'God-bearer', and as 'all-holy' (a term often used since about 750), the doctrine of her 'immaculate conception' has never been defined for the Orthodox as it was for the Catholics in 1854, partly because 'immaculate' refers to her freedom from 'original' sin as understood in the west but not in Orthodoxy. The doctrine of her 'assumption body and soul' into heaven has also not been defined for the Orthodox as it was for the Catholics in 1950 although belief in the event seems to have been general in the churches of the east since about 650. It has become customary for the Orthodox to refer neither to the death nor to the 'assumption' of Mary but to her 'falling asleep'. So the legacy of the seven ecumenical councils accepted by the Orthodox concerns Jesus himself. Although it may be thought that divine inspiration did not completely obliterate the human nature of emperors and churchmen, we may end the story with words written by Karl Rahner in the 1970s. 'The legitimacy and permanent validity of the classical Christology lies in the fact that it prevents Jesus from being reduced merely to someone in a line of prophets, religious geniuses and reformers . . . Positively, it clarifies the fact that in Jesus God has turned to us in such a unique and unsurpassable way that in him he has given himself absolutely.'

Survival and Fall

Right down to 1453 many people in Constantinople were, it seems, sincerely convinced that their city was 'God-defended', that their 'Christ-loving' emperor was anointed to reign over all the kings of the earth and that their religion was the only reliable guide to deification in heaven. On earth miracles of deliverance would come in the future as in the past, if only the faith was kept. There were many dangers but the greatest was to change the traditions, for as Patriarch Photius had explained, 'even the smallest neglect of the traditions leads to the complete denial of all doctrine'.

For a period this continuing confidence in the empire's religion seemed to be rewarded by a measure of recovery in its material position. The empires of the Arabs to the east and of Charlemagne to the west both disintegrated. The Macedonian dynasty in Constantinople (867–1056) secured a series of military victories: under it the empire advanced into the Balkans, Armenia and Syria and recovered the islands of the Mediterranean previously lost. Three able emperors of the Comnenian dynasty (1081–1180) achieved some stability and prosperity with a flowering of culture. In the Church the disputes about the natures and wills of Christ were subdued, partly because Constantinople now possessed the only patriarch with real power. There were trials for heresy but the centre of theological discussion gradually shifted to the question of how the mystical experiences of the monks (and some others) were to be interpreted. The claim that in trances it was possible to enter 'uncreated' light was attacked by some critics as being incompatible with humility before God and before the Church of God with its careful organization of clergy, sacraments and doctrines, but when the controversy came to a head in 1341 the bishops backed the mystics and the leading critic (Barlaam) fled to the west. It was the proud teaching of the monks' spokesman, Gregory Palamas, that 'the Son of God becomes one single body with us and makes us a temple of the undivided Divinity'—and the Byzantine Church agreed.

However, the earthly facts were increasingly ugly. From the eleventh century onwards Constantinople shrank in its control of territory, lost command of the sea, declined in commerce, had a government often desperate for cash, and depended for its defence on the reduced strength of its army and navy and, in the last resort, on its walls. And Constantinople was becoming isolated from the west which, in contrast, was prospering. In 1054 there was an ominous drama. A mission was sent from Rome to Constantinople, whose patriarch had closed down western visitors' churches in retaliation for the suppression of 'Greek' customs by 'Latins' elsewhere. Rome's envoys were supposed to rebuke and convert the patriarch and to assert the claims of the papacy to be the head of all the world's churches— and at the same time to enlist the emperor's help against the Norman invaders in Sicily and southern Italy who held the pope prisoner. It was a doomed mission. Its objectives were too mixed, its arrogance was too plain. Tempers flared. Cardinal Humbert excommunicated the patriarch, who in response excommunicated whoever had written the letter alleged to be papal (which he declared a forgery). This incident, which was not widely noticed at the time, did not mean a complete schism between the Christians of east and west, but the split was widening and the extent of the misunderstanding could be seen in the cardinal's other behaviour. Not knowing that in fact the Orthodox had the older customs, he accused the patriarch of heretical innovations: excluding *Filioque* from the creed, allowing married priests, having no daily Mass, and in the Liturgy using ordinary leavened bread and wine without water (for about 300 years Catholics in the west had used bread which was unleavened). He returned to Rome full of indignation.

The year 1071 brought material disasters to the Byzantines. The Normans took their last stronghold in southern Italy, this time with the papacy's blessing. In the same year the defeat of a Byzantine army of mercenaries at Manzikert opened Asia Minor, Armenia and Georgia to the Seljuk Turks, Muslims recently nomadic in Asia and now as aggressive as the Arabs had been. They had already taken Baghdad and they ruled over Iraq, Iran and part of Syria in the name of the decadent Abbasid caliphs. For a time it seemed possible that they would enter Europe as the Arabs had done. However, attention switched to conflicts between Muslims. The Turks and the Arabs were far from united. The Fatimids, who were Shi'ites and therefore heretics, had taken control in Egypt. In Asia Minor and Syria Islam was fragmented because the local rulers became absorbed in their rivalries. Such divisions which had temporarily deprived Islam of its greatest asset, its unity, encouraged hopes that Christians in east and west might combine to restore all that had been lost to Christian rule. When in 1095 Pope Urban II and other preachers aroused an extraordinary enthusiasm for the First Crusade, it was after an appeal from the Byzantine emperor. The declared aim was to throw the heathen out of 'our lands' and at least the pope's response to the emperor showed that the excommunications of 1054 had been largely forgotten. But in the event, the crusade made the relationship between east and west worse.

No proper arrangements were made for the discipline or provisioning of some 50,000 'pilgrims' who set out to restore its former empire to Byzantium and to end up victorious in Jerusalem. Their leaders were a mixture of non-military visionaries such as Peter the Hermit and extremely military, but disunited, lords and knights. The people who rallied to such leaders were sacrificing and risking much to 'take the cross' and were inflamed by rhetoric about avenging insults to Christ, so that their first action was to perpetrate the first holocaust of Jews in European history, in massacres in the Rhineland. They had no spare cash and needed funds, so that they pillaged the countryside and did other damage as they marched to Constantinople. The Hungarians killed large numbers of them in retaliation. The emperor had not been adequately consulted and was suspicious of the intentions of the leaders. Refusing what would probably have been the empty title of their commander-in-chief, he made them swear oaths of loyalty to him before he would produce money for provisions and then contributed only half-hearted and short-lived military help. His daughter Anna made a record of her reactions to them: she admired their bodies and despised their minds. The embittered crusaders suffered large losses at the hands of the Turks but in the end had success which they thought miraculous. Enough of them fought their way along the southern coast of Asia Minor, through Antioch and Edessa, to Palestine. Some of them became so famished that cannibalism was reported. But they arrived within sight of Jerusalem. These Christians, whose badge was a red cross and whose cry was 'God wills it!', went through devotions on the Mount of Olives above Gethsemane. Then they entered the Holy City. They massacred many Muslims along with some Jews and Christians and it was gleefully reported that the site of the temple became ankle-deep in blood. Jerusalem was at last under the control of the followers of Jesus.

They now refused to restore their conquests beyond the western region of Asia Minor to the Byzantine empire, which they accurately said had contributed little. As they set up colonies more fragile than the splendid new churches which suggested a permanent occupation, they installed Latin patriarchs and clergy. They encouraged groups to break away from Orthodoxy into obedience to the papacy. (One such, the Maronites, still survives in Lebanon. Already tainted by the 'heresy' of believing that Christ had one will, it accepted the papacy in 1181.) Only the Catholic minority had full rights under their laws. Such actions split west and east much more decisively than the hysterics of 1054 had done. Further crusades included major efforts in 1147 and 1190, but within a century of the excited launch of the first crusade the conquests of Palestine had been reduced to a few strongholds on the coast. Saladin had arisen to restore the might, and most of the unity, of Islam and had recaptured Jerusalem without any massacre. Glittering Christian armies had come to grief in Asia Minor or Galilee and a seaborne crusader, Richard the 'Lion-hearted' king of England, had added to the takeover of Byzantine territory by seizing Cyprus.

In the 1120s crusaders from Venice had ravaged some of the empire's remaining possessions on their way to and from the Holy Land (in revenge for a curtailment of their commercial privileges) and in 1204 the great fourth crusade inflicted damage on Constantinople from which neither the city itself nor its feelings about the west ever recovered. The expedition was bound for Egypt, now seen to be the centre of Muslim power, in Venetian ships. However, since only half the number expected had reported for the voyage the crusaders had not raised the funds needed to reimburse Venice for the transport they had booked and, being debtors, they were now obliged to do Venice's work. They were diverted to Constantinople in order to place on the throne the son of an emperor who had been deposed as being too pro-Venetian. This son was first reluctantly accepted, and then murdered, by the Byzantines. On Good Friday the crusaders stormed the city and inflicted on it the fate of Jerusalem. They massacred, raped and looted for three days. Among the many buildings burned to the ground was the imperial library with its irreplaceable contents including most of ancient Greek literature. They put a prostitute on the patriarch's throne in Hagia Sophia. Then a new emperor (Baldwin, count of Flanders) and a new patriarch (a Venetian nobleman) were installed. Venice took possession of a string of ports and islands and other westerners occupied most of Greece and Macedonia.

In 1212 the dream of liberating Jerusalem by innocence rather than force excited the 'children's crusade', so called from the adolescence of most of its members: those who actually sailed from Italy did so as slaves bound for North Africa. In the same year the pope called for another crusade by adults (the fifth), which reached Egypt but had to withdraw. An unofficial crusade led by the western emperor Frederick II had more success: in alarm at the prospect of another invasion of Egypt, its sultan bought Frederick off by the surrender of Jerusalem and its neighbourhood in 1229. But the success was not permanent and the efforts of other crusading expeditions could not make it so. Muslims recaptured Jerusalem in 1244 and remained as its rulers until 1917. The crusaders' strongholds on the coast were now refortified, but the last of these fell in 1291. Fresh crusades against Islam were talked about and once or twice materialized: in 1365 crusaders took Alexandria, looted it and left it. But from the Byzantine viewpoint the idea of a crusade now meant a threat, not a rescue, from the west.

When another Byzantine dynasty, the hard-headed Palaeologi, recovered control of Constantinople and the small surrounding region in 1261, they relied on a fleet supplied by Venice's rival Genoa and in return had to hand over to the Genoese almost all the fees levied from ships passing through the straits of the Bosphorus. They also relied on help from the Ottoman Turks, who now ruled most of Asia Minor. It seemed obvious that any hope of surviving depended on reaching an agreement with the papacy. The Turks were bound to attack one day but the immediate threat was that Charles of Anjou, who then ruled Sicily and much of Italy under the overlordship of the pope, would launch another 'crusade' with a papal blessing in order to restore Constantinople to 'Latin' rule. Eventually a pope, Gregory X, was elected who was more interested in sponsoring a crusade to recover Jersualem. He was delighted when Michael Palaeologus promised to secure the reunion of Catholics and Orthodox on the papacy's terms for the benefit of that glorious enterprise. In 1274 a council assembled in Lyon. The Greek delegates arrived; the elaborate proofs of their errors provided by the great mind of Thomas Aquinas were not required; the disputed doctrine of *Filioque* was declared to be part of the Catholic faith; within a fortnight the pope was able to ratify the reunion. Church bells rang in far-off England. Amid the excited joy Charles of Anjou had to swallow his disappointment. But no crusade against Islam proved possible. On the contrary, a later pope encouraged Charles to revive his anti-Byzantine plans and in 1281 excommunicated Michael Palaeologus although that emperor had been doing his brutal best to impose the reunion on his subjects. After his death a new emperor formally annulled the agreements of 1274, which had never been more than superficial.

It would have been truly miraculous had there been any other outcome. Neither the remnant of Byzantium nor the Catholic west was genuinely interested in an exploration of the theological questions with a view to unity in faith. Nor were they willing to agree to differ on non-essentials. The days were now distant when the Roman church had used Greek and when the administration and army of the Byzantine empire had used Latin. Two Christian cultures had grown, very unequal in power and scarcely knowing each other. Not much of Byzantine theology had a substantial impact outside its own region and before scholars became refugees in Italy (from the 1390s onwards) not much of the Byzantine heritage from ancient Greece was translated directly from Greek into Latin. (More usually it was transmitted through translations from Greek into Syriac and from Syriac into Arabic and thence into Latin through Sicily or Spain.) Not many theologians in the west took the trouble to learn Greek and Dante, the medieval west's greatest poet, fascinated by the ancient world, never did. And while the discovery of Aristotle's philosophy helped to stimulate an outburst of new theology in the universities of the west—reasoning with a bold freedom although it was in order to understand the implications of a faith which was taken for granted—similar attempts in Constantinople were halted by the authorities of Church and State. It was maintained that theologians should learn not by disputation but by prayer and the study of the Scriptures and the Greek Fathers. In the fourteenth century some of the most significant works of Latin theology were to be translated for study by Byzantine theologians, but the study was made by the few. As political power or security diminished or vanished, most of the faithful clung all the more firmly to their traditional faith and pictured Christ, his mother and his saints, in a new beauty. All the coming destruction of Constantinople was to be survived by the mosaics in the little church of Chora, restored in 1315–20 at the expense of the empire's leading civil servant. In John Beckwith's words, these mosaics 'offer with considerable freedom of expression the intimacy of a living faith transfigured by gold and brilliant colour, luminous, exquisite and serene'.

It was the beauty of a sunset. Byzantine emperors had learned that the Catholic west would exact a very high price for any military protection, yet without such protection, or failing that a major miracle, the coming of the dark was only a matter of time. Two of them tried again to see whether a surrender of their religious heritage would be enough to secure an alliance. In a ceremony in Rome in 1369 the emperor John V submitted to the claims of the papacy: no Orthodox clergy were present but there was talk of another ecumenical council to agree the terms of a reunion of the churches. Instead of pursuing that idea, however, the pope retreated from the disorders of Italy to the safety of Avignon in France, where he soon died. In January 1438 an ecumenical council did open, in Ferrara in Italy, and many months of theological debate followed. This time the Orthodox were well equipped to argue against the west's insistence on the *Filioque* clause in the creed, on purgatory as a condition between heaven and hell, and on other beliefs and practices developed in the years apart, and the discussion was so prolonged that the pope had to announce that he could no longer afford to finance it. Fortunately the city of Florence was willing to display its wealth and beauty and the council moved there at its invitation. While in Florence the Orthodox were reminded by the Byzantine emperor John VIII that they could not argue against the fact that only their troubles with the Mongols in their rear were preventing the Ottoman Turks from bringing their men, ships and guns to the walls of Constantinople. The emperor now insisted on the crucial step, acceptance of the papacy. The full theological surrender then became inevitable and almost all the Orthodox signed it, in July 1439.

However, if the emperor thought that theological surrender was a price worth paying for military survival, many in Constantinople disagreed. Many feared that if the Latins were to defeat the Turks after reaching this agreement they would remain in possession of the city as well as of the theological field. A prominent official announced that he would prefer to see a Turkish sultan's turban rather than a Latin bishop's mitre. There was indignation that the west had driven such an unequal bargain when asked for help against the heathen and the anger increased when it was seen that the divisions within the west meant that even if a pope were to call for another crusade to rescue Contantinople his call would go unheeded. Venice was finding that trade with the Turks was far more profitable than ferrying crusaders, and western experts in the new guns found employment in the development of the Turks' artillery. So when the one-sided treaty of 1439 was published in Constantinople after a long and nervous delay, a storm of fury about its surrender to the Latins persuaded most of its advocates to flee to the west. But while the artillery was preparing to breach walls which had been considered impregnable, in the final hours before the fall of Constantinople on 29 May 1453, there was an event which might have changed history had it occurred much earlier: Orthodox and Catholics joined in the Eucharist in the great church of Hagia Sophia, under the heaven-like dome, and this united prayer continued all night.

As daylight came and the last of the emperors went from his communion to a fighting death, the Byzantine empire ended: more than a thousand years were over. But the story spread that he was turned to marble and would one day again live and reign; and in fact the history of his empire's influence was far from over. During the long sunset of imperial power the patriarchs of Constantinople had presided over an Orthodoxy which had got its public worship and its life of prayer into solid shapes. These shapes were to survive, almost like marble, when the Byzantine empire was no more than a haunting memory.

4

❧❧❧❧

Orthodoxy after Byzantium

Orthodoxy for the Slavs

'MY son', wrote a patriarch of Constantinople to a grand duke of Moscow in 1393, 'it is not possible to have the Church without the empire.' And having the Church plus the empire meant accepting that kind of lofty exhortation from Constantinople. A little earlier another patriarch had reminded some Russians who were asserting their independence that 'God has appointed Our Humility as the leader of all Christians'. These were claims with no strong foundation in biblical or later theology but they arose out of the history of Orthodoxy's influence on the Russians and other Slav peoples.

As we have seen, Church and Empire were linked so closely in the Byzantine scheme of things that evangelism outside the empire was not given a high priority and the missionaries who were most adventurous were the Arians, Nestorians and Monophysites who did not have to recommend the claims of the emperor as well as those of Christ. Some evangelism was done: indeed, Justinian decreed that the pagan tribes on the empire's frontiers should be converted. But such tribesmen were usually regarded as 'barbarians' and what their conversion might involve was seen early on, when Constantine's son Constantius ordered the princes of far-off Ethiopia to adopt the theology which he favoured. Naturally, such claims were resisted. In the Caucasus most of the nobility of the Khazars saw that they needed both a new religion and an alliance (no more) with the empire, so they became Jews. In North Africa the nomadic Berbers on the fringes of the Romanized farmland retained their own version of paganism, or sometimes their own version of Christianity (Donatism), until they adopted their own version of Islam. And, as we have already noted, Islam arose in deserts beyond the reach of Byzantine power and Byzantine evangelism. There was an Arab version of Orthodoxy, for the land near the Persian empire was of strategic importance and its inhabitants were made allies and often converts until they became Nestorians or Monophysites, but the sand lying to the south aroused very little interest.

The greatest success of Byzantine evangelism was in the north. It was secured by developing a kind of Orthodoxy which did not use Greek and which did not involve a submission to Constantinople. But that kind of success was not intended from the beginning by the authorities and was not swift.

In an expansion of Byzantine security and trade as well as religion four peoples living around the Black Sea were converted and the city of Cherson was established in the Crimea as a secure base for further advance. But during the seventh century the Balkans passed out of the empire into the hands of more obstinately pagan invaders—Avars, Slavs and Bulgars. The Avars allied with the Persians to besiege Constantinople, which was saved only by the use of 'Greek fire', an incendiary mixture of petrol and other substances which was to come to the rescue on many later occasions. But the power of the Avars was eventually destroyed by the western emperor Charlemagne and in the Balkans the Bulgars presented the biggest long-term menace to the Byzantines. The bulk of that people was not Christianized until the Byzantines under Basil I conquered and converted them in the second half of the ninth century, their prince (khan) having in the meanwhile converted a defeated emperor's skull into a drinking cup. Even then the change of religion did not stop wars between Bulgars and Byzantines until the eleventh century, partly because much of the Bulgar aristocracy remained pagan while the Slavs over whom they ruled accepted Orthodoxy. These two and a half centuries (approximately 625–875) when Constantinople lived in fear of Balkan 'barbarians' left a lasting mark in history, for the Via Egnatia, the great Roman road which ran from Constantinople to the Adriatic coast, was no longer the link between east and west and travel by sea was slower and more perilous. It was in this period that the eastern empire drastically reduced its use of Latin. Greek became its official and dominant language, which the authorities tried to impose on conquered Slavs both in church and in daily life.

The attempt to make the Balkans speak Greek and think Byzantine was dangerous. It was for some time uncertain whether the Balkans would come under the ecclesiastical jurisdiction of Constantinople or Rome; while most of the land which became Romania became Orthodox, in the end the Magyars in Hungary established their rule over Croatia, Dalmatia and Transylvania and helped to make that an area which in religion as in geography was close to Italy. Although the Serbs were Orthodox they declared their ecclesiastical independence in the thirteenth century and attempted to establish their own empire in the fourteenth. In Bulgaria resentment against increasing Byzantine domination was such that in the tenth century it gave rise to a movement of popular protest and action inspired by a Slav priest, Bogomil. As part of an escape from the official hierarchy of bishops controlling sacraments, he urged Christians to confess their sins to each other not to a priest—and, if they wished to be 'perfect', to reject both meat and marriage because both were associated with sexual intercourse. In many ways this was a revival of the Gnostic and Manichean heresies which Orthodoxy hoped had been crushed, but it was also like the Donatist movement in that it turned against the rich. It spread all over the Balkans and when its missionaries were scattered by Byzantine persecution it provided a creed for the medieval puritans known as the Cathars (from the Greek for 'pure'). The spread of this movement in northern Italy and the south of France was countered only by panic-stricken persecution and preaching and for two hundred years the Bogomils provided the main religion of Bosnia.

How, then, are we to account for the success of Orthodoxy in the Balkans, which was lasting although limited?

A change occurred which made it possible for Byzantine Orthodoxy to respect the cultures of different peoples in the Balkans as the cultures of the Middle East had not been respected. In 863 Photius, a patriarch of energy well aware of the loss of land to the Muslims, was encouraged by the emperor to respond to an invitation from the ruler of Moravia, to the north-west of Bulgaria. This king was alarmed by the growing influence of Christian missionaries from Germany who used Latin: they were at work in adjacent Bohemia, whose ruler became a Christian in 894. If Moravia was to become Christian, he preferred that the political influence should come from Byzantium and that the language should be the native Slavonic. So Photius, although himself totally wedded to the Greek language and heritage, sent Constantine, who later took the name of Cyril, and his brother Methodius, who had spoken Slavonic since their boyhood in Greece. The mission failed in Moravia; it could not hold out against the Franks in Germany on the one side and the Magyars on the other. Approval in Rome (where Cyril died in 869) could not rescue it. But the language was put into writing by Cyril (an outstanding scholar) and the alphabet which he invented was later simplified and became 'Cyrillic'. These developments had momentous consequences, going far beyond the actual use of 'Old Church Slavonic' in worship which had precedents in the Orthodox use of languages other than Greek in eight other areas. A whole Christian Slavonic culture developed around the language. As Dimitri Obolensky put it, Cyril and Methodius 'transmitted to the Slavs the idea that underlies the whole of their missionary work: the idea that every nation has its own particular gifts and every people its legitimate calling within the universal Church'. That was an idea which had to struggle against the strong tendency of the Byzantine elite to regard all peoples not speaking Greek as barbarians and against the decision in Rome when Methodius had died to end the brief approval of the use of Slavonic in church.

Byzantine rule in Bulgaria and Serbia was ended when Constantinople fell in 1204 to the western Catholic 'crusaders'. As the Bulgarian and Serb kings took themselves and their kingdoms into obedience to the papacy, it looked as if Orthodoxy in the Balkans was finished. But in response the Byzantine Church granted some independence to the churches of these two politically independent nations and those concessions, together with the continuing use of Slavonic (or the local language in Romania) in worship, were enough to make sure that the main faith of the Balkan peoples remained Orthodox. That remained the situation in those parts of Greece which were occupied by the Franks and the Venetians who imported the western kind of Catholicism—and when the military supremacy of the Ottoman Turks had been won at Kosovo in 1389 and re-established after reverses by the conqueror of Constantinople.

These Turks ruled the Balkans as part of a great empire. Not before the 1680s was their expansion checked when they were thrown back from the walls of Vienna and out of the great plain of Hungary. Not until the 1870s were independent kingdoms recognized after rebellions in Serbia and Romania. Under Turkish rule, usually material conditions for most of the people were better, or no worse, than before. Many Christians accepted Islam for the mixture of reasons which had already made the Middle East and Asia Minor (now 'Turkey') so largely Muslim, and many Turks became settlers. This permanently changed Bosnia and Albania. But the Slavonic-speaking Orthodox Churches were now secure enough to become symbols and centres of the survival of a popular (particularly rural) Christian culture, ready to fuel Balkan nationalism when the Ottoman empire weakened and became bankrupt in the nineteenth century. Through the years of foreign rule the Liturgy gathered people willing to accept higher taxation, a lower social status and a distinctive dress, and the monasteries defied the conquerors' belief that Islam was the final religion. The Turks could forbid the churches to hold public processions or to ring bells but they could not forbid Orthodoxy.

Moreover, the acceptance of the Slav language and culture had great consequences outside the Balkans and beyond the reach of the Turks. In its various dialects the language united peoples to the north of the Danube, towards the sea named after the ethnically different Balts but also across the steppes towards the great rivers in the east. In this region the western Slavs in Poland became Catholics hearing Latin in church, but the eastern Slavs became Orthodox hearing Slavonic. And among the eastern Slavs were, and are, the Russians. It was because they became Christians that the Russians became Europeans. But they became Europeans with a difference, because their Slav form of Christianity was connected with Constantinople not Rome.

The Russian Church

Old Church Slavonic has remained the language of the Liturgy in the Russian Orthodox Church and in the 1990s the Russian alphabet is still Cyrillic. But there have been some developments peculiar to Russia. Not only did the Russians build churches somewhat different from those of the Byzantines: in this land of forests they usually built in wood which they could carve and paint and their onion-shaped domes took account of the snow. There were deeper changes. The harshness of the land—of its weather, of its distances—evoked the identification of most of the Church, specially of its spiritual teachers, with the sufferings of the peasants who worked the land. In the Byzantine empire the tradition had been that the best form of holiness was a monk's self-denial—a tradition which remained strong in Russia—but Christ himself had been increasingly depicted as *Pantokrator*, the All-Ruler, and praised in hymns as 'God clothed in flesh'. Now a Russian Christ was known, close to peasants and crowned with thorns, the suffering God. This development was very remarkable in Orthodoxy: in the fourth century Bishop Eusebius of Caesarea had maintained that the divine Word was affected by the body's crucifixion no more than a musician was affected by the destruction of his instrument. At the same time, in Russia the Church was subordinated to the state more firmly than it was in Byzantium. One reason was that the clergy and faithful laity were less educated, but it was also the case that the very size of the land strengthened the belief that if it was ever to enjoy the advantages of unity under a stable government the power at the centre had to be a despotism. The leadership of the Church should therefore obey without even the limited scope for criticism or a coup that existed in Constantinople. The faithful peasants suffered as Christ had suffered, but it was believed that they would suffer even more if Russia was not ruled by an autocrat.

The merit of Russian spirituality can be illustrated by two well-known sayings. 'There can be no Church without love', said John of Kronstadt. 'Acquire inward peace and thousands around you will find their salvation', said Seraphim of Sarov. But even such sayings had ambiguous implications for Russia. John was the saintly parish priest of a naval town, a man of prayer, a charismatic pastor whose only touch of unorthodoxy was his advocacy of frequent communions during liturgies which he made somewhat informal by his ecstatic outbursts of love for God. He loved the tsars as he loved his parishioners and was loyal to their policies. Summoned to the deathbed of the reactionary Alexander III in 1894, he could not face the fact that he was bringing the sacraments to a dying despotism. And the spiritual peace spread to many visitors by Seraphim, an austere hermit and advanced mystic, encouraged (however unintentionally) the acceptance of a regime already indefensible morally before that saint died in 1832.

It does not seem merely sentimental to say that the early years of Russian Christianity set this tone of dependence on strong princes and devout peasants. In the ninth century the amazing expansion of the Vikings reached down the great rivers to the Black Sea and over it to Constantinople. Once they tried to loot that richly tempting city; year by year they succeeded in trading; and in the 860s they accepted from there a missionary bishop, to match the mission to Moravia. As was the case in Moravia, that early mission could not flourish; it was destroyed by a new Viking dynasty. But in the next century a princess who ruled the Russians descended from the Vikings was baptized in Constantinople and in the late 980s a prince, Vladimir, who had captured the Byzantine outpost of Cherson, decided that further war would be less profitable than an alliance to trade which would include his marriage to the emperor's sister and his own baptism as part of the bargain. That began a period of close ecclesiastical links over the Black Sea and until the 1240s the chief bishops in Kiev were almost always Greeks sent from Constantinople, although Slavonic was the Church's language and so the Church's culture was not Greek.

Two of Vladimir's sons, Boris and Gleb, were to become the Russian Church's first saints because they preferred death to civil war when assassins were sent by a brother. Vladimir (also reckoned a saint) used his power to order the baptism of his whole people and he took a share in the work of Christian instruction. For many years Kiev was the centre of a prosperous and remarkably Christian society which avoided the Byzantine frequency of executions and mutilations. It cared for the poor and its monks identified with them. In the Monastery of the Caves the first Russian monastic saint, Theodosius, told his monks to 'obey one another' and was famous for his own shabby dress but warned the rich about eternal punishment.

Kiev's dominance was founded on waters—on the north–south water-way which brought trade down from the Baltic to the Black Sea, and on the water of baptism which without too much Greek colouring brought Orthodoxy and civilization up from Constantinople. The second kind of water had the more lasting influence. Although Tartar invaders from the east (a branch of the Mongols) conquered the land, massacred many of its inhabitants and destroyed Kiev in 1240, they did not settle down to farm, being proudly content with their nomadic traditions. Nor did they attempt to replace the people's version of Christianity, being tolerantly contemptuous of all religions not their own. What they did want was money, in large quantities, and that helped to keep Russia poor because their dominance lasted until 1380. In the same period invaders came from the west: they were defeated by Alexander Nevsky, the heroic and devout prince of Novgorod in the north. However, in the end the 'gathering' of the Russians against the Tartars, and against invaders who were Polish or Lithuanian Catholics or pagans, was led by the princes not of Novgorod but of Moscow. The 'metropolitan' who led all Russia's Christians was based there from 1328. Now independent politically, and theologically indignant when the Byzantines tried to save themselves from the Turks by surrendering to the western Catholics, the Russians elected their own metropolitan from 1448 without waiting for word from Constantinople. In 1589 the older Orthodox centres had to recognize him as a patriarch. A tension had begun between Moscow and Constantinople which was to last for more than four hundred years.

In the sixteenth century a new idea provided a basis for the Russian alliance of Church and State: Moscow was 'the third Rome'. The first Rome had fallen into heresy as the Latins adopted the *Filioque* clause in the creed and other novelties. Constantinople, the second Rome, had also fallen by agreeing to a union with the heretical Latins, even before its fall to the Turks. But in the same century this proud new Russian ideology underwent two tests. In the Church a movement of 'non-possessors' advocated the end of the ownership by the monasteries of estates and serfs: monks ought to concentrate on intense mental prayer and humility. Such ideas were defeated by the arguments that the monasteries had to maintain dignified worship and had to attract well-born and educated monks who were capable of becoming bishops. The bishops made sure that the state supported these arguments. Then, in the state, a fresh challenge arose from the personality of Ivan the Terrible. A metropolitan who denounced his crimes became the victim of one. But non-resistance was general until someone had the sense to poison that mad 'Caesar' (*tsar*). The Russian Church's combination of characteristics was emerging: at the top were the possessors, at the (much larger) bottom were the suffering, praying poor and the priests who 'served' the Liturgy which was the weekly glimpse of glory. What was missing was what had been present in Byzantium: an educated middle class.

It seemed ever more necessary that the power of the tsar (symbolized by the adoption of the Byzantine emperors' double-headed eagle) should be supreme and sanctified; that the land-owning aristocrats should derive their own power over the peasants from their services to him; and that the people should obey him even more completely than the Byzantines had obeyed their emperor. The dismaying alternative was seen in the anarchy of the time of troubles before the first of the Romanovs (a patriarch's son) was elected to the throne in 1603. The tsars now spent much of their time in church and in the 1650s the Moscow which they policed was as puritan as Oliver Cromwell's London. They were also successful in battle (like Cromwell), in a process which extended their rule into the Ukraine and the south; in 1685 the metropolitans of Kiev were placed firmly under Moscow's control. In the 1660s a forceful patriarch of Moscow, Nikon, revised details of church life unaltered since the eleventh century. The purpose was to keep in step with Orthodoxy as now practised in Constantinople and in Greece, for behind the patriarch stood a tsar with ambitions to take the Balkans over from the Turks. (The reforms concerned questions such as how many fingers should be used when blessing and how many Alleluias should be sung.) The power of the state made the changes permanent, but they were enough to make the Old Believers withdraw from the Church into their own meetings, into the far north of Siberia and sometimes into suicide. Such dissenters were cruelly persecuted but when Nikon developed ideas about the revision of the Church–State relationship in the Church's favour he was deposed. Russia's monarchy was to remain despotic; Russia's piety was to remain medieval.

This schism weakened the official Church and exposed it to a more ruthlessly modernizing programme. As the eighteenth century with its 'Enlightenment' began Peter the Great looked to the west and created St Petersburg as his capital: it had access to the Baltic Sea and psychologically it was to be a city more modern and more ordered than Paris or London. This rejection of Moscow and all that it represented in history and religion was a decision as drastic as Constantine's move from Rome to Constantinople, but Peter felt nothing except contempt for what survived of the Byzantine tradition. Although cautious about giving too much offence to the people's piety, he had no intention of listening to complaints by bishops. After 1700 no patriarch was appointed and after 1721 all church affairs were strictly supervised by a 'Holy Synod' appointed by the state. In practice a state official (the 'chief procurator') appointed and controlled the bishops. From the Orthodox there were almost no protests. Thousands of Old Believers set fire to themselves rather than witness this degradation of the Church but their shortage of priests posed a dilemma for those who lived on: either they must conform to state-controlled Orthodoxy, or they must make do with a small supply of dissident priests, or they must become the first of the many Russian sects which were to meet without priests. The Holy Synod remained in control until 1917, enforcing a state religion which developed with the motto 'Orthodoxy, Autocracy, Nationality'.

Priests were now appointed to parishes without consulting the people and ordered to report any treasonable intentions, even when confessed sacramentally. The gentry were forbidden to seek ordination without special permission, rarely granted. Restrictions were imposed on the 'useless' monasteries, much of their wealth was confiscated and women under fifty were forbidden to become nuns. The estates taken from the Church under Catherine the Great covered land so vast that it had been worked by about two million peasants. The compensation paid for this massive change of ownership in 1764 was inadequate to support the clergy in that century and became more so as inflation reduced its value.

In the nineteenth century Russian religion presented a gigantic paradox. Apart from the unorthodox idealism or hard-boiled scepticism in an educated and largely westernized elite, this people was as devoutly Christian as any people has ever been. Prayer as well as good behaviour was often taken very seriously; fasts as well as festivals were observed; the Liturgy was loved; the local priest was close to the people, often born locally, often working his own fields, often in his parishioners' fields and homes with his blessings; and the number of monasteries doubled in the nineteenth century. One word says it all: the usual word for 'peasant' was 'Christian' in Russian. But the picture of Holy Russia was not the whole picture. There were dangers in the fact that because a tsar (Nicholas I) had been against it, the whole Bible was not translated into contemporary Russian before 1875. Not only had the Church largely lost the intellectual elite. The village priest was very often a priest's son who had been placed by his family in a seminary where he was taught little except the traditions and basic skills of his inherited profession. If the laity wished to discuss spiritual problems at any depth, they turned to a *starets*. These were senior and holy monks who made themselves available as counsellors, either in the monasteries or sometimes as travelling apostles. An ominous development in parish life was resentment about the priests' demands for fees for church services in order that their families might eat. If the priests were superior only through their ability to provide rites, peasants who were themselves short of cash could be cynical. Bishops also complained about the priests, who in their turn grumbled that the bishops had been sheltered from parish life in monasteries. The authorities of the state had no real interest in various proposals for reform which lapsed.

Dostoevsky portrayed a *starets* in *The Brothers Karamazov*, contrasting his gentle sanctity with the Catholic style of control symbolized by the Grand Inquisitor. But no more than the Inquisitor could the holy man actually answer the atheists in the Karamazov family. For Dostoevsky himself there was a tension between a belief in the Messianic mission of the Slavs and his own share in the sophistication of the 'corrupt' west (he was a compulsive gambler). He agreed with much that the 'Slavophiles' said: against atheism it was necessary to maintain the 'wisdom' of 'rational believing', against materialism 'wholeness of the spirit', against individualism a belief that 'souls' could flourish only if rooted in the community life of the village around the church. As a young man he had been fascinated by revolutionary socialism, but this he now rejected while also lacking in any conviction about the importance to Russia of parliamentary and legal institutions. But he could not accept other aspects of the cult of being a Slav. He could never believe easily in the goodness of God: the amount of suffering in the world made that impossible, even if one thought only of the suffering of innocent children. His final voice uttered his 'Hosanna raised in the furnace of doubt' because he reached an acceptance of reality as making for tragedy as well as beauty. He could never believe easily in the brave freedom of the spirit: he saw people trapped in their material circumstances and in their own temperaments and the only solution which he saw was that we must forgive each other. And he could never share the nostalgia and snobbery of ultra-conservative Slavophiles such as Leontyev, who advocated the fear of God as the answer to 'the Antichrist of democracy' and deplored even the degree of modernization embodied in St Petersburg. Dostoevsky's heart was with the often pathetic individuals—criminals to the state, non-believers to the Church—of the kind he had met in prison. They were the blessed children of God and the Russian Christ was supremely the Christ of compassion.

The holy men whom Dostoevsky admired without imitation could also not begin to address the social problems which troubled him and many others who were at one time or another classified as revolutionaries. How could the Christian among the Karamazovs (Alyosha) avert disaster? How could a Christlike 'idiot' defeat power? These problems tormented Dostoevsky's rival as a novelist, Tolstoy, who also in the end gave his praise to the cross-bearing peasant, to the pilgrim on a long road to a monastery. During his own special kind of pilgrimage, with a spiritual crisis in 1879, he turned to the ethical perfectionism, including pacifism, of the Sermon on the Mount and right away from his background as an aristocrat, soldier, family man and author of *War and Peace* and *Anna Karenina*. He now felt compelled to attack the Orthodox Church and was excommunicated by it. And in reality he was no longer an Orthodox believer. He cared little for the traditional creed: even before his conversion to his new faith, religion for him as for Dostoevsky had meant a relationship with an Infinite beyond understanding, with a morality consisting chiefly of compassion.

We have to ask why a spiritual tradition which had a strength seldom matched in Christian history produced not only unquestionable sanctity but also the impotent agonies in the minds of Dostoevsky, Tolstoy and many nineteenth-century contemporaries who, with them, foresaw catastrophe for the whole regime without being able to prevent it. The answer made simple by later events is that the Church was tied to an unrevised system and to a doomed state. Often Russian literature in its greatest age became a substitute for the Church's doctrines and the struggle for a new society a substitute for the Church's life, yet their hostility to the Church divided the educated from the peasants they were trying to liberate. For Tolstoy himself life was full of paradoxes and dilemmas. To the end he wrote marvellously about the virtues of the peasants who suffered, of women who were crushed in a man's world—but to the end he was himself dictatorial, ungrateful and very unkind to his long-suffering wife, unable to free himself from his inheritance of privilege until he fled on that last journey to the railway station where he died of pneumonia. And to this situation the state-controlled Church could offer little except the repetition of its own Byzantine tradition of faith and worship—which was, however, for many (as not for Tolstoy) consoling. In its own way the Church practised compassion but in the absence of justice compassion was not enough. The most influential figure in its life between 1880 and 1905 was Constantine Pobedonostsev, a lawyer who dominated the Holy Synod as its chief procurator in succession to a general. He was a complete conservative.

There were false dawns. In 1861 the serfs, who had been virtually slaves, had their legal status improved and were given some land, and the tsar (Alexander II) was encouraged by the Church to plan further progress. He was, however, assassinated and his successor was an unyielding reactionary. In the early years of the twentieth century the economy was becoming more productive because more westernized and at last the middle class was growing. The most radical of the intellectuals still saw no alternative to the destruction of the whole system of Church and State, God and tsar; but they were now engaged in an argument by other intellectuals who had become Orthodox believers and who hoped that the system could be improved by more freedom and justice as the best faithfulness. In 1904 a collection of essays called *Signposts* pointed to a better future and many of the clergy in the towns seemed willing to move along a comparatively new road. In 1905 there were demonstrations in St Petersburg, singing hymns and carrying icons. The crowd appealed to the weak tsar in the belief that the sanctity of the crown might outweigh the stupidity and isolation of its recent wearers. The nineteenth-century tsars were far more devout than Peter the Great and Catherine the Great had been, and now their equally devout subjects hoped for greatness in Christianity applied to government. Bullets replied. At the same time there were public proposals for the restoration of self-government to the Church under elected bishops. These hopes, too, had no large result; the Church was not united in demanding changes and those who wanted them had no great leadership.

Calamities now followed as in a classic tragedy: the concessions to parliamentary democracy which produced no adequate reforms, the wars with Japan and Germany, the politically disastrous influence of the faith-healer Rasputin over the imperial family, the revolutions after the defeats, the Bolshevik seizure of power, the execution of the tsar and his family, the Communist state, the brutal and deadly treatment of the privileged and the peasants, the systematic persecution of the Church. By 1941 the Communists had closed all monasteries and seminaries and all but some 4,000 of the 57,000 churches which had been open and loved in 1914. Any trace of defiance by bishops or clergy, or outstanding laity, was met by imprisonment or execution and tens of thousands were killed. When in prison many of these martyrs turned out to be saints in the highest tradition. The persecution launched by Lenin confiscated all church property, prohibited all Christian education outside the home and the pulpit and made even worship in a church depend on the state granting a lease which could be cancelled with the pretext that the building was needed for more important purposes. Under the Law on Religious Associations Stalin made it a crime for the Church to do charitable or educational work or to hold without special permission any meeting which was not a traditional act of worship. Clergy who wished to function legally had to be licensed and sermons had to be confined to religious devotion. The identities of worshippers were noted by the hostile police and believers found it very hard to get higher education or good jobs.

In response many of the people kept alive belief in God and the observance of customs such as baptism to an extent which infuriated and perplexed their Communist rulers; when the end came, about a third of the population of the Soviet Union remained 'believers' and although the results of the 1936 census were never published it was reported that at the height of the persecution more than half of the people had been brave enough to describe themselves as 'religious' in some sense. But the story would not be complete if it did not include some mention of embarrassing problems. While many people disbelieved the new Marxist creed and the often puerile propaganda of the atheists, Communism educated the people of Russia for the first time and the failure of the Church's leadership to update itself intellectually could not be ignored. While many people respected the suffering of the clergy and other believers, it could not be forgotten that the influence of the Church had, until towards the end, supported the tsarist system despite what was now very widely seen as its flagrant injustice. Only after the tsar's abdication in 1917 had the Church been allowed to elect a patriarch and to begin to reform itself under Kerensky's short-lived government, and even after the start of Lenin's persecution of religion in 1918 the 'Living Church' movement which tried to combine Orthodoxy, socialism and church reform had gained a good deal of support among the genuinely devout. Moreover, after 1925 most of the bishops who were still alive and free to function in public advocated collaboration with the new state, more or less as they had co-operated with the old regime. That dismayed the more heroic of the faithful, many of whom formed an underground of dissenters. The collaborating bishops adhered to the Byzantine tradition of respecting the state but they could also argue—probably with no real alternative, but perhaps against the protests of their own consciences—that they were undergoing a kind of martyrdom by their acceptance of compromises needed if any bishops were to be allowed to exercise any leadership and if any churches were to be kept open for the Liturgy. Towards the end of his sad life Tikhon, the patriarch who had been imprisoned, had himself urged this policy.

When Hitler sealed his own fate by invading the Soviet Union the bishops' policy of collaboration with the government seemed to pay—at last. The Church threw itself into 'the great patriotic war' and Stalin, who had thought that he was being cleverly realistic in concluding a non-aggression pact with the Nazis, now reached a similar agreement with the Orthodox, seeing that a possible alternative was a welcome by the persecuted to the invaders as liberators. Concessions to the Church in 1943 included permission to elect a new patriarch, Sergius, who had promised loyalty to the regime on his release from prison in 1927 and who before his death in 1944 claimed that he had lived to see the 'freedom of religion' which was celebrated in Soviet propaganda for export.

After the war this uneasy situation continued and Stalin's successors were glad to see representatives of the Church (whose appointments they had approved) advocating on international stages 'peace' as interpreted by Communism. But the tension came to the surface in 1959–64, when under Khrushchev severe persecution was resumed. The surviving churches (less than half the number open in 1950) were placed under councils elected by the whole neighbourhood, on which the clergy had no power, and it was often after cynical 'petitions' to the authorities from these councils that about two-thirds of the buildings were closed as centres of worship or demolished. The patriarch Alexis refrained from any public protest and after his death in 1970 his successor, Pimen, continued the policy of discretion while the 1975 law about religion still codified drastic restrictions. Many of the faithful ceased to trust the bishops but did take heart from the courage of a new generation of martyrs in the prison camps, who included many members of the Orthodox or Baptist congregations which met in secret.

The Church was eventually rescued. The Communist system collapsed not only because the economy under bureaucratic control was inefficient but also because the official ideology which included atheism failed to take account of the deepest feelings of the Russian people, which often still included religious instincts. Khrushchev's exposure of Stalin's crimes and mistakes was an important factor in the decay of the very system which he hoped to reinvigorate so that it would become fit enough to 'bury' capitalism. Having denounced Stalin, he made one of his own mistakes by alienating the Christians. People were still patriotic and had little or no wish to return to the old days, but the crude propaganda of atheism had become a boring part of Marxist indoctrination; Communist ceremonies had turned out to lack the mystique of the Orthodox Liturgy; the hope of a classless society which had not arrived and which seemed likely never to arrive had proved to be no consolation for the end of the hope of heaven; cynicism and vodka were also ultimately unsatisfactory. The might of the Red Army, the status of a nuclear superpower and the technical brilliance of the journeys into outer space were facts to feed pride, and the Union and its satellite republics in eastern Europe constituted the last great empire on earth, but it was an empire full of discontent which needed to be suppressed by further military expenditure. In Moscow Red Square was marched over in the military parades but it had become possible to hope that the churches still standing in the Kremlin would be there when the troops and tanks had melted away; that the Virgin would be honoured when pilgrims no longer went to Lenin's tomb. Gradually most restrictions on church life were lifted and the relaxation of censorship and intimidation changed the political climate. Shortly after the celebration of a thousand years of Russian Orthodoxy in 1988 Communism was overthrown and the Soviet Union was broken up with a sudden completeness, to be succeeded by a time of spiritual as well as economic chaos.

Under Communist rulers old and incompetent, or under successors younger but even weaker, or under the uncertain presidency of Boris Yeltsin, there was no strong state with clear policies. The direction being taken by Russian Orthodoxy was also unclear. The political confusion was matched by a riot of new religious or semi-religious movements (some imported from the west), called by the Orthodox 'sects' or 'cults'. Should the chaos be met by modernization in the Church as well as in the economy? Or as churches and monasteries were restored, could a new generation be attracted to the security of a strongly patriotic traditionalism in religion, accompanied perhaps by a return to authoritarianism in the state? In the middle of the 1990s there were Russian churchmen who argued that the clock should be turned back by restoring both the material wealth and the spiritual attitudes of the Church as it had been established before 1917, although others who seemed to be in the minority wanted a (perhaps radical) renewal of religion in a modern or postmodern society. It was a revival of the old debate between westernizers and Slavophiles, between Russians who envied the material riches and the freedoms of the modern world and those who valued more highly Russia's own traditions which included a submission to political and religious authority. 1996 brought two significant events. In the election for the presidency more than a third of the voters in the diminished territory of Russia supported the Communist candidate in protest against the failures of the Yeltsin government or non-government. In the same year the patriarch of Moscow announced that he was no longer in communion with the patriarch of Constantinople. The relationship was patched up but he was protesting against the latter's recognition of the independence of an Estonian Orthodox Church. Evidently Moscow still wished to control all the Orthodox living in the former Soviet Union, an attitude which might imply some reluctance to accept as final the dissolution of that union. Both events were warnings against any confident predictions about the future. In the parishes church life has been rebuilt by the energy of clergy and laity, and some 350 monasteries have resumed the life of prayer, but in Church and State leadership has been lacking.

Nicholas Zernov, a great interpreter of Russian Orthodoxy to English-speaking Christians, wrote in 1963: 'The fundamental conviction of the Russian religious mind is the recognition of the potential holiness of matter, the unity and sacredness of the entire creation, and Man's call to participate in the divine plan for its ultimate transfiguration. These ideas can be grasped under the name of *Hagia Sophia*, Holy Wisdom, the vision of which has never faded out in the long evolution of Russian Christianity.' He referred to the mystical theology of Dostoevsky's friend Vladimir Solovyev, who believed Holy Wisdom to be 'the hidden soul of the created world', and to the somewhat more down-to-earth vision of the twentieth-century Bulgakov. Essentially the same attitude to the world can be expressed in a theology which is now slightly easier for most people to understand: the theology which sees the resurrection of Christ as the beginning of a new creation, traditionally celebrated in Russia by the Easter night vigil in church, the lighting of innumerable candles, the ringing of almost as many bells, the feast on the return home, always with the response 'He is risen indeed!' After a thousand years of the world-glorifying religious tradition which Zernov rightly praised, much of the vast Russian land makes a sorry spectacle because the Communists failed to release its potential prosperity and polluted it physically as well as spiritually during their failure. A devastated land, a people confused or in despair: that is the tragic reality in the 1990s. But Russian Christians, who have endured so much, have retained the ability to hope—and to hope for leaders not so unworthy of them as the tsars and their successors.

Orthodoxy Survives

A dependence on the state which owed something to the Byzantine legacy may also be seen in the Greek Church. From the eighth century it was under the patriarch of Constantinople and during Turkish occupation from

1503 this relationship increased, for it often suited the Turks to treat the Christians as a *milet* (community) under their own ethnarch (community leader), the patriarch. In Greece as elsewhere, the treatment of Christians fluctuated: there were some martyrdoms and some forced conversions to Islam but the Turks were interested less in converts than in taxpayers paying up without disturbances. Patriarchs had to collect and pay large sums to the government in order to secure appointment; thus they could be first corrupted and then replaced. Of 159 patriarchs under the Turks, only 21 died natural deaths while still in office. Under the patriarch in the Phanar district of Istanbul his lay officials (the Phanariots) had considerable powers over their fellow-Christians. They also paid large bribes to the Turks but they and their families could grow rich. Bishops were similarly dependent on the state but had few powers over the parishes, where clergy were without training. As in the Balkans, the survival of the national spirit depended largely on the quiet continuity of the Liturgy and the monasteries. In 1782 two Greek scholars edited a large collection of spiritual teachings from the past, published it in Venice and called it 'The Love of Beauty' (*Philokalia*).

The history of leadership in the Greek and Balkan Churches has continued to be full of problems—but the love of many for the beauty in the Orthodox tradition has also continued.

Towards the end of the Turkish occupation of Greece a patriarch addressed a 'paternal exhortation' to the faithful urging acceptance of the Sultan's God-given authority but a successor in that tarnished patriarchate was hanged by the Turks when the exhortation was seen to have failed and revolts broke out in the 1820s with some support by bishops and clergy. After independence there has been a history of varying degrees of control by the national governments of Greece and the Balkans and under some regimes this has reactivated memories of humiliation under the Turkish empire. Between the world wars in Bulgaria, for example, the leadership of the Church seemed to be identified with an almost Fascist regime and after the second world war it kept quiet under Communism. In Romania a numerically strong church under a patriarch with an exceptionally strong personality (Justinian) seemed to have worked out an acceptable future for Orthodoxy under 'socialism' but his successor was exceptionally timid in his applause for the megalomania of the Communist dictator; in 1938 a patriarch had served as prime minister under a very different dictator, King Carol II. And whatever the government might be, it became clear that Orthodoxy in the nation could not be under foreign jurisdiction. Very reluctantly patriarchs of Constantinople who had extended their jurisdiction under the Turks had to agree that the national churches should be 'autocephalous' (self-governing) as in Russia—in Serbia first, then in Greece, then in Romania, finally in

Bulgaria. More calamitously, almost all the Greeks in Turkey were driven out of that country in the 1920s. In his own area the jurisdiction of the patriarch of Constantinople was reduced to the shadow of a shadow.

However, in the Balkans and Greece as in Russia, Orthodoxy has remained remarkably strong in its appeal to the hearts of the people. In Greece, for example, churchgoing has declined since the second world war and the bishops have, on the whole, not provided effective leadership, being divided by disputes which seem to have been largely personal and handicapped by a conservatism which seems to have been insensitive. But both in the towns and in the countryside the clergy have become better educated and more active and congregations often include plenty of young people. Only in recruitment for the monasteries, and then only in the case of the men, has there been an obvious drop. The links with the state have been somewhat loosened since the 1970s: civil marriage has been introduced and abortion has been legalized. But so far there has been no great public demand for the end of the customs by which the state pays the clergy and funds their training, and a large network of charities is related to the Church. The *Zoe* (Life) movement of the laity has been active in charitable and educational work since the 1910s. Still in the 1990s almost all the Greeks are baptized and consider that the Orthodox tradition is inseparable from their national identity—an identity now firmly linked with the democratic and liberal ethos of the European Union.

A Renewed Orthodoxy?

In the years to come, when Christianity is less likely to be used as a cement to bind a society together, governments will probably have less interest in trying to control the daily life of the Church; and since the sense that Christians are an international minority may be expected to grow, there are likely to be fewer Orthodox regrets over the separation of the Church and State. Such a change from the Byzantine model could recognize the lesson of history which teaches that Orthodoxy does not in fact depend on state support. The strength of the Church has been in the lives of the faithful, fed by the Liturgy and the 'prayer of the heart'. The Byzantine union of Church and State might dismiss movements of theological dissent as heretics, but these heretics could spread the Liturgy and the prayer far beyond the empire. Mongols, Turks or Communists might regard the post-Byzantine Church as a community to be taxed or as a superstition to be eradicated, but if faith was strong enough in the hearts of enough people enough of the Church could survive. That has also been proved true of the Coptic Church in Egypt under Islam and of the Ethiopian Church under Marxism. But it will take time for Orthodoxy to adjust to the withdrawal of the state from church affairs.

The monasteries have also become a less reliable source of strength. The confiscation of their estates and the closure of their main buildings have been major blows inflicted by states. But that has not been the main problem. Poverty could never kill the ideals of monks and they have returned to some restored monasteries, conspicuously in Russia. The tradition suffers, however, when too few Christians feel the compulsion of conscience to give their lives to prayer in the monastic style and this, too, has happened, although not a few women and men who are impressive and full of energy have recently come forward. The causes are obvious: universal schooling has made the young dissatisfied with the intellectual diet in most Orthodox monasteries; higher material living standards have been accompanied by a Christian emphasis on the goodness of sexuality and the rest of creation; practical service to society has been stressed; the reality of the choice between heaven and hell has become less vivid; the Christian life is no longer seen as a battle with devils trying to topple the monk from his ascent of the ladder to heaven. In this situation it may be questioned whether it is wise to continue to recruit almost all bishops from the monks and, in a further tribute to monastic ideals, not to allow parish priests to marry after ordination or to remarry if widowed. When marriage has more prestige than monasticism a new phenomenon has arrived in Orthodoxy.

The decline in churchgoing is not a problem limited to Orthodoxy, but here special questions are beginning to be raised. Modern people need a special motivation if they are to enjoy services dating from a very different era. In the past this motivation has often been present: the confidently traditional drama of the Liturgy was the focus of a patriotic or ethnic, as well as religious, community. But the spread of the practice of frequent communion and the use of modern languages may be signs that the Liturgy will be revised continuously as people who have inherited Orthodoxy feel at home in the idioms of modern societies and willing to learn from other Christian traditions.

Orthodoxy has not so far produced any influential theologian who has given a convincing lead in the restatement of the terms in which faith is expressed through doctrines. In the seventeenth century Cyril Lucaris developed a Protestant version of faith but made an improbable patriarch of Alexandria and Constantinople and his murder was less surprising. Peter Mogila, who was metropolitan of Kiev, more cautiously attempted to restate the tradition with reference to Catholic doctrines, to no lasting effect. In the eighteenth and nineteenth centuries there were westernizers in theology as in art or music, but they were attacked by Slavophiles such as Alexis Khomyakov and ignored by the bulk of the faithful. Vladimir Solovyev attempted an independent approach in his *Russia and the Universal Church* (1889), trying to combine the best of Orthodoxy and Catholicism, but he was forbidden to write any more on religious questions and he has had no successor so daringly creative. In the twentieth century Russian theologians of the stature of Bulgakov and Lossky, Florovsky and Meyendorff, worked in the west and did much to explain their heritage to a new public, but even their combination of wide knowledge with deep spirituality could achieve little more than the beginning of a dialogue between Orthodoxy and modernity. Nicholas Berdyaev, who worked on the social questions of the 1930s, wisely applied Orthodoxy rather than arguing about it. Such writers demonstrated the superiority of Orthodoxy to Communism and to western individualism; they proved its strength as a source of inspiration for faith in God and in the spiritual dignity of Man; but it was impossible for them to be more than pioneers in the development of a modern Orthodoxy in an ecumenical setting. That was impossible because of their great loyalty to their own spiritual tradition, then under persecution. Thus Bulgakov's fine exposition of *The Orthodox Church*, which in the 1930s introduced to readers of French or English the Russian ideal of *sobornost* (agreement reached through consultation), began defiantly: 'Orthodoxy is the Church of Christ on earth.'

For the necessary dialogues to be creative, it seems essential not only that other Christians should be ready to receive the spiritual treasures of Orthodoxy but also that the Orthodox bishops should be ready to encourage their theologians and their thoughtful clergy and laity to exercise more freedom—of course, responsibly. In particular it seems important, although not easy, to accept that doctrines and practices which have been venerated and defended, often at great cost, as the 'Apostolic Tradition' have in fact developed in the circumstances of history long after the days of Jesus of Nazareth and the apostles. That demonstrable fact does not automatically condemn all the developments which we have been studying, but it may mean that it is right to examine them afresh, to 're-receive them' as some Orthodox theologians have advocated, trying to restate for a very different age what was expressed and safeguarded in the old doctrines and customs. And that is no easy task; it calls for many dialogues between Christians.

In 1755, so far from reopening a dialogue, the patriarchs of Constantinople, Alexandria and Jerusalem agreed that any Roman Catholics becoming Orthodox must be baptized afresh, so deplorably heretical were western additions to 'the faith of the Fathers'. Two hundred and twelve years later Pope Paul VI and Athenagoras, who as patriarch of Constantinople 1948–72 did much to restore the international prestige of that office, cancelled the excommunications of 1054. After this symbolic act theological dialogues were opened but their conclusions were like the results of the 'councils of reunion' in the Middle Ages: on the central doctrines there was sufficient agreement to make 'communion' proper in principle and it was also agreed that minor customs might vary, but no lasting agreement was possible over the claims of the papacy. The dialogues were suspended in 1992 when the appointment by Rome of five Catholic bishops to minister to Catholics in the former Soviet Union was attacked as an intrusion into Orthodox territory. At the same time the historic Ukraine problem caused great bitterness. In 1596 papal authority had been acknowledged by many of the Orthodox under Polish pressure. In 1946 the dominance of the Russian Orthodox Church had been restored as part of the Russian victory in the world war. And now that Ukraine was an independent state, Orthodox and Catholics struggled for the mastery over its religious future.

Other dialogues were held with representatives of the ancient 'Church of the East' and the 'Oriental Orthodox'. A theologians' consensus was reached that in the past both sides had meant to affirm the same truths while differing over words. A joint statement in 1990 declared that the Son united his 'divine uncreated nature with its natural will and energy' to 'human nature, with its natural will and energy', but also that these two natures, wills and energies 'are distinguished in thought alone', so that 'the Son who wills and acts is always the one *hypostasis* of the Logos incarnate'. Disastrous controversies and schisms could have been avoided had that agreement been reached in, say, 490 and it remains to be seen whether it has been reached too late. Dialogues with Anglicans also promised well but it remains to be seen how they will recover from the distress caused by the Anglican ordinations of women priests.

In sharp contrast with Roman Catholicism, Eastern Orthodoxy has become disorganized. It has not yet been able to escape the dominance of its Byzantine or tsarist past and was, indeed, not free to do so while Turks or Communists controlled its heartlands. Some need for renewal was acknowledged in the 1960s when preparations were begun for a 'Great and Holy Council' of bishops but the next thirty years saw few concrete results. What seems to be needed is a council which will do for Orthodoxy what the Second Vatican Council did for Roman Catholicism, but the difficulties should not be underestimated. Even the old question of the dating of Easter in conformity with the custom of most Christians would revive tensions. Even the new question of whether women may be deacons would arouse new fears of secular-minded feminism. And even proposals to revise the boundaries of jurisdictions would be disturbing. Many memories of past controversies would be revived as warnings. But as John Meyendorff wrote in 1985: 'Unless the visible reality of our church life becomes consistent with that communion which is revealed to us in the Eucharist, unless our ecclesiastical structures—especially here in the west—conform themselves to that which the Church truly is, unless the eucharistic nature of the Church is freed from the facade of the anachronism and the ethnic politics which hide it today, no ecumenical witness, no authentic witness to the world, is possible.'

Recent Orthodox theologians, among them Christos Yannaras and John Zizioulas, have put great emphasis on the communion of the 'persons' of the Trinity in eternal love as the best model for human relationships in the Church, in society and even in politics. No icon is more famous in the 1990s than Rublev's *Holy Trinity*, painted about 1410: showing three angels in communion, it hints at the mystery of the Three-in-One. And while most people may not feel able to enter into such depths of theology and art, it is certain that as it enters the third Christian millennium the world, when it looks to Christians at all, is looking to see whether they hold the secret of human unity. Do they love one another enough to increase or restore communion with one another and to learn by listening? Do they love the rest of humanity sufficiently to explain themselves to those unfamiliar with their traditions? And since how the Church lives is always more influential than how it speaks, can Christians so arrange life in the Church (where they can decide things) that it will be a model to the rest of society?

Such challenges have to be answered mainly in the lives of the people who are the Church, and there Orthodoxy has had a fine record. Over many centuries many Christians quietly demonstrated that the Islam of their conquerors did not possess a complete revelation. It did not reveal the full spiritual dignity of the woman or the man who shared the flesh which had been taken by the Son and who could cling to the hope of sharing the glory of God with all the saints. In the twentieth century, under persecution more severe than the pressures experienced under Islam, courageously persistent Christian believers were the people who, more than any other group, practised the virtues which maintained an alternative to the Communist Party. This alternative was not so materialistic as the Communists were, both in their philosophy and in their daily behaviour. It did not automatically sacrifice the individual to the state, or undermine the life of the family, or stifle creativity, or wreck both personal relations and the person's own integrity by the constant fear and the need to lie. But as prophets in every age have declared, the Church is not merely private. It is meant to witness to justice in society. In the 1930s Bulgakov wrote: 'When the iron grasp of godless Communism, which would strangle all life, has ended, the Russian Church will not fail to apply in the realm of social Christianity the lessons it has learned in the present time of spiritual testing.' In the 1990s the hour for which he could only hope has struck. What, then, has Orthodoxy to say about the right shape of society, now accepting democracy? It is a question which only the Orthodox can answer, developing their great tradition for a new age. The essential point made by an Orthodox theologian writing in the 1990s on *Ethics after Christendom*, Vigan Guroian, was a repetition of Bulgakov's plea: 'my Church needs to retrieve its rich liturgical tradition and then apply this tradition in a lively way to life in contemporary societies.'

Orthodoxy has avoided the standardization in church life which in Catholicism goes awkwardly with the recent teaching that it is wrong in society to have a strict control from the top (the teaching about 'subsidiarity'). But it is widely agreed that Orthodoxy's canon law needs to be updated. There, too, any revision will run up against very difficult questions. To what extent is it right for a synod of bishops, or a 'spiritual father', or the conscience of an individual, to allow a deviation from a general rule in accordance with the traditional teaching about 'economy'? What is the relevance of the old theological principle that there should be 'one bishop in one place', that diocesan bishop being under the presidency of the nearest metropolitan or patriarch? Does that principle mean that Roman Catholic or non-Chalcedonian bishops should be denied all recognition in lands traditionally Orthodox? Does it mean that it is right to continue to refuse communion to Christians who belong to other churches? Even in the question about patriarchs there are now major problems. The ancient patriarchates retain their prestige but have relatively small numbers of Orthodox living close to them. It seems curious that the patriarch of Alexandria, with a flock of perhaps a hundred thousand in Egypt, should still rank so high in the Orthodox world, although ideally this ancient African bishopric might become a centre of Christian vitality in the whole continent (it already has some links with the south). It is even more curious that the patriarch of Antioch, now based in Damascus, should be the patriarch acknowledged by some 300,000 Americans. It is sad that the numerous Orthodox of Australia should have no patriarch nearer than the Middle East. It is also sad that the patriarchate of Jerusalem, which inevitably has a status depending more on history than on current pastoral responsibility, should have been the focus of disputes between Greeks and Arabs.

The history of Orthodoxy in the USA has resulted in overlapping jurisdictions, based on ethnic groups and therefore related to the various ancient patriarchates or to national churches in Europe—an arrangement which, since Americans are Americans, does not commend Orthodoxy to a patriotic nation which is the most important in the world and in the Christian world. Not until 1866 was the first Orthodox parish organized (in New Orleans) and not until 1872 did the Russian bishop move from Alaska to San Francisco. Later he moved to New York—only to find that the total Orthodox community was to be divided. The prospect of unity around a Russian bishop was destroyed both by ethnic groups becoming more conscious of their European origins (but dividing again in many cases) and also by the White versus Red split in the Russians, healed only in 1970. The largest Orthodox group has been not Russian but Greek (some two million out of about 3.5 million). It has been troubled by divisions. Its membership has ranged from nostalgic monarchists to those who have believed that not even the tension between Greek and Russian should prevent the emergence of a united and thoroughly American community worthy of being called the Orthodox Church in America. That title has been used since 1970 by the originally Russian 'jurisdiction', granted 'autocephaly' by Moscow despite protests from Constantinople, whose patriarch claims the exclusive right to bestow this independence. Co-operation between these ethnic groups has grown but to an outsider it must seem possible that the time will come for the unifying establishment of a patriarchate of New York, with a determination to lead a renewal.

These appear to be a few of the problems which would call for attention were Orthodoxy to embark on a renewal comparable with that undertaken by the Roman Catholic Church during and since the Second Vatican Council. But to say this is not to say that Orthodoxy can be expected to copy Catholicism or Protestantism, as to some extent it did during the age of the Reformations with unfortunate consequences. History has not left the west in a position to preach to the east, as Russian resistance to Catholic or Protestant expansionism has shown forcibly in the 1990s. Even indisputably Christian words such as 'evangelism' can arouse hostility when spoken by westerners in connection with traditionally Orthodox countries: such words can seem to refer to stealing sheep from their shepherds. Catholic or Protestant missionary work has done something to stimulate the various ancient Christian communities in the Middle East—but these communities became so defensively conservative in societies which treated them as disloyal partly because of the damage done by the medieval 'crusades' from the west and since then western Christianity has been associated with colonialism. Catholic or Protestant church life has set something of an example to the Orthodox by its energetic efficiency and by its active theology—but the west, either medieval or modern, has not been superior to Orthodox spirituality, which is what really counts. And the Orthodox have many facts on their side when they refuse to accept that their present position is worse than Catholicism's or Protestantism's in institutional terms: except as a result of persecution they do not have an acute shortage of clergy, and they are not profoundly disunited.

If Orthodoxy cannot be asked to imitate either Catholicism or Protestantism, how is it possible to hope for its renewal? The answer coming from within Orthodoxy appears to be this. It is not out of keeping with 'tradition' to hope and pray for renewal through the 're-reception' of some of the traditions, for at the heart of Orthodoxy has been a vision more golden and more permanent than any ethnic or denominational conservatism. Tradition has taught that the Eucharist is only a foretaste of a kingdom to come, the kingdom of God, and has spoken of the hope that a whole society may be just and loving around a Christlike Church. It is understandable that Orthodox believers driven from their homelands by poverty or persecution should wish to conserve their traditions. But many of the children of these homesick exiles have now settled down to become citizens of new societies where the future is considerably more interesting than the past. It is also understandable that when believers were being persecuted they grew isolated and became rigid in defiance of their oppressors. They lacked the freedom, the resources and the incentives needed for fresh thinking. But at the end of the twentieth Christian century the long martyrdom of Orthodoxy seems to have ceased. The time has, it seems, come for a new outburst of energy, of debate and reconstruction, which for a new age would be better than nostalgia. This would also be better than any surrender to modernism and onlookers need always to remember how many reasons the Orthodox have for not making the nineteenth and twentieth centuries their golden age. The postmodern mood which has appeared on the eve of a new century, however, includes what should interest the Orthodox: an acknowledgement that people need not be thought fools if they prefer to be traditional in at least some ways.

It would be a tragedy if Orthodoxy, having achieved so much and suffered so much, were now to think renewal impossible without an emperor or tsar to lead it. But God, said Gregory of Nyssa, when explaining why Moses struck the rock in the wilderness, 'is like a spring of perpetually fresh water'. And the history of Orthodoxy, including its history in the twentieth Christian century, shows saints and the more ordinary millions being carried along by a great river.

5

cɔeɔeɔeɔ

Medieval Catholicism

The Spirit of Catholicism

MANY Christians who do not accept the pope's jurisdiction—most numerously, the Eastern Orthodox—insist that they, too, are Catholics. But in everyday speech the word usually refers to the Roman Catholic Church, which in the 1990s has baptized almost a thousand million of the living.

Its differences from Eastern Orthodoxy should not be exaggerated. Both traditions are based firmly on the Bible as interpreted by bishops who have continued to embody something of the spirit of Roman law and government. In both traditions terms familiar to the old Greek philosophers have been used to express doctrines. In both traditions church life for the people has been largely a matter of receiving the benefits of the sacraments: the number of these is not defined by Orthodoxy but for Catholics the standard seven are baptism, the Eucharist, the confirmation of the baptized, the confession of sins, ordination, matrimony and the anointing of the seriously sick ('unction'), in a list going back to Peter Lombard in the twelfth century. In particular the fully faithful laity feel 'obliged' and glad to attend the Eucharist ('Mass' to Catholics since the sixth century) every Sunday. They supplement it by traditional prayers in private, often prayers used by saints in past centuries. In both traditions the heritage of spirituality is very rich. One expression of it is the number and importance of those whose lives are 'religious' in the special sense of being lived in a religious 'order' with a discipline of prayer. In the Catholic Church of the 1990s almost a million women and men belong to a variety of 'orders'.

But a visit to the Mass will show differences between Catholicism and Orthodoxy. 'Mass' comes from *missa*, the 'sending' of the faithful in the final blessing, and this service has often been regarded as a blessing on the congregation, rather than as *leitourgia*, 'work' by it; in the Middle Ages, and sometimes later, Catholics spoke of 'hearing Mass'. The presiding priest who 'gives the blessing' is likely to be more visible and prominent than in the Orthodox Liturgy and the emphasis on the name in prayer, with perhaps a photograph on the wall, is likely to display the ultimate human source of his authority, the pope in Rome. In the words to which the Orthodox representatives agreed in 1439, although reluctantly and temporarily: as the successor of St Peter the pope exercises 'the full power of nourishing, ruling and governing the universal Church'. Other Roman Catholic bishops are therefore the pope's subordinates and in that respect they have less authority than do Orthodox bishops, but the priests in the parishes are in effect their deputies and so locally they are powerful. That does not mean that the priest has a low status in relation to the laity. On the contrary, he is essential. Recently the worship has become more congregational, the custom of the regular confession of sins to a priest has diminished and the number of priests in proportion to the laity has become much smaller, but still there are about 400,000 priests in the Church of the 1990s and still they are essential. In this tradition the priest's most important role has been to 'offer sacrifice' in the Mass, pleading to the Father the merits of Christ's self-sacrifice in death. The presence of Christ in the bread and wine after their consecration by the priest has been defined more precisely than in Orthodoxy: it is presence by 'transubstantiation'. The priest has full authority to convey God's forgiveness to penitent sinners. And the priest is expected to preach, expounding a clear, authoritative system of doctrine which covers a wide field of faith and ethics. This doctrine is derived from the Bible but also from 'natural' law and it is defined in a continuous tradition by the *magisterium*—by the pope at the head of the bishops who have been in communion with him and with each other in many ways. Bishops in communion with Rome have met in fourteen 'ecumenical' councils since 787, the last such council to be recognized by the Orthodox. The Second Vatican Council, meeting in the 1960s, demonstrated once again that in Catholicism 'tradition' can develop to an extent which so far has not been found either possible or desirable in Orthodoxy.

The main tradition of private prayer for Catholics includes what is almost preaching to oneself, being the devout study and absorption of a message in the Bible. Other aspects of Catholic spirituality have also had more precision than is traditional in Orthodoxy, although for many Catholics this precision has recently decreased. The consecrated bread and wine are made the focus of adoration outside, as well as within, the Mass. Beliefs about the glory of the Virgin Mary as 'immaculate' from the moment of her conception and 'assumed' into heaven 'body and soul' have been made official doctrines and in 1992 the *Catechism of the Catholic Church* repeated the teaching that she was always free of personal sin and perpetually a virgin, 'even while giving birth'. It is clearer in Catholicism than in Orthodoxy who is a saint: he or she is 'canonized' by the pope, who can act without waiting for centuries to pass. It is also clearer what occurs after death: in addition to heaven or hell there is the condition of 'purgatory' and the sinners being purged in it may be liberated into heaven with the assistance of the prayers of the Church on earth, particularly in the Mass. Orthodoxy has also encouraged prayers for the dead but has felt unable to be dogmatic about the nature of purgatory.

It cannot be said of this tradition, as is said of Orthodoxy, that the faithful laity guard its life and doctrines. Here the acknowledged guardians of the faith are the pope and the bishops and the laity have often been regarded as learners. This purposeful control by a hierarchy has been immensely successful. Many good and holy people have loved, and do love, this church not only because it is the form in which they have received the Christian heritage, usually from their earliest years, but also because it is authoritative. They may be glad to accept the tradition that Christ promised the 'Spirit of truth' to guide the Church, particularly the apostles and the bishops who are their successors, since Scripture needs trustworthy interpretation. They may feel that they have enough to worry about without debating the truth of what the Church teaches or the validity of what the Church practises as its tradition: such matters are best left to the religious experts. This obedient group has included, and still includes, saints whose only real worry is about their own sins and who welcome a strong discipline as the framework for the struggle to lead a holy life. The contented group has also included some sophisticated intellectuals who think that faith is needed but is a leap in the dark of uncertainty, so that a firm guide is indispensable if the leap is to end safely. Yet not all Roman Catholics are equally obedient to Rome, for the character of this tradition is a paradox.

There is, to be sure, official certainty about the organization of life and thought; one can know by looking it up in a book where the Church stands and what it teaches officially, in some detail. This contrasts sharply with the confusion in much of Protestantism. But often a closer inspection reveals a generous inclusion of sinful and unorthodox humanity. This Catholicism exhibits its saints as models but its leaders have often granted that it is not made up of saints exclusively and that 'the Faith' taught has not been received by all. It has stressed the sinfulness of human nature to a degree not found in Orthodoxy, and in practice it operates on the basis that not all who have been baptized, or who attend the Mass, are heroically pure either in belief or in behaviour. Thus the Church has stressed that its sacraments depend for their validity not on the orthodoxy and holiness of the priest administering them, nor on the opinions of the laity receiving them, but on the faith of the Church itself. What makes sacraments 'valid' is the intention 'to do as the Church does'—of course, normally using words and actions which the Church has authorized. And the Church has pursued a strategy of blessing the 'folk religion' which concentrates on the human experiences of birth and death, of family, community and celebration, of everyday fears and needs, and which offers the security of traditional rites and images without asking too many questions. Blessing and lifting up the people's religious instincts has involved the active, creative patronage of architecture, art and music, with masterpieces as sublime as may be found anywhere in the history of the world. But it has also quite often meant the practical acceptance of what may be called (if critics incline to be harsh) popular religious customs containing elements of paganism, superstition or magic which are not blessed by Scripture; and Catholic religious art has sometimes been loved by the people rather than by aesthetic experts.

Many Protestants have therefore protested that popular Catholicism is scarcely Bible-based. They have also protested at attempts by the authorities of the Church to eliminate the heresy which denies official doctrines because those attempts have been made through the exercise of worldly power, the most notorious example being the Inquisition which handed heretics over to the state for burning. Thus Catholicism, when it is not being too popular in the eyes of its critics, can be denounced for its long record of persecution or intolerance, crushing the people. The paradox arises because the Church has been concerned both to teach what is true authoritatively and to use what is popular pastorally. Yet many Catholics have also protested against both the semi-paganism and the persecutions, and many prophets including theologians have arisen with a mission to put things right. It has plainly been the Church's long-term intention to be inclusive while setting an example of faithfulness to Christ and to be institutional without smothering the life of the spirit. In this, the Church has often been successful; otherwise it could not have been a mother and a teacher to so many saints, famous or known only locally.

To understand this tradition we need to look at its history. Just as Eastern Orthodoxy is full of memories of the Byzantine empire, so this Catholicism inherits the legacy of the Middle Ages in the west. The word 'Middle' in this connection has been traced back to the 1460s but began to be used more prominently in the sixteenth century. It may suggest dismissively that a period neither modern nor ancient lay between the achievements of two superior ages, but in fact this medieval period had its own immense achievements in western Europe. It created a civilization never imagined by Paul when (according to the Acts of the Apostles) he had his dream on the coast of Asia Minor, of a Macedonian saying 'come across and help us'.

In the fifth Christian century the Roman empire in the west could not resist invasions by barbarians who were either pagan or heretically Arian and even the Romanized population had not been thoroughly Christianized. It was left to the Catholic clergy to conserve what remained of the old civilization, to maintain the Church as an alternative society within its own beliefs, values and laws, and gradually to build a new society. This the clergy did. They owed much to the support of emperors, kings and local lords, but not to the same extent as in the east. There, as we have seen, the empire survived although diminished by the Muslim conquests and the Orthodox Church was that empire's religious aspect until 1453. The Church in the west was different. As F. W. Maitland put it bluntly, 'the medieval Church was a state', and as another great historian, R. W. Southern, added: 'the Church was not only a state, it was *the* state; it was not only *a* society, it was *the* society—the human *societas perfecta*.' But the Church's clergy-dominated triumph was not the whole story. Because it was necessary first to make the west nominally Christian and then to deal with a new society which grew in numbers and vigour, the Church as it rose to the challenges became less conservative than Eastern Orthodoxy. It produced many new developments in its own life—developments which linked it with the society and culture around it at the cost of some links with the earlier Christian centuries. Its official doctrine was taught with authority but if it was to be popular it could not afford to reject everything that the people wanted. So it came to need purification by reforms. And many reforms came, further demonstrating this tradition's vitality.

The character of medieval Catholicism as both institutional and inclusive resulted in another phenomenon which deserves a brief introductory mention. The ordained leaders of the Church asserted their rights in no uncertain manner, including the right to dominate political rulers, or at least to arbitrate in their disputes. But in the long term they were not able to enforce these rights against the men who had power and prestige in the states. An emperor could refuse to be controlled by a pope; a king could insist that a bishop was his subject; a city could object to the excessive numbers of clergy who walked its streets, particularly if they demanded money; the Church's own coercive power was limited. So two sources of authority, the *sacerdotium* which in practice meant the pope and the bishops, and the *regnum* which in practice meant the king, the lay barons or the rulers of cities, were available to people who could prefer the one to the other according to the circumstances. Despite its unity which strikes the modern eye as being very strange, Christendom was never so unified as churchmen or statesmen wished in their rival ambitions and theories. The Church had to include cities and nations with substantial independence. The state had to acknowledge that it did not embrace all life. Thus the Middle Ages in the west unintentionally contained some of the seeds of modern pluralism.

Of course the Middle Ages did not produce many of the features of a modern society: life was then considerably closer to the earth and to early death, and the clergy were much more powerful, partly because they were believed to be in charge of admission to the life after death, partly because they were known to be more educated and skilled in the subtler activities of this life. And of course the culture of the Middle Ages until the Renaissance did not reach the level of elegance and sophistication which had been achieved by the elite in the Greek and Roman world of antiquity. But there was a rich creativity producing complexity in this medieval period which is obscured when it is described, in praise or blame, simply as the time of the Church's triumph or as the 'Age of Faith'. The liveliness which Roman Catholicism has inherited can be indicated more accurately by reference to a festival which the Middle Ages in the west made popular. We can picture the leaders of the medieval society, and of the worldwide Roman Catholic Church which developed out of it, as being like kings with more than a touch of grandeur or like shepherds who have to use some whistles, and perhaps dogs, if they are to get the sheep where they ought to be. Such leadership has been clothed in spiritual authority and often in worldly power, but also in many beauties of myth and ritual. It has managed to lead very large numbers of people, walking or stumbling along a variety of paths through many forms of darkness, to a light which they are capable of seeing. In that light the people find something both reassuringly familiar and so mysterious that the natural response becomes worship even if things and actions, rather than words, are the means of worship. With its medieval heritage, the Roman Catholic Church has been well called the Church of Christmas.

Bishop and Emperor

In preparation for the Middle Ages in the west the 380s were the decisive decade and the leading actors in the drama were Ambrose the bishop and Theodosius the emperor. The scene was Milan, for a hundred years from 305 the capital of the western half of the Roman empire.

Ambrose was the son of Roman aristocrats. When present at the election of a new bishop, he had been at the head of troops to keep order in his capacity as the governor of the city and its region. He found himself elected and eventually agreed to accept the position, but he needed to be baptized and ordained as a priest before he could get to work as a bishop. His age was then 34. To his continuing masterfulness he now added an austere piety and an understanding of what ordinary Catholics wanted. His Catholicism included the faith of Nicaea, his writings conveyed the conclusions of Greek theology to the west in clear Latin, and his sermons included no hesitations. He continued to take the lead in the city's life and to regard himself as at least the equal of the empire's grandees; he stressed the solemn significance of the Church's sacraments; he encouraged the cult of the relics of the Church's martyrs and was excited when some relics were unearthed to form the centrepiece of his own cathedral; he wrote hymns to add to the biblical psalms; he taught morality firmly, holding that 'penance', then understood as the public reconciliation to the Church of a sinner who had been excommunicated, could take place only once in a lifetime—and not offering absolution for sins confessed privately. He also wrote a book about the duties of the clergy and by his example set a new standard for Catholic bishops.

Even in his lifetime he was regarded as a saint. Before this period the only widely acknowledged saints other than those in the Bible had been the martyrs and the hermits or monks. Such Christians had escaped from the wicked world either through death or through the killing of self-will. Now kings, bishops, abbots and others were to receive the Church's highest honours and they were to be praised for changing the world. Bishops proudly brought the relics of the martyrs from the *martyria* in the suburbs to the centres of cities. They also brought the Church for which the martyrs had died into the centre of the world's life—even, in the west, into a certain superiority over emperors. In 378 the Goths, forced to migrate into the Roman Balkans by the pressure of the Huns on their former territory, fought and destroyed much of the Roman army and killed the emperor Valens. In the east the empire rallied but in the west the pressure of the barbarians was now such that the emperors needed all the help they could get from the Catholic Church. The time of the bishops had come.

In 380 the emperor in the west was the young Gratian, who in that year asked the great bishop of Milan to instruct him fully in the Catholic faith as defined by the council of Nicaea. He was determined to make it compulsory throughout his territory, in collaboration with the Spanish general Theodosius whom he had appointed emperor in the east. But he was murdered, as was his young successor, and in the early years of that successor's reign his mother who acted as regent was an Arian. Amid these uncertainties Ambrose's authority increased. He successfully defied the Arian regent's order to hand over a church for heretical use; he threatened to excommunicate Theodosius for ordering the local bishop to rebuild a synagogue which a Catholic mob had destroyed and the emperor cancelled the order; in 390 he did excommunicate him for ordering a massacre, until the emperor had repented publicly. Such assertions of moral authority sound like a rehearsal for the medieval papacy. When the Arian regent's troops had surrounded his cathedral, Ambrose preached that 'the emperor is in the Church, not over it'. When Theodosius tried to compensate Jews for Christian vandalism, Ambrose protested that a proposal contrary to true religion was invalid. When the emperor was still thinking that a massacre of rioters was in keeping with imperial tradition, he was reminded: 'Remember you are a mortal man!' And he accepted these rebukes. The explanation turns partly on Ambrose's personality, but also on the fact that Theodosius knew that in the west his own position was weak, both Arianism and paganism were strong and barbarians were ready to invade: as the Catholic emperor he had to acknowledge some dependence on the Catholic bishops. His supremacy was not established until he had defeated the usurper Eugenius who had started to bring back paganism, in the autumn of 394—and six months later he was dead.

On his death the Roman empire was divided for the last time: now the west could no longer draw on the wealth and power of the east. Two years later Ambrose died. Within ten years large numbers of Germanic tribesmen had crossed the Rhine into Romanized Gaul. In 410 the Britons were told that the western empire could no longer defend them from raiders across the North Sea. And in that year the Goths sacked Rome. This sensation suddenly made it clear that imperial Rome, believed to be *Roma aeterna*, was dying. The reaction was courageous only in the mind of Augustine, whom Ambrose had baptized as the celebration of Easter began in 387.

Augustine

We do not need to claim that Augustine was the first to think all the thoughts with which his great name was to be associated, or that every theologian in the Middle Ages was to agree with every word that he wrote, or that most people actually read him. But he acquired an authority in the medieval west larger than any other theologian's. In the ninth century when Radbertus and Ratramnus disputed over the nature of the Eucharist, or Gottschalk and Hincmar over predestination to hell, or Gottschalk and Erigena over the probable size of the population of hell, much of the argument turned on the right interpretation of Augustine's teaching. In 1150 Peter Lombard completed a series of answers to theological questions, his *Sentences*. It became the basic text book of medieval theology and in the universities all who aspired to be 'masters' were expected to offer lectures commenting on it. More than a thousand of its quotations were from Augustine's actual or supposed works, more than double the number of the references to all the other Fathers. At about the same time Bishop Otto of Freising wrote a widely used history of Church and State. Its theme and its title (*The Two Cities*) were derived from Augustine although after completing that book this bishop, who was an emperor's uncle, became more optimistic than Augustine ever was about the possibility of a truly Christian Church and a truly Christian empire together building the City of God.

Among the greatest minds of the Middle Ages, Anselm defended himself by the protest that he had said nothing in his *Monologion* that Augustine had not said long before him and Bonaventure declared that Augustine had combined *scientia* (knowledge) and wisdom more completely than any other Father of the Church. Thomas Aquinas thought of himself as a disciple in conversation with him although his critics claimed to be more faithfully Augustinian. One of the most prominent of these critics, Gregory of Rimini, belonged to the 'Augustinian' order of clergy and was a leader of the 'modern Augustinian' movement in theology. John Wyclif and John Hus claimed that their pre-Reformation 'heresies' were based on Augustine's teaching because the true Church consists of the few who are predestined to enter heaven. In a very different vein Petrarch, a forerunner of the Renaissance, wrote an autobiography consisting of three dialogues with Augustine. And these great men of the Middle Ages were far from being the last to think in the shadow of this giant. His vision of Christianity was to be decisive (although differently applied) for the Reformations masterminded by Luther and Calvin. Among Catholics, when Pascal sold his library in order to raise money for the poor he kept 'the Bible, St Augustine and a few other books'—and incessantly Catholics more conventional than Pascal quoted him as an authority. And even in modern times, when his theology has often been condemned for reaching inhumane conclusions, he has continued to interest by his revelations of his own humanity.

He was born in 354 and the easiest access to his life before 400 is provided by his *Confessions*, the autobiography which he wrote not long after his return to the North Africa of his youth. It is a book which has never lost its appeal. Even in the overlong epilogue which explores conundrums such as the meanings of 'time' and 'creation', something about him, and about us, may be learned. Time, he says, does not exist in eternity, and it has scarcely existed since it was created along with the world: the past is no more, the future is not yet, the present is a fleeting instant. We have met a man who is fascinated when he thinks he glimpses what is timeless amid the changes and chances of life; and perhaps we have met our own deepest selves. Creation, he says, is the act of the Creator and what is created must be less than perfect: 'all things are beautiful because you made them, but you are inexpressibly more beautiful.' It is not so strange after all that the climax of the *Confessions* is a meditation on the first chapter of Genesis, for Augustine, too, has been created—first out of nothing, then out of chaos.

His story about time lived by himself hints continuously at lessons to be learned about all human life. Infants cry because they are both self-centred and disappointed. Schoolboys are beaten by adults whose own serious business is a more disastrous game. Adolescents rebel simply in order to rebel; the stolen pear is sweet because it is stolen, like the forbidden fruit which Adam ate. Augustine's rebellion was against parents (of course)—an ill-tempered father who was for most of his life a pagan and a possessive mother. So he became a Manichee and was thrown out of home. The Manichees suited him for a time: they poured scorn on biblical fundamentalism but were religious in an exciting way, assuring him that his exploding sexuality was not the fault of his will. He wanted sex because his pure spirit was temporarily imprisoned in a body and thus under the power of Darkness and the Devil; and as a 'hearer' he could have sex. But he was exceptionally clever, like the unintended son who arrived to him and to the concubine taken as was customary; and his mind was refined by an education in the Latin classics, producing through Vergil a sensitivity to emotions and through Cicero a love of well-phrased philosophy. His ambition grew at the same pace, for at this stage the rule of the world seemed open to men who had been born obscurely. But when he went to Rome and Milan to teach the material he had learned and to begin a brilliant career as public orator at the intellectually active court of the young emperor of the west (on the recommendation of Symmachus, the definitely pagan governor of Rome), he found something for which he did not know he had been looking.

There now occurred a conversion which seems to have been like that of Cyprian, the bishop who was still remembered in Carthage. Writing to a friend, Cyprian had recalled his thoughts in the 'gloomy night' before he could decide to seek baptism. 'How is so great a conversion possible?' he had asked himself. It would mean abandoning his dreams of a provincial's share in the glory of Rome: 'great banquets . . . costly clothing of gold and purple . . . crowds of dependants'. It was true that the empire which had made Cyprian a martyr was now nominally Christian, and it was also true that because of his ambition to rise in that empire Augustine could be persuaded to send his low-born mistress back to North Africa (we do not know her name), so that it became theoretically possible for him to conform to the imperial creed of Catholicism, to marry a woman whose dowry would enable him to buy a post in the government, and to expect the banquets, the robes and the dependants to follow. His mother found a suitable bride for him (then aged twelve). But the decision to part with his mistress was very painful: 'my heart', he remembered, 'was torn where it had stuck to her.' They had defied the Manichees' hostility to sex, and had ignored the inconvenience of an illegitimate baby to an ambitious young father and insecure young mother, by naming their son 'God-given' (Adeodatus). There was also great pain in the decision to part with worldly ambition. To other men in that age becoming a Catholic could further a career: to Augustine it meant renunciation. The pain of his journey into an uncertain future ('stumbling, hurrying, hesitating') made him ill with asthma. His account of the climax may, however, owe something to a gift which remained with him: the gift for a dramatic phrase. He says that he heard a child's voice in a garden: 'take, read.' He read Paul in the Scriptures: 'make no provision for the flesh.'

He became persuaded that God would so strengthen his will that he could control his desires and ambitions. In the past 'it was I who willed'—for 'what are we but our wills?' Now conversion meant celibacy: 'if bodies please you, praise God for them and direct your love to their Maker.' This was no easy act of the human will: it depended on prior action by the will of God. He made his *Confessions* one long prayer to God, in contrast with the *Meditations* which the Stoic philosopher-emperor Marcus Aurelius addressed to himself with a great respect for his audience. It never ceased to amaze Augustine that he had been chosen by God. Yet it was also his vocation to reason philosophically about the God who had chosen him. Before his baptism he spent some time in a retreat, from which issued books more tranquil than much of his later writing. They demonstrated the supreme importance of happiness and its ultimate impossibility except in immortality; the unavoidable need to make personal decisions about the great mysteries surrounding human life and death; and the reasonableness of the belief that human life, like the rest of the universe, is in the hands of a Creator who controls and sustains even in death. Augustine was never to be idle but deep down his heart was no longer restless. He had found not a career but eternity; not a wife but Beauty, so old, so new. That was the background when he wrote famous words which have often been misinterpreted: 'Love God and then do what is your will.' And all of the life on which he now embarked was for him a voyage into eternity. After his baptism he intended to return to his home town in Africa, Thagaste, to live quietly with his widowed mother Monica. They were held up in Ostia, the port of Rome, and looking out of a window into a garden they talked about heaven, where there would be no 'tumult of the flesh', no 'earth and sea and air', no 'dreams and images', no words, only 'Himself'. Within a fortnight Monica was dead. And when he came to die, this man who had loved a woman, who always enjoyed friendship and discussion, asked to be left alone, as Monica had asked.

To the end he remained something of a Platonist. All that exists is essentially good because it has come from the supremely good Creator: so he believed as a Catholic Christian. But what is created cannot be perfect, pure or satisfactory. In the realm of thought, 'no pure truths can be expected from the senses' since created matter is 'almost nothing'. In human life, a decision, a *conversio*, has to be made to 'use' the body so that there may be immortal union with the Creator. Evil arises when the creation is chosen instead of the Creator, but God's grace works for the right decision, in the depths of the 'memory' which is an 'immense palace' storing all life's experience.

God is even more mysterious than our deep selves: 'If you understand, this is not God.' But if people will only withdraw into the 'immense palace' ('do not go outside, enter into yourself'), there they will find the proof against total scepticism ('I know that I am'); and there they will find that their own personality is the God-given mirror of God ('if I know myself, I shall know you'). Truth, beauty and goodness are not merely the convenient arrangements of material things in human thought. Truth calls us to seek it through the opinions which we think more or less true; beauty is glimpsed through visible people or objects which are more or less lovely; perfection is hinted at as we admire things or actions which are more or less good. Plato had written about 'forms' or 'ideas' as being more real and permanent than the individual realities, all imperfect and changing, which we perceive with our senses: that had been his answer to the scepticism of the Athenians of his day. Now Augustine developed Platonism so that truly to know oneself, really to explore that 'immense palace' of the self, is to find God, who alone is truly real and permanent. 'In the flash of a trembling glance my mind came to Absolute Being, to that which truly is.' And to know oneself is to begin to understand how Absolute Being has a simplicity which is not without complexity. As a human being is one unit, so Father, Son and Spirit share the one 'substance' (as Tertullian had already taught in North Africa). But a human being has mind, knowledge and love—and so does God. The Father is somewhat like the masterful, ordering human intellect; the Son somewhat like precise knowledge; the Spirit somewhat like the love which unites people. The Father is somewhat like the memory from which all thinking comes; the Son somewhat like the understanding which clarifies and articulates; the Spirit somewhat like the will which desires and, because it desires, acts. That is why God can say in Genesis 1:26: 'Let us make Man in our image and likeness.' Of course it has proved possible to doubt the value of these comparisons, but we can at least see here what Augustine thought about the image of God in humankind.

The greatest human need is to know, obey, enjoy and love God. No moral decision can be 'just' in God's eyes if it merely weighs alternatives and acts in human strength. To be right is to want to do God's will in dependence on his power. No human achievement is worth much, but 'God, when co-operating with us, perfects what he began' and 'when God rewards our merits he crowns his gifts'. The only finally wise aim is to desire heaven and 'he who is a Christian for any reason other than that he may receive God's ultimate promises is not a Christian'. All words are 'signs' pointing to 'things' and all Christian words point to God, the only ultimate reality. Augustine's very wordy book *The City of God*, which took him thirteen years to write, ends: 'There we shall rest and see, we shall see and love, we shall love and praise. That is what shall be in the end without end. For what is our end but to arrive at the kingdom which has no end?'

That was the heart of his teaching. But he also taught his contemporaries and the future by his active life. When he returned to his roots in North Africa it was in order to serve the Catholic Church. He founded an informal monastery but did not persist in his desire to spend his life in contemplation and philosophy. He accepted ordination first as a priest and then as a bishop, with a bishopric far less prominent than Cyprian's Carthage or Ambrose's Milan: he was now the chief pastor of the region around the port of Hippo (in modern Algeria). It was a place where nobody was his academic equal and probably few understood him at any depth. Even now he surrounded himself with a kind of monastery, for he insisted that nearby clergy should be unmarried and live together with him as his *familia*. But he usually preached several times a week to non-intellectuals and almost every day he sat as the arbitrator in quarrels which were personal or financial, not theological, since a bishop was now used for this purpose even by non-Catholics. And that was his life for 35 years. What he taught by living it, and by his sermons, was that the Church's sacraments can reach where intellectual arguments cannot. Baptism marks or 'seals' a sinner as belonging to Christ. The Eucharist gives the 'body' of Christ in order that Christians (including young children) may become that 'body' in another sense: 'it is the mystery of yourselves that you receive.' A sacrament is a physical 'sign' pointing beyond itself to a 'sacred thing', but somehow (Augustine does not precisely define how) it communicates that thing. The result is that the baptized, eucharistic people becomes *totus Christus*, Christ alive not only in himself but also in his 'members', in human limbs. When the bishop addressed that very human congregation in Hippo, he saw Christ if he looked carefully enough.

Had that been all that Augustine taught, his legacy to the Middle Ages would have been almost flawless in the eyes of most modern Christians. But it was not. His years under pressure as a bishop took their toll. To the end he believed as he wrote in *The City of God*: 'God has made the mortal race of Man the loveliest of all mortal things on earth.' But while a bishop he gave more and more emphasis to the truth that Man needs to be saved.

He often called the Bible which he had once despised 'the foundation' because it was the message of salvation. In his treatise on *Christian Doctrine* he even boasted that 'whatever may be found elsewhere, if it is useful, is found there'. Modern scholars have lamented that his circumstances prevented him from more thorough studies 'elsewhere': he was not at ease in the Greek language or eastern theology, he knew little of Aristotle, not much of Plato, not all of Plotinus. But it is fairer to concentrate on his handling of the Bible itself. He applied to it his acute intelligence and his non-biblical knowledge, which was large by the standards of his time. He spotted in it some inconsistencies and some silences. He saw that the 'days' of the creation in Genesis were not literally days and that in them God's creatures were not all perfectly developed. His basic understanding of a *miraculum* was that by God's decision special events reveal hitherto unknown powers in his creation and that ordinary events are also marvellous since 'the miracle is the order' and 'greater than any miracle performed by Man is Man himself'. However, as a man of his time he did accept as literally true some parts of the Bible and of contemporary 'knowledge' which to most modern eyes are not factual. For example, he believed the story that 72 men when set to translate the Hebrew Bible into Greek without consulting each other came up with exactly the same text (the Septuagint). His contemporary Jerome, an accomplished linguist, produced a new Latin translation which was to be regarded as the official version from the eighth century and was to be called the 'Vulgate' from the sixteenth, but Augustine did not care to get at the original Hebrew and Greek: the old Latin Bible, translated in the second century, was good enough for him. This meant that some of his favourite texts were mistranslations. 'Unless you have believed you will not understand' did not accurately reproduce the Hebrew of Isaiah 7:9 and his use of Romans 5:12 wrongly enlisted Paul in support of his theory of 'original sin'. According to this theory, 'in Adam' all sinned before being born—but in the Greek Paul wrote merely 'because of Adam'. His theology gave far more prominence than the Bible did to the Fall of Adam (as he believed, six thousand years before his own time). Adam's 'original' sin was believed by him to justify the infliction of the punishment of suffering on every human individual—and he did not fully listen to Job's protest against the smoothly convenient theory which blames all that an individual suffers on sinfulness.

In harsh controversies while a bishop he reluctantly lent his name to violence although probably his true character came out in his dislike of capital punishment. This was partly because he had to deal with the Donatists who, when he returned to North Africa, outnumbered the Catholics. In character they were not unlike the Muslims who were in the end to drive Christianity out of the region: simple, severe and prone to use force. But to him they were at worst fanatical terrorists and at best uneducated provincials, obsessed by the memory of the distant age of the martyrs and now obviously wrong: 'untroubled, the world judges' such people. For a time he responded calmly. He snubbed their personal attacks by not mentioning them in the *Confessions* which he wrote in order to reassure Catholics that his conversion had been painfully genuine. He snubbed their rejection of all Catholic sacraments by teaching (unlike Cyprian) that baptisms by schismatics, if trinitarian, are valid, explaining that what makes a sacrament valid is not the purity or orthodoxy of the individual but the grace of God received through the enactment of a rite agreeing essentially with Catholic doctrine. But he did not say that the Donatists' sacraments were beneficial. In the end this restrained rebuke to their holier-than-thou puritanism was to bring fresh dangers, for along this line a sacrament might be seen almost as a machine dispensing grace, and Christians might forget the vision of the gracious God in a personal relationship with the human person. And his restraint was not inexhaustible when Donatist bishops were very rude to him, and to Catholics in general, at a conference called in the hope of reconciliation, and when the violence of their followers became extensive. He now accepted the need to exterminate these pests by heavy fines, by tough police action and by the denial of access to the courts. There were to be no executions of Donatists as such: the Catholics did not want to make more martyrs. But the persecution was such that there were many suicides. Augustine quoted, or misquoted, a parable of Jesus: 'compel people to come in' (Luke 14:23). And eventually the Donatists were compelled—by the Roman state and later on, more completely, by the Byzantines.

Augustine's alliance with the authorities of the state also led him to propound the influential doctrine of the 'just war'. Hitherto the Church had been either unwilling or confused when invited to say that Christians could be soldiers. From an early date some Christians had served in the army, but preferably as policemen without shedding blood. Now that the empire was becoming Christian, could Christians fight, and if necessary kill, in its service? Augustine gave a momentously affirmative answer to that question. He added important qualifications: the war must be declared by the proper authority, intended for the defence of proper rights and waged by means as merciful as possible. This has often been thought a sensible answer, for the empire had to deal with invasions and its many Christian subjects could not be completely detached. But Augustine's answer was to be misused in the centuries to come, justifying wars fought for purposes and with methods other than those which he accepted.

In the development of rather too much muscle in the Catholic Church a summary of trinitarian theology in a creed called 'Athanasian' but actually Augustinian was to have a sinister influence. That creed announced that 'whoever wishes to be saved must believe' doctrines which it sets out in some detail, the only alternative being to 'perish everlastingly'. These doctrines stress the essential unity of God, as Augustine did, but they do not repeat the equal emphasis on God's unfathomable mystery. The creed seems to have been composed in the south of France about half a century after his death in an attempt to simplify his teaching for the ordinary faithful. It was gradually accepted in the western (not the eastern) Church as one of the authoritative creeds and in the west, during and after the Middle Ages, it was more influential than any other document in spreading the idea that any dissent from officially endorsed dogmas deserves eternal punishment in hell—an idea which was to encourage the further belief that the fire which burns a heretic on earth is comparatively merciful.

At the same time popular religion was to separate the Father and the Son for most readily understandable purposes (did not the Son experience the Father's wrath on the cross?), neglecting the Spirit but exalting the more attractive Virgin to a status difficult to distinguish from divinity. Augustine's own teaching was, of course, far more deeply thoughtful and Christian. When he distinguished between the Three he did so with frequently expressed hesitations, for most profoundly he believed in the One ('God alone is simple'). He was well aware of the dangers in using the Latin term *persona* as the equivalent of the Greek *hypostasis*. He used it, he said, only because to keep silent would be even more dangerous. After his death he was to contribute decisively to the council of Chalcedon through the 'tome' sent to it by Pope Leo, for the key phrase about Christ, 'two natures in one person', was derived from Augustine. Another of his contributions, as his 'human weakness' tried to penetrate the divine mystery, was to emphasize that the Three who are equally eternal, perfect and almighty may be distinguished by their relationships. The Father 'begets', the Son is 'begotten' by the Father, the Spirit 'proceeds' from both by one and the same operation. Thus the Father is the Lover, the Son the Beloved, the Spirit the Love. All the work of God is done by all the Three, and the Three are more united than are the memory, understanding and will in a human person, but the Church is right to respond to the revelation in Scripture by using the three names to identify aspects or parts of the life and work of the One: creation, salvation and inspiration.

That teaching is characteristic of Augustine. Always relationships were important to him; always the relationship of love is the supreme activity. However, use was made of his trinitarian teaching as the relationship between east and west in the Church was poisoned and destroyed. Although he was not familiar with Greek theology there is no evidence that he wished to differ from the doctrine carefully propounded by the three Cappadocian bishops in preparation for the council of 381. He was as zealous as they were in defence of the divine unity. But the doctrine that the Spirit proceeds 'from the Father and the Son' could be extracted from his complex theology—and was so extracted in the confession of 'Catholic' faith made by the Visigothic king of Spain when formally converted from Arianism in 589. As we have seen, this '*Filioque* clause' then made its way through approval by the emperor Charlemagne to reluctant acceptance in Rome, but it aroused the indignation of the Orthodox east. Another reason why Augustine has never been recognized by the Orthodox as an authoritative 'doctor' (teacher) of the Church was his teaching that every newborn infant inherits the guilt of Adam's 'original' sin. The teachers revered in the east did indeed say that Adam's sin had tragically weakened humanity's original goodness but they never held Augustine's gloomier theory.

One of his theological battles was against Pelagius who after early years in Britain had moved to Rome, becoming a spiritual counsellor to men and women of the aristocratic class who were beginning to take Christianity seriously. He urged them to forget their pagan customs and to seek 'perfection', promising that they would be 'assisted' by divine help conveyed through Christ's teaching and example. Later Pelagius took this message to Palestine, urging fellow Christians to walk strongly in the Lord's footsteps.

Up to a point this was also teaching which a younger Augustine had believed and had urged on others, as he was now firmly reminded. But being an older man, soured by the observation of too many moral failures, he attacked the emphasis of Pelagius on humanity's glorious and merely 'assisted' potential. It seemed a fatal concession to human pride and a disastrous underestimate of what God gives. The Christian, he replied to Pelagian optimism, 'receives the Holy Spirit' and only through that unmerited gift is given the love for, and delight in, 'that supreme and unchanging good which is God'. In the *Confessions* he remembered how reluctant he had been to be holy ('Give me chastity but not yet!') until he had reached a prayer of surrender ('Give what you command and command what you will!'). As Pelagius read that prayer, it was his turn to be shocked. 'God', was his reply, 'would not command what he knew we cannot perform.'

As the controversy intensified both men moved to extreme positions. Pelagius and his admirers said things which could be interpreted as the denial of the Christian's reliance on the mercy and grace of God. But Augustine so emphasized humanity's inherited guilt and personal impotence that he seemed to forget some of what he had himself taught when full of joy at his liberation from the gloom of the Manichees. He had described evil as 'the absence of good' since all God's creation is essentially good: evil is, so to speak, a hole in the creation, a hole which is inevitable because the good creation, not being God, cannot be perfect. But by that he never meant that evil is an illusion (a hole can do great damage) and increasingly he saw evil as the opposite of all that is good, an opposite which may be chosen precisely because it is evil. Indeed, he now insisted that since the ability to choose the good without God's grace was lost at the Fall, the choice of evil has become normal for humanity. He had taught that really to look inside the human mind is to see a mirror reflecting the Trinity, but now when he looked inside himself he saw much that needed penitence and when he looked around him although he saw the Body of Christ he did not see many individuals who could easily become saints. To be a saint is such a miracle that it is possible only because God wills and achieves it: 'He orders all that he wills.' The bishop of Hippo compared the Church to a hospital.

Augustine now developed another epigram in the *Confessions*: 'what one does is sin, what one suffers is punishment.' He did not do so with quite the brutality of the ninth-century monk Gottschalk, who was to teach that God predestines many to hell, so that Christ lived and died in order to save the elect and no one else; that Augustinian extremist was to express himself so crudely that he incurred the Church's condemnation in 849. But it is possible to draw out of Augustine's own teaching the doctrine that, with the exception of a minority chosen in order to make up the number of the angels who fell, the bulk of humanity is so chained by inherited guilt, is individually so inclined to evil, and is so firmly left by God in that state without adequate illumination or grace, that it deserves a hard life and an endless hell. Augustine considered it clear that 'God works in people's hearts to incline their wills in whatsoever way he himself wills: either to good in accordance with his mercy or to evil according with their evil merits'. And he taught that in the minority which escapes hell few escape some painful purification after death. The noun *purgatorium* was not used before the twelfth century when the doctrine of purgatory was developed in detail with an emphasis on punishment, but Augustine wrote about the 'purgatorial' fire ('more terrible than anything a man can suffer in this life') which can purify Christians who have already expressed their penitence before death. In his expectation for almost everyone, 'after this life there will be either the purgatorial fire or eternal pain'. With this view of the nature and destiny of Man he inspired a successful campaign to suppress the more cheerful Pelagians. Having enrolled the bishop of Rome as well as the imperial authority against Pelagius he could claim *causa finita*, 'the argument is over'. And when he wrote his *Reconsiderations*, towards the end of his life, he looked back on this dispute with satisfaction. 'I laboured on behalf of free will, but the grace of God won the day.'

What he now meant by 'the grace of God' became clear when he had to deal with Julian of Eclanum. A bishop's son, himself happily married and a good pastor, Julian had been exiled during the government's purge of Pelagians under pressure from Augustine. He now attacked his enemy as a windbag who did not know about life, particularly not about married life. In response Augustine was not as hostile to marriage as was (for example) Jerome, who told one correspondent that the best reason for marriage was that it produced virgins. Christians may marry for the world needs children and people need companionship which can enter calmer waters in old age. The marriage of Adam and Eve before the Fall, including some sex, must have been perfect. But when he wrote for nuns a book to explain *The Good of Marriage* he accompanied it by another on the superior state of *Holy Virginity*. In his abusive replies to Julian of Eclanum he distanced himself further from any full approval of sexuality as known since Adam's Fall. Sex is now stained by lust, so that all babies without exception are born with that stain. If they die unbaptized they must go to hell, although not to suffer the worst punishments. If they are baptized the guilt which they inherit from Adam is washed away—but God's just punishment for Adam's 'original' sin continues, as does their own tendency to sin, particularly through lust. So they too will end up in hell unless they have first been predestined to heaven—and most of those so predestined will find heaven attainable only through the purging fire.

Commentators inclined to defend Augustine have been able to point out that he did not denounce sexuality altogether. That point is accurate. It has also been observed that when he denounced the pagan world for being no more moral than its gods in its sex life, and for taking pleasure in public displays of sexual perversions, he was agreeing with a long line of Christians. That point is fair. But he was one of the many moralists in the ancient world who believed that the sexual act should be intended exclusively for the calm procreation of children within marriage, not for pleasure. This meant that most of the physical expressions of sexuality which human nature has desired were judged to be guilty. It did not mean that they ceased, but as moral theology became more elaborate they could be regarded by a spiritual counsellor, or by the individual Christian's conscience, as 'mortal' sins deserving hell, or at least as venial sins to be punished somewhat more mercifully. This difference between 'venial' and 'mortal' developed out of Augustine's distinction between 'slight' or 'daily' sins and serious 'crimes' against God. He regarded sex-for-pleasure as only a venial sin, but even so his attitude to sex was more negative than any teaching to be found in the New Testament or in the Orthodox tradition. Henry Chadwick's verdict is balanced: 'By his stress on concupiscence (uncontrolled desire) he set the west on the path to identifying sin with sex; that was not his intention.'

Augustine also had to respond to invasions by barbarians. *The City of God* was begun as a reply to the accusation that the sack of Rome by barbarians in 410 had been brought about because the Christians had dishonoured the pagan gods who had made the Roman empire worldwide and its capital majestically invulnerable. As he lay dying twenty years later he could hear the sounds of the Vandals' siege of his own city. But his big book—too big to be fully organized—dealt with many subjects without ever admitting that there was some truth in the charge that the Christians had undermined the empire. They had indeed helped to destroy the pagan empire's psychological strength, and at least in the western half of the empire they had not yet replaced it by contributions great enough to build a new society. The Canadian scholar C. N. Cochrane published a penetrating analysis of *Christianity and Classical Culture* when Europe was entering a dark age in 1939 because it had not united against barbarians. He observed that the notion that 'it was possible to attain a goal of permanent security, peace and freedom through political action ... was one which Christians denounced with uniform vigour and consistency. To them the state, so far from being the supreme instrument of human emancipation and perfectibility, was a strait-jacket to be justified at least as a remedy for sin.' This was one of the reasons, Cochrane showed, why 'when the barbarians descended like vultures upon the empire, it was to pluck out the eyes of a corpse'. In *The City of God* Augustine took a semi-detached view of the empire and his life had already shown how far he had moved away from *romanitas*. He had exalted the monastery above the army, penitence above honour, humility above manliness and virginity above marriage and motherhood, and in the crisis of his life he had rejected the prospect of a career in the service of the empire.

This attitude to the empire was in some ways valuable to the future of the Church (as Cochrane fully recognized). It enabled Augustine and others not to identify Christianity with a half-Christianized empire and not to get bogged down in detailed arguments about whether or not the disasters since the empire had become nominally Christian had been greater than previous calamities. He did try to show at some length that disasters were nothing new and had not been prevented by the old gods, but he left the handling of more detailed evidence to a history by a disciple, Orosius. His aloofness also enabled him to avoid the naive enthusiasm about a Christian empire to which Orosius succumbed. Augustine granted that under pagan or Christian rulers the empire had brought to many the blessings of justice and peace and had therefore deserved obedience. But as the lust for pleasure had corrupted sex, so the lust for power had corrupted government and the empire inherited by Christians had been based on pride thinly concealed as dignity, on conquest and exploitation thinly concealed as benevolence. 'A kingdom without justice', he wrote, 'is a mere burglary.' *The City of God* would always be a warning to Christians to be discriminating in their support of earthly states, to distinguish between the realms of God and of Caesar. The great book began by observing that the barbarians had spared the churches and those in them while they pillaged, raped and murdered in Rome. Its whole tone was different from Jerome's lament that 'the city which conquered the world is conquered itself'—words dictated (he said) amid sobs. But Augustine's distancing of the gospel from the state could be one-sidedly interpreted so as to increase the danger that the western Church would identify itself with the kingdom of God and try to dominate states— as, in fact, occurred in the Middle Ages.

Augustine did not intend that crude conclusion any more than he intended to condemn all sexuality. He was sure that the clue to the meaning of history was to be found in the Bible, not in imperial propaganda or in extravagant claims for the Church. History is not the story of steady progress. Nor is it a repeating cycle of events ruled by chance or fate and ultimately meaningless. Nor is it an advertisement for one institution, political or ecclesiastical. It is the story of two 'cities' (meaning societies), two loves, two futures. The City of Earth, founded by Cain the murderer, is symbolized by Babylon or Rome. It is motivated by a love for self and therefore for evil. Its history will soon move towards the reign of Antichrist and then it will be judged and it will end up in hell. In contrast, the City of God, founded by Abel the saint, is symbolized by Jerusalem or by the Catholic Church, which is now its 'shadow' on earth. It is motivated by love for God and good. In the end it will be purified. But not all Catholic Christians are its true members. As is declared in Revelation 7:4, the true citizens of the City of God are the 'elect', chosen by God to enjoy heaven. As for other souls, the 'damned mass' outside or inside membership of the Church on earth, the relevant questions, discussed at some length, are how fire can be applied to devils who are not physical, how the resurrected physical bodies of human beings can be burned without being consumed and how the blessed can rejoice at an exhibition of God's justice which at first sight will not be pleasant.

We know more about Augustine than about anyone else in antiquity and he is widely agreed to have had great strengths. He was realistic about the human inclination to evil and about the imperfections of all human societies including empires and churches. He taught Christians not to weep for too long over the decline and fall of the Roman empire and he taught them a faith on which a new society would one day be built. At its best, it was a faith in God as supremely real and supremely desirable. He combined the Bible and Platonism more successfully than Origen had managed. Ideas which he phrased with great skill were to be accepted by almost all the leading thinkers of Europe until after the Enlightenment in the eighteenth century. Étienne Gilson has summed them up: 'the existence of one single God, infinite in being and power, free creator of heaven and earth, conserving the world by his all-powerful will and acting as a Providence for man whose soul can be proved to be spiritual in nature'. A glorious hymn praising God in a confident Church, *Te Deum Laudamus*, was probably written by a contemporary bishop, and Augustine showed how this God could be loved with all the mind. He was no less eloquent about *caritas* as the divinely inspired love of the neighbour.

Yet it may be questioned whether his theology was entirely dominated by the character of God as presented by Jesus. His increasing gloom about the spiritual prospects of the human majority did not make it clear why a compassionate Father stands at the centre of the Christian Bible and why the Saviour representing the Father was called the friend of sinners. He certainly did justice to the warnings of Jesus, to the theme in the gospels that 'many are called but few chosen', but his grim message to the majority was perhaps closer to John the Baptist's. He was of course entitled to cite Paul's conviction that choice by God is needed before anyone can be called, justified and glorified; that God shows mercy as he chooses and makes people stubborn as he chooses. He was of course also entitled to repeat Paul's fear that there might be objects due for destruction, as defective pots are thrown away by the potter who ought not to be rebuked for the decision. But he and his most austere disciples had to explain away Paul's hope that (as he wrote to Corinth) 'God will be all in all' at the end, that (as he wrote to Rome) 'God's purpose in condemning all was to show mercy to all . . . How unsearchable are his judgements, how untraceable his ways!'

After Augustine's death Prosper of Aquitaine did his best to have the whole of his teaching accepted in Rome and elsewhere, but he saw that predestination by God to hell would never be believed by all and he changed his own mind. When a council of western bishops in Orange endorsed Augustine's position against Pelagius in 529, it was with this exception. It became the usual belief that God, who knows everything, knows who is going to hell but does not predetermine it. (As Anselm was to teach, 'God foreknows that I am going to sin without making that inescapable'.) This decision that heaven was attainable by everyone was to be necessary if the Church on earth was to be for the many not for the few—as Augustine himself had wished in his controversy with the Donatists. A saying attributed (falsely) to Ambrose was often repeated: 'God will not deny his grace to those who do what is in them.' But there was to be a considerable defence of predestination to hell and those who rejected it had to worry about its advocacy by Augustine. As Jaroslav Pelikan wrote about the discussion which took place in medieval theology, 'what was embarrassing about Augustine on the real presence in the Eucharist was his vagueness' but 'what was embarrassing about him on predestination was his clarity'. And what survived strongly from the great man's teaching in this field was his conviction that, whether or not they were predestined to it, most people would find that hell was their destiny. They would not do much good or get much grace: they had inherited guilt from Adam and in the exercise of what freedom they had they had added to this guilt. Placed by Adam on the broad road to hell, they had deliberately speeded. Medieval preachers would predict that the saved among the damned might be one in a thousand or in ten thousand, or in a hundred thousand; or that they would be like Noah's ark in relation to a flooded world. The medieval Church urged one and all to try for heaven but offered no promise that many would get there.

Medieval people who took a pride in being human were often to be slapped down and reminded in particular of the guilt associated with their unavoidable sexuality. People were to fear the endless torments of hell, for themselves and those they loved, and were to pay many monks to intercede for them and many priests to offer 'this my sacrifice and yours' on their behalf, propitiating an angry God. Even when the Renaissance had brought in more humanism, Christ was to be the sternly strict Judge of the last day which would be the 'day of wrath', the Judge whose more humane mother had to be invoked as intercessor. From the twelfth century in the west he was also to be thought of as being touchingly human in his cradle and on his cross, and as such he was to be loved; but the chief thought even then was to be gratitude that he had become human in order to be the Victim, the Sacrifice, and thus to meet the demands of divine justice. The word for the bread which became his body in the Mass (the 'host' in English) was to be *hostia*, 'victim'. And even that divine Victim's self-sacrifice was not to be thought able to save from endless torments the vast majority of the sons and daughters of Adam and Eve, the many millions who had been conceived and born in sin even before they chose to become sinners. In 1439 the council of Florence taught that all unbaptized adults must go to hell even if they have committed no personal sin, because they have inherited 'original' sin from Adam.

Celts and Catholics

It is astonishing that in ages so dark it was believed by some people that the gospel of Jesus could be spread without relying on the advantages given to the Church by material wealth and the use of force and fear. Yet that kind of Christianity was developed by some Celts.

The eastern Celts lived in Gaul and their Christianization, a process neither rapid nor complete, was led by city-based bishops with impressive cathedrals and even more impressive powers of local leadership, and by monasteries with considerable endowments. But other Celts lived on the western margins of the Roman world, in Ireland, Scotland, Wales and Brittany. Although Ireland had never been conquered by the Romans, somehow Christianity reached it. In the fifth century a bishop was sent to its few Christians from Rome and, more influentially, Patrick who had been taken to the island as a kidnapped boy returned as a missionary bishop; the faith which had meant little to him as the son of a well-to-do clergyman grew as he prayed while herding pigs or was awake 'before dawn in all weathers, snow, frost and rain'. He wrote his *Confessions* about 450. That autobiography, together with a letter begging a British warlord to return some Irish Christians captured and made slaves, shows why the strength of his faith and character appealed, and the next century supplies abundant evidence that bishops developing his work in Ireland were now unlike those in Gaul.

These western Celts had few towns over which bishops could rule. Their bishops were often mere monks appointed to be ordainers of the necessary priests. Their monasteries were usually only circles of wattle, or wooden or rough-stone huts, used as the headquarters of prayer, evangelism and pastoral care, although in Ireland some of these centres amounted to villages. Their abbots usually belonged to the highest families and for social as well as religious reasons could exercise a firm control, and in Ireland where the monastery had been given substantial estates these were controlled by laymen of aristocratic birth. Life was as often comfortless for these monks as for their neighbours; it was said that in Wales David made his monks drag their own ploughs. But as other Celts living without comforts hammered out jewellery with intricate designs, so these monks 'illuminated' (decorated) copies of the gospels with a marvellous art; most marvellously the *Book of Kells* now in Dublin. Trading links with Mediterranean ports were reflected in the art, but more importantly the unending lines meant eternity in these books made amid the wind, the rain and the cold. And often the hard life in the monastery did not seem hard enough. Remarkable numbers of monks undertook 'pilgrimage for the love of God', meaning exile in a strange land in order to pray and do penance, and incidentally in order to influence strangers by their lives more than their words. This expansion brought the princely Columba to the island of Iona which became a base for missions to the Scots. It took Aidan to the island around Lindisfarne in the North Sea, the Iona of England. It took others to Iceland, to Greenland and (it seems) to North America. And from 590 it took Columbanus to the eastern Celts, to Switzerland and to northern Italy. The monks who accompanied him could be beaten for talking at meals or smiling during services, and this formidable abbot never hesitated to criticize the laxity of the Christian life which he encountered locally, but he touched the hearts of many, as was shown by the welcomes and the gifts attracted by this austere foreigner with strange customs. In northern England a Celtic saint, Aidan, was given a fine horse by a king but gave it away to the first poor man he met, explaining that the man was a son of God and the horse the son of a mare. Missionary monks were wise to walk.

The Celts loyally used the Catholic Church's Latin in the Mass but their hymns and prayers in their own languages show a sense of the power of the Father and the presence of the victorious Christ in the whole of nature and in all neighbours. ('If you wish to understand the Creator', said Columbanus, 'understand the creation.') Much in this earthy spirituality was inherited from rural paganism, but in its Christ-centred transformation it celebrated the natural world with a fresh joy and a lyrical beauty. The Celts believed as strongly as did other Christians that devils were everywhere, but it was also believed very strongly that Christ had conquered them and made the creation clean. Like other Christians the Celts could confess their sins in public, but at least some of them, in monasteries, confessed regularly to 'soul friends' (not necessarily priests): in that way their souls might be kept clean. And the practice of making a detailed private confession was one of the few Celtic customs that survived, with one change: the confession must be made to a Catholic priest. The practice was humane in that the confession was private but it did not follow that the Christian Celts were lenient. Penances were adjusted to sins which were described and classified with an open-eyed realism in the manuals called 'penitentials'. The sins were not treated lightly; nor were the penances.

When they came into contact with Catholics, however, these Celts found themselves condemned. They had no centre equivalent to the papacy and no doctrinal system of their own: what they had was a collection of customs which could vary from place to place and from time to time. Their willingness to forgive sins confessed privately seemed to lower moral standards and Spanish bishops condemned their innovation as 'detestable'. Their dating of Easter had become out of date: did they intend to be in harmony with other Christians? Their clergy had their heads shaved in the style of the druids of paganism: were they pagans at heart? Their priests might be married and women might preside over mixed communities of monks and nuns: their attitudes to such dangers seemed insufficiently Augustinian. Their bishops did not need to be consecrated by three others, and could be without jurisdiction; therefore they might not be valid. What was beyond dispute, however, was that the Celtic Christians lacked the organization needed to rally against a ruthless onslaught of brute strength. When Viking raiders destroyed their key monasteries (often placed so as to be convenient to sailors) the loss was devastating, spiritually as well as materially. When kings turned to Catholicism as being more prestigious Celtic spokesmen had to retreat, as some did to Ireland when it was decided in 664 that the English kingdom of Northumbria should accept Roman customs. The religion of Anglo-Saxon England retained its own character, mainly because this was an island on the edge of a developing Catholic world, but many royal and other pilgrimages demonstrated that the link with Rome was valued. Indeed, the custom of sending 'Peter's Pence' as a regular gift to the pope—a custom which was to become almost universal among Catholics—originated in the loyalty of Anglo-Saxon England. The Normans brought Catholicism in its latest shape to England and Scotland in the eleventh century, and in the twelfth Ireland was invaded from England with much the same results in church life. Celtic Christianity survived but only on the margins of the Catholic west. By the end of the twelfth century the Catholic style of organization had been accepted in Ireland, a change which was assisted by the English invasion.

Antichrist did not come to the west as many had expected, but great disasters did. When the pathetic Romulus had been deposed in 476 the Goths who now constituted the bulk of the 'Roman' army in Italy did not trouble to elect another puppet emperor. Barbarians devastated in wave after wave; plagues struck; from 400 to 800 the worse weather, a little ice age, produced famines; such knowledge and skills as the Romans had spread largely disappeared. The Church's task outside the monasteries was to deal with people who, whether or not they were baptized as Catholics or Arians, remained largely pagan in mentality and downtrodden in their lives. This was an age when violence often reigned in the countryside; when 'justice' might consist of the accused being thrown into a river and acquitted if he or she survived without floating quickly; when survival on earth in a peasant's hut through the winter was a battle against time as the normally meagre supply of food vanished; when often the alternative to anarchy or destitution was becoming a 'serf' (from the Latin *servus*, 'slave'). In exchange for some protection by the lord and his mounted retainers, and perhaps for the use of a plough, a cart or an oven, a previously free tenant (in Latin, *colonus*) tied himself, his family and his descendants to a local lord or monastery. He now owed much of his labour to that lord. In the rest of his time he could work his own bit of land but part of his produce had to go to the lord and even the soil could be taken away from him. He could not travel, or grind his corn at any mill other than the lord's, or marry his daughter off without the lord's permission. The Church accepted this institution of serfdom as it had accepted Roman slavery. Every serf was warned that disobedience was sin and no serf could be ordained priest unless first freed by his lord. Other peasants were tied to the lords for labour services, although not by the inherited bondage of serfdom. All were called in English 'villeins', a word which recalled the slaves who had worked the estate around the Roman villa.

Life in the towns was also grim. Many of the cities, including Rome, became depopulated. The decay of the Roman empire's network of military roads meant that only towns on seas or rivers could trade—and even then trade was hampered by many factors including the absence of coins. So people had to move nearer to food. The Roman emperors had forced the richer citizens to maintain, as well as to adorn, cities as the showplaces of civilization. Now the remaining townspeople turned to the Christian bishops who were expected to organize relief for the poor and such defence as was possible behind the broken walls. Such a society found the institutions and ceremonies of Catholicism more protective than all the charms of Celtic Christianity. Devils seemed to be everywhere, in the air and in people's lives, and when people suffered or sinned under this empire of evil it was not easy to find relief. If families could not help during disasters no one would. Medicine had become more primitively magical than in Roman days and people who did not wish to die young were eager for a magic which might be less ineffective.

The Catholic Church did not offer easy comfort. If sins were serious, specially if they had been public, before absolution the sinner still had to make a public confession and undergo a severe period of fasting or pilgrimage as a penance. To enlist monks to perform some of the penance on one's behalf was too expensive for the average sinner. Angels who did not need to be paid could help against the devils: a bishop had a vision of the archangel Michael promising such help in the eighth century and in his honour built a church on Mont St Michel, a rocky island around which tides of the Atlantic swirled. This became a great centre for medieval pilgrims. But other dreams in these dark ages were filled by large numbers being escorted by devils to hell. Who could rescue them? The Anglo-Saxon poem *The Dream of the Rood* saw Christ as a young warrior mounting the cross and the tenth century brought a spread of crucifixes on which the Saviour was depicted as a clothed knight, tough in his battle against the devils. In theory the Christian could now receive strength for his or her own battles through the service of 'confirmation' with its solemn anointing and prayer as the bishop placed his hands on the head (which custom often made a seven-year-old head). But in practice it was often hard to get near a bishop and help could be sought from objects stranger and more uncanny than a bishop's hands. In the Mass the bread became the Saviour's body and the wine his blood, in changes which almost everyone regarded as somehow physical although invisible, and the presbyter who was the instrument of this miracle was now a *sacerdos*, the old Latin word for the pagan priest. The most prized possession of a church was often bones believed to be a saint's. To be near those bones was to be near glory and to be given some hope, for saints had been Christ's companions in battle, their souls already shared his victory in heaven and one day their bodies would be raised in physical splendour. The discovery of the bones of the apostle James resting unexpectedly in Compostela on the Atlantic coast raised the morale needed for the Christian reconquest of Spain. At the end of one of the pilgrim's roads to this shrine, the body of Mary of Magdala made the abbey of Vézelay another centre of prayer and hope, almost in the centre of a turbulent Gaul (France). Other bones were not discovered but stolen: when the ambitious traders of Venice wanted a spiritual centre, they took bones believed to be those of St Mark from Alexandria. And in the belief that burning a Christian's body did not assist the hope of physical resurrection, the Church did all it could to end the pagan practice of cremation.

The Church which made the Mass and the saints' relics available as a refuge for frightened sinners was sure that when addressed to that public its teachings had to be firm and its warnings fearsome. It had to offer what the pagan priests had promised: security, healing, food, children, a better life after death. It had to threaten everlasting torments as punishment for disobedience to what it commanded as belief and behaviour. But in practice it had to tolerate the survival of many pagan customs, for the people were still at least half-pagan. This involved a massive change from earlier Christian attitudes but few people were in a position to know. They could not understand the Mass, said by the priest in Latin with his back to the people. They could not read a Bible although they might admire the costly beauty of its cover.

Makers of the Middle Ages

We can find a path through these dark centuries by the help of lights held up by some great men, chiefly Benedict and Gregory the Great, Boniface and Charles the Great. All four revered Augustine. He had started informal monasteries and a letter he wrote to a sister who became a nun was to guide the many Augustinian canons and monks in the Middle Ages, but Benedict's 'rule' was to do more: it was to organize medieval monasticism. Augustine had made much of being the Catholic bishop of Hippo, but Gregory the Great (Benedict's biographer and like him a great organizer) was to demonstrate how much more could be done by a bishop of Rome. Augustine had fought to make North Africa Catholic, but it was not to be so permanently; when it was lost, Boniface's mission in central Europe built a replacement. And Charles the Great was said by his biographer Einhard to have loved Augustine's books. Whether or not he understood them, he built a Christian empire in the west, the forerunner of a civilization for which Augustine had not dared to hope.

Benedict of Nursia was born half a century after Augustine's death. His experience of student life in Rome drove him into a cave but his experience as a hermit convinced him that monks (a word originally referring to the hermits who lived *monos*, alone) would be safer if they lived together in communities which would be small, humble and still separated from the world. He had no intention of founding a large organization but he did begin a dozen or so little monasteries almost entirely for laymen such as himself. The largest was at Monte Cassino between Rome and Naples, but it was destroyed by the Lombards soon after his death. For these monks he drew up a rule of life, one of the most influential documents in history.

It was quite short, much shorter than the 'rule of Basil' for the monks of Orthodoxy, and was often learned by heart. It had much in common with another rule, almost certainly earlier, which was anonymous, but Benedict's own rule reduced the material by two-thirds and was a model of the Roman ability to legislate. We therefore have to understand why this rule which so firmly legislated for a very simple life of prayer and poverty was to be revered and used, if not completely obeyed, by monks who were often musical and scholarly, keen to build large and beautiful churches, willing to spend half their waking hours at formal services in them and accepting the need to own large estates in order to finance the monastery's great dignity.

The rule imposed no austerity as strict as that of the eastern hermits or the Celtic monks. It demanded the renunciation of all private possessions, of all sexual activity and of all self-will, for the 'labour of obedience' was necessary if monks were to fight in the spiritual warfare against devils. But the abbot to whom obedience was due (under God) was to be elected by his brethren in the monastery, not imposed by any outsider, and Benedict wrote a rule for 'beginners in the service of the Lord', with nothing 'too difficult or grievous'. With characteristic practicality he laid down an adequate diet (four cooked dishes a day without meat, other vegetables or fruit when available, a pound of bread and almost a pint of rough wine, to be supplemented if necessary in cold or heat). He put great emphasis on the care of the sick, who were allowed meat and frequent baths. By the standards of the time this was not a harsh life and since the rule was simple and short it did not forbid what it did not order, so that it was later thought by many to allow room for developments in the direction of comfort.

The rule urged courtesy: monks must 'bear with patience the weakness of others, whether of body or behaviour'. The result was a friendship seldom known in a brutal world and it was to be on the whole congenial to men from well-off families, often younger sons placed in monasteries at the age of seven ('oblates'). The rule allocated six and a half hours of the monk's day to manual work, necessary if the monastery was to support itself. The principle that 'to work is to pray' was to be held to justify intellectual labours when the monks used bonded serfs or hired labourers to do the sweaty work in their fields. The rule itself envisaged *lectio divina* (meditative reading of the Scriptures or of commentaries on them by approved authors) occupying about four hours a day, and it ordered that 'during Lent they are each to take one book of the Bible and read the whole of it from beginning to end'. Such a regime assumed literacy, uncommon in that age, but some monks were to be more ambitious, developing libraries and even writing their own books while others made fresh copies of the Bible and the works of the Fathers. As they grew, the libraries of the more scholarly monasteries included copies of Latin (and even Greek) classics which would have been lost without this custody. Monastic schools taught the novices how to read and write Latin and had a slightly wider influence, for some novices could return to the world without becoming monks. Later some well-born children were to be allowed to sit alongside the novices.

For Benedict as for all true Benedictines the main work was the *opus Dei*, the 'work of God' which was the worship of God in at least seven services a day. That should enable any monk to find God, the supreme purpose of life, and to give thanks. The rule called for *stabilitas loci*, residence in one monastery until death, in contrast with the belief that an advanced monk ought to become a solitary hermit. And the paradoxical result of these provisions for a life of self-sacrificing worship was that a Benedictine monastery could become rich. Worldly men who were themselves rich could endow the monastery as a place where the monk ('he who weeps') could pray for other men's souls as well as for his own—and, incidentally, where the benefactor's family could be honoured in the future on earth. And the stability of the monks, generation after generation, made the monastery an institution to which endowments could be entrusted. Thus it came to be taken for granted that the medieval society would consist of the 'three estates', *oratores, bellatores, laboratores*, those who prayed, those who fought and those who toiled in the fields. The peasants should support the fighters whose physical protection they needed and the fighters should support the monks (and other clergy) whose prayers were specially needed because fighting was no game. And increasingly the monks became priests, for the most valuable prayer was the offering of the Mass for the benefit of the living and the dead.

Benedict's most truly distinguished contemporary was Boethius, who has been called the schoolmaster of the Middle Ages. He translated some of Aristotle into Latin, planned to translate more and had the ambition to make a synthesis of his whole philosophy and Plato's, inclining towards Plato. Instead of achieving that impossible feat he wrote his own short books on subjects ranging from musical theory to trinitarian theology and served the state in high office under Theodoric, the Arian king of the Goths in Italy. So he bequeathed a rich legacy of conserved knowledge and logical reasoning, and he led an exemplary life although he was no monk. Accused of treasonable intrigues with the Byzantines, while awaiting execution (he was clubbed to death) he wrote *The Consolation of Philosophy*. The ultimate consolation, the true liberation, is found in the knowledge of the reality of God: whatever befalls in human life, God never changes or loses control. Eternity remains 'the complete, simultaneous and perfect possession of unending life' and beatitude in eternity is 'a condition made perfect by the union of all that is good'. A person can enjoy such beatitude because a person is 'an individual substance of a rational nature'; immortality, the survival of bodily death by this substance, is therefore a part of being a person. In many ways the book is close to Augustine's earlier writing (although it is more the work of a trained philosopher) and the absence of any mention of Christ has been explained by the reminder that its subject was the knowledge of God and eternity by calm reasoning: here one lady, Philosophy, comes to the rescue against the unreliable blandishments of another, Fortune. But it remains an extraordinary tribute to the spiritual power of Platonic philosophy that on the brink of eternity this great Christian writer did not write about Christ.

This was a world in which the brain of Boethius could be destroyed by a piece of wood wielded by a barbarian—and the very fine brain of Boethius was not typical of the bulk of humanity. In such a world the Church was more quickly influenced by Sidonius Apollinaris, a scholar but no philosopher. For some years he tried to escape from a dismal and dangerous age by literary pursuits in a rural retreat. Then he threw himself into the work of the bishop of his area in Gaul. His willingness to be the pastor, teacher and leader of non-intellectuals was a foretaste of what was to come. Men of outstanding status and ability could become bishops; well-off people could become monks and nuns under the rule of Benedict; large Roman villas were being turned into monasteries; the western empire's resurrection was to be into a society dominated by the Latin-speaking clergy. And the visible signs of this process began to multiply. The vestments worn by the clergy in church were adapted from the best clothes of the rich. The more important churches built before the thirteenth century, and sometimes during it, were to be Romanesque in style: massive walls and rounded arches were to reproduce the old imperial architecture, almost as if the great new churches were God's fortresses. On the capitals of pillars strange, contorted beasts could be carved, for this was still a frightened world full of devils and its imagination was unhappy. It was also a poor world, which in contrast with the Byzantine east could not afford mosaics or skilled painting. But the gold and the incense in these dark churches could be reminders that these were palaces prepared for Christ the King, who would surely see the poverty and the terror around the church's walls and return to judge and to reign.

In 590, about fifty years after the death of Benedict, Gregory the Great accepted the bishopric of Rome at the age of fifty. He was reluctant to do so. He came from a wealthy family which had already provided two popes and had himself been governor of the city of Rome, but he had felt called to be an austere and contemplative monk. When he had agreed to serve as ambassador for the papacy in Constantinople he had not troubled to learn Greek and the chief result of his time in the eastern capital had been a commentary on the moral lessons to be derived from the lonely sufferings of Job. While pope he used his monks as his agents. But he was a born administrator and communicator. Some other bishops of the age were also large-scale landowners: the Church kept written records of its ownership and management and the donors of these lands escaped taxation on them while enjoying quiet privileges as a result of their gifts, not only the privilege of the clergy's prayers. But Gregory was the greatest landlord among the bishops, as Rome was the supreme bishopric in the west. As early as AD 200 a Roman presbyter, Gaius, had boasted to a visitor from Asia Minor that there were monuments in the city to the great apostles who had founded the Roman Church—to Peter on the Vatican hill, to Paul on the road to Ostia. In almost four hundred years since that boast bishops of Rome had increased their prestige as well as their financial strength and Gregory, a Roman of the Romans, knew how to use these assets.

He attended to the detailed government of the estates given to the papacy: these had fallen into disorder, not least because of the Byzantine campaigns in Italy. The new income enabled him to provide paternally for the numerous poor. He concluded a separate agreement with the Lombard invaders, bribing them to spare Rome, planning their conversion to Catholicism (he sent impressive gifts to their king and queen), and meanwhile organizing troops to keep order under his own control. On his tomb he was called by an almost imperial title: 'the consul of God'. But he was not clumsy. He was careful to be diplomatic about the dignity of the Byzantine emperor; he paid taxes and made compliments. While protesting against the patriarch of Constantinople's claim to be 'ecumenical' (meaning imperial) because he insisted on the superior dignity of Rome, he disclaimed any jurisdiction in the east. He was, he assured the eastern bishops, their brother and morally their inferior. Even in the west, where he was the sole patriarch, he acted diplomatically, calling himself the 'servant of the servants of God'. He had good reason to be cautious: in 418 Augustine had taken part in a synod of North African bishops which forbade clergy to appeal against their decisions to Rome. But such was Gregory's well-earned prestige that he faced very little opposition. Almost five hundred of his letters survive. They are models of efficiency combined with tact. Other bishops turned to him because he knew the right answers.

His teaching was based on the Bible and Augustine but he organized those authorities, illustrated them by anecdotes and related them to current questions so as to provide doctrines which simple minds could grasp. He wrote a book on *Pastoral Care* in order to remind his fellow bishops that 'the art of arts is the guidance of souls'. It was to influence many generations with its ideals ('the ruler should be the near neighbour to everyone in sympathy and exalted above all in contemplation') and in the ninth century King Alfred had it translated into Old English along with the *Consolation* of Boethius. To the people Gregory gave assurances that prayers are answered by miracles. Benedict's miracles interested him more than any other feature of that saint's life. But his view of human nature was no more cheerful than Augustine's. He it was who first made the deadly sins seven: pride, envy, anger, avarice, gluttony, sloth and lust. He understood the book of Job not as a human protest against inherited disasters but as a call to accept sufferings in time or eternity, as God's just punishment of sinfulness. Even people whose own sins have not deserved death inherit Adam's sin and are 'born condemned sinners'. Thus Gregory echoed Augustine—and he popularized a theory put forward by eastern theologians but repeated by Augustine, about how God the Father achieved the salvation of those whom he wished to save; a neat theory which was to be standard until Anselm demolished it five centuries later. Since Adam chose to obey the Devil rather than the Father, the Devil now had rights over all Adam's descendants. But God the Father sent God the Son, who had never made that fatal choice. Not understanding his identity, the Devil made the innocent Son suffer on the cross. Thereby the Devil went beyond his rights and lost them all; and the Father could at last forgive those sinners whom he wished to forgive. To illustrate this theory it could be said that the cross was like a hook to catch a fish: the Devil was attracted to the bait and swam into disaster.

For Gregory as for the earlier teachers the Son's death is renewed in the Mass, where 'he suffers again for us' and the Father is again 'reconciled to us'. The Mass is itself a sacrifice and a miracle and it can be offered to the Father so as to secure further miracles of deliverance from the 'purging fires' in which some of the dead suffer. In the Middle Ages it was to be believed that Gregory's own prayers had liberated the emperor Trajan from purgatory. It was particularly on the subjects of the Mass and purgatory that Gregory supplemented Augustine. He was sure that few people would end up in heaven, but equally sure that it was the duty of the Catholic Church to spread its gospel in the short time remaining before the end of the world, in the hope that the message would reach any whom God wanted to share in his eternal bliss.

Since he was mission-minded in that sense, he took good care to be on good terms with Reccared, the formerly Arian king of the Visigoths ruling Spain, who led his people into Catholicism in the 580s. He also sent a Roman monk named Augustine to begin from the south the conversion of the pagan Anglo-Saxons who had occupied England; he reached Canterbury in 597 and was welcomed by the local king, who had married a Christian princess brought over from Gaul. Drawing on memories of the earlier Roman occupation, Gregory had formed excessively ambitious plans for the rapid division of the island into Catholic dioceses, but when informed about the realities he had the wisdom to advise Augustine to use the customs of other churches without copying Rome exclusively and also to use pagan temples for Christian worship where that seemed sensible. Even so, the mission faced many obstacles. Celtic Christians viewed it as a form of imperialism. It suffered reverses as pagan kings checked its expansion and as Christian kings relapsed into paganism. But in the end it produced a Christian people. In Northumbria Bede, another monk, wrote a history of the conversion ending in 731: it was the first book to cover England as a whole although the difficulty of collecting information made the coverage patchy.

In theology Bede was stoutly Augustinian through his loyalty to Gregory the Great. And some of the English became eager to take Catholic Christianity back to the mainland from which their ancestors had come.

Little more than a hundred years after Gregory's death in 604 an English monk set sail from London to be a missionary among the much feared Frisians, whose slow conversion had been led by another Englishman, Willibrord the first bishop of Utrecht. That was itself a remarkable demonstration of the effects of the conversion of England, but more was to come. Feeling the challenge of new territory, he was made a missionary bishop in Rome, taking the Latin name Englished as Boniface, and his work was to organize a new Catholic church in Bavaria and elsewhere, based on strong bishoprics as well as on monasteries. In everything he relied on the authority and guidance of Rome's own bishops and particularly on the writings of Gregory. When in his seventies he went back to missionary work among the obstinate Frisians, who murdered him.

Gregory had demonstrated what could be done by a bishop of Rome who possessed ability and moral stature and Boniface had shown that the Church could gain a sense of direction by looking to Gregory and his successors. But the mission in Germany also depended on the support provided by the Frankish monarchy whose power had spread over much of Europe from Gaul.

Gaul had fallen under the rule of the Visigoths and Burgundians, in religion Arians, in reality harsh exploiters. The people had been half-Romanized and half-squalid, half-Christian and half-pagan. Any civilizing influence on them had come from the Catholic bishops. In many cases it had been a spiritual influence, honouring in particular the memory of Martin, a former Roman soldier, who around 370 became bishop of Tours. He never ceased to devote much time to solitary prayer in the cave which was his home and when he toured the countryside, preaching in the style of the Celtic saints, it was on foot or occasionally on a donkey like Christ himself, but he did not hesitate to drive out devils and to destroy pagan shrines. A biography by a disciple was to impress many and his tomb was to become a centre of pilgrimage and of widely reported and rewarded miracles. But at a more worldly level most of the Catholic bishops of Gaul had been useful as the chief upholders of what remained of the Roman style of life, teaching, judging and organizing, and in effect running cities. And the Church's position had been transformed first by the arrival of a new group of energetic barbarians, the Franks, and then by the conversion to Catholicism of one of their chiefs, Clovis, during the 490s.

A man as shrewd as he was brutal, Clovis took his first step towards civilization by marrying a Burgundian princess who was as Christian as she was charming and in the 490s he saw the advantages of becoming a Catholic:

in addition to securing St Peter's support at the gates of heaven, the Franks would be entitled to wage war on the Arian Visigoths and Burgundians and to enjoy the support of the Catholic bishops in ruling the Catholic peasants. When he had been baptized these ambitions were gradually fulfilled. He and his sons drove the Visigoths out of what was now Francia, into Spain. From the sixth century to the tenth the rulers of the Franks were the most powerful men in western Europe and in alliance with them the Church gained some confidence while not forgetting the cross. Venantius Fortunatus wrote hymns about the cross which have never been forgotten: 'Sing my tongue, the glorious battle' and 'The royal banners forward go'. Bishop Gregory of Tours wrote a *History of the Franks* which was honest about the continuing confusion and violence, yet hopeful about the Church's spiritual power as it followed its own banners. Caesarius, a great missionary bishop of Arles for forty years from 503, warned the people: 'You reign with Christ or you die with the Devil!'

It could look as if the Devil was winning. The descendants of Clovis did not have his ability although they shared his brutality, and the civil wars were very cruel and very destructive. The Church suffered along with others: for more than a hundred years from 683 Arles had no bishop and many cities experienced similar vacancies. Things improved when power fell into the hands of the family which produced Charles Martel ('the Hammer'). He began to organize an army which would be loyal to him because its subordinate commanders owed their lands to his favour—and which could be turned against the whole country's enemies because Franks and Celts had settled down to live together. In 732 he turned back the Arabs who had been going to plunder the shrine of Martin of Tours: it was their first reverse in Europe and it taught them to be content with the control of the Mediterranean and the warmer lands around it. His son, Pepin the Short, was anointed king by Pope Stephen II in the abbey of St Denis near Paris in 754. It was a mutually profitable bargain. Popes were to derive far greater benefits from this alliance than they had ever obtained from the Byzantine emperors. In the immediate future Pope Stephen was to be rewarded by the beginnings of the papal state in Italy, for Pepin promised to throw the Lombard invaders out of Ravenna, Rimini and a considerable area around those cities—and he kept his word. In return, the new king of the Franks received the pope's approval of his overthrow of the Merovingian dynasty. There was now a blessing on the transfer to him and his descendants of a tradition of sacred monarchy which had survived the years of chaos in what had become Francia. Pepin had already been anointed by Boniface but a pope's action seemed more authoritative.

At this time, or not long afterwards, the papal court produced the Donation of Constantine, a document almost always treated as authentic until the fifteenth century. It was a forgery purporting to show that in 317 Constantine had bestowed the city of Rome and all the 'provinces, territories and cities' of all Italy and the western 'regions' on Rome's bishop, together with some royal insignia. It was said that the bishop (Silvester) had miraculously cured the emperor of leprosy. The immediate purpose of the forgery was to justify the pope's claim to Italian territory which the Lombards had seized. In the Middle Ages, however, the Donation was to be used to establish the pope's right to make and unmake all the political rulers of the west. In 1001 the emperor Otto III, who resisted the papacy's growing power, called it 'fictitious and fantastic', but not many dared to agree with him.

Another forgery, known to modern scholars as the False Decretals, was manufactured in France in the middle of the ninth century. Its invention of decrees by earlier church councils was intended to justify the alliance of the local clergy with the pope against the powerful archbishops of the time. This, like the Donation, was accepted because people accepted the fact that the bishop of Rome held a unique position in an age when even kings as tough as Pepin wanted a legitimate bishop to bestow a legitimate and mighty blessing. But while the Donation of Constantine was usually accepted in theory, in practice popes were not allowed unlimited political power. Certainly subordination to a bishop of Rome was not accepted by Pepin the Short's son, Charles the Great, better known as Charlemagne

Like all successful rulers of the Franks Charles was essentially a warrior; he could read, but try as he would he could not learn to write. He inherited a large kingdom and extended it when his brother died and when he was the victor in the wars which took up his main energies through most of his reign (768–814). In the end his empire covered almost the whole of France, West Germany, Bavaria, North Italy, Switzerland, Belgium and the Netherlands, and his overlordship was acknowledged by surrounding peoples. His conquest of the Saxons was slow, and bloody during and after the many battles: having been conquered, any Saxon refusing baptism, or eating meat in Lent, or stealing from a church, became liable to execution. He crushed the pagan Avars in the east, he destroyed what was left of the Lombard kingdom in Italy and he was involved in the hard beginnings of the Christian re-conquest of Spain. To sustain these campaigns he developed feudalism, attaching the obligation to provide equipped soldiers to the ownership of defined lands; to sustain his control over dukes and counts he appointed travelling *missi* (inspectors); to lead his church he appointed bishops of quality; to support the clergy he ordered the compulsory collection of tithes (a tenth of the produce); and to staff the limited revival of Roman order he developed some education through the monasteries and through his palace's school for the sons of the aristocracy. At the top of the political system the grandest men took oaths of allegiance to this ruler, feasted and sported under his eye when not on campaigns under his generalship, and had their sons trained to serve in his empire. Lower down the social scale, folk vowed obedience to landlords and at the bottom there were still vows, for at baptisms 'godparents' now vowed allegiance to Christ on behalf of the infant at the font. To educate the leadership of this organized empire Charles drew together scholars from far and wide, headed by Alcuin of York who had the courage to protest (although in vain) against the practice of compelling uninstructed pagans to be baptized and to pay tithes. As practical steps towards a civilized Europe a clearer handwriting was encouraged (the ancestor of the letters used to print this book), as was a clearer method of dating, by the calculation of a year as *Anno Domini*, 'the year of the Lord'. And a 'proper' pronunciation of Latin was made standard at the top of Church and State, leaving the popular forms of Latin to evolve into the 'Romance' languages such as French.

This Christian empire was based on privileges given to the Catholic Church in exchange for its support. Charles encouraged local lords to provide churches in all large villages and issued an *admonitio* to guide the clergy. Although his sex life was not austere, he attended services several times a day when possible, happily compared himself with the good kings in the Old Testament, and presided grandly over services in the chapel (which has survived) in his palace in Aachen. 'The pagans are wrong, the Christians are right!' That is the shout of an archbishop who charges into battle in the eleventh-century *Song of Roland*, which added glamour to Charles's first campaign in Spain (in 778). The battle was in fact a defeat, for the Christians were ambushed while retreating, but the militant bishop's cry proclaims the confidence of the Carolingian union of Church and State. In medieval folklore Charles became *Carolus Maximus*, Charlemagne, a miracle-working saint, the founder of the 'Holy Roman' empire.

His coronation as 'emperor of the Romans' by Pope Leo III in Rome on Christmas Day 800 dramatized this revival of Christian imperialism. Like the earlier anointing of Pepin, it brought benefits to both sides. The pope secured the favour of the man who was now the master of Italy—and he needed it: a faction in Rome which had opposed his election was doing its violent best to get rid of him. But Charles also gained: he could now claim to be the equal of the emperor in Constantinople. He professed to be surprised by the pope's action but more significantly accepted the honour and did so on his own terms. When he repeated the coronation later he crowned himself: he was not going to be indebted to any bishop. Four years previously he had told Leo that it was a bishop's duty to 'lift up his hands in prayer under the leadership of God', while a king's duty was to protect the Church from invaders and heretics, clearly implying that the king decided for himself how to do it. Not for nothing was he a giant of a man: his skeleton, unearthed in 1861, was seven feet tall.

It therefore seems possible that had the empire of Charlemagne survived the Catholic west might have been more like the Byzantine east, with a Christian emperor clearly on top of Church and State, and a continuing Carolingian empire might have been a great deal more impressive than what was left of Byzantium after the conquests of Islam. (One reason why Charlemagne could be called 'emperor' was the weakness of protests from the battered east: in Henri Pirenne's verdict, 'without Muhammad Charlemagne would have been inconceivable'.) But that was not to be. Within fifty years of his coronation his empire split up into three sections: Germany, France and the 'Middle Kingdom'. The Holy Roman empire, mainly Germanic, was revived when a prince of the Saxons who were now stout Christians, Otto I, was crowned in Rome in 962. Otto III took his own coronation so seriously that he spent most of his short reign in Rome and planned to make it his capital, but he soon died and no Ottonian ruler could revive the full majesty of Charlemagne's power. In France the Capetian dynasty which replaced the decayed Carolingians in 911 had even less power, and the region which had been intended to form the Middle Kingdom never developed into a proper state. Much of the wealth in it passed into the hands of bishops, illustrating the tendency in the Middle Ages for the Church to have many more privileges than Charlemagne had intended.

Europe as Christendom

A Burgundian scholar noted that around AD 1000 much of western Europe was being covered with a 'white robe' consisting of churches in stone, built or rebuilt with recovered skills. There was some excitement about the thought that Christ might begin his reign on earth in this appropriate year; a real Christian was emperor (Otto III) and the cleverest man in Europe was pope (Silvester II). But the optimism came and went, as did the thousandth anniversary of Christ's resurrection. At any rate the ages of darkness after the collapse of the Roman empire seemed to be coming to an end. In the year 1000 the little parliament of Iceland decided to accept Christianity and about this time an English monk baptized the king of Sweden (Olov). Europe was now defining and defending itself against Islam: the first mention of *Europeenses* has been traced to a Spanish chronicler referring to the defeat of the Arab army near Poitiers in 732 and Charlemagne was called 'Father of Europe' by his contemporaries. Islam still presented a threat: Muslim pirates were dreaded and Muslim soldiers occupied most of Spain with the islands of Majorca, Corsica, Sardinia, Malta, Sicily, Cyprus and Crete. But Abbasid caliphs moved the centre of Islam east to Baghdad, the heart of Muslim-Persian wealth and culture for some five hundred years. The Muslim rulers nearer to Europe were thereafter in conflict with each other, whether or not they acknowledged the Abbasids as their superiors. Europe had a breathing space and the continuing control of the Mediterranean by Islam stimulated trade in the previously backward north of the continent. Other developments followed trade.

Although for a time the Vikings from the north and Magyars from the east were as terrifying as the Muslims had been, eventually they were absorbed by becoming Catholic Christians, at least nominally. In Scandinavia there was little response to early missionary work led by the monk Anskar, bishop of Hamburg and Bremen, before his death in 865 but in England in 878 the Viking chief accepted baptism as part of a treaty with an outstanding Christian king, Alfred. The conversion of the other Danes settling in England followed quietly and when the Danes later ruled the whole of the country it was under another great Christian king, Canute. In the Vikings' homelands Christianization was slower, partly because the kings had less power, but it was accomplished—in Denmark by King Harald Blue Tooth about 950, in Norway by a king and 'saint', Olaf, who was conspicuously brutal, in Sweden in a more peaceful process which was complete only in the twelfth century. Following the example set by Boniface in Germany, Anglo-Saxon mission-aries founded the bishoprics from which the Church's work radiated, from Trondheim in the Norwegian north through Uppsala and Lund in Sweden to Schleswig in Denmark. The Norsemen who cut deep into the north of France became Catholics when their leader Rollo had made a treaty with the Capetian king in 911. These 'Normans' were now as pious in support of bishops and monks as they remained fierce in their civil wars and in their conquest of further lands—of England from the Anglo-Saxons, of Sicily from the Muslims, of southern Italy from the Byzantines. So the north returned to the Mediterranean.

For a time it looked as if the Magyars might sweep across the centre of Europe but they were pushed back into the Hungarian plain by the emperor Otto I in 955. Some thirty years later their chief was baptized by the bishop of Prague and in the year 1000 his son, who became St Stephen, was given the title of king by the pope. Beginning at Esztergom, bishoprics were set up to instruct his growing kingdom. Otto also commanded military and ecclesiastical operations against the pagans to the north of the Magyars. The archbishopric of Magdeburg was established as a base for colonization and evangelism. In the 960s a Polish prince, Mieszko, was baptized after marrying a Christian princess and putting away his seven pagan wives; the military aristocracy and the people followed in a pattern which was by now familiar and he and his son were able to unite all the Polish tribes. There were pagan revivals in Hungary, Poland and elsewhere, but none proved permanent.

The pagan Wends between Poland and Germany were more difficult to convert until in 1147 a famous preacher (Bernard of Clairvaux) urged mostly Saxon crusaders who had been thinking of activity against Muslims in the east to wage war across the river Elbe instead. They were, he preached, not to rest until either the religion or the nation of the Wends had been exterminated. The Wends chose to accept Catholicism when, within twenty years of Bernard's call, their last pagan temple had been destroyed. By the middle of the next century Catholic Europe was colonizing beyond the Elbe, beyond the Oder, beyond the Vistula.

Pope Innocent III announced that crusading against pagans in the Baltic was a satisfactory substitute for war against the Muslim east. The offer was taken up by the Teutonic knights whose work had originated in a field hospital in Palestine. From 1231 they concentrated on the more profitable conquest of Prussia and the Baltic region of Livonia, which was held to belong to Mary as the Holy Land of Palestine belonged to her Son. Each campaigning season found knights from many parts of western Europe gathering for hospitality and adventure in their new headquarters, a castle which covered five acres. Under papal patronage they achieved great success by building other castles with forced labour, exercising their rule with notorious cruelty and settling Christian colonists and missionaries among the defeated and bewildered natives. New lands were farmed and new towns created, but the knights were not popular. Their power was not broken until they were defeated by an army of Lithuanians and Poles in 1410. The Brothers of the Sword were a similar order, half monks, half thugs, but were suppressed when their atrocities seemed excessive.

The Christian reconquest of Spain was also a prolonged operation, with many of the features of a crusade. To those who died in the struggle to liberate a land which had been seized by the heathen, heaven was promised; to those who survived and conquered, there was the promise of the land itself. Victories began in the eleventh century and Toledo was entered in 1085. After a major victory in 1212 Cordoba fell in 1236 and Seville a dozen years later but the Muslim kingdom of Granada survived in the south until 1492. The completion of the reconquest was delayed by difficulties in ruling and farming and by the diversion of the kings of Aragon to the easier occupation of the Balearic islands, so that for many years the Christians had to be content with receiving a financial tribute from the wealthy civilization of Granada.

Unlike the pagans on Europe's eastern frontier the Moors were skilled both in war and in the arts of peace, as some of their palaces and gardens testify to this day. They were disunited and prone to civil war, but so were the Christians. After many internal disputes, Castile (the central kingdom) was united with Leon only in 1230 and with Aragon only in 1479. The slow victory over the Muslim warriors would have been impossible had the Christians' war effort not been strengthened by fighters and settlers drawn from many parts of Europe and by repeated papal assurances that this was a holy war. As a result the Catholicism which gradually covered Spain adopted the customs which had become international and had been authorized by Rome, and the less tidy and more tolerant 'Mozarabic' customs which had sustained the Christians under Moorish rule almost completely disappeared. Finally a strictly disciplined, fervently believed, form of triumphant Catholicism was given a monopoly: no other religion was to be allowed to pollute the reconquered land. Jews and Muslims were given the choice between conversion and exile. For some of these unfortunates conversion was shallow but the Inquisition did its best to hunt down all such heretics. Even those who sincerely abandoned their ancestors' religion found themselves discriminated against because their blood was not pure.

We can see that medieval Catholicism was not spread by a complete reliance on the words which had been spoken in Galilee. Here was a mixture of evangelism and violence, of conversion and colonial settlement, and it is inevitable that the true history of Europe's 'conversion' should remind a modern reader of the mixture of guns and sermons in the modern story of European colonialism. Indeed, the medieval campaigns and the modern colonialism formed a single process, for after their *Reconquista* the Portuguese and the Spanish, full of the self-confidence of victory and firmly believing that God would continue to reward their courage but also conscious that they were not yet rich by Muslim standards, went straight on to the exploration of the routes to 'the Indies' around Africa and across the Atlantic. They did so seeking to reach the wealth of Asia without going through the territory still under Islam but also seeking (or so they often said) to preach the Catholic faith which had already inspired their triumph. The year in which Granada was at last taken and the Jews were expelled from Spain was the year in which Columbus discovered islands which turned out to belong to a new world. But revulsion about some of the methods by which the Christianization of Europe was achieved as a prelude to the Europeanization of the world should not blind us to its historical significance. The Anglo-Saxons used the word *Christendom*, meaning an area under the rule of Christ. It meant the same as the Latin *Christianitas*. It also meant almost exactly the same as *Europa*, for the underdeveloped projection of Asia into the Atlantic unexpectedly became the centre of Christianity's expansion to the ends of the earth.

Popes, Priests and Kings

The three most important factors in the development of the papacy were the prominence of Peter among the apostles of Jesus; the prestige of 'Eternal Rome' as the capital of an empire which from end to end had covered some three thousand miles; and the absence in the west after the fourth century of anything like the continuous power of the Byzantine emperor.

We have already noticed the leading role taken by Peter in the first stages of the Christian mission before the emergence of James the brother of Jesus at the head of the church in Jerusalem. Peter then became the leader of the mission to the Jews outside Jerusalem. When the gospels were written he was often close to the centre as the spokesman of the disciples. He was, it seems, not without his human weaknesses (a point stressed in the gospel of Mark, possibly because Peter had always told him to be honest about it), but great promises were also included in these traditions. Matthew recorded the tradition that Jesus gave this outstanding disciple a name which meant Rock and said: 'Upon this rock I will build my Church and the powers of death shall never conquer it. I will give you the keys of the kingdom of Heaven; what you bind on earth shall be bound in heaven, and what you loose on earth shall be loosed in heaven.' The epilogue to John's gospel included another commission, this time after the resurrection: 'Feed my lambs, tend my sheep, feed my sheep.' This gospel also contained the risen Lord's commission to the disciples including Peter: 'Receive the Holy Spirit! If you forgive anyone's sins, they are forgiven; if you pronounce them unforgiven, unforgiven they remain.'

The significance of these sayings has been disputed. When the Matthean promise mentions *ekklesia*, Englished as 'Church', it is one of the only two instances in which that word is used in the New Testament's gospels. The Johannine epilogue gives more prominence to Peter than he receives in the rest of the gospel and even in this epilogue Peter is rebuked because he is curious about the future of the anonymous 'disciple whom Jesus loved'. The power to forgive sins is also not without its problems. The sterner belief that after baptism serious sins could not be forgiven by anyone on earth is taught in the Letters of John and to Hebrews. In the Letter of James Christians are told to 'send for the elders of the congregation' when seriously sick but to 'confess your sins to one another'. It is not known when the system by which serious sinners had to become excommunicated penitents before being forgiven by the Church emerged. Many modern scholars, Catholics as well as Protestants, have therefore concluded that these sayings originated not with the historical Jesus but in the developing life of Early Catholicism. They reflect the importance of Peter in the life of the church in Antioch if

Matthew's gospel was written there, and they also indicate disagreement about the forgiveness of sins between, and even within, the early Christian communities.

But the sayings certainly are significant. It is clear that they refer to the power of the apostles, led by Peter at least initially and in the later mission to the Jews of the Diaspora, to proclaim the gospel with its promise of forgiveness, to baptize and to care for young and old, the beginners and the mature, in the new fellowship. This power was believed to derive from the risen Christ and therefore from the Spirit of God, and the letters of Paul are among the evidence that it was a strong reality. The nickname 'Rock' for Simon, son of Jonah, indicates an early and unique importance, confirmed by references in Paul's letters, and the words 'bind' and 'loose' point to a background in Judaism, where rabbis were said to bind and loose when they taught what was in keeping with the religious law.

The fragmentary evidence in the New Testament therefore suggests that Peter's leadership, although not unlimited, was a fact. Equally important for the future was his martyrdom in the empire's capital—along with Paul who had addressed to Rome his longest and most carefully composed letter. Some thirty years later the church in Rome was reminding Corinth of its proud links with these two great apostles and martyrs. From the middle of the second century the evidence is clear that a single bishop presided over the Roman Christians. Irenaeus taught that 'every church must be in harmony with this church because of its more powerful pre-eminence' and it became the general conviction that the position of Rome was unique. That did not stop Irenaeus from disagreeing with a bishop of Rome who attempted to decide the date on which Easter should be celebrated in Asia Minor. Nor (as we have noted) did it stop the bishops of the eastern churches, or of North Africa, from making their own decisions. But in the west the bishop of Rome was the only patriarch and even in the east no other bishop could be acclaimed as 'the voice of Peter'—the cry which greeted Pope Leo the Great's letter to the council of Chalcedon in 451. The evidence of the history of these early Christian centuries suggests a status for Rome more informal than many Catholics have claimed but higher than many Orthodox and Protestants have granted.

The trouble, of course, was that the history of the bishops of Rome was affected by personalities and events as well as by traditions and ideals. Damasus I, for example, was bishop only because his supporters had massacred the supporters of his rival in the election of 366. He did much to attract and spread wealth, building churches, restoring catacombs and exercising magnificent hospitality. He often referred to Rome as 'the apostolic see' and Theodosius the Great, when he made Christianity the religion of the eastern empire in 380, defined it as the creed once taught by

Peter in Rome and now by the bishops of Rome and Alexandria. Yet Damasus never entirely lived down the circumstances in which he had been elected and his successor Siricius also faced difficulties. He was the first bishop of Rome to be called 'pope' (which meant 'father') and the first to issue *decretalia* in the style of the emperor's decrees, and Ambrose of Milan acknowledged his seniority; yet in fact Ambrose overshadowed him. Not even Leo the Great could quash Constantinople's claim to near-equality with Rome and not even the saintly Gelasius, the first pope known to have been saluted as the 'vicar' (deputy) of Christ, could prevent the many brawls which accompanied the election or deposition of popes and antipopes after his death in 496.

Popes were often in an unhappy position as they had to respond both to kings of the Goths and to emperors of Byzantium. The last emperor to visit Rome from Byzantium, in 663, had the metal which strengthened its most famous buildings removed: he needed it for armaments but did not need the pope's good will. As we have seen, Gregory the Great expanded the papacy's role and Stephen II allied it with the Frankish monarchy. Nicholas I, elected in 858, deposed archbishops of Ravenna, Cologne and Trier, countermanded the mighty archbishop of Reims and tried to depose Photius from the patriarchate of Constantinople. But the progress of papal Rome, thus resumed, was not sustained. His successor, who had married before ordination, experienced the murder of his wife and daughter and the next pope was himself assassinated. By the tenth century the city had lost all visible pre-eminence except in its custodianship of the relics of Peter and Paul and the decaying monuments of imperial glory. It had become a depopulated slum controlled by feuding families of local landowners. The papacy was by now well-endowed financially, but for that very reason was fought over by the factions in elections which for almost a century and a half produced a line of popes or antipopes often related to each other but seldom fit to hold the office. Most did not sink quite to the level reached at the beginning of this period, in the years 896 and 897. When a priest who had been deposed for immorality was elected pope but died of gout after fifteen days, or a pope was confined to a monastery after four months, or a pope who was later strangled presided over the mock trial of the corpse of a predecessor which was mutilated and thrown into the Tiber, it was not easy to hear the voice of Peter.

It was a German emperor, Henry III of the new Salian dynasty, who ended the scandals of papal Rome in his own time and in 1049 nominated one of his own kinsmen to be Leo IX. This worthy pope was a reformer within the limits imposed by the absence of training for the parish priests and by the almost total lack of schools. What did seem possible was a bold campaign to remove the clergy from entanglements in the world of the laity, making parish priests more like the monks among whom this limited reform first gathered impetus. Already a very important custom had spread to the priests in the parishes from the priests who now constituted the majority of the monks—the custom of 'saying Mass' every morning, with if need be only a single server as the congregation. This had become any priest's central duty. Another duty was to hear the confessions of sinners, order a suitable penance and absolve on the condition that the penance would be completed—a duty which since the sixth century had been discharged privately in the priest's house, but was now transferred to the church building. So from the altar the priest moved to a tribunal where the laity would be judged: his role was awesomely sacred. Believing this, the new pope denounced and removed bishops who by paying for their elections had committed the sin of simony and were not fit to be the spiritual fathers of priests. He also tried to get rid of priests who by marrying or cohabiting had sinned against the vision of the Church as the Bride of Christ, the bride to whom every priest ought to be totally devoted.

No doubt this reforming pope wanted bishops and priests to be more worthy in a general sense, but the special motive of his campaigns was shown when he also condemned Berengar of Tours, a monk who had suggested that in the Mass the bread and wine became Christ's body and blood in a way which was more symbolic than physical. Another monk, Lanfranc of Bec, who in England was William the Conqueror's archbishop of Canterbury, rebuked the suggestion theologically. When papal displeasure was added Berengar took an oath that he agreed that the consecrated bread and the wine 'are physically taken up and broken in the hands of the priest and crushed by the teeth of the faithful, not only sacramentally but in truth'. According to an Englishman who heard him (Eadmer), a later pope who belonged to this reforming movement (Urban II) taught that 'the priest has the power to create the God who is the Creator of all things and to offer him to God the Father for the redemption and salvation of the whole world'. It was intolerable to the reformers that a priest with this supernatural power should bribe and copulate like other men. Such practices could not be stopped overnight: some priests seeking senior positions continued to enter into financial arrangements and some at every level who sought female company continued to get it. But those who bought bishoprics faced the risks of exposure, unpopularity and deposition, and priests who wanted to marry could not do so legally.

Leo IX was the first pope to tour France and Germany: it was in order to preach *libertas ecclesiae*, 'freedom for the Church', and he got a response. Many clergy were troubled in conscience and the cause enjoyed popularity with at least some of the laity: in Milan there was an explosion of popular anger against priests who seemed so worldly that their sacraments could not be valid. He also drew to himself men of ability and determination who would continue the struggle. One was Cardinal Humbert, whose angry upholding of the claims of Rome brought about the half-break with Constantinople in 1054 and led him to insist on his return to the west that just as laymen should obey kings, so kings should obey bishops—in particular bishops of Rome. From 1059 onwards popes were crowned with the *tiara*, a tall cap which enabled a king's crown to be added to a bishop's mitre. The custom was to continue for nine hundred years.

Another official was Cardinal Hildebrand, who ran the administration under Leo and shaped policy under his successors. Although short and ugly, he had a great vision. When elected pope in 1073 he did not wait for the emperor's approval and renamed himself after Gregory the Great. As Gregory VII he was determined to complete the reform by securing the independence of himself and of all the clergy under him. It was not long before he formally recorded his programme, denying the right of any layman to 'invest' a cleric and asserting his own right to depose any cleric or layman including the emperor. This *Dictatus* made clear his vision of the glory of the Roman church: 'Established by God alone, it never has erred and never will err to all eternity.' No one at all may judge a pope, or appeal against his rulings, or argue that a synod may act without his authority; and any pope is 'made holy by the merits of St Peter'. Armed with this vision, the new pope was prepared to defy the whole lay world in order to move the priesthood from its control and he saw that the power of kings and lords to interfere in ecclesiastical revenues and appointments provided the decisive battleground.

In the parishes new feelings about the dignity of the priesthood were already changing the old pattern of lay control. Landowners had claimed that since they had provided the churches they owned them and were entitled to a large stake in the tithes which were the profits. In this eleventh century many laymen transferred their shares in these tithes to monasteries; by the 1060s Benedict's old monastery, Monte Cassino, now restored magnificently, had been given the tithes of 560 parishes. The new arrangement did not benefit the priests who did the pastoral work in parishes (the 'vicars' or 'curates') but it was achieved peacefully. In contrast, a collision was the result of the proposal to alter the procedures surrounding the appointment of bishops and abbots in order to exclude any idea that they depended on kings.

The new emperor, Henry IV, a man as proud as the pope and still in his twenties, objected so strenuously that he deliberately appointed bishops in Italy as well as Germany and summoned the pope to abdicate. Gregory then excommunicated him, releasing his subjects from allegiance—an unprecedented move which so alarmed Henry that before gaining the pope's pardon he went through an exhibition of barefoot penitence at Canossa in the dead of winter (1077). Three years later, when the quarrel had resumed,

Gregory recognized Henry's chief rival as king and planned to crown him as emperor. This time the response was different. Henry got the bishops under his control to elect an antipope and occupied Rome, from which Gregory had to be rescued by a Norman army which took the opportunity to sack the city. Gregory did not live long after his enforced flight and his successors depended on the Normans.

When a settlement was reached by another pope with another emperor in 1122, it conceded the latter's right to be suggestively present at elections of bishops and abbots within the empire. Emperors and other kings were now acknowledged to be entitled to 'invest' bishops and abbots with their lands. Such concessions by the Church were inevitable since these estates, like all others, carried with them the obligation to provide armed men for the army, so that their holders' reliability was politically important. Moreover, many lay lords were still entitled to appoint priests to parishes. This system survived to the end of the Middle Ages and beyond, but elections to the leadership of the Church were now to be free of secular control, at least nominally. In order to symbolize this change, the lay power lost the right to 'invest' the new bishop or abbot with the ring that meant marriage to Christ and his Church, and with the staff that meant the pastoral work of a shepherd of Christ's flock; and there could be an appeal to the pope if the validity of an election of a bishop or abbot was disputed.

The next drama in the tension between Church and State concerned the scope of the Church's courts in England. Archbishop Thomas Becket insisted that all 'tonsured clerks' (priests and larger numbers in lesser 'orders') must be tried and sentenced in the bishop's court, not sentenced in the king's, even for crimes of violence. He had precedents on his side: in earlier days an archdeacon accused of murdering an archbishop of York by adding poison to the wine at Mass had been dealt with by a church court. According to such claims, the royal justices would have to rest content with the hope that such criminals would be deposed from holy orders and so would not escape after a second crime—but they suspected that a mere oath of innocence might be accepted and that after any conviction the bishop's prison would not be too uncomfortable. The royal demand was that royal courts should do the sentencing. But in 1170 the archbishop was murdered by knights encouraged by his king (Henry II) in a fit of temper and the scandal forced the king to do penance publicly. After these sensations the ultimate settlement was a compromise in England as in the rest of Europe—as most of Becket's fellow bishops had wanted all along. On the one hand, the king's courts found quiet ways of extending their ability to punish serious crimes such as murder or treason. On the other hand, lighter sentences for minor crimes might be obtained by pleading the 'benefit of clergy', displaying the ability to sign one's name and to read out some of the Bible. It was no great problem that criminals might find sanctuary in churches: they could not stay there comfortably or permanently and in the end if not arrested they had to leave the country as penitential pilgrims.

It was agreed that church courts should have jurisdiction in all disputes about marriages and wills and (in theory at least) all offences against morality. And the Church was left to settle the frequent disputes about its own very extensive property. These cases could be decided locally by judges who were the pope's delegates, but many went either directly or on appeal to Rome, where a bureaucracy more efficient than a king's developed in these years. It was now presided over by the cardinals (bishops and priests nominally in charge of the city's main churches). In 1059 it had been laid down that these cardinals alone should elect popes (thus excluding both the Roman mob and the distant emperor) and between 1050 and 1350 the officials under their supervision multiplied tenfold. About 1150 the Church's canon law was codified by Gratian, a monk in Bologna. It included 3,458 texts. One of them was the decree of the Second Lateran Council of 1139 making all the wives of the clergy mere concubines and all their children serfs, the property of the Church. Such were some of the legal foundations of the power of the pope and the bishops over a large, but not unlimited, part of medieval life.

Crusades and Chivalry

Something about the character of the early medieval west may be learned if we try to understand why there was such a response to the appeal of Pope Urban II in 1095 which launched the crusade whose climax was the capture of Jerusalem.

Jerusalem had never ceased to be a holy city in the hearts of informed Christians and many pilgrims had continued to make the arduous journey to see it, but there had been no overwhelming excitement about the fact that it had been in Muslim hands for four centuries and a half. Why, then, was a crusade to liberate it launched at this time, and why did an appeal which has so often seemed crazy or wicked to historians succeed in attracting large numbers who faced dire hardships and considerable expenses? One of the reasons why these crusades failed to secure their conquests was that relatively few of the crusaders remained in the east when the fighting was temporarily over: why, then, did such numbers assemble and go when the call to crusading was new? In the centuries to come those crusaders who did remain, to run and defend the little 'Latin' enclaves surrounded by Muslims, were to be supported by gifts rather than in person, or by talk rather than by action: why, then, was there now so much hysteria?

The main answer is, it seems, not to be found in any western eagerness to assist their fellow Christians in the Byzantine empire. In his speeches the pope used an appeal for aid from Alexius, the eastern emperor, but as we have already seen events made it clear that the two never worked out how to collaborate. Alexius wanted to make sure of the defence of what remained of his empire but was not particularly interested in the liberation of Palestine. Little more than a hundred years later, a 'crusade' from the west was to sack Constantinople and to occupy much of its empire. Nor does it seem that the west was so well informed about the politics of the east that it fully appreciated the opportunity presented by the recent divisions between the Muslims. This was not stressed by the pope. The main answer to our questions seems to lie in the fact that through the bishops assembled for a council at Clermont in France a pope appealed to knights.

Urban was a son of a French aristocratic family who became a monk of Cluny and then a cardinal who supported Gregory VII in his struggle against the western emperor. The cardinals who elected him pope in 1088 could not do so in Rome, then in the possession of the imperially supported antipope who was not to be driven out of the city for another ten years. Urban attempted to strengthen his position by a closer relationship with the Byzantine emperor and by a dramatic initiative which would be popular in France. No doubt genuine ideals were mixed with his own interests as he announced that his message came from God and no doubt many who heard it understood 'Take up the cross' as an authentic call to Christian discipleship. But it seems relevant that in practical terms the success of a military expedition would depend neither on idealism nor on support by peasants. Pope Gregory had dreamed of leading a crusade to the east: now Urban saw how to translate that dream into reality, although his own role would be inspirational rather than military. His appeal was addressed through the bishops to knights, or would-be knights, mostly younger sons, who were surplus to the requirements of the social system within Europe. They had become guilty of many violent sins—murder, rape, robbery—because they did not possess the estates to which they thought their class was entitled: increasingly, these went to the eldest son. Now they could be offered both forgiveness and land if they left Europe, and if nobles or peasants were influenced by the enthusiasm of these consecrated knights they, too, could be blessed as they disappeared. They could be replaced.

As we have seen, in the early centuries Christian spokesmen had given no approval to violence, saving their admiration for the non-resisting martyrs who were called the 'soldiers of Christ'. The martyred Justin had declared that 'we who were filled with war now farm piety, righteousness and love'. When the empire had become nominally Christian, it had become the turn of the monks to be honoured as Christ's true soldiers. Service in the imperial army had then been approved but when in the tenth century an abbot of

Cluny wrote the first biography of a knight he made it sound as if he had been a monk at heart all along. As late as 1066 the Norman knights who accompanied the Conqueror in his papally approved invasion of England incurred penances if they killed—or that was the Church's theory. But the problem was that considerable numbers of the baptized were professional warriors under no squeamish illusion that they could avoid killing: these included the Normans. Mounted on trained horses with saddles and spurs, protected by helmets, shields and chain-mail, they could and did thunder into the attack wielding swords, lances and clubs. In France bishops tried to reduce the violence by persuading the knights in some areas to accept the 'peace of God' or the 'truce of God', limiting in the one case the targets, and in the other the days, when fighting was not too great a sin. But the violence continued.

Now the energies of many knights could be diverted to adventures which could be celebrated as romantic and prestigious, even as holy, in the *chansons* of the troubadours. The papacy guaranteed protection from lawsuits during a crusader's absence, subsidies from funds raised by a tax on the clergy if the local ruler co-operated, the forgiveness of repented sins with the crusade counting as the necessary penance, and the heavenly Jerusalem as the reward of a crusader who sacrificed his earthly life. The Europeans did not yet possess a fleet capable of transporting an army and the first crusade suffered greatly as it fought its way through Asia Minor to Jerusalem (and made others suffer). The capture of the Holy City seemed to be a miracle which proved God's own approval of the whole enterprise, but many of those who had responded to Pope Urban's call with enthusiasm died or were disappointed by the material results and when the 'Saracens' (Muslims) had recovered their unity and military might in the 1130s the disasters of the Christians began. However, for some knights solid wealth could be obtained in the temporarily conquered lands of the east ('Outremer'), including much of Greece after 1204, and to others who remained in Europe the crusades brought a new glamour. The *milites* of a society very close to barbarism became, at least in theory, the *chevaliers* of a Christian civilization. From the realities of the ferocious fighting of the cavalry grew the ideals and fantasies of medieval chivalry.

In formal ceremonies knights could now take their swords from altars after prayer, fasting and a bath, with a solemn oath to deliver, rather than oppress, the innocent; and even when a knight was 'dubbed' with a ceremony less religious, his elevation was still thought to have some moral content. A literature arose which catered for this market. In its best known stories King Arthur's knights are not saints, but neither are they complete scoundrels. It was a progress of a sort when the 'epic' celebrating a blind loyalty to a fighting group was rivalled by the stories and songs of 'romance', glorifying an individual's search for honour and love. Now honour was said to consist in obedience to a moral code, not merely in the possession of power, and love meant that a knight was expected to rescue a maiden in distress or to sigh for an older lady (usually not his wife) instead of raping her. Adventure was said to lie in the knight's quest for the holy grail (variously understood as the cup used at the Last Supper or as the dish in which Joseph of Arimathea had collected the blood falling from the crucified Christ) instead of the hunt for earthly wealth. Or it could lie in battles against Muslims. In the most famous poem about chivalry, before he dies Roland has time to pay homage to God. He has his reward: angels carry his soul from the Spanish battlefield to heaven. It was inevitable that the Church's and the poets' success in idealizing and sanctifying knighthood by such propaganda should be limited. Many knights remained thugs. Next to sex, hunting and hawking, their favourite sport was provided by tournaments. In these jousts between individuals or battles between groups, with excited ladies looking on, those who lost and had not been killed were usually expected to hand over horse, armour and cash to the victors. After some two hundred years of condemnation the Church accepted the tournaments in 1316. But something was done to limit the violence of the knights, or at least to divert it into war against those regarded as the Church's own enemies.

Religious orders were formed where knights no longer needed to subsidize monks in order to win the Church's favour: they could become monks themselves, in some sense, while continuing to be knights, for they were now engaged in violence which the Church blessed. A much admired monastic saint who applied the 'courtly love' tradition to mystical relationships with Christ and Mary, Bernard of Clairvaux, assured these sacred knights that 'to kill someone for the sake of Christ, or to wish to undergo death, is not only completely free of sin, but even highly praiseworthy and deserving of reward'.

The history of the Knights Templar mixed idealism with sordid realities. Formed in 1119 to defend pilgrims on the dangerous roads of Palestine, their rule was drawn up by Bernard. Unless they were on military service or recovering from it, knights and sergeants alike were to be quiet and to listen to clergy singing the monastic services and reading out religious books. Their name was derived from the house granted to them near the site of the temple in Jerusalem. The papacy and many lay benefactors showered privileges and wealth on them and they attracted many recruits. An international order, they began to be international bankers and their wealth grew as their involvement in the crusades diminished and vanished. That was their downfall. A brutally ruthless French king, Philip the Fair, arrested them and confiscated their assets in 1307. They were accused of a remarkable number of crimes, sins and heresies; confessions were extracted by torture;

the grand master was among the knights who were burned alive; and under French pressure, a pope and a bishops' council suppressed the whole order, most of whose funds remained in royal hands. Only one allegation seems to be worth a moment's thought: the order was accused of encouraging sodomy. This story was part of what seems to have been a growing hostility to homosexual practices in society at large. It seems very likely that feelings (at least) of this kind coloured some friendships in monasteries and were less controlled in semi-monastic orders of unmarried soldiers, but when monks were accused after the Church's own inspections usually women were involved. Most of the French royal propaganda against the Templars was probably one more example of the age-old habit of attributing sexual promiscuity to people being persecuted.

The Hospitallers were more fortunate, partly because they never entirely lost their connection with hospitals, begun in Jerusalem before the crusaders arrived. They, too, attracted endowments and privileges, and were authorized as a semi-monastic order (the Knights of St John). When they had been drawn into the military life by defending pilgrims they provided garrisons for crusaders' castles. When no such castles were left, they captured Rhodes from the Byzantines and held it until 1523. They were then given Malta and kept it until 1798. They ended up as an international charity, the Order of St John of Jerusalem.

The Power of the Papacy

The power to authorize a crusade belonged to the papacy alone, and that custom illustrated the uniqueness of the authority claimed and mostly acknowledged. Yet normally the pope, like any other medieval king, was expected to rely on his own rights and possessions: taxes were legitimate only if absolutely necessary to meet emergencies. So he was forced to develop his financial rights. At this stage he had to rely mainly on payments by nations of which he was the feudal overlord and on profits derived from his own lands. In addition he was entitled to 'annates'—the first year's income of a bishop, abbot or priest in whose appointment his officials had been involved, either because he claimed the right to appoint or because the appointment had been disputed or needed confirmation. He was also entitled to regular visits by archbishops and some abbots, who could commute this duty for money. And occasionally he could collect as much as a tenth of the income on every benefice (usually after sharing it with the local ruler). Such a tithe was justified on the occasion of a crusade and the temptation was strong to launch a 'crusade' against political enemies.

Rome was seldom a secure base for the rule of an Italian kingdom. As the economy of the city recovered, so did its claim to civic independence. Increasingly the bishops of Rome preferred to live away from such troubles in their other castles but in the 'lands of St Peter' nowhere offered complete security. In the north the cities were now prospering, like Rome, but in them, too, there was almost continuous turbulence. Both popes and emperors claimed rights and bitterly rival parties, the Guelfs and the Ghibellines, were supporters. The cities were also riven by internal conflicts, between classes and between factions of the powerful. In the south and in Sicily the end of Norman rule in 1189 brought fresh problems, for here the pope was nominally overlord but never had the military strength needed to govern.

In such circumstances the papacy's involvement in politics and violence was probably inevitable, but it damaged its religious authority. In theory the pope was the sacred centre of Christian unity, at least in the west, but he often functioned as one prince among rivals and as the one who cheated in the competition for power by fighting with weapons which were meant to be reserved as rebukes of the utmost solemnity for sins of the deepest wickedness. Excommunication excluded a sinner from the Church's sacraments and the company of Christians, and it was feared all the more because it was believed to exclude from heaven. An interdict excommunicated a whole nation, although it was usually modified to allow infants to be baptized and the dying to be absolved. A crusade summoned all Christians to rescue the Holy Land from the infidels. Such weapons could hurt the papacy when wielded for its own short-term political purposes.

Innocent III, an earlier pope's nephew, himself a graduate in theology and law, joined the papacy's staff as a cardinal at the age of thirty and was only seven years older, and not yet a priest, when he was elected in 1198 to begin a reign of eighteen years as pope. Now he was, he declared, 'above all men, judge of all and to be judged by none except the Lord'. His understanding of the papacy's rights included political supremacy and he soon seized an opportunity presented by a lack of clarity in the procedure for electing a 'king of the Romans' whom the pope would be more or less obliged to crown as emperor.

Innocent was delighted to be arbitrator when two rivals, both claiming to have been elected by the German princes, applied to him for the imperial crown. He chose the one who promised to support him in Italy, only to find that this favourite invaded Italy and had to be excommunicated and deposed. He eventually backed Frederick II. It turned out to be another mistake, for this Frederick inherited from his grandfather Frederick Barbarossa (Redbeard) a network of rights in northern Italy, and from his father, Henry VI, who had married the heiress, the actual possession of the Regno, the kingdom in the south. His aim was now to combine north and south as a secure basis for an emperor's power, squeezing the papacy.

In its response to this threat the papacy had to sacrifice large expenditure and much of its credibility as a religious force. It also had to sacrifice its hopes that an emperor might at last provide the strong leadership which was vital to any hopes of a successful crusade against Islam. Frederick Barbarossa had given some unity to the third crusade but had been drowned in an accident in Armenia. Neither Philip Augustus of France nor Richard the Lionheart of England had proved able to out-general Saladin, who emerged from the battles as the lord of Jerusalem and the most powerful figure in Islam. After Innocent's death in 1216 Frederick II promised to lead another great expedition, but being nervous about the new pope's intentions in Italy withdrew and was excommunicated. He then did go east, and by negotiation (Saladin being dead) secured the temporary restoration of Christian rule in Jerusalem, but he rapidly abandoned the Holy City in order to defend Sicily against an invasion instigated by the pope.

The struggle for power in Italy, which was disgraced by atrocities on both sides, was not over when Frederick died in 1250, and it was accompanied by a fierce propaganda war that continued long after his death. Frederick fascinated people. He was called 'the wonder of the world' and stories that he was not dead, or would rise from the dead, circulated for centuries after his exit from the world. As cruel as he was clever, and as licentious as he was eloquent, he seems to have believed what his supporters said about him. Papal propaganda treated him as a monster but the propaganda in his own cause, widely circulated to high and low, depicted the popes as the arrogant enemies of divinely appointed monarchs. The papacy was further discredited when in order to get rid of Frederick's heirs the king of France's brother, Charles of Anjou, was imported to lead another 'crusade' in Italy. In the 1260s Charles defeated Frederick's illegitimate son Manfred and defeated and executed his young grandson Conradin, but the French made themselves so unpopular that many were massacred by the Sicilians in 1282, beginning a century when the island was disputed and devastated.

Innocent and his successors had shown that they could often be strong enough to defeat their political enemies by 'crusades'. In the process they had made sure that the western emperors would never become the hereditary lords of Europe, with a large kingdom of their own. But just as emperors were to remain elected rulers with limited powers, so would popes. They would not even be able to dominate Italy, which remained divided until in 1870 popes ceased to rule Rome. In religion they might be 'judged by none except the Lord'. But in politics and war they could be defeated.

Innocent often spoke of his concern for Christian unity, in particular of his burning desire that under his leadership all Christians should unite to recover the Jerusalem which had been lost only a year before he became pope. He was delighted when what remained of the ancient Christian kingdom of Armenia acknowledged his authority as the vicar of Christ. But in the event, the 'Great Crusade' which he sponsored was diverted to attack the Hungarians on behalf of the Venetians. He excommunicated those responsible, but took no action when his edict was ignored. Then, as we have seen, the 'crusaders' destroyed all hope of the west's reunion with the Christian east when they sacked Constantinople in 1204. Innocent lamented this further outrage, but rejoiced when it seemed to result in the triumph of the Latin Church. When a group of the defeated Orthodox offered to accept his appointment of a new patriarch on the condition that eastern customs would be protected, the offer was refused. To Innocent Christian unity meant complete submission.

The 'crusade' which achieved the largest, because most brutal, success was waged in the south of France, an area which had for long enjoyed neither strong government nor a high level of church life. A powerful influence, defying landlords and bishops alike, was exerted by the Cathars or Albigenses (from Albi, a stronghold of the movement). Some of their leaders, the *parfaits*, were women. Some came from the nobility, but most earned their living in humble jobs. All seemed more self-sacrificing, more spiritual and more impressive than the local clergy, and the fact that their ultra-puritan teachings, denouncing the physical as evil, bore more resemblance to the Gnostics and Manichees of earlier centuries than to the Bible did not trouble most of their hearers, who could not read and who were not usually expected to become puritans before they were on their deathbeds. Their myths were exciting. When a peasant or an artisan received the *consolamentum* from a *parfait*, usually before dying, he became for the first time in his life fully entitled to say the Lord's Prayer and he knew that the spirit in him, soon to go to heaven, had wandered from body to body since the Fall. Christ, being spiritual, could not have had an ordinary human body and true Christians should have as little as possible to do with the appetites which dragged them down. The *parfaits* set a fascinating example, whether or not it was followed: they moved among the people earning small sums, yet they avoided sex and did not eat the products of sex such as meat or eggs. So their doctrine seemed more interesting than the Catholicism of the all-too-human parish clergy. And their network proved too tough for the local bishops to break. In due course they developed their own bishops, priests and deacons (not including women), but a spirit going deeper than any organization preserved their appeal.

Innocent sent an envoy to investigate. He was murdered in 1208. The pope thereupon released the fury of twenty years of 'crusade'. Like the crusades in the east these expeditions were led by lords willing to take over the lands of their enemies as earthly rewards; the most prominent among them was Simon of Montfort. Indiscriminate massacres followed. So did large-scale burnings of heretics. Innocent then told the bishops to conduct small-scale 'inquisitions' which meant enquiring into the existence of heretics instead of waiting for complaints.

After his death, in 1233, specially appointed inquisitors received further authorization from the papacy and their activities became more frequent and severe in many (although not all) parts of medieval Europe. In contrast with the care which medieval justice normally took about the rights of the accused, here those reported by their parish priests or neighbours, or by spies, could not call their own witnesses and were seldom helped by advocates committed to their defence; the lawyers they needed were themselves frightened of being thought heretical. They faced trained theologians who kept careful records of earlier cases, were convinced that it was their duty to save humanity from the fires of hell and were assisted by juries of impeccable orthodoxy. Normally these inquisitors worked by tireless questioning and argument between spells of often harsh imprisonment, but from 1252 they were allowed to use torture. If the accused remained obstinate in grave heresies, their goods were confiscated and they were imprisoned for life or handed over to the local authorities to be burned; this had been the fate of condemned heretics since the first burning in 1022, and the last was to be in Spain in 1781. Those who repented of heresy under this treatment—the majority—were given warnings and penances such as arduous pilgrimages.

Innocent also got entangled in the vigorous, although less violent, politics of England. The election of an archbishop of Canterbury began it: the monks naively elected one of their brethren; King John demanded the election of a bishop he trusted; the pope, when appealed to, appointed his own candidate, Cardinal Langton. John's refusal to accept the verdict was punished by an 'interdict' which forbade almost all public worship in his kingdom. After five years he capitulated and England became one of a number of kingdoms paying sizeable annual tributes in cash to Innocent as overlord. The pope thereupon supported the king against his barons, led by Langton, who extracted Magna Carta from John in order to limit the discredited monarchy's power; the barons were, Innocent pronounced, 'worse than the Saracens'. The French seized the moment to launch a victorious war, conquering Normandy. The great pope had given England an archbishop more worthy of the post than either of the two previous nominees, but his subsequent conduct had given to the English reasons which could be remembered to resist the papacy's 'plenitude of power'.

When elected pope in 1294 Boniface VIII set himself to restore this plenitude. He succeeded a monk and miraculous healer in his eighties. The election of Celestine V had been a sensational reminder that the papacy was still regarded as a spiritual centre, but the old man had soon been persuaded to abdicate from responsibilities for which he had no competence.

Boniface was in character utterly different from that 'angel pope'. He had spent many years as the papacy's leading lawyer, impatient with the fumblings of eight short-lived popes since the great Gregory X, and his main interests were legal and political, while keeping an eye on finance. In some ways his nine years as pope repeated the success of the equally masterful Innocent III. He presided over reforms in the Church's law and central administration. He encouraged scholars and artists. He brought floods of visitors to Rome by proclaiming 1300 as a 'jubilee' year, with promises ('indulgences') to pilgrims normally reserved to crusaders: a devout pilgrimage would itself be the penance due for sins and there would be no further punishment in this world or the next. He launched a 'crusade' against a Sicily which was now asserting its independence, paying French troops with money extracted from the clergy. But he was far from modest about such successes, commissioning many statues of himself although leaving behind no evidence that he had a single friend. The language he used in order to bully those around him was brutal. The language he used for the papacy's traditional claims was boastful beyond anything seen before or after. And by a monumental misjudgement his most lofty boasting was directed against one of the toughest of medieval kings, Philip the Fair of France.

Philip felt unable to tax the French laity in order to pay for the suppression of a revolt in Flanders. Without papal permission he therefore imposed a tax on the clergy. The furious Boniface could reply that this move was against the Church's law, but he also proclaimed that it was a plot by the laity against the interests of the clergy. He had to yield in the end, but when Philip arrested a bishop regarded as a traitor this angry pope reasserted his power to excommunicate and depose any mere king, announcing that no human being could hope for salvation unless in communion with the bishop of Rome. And as he opened this war with France he had no secure base in Italy, for his naked determination to finance the rise of his family had aroused the hatred of the Colonna clan. He called for yet another 'crusade' in Italy, excommunicated the Colonna cardinals, destroyed the Colonna castles and razed the Colonna stronghold of Palestrina to the ground. He prepared against the French king the final blow, a decree of deposition. However, mercenaries assembled by the Colonnas and paid by the French forced their way into his palace in the town where he had been born, Anagni, in order to kidnap him for trial by a council which Philip was planning in France. He was rescued by the townsmen, only to die in deep shock a few weeks later.

Such dramas stirred political thought, particularly in Italy, and a great poet was one thinker. In his treatise on *Monarchy* Dante's glowing ideal was that the emperor, God-fearing in his righteousness but God-like in his strength, should rule the whole world. This imperial paragon would support the ethics taught by philosophy and natural to humanity, and so would bring well-being and happiness to all. He would not be tempted to invade anyone else's jurisdiction because all the other rulers on earth would be clearly subject to him, but he would place total power at the service of total justice. And he would then be the Roman emperor, for Rome had been appointed by God to rule the world in the 'tranquillity of peace'; Christ himself had been content to live and die as the Roman emperor's subject. Under the pope the Church would be confined to spiritual functions, but would preach and demonstrate faith, hope and love as the ways to the joys of Paradise. A slightly later Italian thinker, Marsilio, produced a theory which reflected his own background in the independence of the city of Padua. He argued that political power ought to rest with the wiser and elder (*sanior et senior*) among the people, while the clergy were to be confined to religion, about which he was less eloquent than Dante. He attacked the claim of the pope to be St Peter's successor (which Dante had accepted) but was slow to advocate the claims of emperors. For him the nearest equivalent on earth to the City of God was a city.

However, the political realities were very different from such theories. For almost a quarter of a century, from 1250, it was demonstrated that Europe could manage without any effective emperor at all. Dante's dream arose at the time of the armed attempt by Henry VII to revive the imperial power in Italy, an attempt ended by the papacy and malaria in 1313. Later emperors became virtually the presidents of Germany, elected by the leading nobles and aristocratic bishops whose decisions favoured candidates with little power and after 1338 could not be overturned by popes. And Germany's interests turned away from the south, to the north and the east. In Italy the cities which Marsilio had idealized became prey to fights between factions. As Dante knew from his own very bitter experience, these often resulted in the takeover of power by the men who, whether or not they were wiser, had more financial or military muscle. Outside Germany and Italy the future lay with the national monarchies, although kings encountered many obstacles on the way to that future. Spain slowly became one nation. Kings of France eventually resumed the extension of their power: the ability of Philip the Fair to organize national resistance to Boniface had been an ominous precedent. England coalesced more easily on its island, despite the disastrous ambitions of several of its kings to conquer France. Such monarchies could claim their own Christian sacredness and could employ armies of officials, and field armies of soldiers, larger than those at the disposal of any pope.

Yet the papacy and the Church which it governed still controlled much of the mind of the Middle Ages. The pope was the supreme teacher of a faith which almost no one contradicted in public. We cannot tell how many doubts or denials were private. Those we know about were usually reported by enemies and may not have expressed any considered non-Christian philosophy. How many peasants thought that the priest was untruthful as well as too comfortable? Did the academic debates about the interpretation of received doctrines conceal a more profound scepticism, sometimes or often? We cannot know. We do know that Christian faith was the social convention. Thus Frederick II was often said by churchmen to be a heretic, even an atheist, but according to his legislation heresy was a crime punishable by death. Boniface VIII was said to have made cynical remarks about the faith he was supposed to teach, but the evidence or gossip was collected by his enemy Philip the Fair, who professed to be deeply shocked. And we also know that with the consent of the rest of the society the Church had immense material wealth. It has been calculated that by 1200 the clergy controlled about a fifth of the land of western Europe and received about a tenth of its gross income. Boniface had been mistaken to think that kings could afford to exempt such a class from all taxes and during the rest of the Middle Ages a settlement worked: under pressure from kings the clergy volunteered their own financial gifts which were often larger than the normal taxes. But the wealth itself was never confiscated. Much evidence survives of cynicism about this privileged class whose founders had been fishermen in Galilee and quite often the disapproval led to protests against such riches, even to the voluntary adoption of Christian poverty, but most people got on with their humble existence against the background of the great fact of Christendom, with its authorities in Church or State permanent although remote. Most people found it impossible to imagine a very different Church.

Cathedrals and Towns

The life of this medieval society, full of tensions and violence but in the last analysis united, was dramatized in the life of Thomas Becket, before and after his murder in 1174.

His fame after that final drama had the result that we can know much about his previous performances in strikingly different roles. As a young Norman brought up in London he found in himself energies which were satisfied neither by a love of sport nor by student days in Paris and Bologna: he could organize, he was ambitious. It seemed natural to pursue a career in the Church. Somehow he inserted himself into the household of the archbishop of Canterbury and became an efficient archdeacon. Then he rose to being a servant of the crown, as chancellor, and was a brilliant success. As a civil servant he could administer anything effectively; as a courtier he threw himself into the display, the feasting, the hunting and the fighting. He was a knight among knights and as the king's man he became the king's friend. Imposed by Henry II on the Church as archbishop, he was ordained as a priest and to the surprise of all changed his character. As a thorough churchman he became the totally obstinate defender of the powers of the church courts, of the privileges of his archbishopric and of obedience to the pope—who was, however, not anxious to defend him against the king. The king's anger at the betrayal became hatred. Becket's own idea of the role of an archbishop did not involve the control of his sharp tongue but he was chaste and austere. In exile he lived as a monk and scourged himself. As he accepted death from the king's knights in his own cathedral he was a model martyr. Even now he was not loved and his many critics pointed out how easily he could have escaped martyrdom. But criticism had to be softly spoken, for he was admired. 'Great he was in truth, always and everywhere', wrote a contemporary, 'great in the palace, great at the altar and singularly great at his journey's end.'

Placed in a shrine covered by precious metals and jewels, his bones became the centre of believers' healings depicted in very beautiful stained glass brought to Canterbury from Chartres in the 1220s. As pilgrims came to St Thomas of Canterbury he rose to his supreme, and strangest, role: he was now the hero of English popular religion. In the 1380s the custom of telling 'tales' on the pilgrims' way was used by Geoffrey Chaucer to make the first masterpiece of literature in English. Chaucer, whose main work was as a civil servant, shared the pilgrims' holiday mood: he was sometimes bawdy, sometimes anticlerical (the pardoner who retails for a price the Church's power to forgive sinners is presented as an exceptionally repulsive sinner), but almost always he is genial and compassionate, celebrating what John Dryden was to call 'God's plenty'. He included in the company genuine Christians, among them a 'gentle' knight and a 'poor parson of the town'; he wrote out a thoroughly conventional sermon and presented it without irony as the parson's tale. But he stopped his *Canterbury Tales* before this mixed and outspoken band of pilgrims reached the shrine of this 'holy, blissful martyr'. Did he fall silent in reverence? Or was Geoffrey Chaucer embarrassed by the theatricality of Thomas Becket, alive or dead?

Four years after that sensational martyrdom a fire destroyed the eastern half of Canterbury Cathedral apart from the Norman crypt. With the prospect of profitable pilgrimages the opportunity was seized to rebuild in the new French style, with larger windows, detached shafts, pointed arches and ribbed vaults. This style was to be called 'Gothic' by men of the Renaissance who despised its lack of the restrained elegance which they attributed to ancient Greece and Rome and tried to associate it with the barbarian Goths. In fact this medieval style was influenced by the rebuilding of the church of St Denis near Paris, finished in 1144.

That project could be afforded because the church housed the tombs of the French kings and because the adjacent monastery's abbot, Suger, was virtually the regent in the absence of a commanding king. As he explained in widely circulated writings, Suger had thought it all out. He wanted as much beauty as possible to surround both the Mass and the sacred monarchy; and he wanted it to be the beauty of light. Doorways richly carved with biblical subjects invited pilgrims into a well lit church; walls were becoming surrounds for windows and the arches incorporated in them were in three storeys, permitting endless variations in design. The light enabled gold and jewels to glitter and fabrics to glow. An ambulatory led the pilgrims to the saint's shrine, the devotional climax of a series of chapels. Vertical shafts and pointed arches led the pilgrims' eyes up to the vaults and it was Suger's hope that the beauty would elevate souls to 'that which is truly beautiful'. He believed that the St Denis (Dionysius) buried in this church was also the author of a mystical treatise on the light of God.

This style was now used in Canterbury although the French architect who began the new work also began the English tradition of being comparatively cautious. The English did not aspire to reach the extraordinary height of the cathedrals in Amiens and Beauvais (the vaults in the latter fell down). Instead they built cathedrals large on the ground and surrounded them with large 'closes' behind walls. They developed new versions of the French style— 'Early English' as in Salisbury, 'Decorated' as in Exeter, 'Perpendicular' as in Gloucester—but they did not copy the 'flamboyant' exuberance of Rouen. However, the style was always essentially the same in the best buildings of Europe—in Chartres or Reims, in Ulm or Prague, in Uppsala or Siena.

In Cologne the Gothic cathedral built around relics believed to be those of the biblical Magi was so vast that, begun in 1248, it was abandoned in 1560 and not completed until 1880. In 1385 Gian Galeazzo Visconti celebrated his successful overthrow of his uncle in the control of Milan by beginning a vast new cathedral faced with marble, eventually to be adorned by a forest of pinnacles and more than two thousand statues. In Spain this style could celebrate reconquest from the Muslims magnificently, as when the canons in Seville resolved in 1401 to begin the building of a cathedral so great that those who saw it completed would think them crazy. More normally, benefactors wished to advertise their wealth and power; the mobile architects and masons (there was no clear distinction) wished for jobs and for chances to exercise their remarkable skills; ordinary folk were swept into the enthusiasm to raise spectacular symbols of their communities and great shrines where prayers could be offered for their souls; and probably for almost everyone, in all classes, a factor was the desire to offer praise to God. The work was as careful where it could not be seen as where it could be admired. The smiles on the faces of angels were sculpted by masons who did not work only for money.

This architecture exhibited harmony. Designed with the new skills of geometry and arithmetic, standing up because it was successful engineering, a great church offered back to the Creator the harmony of the cosmos. Medieval people were told that all nature could teach an abundance of religious and moral lessons because it had all been created by the God comprehensively explained by the Bible and the Church; and here was a building full of symbolism which the faithful could recognize. The stories of Christ and the saints, directly revealing God, were carved or painted here as the 'Bible of the poor' who could not read. The great church dwarfed individualism, being the intelligible and acceptable construction of a united culture, but it also gave scope for some excitement and daring within the agreed structure. About five hundred medieval cathedrals can still be seen in western Europe and no two are exactly alike.

The most conspicuous feature of the 'Gothic' style is its fascination with light and height—light pouring down from heaven, height rising up to it. That is what most obviously distinguishes it from other styles. In a Byzantine church the dome represents heaven and the icons represent Christ, his mother and his saints; but the building is seldom tall enough to be a ladder to the saints in heaven. In a Romanesque church the worshipper may find refuge from a physically and spiritually dangerous world; but there is no visible promise of admission to a realm of light, a better world above. In a great Gothic church, however, light and height proclaim that Christendom has come out of material poverty and spiritual darkness and that Christians can be assured of the possibility of a climb to Paradise. Moreover, a great Gothic church communicates even to those who do not go inside, for the magnificence of the exterior, particularly in its array of statues, can suggest a rich relationship with its city or other neighbourhood. In places there was a custom for an annual gathering of large numbers from the parishes in the cathedral and much more often prayers would be offered by pilgrims, but in general the worship in a great church was the business of clergy, monks or choir, not of the laity. The main connection with the laity was through the building, which was raised and adorned to be worship on behalf of a community. The west towers of Laon feature statues of bulls looking down the hill to the fields. The cathedral's interior could also be evidence of the variety of the links between the Church and the community: chapels were given by fraternities and in the windows of Chartres 43 trades are represented. This is architecture which is part of a whole society which (at least officially) shares the Church's confidence that heaven is accessible. In the

Florence of the 1420s Brunelleschi will exhibit the Renaissance style in the rebuilding of San Lorenzo as the parish church of the Medicis; then the arches will be round, the roof flat, statues absent, the facade left for a future generation to complete. (It has never been completed, although Michelangelo drew up plans for it.) All this is going to announce that the citizens who go inside will find a Christian temple as beautifully proportioned as any Greek or Roman temple, with its restrained elegance articulating the rational order in the world. But such a temple will no longer say on behalf of a civilization that the Catholic Church provides a gateway into light and a ladder up to heaven.

That high medieval confidence would have been less likely if the west had not reached a level of material prosperity inconceivable in the previous dark ages of hunger and fear. It seems probable that the population of western Europe, which had declined as the Roman empire died, more than doubled between 940 and 1340 (the best guess seems to be that it grew from about twenty to about fifty million). This was mainly because there was more food, although many thousands still died if the local harvest failed. The climate was usually better and for seven hundred years Europe largely escaped Asia's plagues. Scrublands, woodlands and swamps were cleared for agriculture; in northern Europe, allowing one field in three (instead of one in every two) to lie fallow for a year further improved production; heavier and more numerous ploughs were drawn by horses made more efficient by shoes and harnesses; more vegetables provided protein for the poor; more water mills did the grinding of grain; more roads could be used (although inferior to the Roman roads); more markets helped sellers and buyers; money became much more important in exchanges and wages; safer means of banking and transmitting it developed. These were three hundred years of economic progress, feeding subsistence for the many and a few luxuries for the privileged. A new Europe had arisen, different not only from the dark ages but also from the Roman empire where dependence on slave labour had made technological progress seem unnecessary. And as part of this renewal of Europe, cities which had shrunk into villages amid ruins expanded into prosperity and new towns were founded.

Towns old or new, often growing around great churches, offered markets and attracted inhabitants who accepted the overcrowding and the riots, the noise and the dirt, because life behind the walls was better than the conditions in the countryside where most peasants were still tied to their lords. These towns had to organize themselves if they were to trade, manufacture and prosper, and as they grew prosperous they could purchase from kings, bishops or lords charters which conceded 'liberties'. And some of the energy visible in the towns was seen elsewhere. Not only did more sons survive in the landowning class: peasants, too, now suffered from hunger for land and so were willing to move as colonists, although preferably not to move far.

Such unprecedented growth brought problems. By 1250 there was not enough profitable agricultural land for everyone who wanted it, even after the success of the great labours in reclamation and colonization, and in the suburbs of the towns there were many thousands who found urban life very far from Paradise. Men were noticing (if not understanding) the problems of unemployment and inflation: too many people wanted better wages, too much money chased the still limited supply of goods. But the responses of the Church showed that it was still on top of a society bursting with energy.

The Church at its Height

In November 1215 the work of the Fourth Lateran Council took only three weeks although the assembled multitude of bishops and abbots was required to pass no fewer than 71 decrees. Meeting in his palace in Rome, his presidency over this council was the most lasting achievement of the most imperious of popes, Innocent III. Not all the decrees were effective: in the event, privileges were granted to new religious orders because bishops did not train and finance enough preachers to address the new population. But the council agreed on a large programme of reforms and this was not altogether in vain.

There should be annual synods in all provinces (groups of dioceses) and all monasteries and religious orders should have regular inspections or self-examinations by their own 'chapters' (meetings where chapters from their rules would be read out). The council insisted on the dignity and discipline of the clergy. They were to be appointed to their parishes or other 'benefices' within three months of the vacancy but subject to the bishop's approval. They were to be sure of receiving tithes from parishioners but were not to solicit or accept fees for their services. They were not to go hunting, to wear colourful everyday clothes, to sport buckles on their shoes. They were to put away their concubines (a rule which proved specially hard to enforce). A short new summary of doctrine provided a basis for their instruction of their flocks, and it included the 'transubstantiation' of the bread and wine by the priest's words in the Mass. The custom had already been established that the holy wine should not be offered to the laity for fear of spills and it was explained that the consecrated bread also contained the 'substance' of the blood, by 'concomitance'. Since the words recalling the Last Supper were said silently or in a low voice, the climax of the Mass for the laity would be the elevation of the white wafer of unleavened bread (the 'host') by the priest after the ringing of a bell. The people would now 'gaze at God' with acclamations spoken or silent, although they often felt free to leave the church after that. But in 1215 the council's most important decree made it compulsory for all adult Christians who were not excommunicate to confess all their sins (not only 'mortal' sins deserving hell) to their own priest before receiving the consecrated bread in the Mass at least once a year, at Easter.

This rule, establishing a new religious link between the parish priest and every parishioner, was part of a general tendency to clarify laws. The clergy were now forbidden to certify the results of the primitive trials by 'ordeal' using fire or water, with the result that these mockeries of justice, previously frequent, had almost entirely ceased by the end of the century. (The attempt to stop clergy acting as judges in ordinary courts was, however, less successful because they were still needed for that purpose.) Another new law provided that new saints and new relics of old saints were not to be venerated without papal permission, although the love of saints and their relics overcame this restriction.

Marriage was now seen as more than a civil, and perhaps temporary, arrangement: it was a Christian sacrament. The exchange of vows before the priest in the porch of the church was becoming usual and was more often followed by a nuptial Mass. (In Italy, however, it remained the custom that the vows were exchanged before a legal official, the notary.) Any marriage between Christians who before it were not too closely related, who publicly consented to it and who consummated it by intercourse, was valid and therefore indissoluble. There was no relaxation in the condemnation of offences against marriage such as adultery, divorce, abortion, contraception and homosexual practices. The use of sex within marriage was now being affirmed more realistically, although its fruit in children was still regarded as its main justification. However, a host of human problems might complicate this clear picture. Moral lapses were to be confessed to the priest, but legal questions arose about precisely which marriages were valid and these were to be answered by the bishop or by 'dispensations' from the pope.

Parish churches were becoming the places where children were normally baptized: parents no longer had to take their babies to the 'mother' churches. Children were now being named after saints but were not being given communion before the age when they could be 'confirmed' by the bishop after instruction by the priest. For girls the age was usually now about twelve, for boys about fifteen. It was hoped that parish priests would be capable of teaching these children, supplementing parents and godparents; and in theory children should not receive Holy Communion until after this 'confirmation' although since bishops did not always make themselves available to villagers the practice might be different.

In theory all the secrets of a parish were to be laid before its pastor, whose new authority was shown in the formula replacing the earlier prayer after the confession: 'I absolve you.' Penances were still imposed as the condition of forgiveness but were being varied according to the circumstances, as discussed in many books to guide priests. They were becoming more workable for the ordinary sinner: indeed, it was becoming possible to commute them by less painful actions or gifts. Thus Christendom was being strengthened by changes which were mostly realistic at the level of the parish. But to show how united and how exclusive it was, any Muslim or Jew remaining in western Europe after the violence connected with the crusades was ordered to wear distinctive dress, usually a yellow circle on the chest.

Western Christendom was greatly enriched by Islam. Many devices, luxuries and words were imported and the beauty of Venice was built on the profits of trade with the Muslims. Specially in Sicily and Spain much was learned from Muslim scholars who had access to the intellectual legacy of ancient Greece. But attitudes to the religion of Islam were almost always complacently arrogant and in their usual practice Christians, when they had the power to do so, treated Muslims at least as badly as Muslims treated Christians after an initial period of toleration. The Prophet's character was blackened and although the Quran was translated into Latin in the 1140s it was not respected. Some Christians attempted to convert Muslims: the bravest and most intelligent of them was Raymond Lull. To encourage his fellow Christians into a deeper devotion he wrote mystically about the Lover and the Beloved and he saw that the crusades were no way to draw Muslims into this love. But he also believed that the entire Christian faith could be proved by reason alone and the example and encouragement which he gave to studying the language and literature of Islam were all designed to assist a preacher in the refutation of obvious errors made by the Prophet. He sought to argue with intellectuals but those who came across him found him offensive and what ordinary Muslims heard when a Christian preached was the enmity in the Spaniards' battle cry: 'St James, Killer of Moors!' Lull was stoned to death in North Africa, about 1315.

In the early Middle Ages 'Christian' attitudes to the Jews were not thoroughly hostile. Augustine and Gregory the Great taught that Jews ought to be protected because their conversion was necessary before Christ could return to reign on earth, as Paul had told the Romans. Another scholarly bishop, Isidore, presided over a council in Spain in 633 which decreed that Jews must not be compelled to be baptized and he wrote a treatise which was the most persuasive presentation so far achieved of the peaceful Christian appeal to Jews. Carolingian and other rulers encouraged Jews to contribute to the economy by doing jobs which Christians were not yet able to do and by lending money. Jews were forbidden to convert Christians and there were incidents when anti-Jewish prejudice surfaced, but the major horrors began only when the crusades began. Leaders of crusaders on their way to

Jerusalem could instigate massacres with the cry that it would be wrong to avenge the Muslim capture of Christ's tomb without first avenging his death on the Jews who (it was said) had killed him. In those riots many Jews committed suicide rather than accept the forced baptisms which were still contrary to the official Church's teaching.

Such exhibitions of popular hysteria left the remaining Jews vulnerable. At this time legislation led by Theodosius the Great was revived and enforced: Jews were not to own land or to work as artisans in trades. Their response to this discrimination was to live in their own district of the town, the ghetto, and to concentrate on the trade of the moneylender. That occupation was denied to good Catholics because the Hebrew Bible had prohibited the taking of usury, defined by Gratian around 1140 as 'asking for more than is given'. The great council of 1215 reinforced this prohibition. But the Scriptures had allowed Jews to lend to Gentiles, a concession which was interpreted as meaning that they could lend money on interest to Christians, particularly to kings, who were often in need of it. Kings, German princes or Italian cities therefore became the protectors and even the owners of Jews, often rescuing them from attacks which the papacy also condemned. But their status meant that kings and others could cancel indebtedness by demanding ransoms or by expelling Jews, as happened in France several times (finally in 1394) and in England in 1290; and gradually Christians became moneylenders with more resources than the Jews, whatever the Church might say about usury. When the Black Death and other plagues came in the fourteenth century the Jews formed a segregated and unpopular group that could be sacrificed as a scapegoat in any return of popular hysteria. The Middle Ages became full of stories that the Jews insulted Christian beliefs and practices, crucified and ate Christian children, poisoned wells, seduced maidens and were in general the allies of Satan. At the end of the fifteenth century the worst period of the medieval treatment of the Jews began: the expulsion of the unbaptized from Spain was copied elsewhere, and in the places still allowed to them they were more insecure. The sixteenth century saw the unwilling exodus to the east, to Poland and Russia, where the skills of this talented race were still needed. But in those lands, too, they were to be persecuted in the name of Jesus of Nazareth.

Towards believing Christians, however, in practice attitudes became more relaxed than before. The medieval society largely tolerated sinful behaviour and the medieval Church forgave it when it was confessed. What could not be tolerated was heresy in belief, for that destroyed the society's unity more disastrously than did the sins of the flesh.

Clergy continued to be all too human, as could be pointed out by indignant saints or mocking fellow sinners, and the newly intimate contacts between priests and penitents were fertile ground for gossip about further sins. Sexual behaviour which the Church condemned did not stop and the growth of legislation included the licensing of many town brothels or red light districts. Fornication by young bachelors seems to have been taken for granted and by no means everyone agreed that the priest should decide who was married to whom. Imagination and expenditure were lavished on fashions in female or male dress which were often sexually provocative. The spoken or written entertainment appreciated by all classes usually had a sexual content: Jean de Meung's continuation of the *Romance of the Rose* urged the rich to be fruitful in many beds and tavern songs celebrated the effects of drink on the less rich. The powerful passed laws against the lowly who dressed in imitation of their betters, but the luxury of the display by the powerful made more of an impression.

For the social pleasantries the churches were available almost as readily as the taverns. Parties ('church ales') were held in churchyards or the naves of churches. Some foolery was accepted when boys acted as bishops or men who sang the services staged mildly obscene parodies. While they recited their psalms monks could prop themselves up by using 'misericords', seats with often humorous or grotesque carvings beneath them; and high above them rain spouted out of the mouth of stone gargoyles, each one a joke. The Bible, doctrine and morality were popularized by plays which the laity enjoyed performing or watching, and these included comic or sensational incidents. The twelve days after Christmas became a merry time; *caroles*, songs to which people could dance, were often sung then. The many saints' days were often days off work and pilgrimages provided other holidays. In practice much rural magic or semi-magic was taken into Catholic shapes, as in the blessing of crops or the devout use of holy wells.

The point was made again and again that Christ and his saints were human: Christ on his mother's knees was being shown as a baby more or less normal, Christ on his cross as a man in pain. And they came near to people in their daily lives. Many stories told of miracles when a doubter or sinner was given a vision of Christ, perhaps as a bleeding corpse or as a baby, present in the wafer as it was elevated during Mass. Another popular legend was about a smart young hunter whose life was changed by seeing a crucifix between the antlers of a deer. About 1260 the *Golden Legend* was compiled by a future archbishop of Genoa: it enjoyed the largest medieval circulation of any book apart from the Bible because of its picturesque stories of the saints in everyday surroundings. Saints' relics were still collected, but often for domestic use and with less of the sense of awe characteristic of an earlier age.

Since the days of Augustine and Gregory the Great it had been believed somewhat imprecisely that the prayers of the Church on earth could reduce the suffering after death of Christians who were not destined for hell but were also not ready for heaven. In the tenth century the annual observance of All Souls Day spread from the great abbey of Cluny. Towards the end of the twelfth century this tradition became clearer and more prominent. Theologians worked out the detailed doctrine of purgatory; preachers imagined the horrific pains, more intense than any suffering on earth, which could be ended quite easily by the prayers of those listening to them; there were many nightmares about the agonies of the beloved dead and ghosts made known their agreement with the preachers. No doubt such beliefs often caused anxiety or terror but they offered hope to, and about, people who were not saints and who were accustomed to pain in their lives before death. When in the Second Council of Lyon in 1274 Catholic doctrine had to be defined in order that the Eastern Orthodox representatives might temporarily agree with it, the belief that some souls are 'purged by penalties' after their deaths was one of the non-negotiable items.

Art and books were, of course, paid for by the rich. How everyday life actually felt for most medieval people is hard to say. The seasonal labours of the countryside are depicted beautifully in some of the prayer books ('books of hours') which were among the luxuries of the rich, but we cannot see the sweat or the mud or shiver in the cold. Some wills survive listing the goods of the richer peasants but the average little wooden house has not survived. Usually aerial photographs are needed even to trace the pattern of the medieval fields and the poorest tenth of the population has remained submerged. Some records of law courts survive giving the memories of the accused and the witnesses, but medieval people did not spend their whole lives committing crimes. Some personal letters survive, but few medieval people wrote letters. So general views of the Middle Ages have often been either absurdly romantic or absurdly hostile and despite the labours of many 'social' historians only in recent years have two books, about a community and an individual, been really illuminating for non-specialists. Through a book of 1979 light has come from the records of a detailed inquisition by the local bishop in 1318–25 into heresy in Montaillou, a village in the Pyrenees. This was less isolated than some other villages because shepherds met each other in the surrounding fields, but it was a close community of some forty houses full of gossip, friendships and feuds. It enjoyed theological arguments while being very far from the expert clarity of the theologians. It was also full of sexual laxity in which the parish priest joined. Before the Inquisition probed and punished, life seems to have been quite agreeable although unheroic. Almost all the parishioners confessed their sins before Easter to the lecherous priest who privately admitted that he carried out his duties for the sake of the income. Yet the visiting Cathar *parfaits* were respected precisely because they were mysteriously perfect in their morals. And vivid evidence about a very different part of the medieval society, the life of a merchant, was published in 1957. It was derived from some 150,000 letters written by, or to, a merchant of Prato near Florence, Francesco Datini, who died in 1410. He, too, was not chaste: he was not faithful to his wife or always polite. His motto was honest: 'for God and profit'. To God he addressed many prayers and a very large bequest: he left his fortune to found a charity for the poor. To profit he dedicated his life in greed, anxiety and overwork.

What these two books and other studies suggest, unsurprisingly, is that whatever the theories might be everyday human nature was neither saintly nor devilish, life on earth neither hell nor heaven. It is easier to know what the medieval society admired in theory. This was set out in a biography of Louis IX, a king who was declared a saint by Boniface VIII, thus confirming the title 'Most Christian' used by all kings of France after an earlier declaration by Innocent III. His life was recounted in a fairly lifelike fashion by the lord of Joinville who had known him well. We also have the evidence provided by his written advice to two of his many children.

We meet a king of France devoted to his royal duties from the age of twelve, a model to monks in his self-discipline, always anxious to see justice done, and for all that a man of tact, humour and charm. He frequently sought guidance from the clergy and gave expensive patronage to churches and charities; yet he was not afraid to protest when the papacy seemed to be taking too much money out of France. His ideas about Christian monarchy were shown in his dealings with his brother-in-law, Henry III, the far less effective king of England. He defeated almost all Henry's claims in France but supported him against his barons at home. He applauded his expenditure on (and personal interest in) religious architecture and art, including the reconstruction of part of Westminster Abbey.

Louis purchased what were believed to be Christ's crown of thorns and the miraculous imprint of his face on a cloth and in their honour built a nifty marvel of stone and glass, the Sainte Chapelle in the middle of Paris near the new cathedral of Notre Dame. And he believed it to be his duty to endure thorns in his own life. In 1248–54 he experienced the total failure of the sixth crusade, which he led into the sands of Egypt, believed to begin the road to the reconquest of the Holy Land. One part of the disaster was the cost to France, including the raising of a huge payment to ransom prisoners of war, but the experience only strengthened this royal saint's determination. Back in France he extracted money for crusades from the Jews among others, borrowed what he could not get, and meanwhile threw himself into the 'crusade' against the Albigenses which extended his kingdom as well as the Catholic faith. In the summer of 1270 he at last embarked on the seventh and last crusade to be aimed at the east. This time he went via a siege of Tunis, where he soon died of dysentery, repeating 'Jerusalem! Jerusalem!'

Among all the kings of the Middle Ages Louis was admired most widely because he seemed to embody all the ideals. And if we regret the limitations of those ideals, we may notice the old woman of Acre who was spotted during a crusade and mentioned by the lord of Joinville. She carried a brazier of coals and a bucket of water, explaining that she wished to set fire to heaven and to put out the fire of hell, because people ought to love God for his own sake.

New Movements

We have more evidence about the religious orders. In them may be found traces of the love which that old woman wanted. Anyway, they wrote most of the literature, produced most of the official saints and enjoyed the patronage of Christian kings such as St Louis.

In the ninth century an abbot under imperial patronage, Benedict of Aniane, led the successful campaign to use the rule of the original Benedict to regulate all monasteries, with the changes in the founder's intentions which we have noted. But the largest changes followed the foundation of the abbey of Cluny in 910 by a duke who did not insist on his family's rights over its future. It was dedicated to St Peter and in 1024 placed directly under the papacy. Before long the abbey acquired more prestige than the papacy itself. It exercised a decisive influence over the reforming movement inaugurated by Leo IX. By the end of the eleventh century it had three hundred monks, its church was the largest building in Europe and some six hundred monasteries looked to it for inspiration. Either they were priories under the one abbot or they were abbeys pledged to follow Benedict's rule as interpreted by Cluny. Yet this interpretation became increasingly a new development. Many of the inmates of these monasteries were children deposited by their parents. Not a few of the adults had been admitted as monks after less than the year as a novice which Benedict had prescribed. As endowments grew with ever closer links with the aristocracy, and as the monastic estates flourished, these monks began to live in what Benedict would have thought was luxury. Instead of a balanced diet of work which would include private prayer, reading and manual labour, they became almost totally absorbed in the (sometimes bored or hasty) recitation of services in churches which were as elaborate as could be afforded. For many years Cluny had very impressive and long-lived abbots. But the quality of leadership and of self-discipline declined—as did the income in comparison with the expenditure. And the twelfth century saw the beginnings of a development which further reduced the income: people able and wanting to endow the saying of Masses for the dead could now begin to do it through local 'chantries' and did not need the monks.

There seems to have been no great scandal in that kind of life, but inevitably men arose who felt called to greater austerity, many living as hermits, others not permitting their communities any laxity which Benedict had not explicitly authorized. In the Alps the Grande Chartreuse survived as the most austere of the experiments: there the monks spent most of their time in silent prayer, each in his own cottage. But the biggest movement came when monks seeking 'perfection' walked out of one monastery to found another in Cîteaux (also in Burgundy) in 1098.

These Cistercians became known as the 'white' monks because their 'habits' (robes) were undyed in distinction from the older Benedictines' black. They insisted that new monks should be adults prepared to be trained for a life under a strict discipline and without any material comforts. Three of the original Benedictine principles were developed. Private prayer encouraged a fervently personal devotion to Jesus and his mother (with no distraction by the possession of relics); a shared involvement in a tough adventure, with more time outside the formal worship in church, encouraged a new depth of friendship; and manual labour was once more essential, with monks setting an example although many thousand *conversi* or illiterate lay brothers were enrolled to do most of the work. (These were recruited from young men who sacrificed marriage but would otherwise have probably been unemployed.) Leadership as creative as any in Benedictine history was given by abbots, most notably by Bernard, a young nobleman who after two years in Cîteaux was sent to found his own monastery in Clairvaux in 1115. Characteristically, he had brought his brothers with him when he became a monk.

When he died in 1153 there were 539 Cistercian monasteries, not all under a single abbot but standardized by a 'chapter' of abbots. Helped by the fact that Pope Eugenius III had been his pupil but mainly through his own eloquence as preacher, counsellor and letter-writer, Bernard had become the spiritual leader of Christendom. His physical self-denials wrecked his health but his passion for God and the Church raised Catholicism, or at least its elite, to a new level of emotional intensity. It is clear that he experienced a mystical union with God, although he always insisted that both in mortal life and in eternity's 'beatific vision' the union was a harmony of wills, not a confusion of substances. It was the fruit of love on both the divine and the human sides, not an achievement through spiritual exercises. About eighty of his sermons which survive use the erotic poetry of the Song of Songs in the Bible and apply it to the love between God and Man, between Christ and the Christian—or, if Christ is too frightening, between the Christian and Christ's mother ('she will listen to you, the Son to her, the Father to him'). Monks were enthralled by this spiritual equivalent of the courtly love between knight and lady which so interested some of the monks' brothers who were out in the world.

As was inevitable, the Cistercian story was partly a record of human nature being less than saintly. Towards the Cluniacs the Cistercians could be self-righteous—although the abbot of Cluny who pointed this out in response to Bernard's strictures also introduced his own quiet reforms. Towards those who did not share his uncompromising faith, Bernard could be very hard: he attacked the philosopher Abelard to whom Cluny gave a final shelter, he lobbied against bishops or candidates for bishoprics of whom the Cistercians disapproved, he promoted the calamitous second crusade against the Muslims and, as we have seen, he urged Christian knights to kill pagans in Europe. Moreover, the Cistercians themselves became almost as wealthy as the Cluniacs. Choosing remote sites, they farmed virgin lands efficiently. If villages stood in the way of their methods, they could be abolished. As peasants became less willing to accept food and shelter instead of wages, and as estates became wider by development or purchase, labourers were hired and there were disputes about how to treat and pay them, resulting in strikes. The Cistercians transformed waste lands in France, Flanders, Yorkshire, Germany, the Baltic lands, Bohemia, Hungary and Poland; sheep, cattle, iron mines and rich crops added to the wealth of Europe; but in the end, these entrepreneurs who produced and traded acquired a reputation as grasping businessmen who did well for themselves. And with the wealth came a relaxation of the old austerity. Some Cistercian, like Benedictine, monasteries looked like gentlemen's clubs. It was an example of a pattern: disciplined work brings material as well as moral rewards, and thus fresh temptations.

The hour had struck for adventures in heroic discipleship of a more definitely lay character. These included experiments in religion for women.

It was one of the tragedies of the Middle Ages that the male-dominated Church could never work out a sufficiently positive role for women. The relevant volume of a history of women published in 1992 has the apt title: *Silences of the Middle Ages*. Almost all the clergy seem to have shared this society's general attitude: the daughters of Eve were temptresses, being sexually voracious but otherwise weak-minded, and should be married off by their families while still in their teens (to men often some ten years older), should produce at least five children each, should watch many of these die before adulthood, should make themselves additionally useful by embroidery for the better-off or by spinning or farm work for the others, should not be spoiled by being educated and should not be allowed to manage any property which might be theirs, being instead transferred like servants from fathers to husbands. Life was often more pleasant for women in the nobility, of course, but their essential functions as women remained the same and they had their own problems in that they were married off for reasons of politics or finance to men whose skill was in fighting, often to the death. The songs of the Middle Ages, if glamorous, were often about unhappily married ladies who welcomed adultery in word or deed; or if popular these songs were often frankly lewd in their contempt for women. But there was an alternative to marriage and childbearing for women who did not wish to become nuns: prostitution, of which the authorities took a relaxed view if the customers were not known to be ordained or married.

Nevertheless, many women wished to enter convents. Some were widows, some were spinsters and some were unhappily married, but that did not exclude a religious motivation for many. By 1500 there were 654 convents for women Cistercians (with 730 for men). A twelfth-century Benedictine abbess, Hildegard of Bingen, Christianity's first woman theologian, reached out from her Rhineland convent by many journeys and by letters and books despite many male attempts to silence her. She taught a theology which included scientific knowledge rare in her day. She had many other talents as an artist, poet, musician and healer, yet she dedicated all these gifts (unequalled among men when she died in 1136) to the teaching of a spirituality based on a direct and essentially simple vision of God. For her God is present with overwhelming power in nature as well as in salvation, and one day God will prove that power by the condemnation and destruction of all evil. Despite this impressive example of what women had in them to contribute to the Church, many religious houses for women had to struggle for existence. Some were endowed in the expectation that the daughters of the rich would find a good life in them, but some other benefactors did not favour monasteries where many Masses could not be promised. A religious house for women was thought to need men to say Mass, to direct souls and to do many practical jobs; yet men could not be allowed to live near temptation. Some unmarried women therefore came to live and pray together in little houses of their own. They hoped to escape condemnation by devoting many hours to prayer (they began the devotion of the 'sacred heart' of Jesus), by caring for the sick and by supporting themselves by hard work in simple crafts. When necessary they hoped for charity.

Such were the Beguines. They began in Liège later in the twelfth century, with the support of a priest called le Bègue ('the Stammerer'), but their real founder was Mary of Oignies, who certainly did not stammer as she inspired other women. They spread to many towns in northern Europe but they were suspected. They did not take the vows which nuns took, and it was alleged that this was in order that they might be free to reclaim their property or marry. It was, of course, also alleged that their advocacy of a 'free spirit' concealed free sex. Being women they had little or no formal education, so that in their ignorance they might fall into heresy. They were told to accept clerical supervision and those who refused were persecuted. In 1310 Marguerite Porete was burned for refusing to withdraw her *Mirror for Simple Souls*, a book which taught love as the road to God without much dependence on the Bible or the Church. A more highly born mystic among the Beguines, Mechthild of Magdeburg, escaped death, but was forced to enter a convent. Her best known book invited its readers to enter 'the light flowing from the Godhead' without too much attention to lesser lights. Since so many suspicions surrounded these deviant women, it is surprising that their numbers began to decline only after 1450.

Probably almost all the accusations made against the Beguines arose in men's unclean imaginations, but it is harder to know what to make of the Beghards. These were men from whom the English word 'beggar' is derived. They were often in trouble with the authorities and the locals as they wandered around, begging aggressively while they shouted religious slogans, and it seems likely that some had chosen the open road as an escape from the tedium of work, marriage or other conformity. The Beghards had dropped out of medieval society and they paid the price. But it was a religious age and it is hard to believe that many were so dangerously non-Christian as was often alleged. Heresy was risked when, like the Beguines, these men attempted a do-it-yourself mysticism—but the vision of an organized campaign against the Church in the name of the 'free spirit' seems to have been largely a nightmare in the minds of the higher clergy.

The Augustinian canons were priests under the control of the local bishop and were far less open to sensational accusations. Some of their houses and churches were substantial (some were cathedrals) and some were 'regular' (under a monastic rule), producing an influential school of mystical prayer in twelfth-century Paris; many founded little schools, hospitals and burial grounds. All were willing to combine the corporate prayer characteristic of the Benedictine tradition with pastoral work in the towns, listening to confessions and personal problems, saying Mass, preaching, baptizing. So the Augustinians, although never obtrusive, were numerous and popular.

More definitely lay movements which chose poverty but avoided controversy included the Humiliati. These were men who lived with their families, earned their living by humble jobs, dressed in undyed clothes, ate sparingly and came together to pray. Mostly in the towns of northern Italy, they offered a quiet protest against Christian involvement in usury and other money-making. Some priests and unmarried laity joined this movement and lived together in little houses. In 1201 Innocent III organized the Humiliati into three 'orders' (clergy, laity and married 'tertiaries') and even allowed them to preach morality in public, although not doctrine.

Another new movement became controversial. In 1179 Pope Alexander III granted the request of Peter Valdes, formerly a rich merchant and banker in Lyon, to be authorized to lead a movement of 'poor men' after a dramatic conversion. But the movement soon split. The authorities thought that they were being generous to permit some of these poor men to speak in public if allowed by the bishops and parish priests after tests for orthodoxy. Valdes always claimed that he was orthodox, but he was among those who rejected such control. As the movement spread it offered women among others the opportunity to be trained for simple, mainly ethical, preaching based on translations of parts of the Bible, with or without blessings by bishops. But a further development left Valdes behind as comparatively conservative. Some of these lay preachers began to say Mass and to hear confessions when no Catholic priest seemed available or suitable. Some were evangelists and pastors in villages where Catholicism was not strong. Some, particularly in the towns of northern Italy, resembled the Humiliati in character but were far more radical in protesting against a Church which was too rich.

Dominicans and Franciscans

A much more respectable and important order of preachers choosing poverty was founded by a major saint, Dominic Guzman. It arose out of the slowly perceived need to convert the Catholic heretics in the south of France by instruction, in addition to the use of force and terror. Dominic, who had been a canon of a cathedral in Spain which strictly observed the Augustinian rule, joined the Catholic preachers but saw that little impression would be made by men not so self-denying as the heretics' own leaders. He accepted poverty for himself and commended his example to Cistercian abbots who had attempted to be missionaries accompanied by servants. A small movement gathered around him and was authorized by Innocent III on the understanding that it would be Augustinian like its founder. But Dominic had bigger ideas. During years of travel he began to organize a new international order of preachers. There were to be priories where 'friars' (brothers) were to be trained and based in a single pattern. Each priory was to be accountable to a provincial 'chapter' and through its head to an annual chapter of the priors of the whole order, and other friars were to be charged with the duty to report on the conduct of the priors. This was government with the consent of the governed and it seems to have had some influence on the gradual development of parliaments in which kings secured the counsel and consent of representatives of at least some of their subjects. It seems probable that this ambitious idea of a large order of preaching beggars was influenced by some contact with the success of Francis of Assisi, whom Dominic met during the Lateran Council of 1215.

Francis outstripped Dominic, both as an innovator and as a popular hero.

He never lost the charm which had earned the nickname Francesco because he had seemed so Frenchified as an elegant, young man-about-town. Some of the stories later told about him had already been told about other holy men but their very beauty testifies to his appeal to affections, imaginations and consciences. Others before him had shared the ambition to 'follow the naked Christ naked', but a gift for drama was displayed when he literally stripped himself when accused of theft by his exasperated father before the bishop (he had taken some cloth from his father's shop in order to raise money to 'repair my church' as ordered by a voice from a crucifix). Hastily made decent by the bishop while his clothes lay at his father's feet, he was turning completely to the Church, away from the materialism and snobbery of the rich in the towns. But he was never a priest and he did not turn to any established institution or lifestyle. It took some time for him to discover his new vocation.

He was thunderstruck, as Antony of Egypt had been at the very start of Christian monasticism, when he heard a priest read out the instructions of Jesus to his first disciples. He saw that he had to repair the living Church by new actions as well as by old words. He kissed a leper, and years later he invented the Christmas crib by placing animals around the altar at Midnight Mass. Being determined to prove that while he preached the gospel he was not more sheltered than his Master or his audience, he renounced every kind of possession. He and other 'friars minor' (little brothers) did not need to own any base: they would be at home everywhere. They did not need incomes: they would get food in exchange for doing little jobs, and if that failed, they would beg. They did not need books: their lives of prayer and love would teach them and teach others. He made this destitution sound glamorous by calling it Lady Poverty. He went on various ill-considered expeditions, including a journey to Egypt where he hoped to convert one of the finest and strongest of Muslims, Saladin, in the midst of an invasion by the crusaders. But for all his naivety and eccentricity he never doubted that the Lord had called many to walk behind him in the adventure. The many were to include Clare, the daughter of a noble family, who began the Second Order (the 'Poor Clares') and entered a life of prayer, great austerity and an illness lasting almost thirty years. This order soon included saints of the quality of Elizabeth of Hungary, a princess by birth and marriage, who as a widow lived in poverty serving the poor and the sick in Marburg. Her cousin, Agnes of Bohemia, also became a Poor Clare, presiding over the convent which she and her brother Wenceslas (the 'good King' of the carol) had built in Prague. Other Franciscans in the Third Order could follow in the way according to their circumstances, which might include marriage and ownership. At an early stage Francis persuaded a far from Franciscan pope, Innocent III, to approve informally a rule of life consisting of little but quotations from the New Testament. Towards the end of his life he grew deeply fearful that this would not be enough to preserve his vision. He did not hesitate to demand obedience to a more detailed rule which he drew up, and supplemented it by a personal testament to be read out, as he hoped, whenever the friars gathered in 'chapter' to the end of time. Nor did he hesitate to differ from Benedict's rule for monks. In his order there was to be joy and laughter but no question of anything which the poor might regard as luxury; the friars were not to commit themselves to one house but were to move around; they were not to own books other than those needed for services; any friar elected to lead his brothers was to be their 'minister' (servant), not their superior; all who came on these terms were to be welcomed into the order with little or no training; a depth of contemplative prayer was not to be incompatible with a vulgar evangelism.

Being unencumbered by possessions and often outdoors although his main mission was to the poor in the towns, Francis became a poet of nature. He got the brothers to sing of sun and moon, earth, fire and water as members of their own new family. It was said that he preached to the birds. But his life was no rural idyll. He added to this Canticle of the Creation a verse in praise of 'our sister, the death of the body'. Two years before his death his body ('Brother Ass') received the wounds of crucifixion, the *stigmata*: he had increasingly chosen to be alone in prayer and that was the physical effect of his union with his Lord amid his own agony of fear about the future of his vision. When he died in 1226 he was once more naked, on a bed of ashes in a hut. Two years later a close friend who was now pope, Gregory IX, declared him a saint without waiting for further evidence.

It is a story which has never ceased to appeal, but in it lay the seeds of tragedy, exactly as Francis had feared. He had made his first recruit, Bernard, not by talking to him but by being overheard as he talked with God. He had said again and again, through the night, 'My God and my all'. He had consistently refused to equip the friars with anything except faith, hope and love. He had been surprised when friars sent to Germany with no letters of commendation and no knowledge of German were thrown into prison as vagrants and when friars sent to Morocco were executed for insisting on preaching against Islam (with abuse of the Prophet) despite many warnings. He would have approved of bold but excessively optimistic missions which took friars into Mongolia. In 1246 John of Plano Carpini conveyed a message from the pope urging the Mongols to become peaceful and Catholic; the Great Khan's reaction was to urge the pope to submit to him. A little later William of Rubruk debated religious claims at the court of another Great Khan, but inconclusively. Francis wanted the friars to preach in European towns but did not allow them to have their own churches to use if the local clergy grew resentful. He had wanted them to preach orthodoxy but had not permitted any facilities for study. He wanted them to be very like the first followers of Christ but had ignored all the differences between the situation of the apostles and the thirteenth Christian century.

So what had happened to the rule of Benedict—which had also been intended to recover the 'apostolic life'—happened to the rule of Francis. Although he had instructed the friars never to seek privileges from the papacy, they became dependent on protection by the popes, and in the end vulnerable to their displeasure. In 1215 Innocent III rescued the order in its infancy: when the bishops' council had decreed that no new orders should be allowed, he decreed that it was not new. In 1274 a council of bishops and abbots in Lyon secured the suppression of several smaller orders of friars, but through papal protection the Franciscans and Dominicans again escaped. Francis had prohibited the ownership of convents, churches and libraries but the papacy solved the problem temporarily by accepting nominal ownership for itself and by allowing 'spiritual friends' to be other nominal owners. The Franciscans still begged but did not now refuse large or regular gifts. Like the bishops or the monks they could be accused of being money-minded and the accusation disturbed them because they remembered Francis.

Other new orders were encouraged by the success of these friars to choose poverty, to defy the bishops' prohibition of novelties, and to gain the papacy's protection. Men and women called Carmelites, whose austere lives had begun in Palestine with memories of Elijah on Mount Carmel, came west after the failure of the crusades and were reorganized as an order of 'mendicants' (beggars). Italian hermits and canons who interpreted the Augustinian rule with exceptional austerity became the nucleus of a new order of 'Austin friars'. But because Francis had been Francis, the Franciscans experienced unique conflicts and suffering.

Acknowledging his own incompetence as an organizer, he had appointed Elias as his deputy. Rapidly after his death Elias collaborated with the pope in building in Assisi a magnificent basilica beside a large convent, and in it the saint's body was placed beneath paintings by the leading artists of the day: from that time to this, it has been a centre of pilgrimage. A few weeks after this burial, however, the pope decreed that the saint's last testament should not bind the friars. Elias continued to be a superb organizer, but he lacked the saint's charisma as he lacked his love of poverty. He was deposed from the leadership in 1239 but soon it was agreed that candidates for the order must be either clerics or else unusually qualified laymen. Recruits were sought among the students in the universities, then reckoned as clerics. Then the Franciscans became university lecturers, often the most respected since they combined intellect with idealism, did not teach for money, did not strike and did not leave the university for a better job. In Oxford a Franciscan, Roger Bacon, was the best scientist yet to appear in Europe.

These developments, however unavoidable, ruined the original vision ('O Paris, you have destroyed Assisi!' cried Brother Giles) and the 'Spirituals' put this point with passion to the 'Conventuals' who accepted the need to use their own convents, churches and libraries. For a time the leadership of a friar who was given the name of Bonaventure held the two sides together. He was a sophisticated theologian who had been the most distinguished teacher in Paris and who now consolidated the transformation of the order into a large society of educated priests living in convents. But he was also a holy man, indeed an advanced mystic, and he eloquently defended the Franciscan vocation to humility and poverty. He wrote what became the official life of Francis. He combined the roles of scholar and friar so successfully that his systematic theology, praising the light of God present in all nature and in all human reasoning as well as in Christ, may be said to be the Canticle of the Creation intellectualized. ('The creation', he wrote, 'is like a book in which the Trinity may be read.') His elaborate account of Christian prayer as the ascent of the soul to God echoed the story of the journey of Francis to the *stigmata*. His emphasis that the Christian needs to act by the conformity of his will to the will of God went back to the conversion in Assisi as well as forwards into much later Franciscan philosophy. But a split could not be prevented. The Conventuals may have had common sense on their side, but the Spirituals could appeal to the last testament of Francis himself and to the teaching of Scripture about apostolic poverty declared by a pope in 1279 to be revealed truth. The atmosphere of excitement was given oxygen by the prophecies of an Italian monk, Joachim of Fiore. He had predicted in the 1180s that the 'Age of the Spirit' would arrive before long and would produce a new kind of monk, serving and inspiring the people without earthly wealth. The Spirit would replace the Church of Peter by the Church of John. That could mean the replacement of popes by revolutionaries.

The actual split was brought about by John XXII, a pope who feared that the Spirituals were undermining the social order over which the papacy was expected to preside. He condemned them in 1317 and a severe persecution began. Five years later he went against the papacy's previous decisions and refused to be responsible for the theoretical ownership of the Franciscan houses: the friars or their supporters must be responsible themselves. In 1323 he pronounced that it was a heresy to believe that Christ and his apostles had lacked possessions. The current 'minister general' now led a small breakaway group of protesters and in the 1360s, when the dust had settled, a larger movement of 'Observant' Franciscans began, observing the rule of Francis strictly. It was not fully acknowledged by the papacy until 1517 and was not reunited with the Conventuals for almost another four hundred years.

Like the Franciscans the Dominicans aroused the jealousy of monks, parish priests and university lecturers. It was said that all the friars were too willing to become bishops and too friendly with kings and merchants despite their talk about humility, and that their churches could be large and handsome because they had promised a comprehensive pardon and a dignified burial to sinners who ought to have done arduous penance. And certainly when the friars, Dominican or Franciscan, heard confessions they gave advice which was more sophisticated, and more persuasive, than the earlier sweeping condemnations of business as necessitating the sins of usury and profiteering. Usury was now said by pastors sympathetic with merchants to consist in the exploitation of the distress of one individual by another who was in a position to make a charitable gift. Profiteering was charging too high a price. Sins so defined were still condemned. It was, however, permissible for a banker to receive compensation for placing money at the disposal of a ruler or trader well able to reward him—and for a merchant to set a 'just price' by buying the material cheaply and charging for every kind of labour. The merchant who sinned by interpreting these concessions too liberally could make amends by gifts to the Church or the poor. Being grateful for these assurances, the businessmen of Florence, a city which specialized in banking and the luxury trades, devoted some of their profits to building the large and very lovely churches of Santa Maria Novella and Santa Croce for the Dominicans and the Franciscans. In every town there were 'guilds' maintaining monopolies and standards of training and work in their own interests but, as they claimed, also in the interests of commoners. These derived self-esteem from their association with a favourite church but were compelled to listen to the moral advice of friars and other priests. This consecration of civic life and trade, and of capitalism, was not what Francis had intended when he walked out of Assisi, but it meant that the medieval Church had up to a point succeeded in accepting and moralizing commerce like knighthood and since the priests who thus came to terms with the world remained without their own money they continued to enjoy sincere respect.

The Dominicans also grew in numbers and outreach, although never so fast as the Franciscans. This meant that the fine plan for a 'general chapter' each year to which each prior would walk proved unworkable—and that their convents were usually large and scarcely an exhibition of poverty. Many of them became scholars as their founder had intended, but they remained the Order of Preachers: their scholarship prepared for the pulpit, not for academic cleverness and independence. This meant that although new entrants needed to be trained as theologians in the universities they had to be sheltered from preliminary student life, so that a network of Dominican 'arts' courses had to be established. Naturally the universities did not welcome this. And the Dominicans obeyed the will of the papacy that they should be Inquisitors. This meant that they became hated by many as the methods used to hunt out Cathars were adopted throughout France and Italy and in other parts of Christendom.

It was the tragedy of the Franciscans that instead of treading their founder's road with Lady Poverty most of them felt obliged to imitate the scholarly Dominicans who rightly needed more material assets if they were to do their work. And it was the tragedy of the Dominicans that, having been given the work of passing to others by argument what they had contemplated in prayer and study, with as little property as possible in order not to alienate the poor, some of the best known ended up as they did—bullying defenceless peasants, inflicting tortures in order to extract predetermined confessions, handing over some of their victims to be chained to a stake and burned alive. The great ideals and the great tragedies of their betrayal created great literature— the speeches by Bonaventure (praising Dominic) and Aquinas (praising Francis) in Dante's *Divine Comedy*, but also the legend of the Grand Inquisitor, a Dominican, who is confronted and in the end kissed by Christ in Dostoevsky's *The Brothers Karamazov*. We may also find some consolation in the fact that friars were among the great medieval thinkers.

Faith and Reason

For educated Christians in the early Middle Ages, and for those whom this tiny minority tried to instruct, the union of faith and reason was taken for granted since all the available authorities seemed to agree. That was the tradition in the monasteries where Augustine and some other Fathers, and some remnants of pre-Christian thought acceptable to the Church, were studied with a reverence almost as great as that given to the Bible. The intellectual work of the monk and of the monk's pupil was to meditate on this unquestionable heritage, to 'chew the cud' as reading was often described. Study was not very different from worship. Christians of the present age were, it was said, like dwarfs sitting on the shoulders of giants. But we have already looked at some of the ways in which monasteries under the rule of Benedict were supplemented or replaced by a greater vitality and variety and now we have to see the consequences of a linked change: the monastic schools, which had been intended chiefly for the training of boys to be monks but had sometimes included the brighter sons of the rich, were outstripped by schools linked with the cathedrals in the turbulent towns.

Eventually some of the schools in the towns developed into 'universities' (meaning guilds of students at first without their own buildings or regulations but with just enough money to pay fees to lecturers). The university of Paris developed out of the school run by the cathedral of Notre Dame and the first privilege granted to its students, by a king in 1200, promised its students that if they rioted they would be tried in the bishop's court. The university of Bologna, specializing in law, had been recognized a little earlier; Oxford and Cambridge were later offshoots of Paris. In these early days the universities gave little trouble to the Church which most of their students were going to serve. But the days came when young monks and priests-to-be were sent to a university for their education and when the university of Paris would regard itself as Christendom's intellectual centre, with a responsibility to give guidance in doctrine, and it was found that in such places where questions were not unknown there was not the intellectual security which could nourish intense devotion—as Bernard's hostility to Paris made very clear. There was not even the training in Latin elegance which had shaped some of the Cistercians (most conspicuously Bernard) or Franciscans (most conspicuously Bonaventure) as they advocated a mystical holiness in a language of which the great pagan orators would not have been ashamed. The slow recovery of the philosophy of Aristotle, mainly through the Muslims of Sicily and Spain, brought to western Catholicism not only a larger body of scientific knowledge, or of what was believed to be knowledge. It also made available fascinating new tools of logic, of the arts, of thought and argument. Silvester II, who was appointed by an admiring emperor as the first French pope in 999, had taught logic, mathematics and music along with the Bible and the Fathers while master of the cathedral school in Reims and the rumour spread that he had made a pact with the Devil. His pupil Fulbert opened the cathedral school in Chartres before becoming its bishop. Fulbert's pupil Berengar, who was for a time the schoolmaster of the great monastery near Tours, had unusual views about the Mass, although he recanted and became a hermit. There was danger in the air.

In the teaching of Anselm, who became archbishop of Canterbury in 1093, may be found not only one of the cleverest expositions of the medieval union of faith and reason but also some new thinking. He combined orthodoxy with a remarkable streak of independence.

Anselm was an innovator in comparison with Lanfranc, a fellow Lombard who was his teacher and his predecessor as abbot of Bec in Normandy and as archbishop of Canterbury in Norman-ruled England. Lanfranc had refuted Berengar with arguments which showed his own training as a lawyer. In Bec he had taught the sons of the nobility alongside young monks and with unquestionable authority he had taught them the Bible and the Fathers. Anselm, in contrast, restricted his teaching to monks who might appreciate his policy of making them think for themselves. Some monks (at least) responded with delight, but when he submitted his first book to Lanfranc's scrutiny he found that his senior was shocked by how seldom he quoted the sacred authorities. His own style was to use logic in words as simple and as fresh as their difficult subject-matter allowed.

The result was never a disagreement with the Catholic Church and the one critic who accused him of heresy was easily demolished. While an archbishop he incurred the wrath of his king because he was so loyal to his pope. As an author he argued against the theologians of the east in defence of the west's traditions. The central beliefs which the west shared with the east could be proved, he believed, as the necessary results of reasoning, admittedly after being accepted on the authority of the Bible and the Church. 'I believe in order that I may understand', he wrote, and his advice to others was 'if he can understand let the Christian rejoice but if not, let him revere'. But his style allowed for some individualism: when he wrote prayers, he circulated them as his own and they were the prayers of 'I', not of 'we'. His style also allowed for some developments in the theological tradition under the pressure of logical questions, particularly in two fields.

His *Proslogion* resulted from a desire to find a proof of the reality of God simpler than the traditional proofs taught by Augustine (for example), which he fully accepted. He argued that the idea of God is the idea of 'that than which no greater can be conceived'. But if this is thought to be an idea which is real only in the mind, then the idea of a God who is real outside the mind is greater. Therefore it is impossible to think about God seriously without thinking that his reality is more than an idea. When a monk raised the objection that it is possible to think about an island which does not exist, Anselm was pleased because it gave him the opportunity to explain that his proof applied only to the reality of God, for the very idea of God is the idea of 'necessary being' and that is different from the existence of a mere island. His logic was, in fact, so well-wrought that it has never ceased to interest philosophers, but it may be enough for students of history to observe that the whole book was in character akin to the prayers which he also published for the benefit of Catholic believers. To him, as to countless other monks, God's reality was indeed obvious. Only a fool could deny it. Without it, prayer would yield no results; morality would be as pointless as prayer; the medieval society would revert to the violence from which it was beginning to emerge; heaven would be closed to all, not merely to most. But in Anselm's heart there was special love for the God-filled life of a monk. As a young man he had left home deeply unhappy and confused. In Bec he had found a family to which he could belong: the family of faith.

Twenty years later, now an archbishop but given the leisure of exile, he completed another famous book, this time explaining why it had been necessary for God, the Son, to become Man. Anselm had found arguments with a coarse king and a brutal baronage totally uncongenial but his involvement in Anglo-Norman feudalism had helped him to teach a new way of stating the truth of the incarnation. His emphasis was on justice, 'being what one ought to be'; to him freedom was the ability not to be unjust. A kind of justice, the insistence that everyone is entitled to respect for his 'honour', bound together kings, overlords, tenants and serfs. A greater justice ought to unite God, angels and humanity. But some of the angels had rebelled and so had Adam, and after Adam's affront to his honour God's justice had to be satisfied much as a king or other lord had to be satisfied after a rebellion: an adequate penalty had to be paid by the transgressor or his family. The honour of the Lord God was at stake. To belittle this was, he maintained, to deny the enormity of sin. The difficulty was that no human recompense for rebellion against God could be satisfactory, for the sacrifice of all the creation could not satisfy God's just wrath. The payment needed could be provided only by God the Son after incarnation. As God he is greater than the creation but as Man he belongs to the human family of sinners while being himself completely innocent. So the satisfactory payment is made on the cross, where the Son is willing to abandon the immortality to which he is entitled.

Anselm quietly disagreed with Augustine about a number of doctrines. For him the sacrifice offered by the Son to the Father was a death needed to appease the Father, whereas for Augustine 'sacrifice is offered in every act which is designed to unite us with God in a holy fellowship'. Anselm also rejected the theory that Christ on the cross had freed humanity by paying a ransom to the Devil: with his acute sense of justice, he was sure that the Devil was a usurper who deserved no ransom because he had no legitimate rights. And he disagreed with Augustine's belief that concupiscence or lust is central in 'original' sin: his sense of justice made him see Adam's general rebellion against God's justice as the great disaster. But his willingness to dissent from Augustine invited other theologians to criticize him and many have done so. Those who wished to do him justice have had to grant that his theology was not entirely derived from feudalism. At least as relevant was the Church's own system of penances, where a kind of payment in suffering had to compensate for every sin. Nor was his theory based on any idea that God is too angry to forgive and be satisfied by Man: the basic idea is that God the Holy Trinity provides the sacrifice which restores the 'rightness' of divine justice. Yet the theory could easily be debased into being a suggestion of a legal transaction between Father and Son, or between God and Man, under a system which demanded the death in agony of a totally innocent victim; and when so understood, the theory could be denounced as being monstrously unjust.

When Anselm died in 1109 Peter Abelard was already thirty years old. His character was utterly different. Although he could never bring himself to contradict the Bible or the Church outright, he was plainly eager to expose the deficiencies of his seniors who expounded these authorities. Born into the minor nobility of Brittany, he was (as he later recalled) ambitious for money and fame, and he rode into theological disputes like a knight overthrowing opponents in a tournament. He specialized in humiliating venerable teachers and when he began lecturing himself (for fees), his method increased his popularity with students. He would read out extracts from the set books but would then raise questions about shades of difference between them, and finally deliver his own verdict, his 'sentence'. This was to be the standard method of teaching in the 'scholastic' method of the universities, with formal disputations leading to the higher degrees, but Abelard's was an early and cocksure performance and it caused a sensation with the claim that 'by doubting, we come to questioning and by questioning we perceive the truth'. He published a collection of 158 quotations from the Fathers which seemed to contradict each other (*Sic et Non*) and his own writings presented a theology which also startled the conventional. He stated that 'the Holy Fathers sometimes propounded, or even wrote down, what they thought was true but was not in fact true'. That could not be said about the Bible: if a statement in it seems 'absurd', it is the fault of the copyist, the translator or the ignorant reader. But what does the Bible teach? Abelard interpreted it as saying that Christian morality is not obedience to moral laws defined by the Church: it depends on one motive, love for God. 'Sin is contempt for God or consent to evil, and the love of God which calls forth our grief allows no vice.' The crucial thing about the cross is that it demonstrates God's love, not the satisfaction of his own rights or of the Devil's. It was 'a unique act of God's grace' that 'his Son has taken our nature upon himself and persevered in it, teaching us by word and example even unto death'. Thus 'God has more fully bound us to himself by love with the result that our hearts should be enflamed by such a gift of divine grace and true love should not now shrink from enduring anything for his sake'.

To Abelard's critics this interpretation of the Bible seemed disastrously inadequate. They insisted on the biblical passages which present the death of Jesus as an objective sacrifice, ransom or victory, and a furious Bernard quoted the words repeated at every Mass about the blood 'shed for you and for many for the forgiveness of sins'. And when Abelard applied his sharp mind to traditional doctrine about the Trinity, he so stressed the unity of the Three that he earned condemnation by two councils of bishops. It did not help his cause when his brightest pupil, Arnold of Brescia, was invited by an over-generous pope to study in Rome in order to cure him of radicalism. Instead of imbibing orthodoxy this young man led a revolutionary commune which expelled the pope and ran its own church with a drastically simplified organization and doctrine. When papal troops recaptured the city he was executed.

The disaster which cut deepest into Abelard's heart arose from an encounter between what he called 'my exceptional good looks as well as my great reputation' and a woman who 'did not rank last in beauty, while in learning she stood supreme'—and who was seventeen years younger and either an orphan or illegitimate. He fell in love. He persuaded Heloise's uncle, a canon of Notre Dame cathedral in Paris, to allow him to lodge in their house and to teach her instead of paying rent. He seduced her, she became pregnant and they went through a secret marriage. She never ceased to love him, but persuaded him (if he needed persuading) that his career, which seemed incompatible with marriage, must come first. She retreated to a convent. Her uncle, already enraged, thought that the tutor who had got her into trouble was abandoning her, and hired thugs who castrated him. Abelard then became a monk, in the monastery of St Denis, and lived to write letters of holy counsel to Heloise, which survived together with her humble and edifying replies which some sceptical scholars think he wrote. Later she became an abbess, but even in those years of holy dignity her letters say that she was still dreaming about his embraces. She was buried beside him.

He had to leave St Denis because he had caused outrage by his demonstration that the founder of that royal and rich monastery had not been the Athenian, Dionysius, mentioned in the Acts of the Apostles. When he took refuge in a little oratory in the countryside further controversy dogged him: experts in orthodoxy were shocked when he dedicated it to the Holy Spirit and the locals were indignant when students flocking to listen to the famous lecturer indulged in unspiritual relaxations. Foolishly agreeing to become the abbot of a little monastery back in Brittany, he was nearly murdered by the monks he tried to reform. He poured out his laments in a *History of My Calamities*. Eventually he found a calm home with the charitable, intelligent and well-behaved monks of Cluny. His last book was a debate between a Christian, a Jew and a philosopher. To the end, theology was for him a task somewhat different from what had been expressed by the Greek word *sophia* or the Latin word *scientia*. It was not chiefly the expression of the 'wisdom' which came from the prayerful contemplation of the revelation given in the Bible and the Church. Nor was it the ordering of the 'knowledge' so derived. It was the discipline of hearing questions about these authorities; of answering them with all possible courage and intellect; of caring for the truth more than for any tradition and of finding God's love as the greatest truth.

Aquinas and After

Some 75 years of theological debate separated Abelard's death in 1142 from the birth of Thomas of Aquino, a thinker who initially alarmed the orthodox but eventually persuaded them that what he thought was orthodoxy.

Aquinas was born into a rich family in the Italian kingdom ruled by Frederick II, and sent as a boy to the Benedictines of Monte Cassino. He began his study of Aristotle in the new university of Naples and when he had insisted on joining the Dominican order (to his family's dismay) he had the privilege of being taught by a scholar already known to his contemporaries as Albert the Great. His temperament was placid, as is suggested by his nickname 'the Dumb Ox'. His piety was straightforward and he wrote devotional hymns which have been used widely from that day to this. He inherited from Augustine an approach both biblical and philosophical but took a more hopeful view of what people could learn about God by looking at his creatures. He also shared with Augustine the belief that God has already decided the number of people who will be saved, but he was more hopeful that the number would reflect God's mercy. He inherited from Anselm an insistence on reasoning rather than merely quoting, but he had the confidence to sort out a much wider range of subjects with a much greater ease. He inherited from Abelard a developed skill in answering questions by arguments, but he had the wisdom not to get involved in indiscretions and calamities.

This was a time when the study of Aristotle's logic formed the centre of the 'Arts' course which prepared undergraduates for the professions or the higher degrees and the main challenge which Aquinas faced came from the interpretation of Aristotle by Ibn Rushd, in Latin Averroes. He had been exiled from Cordoba in Muslim Spain for teaching that there were two supreme sources of truth: Allah's revelation to the Prophet is decisive, at least for ordinary people, but Aristotle's reasoning (with touches of Platonism) can guide the philosophically minded. Thus he developed an unorthodoxy already put alarmingly by Ibn Sina (in Latin Avicenna). For some Muslim philosophers the emphasis on the majestic otherness of God has led to the teaching that all events are directly caused by God without any secondary causes in nature, but the philosophy with which the names of Avicenna and Averroes are associated did not take that line. Here God is the Unmoved Mover. The divine perfection is the beginning of all existence and all existence desires, aims and tends to return to it, but the Mover takes no initiative after the initial move which was the creation. After that God is content to be a magnet and what is ultimately valuable in his creation is what can return to his eternity. That is a severely restricted category. It excludes 'matter' because matter is mere 'potentiality': what really matters, so to speak, is the 'form' of the matter. For example, the 'form' of a human body is the more precious soul. But a 'form' is common to a whole species and the human soul is a spiritual and intellectual life common to all humanity. God is not concerned to save individuals by his providence, although he is willing that humanity in general should be drawn back to its origin in him. When an individual's body dies its surviving form, the soul, is not individual.

It was the task of Thomas Aquinas to meet this challenge. He met it by thinking as a Christian about God. Many others had done that before him, but he did it with an unprecedented thoroughness and with explicit reference to the new questions. Among his many books two stand supreme. A *Summa*, or manual, which he compiled (in the first instance, it seems, for the benefit of other Dominicans) was *Against the Gentiles*, working out a reasoned faith which could, he hoped, convince 'unbelievers' such as the Muslims and Jews of Spain. But even his longer *Summa*, written in Naples and not complete when he died in 1274, had the Averroist challenge in mind. These works are voluminous, they read like lecture notes and they are not easy to absorb without the lecturer's explanations, but it may prove possible to sum up their essential message.

Aquinas relied on a combination of the Bible as officially interpreted by western Catholicism (all of which he accepted as God's self-revelation in words without error) with as much of Aristotle's logic as was compatible with that divine authority. Inevitably the two sources of his thinking came together in the depths of his mind, but he did what he could to distinguish them carefully. He did not want faith to claim too much.

He denied Anselm's claim that it is impossible to think of God as the greatest Being without admitting his reality: he thought it theoretically possible that a philosopher confined to abstract reasoning could reach a different conclusion, although like Anselm he accepted the more traditional proofs of God's existence. He also denied Anselm's claim that the incarnation was demonstrably necessary because God had to have his justice satisfied before he could forgive: thinking showed that God could have chosen to forgive in another way, although this way was appropriate. The doctrine of the Trinity was not the inescapable result of logic, as some had claimed: it depended on the revelation in the Bible although the Church had interpreted this reasonably. And Aquinas criticized some opinions current in the Church as being unreasonable. He did not endorse Augustine's link between guilt and sex. He was more restrained than the Franciscans when he taught about Mary. He did not support the claim of some bishops that they constituted an 'order' superior to the priests: the Mass is the supreme sacrament and so the priest who makes it possible has no superior in 'order', only in 'jurisdiction'. The priest effects a miraculous change in the 'substance' of the bread and wine. 'Substance' is a category derived from Aristotle. It means what lies beneath the 'accidents' such as size, shape, weight, colour or taste. For Aquinas the substance can be changed because of the repetition of the words with which the Lord instituted the Mass, but the accidents—the physical properties—of bread and wine remain the same.

He was cautious about what could be discerned or proved by human reasoning, for everything in the mind has been put there by the senses: God is not an object within the reach of the senses, not even a 'person' in the ordinary sense of the word, and can be thought about only by comparison ('analogy') with the things and people perceived by the senses. He felt unable to answer the question whether the world was created in time or eternity: he had not been there and the Bible gave no clear answer. But for him God must be infinitely greater than the Unmoved Mover. Unlike all his creatures, God does not have a limited 'potential': he is the one, self-caused, all-perfect, 'pure act'. Everything that exists in a lesser fashion is created by him, so that however imperfectly it reveals something of what he is. It can reveal this because nature is orderly and its Creator is not a mass of contradictions. Although he is totally free to do anything that is not self-contradictory, God has decided to act in certain ways and has ordained that he will adhere to them. Although he does not need it in order to be himself, for his perfection lacks nothing, he loves what he has made. Although he is himself not one good thing but complete Goodness, what he loves is the good which is present in everything. Existence is itself good, but God has made all creatures exist in such a manner that they will, if they are true to their own natures, seek to be and do what he wishes, because what he wishes is their perfection. Although he never changes, he is supremely alive and active in his dealings with these creatures. He permits evil to exist in a creation which has to be less than perfect: otherwise it would be divine, not created. He permits human beings to choose evil because he has decreed that their wills shall be free, but he refuses to write off his partly evil creation. He is the Creator of matter and so of individuals, not merely of 'forms' or 'universals' such as 'humanity'. He is the ultimate cause of all events in nature, not merely of miracles; and he controls all human history. He wishes the needs of humanity to be laid before him in prayer. Through the work of the Son and the Spirit, he rejoices to save those human individuals whom he has chosen to save. The sacraments of the Church 'do cause grace'. Love pours out from God, who is aptly called Father.

A doctrine about Man in society results. Following Aristotle ('the Philosopher'), Aquinas denied the Platonic theory that the soul is like a sailor in a ship, using the body but happily surviving its death. But he also denied the Averroist theory that the one soul is shared by all humanity. The soul is the life which God causes in a body as its 'form', so that soul and body are the spiritual and physical aspects of an individual's reality. Although all animals have souls, the human animal is unique in having a soul capable of reasoning and understanding and therefore capable of seeing and enjoying God. The soul is, however, not complete without the body—a problem which Aquinas thought he had solved by looking forward to the miraculous resurrection of the saints' bodies.

He also followed Aristotle in teaching that Man is always 'a political and social animal' and that subordination to a government is natural, not a part of God's punishment after the Fall. Thus he reduced Augustine's gloomy verdict on the City of Earth. The state is inferior to the Church but the Church may not act against it unless it causes sin. Its laws may be broken if they are unjust, but only if the rebellion does not result in a worse disaster. Its citizens even have a right to share in the election of a monarch, although the ideal remains the Christian king who keeps his oaths taken at his coronation.

Some parts in his system were new and it was not received with universal acclaim. Some fellow philosophers protested that it was not faithful enough to Aristotle, and some remained more or less Averroist. But Aquinas was not named when two archbishops of Canterbury warned the philosophers of Oxford against heresy, and when 232 propositions were condemned by the bishop of Paris the attack voiced a general unease about the use of so much pagan philosophy, without naming names. The bishops insisted that God is revealed as all-powerful and all-knowing; that Man has free will; that the soul is separate from the body and therefore able to enter heaven in glory, even before the body's resurrection. For a time it seemed possible that the conservative reaction would discredit Aquinas but the Dominicans made him their official theologian in 1314, and nine years later he was officially declared to be a saint. In 1346 a pope criticized the university of Paris for not studying Aristotle enough.

For a time the Franciscans forbade their students to study Aquinas and many of his conclusions were rejected by two of their friars who had taught in Oxford and Paris, John Duns the Scot and William of Ockham (a village in England). The one died in 1308, the other during the Black Death of 1349. They went much further in limiting the scope of reason. They had no wish to deny Catholic doctrine but for them its truth lay in its revelation to believers of what God had in fact chosen to be and to do. It did not lie in propositions which could often be shown to be the necessary consequences of realities which anyone with the ability to reason ought to be able to see.

John Duns became known as a 'subtle' theologian, but we may be getting at the centre of his complex philosophical system if we remember the simple prayer of Francis to 'my God and my all'. In this system God is infinite being and absolute power, and he is free to do whatever is not self-contradictory.

As things are he has 'ordained' to exercise his power in a certain way. All creation and all history are ordered by his free decision to love what he has made. His love is so great that the incarnation would have occurred even if Adam had not sinned and the atonement would have been possible even if Christ had not died. His commandments are good not so much because they seek our good (he could have chosen to issue other commandments) but because it is his will that we should obey them as aspects of our love for him. The beatitude of the saints in heaven consists not in their vision of God from which love follows (as Aquinas had thought) but in the love which leads to the vision. And all this is known solely because God has chosen to reveal it: 'our theology does not deal with anything except what is contained in Scripture or may be drawn out of it.'

William of Ockham worked out his own philosophy in rebellion not only against Anselm and Aquinas but also against the systematic thought of John Duns. He was, like Abelard, a born rebel. As a 'Spiritual' Franciscan he rebelled against John XXII's ruling against the order's poverty: in his view that ruling made the pope a heretic. He fled to the court of the emperor and from there poured out a stream of pamphlets arguing that the Church should have no wealth and no power over the state, and that if a pope erred the emperor ought to convene a council which would depose him. In philosophy he agreed with John Duns that God's commandments are good because they are what God has decided. But he had no respect for claims that the human mind can understand the divine Being as a logical necessity and that the 'universals' in created beings are more real than any individual. He insisted that 'no universal exists in any way whatsoever outside the mind of the knower', universals such as 'humanity' or 'horsiness' being no more than ideas about similarities between people or things. And people on earth cannot even fully understand what does exist. Our perceptions are intuitions of greater or less accuracy in accounting for the evidence which we experience. They result in names we give to the real people or things, so that this philosophy has been called Nominalism although to the late Middle Ages it was simply the *via moderna*, the 'new way'. People and things are what they are because God has made them so, beyond our understanding. Really to believe in God is to believe that just as human reason cannot reach understanding so human goodness cannot reach holiness; that God is absolutely sovereign; that he reveals his existence and character to those whom he chooses; and that he follows that revelation with grace enough to rescue the chosen from sin and death.

These two radically minded Franciscans, while differing as philosophers, both indicated the end of the assured marriage between faith and reason. As the direction taken by Christian thought since the time of Augustine was reversed, Nominalism became the intellectual fashion. The papacy condemned it but other philosophers developed its radicalism. In the fifteenth century the leading teacher in Paris, John Gerson, had to beg his colleagues not to waste time on such philosophical disputes which had little connection with the challenges of the Christian life or with the urgent needs of the Church. In the sixteenth century the whole of scholastic philosophy was to be ridiculed or denounced. Those who still wrestled with the theology of John Duns were to be called 'dunces' and Nominalists were to be told to study the Bible as the answer to the religious uncertainty from which they ought to escape. The mood was to be very different from the mood of the theologians whose ambition had been to reconcile faith and reason by hard philosophical thought.

Modern theologians have tended to agree that for all his apparently flawless and timeless assurance Aquinas was in fact a product of his place and time, and that for all his apparently logical argumentation he took for granted a large doctrinal system plus the firm belief that heretics deserved death. It is improbable that he ever had a real discussion with a living Jew or Muslim, let alone with an atheist. He not only defended all the teachings of the Catholic west against the Eastern Orthodox; he also accepted common opinions which appeared to be confirmed by the authority of Aristotle. These were particularly unfortunate when they were opinions about the nature of women. From the 1560s Roman Catholics tended to feel obliged to defend almost all that Aquinas had taught, but the system of Thomism had to become 'Neo-Thomism' as some disciples faced up to modern questions and in the 1960s a long reign over the mind of the Catholic Church ended. And this dethronement supplies a special reason to remember the day when Aquinas said that he would write (or dictate) no more because what had been written seemed to him 'like straw'. Perhaps he had had a mystical experience; perhaps he had had a stroke after many years of overwork; perhaps he was simply tired and ready to die, as he soon did while still in his forties. Yet this man who was so aware of the limitations of the human mind had provided a magnificently reasonable account of what western Catholics officially believed for a long time.

The Late Medieval Church

In the late Middle Ages there was little dissent from a Catholicism which had achieved the feat of being both official and popular. Kings and their servants might complain about the political and financial activities of popes and bishops but they displayed no wish to be thought heretical. Theologians might debate about the manner in which the Catholic faith was true, but that it was true they did not question. Priests might complain about their superiors, but they did not resign. People might grumble about priests, but they went to church. At least, that was the general picture.

The reluctance to dispute at a basic level had at least one tragic consequence. Between the middle of the fifteenth and the middle of the seventeenth century about 50,000 people, three-quarters of them women, suffered cruel deaths often preceded by torture because there was not enough official resistance to the popular belief that disasters were being caused by witches. The clergy deserve some of the blame for this evil although they seldom initiated the arrests and trials. In 1482 Pope Innocent VIII bestowed his blessing on witch-hunts, alleging among other things that these demon-possessed people made men impotent (although several children bore witness to his own exemption from this fate). Next year two German Dominicans cited this authority when they published their sensational *Hammer of Witches*, a book which had a wide and long influence. Modern scholars investigating the surviving evidence have agreed that the accusations arose out of neighbours' fears of women (particularly old or single women) or men who seemed strange and sinister. When these witches confessed to having made a pact with the Devil, or to having had sexual intercourse with him, or to having performed a blasphemous and obscene parody of the Mass, they were agreeing with the foul imaginations of their tormentors, often under torture. But it has proved difficult to tell why this craze flourished in some times and places and not in others. General theories that it was a time of religious or social ferment have proved difficult to substantiate about the fifteenth century: there was unsettlement but not to an extraordinary extent. It has also proved difficult to link the phenomenon with Catholicism exclusively, since it was encouraged by Luther and Calvin and flourished during the seventeenth century in Protestant areas such as Sweden, Scotland, England and New England as well as in some (not all) Catholic countries. Much probably depended on the hysteria of some accusers and the terror of some of the accused: hysteria and terror which were infectious. Although there were some later executions, the worst was over for Catholics and Protestants alike by the 1660s. The disgrace attaching to the late Middle Ages is that the intensity of this epidemic of evil began then and was not stopped by the leaders of a religion which was supposed to be rational and humane.

But not all the support given to popular religion in the late Middle Ages had such terrible consequences. It was widely thought and believed that making the sign of the cross, not a very difficult exercise, would terrify devils. While the fear of devils was strong so was the faith in angels, lovely and friendly beings eager to bring supernatural help. Although the wall-paintings of the Doom, showing devils directing naked sinners into everlasting torments, were of course fearful, the images of a joyful faith filled churches at the expense of donors rich or modest. For example, almost every church had a large carving of the crucifixion on the 'rood' (a beam across the church) with Mary and John alongside Christ. Late medieval art did not create many great churches: there was now no need for many more such buildings. What it did create in comparatively small images was to be denounced, and often smashed, by Protestants who thought it evil idolatry, and although in the Catholic world (as in the Orthodox) images proved too popular to be suppressed they were often to be in the more theatrical style of Mannerism and the Baroque. But the art which survives from the centuries when the Middle Ages are said to have been 'declining' suggests very powerfully that the Christian imagination was then not diseased or exhausted. Such art was produced by a society where genuine piety could inspire the artist or the patron and where the community loved and used the work of the artist (who was usually anonymous) because the authorized symbols of religion were also the popular symbols of the community itself.

Theologians did not always agree about the precise connection between God and this popular religion which celebrated human goodness and human skill. Thomas Aquinas taught that God rewards human merits even when he can only foresee them in his wisdom, but William of Ockham maintained that God decided whom to save without regard for their merits and Gregory of Rimini said that God saves some from hell despite their merits. However, the discussions of the theologians suggested to most people who were aware of them that the priority of God's grace could be combined with a general acknowledgement of human virtues. Leaving the more austere theologians in a minority, the usual belief was that God inspires any turning towards him and towards goodness, but once that turning is made, once there is a willingness 'to do what lies in me', God can be trusted to fulfil his promise to supply further grace. That enables the Christian to be really good by forming 'created habits of grace', which God rewards with heaven. (There was a reference to Aristotle's teaching that virtues are formed by habits.) This grace reaches the Christian through the Catholic Church, in particular through the Scriptures and the sacraments. The gift of grace could be nullified if a mortal sin was 'interposed'—but it could be restored. Gerhard Ebeling has summed it up: 'The Church's teaching, and scholastic theology in general, asserted as self-evident that the grace, infused in the first place in baptism and renewed after each mortal sin in the sacrament of penance, inhered in the person who received it as a new supernatural faculty enabling him to live a saintly life, even though still imperfectly.'

It was becoming slightly less rare for the Christian life to be helped by reading. Although probably still confined to less than 5 per cent of the population, literacy was spreading through the greatly increased number of schools. Businessmen became aware that there was a market for a flood of religious books—books translating the biblical passages and read during Mass, books of 'hours' (prayers for use by the laity), books to give advice to godparents and others about their Christian duties. In Mainz in the 1450s Johann Gutenberg began to print by using movable type on paper. It made a vast difference to the availability of the Bible in Latin or translated from it, for in the earlier Middle Ages the skins of three hundred sheep and many more man-hours had been needed to make a hand-written Bible on parchment. Between 1450 and 1500 there were about a hundred printings of the Bible on paper. But that did not cause great excitement; Gutenberg had great financial problems. The Bible remained an expensive luxury in the eyes of most people. Few could read any language. If they could read a Latin Bible they would have to use the Vulgate, the translation made by Jerome in the fourth century with revisions made in Paris in 1226. Probably the most used copies were those printed for lecturers and students in the universities, with spaces between the lines for copying down quotations from lesser authorities. Armed with this annotated Bible, a churchman ought to know what to teach to the illiterate.

The situation did not worry the bishops; they were convinced that the Vulgate which had been the spiritual food of so many saints ought to remain the authorized version. There was no proposal to revise it although many of its translations from the Hebrew or Greek were beginning to be known to be inaccurate. There was no complete ban on translating it, but in England no translation was approved and elsewhere none was much encouraged. Not unreasonably it was feared that the laity reading the Bible without the Church's detailed guidance might become confused or heretical. Far stronger support was given to popular dramatizations of the Bible. 'Miracle' and 'passion' plays made the great events alive again. 'Morality' plays turned the biblical ethics into stories which everyone could understand, with touches of simple humour. These plays were performed by the guilds of tradesmen or other fraternities and were enjoyed by large audiences in the open air.

Although popular religion was full of echoes from the Bible, these were accompanied by many sounds from other sources. The authorities of Church and State, who could use fury and violence against the outright denial of official doctrine, were in practice far more tolerant of habits which many earlier Christians would have rejected as pagan—and were far more willing to attach to the forgiveness of sins penalties ('penances') which earlier Christians would have regarded as trivial.

In the late Middle Ages most people seem to have confessed their sins to a priest, and to have communicated at Mass, only once a year, usually at Easter, although many appear to have neglected to reach even this modest standard. It was still believed that penances had to be performed after the confession and absolution, as an expression of sorrow to God and to 'satisfy' his just wrath, if the forgiveness was to be valid, but by now these acts were usually no more than the recital of psalms or traditional prayers and the real fear was that a far more serious 'temporal penalty' would have to be paid by the sinner after death. This fear could be allayed by obtaining an 'indulgence'. Early in the sixteenth century it became possible to purchase from the papacy a licence to secure from one's favourite priest a full and final remission of all sins when in danger of death, thus guaranteeing entry into heaven. 'Indulgences', designed to remit the 'temporal' penalties which would otherwise punish a more limited range of sins, could be obtained more easily and were printed for wide distribution. For example, a merchant who daily committed the sin of usury could spend some of his profits on the purchase of an indulgence. The explanation of this system provided by a pope in 1343 would have surprised earlier churchmen. It was, however, in keeping with the character of Clement VI, the character of a French nobleman who was not above the profits to be derived from commercial bargains. He disliked disappointing any petitioner and was even happier than usual when petitioners enabled him to finance his sumptuous lifestyle in his fortified new palace in Avignon. He explained that the Church could draw on a 'treasury of merits'. Christ's blood shed on the cross had been 'copious' beyond what was needed to purchase Man's redemption from 'original' sin and the virtues of the saints had been more than the price of their own admission to heaven. The Church could now distribute the surplus to those willing to provide a proof of their penitence. A welcome substitute for the traditional penance was a payment in cash. Yet the Church which used such escapes from moral seriousness by an interpretation of indulgences which was to be drastically revised in 1967 was also the Church which used the great hymn about the final *dies irae* ('day of wrath') written by Thomas of Celano, the friend and biographer of Francis of Assisi. That vision of divine justice was also a plea to Jesus, 'king of awful majesty', to be the 'fount of mercy' remembering his love for sinners shown on his cross: 'let not that labour be in vain.'

If preached in the local language, with gripping stories and other rhetorical attractions, sermons could command audiences and change lives, usually by dramatic warnings of God's punishment of sins in eternity and by enthusiastic announcements of offers of rescue from the otherwise inescapable wrath and hell. Most preachers in this category were friars. Some preacherships were endowed by the laity of the parish churches but usually sermons by parish priests seem to have consisted of matter-of-fact reminders of the Church's traditions and of notices about parish life. Hymns were sung but were far less important than they were to become. Popular religion had its focus in actions, not words.

The heart of the Christian life after baptism was the Mass. This had become for most of the faithful laity a mysterious rite performed by a priest, and people formed an audience which often chattered as he recited the Latin words. Kings and merchants transacted business; wives discussed the neighbours; young men exchanged glances with young women. A moment of unity came not with a communion, or with direct greetings, but when a small board, the *pax*, was passed round to be kissed. Another moment came when (in a custom which had spread everywhere) the consecrated wafer was elevated by the priest for adoration. But increasingly it was now believed that the supernatural power could be available without going through a Mass. Consecrated at a Mass up to seven days previously this 'host' was 'reserved' in a tabernacle or *pyx* (usually hanging above the main altar) or displayed through glass in a 'monstrance', and it could be adored in a service of 'benediction' or carried round the parish or the town in a Corpus Christi procession. The host could be said to be 'God' because it was believed to contain the substances of both the body and the blood of Christ, and this belief was made more secure by many reported visions of bleeding flesh. People whose lives were usually obscure and short were moved by the smallness of the wafer and by the thought of God knowing death. In this period the devotion of the 'stations of the cross' became popular, following Jesus through his humiliation to his self-sacrifice. The devout meditated intensely on his wounds and even simple souls could venerate his 'precious blood'. At its most Christian, the adoration of Christ in the host was expressed in the fourteenth-century prayer *Anima Christi* ('Soul of Christ sanctify me, body of Christ save me . . .').

It was the awesome privilege of the priest to 'offer sacrifice' ('this my sacrifice and yours', he said) which in some sense repeated the sacrifice of himself which Christ had made on the cross. The more times the sacrifice could be made, the more powerful it would be in securing mercy and forgiveness. If asked why it had been necessary for Christ to die so painfully, probably most people would have answered that he had to do so on behalf of humanity in order to satisfy the just wrath of the Father against sin. In popular religion the Father was therefore not loving in any obvious sense, the Son loved to the extent of dying on behalf of sinners, but it was the Mother of God who embodied love most attractively. Sculptures and pictures presented the Son as a corpse on the knees of his tenderly mourning mother. Alternatively, it was popular to see him as a baby on her knees or at her breast. Woodcuts made it possible to pin up such pictures on cottage walls.

When the thought was of humanity glorified, Christ's resurrection was not forgotten but the image of his mother, a model of innocence and loveliness, was celebrated with a joy which outran the official doctrines. The first Latin hymns had been addressed to her in the fifth century and festivals in her honour which had started in the east had been included in the western Church's calendar since late in the eighth century. During the next hundred years the belief had become general that she had been 'assumed' into heavenly glory without passing through the body's decay or the soul's cleansing. Many now also believed that she had been free from sin—from 'original' sin as defined by Augustine and also from personal sin. This belief was harder for the theologians to accept: they gave a higher priority to the belief that Mary's Son was needed as the Reedemer. John Duns opened up a way out by teaching that Mary was saved in anticipation of Christ's merits and in 1439 the council of Basel described this as a 'pious doctrine in conformity with the worship of the Church, the Catholic faith, right reason and holy scripture'. Forty years later an annual festival based on this belief was authorized for optional use. There was less hesitation about the much older belief that Mary's virginity had been perpetual. The natural interest in her family life tended to focus on legends about her parents (Anne and Joachim) and her own childhood. Many believed that her home in Nazareth had been transported by angels to Loreto in Italy, a centre of pilgrimage from the 1470s.

The twelfth century had introduced the biblically based devotion *Ave Maria* ('Hail Mary'), the thirteenth century had begun the ringing of the *Angelus* bell three times a day in order to remind the faithful, and around 1500 a prayer for her intercession in the hour of death was added. The use of the beads of the 'rosary' helped people to recite many an *Ave* while meditating on her life. She was the *mediatrix* of divine grace to sinful humanity. She was the Second Eve as her son was the Second Adam, reopening Paradise. She was to be 'adored' as the Queen of Heaven. Many late medieval theologians extolled her glories while being careful to avoid calling her divine. For practical purposes in popular religion, however, she was often believed to function with much of the power of God and this informal inclusion of the feminine in the Godhead should not be forgotten when we consider why late medieval religion was so popular. Less attention was paid to the Holy Spirit, partly because the image of a fluttering bird was less attractive than the image of the young mother holding up her baby in order that others might share her love for his perfection. When the Annunciation was pictured even the many-splendoured archangel was eclipsed by the beauty of Mary, often with a handsome home in the background. A picture of Mary enthroned, perhaps with the donor and his family kneeling near, brought recognition and delight.

Lesser saints were readily recognized—in sculptures or pictures by the symbols which they carried, in daily life by the miracles which they performed. Saints could always be prayed to in emergencies. St Margaret was begged to erase the pains of childbirth, St Christopher the dangers of travel, St Roch the ravages of disease. In 1505 Luther vowed to become a monk if St Anne rescued him from a thunderstorm—and became one. So anyone could turn to an invisible mother and family in any hour of need. But the visible Church was also always there—and in the foreground. Anthropo-logically speaking, its 'rites of passage' were some of the most impressive in all history. They gave dignity to life's natural turning points, beginning with baptism soon after birth and ending with the anointing on the deathbed with prayers for the soul's journey to heaven. And those rites did not seem to be mere ceremonies. The clergy were the main educators and guides of the baptized, beginning with elementary schooling under the clerk of the parish. Higher schools were usually attached to religious foundations. A university was chartered by the pope, its graduates often looked for employment to the Church, and its theologians always needed it as their only audience: they might dispute about the precise relation between faith and reason but to the public it looked as if what was known by the educated harmonized with what was felt by simple people, who were grateful for the sense of psychological security. The system worked.

People were becoming more conscious of the passing of time but when dates were used they usually referred to the Church's many festivals, including many saints' days. These 'holy days' were about a hundred in the year, although the days when the faithful were supposed to fast were almost equally numerous. Church bells marked the beginning, middle and end of the working day, and were believed to ward off thunderstorms, although there were some clocks, operated by water or, more rarely, by mechanism. The hours were described by references to the Church's daily services, from Lauds as dawn broke to Compline at bedtime, with Matins at midnight. And the ending of time by death did not interrupt the Church's ability to comfort. In 1476 Pope Sixtus IV offered indulgences which clearly remitted punishments for sin after death and many thousands took advantage of this offer. At the same time many gifts and endowments financed Requiem Masses and whole new institutions to pray for the souls of the faithful departed. Kings and nobles paid in their wills for large numbers of Masses to be said for their benefit after their deaths: in England the first of the Tudor dynasty, a monarch often thought to be miserly, paid for ten thousand Masses. The gentry and merchants followed this example as lavishly as could be afforded. Even people who could not pay to be remembered on such a scale were not excluded: it was generally thought that the bare minimum was one Mass soon after death, followed by another on the first anniversary. Many people belonged to fraternities which made sure that care was taken of the welfare of members who died. In late medieval churches some tombs included statues of rotting corpses beneath bishops and other great men carved in their grand robes. Thus the Church preached by word and symbol about death as the doom of all but the setting made it plain that the message was not one of despair. Near to the tomb there was always the Mass.

As people responded to life before death, however, they did not always treat religion as the Church wanted. Specially in the countryside the Church's official routine was mixed up with a more deeply rooted tradition of rites, incantations and charms intended to force supernatural power to act favourably. A phrase from the services in church, or a consecrated host or a small relic of a saint, could be used in this magic. And when things went wrong swear words were usually religious.

Many amusing scandals were told about the clergy and the nuns, usually about the victories of their sexual appetites over their still professed vows of celibacy. Such priests might forfeit respect through their hypocrisy although its causes were well understood and the tales of Boccaccio and Rabelais raised chuckling talk of this kind to the level of literature. Many nuns had an excuse: their families had put them there without any vocation. The financial greed of the clergy was also the topic of much talk, with less humour. It was irritating when the clergy claimed their tithes, a tenth of all agricultural produce, for which they had not sweated in the fields—or when friars begging in the streets brought moral pressure to bear on women worried about feeding their families. It was more than irritating when parishioners were told that a failure to produce a tithe was a mortal sin deserving excommunication on earth and hell in eternity unless absolved by a priest, or when a priest claimed a 'mortuary' as a fee for burying a man's wife, taking perhaps the matrimonial bed or (as was alleged) the equivalent of a month's wages for an unskilled labourer. Although the clergy paid their own taxes to the pope or the king it aroused real resentment that they were not taxed like the laity and were not usually subject to the ordinary courts.

The position which the clergy had come to occupy was, indeed, the most obvious weakness in this popular religion. Men were attracted to ordination in large numbers but in the immaturity of youth. They might be driven by a lifelong sense of a vocation or be blinkered in a passing phase of adolescent piety, or be under pressure to find a job more secure and comfortable than most. Whatever their motives they would find that no official provision was made for their spiritual development or practical training unless they became novices in a religious order. The abler students in the universities could progress to the study of theology rather than logic or medicine, but anything which future parish priests learned about their duties had to be picked up from observation, conversation or books of advice. And the whole system of the Church which they entered with this lack of preparation suggested that pastoral work did not have the highest priority.

The religious orders still had some prestige, at least in their own eyes, but were not controlled by the local bishops because they were not intended to serve in parishes. Some of these 'religious' concentrated exclusively on their own activities in their houses and many rumours circulated that these activities were not always restricted to worship, study and work approved by the monastic rule. Other 'religious'—most notably the friars and many of the Augustinians—made themselves more available to the people but not with a parish priest's regular obligations. Alongside these religious orders a disorganized multitude of 'Mass priests' had appeared. These were attached to cathedrals or colleges, to parish churches or to separate 'chantries' in order to say Requiem Masses. They could do some other work such as teaching, and might well need to do so in order to survive financially, but their priesthood carried with it no duties to the living.

Within the system of dioceses and parishes the bishops and their cathedrals also retained some prestige along with considerable wealth. But in the first half of the sixteenth century a very eloquent silence was to show how feeble most bishops were in the discussion of spiritual or intellectual issues: they could not respond to the challenges of the Renaissance and the Protestant Reformation. This was not because they were absorbed in pastoral work. Many bishops gave their time to occupations other than the oversight of the parishes—in the service of the pope or the king, or in the administration or enjoyment of their own large estates. Some were men of noble birth; some were statesmen or senior civil servants; some were distinguished lawyers. Some, such as the prince-bishops in Germany, were among the richest men in the land. A few bishops effectively ran both Church and State: such were Ximénez de Cisneros in Castile, Georges d'Amboise in France and Thomas Wolsey in England. Ximénez had been a Franciscan friar and even when entrusted with the regency of the kingdom continued to lead a life of prayer and austerity, devoting much of his income to the encouragement of scholarship and education and much of his energy to the reform of laxity in monasteries and among his fellow bishops. Other men with such opportunities were, however, convinced that their lifestyle needed to be supported by being bishops of more than one diocese at the same time (as in Wolsey's notorious case), in a 'plurality' allowed by the papacy in return for a large fee. Other bishops could be almost as poor as their clergy, partly because many dioceses were too small while others were too large: almost half the Catholic bishops of Europe were in Italy, and underpopulated Ireland had more bishops than England plus Wales and Scotland.

The cathedrals maintained the daily round of worship and pilgrimage, almost like monasteries, but the canons who were theoretically responsible might resemble the bishops in having other more absorbing duties or other paid positions in Church or State. Most of their duties could be delegated to more lowly substitutes ('vicars'). In the parishes too many priests were only 'vicars'. These performed duties on behalf of absentee 'rectors' who kept the bulk of the income. Priests might be supported by more than one 'benefice' if a 'dispensation' from the Church's normal law was obtained from the papacy.

In 1265 Pope Clement IV asserted the right to appoint to all bishoprics by 'provisions' and to many lesser benefices by 'collations'. In 1335 Benedict XII claimed the right to appoint to all benefices whatsoever. He was a reformer who did what he could to insist on high standards of pastoral care, but those so appointed were subject to heavy tax (the 'annate') on the first year's income and naturally the appointment could not be arranged without fees, or bribes, to officials. Naturally, too, the system became more complicated because local patrons did not tamely accept their exclusion. In practice kings could usually assert the right to be at least consulted about bishoprics. In Spain and France the monarchs sought, and in the end obtained, a more formal arrangement by which they appointed all bishops. The 'patrons' of parishes were also not easily dismissed: in Germany they and the popes dealt with vacancies occurring in alternate months. It was a system which reinforced the impressions that a church was a piece of property, that a bishop had prior obligations to the pope and the king and that the spiritual welfare of the diocese or the parish was not the decisive consideration. In the eleventh century the papacy had been in the forefront of the campaign to end the scandal of the purchase of offices in the Church. Now papal officials relied on payments for arranging appointments, often in plurality. Under papal leadership bishops had then been exhorted to act decisively as reformers. Now they presided over the system, administering it either personally or more often through deputies, and usually they did not find it very difficult to satisfy their consciences. In England in the 1350s Parliament legislated fiercely against papal 'provisions' and against appeals from English to papal courts. The laws were not strictly enforced but remained available for use.

Reforms were often talked about. The council of Vienne in 1311–12 urged on the Body of Christ 'reform in head and limbs', but no international bishops' councils were held during the rest of that century and when councils did meet and talk they were preoccupied by their struggles with heretics or popes and by their members' defence of their own vested interests. When another Lateran Council met in 1512–17 the talk was still continuing.

Preachers of a stern morality could be heard, alarming but prone to exaggerate vices and to be unrealistic about reforms. These included eloquent saints, Bernardino of Siena among the Observant Franciscans and Vincent Ferrer among the Dominicans. Some priests were not afraid to attack the corruption and lack of care for people in the higher clergy as well as in the higher laity, and their voices too could be heard: in this class was the author of *Piers Plowman* in England, who earned his living saying Requiem Masses in London but had a vision of Christ as a worker. At the extreme of indignation there was Savonarola the Dominican friar in Florence, fascinating even the intellectuals with his austere simplicity, morally compelling the worldly citizens to burn their 'vanities', finally blazing himself as the fire ordered by the pope consumed his body but not the memory of his protest. However, none of these prophets had the power to effect permanent changes.

If we ask how realistic were more official proposals for reform, we can look at the failure of the reforming mission in Germany in the 1450s. Nicholas of Cusa was a man of high spiritual and scholarly stature, now a cardinal commissioned by a worried pope. He ran up against entrenched opposition from bishops and clergy who had no wish to be reformed. He turned for help to the rulers of the little states, but without much response. He had equally little success when asked to review the work of the papacy's officials. He urged the end of licensing pluralities and granting indulgences, accepting a large financial loss. He advocated that a team of three wise men 'should not fear to correct the pope' and that a council of cardinals should meet daily to advise him. Nothing happened.

Another able and influential cardinal, Pierre d'Ailly, wrote much about church reform. He wanted a simpler Church, with fewer images, ceremonies and saints' days; above all, with fewer clerical sins and fewer fees. He wanted fewer religious orders, and these to be controlled by the bishops. He wanted the cathedrals to be centres of theology and education, not mere sources of income for the privileged clergy. He wanted the bishops to be active pastors and to disentangle themselves from politics. He wanted the cardinals to live and work modestly and to elect a non-cardinal as pope in every other vacancy. He wanted the popes to confine excommunications to serious sins and the whole Church to be reformed and guided by regular councils. He wanted many things which he did not get.

The complacency of most of the authorities is understandable. 'Inquisitions' against heretics by papal agents (mostly Dominican friars) or the local bishops were supported both by the local authorities and by the bulk of public opinion. Heretics seemed antisocial. Those who derived good incomes from the system were naturally inclined to accept it while others hoped to benefit from it. Many people used the procedures involving the papacy to get jobs in the Church, to settle legal disputes or to be told officially of the forgiveness of their sins. They often grumbled about the costs but they paid. Many ambitious churchmen collected benefices or petitioned for them: a useful career in the service of the state could be financed in this way and a scholar seemed to deserve such support. Kings asserted their rights but in practice made convenient arrangements with the pope, a fellow king. The laity complained about the demands of the clergy for tithes in the parishes, for fees in the churches or for alms in the streets, but no one worked out how else the clergy could be paid. The numbers and idleness of clergy seemed excessive and some of the most obviously outdated monasteries or nunneries were closed down, but no one could suggest how to stop laypeople wanting to be ordained, or to be made monks or nuns, in such numbers—or how to stop payments being made by the laity, particularly for Requiem Masses. The system survived because most people loved parts of it and few people were determined to end the bits they did not like.

Spirituality

In the late Middle Ages some Christians were utterly serious about faith, prayer and life. They were satisfied neither by the intellectualism of academic theology nor by the commercialization of popular religion. One such was Dante Alighieri (1265–1321), for whom a belief in heaven, purgatory and hell was important not because it was a subject in a course of lectures, or because it could lead sinners to buy the Church's forgiveness at bargain prices, but because it was the logic of the belief that God judges sinners, exacts a penalty for every sin even after forgiveness and shares his own perfection only with the purified. Dante believed that Christ on the cross paid the penalty for Adam's 'original' sin but that every individual's sin deserves a precise punishment and every life is eternally momentous.

He was the first Christian to be a poet truly great in insight as well as in technique, as great as the Vergil who accompanied him in the pilgrimage of his imagination to the edge of Paradise. He disciplined himself in order that he might belong to that very small class. As a young man he worked hard at the poetry of courtly love in the 'sweet new style'. Then he set himself to acquire knowledge and skill in philosophy and theology, presumably using the libraries and scholars in Florence and perhaps taking advantage of the nearest university, in Bologna. But supremely he used for his education the worst disaster of his life, when he was exiled from Florence because Boniface VIII thought him an enemy of the Church: he was promised death by fire if he ever returned. Already his *New Life* had provided his own commentary on his poems about the woman whom he had idealized, Beatrice, who was in fact a banker's wife dead at the age of 24, and he had shown a sensitive mind working on the experience of young beauty and young death. Now he slowly became willing that twenty years of exile should be the time when his mind grew big enough to think about human destiny and original enough to devise a communication which would be remembered by people unmoved by theories.

For a time he was half-drowned by bitterness and by futile plots to recover his political position. He wrote two unfinished books about his growing interests and convictions in philosophy and religion, believing that even those dignified subjects could be treated for a wide public in the Tuscan dialect, not Latin. Then he turned back to poetry and in the same language began his long labour on his *Comedy*, so called not because it was light entertainment but because it ended happily. The *Divine* was added after his death, when commentators began the interpretation of the greatest book of the Middle Ages. He now communicated his religious and moral vision not through the abstractions of the philosophers (although there were many implicit references to Aquinas and largely through him to Aristotle), but through images as concrete as those in popular religion—only his images condemned almost everything in the life around him and in his own past.

At the beginning of his poem, in a dark wood 'in the middle of the journey of our life', he meets three beasts: a lion representing cruel pride, a leopard representing lust for flesh, a wolf representing lust for money. These have been his own sins and they remain the sins of Florence and of the surrounding Italy. As his own sins had been punished and purged by his suffering, so these sins are being punished or purged in the nine descending circles of hell or on the seven ascending terraces of purgatory. Every sin has a punishment or purgation exactly appropriate in manner and duration: such is God's justice. Infants who die without baptism and virtuous pagans are in hell—but in a part of hell where there is no pain. The most deadly sin is pride, the wrong exercise of the free will which is God's greatest gift to Man. Dante is told that 'all things are set in order and that is why the universe is like God' and he quotes Augustine: 'in his will is our peace.' Since pride disrupts this order, it is a far more serious offence against God than are sins of the flesh. Sinners who in their pride had been guilty of treachery or serious heresy, violence or fraud, are tormented in hell while at the bottom, at the earth's icy centre, Satan the 'emperor of the realm of pain' with three mouths endlessly chews the three men who were traitors either to Jesus Christ or to Julius Caesar, respectively the founders of the Catholic Church and the Roman empire. In contrast, the guardian of the entry into purgatory is Cato although the position is unexpected since he was a pagan who committed the sin of suicide: he is there because he was so public-spirited, so concerned for order and justice in society.

Dante was more compassionate than was the average hellfire preacher of his day, for in his *Comedy* the sins being punished in preparation for heaven include 'mortal' sins which had often been said to merit nothing but an eternity in hell. It is also significant that all the punishment, in hell or in purgatory, is tailor-made to fit the individual's outstanding sin, for the birth of purgatory in Dante's imagination belongs to the general movement of the twelfth and thirteenth centuries which has been called the 'birth of individualism'. But on the whole his great poem constitutes an austerely Christian verdict on much in the politics and the life of the Middle Ages, including the papacy and the senior clergy. The only popes found in heaven are the martyrs among the early bishops of Rome plus John XXI, a Portuguese scholar who was pope for only nine months before the ceiling of his study collapsed and killed him. The circle of hell reserved for heretics is occupied by 'Epicureans' who before their deaths denied the soul's immortality, not by any Christians who merely dissented from papal doctrines. Joachim of Fiore and even the Averroist philosopher Siger of Brabant are, indeed, spotted among the saints in heaven despite papal censures.

Dante was himself a rebel against much in the official Catholicism of his time, judging Christians by how they actually behaved. His *Comedy* agreed with his treatise in prose on *Monarchy*: Christendom's moral salvation must come from God through an emperor not a pope, and humanity's climb to heaven must ascend through the practice of justice leading to faith, hope and love, not through the mere repetition of orthodox words. And the end of the climb is not the earthly Church: it is not even the earthly Paradise. There time continues and images taken from daily life are, although transfigured, not abandoned. To enter the unearthly heavens is different, for the soul must pass through a wall of fire where both time and images are destroyed. The vision of God in the highest is a vision of pure light. As a poet Dante still does his best (the Trinity may be pictured as three circles of light) but for him the ultimate truth is that the soul is dazzled by the light.

Yet he was of course a man of the Middle Ages. He glimpsed the divine love, 'the love which moves the sun and the other stars', but his astronomy was medieval. Below the highest heaven are stars which are moved by angels. They move in perfect spheres around the earth whose turbulent affairs they influence heavily. Ulysses cannot reach Mount Purgatory, let alone the highest heaven, because he sails on the ship of pagan knowledge and morality: he is doomed to perish in the Atlantic. Vergil, although allowed to be the guide through hell and purgatory, has to return after this expedition to Limbo, a castle in the most salubrious part of hell where many sighs express 'desire not hope'. The psychology is simple: a single sin so dominates a character that it deserves a just sentence to purgatory or hell. And the theology is simple: no punishment which is just can be cancelled. And if we look critically into Dante's mind (as into Augustine's) we find characteristics which surprise us in a great Christian: a lack of the humility which leaves the judgement to God, a lack of the faith that the Father is willing and able to forgive completely and to save all who are to any extent open to his invitation, the eclipse of the mercy of God by his majesty, his justice. In the *Comedy* Beatrice is hailed on her thrilling appearance with a number of phrases applied to Jesus in the New Testament, but there is a very strange vagueness about the Saviour and his teaching. The poem is set in the week before Easter 1300 but in it we do not really meet the friend of sinners who became the Lord of Good Friday and Easter. It suggests the deepest reason why painful Reformations were to be needed to put Christ back into the centre of Christianity, to liberate God's love from his justice.

In the great tradition of Italian literature Dante's successor was a scholar also steeped in Latin literature, who died in 1374. Like Dante Petrarch attacked what he had seen of the papacy but he had a positive vision of what Christianity had been and could be. To him theology was a branch not of philosophy but of poetry, because it touched the emotions as well as the intellect. The greatest theologian, Augustine, was not an academic source for quotations to support official doctrines but a human being, still alive, still teaching about life. What he got from Augustine was a sense of humanity's sinfulness and of God's amazing will to cross an infinite distance in the determination to reach that misery.

The impression that popular religion needed to be deepened is also left by the teaching of 'Meister' Eckhart.

Born about 1260, he died not long before the papacy's condemnation of some of his opinions in 1329. In some ways he was part of an essentially stable society. He wanted those who welcomed his message to receive Holy Communion frequently, even daily. He was called 'Meister' because he was a 'master' in the academic sense, an accomplished theologian fit to be compared with Thomas Aquinas whom he often quoted. He too was for a time a professor in Paris but his main work was as a busy leader of the Dominican order in Germany. He agreed with Aquinas that action is better than contemplation because it is its fruit, and he defended Martha in comparison with the contemplative Mary in the gospel's story. Much of his teaching was the traditional exhortation to humility and poverty and, as he assured his accusers when he was dismayed to be charged with heresy, all of it was intended to be orthodox and to be subject to the Church's judgement. But big words which were too many to be always safe poured out of his enthusiasm: he admitted in one sermon that he might be asked 'What is this Silence about which you have said so much?' When preaching in German, rather than writing in Latin, he used rhetorical exaggerations which did not become less careless when some of his excited hearers reproduced the spoken words. And some sermons by others were wrongly attributed to him.

From the material which is almost certainly his own the fact emerges that his spirituality, like Dante's, did not entirely depend on his acceptance of the Church's doctrines and practices. It is not obviously wrong to compare him with Platonic, Hindu or Buddhist mystics. Many of those who heard his sermons were women, for by now most of the Beguines had been given Dominican supervisors. The features of their contemplative prayer which had alarmed the authorities can be found in Eckhart, who did on occasions say that the soul had originally been 'God' and could become that again. Man, he proclaimed, is 'truly of God's race and God's kin'. Himself thoroughly intellectual, he distrusted phenomena which could be said to be hysterical—visions, voices, swoonings, *stigmata*—and he did not use the language about loving Christ which could be said to be erotic. But he certainly taught that what mattered was that God the Son should be 'born in me'. He compared the relationship of Man and God with a drop of water being united with a barrel of wine, and he did say explicitly that 'in the breakthrough to God, God and I are one'. 'Study only this', he once advised, 'how to become pregnant with God.' Using mere philosophical expressions, he taught that the Ultimate is pure, simple Being. The power of this Being makes possible the 'essences' of creatures and these remain in the divine Intellect even when the power of this Being has also created a soul and a body. To be reunited with the One, the soul must be free from all bondage to 'this and that'—from reliance on good works or devotional practices and even from grief for sin, from all selfishness and self-consciousness and even from words or images about God. The naked soul must enter the 'desert', the 'darkness', the 'silence of the Godhead' (*Gottheit*) beyond 'God' (*Gott*). In Eckhart's teaching the prayer to the Father 'your will be done' was boldly interpreted as 'may I become He'. The possibility of becoming nothing less than that was the consolation which he offered in a little book written for a queen of Hungary whose father had been murdered, and becoming divine was the adventure which he offered to anyone in church who tried to grasp the storm of his words.

More caution was shown by followers such as the Rhineland mystics, Tauler and Suso. These were fellow Dominicans who guided Catholics along a spiritually safer path. An anonymous treatise written not long after Tauler's death in 1361 promised 'divinization' as the goal but insisted that through the Spirit the Father must do the work of perfecting the soul and that the Son must be imitated in the annihilation of self-will. The stress on the priority of the Trinity's action was such that in the 1510s Luther was to commend that book as reliably biblical and was to publish it as *The German Theology*. Seventy years before this Protestant blessing on medieval mysticism Nicholas of Cusa expounded, as Eckhart had done, the mysteriousness of the God in whom 'contraries coincide'. After the fall of Constantinople he wrote a book to show that the Islamic religion of its conquerors had something in common with Christianity: awe in the presence of this ultimate mystery. His greatest book was called *Learned Ignorance* because he was sure that it was 'learned' to admit to ignorance about the One who thus transcends all human thinking, about the Trinity who transcends all human numbering, about the divine perfection 'beyond the best'. Yet Nicholas accepted all Catholic doctrines as constituting revealed and inspired 'knowledge'. He became a cardinal—and before we accuse him of ambitious insincerity we need to remember what was decreed by the Fourth Lateran

Council in 1215 amid its regulations for church life. The council declared that any likeness between the Creator and a creature is less than the unlikeness. In the medieval Church there was room both for peasants who clung to customs older than Christianity and for the few who thought that the ultimate 'truth' lay beyond human knowledge.

England produced notable mystics during the fourteenth century who prayed and taught within the Catholic framework—Walter Hilton who wrote about the ladder of self-discipline ascending to perfection, Richard Rolle whose writing spread the 'heat, sweetness and song' of advanced prayer, the author of *The Cloud of Unknowing* who promised that the cloud could be pierced by 'darts of love'. The greatest of these mystics was an anonymous woman later called Mother Julian because she was enclosed in a cell attached to St Julian's church in Norwich. She wrote her *Revelations of Divine Love* after contemplating a crucifix during a grave illness and she revised her thoughts after years of meditation. The love, gracious and 'homely', displayed on the cross is the deepest truth about God and she could call Jesus 'mother' (as did others in the Middle Ages). But she always denied any intention to be disloyal to 'Holy Mother Church'. Hers was in a sense a Franciscan spirituality, simple and full of the humility of adoring love, although her book (the first in English by a woman) was much longer than anything which Francis wrote. One of her visions was of 'all that is made' reduced to the size of a hazel nut. She heard the explanation: 'It lasteth, and ever shall, for that God loveth it.'

Somewhat similar was the spirituality of Catherine of Siena although that fiery Italian's vision of Christ did not depend on anyone else's. From an early age Catherine had many intense mystical experiences, culminating in a spiritual 'marriage' with her Lord at the age of twenty and later in a repetition of the *stigmata* received by Francis. She derived from those moments of ecstasy, and from her long study of theologians (particularly Thomas Aquinas), an extensive body of teaching with the key idea that the blindness caused by sin can be overcome by following the light given in baptism, the light of reason given to everyone and the light given when the neighbour is loved at the expense of self-love. She also derived from her experiences the energy needed to lecture the higher clergy about their morals.

Among Franciscans, Dominicans and Augustinians this period saw the spread of 'Observance', a return to the strictness of the original rules. Among monks there was also some renewal, as when the Benedictines of Monte Cassino copied the Cistercians in allowing more time for private prayer and meditation. There was growth in the numbers of the most austere order, the Carthusians. But disputes between the 'Observants' and the more conservative 'Conventuals' split the friars and in most monasteries the numbers sank. Houses of prayer had often become fairly comfortable clubs for priests, including more administrators than mystics and more graduates than thinkers. The spiritually unambitious monks often did not have enough to do: their estates were worked by tenants or hired labour, books were being copied and schools taught by considerable numbers of the laity. These centuries produced no reforming movement which was creative on a large scale and it is significant that the coming age of Protestantism was to see no great lay effort to save the monasteries from destruction.

In the fourteenth century a new and truly creative experiment was made by the Brothers and Sisters of the Common Life. In 1374 Geert de Groote, a graduate of Paris who had been looking forward to a life of comfort, was converted. He was now under the influence of Jan van Ruysbroeck, a Flemish mystic who like Catherine of Siena wrote about the 'spiritual marriage' between the soul and Christ and who persuaded the convert to become a missionary preacher in the diocese of Utrecht. This work, however, involved renouncing both academic sophistication and the endowed priesthood and it did not involve becoming a respectable friar. Instead, Geert de Groote attacked the ecclesiastical establishment on moral grounds and was accused of heresy, with the result that the bishop eventually forbade him to preach. In the 1380s he gathered his followers into small houses in which they lived and prayed, much as the Beguines had done— but they found it easier to earn their livings, partly because most of them were men. They copied books, taught informally and ran hostels for schoolboys.

De Groote's biography was written with admiration by Thomas à Kempis (of Kempen), who as a boy had been one of the Brethren's pupils. He became a secluded monk in the Augustinian order, teaching his brethren about the spiritual life and busying himself with the copying of holy books in this last period before the invention of printing; two Bibles survive in his tiny writing and each occupies ten volumes. He would have been astounded had he known that when printed one of his own books (actually, four pamphlets joined together) was to make him permanently famous. This was *The Imitation of Christ*, first circulated in 1418 and spiritually influential from that day to this. The book was a deeply challenging call to Christian discipleship, a classic on the level of the rule of Benedict, but it was also a book of its own time, becoming the manifesto of the *devotio moderna*. It put Christ's challenge back at the centre of Christianity but assumed that he could be imitated, not only adored as the Saviour of sinners; it intensified the interior life of the Christian, particularly in eucharistic devotion, but without the alarming intensity of the advanced mystics; it was firmly ethical but its emphasis was on humility not heroism; and in one modest way it resembled Eckhart's teaching in that the key to the imitation commanded, and to the peace promised, was total self-surrender. 'What does it profit a man', asked Thomas, 'if he reasons about the high, secret mysteries of the Trinity but lacks meekness and so displeases the Trinity?' The book was never meant to be popular. Its author scarcely ever left his monastery between 1399 and 1471. Written with fellow monks in mind, it assumed the existence of a community in which individuals had to be exhorted to conquer their individualism. Written for a community dedicated to worship and the rest of the religious life in seclusion from the world, it said nothing about a parish priest's pastoral work or about the practical duties of the laity. But the widespread gratitude for it shows that in his own age as in many later periods many Christians were looking for this kind of Christianity and were willing to apply the ideal of Christ-like holiness to their circumstances.

Inevitably most of the evidence about these spiritual movements survives in books or sermons by men. But we get another glimpse of the serious religion of the late Middle Ages if we look at the young Frenchwoman known to the English as Joan of Arc.

Her background was a simple life in an obscure village but precisely because of that she was able to inspire the recovery of the 'holy realm' of France during the English invasion. This peasant girl transformed the morale of the soldiers who came from similar backgrounds when she told them of her conversations with the saints—and she put backbone into their commanders. Having dominated the lifting of the siege at Orleans which turned the tide in the war, she dominated the coronation in Reims which restored sacredness to the monarchy. Captured by the Burgundians, she was sold to their English allies and tried by a court almost entirely composed of Frenchmen collaborating with the English. The bishop of Beauvais presided over the 'justice'. She was tortured and despite her refusal to confess was condemned as a witch. The university of Paris (then under English occupation) added its verdict of guilty. She died by fire in 1431 and although that verdict was reversed in 1456 a long period passed before she was officially canonized as a saint, in 1920. To her last breath she insisted that she really had heard 'voices' when a girl of thirteen, that after this commissioning she was entitled to dress as a man, and that she had no duty to lie or to yield merely because men who were priests had ordered it.

She had not lived for twenty years but her story shows that the men who wrote books or preached were not the only Christians in the late Middle Ages whose religion was a personal communion with the Father, the crucified Christ and the saints.

Premature Reformations

In the fourteenth and fifteenth centuries the stability of the medieval society was shaken by two great disasters and by two great challenges to its religious system.

The Black Death, bubonic plague, was brought by fleas feeding on rats in ships from India. Arriving in 1347, it killed about a third of the population of Europe and the Near East, and did so in a way that was both sudden and unexplained, both agonizing and degrading. Abating in 1350, it returned in the 1370s and at regular intervals until the middle of the fifteenth century. Towns shrank; whole villages were abandoned; many fields no longer grew labour-intensive crops; places where men lived closely together such as universities and monasteries were devastated. One immediate reaction was a collapse of moral conventions: 'tomorrow we die.' Another was an often hysterical intensification of the fear of death and of petitions for escape. The 'dance of death' was often painted or dramatized, showing the grim reaper at work mercilessly. Decaying corpses were carved on tombs beneath the effigies of the great. Flagellants drew fascinated audiences, publicly scourging themselves in penitence and petition.

Another disaster which the Church was powerless to prevent damaged France and England: the war whose most truly heroic figure was Joan of Arc, the Hundred Years' War (1337–1453). England was the aggressor and paid for it by casualties, by pointless expenditure and by the development of an aristocracy which 'retained' little armies under private command, one of the causes of later civil wars (the Wars of the Roses). But English invasions inflicted a temporary ruin on France. The countryside was pillaged; proud knights lay dead on the battlefields or else limped home half aware that their own arrogance had repeatedly brought defeat; the discredited monarchy faced civil war since the dukes of Burgundy, who were virtually kings with their economic base in prosperous Flanders, became the allies of the English. Between battles gangs of ex-soldiers continued to loot and rape in France although some of the English soldiers hired themselves out as feared mercenaries in the smaller wars in Italy. Another disaster for the glamour of crusading chivalry came in Bulgaria, where a French army was cut down by the Ottoman Turks in the battle of Nicopolis in 1396.

The extent of these disasters should not be exaggerated. Medieval armies could do only a limited amount of damage, France recovered and the epidemics, which reduced unemployment and overcrowding, could not stop fertility: after 1450 the population began to climb again and by 1600 had returned to its level in 1300. It seems likely that the Black Death inflicted more permanent damage on Islam than on Christendom until the brutally healthy Turks took over the leadership. But the disasters were large enough to disrupt the social order. Already before 1350 many of the peasants were paid wages by the landlords and had to pay rents, and now there were many disputes about these payments as workers took advantage of the shortage of labour and landlords tried to recoup themselves. Grazing land which had been common to all was now 'enclosed' under private ownership. Food prices rose and this further damaged the towns where the gap widened between the poor and the merchants or employers able to take advantage of the new conditions. Popular revolts erupted dramatically in France in the 1350s, in Florence and other cities in the 1370s, in France, Flanders and England in the 1380s. Bishops sided with the rich and an archbishop of Canterbury was killed in the disturbances, but many of the priests were themselves poor and some became revolutionary agitators. In central and eastern Europe less resistance was offered as landlords made the conditions of serfdom harsher.

Social discontent contributed to new forms of religious heresy. The last burning of a Cathar was in 1330 but for a time the Waldensians seemed to be as dangerous to the Church because they inherited a simple faith from their founder Valdes, whom we have already met. Whereas the *parfaits* who had led the Cathars had expounded myths about the battles between God and Satan, the spirit and the body, and had practised extraordinary austerities, these new heretics preached from the Bible. The central act of the Cathar religion had been the *consolamentum* administered before dying but the Waldensians used the Church's traditional sacraments after simplification in the light of the Bible. The simplicity of their appeal was ominous for the Church but by the sixteenth century persecution had confined them almost entirely to the valleys between the Alps and Italy.

More formidable were two 'heresies' which were started by theologians but gradually became too popular to be exterminated.

A movement which disturbed England sprang out of the teaching of an Oxford theologian, John Wyclif, whose early career gave very few hints that his name was to be revered in cottages and spat out by bishops. His ponderously technical theology recalled, for the few who were aware of it, the teachings of Augustine and Aquinas. But he developed some ideas which were not conservative. To him the great realities were God the Father, Christ and the revelation of the Bible, and he found unrealities in the popular religion of the day. In defiance of the official doctrine of transubstantiation and many practices connected with it, he asserted the continuing reality of the substances of the bread and the wine in the Mass. They became 'efficacious signs' of the body and the blood, not the body and blood themselves, and therefore were not to be adored: real religion must be worship spiritual and truthful. Wyclif was more popular when he attacked the wealth of the higher clergy and in this role he was used in the propaganda of an aristocracy keen to see the Church paying taxes. When he was summoned before the current archbishop of Canterbury, the duke of Lancaster appeared at his side and the archbishop had to take the hint. But before long the lay grandees had no use for Wyclif because his theology about the Mass had become too controversial. All that they could now offer him was personal protection, although his views became more unorthodox still as he grew more frustrated and more angry.

He maintained that the Bible as interpreted by Augustine and other Fathers of the Church was really true and supremely authoritative; that the real Church was invisible, consisting of those predestined by God to receive grace; that the real Church's main task was to preach the Bible. So far, so Augustinian. But Wyclif now went beyond Augustine. Since 'dominion'— all lordship or ownership—is the gift of God, it is rightly enjoyed only by those who are spiritually and morally worthy of it and who live in a state of grace. Whereas the dominion of the lay lords is not to be resisted unless it becomes exceptionally tyrannical, the dominion and wealth of the bishops who are the lords of the Church are evils contrary to the example of the apostles. Priests are entitled to charitable gifts but not to compulsory tithes. They deserve to be paid only if not sinful, 'sin' being defined by Wyclif. And in the end this angry prophet went further still: the immoral or idle priest is no priest, the pope is Antichrist, the whole system over which he presides ought to be abolished and a pure Church established by the state.

Holding such views, Wyclif and his academic disciples had to leave Oxford. He had nothing to do with the Peasants' Revolt in 1381 but after his death three years later middle-class sympathy fell away as the support of the aristocrats had already done: a small rebellion which used Wyclif's name was easily suppressed. Paradoxically, the disturbance which this sophisticated theologian had created survived in the shape of an underground working-class movement, the 'Lollards'. It was fed by a translation of the Bible into the people's language achieved by two of the 'poor priests' who had become his followers. It was moral in a simple, Bible-based way. The bishops felt safe when they largely ignored it, arranging that a few should be burned.

The Hussite movement in Bohemia attracted much more support in every class, and led to more violence, because it was linked much more firmly with the growth of nationalism. Jan (John) Hus was, like Wyclif, a university theologian but he could communicate in a more popular style: in the Bethlehem chapel in Prague he preached about three thousand sermons based on the Bible and Augustine. His message found echoes in a public which, however, was even more interested in its grievances against the rich clergy and against the Germans who seemed to be taking the country over. Contacts with England came when a Bohemian princess married an English king and Wyclif's protests became known. Hus repeated them and was excommunicated. A bishops' council in Constance summoned him to expound his views. His safety had been guaranteed but he was tried and condemned for his association with the Englishman's heresies. His burning in 1415 made him a national hero.

Although united by its hostility to rich clergy and Germans, the Hussite movement soon found itself divided by class. The middle-class and more moderate wing of it, the Utraquists, concentrated on the reform of the Church through the use of the Czech language and the giving of the cup to the laity in the Mass: had not Christ said 'drink this, all of you' and had he not spoken so as to be understood and obeyed? These reformers wanted the clergy to preach more often, and to be stripped of surplus wealth as Christ had commanded, but they intended to be good Catholics. The socially inferior Taborites were far more radical, looking for a new society, a new age and the reign of Christ on earth. They used a very simple form of worship—and, when enemies appeared, the recently invented hand-guns. This division in the ranks of Hussites proved fatal. Many of the moderates were reconciled to the Church when the bishops made a temporary concession by allowing the cup to the laity and in 1434 Utraquist nobles assembled an army which defeated the revolutionary Taborites. A quarter of a century later another group, the 'Unity of the Czech Brethren', emerged and like the Lollards in England kept alive (but flickering in obscurity) what was to become the spirit of the next century's more successful Reformations: a protest against a Catholic Church which could not be recognized in the pages of the Bible.

The Papacy in Trouble

One reason why Wyclif and Hus were able to dent the complacency of the late medieval Catholicism was that the Church had already damaged itself from the inside by uncertainty about its centre, the papacy.

Boniface VIII was succeeded first by a friend who continued his anti-French policy but whose reign was cut short by dysentery, and then by the archbishop of Bordeaux who took the title of Clement V. Feeling insecure in Rome, Clement moved to Avignon. Seventy years passed before the papacy permanently left that town which was separated from the French kingdom only by the river Rhône. Although there were times when popes displeased French kings it was naturally believed that they were under French influence. But many petitioners found it easier to get there than to get to Rome and during the years in Avignon the papal bureaucracy doubled in size in order to cope with the business. Eventually it had to be housed in a palace larger than any in Rome and the profits of this increased business enabled the popes and their officials to live in a style which aroused new quantities of moral indignation, sheer gossip and attacks from people who had not been able to get the favours they wanted. Critics certainly had a point when they complained that a pope ought to set an example by living in the diocese of which he was bishop. Dante condemned Clement for illegality because he subjected the papacy to the French king, comparing him with a harlot paid to make love with a giant. He sent him to hell, joining Boniface who in a very different outbreak of illegality had not acknowledged the French king's just rights.

The Avignonese popes differed in their characters and miniature biographies of them will be one more reminder that medieval people were people. Clement V accumulated a fortune and bequeathed most of it to his family, five of whom he made cardinals. John XXII was hyperactive, spending two-thirds of his income on wars in Italy, denying the right of Ludwig of Bavaria to be emperor, denying also the right of the Franciscans to be without possessions ('a pestiferous novelty') and denying to the saints in heaven the possibility of seeing God ('the beatific vision') before the final, general resurrection. This last opinion had to be corrected by his successor but the Franciscans could secure no redress when they pointed out that as recently as 1279 an earlier pope had supported their right to be poor. The belief that a previous pope could not be corrected, Pope John taught in 1324, was the work of the Devil. Ever an optimist, he sent Dominican bishops to convert the Christians of Persia and India to Catholicism and other envoys to negotiate the submission of the ancient Church of Armenia. Benedict XII was less expansive. A stern Cistercian monk, he had been the inquisitor cleaning up the heresies of the Cathar village of Montaillou. Now he tried to cut down the number of dispensations from the Church's laws which his officials were granting or selling. He also tried to raise the standards of pastoral care by concentrating appointments in his own hands. His successor, Clement VI, was in contrast at home among princes as the smartly fashionable walls of his study in his new palace still show, and he was no more moral than most princes. He lived splendidly but was also a splendidly conservative preacher. He tried to meet expenses by selling indulgences. Innocent VI wished to return to Rome. Urban V did return, temporarily. Gregory XI finally returned in 1378, only to be disillusioned and to die.

In the end, however, all the arguments about whether or not Avignon was more suitable than Rome for the efficient and comfortable work of the medieval papacy were answered by two women. They differed only in their social standing. Bridget of Sweden had been a nobleman's wife and a lady-in-waiting at the royal court before moving to Rome to continue her life of prayer and to serve the poor. Catherine of Siena was the 23rd child in her family, became associated with the Dominicans and felt called by a vision to a public life: she wrote or dictated the forceful *Book of the Divine Providence* and almost four hundred surviving letters. Both women spoke out of the depths of self-denial and contemplative mysticism, Catherine being marked like Francis with the *stigmata* of crucifixion. They were therefore more than a match for worldly ecclesiastics. Both burned with a holy wrath and both proclaimed that the bishop of Rome ought to live in Rome.

Catherine rejoiced when in 1378 Urban VI was elected pope in Rome and she never abandoned his cause. But the election had taken place amid great disorder and under the stress the new pope seems to have lost the balance of his mind. Frightened of his dictatorial instability, almost all the cardinals soon pleaded that they had elected him only because they had been terrified of the Roman mob. They then elected an aristocrat who had been utterly ruthless when in command of the papal army in a war against Florence. While Urban refused to abdicate, this butcher moved what he could of the papacy back to Avignon and was recognized by France and some other nations. The 'Great Schism' had begun, with two popes. In their rivalry successive popes increased expenditure in international propaganda and Italian wars and (partly because they therefore had to become money-grabbers) they reduced the institution's already battered prestige.

Churchmen who wished to rescue the papacy from these popes turned to a doctrine which had been on the margin of medieval theology and canon law: were a pope to become a heretic, he would cease to be a pope. With the support of this doctrine the cardinals united to depose both popes in 1409, but still worse was to come. The two who had been deposed refused to go quietly and when the cardinals' first choice had died they elected (after being bribed) one of their number who was experienced as a pirate, soldier and lover: he took the name of John XXIII. In the end he had to face a council which he had very reluctantly agreed to summon to Constance. After listening to many accusations he fled the city, was brought back, was tried, was sentenced to deposition and was too broken to disagree.

The council now proclaimed its superiority over the whole Church including all popes. After this decree (*Haec Sancta*) it laid down the intervals at which future councils should meet, in the decree *Frequens*. But it failed to establish itself as the Church's effective government. In order to outvote the many Italians who would have supported John XXIII despite everything, it had been divided into 'nations' plus the college of cardinals. Voting was to be by these groups, but the bishops of a nation often looked to their own kings for directions. This symptom of the council's divisions helped the new pope, Martin V, who before election had agreed to its decrees, to restore the papacy to its old power and glory. The senior member of the Colonna family, he needed to be ordained as priest and bishop before he could be crowned as pope and he paid little attention to the council or to the cardinals. Using an iron will and military force, he concentrated on the reconstruction of Rome's ruined buildings and on the reconquest of the papal states as a source of finance for these projects and for the support of other Colonnas. He and his agents had a clear policy while the reformers debated. The German king, Sigismund, who was to be crowned emperor, was away for eighteen months at a time and angered the French by allying himself with the English king, Henry V. Confused discussion took place in five 'nations' (French, Italian, German, Spanish and, to the disgust of the others, also the English) and it turned out to be just that: discussion. Any pope recognized by all Christendom had more prestige than such a debating society and Martin was able to make convenient arrangements with the rulers of the nations.

His successor, Eugenius IV, had more trouble. The Colonnas who had been enriched by Martin joined other Italian enemies and forced him to live in Florence for nine years. A military bishop representing him in the papal states eventually crushed the opposition but he was clearly vulnerable and a council of bishops and abbots convened in Basle in 1431 successfully resisted his overhasty decision to dissolve it. Without dividing into nations this council then produced a sweeping programme of reforms: the powers and income of the papacy were to be reduced and representatives of the universities and the lower clergy were to form the majority in councils which were to be regular and supreme. Offering this vision of a radically changed Catholicism, it succeeded in reconciling most of the Utraquists in Bohemia and seemed about to reconcile the eastern Orthodox. But it was Eugenius who won. The Orthodox preferred to negotiate in Italy rather than Switzerland, and the pope transferred the council first to Ferrara and then to Florence. Many obeyed his instruction to leave Basle because they did not wish to miss the promised reunion of the Church and as the discussions proceeded they agreed that the reunion must be on the basis of Orthodox acceptance of the papacy's claims. Then those who were left in Basle brought back memories of past schisms by electing the duke of Savoy as the last of the antipopes. Eventually the duke abdicated on a pension and the two parts of the council dissolved themselves without much notice by anyone else. Almost all those who had once supported the conciliar movement as the great hope of the Church's reform accepted this anticlimax. The papacy was left in possession of the field.

Yet the conciliar movement was not completely forgotten. Whatever popes might do or say, it was still possible to appeal to a future council against a pope. Kings of France did it; Luther was to do it. The relationship between pope and council had not yet been settled firmly. Indeed, scholars were now adding fresh complications. In his treatise on *Learned Ignorance*, in

1440, Nicholas of Cusa mentioned fascinating speculations: the universe might be infinitely large and the earth might rotate around the sun. But the conciliar movement, with which Nicholas had been identified for a time, had more sharply asked the question whether the Church needed to rotate around the papacy. He himself questioned the authenticity of the Donation of Constantine, a document on which papal claims had for long relied, and a book published almost simultaneously with *Learned Ignorance* went beyond questioning to a learned demonstration that the purported transfer of the western empire to rule by the bishops of Rome was a forgery.

Lorenzo Valla spent nine years as a secretary to popes. His motive in exposing the Donation was not to destroy the papacy: it was to restore its moral position as a centre of unity, with peace between the princes in Italy and reunion with the Christians of the east under a 'holy father'. But this exposure of the fraud was not the only potentially dangerous example of his independence. He published a book noting the defects of the Latin version of the New Testament in comparison with the original Greek. He attacked the claims of monks and friars to be the only 'religious': 'what does it mean to be religious if not to be a Christian?' He wrote a book *On Pleasure*, arguing that to be a Christian was to be truly happy, in this life and the next. Christ's willingness to assume the humility of human flesh and to accept death declared God's love for humanity, 'a love so great that we are constrained to hope'. Shortly before he died in 1457 he delivered a long speech in which he called for an end to the philosophical speculations and arguments of 'Gothic' theology and a return to the 'Christian mystery' revealed in the New Testament: the mystery of this love. So here was a moment of hope that the religion of the late Middle Ages with its 'immense appetite for the divine' (as it was called by Lucien Febvre) might develop into a religion of love between God and Man, a religion with a visible unity held together by the sacraments and institutions of Catholicism but rising freely from hearts and minds beginning to be aware of humanity's capacity for true joys. And in the reformation which Lorenzo Valla envisaged, he took it for granted that this unity would need Rome and its 'holy father'.

The Papacy in the Renaissance

However, instead of leading such a renewal of the Church the papacy now often seemed to be a typical Italian state of the period, glorying in displays and military victories, precisely as Lorenzo Valla had feared.

Around 1550 there was a sense that the achievements of Italian art and architecture in the previous two and half centuries needed to be understood as a completed whole. Giorgio Vasari then claimed that they had amounted to a rebirth reaching the technical standards of the Greeks and Romans, but his decision to write a history of these heroic artists, treating them as personalities, itself bore witness to the fact that the Renaissance had meant more than the recovery of technical skills. There had been enthusiasm for the study of the writings of antiquity, not merely the philosophy of Plato and Aristotle but also the work of the Latin authors who had explored humanity. An *umanista* was now a scholar who in order to discuss and influence human affairs gained eloquence and elegance from the ancients. Like being computer-literate in the twentieth century, that skill did not necessarily involve holding a particular position in religion or philosophy. But the *Renaissance* (a French word) has been understood as referring to a more profound movement of the spirit: 'humanism' (a word coined in 1808), an affirmation of the dignity of Man, body and mind, and of individualism at the expense of the conventions of medieval religion and society. That was the theme of Jakob Burckhardt's influential book of 1860 on *The Civilization of the Renaissance in Italy*. Later scholars have expounded wider themes: the Renaissance outside Italy, the expansion of the European civilization into the other continents, the expansion of knowledge into the beginnings of an understanding of the sun and its planets. The Renaissance has been seen as a vision of a new Europe and a new world, a new humanity and a new universe, and to some extent it was so seen at the time, at least among some of the privileged.

But twentieth-century studies have made it clear that the Renaissance seldom developed into a rebellion against the Church. In Italy, the Renaissance's heartland, everyday church life was left largely unchanged. There were those who made no secret of their contempt for the Church's teachings, but there were not many. Most new works of art were executed with traditional themes for the adornment of churches, and even when the subjects were taken from pagan mythology the lessons which viewers were expected to draw were at least compatible with Catholic doctrine (as when the goddess of love conquers the god of war). Much of the optimism of the 'humanist' elite was supported by a belief in the spiritual nature of Man 'made in the image of God' as Genesis declared, with immortality the logical consequence.

In Italy two well-known humanist scholars stood in the tradition of Lorenzo Valla. Pico della Mirandola prepared a long *Oration on the Dignity of Man* in 1487 while still in his twenties. He wanted to deliver it to a papal commission in order to refute a charge of heresy and although it wandered into many classical and stranger fields its main message was biblical. In effect, the commission let him off with a warning which he heeded. He admired medieval theologians because they sought wisdom heroically and was fascinated by the uncompromising puritanism of a friar, Savonarola; on his deathbed he was clothed as a Dominican. Marsilio Ficino led a small 'Platonic Academy' under the patronage of the Medicis and he led it into speculations about the spiritual nature of all reality and the spiritual unity of all humanity. But he was a faithful priest, enthusiastic when preaching in Florence Cathedral. And these were not the only striking examples of the compatibility of the spirit of the Renaissance with the Christian vision of human dignity. Moreover, even when the discoveries of the Renaissance challenged the medieval vision of this planet there was no great shock to the system. The explorers of the oceans in the 1490s had minds still full of medieval religion and geography. Columbus included the Old Testament in his studies before he set sail and seems to have been completely sincere in his hopes that his discoveries would greatly benefit the Church as well as himself. He encountered a new world thinking it was the edge of 'the Indies' (as Asia was called) or perhaps the earthly Paradise. Copernicus, who by 1530 had discovered that the sun not the earth is the centre of this system of planets, delayed the publication of his calculations until 1543, shortly before his death, because he had no wish to disturb popular beliefs or to get into trouble himself. He need not have worried, for many years passed before notice was taken of his work outside the small circle of astronomers.

Pictures then seen only by the few but now world-famous communicated the hopes of the leading spirits of this time. Beautiful people dance into springtime in a world without demons; angels celebrate above Bethlehem and embrace the sorrowful as demons retreat; richly clad kings with Medici faces pay homage to the Christ child; the crucifixion itself is a calm sacrifice with a delightful landscape behind it; still calm, Christ rises from the tomb at dawn, clutching the banner of victory. As the Renaissance saw things, the world which God made deserves to be loved, analysed and pictured in perspective; the ordered stars deserve to be studied through a telescope; above all, the human body, whose healthy limbs are like the harmony of the Renaissance's new music, deserves to be investigated much more accurately by the surgeon's knife or by the sculptor's chisel making flesh and muscle out of marble. There is nothing wrong with loving, painting and sculpting the naked human body as the Creator's greatest miracle, including the genitals which share his own ability to create always wonderful, always beautiful, life. And there is nothing wrong with marriage. Of course an artist will take pleasure in the adjacent young bodies of Venus and Mars, and the sinners of the Renaissance will take an uninhibited pleasure in each other, but the solemn union of husband and wife in rich robes also calls for celebration.

It might have been possible to make the Renaissance, which included these elements which were at least not hostile to Christianity, more definitely Christian in thought and life. The popes were uniquely well placed to give a lead in that direction as patrons. Rome attracted the leading artists and architects and the papacy provided incomes for scholars. The popes made very high claims to spiritual and moral leadership and the fifteenth century provided two striking examples of willingness to bow to their authority. Instead of clinging to the Orthodox tradition after the failure of reunion plans and the fall of Constantinople in the middle of the century, the ablest of the Byzantine scholars transformed himself from being archbishop of Nicaea to serving the papacy as Cardinal Bessarion. He nearly became pope himself and remained the leader of the Greek scholars who found refuge in Italy until his death in 1472. Instead of going to war over the division of the newly discovered world overseas, Spain and Portugal invited Pope Alexander VI to draw a line on the map in 1493. Although his moral stature as a man was not towering, and the difficulty of his arbitration was shown by the fact that next year it had to be revised by a negotiation between the empires, there was this acknowledgement of the papacy's position above disputes. But in fact the popes, princes within the Italian Renaissance, did not decisively influence it except as players in the game of politics and as patrons of art.

Popes were expected to maintain a bureaucracy large by the standards of that time and a court as impressive as any king's. For this they needed an income drawn from all over Europe, yet the rulers and peoples of the emerging nations were increasing their resistance to the flow of cash to Rome. Apart from the expedient of creating more posts in the bureaucracy in order to sell them, the only alternative was to increase income from the papal states in Italy, which meant popes acting like other Italian princes, including a reliance on members of their own families. These pressures shaped the actions of a dozen popes between 1447 and 1534.

Nicholas V pacified the papal states without too much violence and for the last time crowned an emperor in Rome. He was associated with the treaty of Lodi which in 1454 began forty years of uneasy peace between the 'powers of Italy' although minor wars continued. Himself a scholar, he founded the Vatican Library and was the well-informed patron of Rome's physical transformation. He was followed by an elderly Spaniard, but then by a man better equipped to enjoy the library and the city.

A humanist scholar, Enea Silvio Piccolomini became a secretary to bishops in the council of Basle, to the duke elected as antipope by what remained of that council, and then to the German emperor-to-be. In the intervals of hiring his pen to these different patrons he was a poet and an historian, he fathered several children, he wrote an elegantly erotic novel and a comic play. In his forties he switched to a new life in the service of the papacy, rising rapidly and becoming Pope Pius II in 1458. He now prohibited what he had previously advocated, the possibility of an appeal to a council against a pope. He lived as a handsome although respectable Renaissance figure, building a lovely little city near the village where he had been a boy. He told the cardinals that they had helped to make the priesthood 'an object of scorn' but did nothing about it, concentrating instead on promoting a crusade to go east after reconciliation between Christians. To this he promised his personal leadership. But he died while waiting for ships to arrive from Venice and for soldiers to come to fill them. Still the crusading dream did not die, but later popes were to be equally unable to translate it into concerted European action. Papal policy was to have its focus in Italy. The successor of this would-be crusader was more interested in Rome's buildings and ceremonies. So was Sixtus IV, with more permanent results: he built the Sistine Chapel and founded an excellent choir. Although a Franciscan scholar in his background he became an overambitious politician, trying to overthrow the Medici in Florence and to curb the power of Venice, and he ostentatiously enriched his nephews including the future Pope Julius II: he made six of them cardinals.

The next two popes were insignificant but Alexander VI, a Spaniard by birth, proved highly effective, at least in tidying up the administration, in securing the death of the prophetic Savonarola and in providing for his illegitimate children. One of these, Cesare Borgia, although made a bishop of several sees and a cardinal, was outstanding even among Renaissance princes for cunning and savagery. He was forgiven by his father for murdering his brother and large energies and sums of money were poured into a plan to make him the master of central Italy. Another child was Lucrezia, who was not saved from gossip by being married to three Italian princes.

During Alexander's time as pope Cardinal della Rovere lived in hiding and barely escaped murder, but he did survive and he became Julius II. He commissioned Bramante to design the new St Peter's as Renaissance Rome's greatest masterpiece (replacing the church which had been Europe's most venerated shrine for more than a thousand years) and Michelangelo and Raphael were instructed to adorn the adjacent papal palace. He led armies against his enemies in the papal states (driving Cesare Borgia from Italy), against Venice and against the French—although he had earlier, in 1494, encouraged Charles VII to invade Italy and to conquer Naples. People remembered the spectacle of him as a general in armour; he could not be forgotten, although this megalomaniac's tomb was never completed by Michelangelo. His three illegitimate children could not continue his lifestyle as they were girls. But he bequeathed one fateful legacy: he arranged for the cost of the rebuilding of St Peter's to be met by selling indulgences.

This soldier pope nicknamed 'the Terrible' was succeeded by Leo X, the fat son of Lorenzo the Magnificent of Florence. A cardinal since the age of thirteen, he clearly owed his ecclesiastical career to Medici money rather than to spiritual qualities. The consistency in his life was that as a true Medici he loved art, architecture and Florence, of which he was the effective ruler. In order to secure his native city against attack he concluded the concordat (treaty) of Bologna with Francis I, accepting the king's right to appoint to all the higher offices in the French Church. Later he deserted that expensive alliance in order to come to terms with the new emperor, Charles V. Alarmed by the new French king's sponsorship of a small rival council, he convened an official Lateran Council in Rome but was happy to see it disperse in March 1517 without instituting any serious reforms. Had it continued for a few more months, it would have heard of Martin Luther.

After an interval Leo was followed by his cousin, Clement VII, born illegitimate but brought up by Lorenzo. He, too, was dedicated to the interests of Florence, where he was for many years archbishop. His political manoeuvres while pope went wrong, to the extent that the troops of an enraged emperor, Charles V, sacked Rome and other papal cities in 1527. This war beween pope and emperor, and their awkward relationship which followed, had consequences disastrous for the papacy's position. Clement was now unable to inspire Christian resistance to the Turks who had occupied Belgrade in 1521, just as he was unable to lead action against the spread of Protestantism. He also had no effective role, because no real interest, in the reform of the Church. Of all these popes, only two might have given a lead in that field. Pius III, a nephew of Pius II, had kept his distance from both Alexander and Julius, but he died ten days after his coronation in 1503. Hadrian VI, a Dutch scholar, was emphatic that papal Rome needed drastic reform. However, he died within two years of his election in 1522.

A Christian verdict on the Renaissance seems to emerge not from the notorious history of these popes but from the life of Michelangelo Buonarroti, in Vasari's eyes the greatest of all the artists. He was no theologian and no reformer but his very public art implied much and his private letters and poems said much, specially in his prolonged old age.

He was indeed a man of the Renaissance—and not only in the extraordinary wealth of his talents. He loved human bodies and the people inside them. In his early *Pietà* now in St Peter's the dead young Christ, his victory won, rests on the lap of his equally beautiful and (oddly) young mother. His *David* in Florence displays masculine youth, naked, unashamed and (oddly) uncircumcised, symbolizing that city's defiance of all its enemies. A later statue presented the risen Christ in the same nude strength. And in his seventies Michelangelo became the chief architect of the pope's magnificent new church: his dome still crowns it. But his letters show how little he admired his patrons. He accepted commissions for tombs in marble but the memorials had little emotional connection with the grandees being commemorated: his Moses is like Pope Julius only in being terrifying, the noble figures in the Medicis' church in Florence represent not his ignoble patrons but dusk and dawn, night and day, action and contemplation. He reluctantly accepted the fact that he was also a painter and that popes could order him to work with paint in great discomfort. In the Sistine Chapel the ceiling depicts the degradation effected by human sin together with the hopes offered by biblical prophets and pagan Sibyls, but the final impression given belongs to the Renaissance: because the Creator is glorious, humanity is capable of glory. Then came the time of explicit disillusionment. The wall over the altar was painted more than twenty years later, after the sack of Rome in 1527 which felt like the end of the Renaissance. There Christ is the pitiless Judge sentencing a swirling mass of sinners to hell. His mother turns away: she can say no more. Later sketches explore the living agony of crucifixion, what it has cost Christ to save some who might have joined those sinners. Within a few days of his death, aged almost ninety, he was struggling to finish a last *Pietà*. The Christ in it, now a heavy corpse lifted by his mother, is noble but tragic. That was the outcome of the humanism of the early *Pietà* and the *David*. That was the dusk where the dawn had been the spiritual beauty of the devotional paintings of Fra Angelico and Piero della Francesca, where the glory of peace in the destined year 1500 had been predicted by the ecstasy of Botticelli's *Nativity*.

Under more definitely Christian leadership could the skills which made the Renaissance have done more for the people who do not appear in the glorious pictures? Could the developments in agriculture and industry which were to begin to modernize northern Europe in the sixteenth century have been matched in the south, where the population grew but also, on the whole, grew poorer?

Such questions are suggested by the life of another genius, Leonardo da Vinci. He, too, was very famously a man of the Renaissance. Because he was not happy in the polite literary and artistic conversation which flowed around the grasping Medicis in Florence, he moved to the more honestly brutal court of the Sforzas in Milan. As painter-in-residence he provided scenery for entertainments, plans for military devices, portraits of mistresses and a picture of the Last Supper in oil paint on a damp wall in the refectory of a monastery which was under Sforza patronage, as he was. Other patrons commissioned technically brilliant pictures of the Virgin and other women, who seem finally enigmatic (he was a homosexual). He poured into his private notebooks exact observations of nature and quick but detailed sketches of possible inventions. These were, however, never developed into a science-based technology for the benefit of the people: that seemed inconceivable in the Renaissance. He designed an ideal city of Rome. It was an exercise in dreaming in a style frequent in that age of ideals unrelated to reality, but the nearest he came to papal patronage for his real interests was when he (a man who deplored the folly of war) spent a year as a military engineer in the service of Cesare Borgia. One of his ambitions was to create a great horse in bronze, but the patron of that project preferred to use the bronze for cannons. His late self-portrait in ink, in its art as marvellous as anything he did, seems to be a study in disappointment, as sad as Michelangelo's last *Pietà*.

Three short books written within the first thirty years of the sixteenth century show how Renaissance men could dream about a better society but were imprisoned in the society which existed.

Castiglione's *The Courtier* established the ideal of that society at the well-educated top: talented and polished courtesy was illustrated by conversations ending in a mystical oration on the glories of love. The scene was the court of the duke of Urbino, whose love of art and literature was genuine but who financed the elegance of the court by hiring out himself and his little army as mercenaries. Renaissance Italy imitated ancient Greece not least in its wars between its city-states.

Machiavelli's *The Prince* was the work of a man who conformed to the Church because he believed that religion made itself useful by spreading a civic spirit. He served Florence well and idealized ancient Rome; his next book after *The Prince* was a commentary on Livy's history of republican Rome, his book after that a lament over the decline and fall of republican Florence. 'Experience shows', he wrote, 'that cities have never increased in dominion or riches except while they have enjoyed liberty.' Yet in *The Prince* he praised tyranny and the cruelties and deceptions by which tyrants keep themselves in power. It is therefore uncertain why he allowed that pamphlet to be circulated in manuscript although not printed. Did he half hope for a job under the Medicis, then recently restored to power in Florence? Probably he did—but if so, he was less shrewd about his own interests than were the ruthless men of *The Prince*, Cesare Borgia who outwitted his enemies and Pope Julius who outwitted him. The Medicis did not need his advice about how to be successful and when they were again expelled the restored republic treated him as one who had attempted to collaborate with tyranny. The best explanation seems to be that Machiavelli was a republican in despair both about a republic's chances in the jungle of Renaissance politics and about Italy's chances of living in peace without invasions, but it is also possible that the Renaissance had made him a mature man without any convictions at all.

Thomas More's *Utopia* was also the work of a Renaissance scholar who knew what had gone wrong. He imagined an island across the Atlantic (Cuba?) which would be ruled by justice, not by a tyrant or by a 'conspiracy of rich men'. It would have no lawyers; its laws would be 'very few' because good; its priests would also be few, because holy. Under a prince elected and removable the official religion would be loftily spiritual and all other sincerely held religious beliefs would be tolerated. Gold would be used only in order to make chamber pots, there would be no money and homes would be exchanged with fellow citizens every ten years by lot.

Modern scholars have noted that the author of *Utopia* was a lawyer who was to serve Henry VIII prominently for fifteen years without arranging social reforms, that he was to persecute heretics and that he was to die as a Catholic martyr witnessing against the takeover of the Church in England by that Renaissance prince. These scholars have therefore asked why in 1516 he published *Utopia*, a book full of egalitarian idealism but not of explicit Catholicism. Was it intended to warn contemporaries against impossible dreams? Possibly—but if so, it is strange that it is not more blunt. When an older More attacked heretics he was to be very blunt indeed. Was it a joke? It certainly was high-spirited in comparison with Machiavelli's *Prince* or with the vision of the perfect society of Communism in Plato's *Republic*. But it is likely to have been a joke which was not entirely a joke. Written with elegant humour in Latin, *Utopia* was fiction about an island whose Greek name means 'Nowhere'. But it hinted at the dreams for Church and society of a man who had nearly become a monk. It implied a verdict on medieval Catholicism.

6

⌘⌘⌘

Reformations

The Renewal of Christianity

THERE was no such event as 'the Reformation' if by that is meant a single, simple change. The Protestants were divided and there was also a Catholic Reformation. These changes were destructive. The unity of western Christendom was shattered, apparently for ever: fellow Christians could now be regarded as demonic, as 'Antichrist'. Much beauty in life and art was destroyed, often with brutal vandalism. Many lives were lost. But out of the deaths there were resurrections. Each Reformation exhibited a courage and vitality which astonish us as we remember how much power, physical, emotional and intellectual, had been wielded with how much confidence by the authorities in medieval Catholicism. A claim made at the time was accurate: not only Europe but also Christianity was being renewed.

In each of the Reformations a large part of the impetus was provided by economic and political forces. The centre of European life was moving away from the Mediterranean; both Spain and Sweden now mattered more than Italy or Greece. Nationalism replaced the international order which had been at least the ideal of the Middle Ages. The laity took over much of the wealth of the Church. But as kings and princes rose against pope and emperor, and laymen occupied the lands of bishops and monasteries, other forces were at work. Cities rose against princes or prince bishops; within the cities the poorer rose against the richer and in the countryside peasants rose against landlords; and the middle classes were rising most successfully of all. The German lands in particular, and the long borderlands of the Rhine including Switzerland, were now socially unstable. The word 'Protestant' originated in a protest by five princes and 14 cities against an attempt to halt the confiscation of church lands and other 'religious innovations', in 1529.

Another large part of the impetus for all the Reformations was provided by a psychological change. We have already met strong individuals in earlier periods, with a personal religion, but there is truth in the description of the sixteenth century as the time of the growth of modern individualism. The pride in personal beauty, ability and achievement which had marked the elite in the Renaissance was now deepened into a new strength of self-awareness which could feed the awareness of God, often through a personal sense of guilt. Not only the specially sensitive but many more ordinary people looked into their hearts and souls and wanted a religion which would speak to them in their own depths. They became less satisfied with the old images, more interested in hearing or reading words or in seeing images with a more direct emotional impact; more impatient with rites which were merely communal and traditional; more willing to undergo the pains of some kind of a rebirth; more ready to submit to a new breed of preachers or priests who would be guides; more enthusiastic about the creed which they adopted as true for them. Each Reformation encouraged a more direct encounter between the individual and Jesus Christ as Lord and God, one to one, but the emphasis on the individual could be alleged to be greater than the emphasis on God. Thus it was said that in practice Protestantism suggested that salvation was achieved not by God but by the individual's emotional faith, or that the new form of Catholicism suggested that a more excited participation in the life of the Church was itself a passport to heaven.

However, a theory that these Protestant and Catholic Reformations were nothing but camouflage for economic and political forces, or for a psychological change in the direction of individualism, does not stand up to detailed examination. The pressure of religious customs or convictions was then a reality which a more secular age may not easily appreciate.

Groups with roughly the same economic and political interests did not necessarily have the same religious allegiance. Obviously it was easiest to protest against the jurisdiction of a pope or an emperor if a group became Protestant under strong pressure from its own ruler, but it was possible to pursue national interests while many of the people remained fervently Catholic in religion; thus Catholic Spain acknowledged little papal authority in practice and a French cardinal was second to none among the leaders of the resistance to the Spanish king and the 'Roman' emperor. Obviously it was attractive for laymen simply to become owners of church lands, but it was also possible for elites to make profitable careers within a Catholic system of Church and State. Obviously it was simplest for a city with new ambitions to reject the local bishop, but other cities in Germany, Switzerland and the Rhineland remained Catholic, as did the older Italian and Belgian centres of commerce and capitalism.

The new emphasis on the individual might have either Protestant or Catholic consequences. Each of these Reformations had its teachers who were believed to be inspired and its saints who were believed to live close to

God. In each tradition countless individuals were influenced by these reformers in the depths of the heart and conscience and were willing to suffer as they were faithful to their convictions. Even the princes whose personalities so often shaped the course of events had religious convictions as well as a keen sense of political self-interest. But as we shall often observe in this chapter, the Protestant and Catholic forms of spirituality and holiness which emerged out of these Reformations were so different that to attribute them all merely to an irreligious 'individualism' would be superficial.

If we ask what were the religious forces at work, we find that in their different ways all the Reformations rejected much of the legacy of the Middle Ages, each with its own interpretation of the cry *ad fontes*, 'back to the sources'. Protestants got back to the Bible, in particular to Paul's understanding of faith, while also acknowledging the authority of the creeds of the Church agreed before the division into east and west. Catholics rejuvenated the Church with a transforming sense of the call of Christ to costly discipleship and apostleship. These were authentic renewals which could be revolutionary in their fanatical zeal to blot out the 'idolatry' of the medieval Church, and they led to the process which Milton praised as 'the reforming of Reformation itself' when in the second stage of Protestantism there were fervent protests against medieval elements which had survived the first protests. The revolution in Catholicism was quieter but it changed the face of the Church.

The need to challenge the great strength of western Catholicism in the Middle Ages, to make a break which altered both doctrines and practices, explains why these Reformations were a phenomenon unique in the history of religion. In earlier chapters we noticed the absence of fundamental change in the eastern Orthodox tradition, where despite the insistence of the bishops' councils on definitions of Christ against which 'heretics' protested the common emphasis was on the far less controversial life of worship and prayer. We find much the same stability in the non-Christian religious traditions—and not only in the almost timeless traditions which are called 'tribal' or 'primitive' or 'animist'. Western Christianity's Reformations may be somewhat easier to understand if we briefly consider why other great religions have not been so divided as Christianity has been.

It is true that there are differences within, as well as between, the Hindu and Buddhist traditions. Gautama the Buddha was a reformer and radical simplifier of the religion taught by the Brahmin priests and for this reason the Hindus eventually drove the Buddhists out of India. Within the traditions now separate there were to be many disagreements. Some movements have developed a devotion to a particular god or *Bodhisattva* (saviour), pictured as a person and presented in a story. Others have preferred a meditative religion which is far less of a person-to-person relationship in prayer. But the general tendency of the religious thinkers of Asia has been to agree that the Ultimate Reality has many faces and many names, personal or impersonal, while on the ground popular religion in the Hindu or Buddhist tradition has not differed basically: in the temple or in the home it has been a religion of petitions for blessings. 'Hinduism' is not a systematic 'ism': the term was invented by Europeans in order to point to the reality of the religious life of India. 'Buddhism' has included a diversity almost as great as India's but has also never split because it has never been organized in order to be exclusive on the scale of medieval Catholicism and the post-medieval Reformations. It follows the 'noble eightfold path' taken towards spiritual enlightenment with reverence for the teaching of the Lord Buddha, who said 'work out your own salvation'. These many paths of religion in Asia have thus been in a direction different from the desire to know and obey the one, all-holy and all-real God revealed in history. God has not been defined; the definitions have not been argued about; there has been no Reformation.

Judaism has, of course, resembled Christianity far more closely, but Jews have acknowledged a common identity more readily than Christians. This is partly because 'Judaism' has been less theological, less interested in arguments about ideas, although it has had its theologians from Maimonides downwards. It has been a people, chosen if not by God then by destiny; chosen to suffer and to create. After the destruction of their temple and nation almost all Jews accepted the orthodoxy of the Pharisees, but with new spiritual life injected by mystical or charismatic movements such as Hasidism; under the challenge of modernity some liberal Jews, specially in the Reform movement, went further than other Jews in assimilating themselves to the surrounding society at the expense of loyalty to traditional laws and customs; under the impact of secularism some Jews have abandoned most of their religious heritage. Yet all Jews have been conscious that they are Jews and most have been reluctant to excommunicate each other. We do not need to underestimate these tensions if we conclude that there is no Jewish equivalent to the depth of the divisions within Christianity.

Unlike Judaism, Islam is very numerous, combines many races and has had very large movements within it. In those ways it is like Christianity and therefore a somewhat larger defence of the claim that it has never experienced a Reformation may be in order.

Islam has been clearly articulated in response to the revelation of Allah, the only God; the word *islam* itself means 'submission'. Politically motivated Muslims have gone to war with each other as Christians have done, but theology has not had much of a role in comparison with the controversies and wars of western Christianity. The biggest difference over the right interpretation of the required religious submission has been between the *Sunni* (orthodox) majority and the *Shia* (sect), but that division originated in the murderous disputes about who should be successor to the Prophet and what should be his powers as the community developed; it was not primarily a division about doctrine. The *Shia* who treasured the memory of the murdered Ali were the losers and protesters. When power passed from one dynasty of caliphs to another in AD 750 there was no alteration in theology: the last of the Umayyads was killed reading the Quran, the first of the Abbasids vowed that he would enforce the Prophet's laws with new vigour. In the tenth Christian century the political unity under the Abbasids collapsed but the religious, cultural and economic unity of Islam did not. In the eleventh century the Turks under the Seljuk sultans imposed themselves by military force (as the Arabs had done) but their success owed much to their Islamic orthodoxy. The same was true of their Ottoman successors. In the sixteenth century the national religion of Iran (Persia) became Shi'ite, mainly in order to assert itself against the Ottomans, but in comparison with the eastern and western churches Islam remained united.

In the modern age the religion of Islam has largely escaped internal questioning. For almost all Muslims the Quran has remained God's revelation recited by the Prophet; it is the Word of God as Christ is the Word for Christians, a book officially declared to be 'uncreated' since its perfection must be eternal. This revelation has provided the consensus which is discerned by the scholars and the preachers are expected to be timeless in doctrine. The caliphs, who in their time were sultans rather than popes, were abolished in 1920, since when Islam has had no leader and no council which might endorse fresh doctrines. The Sufis have been less tied than other Muslims to the written tradition, but they have almost always avoided theological arguments and they acquired their name from their woollen clothes, not from any theologian or doctrine. The liberals who have been present in Islamic communities in recent times have accepted some western customs and ideas but have concentrated on practical matters. The Wahhabis are strict conservatives and puritans in Saudi Arabia while in West Africa or Indonesia many Muslims are more relaxed, but from one end of Islam to another there is a unity looking to Mecca, with no sign of a Reformation.

With varying degrees of politeness members of these other great religious communities have criticized the disunity of Christians. With varying degrees of interest in religion, millions in lands with Christian traditions have given the quarrels of the churches as a reason for withdrawing from them all. And many Christians have seen this disunity as a tragedy. In 1688 Jacques Bossuet, a bishop whose motto was *semper eadem* ('always the same'), published a scornful *History of the Variations of the Protestant Churches*, looking back over a scene of chaos and seeing little or no reason why any one heretic should agree with another or why any of the faithful should think that any benefits had been gained from such attempts to change tradition. In more recent times Catholics have listened to Protestants with more respect but still the shattering of unity has seemed a catastrophe—and many Protestants have lost all complacency as they have reflected on their own divided churches' all-too-human origins. In the twentieth Christian century the ecumenical movement has often been praised as an effort to overcome the sad divisions of the sixteenth, and it is surely right to condemn the hatred, cruelties and wars which Christians then inflicted on each other. But as we try to understand, we may ask whether these Reformations were entirely destructive and evil.

The religious questions in dispute concerned the nature of authority and of salvation for Christians and thus concerned matters lying within Christian experience. It seems easier to excuse disputes about such matters than it is to justify the disputes in the Byzantine empire about the natures and wills of Christ and his relationship with the Father 'before all time'. It does not seem unreasonable to think that it was right to protest against some elements in late medieval Catholicism and it seems relevant to reflect that in the second half of the twentieth century the Roman Catholic Church has made many of the changes which the reformers demanded then. But it also seems that it was right for Catholics to reply that Protestantism had proved too destructive, destroying in particular the warmth of the New Testament's teaching about love. That reaction produced the Catholic Reformation, a movement which twentieth-century Protestants have begun to understand as being spiritual, creative and in many ways admirable. All these Reformations brought about some revival and whether or not they sought the 'restoration' of the church life to be seen in the New Testament (which was the objective of, for example, Zwingli) all revived something of the New Testament's spirit. All moved the emphasis to the moral and spiritual life from the performance of ceremonies, as Jesus had done. Like him all rejected the comfortable pride of good people, celebrating instead the wonder of God's mercy. All rejected the arid debates of intellectuals, developing instead a religion heartfelt, fervent, prayerful and related to practical duties. All were strongly marked by local characteristics but all wanted others to share their convictions, for they believed in a Church wider than the city or the nation.

Of course most people still did not have direct access to the Bible. Most could not read. The history of Protestantism makes much of the translations of the Bible and of publications based on them, but recent research has shown the limits of the numbers of copies printed. For Catholics, after 1559 the printing or ownership of a Bible not in Latin required special permission and an application could sometimes arouse the Inquisition's hostility. But another trend in recent research into the realities of local religion has been to show that if Christianity is defined by reference to the Bible much evidence suggests that the peoples of Europe began to be more truly

Christian as a result of these Protestant and Catholic Reformations. All these movements, however human, included Christians who found themselves being stabbed by the sword-like 'Word of God' in Scripture; stabbed to the heart. For the dedicated clergy this meant being trained spiritually and intellectually for a 'ministry' (service) which was far more arduous than the repetition of rituals or the receipt of an income. For the convinced laity the new life meant a share in the 'priesthood of all believers' or at least in the discipline of all disciples. In all these Reformations many individuals experienced conversion with a thoroughness which had previously been the monopoly of the outstanding few. Many gained a personal relationship with the Christ of the New Testament and a renewed vision of the Church as the Body of Christ. And there was often an even larger vision—of nothing less than the kingdom of God on earth. It often seemed then, as it had seemed in the beginning of Christianity, that a great crisis had come, perhaps the Last Days when God would be fully revealed after the worst tribulations. And even if history were to continue, Protestants believed that their nations could at last become truly Christian societies—and Catholic missionaries began to baptize the Americas, Africa and Asia.

In the twentieth century, however, many scholars have been able to reflect on these events from a distance. They have often concluded that the divided Christians all inherited a long history of beliefs about the Bible and the Church which they continued to take for granted while they changed much else. Almost everyone in that sixteenth century thought that the Bible allowed little or no variety of interpretation. Christians who differed from the authorities in their understanding were denounced as 'heretics' who stupidly and malignantly denied 'the pure gospel' or 'the true faith'; and it was inevitable that those attacked should react with indignant appeals to Scripture, or to Scripture supplemented by Catholic traditions believed to date back to the first apostles and so to Jesus himself. And almost everyone believed that the religious organization which was regarded as 'the true Church' was entitled to be the only Church in an area where life ought to be made very difficult for anyone who was arrogant enough, and foolish enough, to dissent. The age of the Reformations was not an age when diversity in the Bible was seen clearly or when diversity in society was willingly tolerated. In these respects the age remained medieval.

Erasmus

Erasmus, the second son of a Dutch priest, born in or around 1466, was defiantly desired by his unmarried parents. He was therefore baptized as Herasmus, a name which meant 'desired' and was to become Desiderius in more scholarly Latin. He was lifted out of the fate awaiting other priests' bastards, however desired, by being sent to a school a hundred miles from his home, where he came under the influence of the Brethren of the Common Life. He was then admitted into an Augustinian monastery, not because he had any vocation to be a devout monk but because it gave him, a penniless and by then orphaned teenager, an opportunity which he used to the full—the chance to read in peace. He drifted into ordination as a priest although neither then nor later does he seem to have attached much importance to that role. Released from his monastery, he was taken under a bishop's patronage and sent for further study to the college in Paris which educated other men we shall meet, John Calvin and Ignatius Loyola. The philosophy and theology taught there bored him and he hated the Spartan life, the lice and the smells, but he could make some necessary money while a student by tutoring rich boys. He developed a lifelong interest in education and one of his pupils invited him to England. He now had the further good fortune to meet John Colet, who was attracting eager youth by his unworldly character and by lecturing on St Paul in Oxford without the usual suffocating comments extracted from the works of the Fathers and the medieval theologians—a 'swarm of flies', as he spoke of them to Erasmus. Colet knew that he was handicapped by not having learned Greek thoroughly and he persuaded his young visitor to become both a master of that language and a popular interpreter of what the Greek said. And soon Erasmus tasted the influence and income which might come from printed words as the editor of a collection of 'adages' (wise sayings culled from the classics) which gradually expanded both in contents and in sales. So despite his start in life, he was well launched by the year 1500.

In the next quarter-century he became the most famous scholar in Europe, not only as an editor and translator but also as a communicator of a version of Christianity which for a time was attractive.

With the help of assistants he achieved many editions or translations of the Greek or Latin classics, but the crowning glory of his command of the ancient languages was an edition of the Greek New Testament accompanied by a fresh translation into elegant Latin. His edition of the Greek had to be based on manuscripts which were not the best, but he later improved it and the Latin version which he based on it shook the supremacy of the Vulgate. He showed, for example, that Matthew 4:17 had called people to 'repent', not to 'do penance' as in the authorized Latin, and that Luke 1:28 had called Mary 'favoured', not 'full of grace'.

By further exertions he enabled or encouraged educated readers of printed books to acquaint themselves directly with the teachings of the western Fathers—Irenaeus and Tertullian, Cyprian and Ambrose, Jerome and Augustine (the last in ten big folio volumes). Previously they had been known to most readers only through quotations. He also edited some eastern Fathers who had become yet more obscured by the medieval western theological systems: Origen, Athanasius, the Cappadocians and John Chrysostom. And in an even bolder departure from the theology which had become conventional, he addressed the educated laity. His 'colloquies' went into many editions. Nominally these imaginary conversations or reflective essays were intended to show schoolboys and other beginners how to write good Latin. Actually they advised people, young or old, how to lead good lives.

He supplied an *Enchiridion of the Christian Soldier*, saying that he had written it 'in a very few days' for the benefit of an 'almost illiterate' reader (actually a manufacturer of armaments whose wife objected to time spent in the arms of other women). The Greek in the title meant either 'Dagger' or 'Handbook' and it went straight to the point about how a Christian ought to live. At least in the printed version the advice given included too many scholarly allusions in Latin, and recommended the study of too many other books, for it to be ideal for use by the man Erasmus said he was addressing. But after its third edition (in 1515) the book was talked about. Translated into many languages, it was bought by many people glad to be treated as a great scholar's equal and to be told that what they needed was more self-respect. There was no emphasis on the formalities of religion: what matters is morality, guided by the Scriptures whose message may be understood by any reasonable person. The book urged the imitation of Christ, but without the self-effacing monasticism of Thomas à Kempis. 'Monasticism', Erasmus wrote, 'is not godliness but a kind of life which is useful or useless according to one's own habits in body or temperament.' For everyone, monk or layman, the Christian life must be a constant battle in which we must 'rely on divine force'. We must first 'know ourselves' and then be determined to fight with the aid of prayer and the Scriptures, so that reason conquers over passions. If we have to fight against lust, for example, we must remember that the act of sex degrades us into behaving like the animals. We must take ourselves more seriously.

This little book did not frontally attack any practices in late medieval religion, merely saying that prayers to the saints (for example) were less important than becoming saintly; but Erasmus could make such attacks. While staying in the house of Thomas More during a later and longer visit to England he wrote a book which he later explained had the same message as his *Enchiridion* but was 'truth with a smile'. Its Latin title could mean either 'Praise of More' or 'Praise of Folly'. There and elsewhere he mocked many features of the everyday Church: the irrelevance of the disputes which fascinated the universities, the idle escapism of monks, the ignorance of parish priests, celibacy not honoured in practice, the pomp of worship in an unintelligible language, the racket of pilgrimages to bogus relics. All were familiar targets but he managed to attack them in a way which was fresh, with gusto but also with a pleasant irony, with a superior morality but without alarming bitterness, and the little book went into six hundred editions. When he wanted, however, his humour could hit and hurt. Almost certainly he was the author of *Julius Excluded*, a conversation between Julius II and an indignant Peter who guards the gate of heaven. But he never admitted responsibility for that blow, as devastating as it was hilarious, and he never wanted to see the papacy demolished. He had been glad to obtain from Julius release from his vows as a monk. He dedicated his New Testament to Leo X, who praised his work and enjoyed his wit.

His styles were so varied, his translations covered such a medley of authors, his laughter was so frequent, and his temperament was so detached, that his own religious position was to some extent ambiguous, like the titles of these books. But some convictions emerged clearly. Faith is the acceptance of spiritual truths; Christ is the Teacher and Example; the 'philosophy of Christ' is quite easy to understand and accept; it brings love, joy and peace; many things which conventional churchmen have thought sacred are comparatively unimportant. Like a good teacher the Church must win hearts by love and shape minds by patience until what is potential in everyone flourishes. He was himself a superb teacher and his sermon on *The Boundless Mercy of God* was published as a summary of his mature faith. It was invulnerably orthodox, yet it put first the command of Jesus to be merciful like the Father.

A man so aware of the goodness in all Christians could not be expected to approve the burning of 'heretics' and when Martin Luther attacked the papacy Erasmus made known his belief that the rebel was orthodox in all the essentials. But a humanist could not be expected to approve of Luther's uncouthness, of the violence which it unleashed, of the abolition of the Latin Mass which had been the centre of devotion for a thousand years, of the destruction of the unity of Christendom, or of the contempt for human goodness.

The patriotism in Protestantism did not interest him. He had a fierce literary quarrel with a German nobleman, Ulrich von Hütten, who had been among his most ardent admirers but who was a propagandist for the formation of a German church. Erasmus would call himself a German or a Swiss when it suited him, but he felt equally entitled to criticize any country (many were his complaints about the local wine or beer), and at heart he was a cosmopolitan humanist, a civilized European, a citizen of the world. His writing about princes was utterly unlike Machiavelli's: he concentrated on the need to educate them so that they would grow up to love justice and peace. His pacifism involved a departure from the theories of Augustine and Aquinas about the 'just war' as legitimate for Christians. (The justice of such a war depends crucially on its being defensive, but in a dispute between princes and nations who can instantly decide which is the aggressor?) Although he accepted an appointment carrying a stipend but no duties as a councillor to the emperor Charles V, he did not share Dante's dream about the emperor's supremacy. He wanted princes to discharge limited responsibilities and advised them against foreign expeditions. They should stay at home and work quietly for the welfare of their subjects. He also refused to say that a mere city council had the right to decide what was the teaching of the Bible and the right ordering of the Church. When the civic authorities did not stop Protestant disturbances in Basle he left that city in disgust after a residence of eight years. It was ironic that he was to receive a Protestant burial in Basle: he had gone back in order to superintend the printing of his edition of Origen.

But there was some common ground between him and the Protestants' appeal to Scripture and their desire for a simple and serious piety firmly based on Scripture. Both he and the Protestants were impatient with the debates which preoccupied many of the professional theologians. Erasmus caricatured the theories about God's 'absolute' power (in contrast with the power which he had chosen to exercise) as being nothing but speculations about whether God might have chosen to be incarnate as an ass or a cucumber. It ought to be enough for a Christian to know how God had actually been revealed. Yet this common ground with the Protestants was smaller than the love which Erasmus had for the Catholic Church. In the Church's large bosom he had prospered; in its long history he had found much to admire and translate; in its unity lay the best hope of avoiding ruinous wars. Also, as he grew older he grew more conservative. So while Protestants hoped that he would come to their aid, Catholics urged him to attack the new heresy.

For a long time he refused: 'I do not know Luther, I know Christ.' But eventually he did write a book, in 1524, and he believed that he had been clever to choose to defend the God-given freedom of the human will rather than doctrines or practices which he could not support so sincerely. He was ready to admit—indeed, to stress—that neither Scripture nor the Church's compulsory doctrine gave clear teaching on this age-old philosophical question about free will, and that any Christian attempt to answer must acknowledge Man's dependence on the wonder of God's grace. But by the same token he argued that Luther was wrong to be inquisitive about things 'hidden, not to say superfluous', and wrong to publish his thoughts on such topics in such a way as to offend good people trying to be Christian in their lives. Although he was polite, his basic objection to Luther's theology was that it did not encourage the Christian pilgrimage to God, since 'by the freedom of the will I understand the power which a man has to apply himself to, or turn away from, that which leads to eternal life'. He compared God with a parent who helps a small child to walk in the right direction. However, he had little sense of the passions which are the bondage of humanity. He was not eloquent about the sheer fascination of things and flesh, about the often victorious power of evil, about the inability even of good people to deserve God's forgiveness, about the wrath of God against all sin great or small, about the grimness of the life which, if all events are controlled by God, seems to teach that God has no great love for us.

Luther's long reply was angry. He compared Man to a donkey, ridden either by God or by Satan. Man does not have a will free enough to choose God. Unless God chooses Man, Man cannot be truly good or free and God cannot be known as loving. To Luther his opponent did not seem to be on fire with love for the God who of his own will chooses those whom he proposes to make good—so perhaps he was in the deepest truth an atheist? Further books by Erasmus were ineffective, because bewildered, defences of his happier position.

He was glad to return to his labours as an editor of the 'golden' theology of the past. He criticized the crudity of the Protestants in many sad letters while not abandoning his own criticisms of the superstitions in popular Catholicism, and he compared himself with the man who caught his death while trying to separate gladiators. His little book on *Preparation for Death* showed what he meant when in 1536 'dear God' was his last words. But within a quarter of a century a pope had forbidden Catholics to read any of his books and by that time among Protestants 'Erasmian' had become a term of abuse for a cowardly traitor to the gospel. Later generations have better understood the dilemmas of this scholar who loved both truth and peace but have seen that his message was never likely to achieve the *reformatio* of religion which he desired.

Zwingli's Reformation

Huldreich Zwingli was a far more determined reformer whose ideas enjoyed political support. He was deeply influenced by the writings of Erasmus which he studied while a parish priest in the 1510s, and influenced even more by his own studies of the Bible in Hebrew and Greek, but he would rise from his chair to go to the pulpit and announce with intense seriousness that in obedience to the Bible the civil authorities should authorize changes in church life.

From boyhood in a remote Swiss village he went to university and ordination, but nothing separated him from the men among whom he had been a boy. He shared their pride that their toughness as soldiers had won Swiss independence from the Habsburg emperor. As a chaplain he shared the trade which they had to enter because of the countryside's poverty: the trade of a mercenary soldier, for hire by anyone. At Marignano in 1515 he was heart-broken when thousands of such mercenaries were massacred by the French while employed by the papacy and he became disgusted by the trade. Nearly dying in an epidemic, he survived with his personal religion deepened. Elected as the 'people's priest' in Zürich, he began to preach straight from the Bible, not depending on the papacy's doctrines but confident that 'the Word of God will follow its course as surely as the Rhine'—at a speed, however, which must be acceptable to the city council.

The council consisted of the more successful businessmen, whose natural tastes were conservative in religion as in politics, but their power was not the only consideration. Meeting four times a week, they actively represented and enforced the unity of a city with some seven thousand inhabitants. To Zwingli that unity was sacred. It was the work of the 'Eternal Wisdom' and the magistrate was the 'minister of God' no less than the preacher. Thus in Lent 1522 he was present when a symbolic sausage was eaten in defiance of the Church's rule about fasting, and in his pulpit he defended the freedom of Christians to eat or not to eat—but he did not eat himself because he obeyed the council. Later that year he joined other clergy in a petition to the bishop for licences to marry. He knew that the petition would be refused and that the bishop would not believe the assurance that these clergy had 'nothing in common with Luther or with anyone else who might harm Christian doctrine'—but he had already married a widow in secret, a baby was on the way and he wanted to show courtesy to authority. He preached against 'images' in the churches but these were not removed until the city council had authorized the action. He preached against the Latin Mass as unscriptural but it was not ended until Holy Week in 1525. The council then agreed to a Lord's Supper using ordinary bread and wine at an ordinary table with the ordinary German language, a simple but solemn meal which became quarterly.

Excited by this change, radicals led by Conrad Greber now denounced the baptism of infants, the taking of oaths and the fighting of wars. Such customs were attacked as being contrary to the New Testament but they were popular and were defended by Zwingli. He had developed his own theology of the sacraments. While the enthusiasts whom he now confronted cared little or nothing for the preservation of unity among the inhabitants of Zürich, he cared a great deal. To him baptism meant admission to the Christian community as circumcision had once admitted to the community of ancient Israel. It did not wash away guilt inherited from Adam but it was the pledge of God's love for that baby, a pledge which invited love in return. It resembled the admission (with oath-taking) of a recruit into a regiment for war and the Lord's Supper was somewhat like an occasion when a regiment remembered a great battle. When the Christian community recalled Christ's victorious death, the Saviour was present not literally in his body but in the mind of the believer. Critics replied that these comparisons degraded the sacraments but it was Zwingli's intention to make them more, not less, spiritual. 'Sacraments', he wrote, 'are signs by which a man proves to the Church that he either aims to be, or is, a soldier of Christ.' And the word 'Christ' had for him many traditional meanings. Christ's death has satisfied the just wrath of the Father and Christ's true Church is invisible, not necessarily consisting of all the baptized, because it consists of those who are 'elect' by the Father's predestination. What really interested Zwingli was a change in church life, not a revolution in theology.

This was a reform of religion which many of the Swiss could understand and welcome. In 1528 Berne joined Zürich in the rejection of the Mass. Next year a Bible was published in a translation by Swiss scholars. It looked as if Zwingli's leadership would be accepted widely and that a strong coalition of 'reformed' states and cities would be constructed.

But that was not to be. Conrad Grebel insisted on baptizing adults who had already been baptized by Catholic priests in infancy; he was arrested and executions began for those guilty of accepting this 'Anabaptism' (re-baptism). Grebel died while escaping from the authorities but the Anabaptist movement spread and a further problem led to a breach with the Lutherans. This was the problem of the Mass. Seeking to unite all Protestants for military purposes, Philip the prince of Hesse drew Zwingli, Luther and other theologians together in his castle in Marburg. The meeting was a disaster. Luther insisted that the bread and wine did not merely 'signify' the body and blood of a Christ whose glorified body was at the right hand of the Father in heaven, as Zwingli argued. To Luther Christ's glorified human nature shared the 'idiom' of his divine nature and was therefore 'ubiquitous', not confined to heaven but able to be present whenever the words 'this is my body' were repeated in the Mass. The 'substance' of the flesh was then present 'in, with and under' the substance of the bread ('consubstantiation'). In Luther's eyes Zwingli's failure to acknowledge this real presence of Christ in the Mass as part of 'the thing given' showed that he was at heart an ignorant 'fanatic' no better than the Anabaptists. So the Lord's Supper concentrated the divisions between Christians.

Finally Zwingli encountered the problem that many of the Swiss, particularly in the poorer and more rural cantons, resisted the ambitions of Zürich. He volunteered for military service during a civil war in 1531 and fell wounded among the defeated soldiers. The Catholics then killed him and scattered his ashes mixed with dung. Later the Swiss cantons nervously recognized each other's right to co-exist with different religious systems and the next religious leader of Zürich, Heinrich Bullinger (Zwingli's son-in-law), proved more adept at securing agreement among the reformed; but the Swiss confederation was never to be 'reformed' as a whole. The statue which honours Zwingli in Zürich correctly displays him with a Bible in the one hand and a sword in the other, for he had belonged to the city with all his heart: he had preached to it and he had died for it in battle. He had set out his interpretation of Scripture in his book of 1525, *True and False Religion*, but had left the practical implications to be decided by the city's council. Other councils, however, could read the Bible differently. So could other leaders of other Reformations. Luther heard of his death with relief, as did Erasmus.

Luther's Reformation

Born within weeks of Zwingli, like him Martin Luther was indebted to Erasmus for making available a printed New Testament in Greek. Luther was also a 'humanist' in the sense that he encouraged education in eloquence by a study of the Greek and Latin classics. He advocated a library for every town and schooling for girls as well as boys. Indeed, his competence in languages went beyond the attainments of Erasmus. He knew Hebrew well, completing a translation of the Old Testament in 1534 and later revising it with the help of fellow scholars for the complete Bible of 1541. Above all he was eloquent in German as well as in Latin. His own thoughts kept printers busier than ever but his most enduring success was his translation of the New Testament into German, first published in 1522. More than any other book it created the modern German language along with German Protestantism.

But the contrasts with both Erasmus and Zwingli were enormous. These were partly due to the fact that Luther was so thoroughly a German. He belonged to a society which had no strong king: in domestic power the Holy Roman emperor was no match for a capable king of France or England. This meant that there was an explosion waiting to happen, for there had been no legislation to limit or prohibit gifts of land to the Church, or papal appointments to positions in the Church, or legal appeals to Rome. And it also meant that there was an opportunity for territorial princes and urban magistrates to become patrons of the preachers they preferred; the councils in the 65 'imperial cities', for example, were directly under the emperor but in practice that did not usually mean much. Intellectually and spiritually Germany was alive. It had many new universities and printing presses and its religious life was taking many new forms, often intensely personal. Luther's personality enabled him to take full advantage of this society into which he had been born. He flourished as a professor in the new university of

Wittenberg and as a best-selling author because his audience was ready for what he had to say. They could understand something of his experience as it boiled up and flooded over. A man is made a theologian, he said, by experience of God, by the heart. That was a message which arose from sources deeper than those which had been tapped either by Erasmus or by Zwingli. It was closer to the theology of William of Ockham, because it too was a message about God's will, sovereign but also gracious: however, Luther's message came not from a theological debate but from the experienced heart.

His experience may have included a fear of his father which influenced or caused his fear of God, as has been suggested, but no evidence has survived that the father, a peasant who prospered as a superior kind of miner in Saxony, was more harsh than other fathers of the time. On the contrary, Luther wrote gratefully about his parents. He was really afraid in the thunderstorm which made him vow to become a monk not a lawyer, but it is hard to think that had the sun continued to shine this young man would have become the kind of layman whom Erasmus praised. He was very deeply troubled by the Church's teaching about hell and determined to be saved from hell. Later he was emphatic that he entered an Augustinian monastery simply in order to escape from hell. Years afterwards he defied all the princes and bishops because, as he said, had he gone against his conscience hell would have been prepared for him. For him the worst fears of life were not about unpopularity but about the endless terrors of hell and the decisive battles of life were not against his human enemies or his own strong passions; they were against the Devil, the prince of hell. Part of the reason was that the medieval Church's emphasis on the cleansing of sinners in purgatory, as an alternative to the irreversible doom of endless torments in hell, increasingly lost its religious seriousness for this profoundly serious man: it was associated with too many abuses in church life. For him the alternative to heaven was hell.

Luther was a model monk except that he troubled his superior, Staupitz, first by joining the conservatives who were resisting minor changes (and who sent him to Rome to plead their case) and then by being for a much longer period in a state of anxiety as to whether he was being scrupulous enough in his holiness. His first Mass as a priest made an exhibition of this acute anxiety. But he was sensibly advised by Staupitz to think more about Christ than about himself and there is no evidence that he was thought to be psychologically unbalanced. Those who knew him best sent him to train as a theologian, to lecture as a professor of Old Testament, to collaborate and debate with other professors and to supervise other monasteries. There is also no evidence that he was more shocked by seeing Renaissance Rome than other naive pilgrims were, or that he abandoned medieval theology as a result of a sudden emotional crisis when back in his monastery. As he recalled, 'the papacy slipped away from me'—and slipped slowly.

In the twentieth century his surviving notes for lectures, particularly on the psalms, have been scrutinized. These manuscripts reveal a gradual development. He already knew the psalms by heart as a monk; now he heard all their answers to the soul through one question, what did they say about Christ? He had already absorbed the strong emphasis of the Nominalist theologians on the majesty and might of the will of God; now he asked insistently and exclusively what Christ revealed about that will. He had already learned from many sources that all the Church's doctrine is derived from Scripture; now he became sure that the restricting logic of Aristotle, traditionally called 'the Master of those who know', should be forgotten while studying the Word of God. Far better, because far more biblical, was the teaching of Augustine; as he wrote with joy to a friend in 1516, 'our theology and St Augustine prosper'.

Scripture is the 'cradle' in which the Saviour lies. Luther had already learned from the mystics to feel very small before God and to contemplate the love of God in the crucified Saviour; now that contemplation became the response of the rescued to the rescuer. In future years he was to call the philosophical theology he had studied a 'theology of glory' and he was to mean by that a condemnation: it had been ridiculously over-ambitious. Now as he concentrated his mind on the New Testament he limited the 'theology of the cross' to a wrestling with Paul's declaration to the church in Rome (1:17) that 'the righteousness of God is revealed'.

At first he hated that phrase, for late medieval religion had left him with the impression that this righteousness is the divine holiness which in relation to sinful humanity results in a law and a demand. Unless this law is kept perfectly, and this demand met completely, humanity is doomed to hell and can be rescued only by the satisfaction of God's justice achieved by Christ and shared with sinners whose penitence is satisfactory. So this text summed up Luther's nightmares. But now he saw that on the cross Christ ('the crucified God') had revealed the one light to which 'we must flee'. The righteousness of God is not a demand but an offer, not a law but a love, so that 'the righteous man lives by the gift of God'. Although he still believed that the crucifixion satisfied God's justice, the gospel was now for him a message about a gracious gift. In theology *gratia* had become almost a substance, received in ways which had to be analysed with many complications. Luther found that in the Bible it is simply God's 'favour'; that it comes from 'outside us' and not through the strengthening of our virtuous habits; that it comes abundantly from God and does not need to be distributed in doses by priests; that it must be received by 'faith' meaning trust long before the growth of 'faith formed by love' which to the medieval theologians had been essential to salvation. Yet outside this revelation of God's love, human experience continues to point in fear to God as the Judge who is unrelenting in his strictness.

Luther's theology was, as he claimed, basically Augustinian. But there were two differences which became sharper as Lutheran orthodoxy made a clear system out of his own expressions which were often more passionate than academic. Augustine had taught that those whom God chooses to save are made righteous by his grace, within their own experience. Lutherans were to teach something different, arising out of a different experience. 'Justification' was to be understood as declaring (not making) a sinner righteous and it was to be based exclusively on the righteousness of Christ, whose merits were 'imputed', not 'imparted', to the sinner. Any 'sanctification' followed as the second stage in this process. And from Luther's experience came another difference. For him as for Augustine, in the end not many are saved. Indeed, he agreed with Augustine that those who are saved depend on the fact that God has chosen, predestined, them. But even in his own depressed old age he usually avoided any firm statement that God predestines (rather than permits) the many to be damned. His experience was somewhat different from Augustine's: his conversion was more definitely to the God revealed on Christ's cross (without Augustine's continuing tendency to Platonism) and consequently his celebration of the benefits won by the cross was more exuberantly triumphant. To him, therefore, Christ's righteousness is different from what Augustine taught in two ways: initially it is 'alien' to the sinner who nevertheless is 'justified' by it, but once it is planted in the believer it has a power to which no limits can be placed.

This was the Luther who felt compelled to speak out in response to an event in which the worst features of late medieval religion and of the Renaissance were combined outrageously.

Albrecht Hohenzollern, a cousin of the margrave of Brandenburg, needed rich bishoprics in order to maintain his princely lifestyle. At the age of 23, in 1513, he was therefore made archbishop of Magdeburg. A year later he was elected to an additional archbishopric, of Mainz. That archdiocese was worried by a large deficit in its account with the papacy, but Albrecht promised to clear the debt. For a large additional sum he was permitted by the papacy to enjoy the revenues of the two archbishoprics together with another income from the rich church of Halberstadt. He received a loan from the Fuggers, who were also bankers to the papacy. But he was not worried about the repayment, for the Fuggers were well equipped to administer the sale of indulgences and this campaign was to be led by a salesman of outstanding energy, the Dominican friar Tetzel. That was a man who would brush aside the refinements of the theologians and announce that when a coin made a clink in the collecting bowl a soul escaped from the torments of purgatory. After paying the Fuggers for their service to the Church, half the proceeds would settle the archbishop's account with them; and the other half would be transmitted to Rome, to pay for the new basilica erected in honour of the Peter who had once wept bitterly after betraying his Master.

Luther drew up 95 'theses' questioning the theological basis of this operation, mainly on the grounds that it obscured the need to repent in order to be forgiven. As the custom was, he nailed this list to a door of the church next to the castle which dominated the new university where he taught biblical studies in the little Saxon town of Wittenberg. This act on 31 October 1517 did not 'begin the Reformation'. It was an invitation to one of the many disputations which were intended to sharpen students' wits and tongues. It raised questions; it did not commit even Luther to the permanent holding of any particular opinion. And its questions were not clearly outside the territory which theologians could legitimately debate under the late medieval system. Condemnation of the trade in indulgences was coming from undeniably orthodox sources—from the theologians in Paris, from the great Cardinal Ximénez in Spain. A few weeks previously Luther had asked a candidate for a higher degree to discuss theses which he had prepared for a disputation, and he had made these public, inviting other theologians' reactions. 'The natural man cannot want God to be God ... We are not made righteous by doing righteous deeds, but when we have been made righteous we do them ... In comparison with the study of theology, the whole of Aristotle is as darkness is to light.' But almost no one had complained or noticed: theologians were expected to debate.

The new theses proved to be different because they included phrases about the appeal to Scripture as decisive—phrases which in this context opened up the possibility of a denial of the authority on which the offer of indulgences was based. And more than theological opinions might be at stake. In the church behind that door were kept thousands of bits of bone or fabric said to be connected with the stories of the Bible and the saints. It was the largest collection of relics north of the Alps. Periodically these treasures were 'exposed' for adoration and more than a million years of exemption from purgatory could be obtained by reciting penitent prayers on these occasions. The academic notice on the door would, if taken seriously, reduce the value of that prize collection while it destabilized the finances of the pope and the princely archbishop. And that might lead to further practical questions. Thesis 49 was ominous: 'Christians should be taught that the pope's pardons are useful if we do not put our trust in them, but extremely harmful if they cause us to lose the fear of God.'

Luther's progress along the road from that point gives the impression of a man being dragged. The small stir in Wittenberg quickly spread through printing. A respectable, if previously unknown, theologian had raised a signal which could start a demonstration against Tetzel's sales campaign. But at first papal Rome refused to take the matter very seriously. Much more interest was taken in the importance of the ruler of that part of Saxony, Frederick the Wise, as an elector of the next Holy Roman emperor in 1519. The papacy was for a time attracted by the idea that Frederick might become emperor, since he was a sound Catholic (he had collected those relics) and not a Habsburg. The last Habsburg emperor, Maximilian, had been married to the heiress of the large possessions of the dukes of Burgundy and had secured the marriage of his own son to the heiress of the kingdoms constituting Spain, so that the accumulation of a power greater than anyone's since Charlemagne caused alarm in Rome. But Frederick was unable to distribute bribes to compete with Maximilian's grandson who was elected as Charles V. The election of a Habsburg thanks to loans from the Fuggers was to influence the course of Luther's life, for the new emperor had too many other involvements to become the head of a German National Church with reforms of church life but without theological innovations. When the empire's Reichstag (parliament) called urgently for a national church council to plan reforms Charles vetoed the idea. Nor was he able to take the lead in a rapid suppression of Luther's heresy. It was only after Luther's death that Charles had won enough victories over the papacy, the French and the Turks to win one against the Protestants—a victory which turned out to be temporary. So there was time for Luther to be dragged into his Reformation. And he was now under the protection of Frederick the Wise, who cared nothing for controversial theology but much for the dignity of his little princedom now that another was emperor—and much for the survival of the best known professor in the little university which he had founded. He was willing to tolerate Luther's repeated attacks on his beloved collection of relics.

Luther's own Augustinian order might have been able to silence him without further fuss, but when its leading members met they found themselves divided. Some of the older men were reluctant to condemn an able and sincere colleague who had been attacked by the Dominicans and some of the younger men welcomed the new theology with enthusiasm. A Dominican cardinal (Cajetan) was sent from Rome and failed to end the disturbance. He could not persuade the Reichstag to agree to a new issue of indulgences in order to finance a new crusade, or Luther to withdraw his objectionable opinions for the sake of peace: neither fatherly counsel nor bullying worked. When Luther offered to keep silent if his opponents would do the same, he must have known that the discussion which he had started could not be quelled. Indeed, a considerable number of devout churchmen, in circles much closer to Rome than Wittenberg could ever be, shared

Luther's convictions that practical reforms were overdue and that a more spiritual religion must inspire them.

'Evangelical' or 'Erasmian' Catholics belonged to groups of this kind in Italy. In Naples Juan de Valdes was the centre of a circle which sought renewal and the author of a theology which quoted Luther without naming him. In Venice a famous pamphlet expounded the benefits of Christ's death in Lutheran terms. The Capuchins, a reformed branch of the Franciscans, were active in many parts of Italy at this time, and in 1541 their leader openly declared himself a Protestant and fled the country. Two reform-minded aristocrats and scholars became cardinals: the Venetian Contarini and the Englishman Pole. Luther mocked them for their ineffectiveness, but both agreed with much of what he said. Contarini tried to reach agreement with him in 1541 and Pole nearly became pope eight years later. However, it was not to be expected that papal Rome would extend a warm welcome to an attempt by a German monk to dispute the financial basis on which St Peter's was being rebuilt gloriously. A favoured theologian (Mazzolini) announced firmly that whatever the pope approved must be approved by all Christians.

After a delay most of Luther's theses were formally condemned in *Exsurge Domine* (1520), a papal verdict which Luther burned publicly. He was then excommunicated. He had already appealed over the pope's head to a future council, but in a disputation a determined conservative, John of Eck, had taunted him with being an admirer of John Hus. Luther had then read Hus and had decided that 'if this was a heretic, I am one ten times more'. He was given a last chance to repent by being summoned before the emperor and the Reichstag in Worms in 1521. He knew that if he did not accept *Exsurge Domine* he was likely to be burned as a heretic (as two Augustinian monks were to be in Brussels two years later), but he declared that he was bound by his conscience unless his opinions could be proved wrong by Scripture or by 'evident reason'.

He escaped from Worms and was saved from the fire by being kidnapped by men who were in fact agents of Frederick the Wise, although that prince disclaimed all knowledge. Hidden for eight months in one of Frederick's castles (the Wartburg), he suffered the inevitable psychological reaction, with the Devil telling him that he had been arrogantly wrong to put his own opinions against the Church and the empire. But among other writings he translated the New Testament. He had become entitled to use the motto which Erasmus had claimed as his own: 'I yield to no one.' When he emerged from that seclusion, resuming his dress as an Augustinian monk, it was in order to sort out the confusion and violence which had broken out in Wittenberg under the influence of the more radical Andreas Karlstadt, his co-defendant at Worms. It was another big risk but as he placed himself

301

'under the protection of God' he must have known that he had already been given the ability to shape a Reformation.

His Reformation was not to be thoroughly radical. In his *Appeal to the Christian Nobility of the German Nation* in 1520 he had advocated changes many of which were also wanted by the Reichstag which had now abandoned him as a heretic. He had said that the higher clergy ought to be less worldly, that their misuse of their spiritual authority ought to be ended, that priests should be allowed to marry and monks and nuns to take vows which were not for life, that the laity should be given the cup and should hear their own language used in the Mass, that theology should be based on the Bible, that the poor should be helped systematically. This pamphlet had, however, been followed by another, on *The Babylonian Captivity of the Church*. This tackled subjects less congenial to the nobles, who had many reasons not to wish to be ranked as Hussite heretics.

Luther now insisted that Christ had instituted the two sacraments of baptism and the Mass (plus the confession of sins including penance, a third which he later withdrew)—but no others. The practical consequences were that the pope and the bishops had no right to make certain important claims. Confirmation by a bishop (when a bishop was available to perform it) was not necessary if the Holy Spirit was to be given fully to the baptized Christian. The ordination of a priest was a ceremony decreed by the Church, not by Christ; priest and layman differed only in function within the Church. The Mass was not a sacrifice to be offered by the priest, frequently in private; it was a sacrament recalling Christ's own sacrifice and ought to be shared fully by Christ's people. The absolution of sins by a priest depending on 'satisfaction' in penance was similarly now distanced from Christ. Hopes of heaven need not depend on it and this method of confessing sins should not be made compulsory. The priest's anointing of the dying ('unction') was also not essential.

A third pamphlet, on *The Freedom of a Christian*, clearly resulted from the religious experience which enabled Luther to demand changes effectively when so many previous complaints had failed. 'The soul', he wrote, 'can do without everything except the Word of God.' That 'Word' includes the call to faith in Christ and the use of his two sacraments, but nothing else belongs to the essential gospel. The Old Testament includes much legislation, the New includes the Sermon on the Mount, and Christians must obey the Ten Commandments and strive to live as taught by the Sermon: 'faith does good works', as Luther had already made clear in a pamphlet on *Good Works*. But Christians are free from any obligation to earn salvation by their own actions. To be saved, all that they need is faith or trust, for 'faith unites the soul with Christ as a bride is united with her bridegroom'.

These last two pamphlets of 1520 had understandably led many to conclude that the intrepid reformer advocated a new start for Christianity, with total liberty apart from the need to have faith. But he now showed unmistakably that he was only a reformer of a tradition, not a revolutionary. He was resolved to rescue both the church and the individual Christian from captivity to the medieval system, but his Reformation was to have its own firm shape.

In Wittenberg he stopped the riots which had been stirred up by Karlstadt's impetuous attacks on customs and objects dear to conservatives: the Mass had been abolished and images smashed. What Luther wanted was the powerful but also patient preaching of 'the Word' and he trusted that any desirable changes would follow in an orderly manner. In many ways he was a conservative alarmed by disorder. In 1522 an attack by men of the impoverished lesser nobility on the rich prince-archbishop of Trier was suppressed by the princes. Luther had encouraged the 'knights' (who had supported him at Worms) but he did not make this public. Two years later equally unsuccessful risings by peasants and urban workers similarly failed to win his support. He wrote two pamphlets. One blamed the peasants' anger on the landlords ('You do nothing but flog and rob your subjects') but advised non-violence, moderation and the force of prayer. 'Suffering, suffering, cross, cross! This and nothing else is the Christian law!' When this plea for reconciliation was ignored he wrote another pamphlet, urging the lords to 'stab, strike, strangle these mad dogs'. He had thrown away any chance of leading the reform of society outside the sphere of private morals, and incidentally he had ensured that the south German countryside would remain predominantly Catholic. And the rebels had a case. The fiery words of some Lutheran preachers lay behind their demands. They offered to withdraw if any point could be shown as contrary to Scripture and the motto on their banners was 'The Word of the Lord endures for ever'. They protested against what remained of medieval serfdom and against new practices by landlords: excessive rents and demands for free labour, fines as arbitrary new punishments, the cancellation of traditional rights to hunt, fish and gather wood. However, Luther did not see social reform as part of his business and he had no intention of allowing a link with rebellion to alienate the patrons of his preaching.

He relied on princes and city councils to support the spread of his understanding of the Word of God and a theology of 'two kingdoms' was gradually clarified. There was to be no such distinction between these two realms as there had been between Augustine's 'two cities': a Christian could live in both kingdoms. Neither was one kingdom to be placed over the other, as in medieval thought about Church and State where the papacy's claim to supremacy had been met by claims to superiority on behalf of emperors, kings or cities. The comparison was now between two honourable kingdoms and two useful hands. With God's right hand (so to speak) he rules the Church which is 'the community of believers'—and Luther could sometimes write or speak rudely about princes (as well as about almost everyone else). But with his left hand God rules the world which is far from being full of believers. He rules states and cities through princes and councillors, judges and executioners, as he rules families through fathers. This left hand shows love by strength, grace by punishments; and princes and city councils have the right to control the externals in church life.

Although Luther clung to the hope that God would reform the whole Catholic Church by the preaching of the Word, in practice much depended on decisions by the political authority. In 1526 he welcomed the decision of the Reichstag that princes should be free to order church life in their own states in accordance with their own consciences 'before God and the emperor'. From 1527 he taught that John Frederick, who had succeeded Frederick the Wise, was right to authorize a visitation of the Saxon churches as an 'emergency bishop'. He accepted the similar control over church life exercised by the magistrates of the cities which accepted his Reformation, beginning with Nuremberg. And he accepted the right of Christians to go to war in defence of justice, not hesitating about the right to kill. Although he delayed until the 1530s before clearly encouraging Protestant princes to take up arms against the emperor, in the end he did so pronounce. And because he grew increasingly aware that survival depended on the power of a few Protestant princes who were morally weak as well as militarily vulnerable, in 1539 he sanctioned and attended the bigamous marriage of Philip, prince of Hesse (Saxony's western neighbour). When Philip, a sincere Lutheran who was unhappily married, announced that he had fallen in love with a lady who refused to be one of his mistresses, Luther could not point to any passage in the Bible explicitly forbidding bigamy. (In accordance with Matthew's gospel he believed that a Christian might divorce an adulterer and presumably marry again, but unfortunately Philip was in no position to cast the first stone at his wife.) It says a lot that Luther tried to keep this advice secret.

In all this he was like Zwingli. But he resisted any conclusion that the Christian's freedom meant the end of every trace of medieval Catholicism in the Church.

He preached the 'priesthood of all believers' and in practice wherever his Reformation was accepted bishops and priests lost wealth and power, but he attached the highest importance to the responsibilities of the preacher and his vast output of teaching material showed how little he trusted in the ability of the untutored individual to interpret Scripture correctly. He preached against monastic vows and with assurances to his friends that he was not being driven by lust married a former Cistercian nun, Katharina von

Bora. He fell in love after the marriage and became the father of six children, but when he and his Kate made their home in the former Augustinian monastery they took in students as lodgers and he held forth in theological table talk which was recorded and published: his marriage was far from being the secular affair which his enemies made it out to be. He preached against any theory that the Mass was a sacrifice to propitiate God and against Requiem Masses and Corpus Christi processions, and he urged that the laity should frequently receive the bread and the wine, but he saw no reason why the weekly Mass should not continue to be called by that name, or why the 'host' should not continue to be a wafer elevated before communion by a priest in the traditional robes surrounded by the traditional statues of Christ and the saints. And as we have seen, he would not listen to Zwingli's theory.

He preached against the belief that the forgiveness of sins depended on confession to a priest, but he was reluctant to see the practice of private confession discarded altogether. An active spiritual counsellor, he confessed his own sins regularly and spent three hours a day in prayer. He preached against canon law's demand for uniformity but published a largely traditional German Mass to guide worship, a Greater Catechism to guide fellow preachers and teachers and a Shorter Catechism to be learned by the laity. In addition to his German Bible he provided popular words and music for hymns. His basic teaching, repeated endlessly, was that the gifts of forgiveness, faith and grace must be received passively. In God's eyes everyone is a sinner but some sinners can be 'justified'—treated by him as righteous; they can then be given faith in him; this faith can then begin to make them righteous. But this insistence on 'justification by grace through faith' did not produce for Luther or for his disciples a passive religion. He insisted that faith made active love possible and called himself 'the doctor (teacher) of good works'. One of his own works was writing with an extraordinary energy and never accepting any payment for it.

As he grew older he was seldom in good health and his depressions returned. He held the belief that the Christian is *simul justus et peccator* ('simultaneously the righteous one and the sinner') and the Church lives by the forgiveness of its sins. But he observed that many sins remained after his Reformation, complaining that even in his own part of Saxony many people still thought like pagans and lived like animals. It became clear that he was not going to convert the Catholic Church or even to unite all the reforming movements. He allowed Philip Melanchthon, a disciple since student days but no believer in hostilities or exaggerations, to draft a number of declarations of faith which were as conservative as possible, most notably the Augsburg Confession which some princes presented to the emperor in 1530 in an attempt to prove that they were not heretics unfit to rule Christians. It was calm in explaining doctrines and making criticisms and there was no direct attack on the papacy. At the instigation of the emperor a real effort was made eleven years later to reach agreement between Protestant and Catholic theologians. Calm discussion showed that much agreement was possible, along a line which was to be taken again when the ecumenical movement began to seek Christian reunion some four hundred years later: God first 'imputes' righteousness to the sinner and then 'imparts' it. But reactions showed that the bridge was not to be crossed. The pope was suspicious that not enough emphasis had been placed on the Church's sacraments as the vehicles of salvation. Luther was suspicious because Man's free will had been thought to co-operate with God.

His book on *The Councils and the Church* (1539) demonstrated that he expected no improvement from any council which a pope might allow. The four great councils in the distant past had been faithful to Scripture and— almost as important—had been convened by emperors. Any future council must be similarly governed by Scripture and must include representatives of the princes to make sure of it. And Luther's last book, published in 1545 as the council of Trent was opening without Protestants or princes, was an unrestrained attack on the papacy. He also directed his anger against a target from which no counter-attack was to be feared, for in his last pamphlet he raved against the Jews. He preferred to see them converted to Christ rather than persecuted, but advocated that if not converted they should be expelled to some land of their own. He was to be quoted in the future as a propagandist of anti-Semitism.

How is such a man to be assessed?

Apart from Jesus, Paul and Augustine no personality has had so great an impact on Christianity and it is not easy to assess him both briefly and objectively. During his old age 'Lutherans' (a term he disliked) began to quarrel about the right interpretation of his teaching. Some were 'Philippists', for Philip Melanchthon did his best to link the message of his master with other contemporary theologies, Catholic or 'Reformed', and with the wisdom of the ages; for example, he was ready to listen to other people's ideas about the Eucharist. He held that many topics which had aroused controversy were *adiaphora* (comparatively unimportant). Others maintained that there must be a distinctively Lutheran theology and style, in the Mass as elsewhere. Melanchthon also developed Luther's emphasis on the permanence of the Ten Commandments and on the believer's good works. But if the Commandments still had to be kept and if good works flowed from faith, did law-abiding goodness amount to *synergia*, co-operation with God? The suggestion so distressed some Lutherans that they insisted that God is not interested in good works, even that they could be dangerous to salvation. It was reported that once at table with Melanchthon Luther had said, as he often did, that 'God saves whom he wills'—but the disciple had dared to reply 'No, God saves whoever wishes to be saved'. Luther had forgiven this reply, but should Lutherans? Or could it be said that the sinner 'justified' by God's decree was not merely treated as righteous but actually made righteous? If so, what became of the advice which Luther had given to Melanchthon in the fateful year 1521, 'Be a sinner and sin strongly, but even more strongly put your faith and your joyous hope in Christ'?

In 1577–80, at the insistence of Lutheran princes alarmed by these disputes, theologians produced a 'Formula of Concord' which most Lutheran leaders or teachers were persuaded to sign. It was agreed that churches should not divide over *adiaphora*, yet the 'right use of the sacraments' is important; that 'good works follow faith', yet the faith through which salvation is received is 'the gift of God'. What was clearly rejected was predestination to hell, since 'Christ calls all sinners'. Disputes about Luther's significance did not end in 1580, however. While Lutheran orthodoxy was to defend his memory and his doctrine against all comers, he was also to be praised in the Enlightenment as an individual who defied authority and in Pietism as a saint with a great heart. More 'liberal' Protestants were to applaud him as an almost Erasmian scholar and pastor who rejected legalism and ritualism, mysticism and metaphysics. 'Romantic' Protestants were to see him as 'the eternal German', unleashing the creative forces of German emotionalism, German nationalism and the German language. For long he was to be seen by Catholics as the almost demonic enemy of the Church, a man who had reduced the Faith to a mere feeling, who had done what he could to destroy Christendom, who had married a nun and had been the father of many disastrous errors. The quest for the historical Luther has been attempted rigorously only in the twentieth century, but still there has been no agreement. Was he a thoroughly medieval figure in his piety as in much of his philosophy, a man trembling under the wrath of God and the power of Satan? Or was he almost a modern existentialist, wrestling alone with a pathological anxiety inherited from childhood? Was he a forerunner of the arrogantly German Nazis, not least in his anti-Semitism? Or was he a man of learning and prayer, a better Catholic than the Renaissance popes who excommunicated him? By the 1990s the appreciation of Luther by many Catholics had so increased that it was hoped (in vain) that this excommunication would be lifted posthumously as a gesture of reconciliation. On the Protestant side more than five hundred years after his birth, much thought was still heavily influenced by Luther. Those who stressed the very personal 'leap of faith' into 'authentic existence' appealed to his authority. So did those who stressed the Christian's duty to pray and work within the ordered life of Church and State, to perform daily duties well and to support the good causes of the day. The difference between these two aspects of Luther (and of Lutheranism) has aroused controversy within the tradition and puzzlement outside it, but it seems possible to agree one thing about this complex personality: he made Christianity a religion for the laity as it had originally been, but without any admixture of pagan magic praying for material benefits. And something more than that may be agreed.

It was both his strength and his weakness that he reduced the idea of 'faith' to fit his experience. That enabled him to stand and to lead when so many others had produced complaints rather than changes. For many, his vision of God made the whole system of the late medieval Church look unconvincing and unimportant. Yet as something was lost in the first-century break with Judaism after Paul's experience of faith, so something was lost in this break with Catholicism. And while those Christians who wished to retain the Jesus movement's original Jewish identity were clearly defeated by history, no such fate awaited sixteenth-century Catholicism. Most of Europe wanted to remain Catholic, not only because of pressures from rulers but also because the 'old religion' was genuinely preferred. In Germany itself distinguished people who were humanist or biblical scholars abandoned Luther when they saw where he was leading. (One such, who ended up helping Eck in the defence of Catholicism, was Reuchlin, the Old Testament scholar who had previously seemed to be a radical at the centre of controversy. And he was Melanchthon's uncle.) Many humbler people were horrified by what they heard about Lutheranism. This was because the experience which was central in Luther's religious life was not central for all Christians. To some extent he admitted this when he said that within the New Testament there were books which he did not value so highly as others because they did not correspond with his experience. The other three gospels were less important than John's, and since the Revelation of John could not have been written by the apostle who recorded the words of Jesus perhaps it ought not to have been included in Holy Scripture. The letter of James which taught that 'a person is justified by works and not by faith alone' was 'straw' in comparison with Paul's letter to the Romans which taught that 'a man is justified by faith apart from works of the law'. Luther derived 'faith alone' from 'Scripture alone' but had to grant that parts of the Bible were dangerously close to the insistence of Catholicism on 'works'. He attacked the Catholic Church for claiming that Scripture needed to be interpreted by it but he insisted that the gospel needed to be 'preached'. That could mean interpreted in the light of a particular understanding of 'faith', or in the light of a formally articulated and agreed 'confession of faith' as Lutheranism became systematic.

Despite some attempts to be modest he once described his eloquence as 'sword, fire and earthquake' and he was not handicapped by any obligation to be calmly precise, balanced and courteous. (He left all that to Melanchthon, the disciple who used that Greek name as if he were an Athenian philosopher.) His own style, full of exaggerations and arresting paradoxes, helped him to touch the emotions and wills of many, not least because he could use their coarse language ('I would eat dung if God demanded it'). But the freedom which he allowed himself to abuse those with whom he disagreed ruined any hopes of reconciliation with Catholics who revered the idea of the papacy. However much they criticized a particular pope, they could not accept that the only link between the papacy and the Bible was the mature Luther's conviction that the pope was the predicted Antichrist. As Alister McGrath has pointed out, 'however positively Luther's contribution to the Reformation is to be evaluated, it must be conceded that he had the universally negative effect of causing authentically Catholic and orthodox views, potentially capable of injecting a new vitality into a tired Church, to be regarded as heretical'. Luther's rudeness also destroyed all hopes that Lutherans might come to terms with Erasmians or with the Swiss reformers. There was never to be a united front demanding reform. And his ravings in print encouraged ruthless men to respond to the pleas of peasants by extra brutality and to persecute defenceless Jews. Thus his vigorous style both created and destroyed, like richly fertile lava pouring out of a volcano. And his explosive theology, so thoroughly personal, both created and destroyed the Church's integrity. His courage made German and Scandinavian Protestantism possible and it can even be said that he saved the papacy and the Catholic Church by challenging them to develop a Catholic Reformation. These were mighty achievements. Yet his understanding of the gospel did not extend to any very clear vision either of the Church or of society and in practice the preaching of that gospel depended on the good will of princes or city councils. So the effect was to leave governments free to control church life and even to command Christian consciences. This outcome was against his own wishes, for he never taught that a Christian should obey 'ungodly' commands, but it was to be a tragic reality.

In the end, to be fair to Luther is to acknowledge supremely his sense of the power of God to create, rule, condemn, forgive and love. In this shattering experience of what 'faith' means when the sinner is face to face with Christ he had what the late medieval system could not offer and what neither Erasmus nor Zwingli possessed. Shortly before his death in 1546 he wrote a brief note. It ended 'we are beggars—that is true'. He had begged and received.

Calvin's Reformation

Jean Calvin had the mind of a lawyer and brought to the work of reform in Christianity's sixteenth century a personality colder than Erasmus, Zwingli or Luther; yet he often compared the experience of hearing God with hearing thunder and he helped many to hear. His very rare powers as an organizer of men and thoughts were totally employed in the service of God as he understood God. He was masterful but not egocentric. It is characteristic that he never told the story of how he was converted from the life of a scholarly, humanist layman within the Catholic world (although no doubt critically within). He ordered that he should be buried in an unmarked grave. He strongly objected to the word 'Calvinist', preferring 'Reformed': he sank his personality in the work of Reformation.

Born in 1509 in the old cathedral city of Noyon in Picardy, he was the son of a man who had risen to be the secretary of the bishop and the business agent of the cathedral's clergy. The boy was educated socially by mixing with the aristocratic bishop's family and intellectually by going to the college in Paris where Erasmus had been miserably poor and bored. This young man, however, was a privileged student financed out of the income of posts in the Church provided by his father's employers. His powers of analysis and argument were sharpened by that 'arts' course in Paris and then by legal studies in Orleans and Bourges; and through his study of Roman law it became his ambition to be a scholar in the classics, like Erasmus. At the age of 23 he produced at his own expense an edition of the little book in which the Stoic philosopher Seneca had vainly urged *clementia* on the emperor Nero. This criticized the earlier edition by Erasmus and seemed to its few readers a conceited although competent exercise. Although in this period Calvin must have become aware that the humanism of classical scholarship could spill over into biblical studies (Jacques Lefèvre d'Etaples had already written commentaries on Paul and had translated the New Testament into French), in his commentary on Seneca there were only four biblical quotations.

In twelve months, 1533–34, the young man changed. At the beginning of that period he attended a meeting as an office-holder in the cathedral of Noyon; by the end he had resigned. (It may well be relevant that his father and brother had been excommunicated, not for any religious or moral offence but because it was alleged that business for the cathedral had been mismanaged.) The only public event was his involvement in an incident in Paris: a friend preached a sermon which seemed too critical of the Church, the authorities suspected that he also was a Lutheran, the two men had to flee. But somehow before the end of 1536 Calvin had so organized his new faith and his rapidly growing passion for self-taught theology that he became the author of two short books in Latin. One was on life after death, the other was the first version of one of the most influential books in the world's history, the *Institutes of the Christian Religion*.

'Institutes' has been the normal attempt to translate into English a word which is untranslatable ('Institution' may be better) but which does indicate that already the author's intention was to organize clearly. In 1536 the material was almost entirely Lutheran although some scholars have detected traces of connections with the Stoicism of Seneca: there was an emphasis on the control of events by God and on the control of people by a ruler 'clement' but firm. Now the young author needed a job. He was offered one in Geneva, a little city which had just accomplished a political and religious breakaway from the Catholic duchy of Savoy and from its own Savoyard bishop. He was to teach Scripture as assistant to the chief Protestant preacher, Farel.

He tried to organize everything in sight. He compiled a 'confession of faith' and wanted the expulsion from the town of anyone who refused to accept it. He worked out a system for the religious education and moral discipline of those, young and old, who would remain. But the citizens had not rejected the duke and the bishop in order to make this young stranger a dictator. He and Farel were the ones who were expelled. He found refuge with an older and a wiser reformer in Strasbourg, Martin Bucer, who taught him much while he acquired his first pastoral experience and a helpful wife. A much longer and improved Latin edition of the *Institutes* appeared and was translated into French. A more workable system of discipline for 'reformed' Christians was derived from the arrangements in Strasbourg. At first Calvin, wounded by his failure, had intended to lead a scholar's life in private, but when Geneva called him back he decided in the end to go, in 1541.

He returned armed with a scheme which he never abandoned, the 'Ecclesiastical Ordinances'. The heart of the system was a 'consistory' of pastors (nine in 1541, more later) and twelve elders. The function of the pastors was to expound the Word of God and Calvin himself preached four times a week in addition to delivering lectures and writing commentaries on most of the Bible. The elders reported anyone whose life was not in accordance with that Word in order that the offender might be rebuked and, if obstinate, publicly excommunicated. It has often been assumed that this imposed on Geneva a theocracy, a tyranny by preachers claiming to be God's spokesmen. That is not wholly accurate. The pastors were appointed and salaried by the magistrates of the Little Council and until 1555 had to accept the council's decisions about excommunication. Before that the pastors could only receive and approve a recommendation from the elders and transmit it to the magistrates. Not until 1559 was Calvin made a citizen entitled to vote in the choice of the Little Council. He never achieved the more frequent celebration of the Lord's Supper which he wanted, so that excommunication applied only to a quarterly event. It could not lead to imprisonment, for Geneva had no prison. Executions took place (normally about ten a year) but were reserved for offences such as murder, treason or witchcraft, then universally agreed to deserve death, and Calvin never persuaded the magistrates to make adultery a capital offence. Excommunication was meant to isolate the culprit and in some cases involved expulsion from the city but there is much evidence that many people in Geneva were ready to mix with those who were sentenced.

It is, however, striking that a city with its share of human passions accepted even this degree of control by preachers. The magistrates of other cities included the citizens' morality among their responsibilities, but Geneva was stricter. An insult to Calvin's preaching might lead to a magistrate walking the streets dressed as a penitent and open disagreement with his theology might lead to exile. At least on paper the laws of Geneva regulated clothing and hairdressing, banned dancing and gambling, and enforced attendance at sermons. In the 1560s there were about five hundred excommunications a year, in a total population of about 25,000; and many more were formally rebuked for quarrelling. We may wonder why Calvin was given the limited power which he was given.

The reasons were not all religious. Geneva had been overtaken by Nuremberg and Lyon as a commercial centre and if it was not to be sucked back into Savoy it now needed loans from other Swiss Protestant cities (to pay for fortifications, for example). But it did not want to be controlled by any of those cities—in particular not by rich Berne, whose army had been indispensable in Geneva's liberation from the Savoyards. Like any other self-respecting city it needed its own system to defeat irreligion and immorality, perhaps somewhat as a modern city needs a successful football team for its morale. Calvin not only supplied this need against opposition from Savoy and Berne. He attracted refugees from Catholic persecution in France, mostly artisans with technical skills such as clock-making, and the city began to prosper as a manufacturing centre. Eventually it was recognized that the richer of these *habitants* ought to be secured as residents by being made *bourgeois* (full citizens) and it was the voting power of these new arrivals that defeated Calvin's critics.

The worst blot on his memory is connected with the burning of Michael Servetus in 1553. A Spaniard, an Erasmian scholar and an outstanding physician, Servetus had been so indiscreet as to publish unorthodox theology about the Trinity (stressing the divine unity) and baptism (to be limited to adults) and then to visit Geneva—it seems, out of curiosity—while escaping from a heretic's fate in France. He had already returned a copy of Calvin's *Institutes* to the author with insulting comments in the margins. Calvin now accused him of dire heresy but did his best to convert him and then to have him beheaded instead of burned, but the sentence was passed by the Little Council (then dominated by Calvin's enemies) after consulting other Swiss Protestant cities, who were unanimous. Neither Calvin nor Geneva intended to leave any impression that 'reform' meant a relaxation of the general attitude of the time to men such as Servetus. A monument erected in 1902 on the site of the execution rightly calls it a mistake belonging to its age. What is surprising is not that Servetus was burned but that Castellio, once Calvin's colleague as a teacher but now expelled after a disagreement, publicly protested against the use of force in matters of religion.

What Calvin regarded as orthodoxy was set out in his *Institutes*, revised and untidily expanded as a result of his many controversies. Successive editions had that character until 1559, when he heroically reduced the material to order despite feeling old and ill and despite increasing bitterness towards any who dared to contradict. The book became the textbook of 'Reformed' (as contrasted with Catholic or Lutheran) Christianity.

It was inspired by the need to avoid the chaos resulting from the interpretation of Scripture by individuals thought competent neither by the trained preachers nor by the powerful magistrates. The first edition was dedicated to Francis I and was intended to show that critics of the late medieval Church could still be sound Christians and loyal Frenchmen. At that time there was some hope, partly because Francis was involved in anti-Habsburg intrigues with Lutheran princes. When it became clear that the kings of France would remain Catholics in accordance with the religion of the majority of their subjects, it was still Calvin's intention to prove that to be 'reformed' did not mean rejecting ordinary decencies and loyalties or abandoning the faith of the Bible and the Fathers. In particular he stood within the Augustinian tradition although he also paid honour to eastern theology as represented by many quotations from John Chrysostom.

By this time the enthusiastic radicalism which had troubled Zwingli and Luther had become still more thorough in its rejection of Catholicism. Prophets arose whose frank intention was to found small sects separate from the world, not large churches adjusted to life within it. Because they all insisted on confining baptism to adult believers and were therefore willing to re-baptize, these sectarians were commonly called, hated and persecuted as 'Anabaptists', but their vision of Christianity saw far beyond baptism. Very simply they tried to reproduce the life of the little communities of baptized believers in the New Testament—with no desire for fashionableness but a call to discipleship, with no formalities in worship but a commitment to participate, with no links with governments but a willingness to be martyred. Such were the Mennonites in the Netherlands, named after Menno Simons. But particularly since persecution removed most of the educated and moderate Anabaptists, more radical men became leaders.

These radicals taught that true Christians were not mere sinners to whom God had imputed an 'alien' righteousness (in the Lutheran phrase). By the grace of God they became saints well before death. It was not necessary to

313

leave it to God to say who were in this category: they were visible on earth, as members of a congregation of saints. Nor was it necessary to obey princes and magistrates; the saints were entitled to rule and if they met tribulations it was in the triumphant cause of the 'kingdom of Christ' soon to be completed. Such doctrines appealed to some who were not at home in their worldly societies, but they shocked Catholics and almost all Protestants alike. The most famous or notorious leader was Thomas Müntzer, once an admirer of Luther, soon his scornful enemy. He taught that revelation came through dreams and ecstasies and that the sword must be used against the ungodly, and he was a victim when the princes massacred the rebellious peasants. In February 1534 'saints' took over the cathedral city of Münster in Westphalia and enforced the observance of what they regarded as biblical legislation, sensationally including communism in material goods and the practice of polygamy. Within six months the profoundly disturbing experiment was ended by the use of greater forces generalled by the bishop.

Calvin resolved to reply to it by better theology. He had converted his own wife, an Anabaptist's widow, and was full of assurance as he expanded the *Institutes*.

The doctrine of God is Augustinian. We must 'leave to God the privilege of knowing himself' (a quotation from Hilary of Poitiers), acknowledging that the Fall has left humanity a 'miserable ruin' with no clear knowledge of the Creator. Admittedly the elementary 'seeds of religion are sown in every heart'—both by the universal understanding that the world is created to be 'the theatre of God's glory' and by the guilty conscience which everywhere produces 'a serious fear of God'. But God is clearly revealed only in the witness to his will provided by the Scriptures—by all the Scriptures (without being as selective as Luther). In a few details there may be mistakes and the Old Testament is inferior to the New, but throughout the Scriptures God speaks and it is the function of the Holy Spirit to open hearts and minds in order that the Word may be heard. It is significant that Lutheranism was famous for its new hymns, but Calvinism for its metrical versions of biblical psalms. Not until Joachim Neander, who died in 1680, did any hymns written by a Calvinist echo the Bible without repeating it closely. In this biblical message the role of law is more important than it is for Luther, but the focus is, of course, on salvation through Christ.

The decisions of the Church's ancient councils about the Trinity and the natures of Christ are endorsed as being faithful to Scripture but what matters most is that the believer should trust in Christ 'the prophet, priest and king' whose death the Father decided to accept as 'satisfaction'. This trust in Christ is like the trust in the Scriptures, the work of the Spirit. Calvin acknowledged the Spirit as the 'Lord and Giver of Life' much more clearly than Luther did (partly because he was more familiar with eastern theology), but he agreed with Luther that no human being can be 'justified' before the throne of God on the basis of his or her own merits. And he disagreed with Erasmus: any element of 'free will' that may be involved in this turning to Christ is so petty that it does not deserve theological consideration.

The distinctive elements in the revised *Institutes* become stronger when Calvin deals with predestination and with the Church's leadership.

As we have seen, he was no innovator when he taught that God has predestined true Christians to heaven. The tradition to that effect went back to the New Testament—to the prayers of Jesus in thanksgiving that the Father had chosen the disciples for glory and to the reminders that Christians had been 'elected' before the creation of the world. But Calvin experienced painfully the rejection by many of the gospel which he preached and with a mind more logical than charitable he refused to endorse any of the suggestions which previous theologians had hoped would sufficiently soften a doctrine truly *horribile* (terrifying). For him God does not merely know in advance whose merits are going to deserve heaven: he decides a person's ultimate fate in the very act of creation, without regard to that person's merits. God does not merely abandon people to the consequences of their wickedness: by his providence he so orders their lives that they end in the hell for which they were always destined. And God's policy cannot be defended morally, for his justice is exalted far above any human distinctions between good and evil. Calvin's hard line on such matters was to cost Calvinism dearly. Within the next hundred years Catholics and Protestants alike repeatedly attacked it as a doctrine which was based on no more than a few words in the much wider gospel taught by Paul and which was contrary to the central teaching of Jesus that the goodness of God the Father ought to be recognized by comparing it with the goodness of people. But to Calvin, 'double predestination' was inescapably logical. No milder doctrine seemed able to account for the choice by God of people who were not saints; nor could it explain the rejection by so many of truths proclaimed by Scripture and conscience.

The offence caused was increased when after his death Dutch Calvinists disputed about the right interpretation of the doctrine without ever denying its truth. Did Christ die in order to provide the divine justice with satisfaction for the sins of all, however few were actually to be saved through their faith—or did he suffer only for the benefit of the few predestined to believe and to be saved? The 'Remonstrants' defending the views of the theologian called in Latin Arminius argued for the first alternative but an international synod in Dort (Dordrecht) in the winter of 1618–19 decided for the more austere doctrine. Did God decree how many would be predestined to heaven or hell before, or after, the Fall of Adam? This question was debated between the Supralapsarians and the Infralapsarians. It may seem amazing that Christian minds were preoccupied by such questions but the dispute expressed social tensions: Amsterdam was unexpectedly conservative (perhaps because Rotterdam was largely Arminian) but on the whole the Arminian preachers were popular with the middle classes, then making money out of peace. They were correspondingly unpopular elsewhere; three hundred were expelled from their pulpits and the leading statesman associated with them was executed for high treason.

For Calvin himself the refinements of the doctrine of predestination were not so important as they became in Holland. 'Where something is neither given nor lawful to know', he wrote, 'to remain ignorant is to be learned.' He was more interested in the application of the doctrine to spiritual questions, with cheerful beliefs which the synod of Dort was to endorse. God deals with individuals; initially their 'depravity' is total but if his grace is given it cannot be resisted; the 'elect' must and can persevere to the end, whatever their trials. In the earlier editions of his *Institutes* the doctrine of predestination was not stressed and later it was not completely dominant. He spent more space in his great book on another conclusion from his experience of difficulties: the need for strong membership and strong leadership in the Church on earth.

For Calvin, faith is the 'steady and certain knowledge of the divine good will towards us, which, being grounded upon the truth of the gracious promises in Christ, is both revealed to our minds and confirmed in our hearts by the Holy Spirit'. Through the believer's faith Christ 'grafts us into his body and makes us not only partakers of all his benefits but also of himself'. While 'justification' depends on Christ's merits not the believer's and is 'the principal article of the Christian religion', yet for the predestined believer 'sanctification' follows through the Holy Spirit's continuing work. One decisive stage in this process of being 'inserted into Christ' is baptism, which is open to children: the child's helplessness dramatizes the helplessness of all before God. The Lord's Supper is also a sacrament and therefore 'an external sign by which the Lord seals on our conscience his promises of good will towards us, in order to sustain the weakness of our faith'. Zwingli was supported in the teaching that a sacrament works spiritually without any change in the 'substance' of bread or wine, but Luther was supported in the teaching that the sacrament is more powerful than Zwingli came to think. 'Sacraments', Calvin wrote, 'do not bestow any grace by themselves, but they announce to us and tell us, and as guarantees and tokens ratify among us, what is given to us by the divine bounty.' Thus in the Lord's Supper 'Jesus Christ truly is given to us under the sign of the bread and wine, even his body and his blood . . . in order that we might be united in one body; secondly, so that being made partakers of his substance we should also feel his virtue'. Always Calvinism, when loyal to its founder, was to be a firmly structured kind of Christianity, with the emphasis not on the free Spirit but on the Scriptures, the sacraments, the making of disciplined saints.

Calvin was (like Luther) convinced that 'wherever we see the Word of God preached purely and listened to, and the sacraments administered according to the institution of Christ, we cannot doubt that a church exists'. It is noteworthy that he did not include any particular form of 'discipline' among these marks of the true Church: the absolute rejection of bishops by Calvinists came later. Although it is not certain that he was ever ordained formally and he never made much of that rite, he wanted pastors to be chosen by other pastors before approval by a congregation and his definition of the Church implied a very high doctrine about the ministry's work. Bucer had persuaded him that the New Testament supplied a firm basis for such a doctrine, as when the letter to the Ephesians (4:11, 12) taught that Christ's 'gifts were that some should be apostles, some prophets, some evangelists, some pastors and teachers, to equip the saints for the work of ministry'. Apostles, prophets and evangelists were not now needed but separate 'orders' of pastors, teachers, elders and deacons were.

He was not always consistent in listing these four categories, particularly since pastors such as himself could also be teachers. He never really faced (although he stated) two facts about early church history: there was then no difference in function between pastors and elders, and out of the *presbyteroi* who were also *episkopoi* one bishop emerged (although not immediately) as the president. But it seems fair to say that by establishing these three or four offices as essential to any well-governed church, he made provision for scriptural principles. He insisted that the ministers of a church must be called and united in fellowship by the Holy Spirit (with a weekly meeting for mutual correction in Geneva) and must be equipped and active in preaching and pastoral care. Others must assist both by educational work (the teachers), by knowing personally Christians in trouble or troublesome (the elders), and by helping the needy (the deacons). It was an ideal fit to be placed beside the Orthodox or Catholic ideal of the priesthood.

Even that brief summary of the *Institutes* may be enough to show how strange it is that Calvinism has been given some or much of the credit or discredit for the emergence of modern capitalism and democracy. Non-Calvinist and non-Christian societies have provided many examples of the kind of thinking or activity for which Calvinism has been praised or blamed in this connection. In contrast, Calvin was not greatly interested in these matters. He never wrote systematically on ethics or politics after his youthful commentary on Seneca. Geneva went into economic decline in the seventeenth century (like most of Switzerland) and one reason was that in its trade, like the rest of its life, it was as tightly regulated as Byzantium: it was no advertisement either for free enterprise or for liberal democracy.

What, then, are we to make of the claim that Calvin was a 'father of the modern world' (Emile Doumergue), to be complimented for that world's liberation of economic energy (Max Weber)? The reply has often been made that Calvin had little or nothing to do with the making of the modern world, for he has been identified with the doctrine that God predestines a few to be 'saved' without regard to their conduct and makes sure that they never resist his 'grace' or forfeit his favour while the rest go to hell. More than any other factor, it was the belief that Calvinism led to this repugnant conclusion that deterred the Church of England (for example) from becoming thoroughly Calvinist as the sixteenth century became the seventeenth. But more than that needs to be said if justice is to be done to the connections which did exist between Calvinism and modernity.

Luther's encouragement of good works after faith had included an influential emphasis on a lay Christian's honourable 'calling' in daily life. Calvin's own theology could be combined with the same emphasis, for in pastoral practice he softened the doctrine of double predestination. He refused to say that any individual could be known to be damned for eternity; God's choice was known to God alone. When asked how one could be sure of one's 'election' to heaven, he would reply by asking about the life on earth: if good, it strongly suggested 'election' by God. Such teaching helped to make many Calvinists confidently active although some were tormented by the fear of hell. Many felt summoned to fight and win in spiritual battles including what has been called the 'conquest of poverty' and it became easy (although contrary to Calvin's own austere teaching) to point to material success as a sign of God's blessing on the honest, industrious, sober and thrifty. It helped that Calvin did not continue the medieval Church's official campaign against receiving interest on investments. He repeated the usual warnings against greed, but also accepted 5 per cent in annual interest as a reasonable reward (like Zwingli, although Luther was more conservative). But the main contribution of Calvinism to modern economic life was more indirect: it lay in the psychological atmosphere. Work was not to be interrupted by many 'holy' days: it was now itself holy. It was not downgraded in comparison with a monk's prayers: it was itself obedience to the will of God. It supported a family and a family's quiet pleasures: that, too, was God's will. Because marriage and childbearing were sacred, weddings and baptisms must take place in the Calvinist 'temple' (medieval practice had been lax although the church was meant to be used) and every father ought to preside over Bible reading and prayers in the home. Any surplus profit made by that breadwinner ought not to be wasted in vanity's display: it should be invested so that God's good creation might produce more wealth. And although Calvin was interested in the glory of God not in wealth, he provided (as Luther did not) an example of achievement by being self-controlled and orderly.

Much the same appears to be true about the connection between Calvinism and democracy. Luther had already encouraged princes and magistrates to regard themselves as God's ministers, almost as bishops. In the last chapter of his *Institutes* Calvin, too, bestowed a blessing on civil government. The form of government which he preferred was the one he knew in Strasbourg or Geneva, where magistrates were elected by full citizens, but as a man who spent much of his life expounding the Old Testament he was certainly not against 'godly' monarchs. 'The Church', he wrote, 'has no sword' and 'the magistrates cannot be resisted without God being resisted'. However, he differed from both Zwingli and Luther in denying to the magistrates any right to decide religious truth: that was the sphere of the pastors who must base themselves on Scripture and scriptural truth was international. This division of responsibilities left open the possibilities that churches might be formed in defiance of the local laws and that pastors might grant the right to resist tyrants. Calvin was nervous about these possibilities and not always consistent. He believed that 'impious rulers are no rulers' and that 'laws govern the magistrate', but in practice he confined the right to resist to 'inferior magistrates' like the councillors in Geneva who had rebelled against the dukes of Savoy or the nobles in France who now protected 'Reformed' Christians. In his last years and after his death in 1564 this loophole in the doctrine of non-resistance could be expanded by Calvinists faced with life-or-death struggles against armed Catholics. So it came to pass that in the nineteenth century Hegel could write: 'This is the essence of the Reformation, Man is in his very nature destined to be free.'

What Calvin regarded as the essence of the Reformation which he organized in theology and church life was the proclamation of the Word of God. He really cared about the training of pastors and preachers. His heart was therefore in the foundation of the Academy of Geneva in 1559. It provided education at lower levels but concentrated on the training of men to preach to the congregations now gathering in France and elsewhere, and it attracted many hundreds of students eager for that hard life. It also attracted distinguished teachers including Theodore de Bèze (Beza), who succeeded Calvin as Geneva's chief pastor and was active in the organization of international Calvinism. Even before the academy's foundation John Knox of Scotland had spent time as a refugee in Geneva and had concluded that this was the best 'school of Christ' since the days of the apostles.

CHRISTIANITY: THE FIRST TWO THOUSAND YEARS

Establishing National Churches

It proved harder than expected to spread these Reformations across Europe, and in many countries the divisions between Lutherans and Calvinists, often bitter, supplied a suggestive contrast with the Catholic unity. Scotland was the nation that went to school in Geneva (so to speak) and even there the full establishment of discipline in the parishes took many years. One of the reasons for that eventual success was the strength of the personalities of John Knox and of his successor in the 'Reformed' leadership, Andrew Melville. But throughout Europe the heady excitements of the days when preachers and writers of the stature of Zwingli, Luther and Calvin had changed history were over. They had no successors who dominated events in the same way and even if there had been a larger supply of great men the work of establishing Reformed churches for ordinary folk would have been even harder than the overthrow of the late medieval Church by the work of pen and pulpit.

Despite the widespread feeling that reforms were needed, it took long to persuade people to adopt a version of Christianity which lacked the glamour and prestige of Catholic history and was much more demanding. No longer would it be sufficient to take part in rituals which were not always obviously different from the age-old superstitions of the pagan countryside. No longer was there comfort to be had from prayers to the beautiful Virgin or a lesser saint who was equally friendly, or from a visit to a statue or shrine which was a local touch of heaven. No longer was it possible to have one's own thoughts while the priest muttered the Mass which had been familiar, and in its way sacred, to many generations in families. To be reformed meant having to listen to sermons in a church which had been stripped of most of its beauty and having to forget many pleasant rituals. It also meant having to think hard, to enter into a personal relationship with a terrifying God, to accept a Saviour as Lord, to be guided by the Bible in a stricter morality, and to be told that hell awaited those who had not been predestined to be saved or had not experienced the profoundly emotional crisis referred to by the new talk about 'faith'. Moreover, the new preacher seemed to be more dictatorial than the old priest.

The old grumbles that reforms were needed could be changed into Reformations when social and political circumstances favoured the new religious message. These circumstances existed when there was enough town life with discussion fed by printed material including the translated Bible; or when political power was concentrated in the hands of princes or city magistrates who wanted to be rid of pope, bishop and privileged clergy; or when power was dispersed into the hands of landowners willing to be the

320

patrons of thoroughgoing reform whether or not they appreciated its spiritual content.

In the Holy Roman empire no emperor could fail to see that he owed the prestige of his position to an association with Rome going back to Charlemagne, however serious might be his political quarrel with a particular pope. This general consideration applied with special force to Charles V, who had been brought up in Catholic Spain and was its king. Although during a war with a pope his troops sacked Rome he never had the slightest wish to lead a German church rejecting the papacy. On the contrary he was a persecutor, as when in Flanders in 1535 officials responsible to him burned William Tyndale, the greatest translator of the English Bible, as the 'heretic' which he certainly was. As soon as he was free of wars with the French and the Turks he turned an army against the German Protestant princes and defeated them at Mühlberg in 1547, afterwards ending the line of Saxon 'electors' whose princely support had been indispensable to Luther. But he soon found that Catholicism could not be imposed on the empire as it could be on Spain. Not only was it impossible to put the clock back in the territories where the structure of the medieval Church had been destroyed; it was also impossible to make the emperor a dictator, for the empire was divided into about a thousand territories or cities. With French subsidies the duke of another part of Saxony whose support had been vital at Mühlberg turned against Charles and the outcome of a renewed war had to be the peace of Augsburg in 1555. What triumphed then was the principle *cuius regio eius religio*, 'the ruler decides the religion'. In one important respect this treaty checked the advance of Luther's Reformation: it meant that the Catholic prince-bishops would retain their positions although by this stage many of the people under their rule wished to be rid of them. But in general the peace provided an opportunity to build up Lutheranism as a working system over two-thirds of Germany, particularly since neither the Anabaptists nor the Calvinists were allowed the same recognition. Charles V saw this and his defeat influenced his decision to abdicate, dividing his overlarge possessions. Spain, the Netherlands and the Italian states under Habsburg rule were transferred to Philip II, a monarch who was profoundly and aggressively a Catholic. Fortunately for the Protestant cause, Philip did not become emperor.

Year after year Lutheran princes could be bishops for many purposes, issuing orders about church life and controlling visitations which brought pressures on pastors and parishioners. Luther's insistence that the two kingdoms, of Christ and of the world, must be sharply distinguished was not included in the orthodoxy which these princes enforced. Histories of theology have concentrated on the somewhat bizarre academic disputes which led to the formulation of Lutheran orthodoxy in this period (using the logic of Aristotle which Luther had declared irrelevant to true religion), but far more important in any history of popular religion is the work reflected in the records of these visitations of parishes. At that local level the new religious system began to work in many territories. It also worked in cities from Constance and Augsburg in the south to Bremen and Hamburg in the north. And of course, princes and councils were rewarded by greater control and often by larger revenues. When Albrecht, margrave of Brandenburg and master of the Teutonic Order, decided to become a Protestant and the first duke of Prussia in the 1520s, he enforced Lutheranism strictly in his domains.

When a successor was converted to Calvinism almost a century later, he did not attempt to alter the church life of his subjects, now firmly Lutheran. The same thing happened in Saxony. But elsewhere a Calvinist prince could build up the stricter religious system which he favoured. This occurred in the lands ruled by the Elector Palatine in the south west. Calvinism was always handicapped by looking and being more austere, but the personality and power of Frederick the Pious, who ruled 1557–76, overcame that handicap to such an extent that a Lutheran son and successor could not reverse his achievement. His capital, Heidelberg, replaced Geneva as Calvinism's intellectual centre. But the achievement was partly due to the toning down of controversial doctrines in the confession of faith produced on his orders in 1562, the Heidelberg Catechism, a mixture of Calvin and Zwingli. It was also due to the rejection of a claim by the pastors to decide excommunications—a rejection justified by a professor who combined theology with medicine, Thomas Luber or in Latin Erastus, the founder of the 'Erastian' belief that the Church should be clearly subordinated to the state. As a working system Protestantism always had to make concessions to political realities.

The story of Protestantism in Scandinavia illustrates this truth. The down-to-earth idea that power and wealth should be taken from the pope and the bishops was welcomed by two Scandinavian kings, Gustav Vasa of Sweden (which then included Finland) and Frederick of Denmark (which then included Norway and Iceland) with the support of most of their nobles in the 1520s.

Gustav had rebelled against Danish rule and although he remained king amid civil wars until his death in 1560 he needed the support of the landowners who in their turn wanted the lands of the rich but discredited bishops. He also needed some Lutherans from Germany (most notably the brothers Petri, the brilliant sons of a blacksmith), to help to run the life and religion of a fairly primitive country. But he did not want the conservative peasants to be unduly disturbed, Stockholm being the only town of considerable size. Not until 1531 was an archbishop appointed to Uppsala without the pope's approval, not until 1571 was a Protestant 'church order' enforced and not until 1593 was the Augsburg Confession of Lutheranism adopted as the national creed. By then Sigismund Vasa, a Catholic who had been elected king of Poland, was king of Sweden also. Not until his expulsion in 1607 was the future of Sweden as a Protestant country secure, with a Church Lutheran in doctrine but conserving bishops and some other features of Catholicism: a Church so thoroughly national that the year 1860 had arrived before the rights of dissenters were fully acknowledged by the state.

Frederick I was elected king of Denmark after the deposition of the brother-in-law of the emperor Charles V. He gradually secured first toleration and then privilege for 'reform', a process completed by the establishment of Lutheran superintendents in place of the bishops after his death in 1533. Not until 1550, however, was there a Danish Bible. The spread of the Reformation to Norway and Iceland was largely a matter of extending Danish control and culture.

England and France had been left by the Middle Ages as Europe's strongest monarchies, as we have observed. In England the Tudor monarchy eventually imposed a modified form of Protestantism. This was in the end accepted by a mostly conservative people because the alternative seemed to be either a renewal of the damaging civil wars of the fifteenth century or else the rule of a Spanish king. In contrast, France suffered almost forty years of civil wars but in the end the conservatism of the majority encouraged the conversion of the Protestant king to Catholicism. It was said maliciously that the only principle involved in his decision was that Paris was worth a Mass.

Another cynical observation was that the Protestant gospel dawned on England in Anne Boleyn's eyes. The remark is true in large measure. Henry VIII needed a new wife not merely to provide pleasure but also to bear a legitimate son in order to ensure the stability of the Tudor monarchy. A Spanish princess, Catherine of Aragon, had been his wife since shortly after his accession to the throne although the marriage had needed a papal dispensation since she was the widow of his elder brother Arthur and had failed to have registered the fact that she and Arthur had never consummated that marriage by intercourse. Henry's many abilities as a Renaissance prince had included the authorship (or at least the signature) of an attack on Luther's sacramental theology which had earned him the title 'Defender of the Faith' from a grateful pope; but they had not included the conception of an heir able to survive infancy. Characteristically he blamed Catherine and trusted that his senior clergy could arrange the cancellation of the dispensation of 1509, thus nullifying her second marriage. The Old Testament supplied contradictory evidence about the legality of marriage with a brother's widow (Deuteronomy disagreed with Leviticus) and in such matters the papacy had been known to oblige a king (Louis XII for example). But Pope Clement proved unwilling, partly because he was at that time the prisoner of Charles V, Catherine's nephew. In order to beget a future king Henry had to summon a parliament, which at his command gradually abolished papal jurisdiction. Actually, another girl was born and, in a further paradox, became the most successful monarch in English history (Elizabeth I).

But Anne's eyes shone with a liveliness which was not merely sexual. She was a member of a family ambitious for advancement and interested in the new religious ideas coming from the mainland of Europe. The ambitions characteristic of the rising laity mattered most, because they provided sufficient support for Henry's rejection of the papacy. In 1533 one of Anne's chaplains, Thomas Cranmer, was allowed by Rome to become archbishop of Canterbury and he pronounced the new marriage valid. By the end of the 1530s Henry had been declared 'Supreme Head' of the Church of England with effective control over it, the privileges of the clergy had been greatly reduced and the monasteries had been dissolved, resulting in the transfer of most of their wealth to the nobility and gentry.

Such a large alteration would probably have been impossible had it not been a time of religious unsettlement, symbolized by the order that the Bible in English should be made available in every parish church. But there was no large conservative reaction. A few Catholics accepted martyrdom rather than Henry's new status, the most notable being Thomas More, Bishop John Fisher and some courageous monks, and there was a brief rebellion in the rural north, but most of the people assented to the alteration—partly because it was their habit to obey and partly because before his death in 1547 (having worked through various wives and politicians) Henry had made it clear that he intended no big alteration in the Catholic tradition. Heretics called Lutheran or Anabaptist had defied Henry like the few Catholic martyrs or the queens and politicians who had lost his favour—and, like them, had paid for it with their lives. The Church of England owed its separation from the Roman Catholic Church to a tyrant who became monstrous.

This attempt at a settlement did not outlive Henry, however. The powerful laity found fresh targets in the Church's wealth, notably in the charities which had provided Masses for the benefit of the dead: some of the money went to new grammar schools. The nobles who dominated the council governing in the name of the boy-king, Edward VI, enriched themselves. But Edward had himself been given Protestant tutors by his father (very oddly) and the intellectual leadership of English religion now became more open to the Protestantism on the mainland. Martin Bucer moved from Strasbourg to teach in Cambridge. Thomas Cranmer produced prayer books in noble English which translated many of the traditional words of devotion but also inclined cautiously to a Calvinist interpretation of 'the

Holy Communion or Lord's Supper'. For many years the Book of Common Prayer was to hold together 'Anglicans', whether these were Catholic or Protestant in their own preferences: provision was made for the Holy Communion every Sunday and on the festivals of the saints, and for Morning or Evening Prayer with all the psalms used once a month and with four lessons from the Bible in every church every day, but this continuity which almost suggested a nation of monks was balanced by Protestant changes in the words of the Mass and by the intention that the service should be held round a table in the middle of the church. Articles of Religion were authorized, occupying roughly (would smoothly be a better word?) the position that was to be adopted elsewhere in the Heidelberg Catechism: Calvinist, but not excessively so.

The death of King Edward in 1553 was followed by a Catholic reaction, mainly because Catherine of Aragon's devoutly Catholic daughter Mary was now the legitimate monarch offering the best hope of stability. Some three hundred Protestants were burned as heretics, including Cranmer who had previously suffered agonies of conscience because of his distress that he, who had followed Henry through thick and thin, now had to disobey a monarch. Under Cardinal Pole as his successor a beginning was made in the reconstruction of Catholicism, but there were obstacles. The powerful laity refused to part with the wealth it had taken over from the institutions of the Church; Pope Paul IV accused Pole of heresy; the Protestant martyrs aroused a certain amount of sympathy; the marriage of Queen Mary to King Philip of Spain was highly unpopular although Philip was for a time at war with the pope. Above all, the Catholic restoration did not have time to take effect. In 1558 the almost simultaneous deaths of the queen and the cardinal left the way open to Anne Boleyn's daughter.

Elizabeth's personal religion seems to have been Erasmian but she was a masterful politician who knew that she had to deal with three hard facts: she must reject the papacy in order to assert her own legitimacy, but the people remained mostly conservative while also patriotic and the intellectuals needed in Church and State were now mostly convinced Protestants. Until her death in 1603 she ruled England with great effectiveness. She was ruthless in a struggle with the papacy, particularly when in 1570 Pius V had released her subjects from allegiance. 'Recusants' who refused to attend their parish churches were fined and marginalized; priests who came bravely from the mainland to sustain the old faith were tracked down, tortured in order to extract confessions and hideously executed; the Catholic cause was thrown into disarray by being connected with treason. The Elizabethan victory culminated in the frustration of a number of plans to assassinate her and to invade from Ireland, and in the defeat of the Spanish Armada in 1588. But the queen was sensitive to public opinion, which was almost as Catholic as it was patriotic. She took care to gather just enough Catholic bishops to consecrate those whom she appointed at the beginning of her reign, and she regretted that most of the senior clergy whom she had to appoint later inclined to Calvinism, like some of the laymen who served her in government. She suspended one archbishop of Canterbury from his functions when he protested against her order to silence Bible-inspired 'prophesying'. The most energetic of the preachers were Calvinist 'Puritans'. All that she could do was to insist that any manifestation of Puritanism that could be called disloyal, even if only potentially, should be suppressed like 'popery'.

All these policies won some intellectual support, most notably from Richard Hooker's *Laws of Ecclesiastical Polity*, the nearest England came to producing a theology to match Luther's or Calvin's. By this stage the theological debate had moved away from Luther's protest against the papacy in the cause of an intensely personal faith: to its spokesman the Church of England seemed calmly orthodox in belief and people who obeyed the pope seemed traitors to the country, at least potentially. The debate was now about the right of the 'godly prince' to order details of church life. Hooker maintained this right against the Puritans who wanted a further, purer Reformation. The ceremonies were not essential to faith but in every nation its ruler had a God-given right to take care of Church and State and in England Elizabeth had spoken with the consent of parliament. Laws must be obeyed, all the more when they preserved valuable traditions from the Catholic past. The church which Hooker defended was planned as the spiritual home of the English people: he recalled the unity of the people of ancient Israel under their own godly prince. It took the *via media*, the 'middle way' between the Catholic and Protestant systems, walking (it claimed) in the light provided by the Bible and 'the ancient Church' but not rejecting the life which was coming from the English version of the Renaissance. In its parish churches, where attendance was compulsory at least in theory, William Shakespeare was to memorize its Book of Common Prayer. In his plays he was to beat a patriotic drum against foreigners from France or Rome and blow the trumpet of humanity against kill-joy Puritans who wanted England to resemble Geneva.

In France the Reformation caused far more suffering, as the self-congratulating English often observed. Calvin never abandoned the hope that all France could be 'reformed' by monarchy and nobility. In his day Marguerite the queen of Navarre (a little kingdom in the far south) was a patron of reform while remaining a Catholic and her example was followed by some of the greatest nobles in France who abandoned the old Church. There was a long history of French objections to papal jurisdiction and now there was hostility to the Habsburg emperors and to Philip of Spain, so that Francis I and Henry II while burning 'heretics' who insulted the Mass in their own country sent aid to the Protestant princes in Germany. The French bishops and senior clergy were almost as exposed as those of Germany to Protestant attacks on their neglect of their pastoral duties. A network of small groups of Protestants met for devotion and debate in the towns. Calvin did his best to instruct them to stop being mere debating societies and to stop attending Mass, but also to stop thinking of a futile rebellion.

For some twenty years after 1559 Catherine de Medici, the widow of King Henry II and the niece of Pope Clement VII, was virtually regent during the reigns of her three ineffective sons. She alternated between policies of persecution and conciliation because her motive was the preservation of national unity under the Catholic monarchy. That was in fact an impossible aim. The nobles called Protestant or 'Huguenot' (a nickname which may have derived from one of the factions in the politics of Geneva) now controlled much of the country in the south, the west and Normandy, with support in many towns. They were opposed by the nobles of the 'Holy' or Catholic League led by the dukes of Guise and with a strong base in Lorraine and Picardy, in the Church and in the bulk of the peasantry. Both parties sought to dominate the central government, by force if necessary. After the failure of an attempted Huguenot coup in 1560 a civil war was begun by the Catholic League. For a time it looked as if the Huguenots would prevail in alliance with the rebels in the Netherlands, but their leaders were massacred during the night beginning St Bartholomew's Day in Paris in 1572. This was followed by more massacres in the provinces and by the resumption of a civil war as the climax of a struggle marked by many atrocities on both sides.

It seemed that three Frances were emerging. There was virtually a Protestant state under Henry, king of Navarre, although it had no clear frontier. What was almost another state was forming under the Catholic League, assisted by the cash or troops of the papacy and Philip of Spain. But the monarchy based on Paris retained some of the prestige of the past and some of the more modern apparatus of government and unity, and the ruin caused by the civil war was increasing the conviction of many that there must be a sovereign with nationwide power. That belief was expounded by a philosophically minded lawyer, Jean Bodin, in a treatise published in 1576 and much reprinted as the manifesto of the *politiques*, the group which wanted political peace at almost any religious price. In answer both Catholics and Protestants now justified rebellion for the sake of the religion about which they were more enthusiastic.

A temporary solution came because Henry of Navarre became the legitimate heir of the crown of France and allied with Henry III, the last of the Valois dynasty, against the Catholic League and its Spanish supporters. The duke of Guise was murdered and in 1589 Henry III met the same fate at the hands of a priest. Within five years Henry of Navarre was able to complete a process necessary in order to found the Bourbon dynasty: conversion to Catholicism, absolution by a reluctant pope, a Catholic coronation and entry into Paris. Four years later his army had expelled the Spaniards and had bribed the Catholic nobles to make peace. He was now in a position to issue the edict of Nantes. With accompanying decrees this gave less than either Catholics or Protestants wanted, but it stopped the killing for twenty years. The Huguenots were allowed the free exercise of their own religion (although not proselytism among Catholics) over most of the country, but because previous edicts granting such toleration had collapsed there were new safeguards. Subsidies were promised not only to pastors but also to troops, with a hundred fortified 'places of refuge' including the great port of La Rochelle; and the Huguenots were to be represented in the judicial settlement of any disputes. Provision was made for Protestant schools, universities and courts and for access to public offices. Henry's own prime minister, Sully, was a Huguenot. It was the king's hope that by these concessions virtually creating a state within a state domestic peace was secured sufficiently for a war against Spain to be possible, but when riding out of Paris to join his troops he was murdered by a Catholic fanatic in 1610. There had been nineteen earlier attempts on his life.

Much suffering was also caused by the Reformation in the Netherlands. Under a regent somewhat like Catherine de Medici groups of Protestants survived persecution and were associated with powerful nobles and town councils. But when he had the power, Philip of Spain certainly had the will to end the 'liberties' which many in the Netherlands now claimed. The leader in these claims was the most powerful nobleman, William the Silent the prince of Orange (an enclave in the south of France), but Philip had Spanish troops and William had the further problem that some of the Protestants alarmed the majority of the people by setting up a regime in Ghent that seemed to resemble Geneva under Calvin's austerity. As the 1570s ended the ten provinces of the south began to accept Philip's government and a Catholic monopoly. The seven provinces in the north, which hitherto had contained no more Protestants than the south, formed their own union which declared independence in 1581. The Mass could no longer be celebrated in public and William identified himself with the Calvinists: three years later he was murdered by a Catholic.

As Protestants migrated to the north ('Holland') they became a minority with economic strength and their new university in Leiden became a centre of intellectual life. They secured a twelve-year truce with Spain in 1609 and when the independence of the Dutch republic was finally recognized in 1648 they were in the majority, entering a time of confidence and wealth. However, their little nation's vitality owed much to their toleration of many religious groups: Calvinism was the official creed and it did not practise toleration within its own ranks, but the pastors were not allowed jurisdiction outside their flocks. The art of the Protestant Netherlands did not celebrate the triumph of any church: it glorified the home, the land and the sea. At its peak in Rembrandt's genius it studied the individual with an all-seeing intensity, depicting also the humanity of the Jesus of the gospels, a man of sorrows and therefore the Saviour. Previously Antwerp had replaced Venice as well as Bruges; it had become Europe's greatest centre for seaborne commerce. Now it was the time for Amsterdam to gather a new wealth from the oceans, defying the Catholic empires by planting trading posts in the Americas, Africa and Asia. And books printed in Amsterdam, defying Catholic and Protestant censorship, took ideas across many frontiers in Europe.

In Scotland a far less tolerant kind of 'reform' was assisted in its early stages by a national alliance with England rather than France. When Mary 'Queen of Scots' married the Dauphin (the heir to the French crown) in 1558 the result was a rising by the 'Lords of the Congregation' and the establishment by the parliament of a national church rejecting papal jurisdiction although also without most of the revenues of the old Church. Calvinism was clear in the 'confession of faith' and 'book of discipline' adopted in 1560. When Mary had been deposed in 1567 after follies as great as any in the history of royalty, a Geneva-type system was gradually built up in the parishes under the supervision of 'kirk sessions' composed of ministers and elders. Now the question was whether the regent (Morton) or the maturing king (James) would be able to supervise these supervisors through the appointment of bishops. In 1584 and again in 1612 bishops were imposed, only to be swept away in 1638 after a 'national covenant'. The outcome was that the kirk session had only two institutions superior to it: the 'presbytery' gathering the ministers and elders of an area and the 'general assembly' which increasingly became the mouthpiece of the Scottish nation. Some Catholics kept the old faith but this 'Presbyterian' church of Scotland became securely established in the nation's life. It was more secure than the Church of England and at a greater distance from the government, for it represented the force of nationalism north of the border, particularly after the union of the crowns of Scotland and England in 1603 and even more so when Scotland's Parliament disappeared in 1707.

In central Europe Protestantism's opportunity came because the advance of the Ottoman Turks meant that no Christian ruler, not even a Habsburg, could afford to concentrate on the suppression of any Christian heresy. In Austria, for example, Luther's Reformation seemed to be well rooted. In 1526 the king of Hungary and Bohemia was defeated and killed by the Turks near Mohacs along with the leading bishops and almost the entire army.

Subsequently most of the Hungarians and Bohemians became Protestants. The Turks now occupied the central third of the Hungarian plain and the eastern principality of Transylvania was left isolated, becoming mainly Protestant in its religion but also sheltering refugees who struggled to maintain Anabaptism or who agreed with Servetus about the Trinity.

In the years 1556–1612 under three cautious Habsburg emperors there was no anti-Protestant zeal: they observed that their Protestant subjects were weakened by theological divisions and like many emperors before them they were not enthusiastic about the papacy. When the Catholic Church had begun to be renewed and to recover its local strength a new and devout king of Bohemia (Ferdinand II) had begun persecution. A Protestant rebellion broke out in 1618, only to be crushed by an international Catholic army two years later. That brief battle on the so-called White Mountain near Prague had momentous consequences: it was followed by the expulsion of Bohemia's Protestants, the conquest of the Palatinate which had supported them, and the election of Ferdinand II as emperor. In panic the Protestants rallied and the Thirty Years' War began.

In the vast territory of Poland and Lithuania (united in 1569) Catholic peasants remained the largest religious group but the kings were elected by the aristocracy with limited powers and such powers as the church courts had exercised over the laity were virtually ended. The weakness of the monarchy and the Church left landowners and their tenants free to secure what amounted to religious toleration even if the theory was lacking. Thus Brethren exiled from Bohemia were allowed to settle and to ally with the native Calvinists. Even people who opposed the official doctrine of the Trinity enjoyed the same liberty until 1658. Religious toleration for others, made formal in 1573, was never completely abandoned and was to be reaffirmed in 1767. However, in the last quarter of the sixteenth century the people began to return to the old Church in droves because the tide began to flow strongly in favour of a Reformation which renewed Catholicism.

The Catholic Reformation

Late in the eighteenth century German scholars began to call it the 'Counter-Reformation' because they concentrated on the recovery for Catholicism of much of Europe including their own country. And indeed for some time Protestants had good reasons for their fears that their Reformations were being undone. Over almost a quarter of Europe the old Church, now renewed, turned back the Protestant tide. By the 1590s the Catholic cause in Poland had made such advances that large numbers of Ukrainians accepted the papal authority in exchange for permission to retain most of the customs to which they had grown used while Orthodox. There was talk of a similar move in Russia. Perhaps the loss of the north to the Protestants would be compensated in the east? And perhaps even the north could be recovered? Catholic hopes for Scandinavia grew dramatically when in 1654 Christina, the eccentric queen of Sweden, abdicated in order to lead a devoutly Catholic and richly cultured life in Rome. Later she tried to become a queen again and did become an atheist, but even so that abdication indicated the powerful appeal of a reformed Rome.

With this change went the response of 'No Popery!' in Protestants who felt threatened. That reaction had its focus in England, where by the end of the sixteenth century most people seem to have accepted a form of Protestantism, whether in the Established Church or outside it. But all four of England's Stuart kings were suspected of being 'Papists' at heart or at least of being insufficiently identified with the threatened Protestants in mainland Europe. Even James I, a Protestant theologian, sought an alliance with Spain and Charles I, executed by the Parliamentarians in circumstances which made him an Anglican martyr, had a Catholic wife. The Protestants' nightmare became a reality when the cynical Charles II became a Catholic on his deathbed and the openly Catholic James II became king in 1685. Replacing him by Protestants caused the English much trouble. 'Non-jurors' who refused to change their oath of obedience to a king who reigned by 'divine right' left the Church of England. Two daughters of that king, Mary and Anne, were convinced Anglicans and were available to be queens, but eventually a Lutheran king who spoke no English had to be imported from Hanover and twice in the eighteenth century Jacobites attempted to restore the Catholic descendants of James II.

Elsewhere the power of monarchs worked in favour of Catholicism without so many complications. Under the Wittelsbachs Bavaria became solidly Catholic and the university of Ingolstadt became an arsenal equipping preachers for the war against Protestant heresies. But the main monument of the Catholic Reformation is the Escorial palace near Madrid, a complex built by Philip II to be the stern centre of his rule over Spain, Portugal, Latin America and (as he hoped) the Netherlands. Much of it was a monastery, much of it a college to train priests, all of it a union of spiritual and secular power. An appartment which was modest by the standards of that time was sufficient for that absolute monarch: there he toiled at papers from his vast kingdom, often far into the night. But this workplace had the supreme advantage of being next to the high altar of the great church.

The emperor Ferdinand II was a model Catholic prince with a dream that he could bring not only Austria, Bohemia and Hungary but also the whole empire back to the true faith. By 1629 he had won enough victories to feel able to demand the restitution of all the Catholic Church's property which had passed into other hands since the 1550s, and the end of the toleration of Calvinists. He might have succeeded in his aims had it not been for factors with which he had not reckoned. Gustavus Adolphus of Sweden (Christina's father) was a king strongly Protestant and territorially ambitious, and he had built up the world's first modern army: he now swept through Germany before he was killed in 1632. The most formidable general opposing him, Wallenstein, was as brilliant and as destructive, but his Catholic employers resented the power he acquired for himself. He was dismissed, murdered and never replaced by any commander of similar ability. And neither of the two major Catholic powers greatly helped the Catholic side in the empire. Spain was by now suffering from financial and general exhaustion. Cardinal Richelieu, the prime minister of France, was more anti-Habsburg than anti-Protestant and he subsidized the Swedish invasion. In 1635 France threw its army into the war in alliance with Sweden and the German Protestants.

Thirteen years later, after four years of negotiation, the two treaties constituting the Peace of Westphalia re-established the principle (if it can be called that) of 1555, 'the ruler decides the religion'. There was a return to the ecclesiastical geography of 1624 with the recognition of Calvinism, the acceptance of the loss of buildings and lands which had been the Catholic Church's property and a new provision against a future ruler altering the religious situation which he had inherited. The pope, whose authority over Catholics in the empire was now restricted, denounced this settlement, which did indeed signal the end of hopes that Protestantism could be destroyed by a 'Counter-Reformation' on the march. The Thirty Years' War ending in 1648 also meant the end of the medieval partnership of pope and emperor—and the end of any unity or great prosperity in Central Europe for another two hundred and more years.

But even if history had been different, even if the Catholic triumphs in Poland and France had been followed in England and Scandinavia, and even if Ferdinand II's dreams of a totally Catholic empire had all come true, the term 'Counter-Reformation' would still be too negative to do justice to the spiritual movement which we are about to consider. This movement was continuous with medieval Catholicism, yet transformed it. Even the term 'Catholic Restoration' is therefore inappropriate: this movement was creative. Some recent historians have revived the term 'Catholic Reformation' and it seems significant that when the Habsburgs sent missions of priests, officials and soldiers to check that their subjects were attending Mass and confession these were called 'Reformation Commissions'.

This Catholic Reformation may be judged as, on the whole, a disaster if our standards of judgement are those of economic development and freedom for the laity to develop a religious and cultural life not dominated by kings and priests. One fact was the economic, political and cultural decline of the

332

south in comparison with the north in Europe, and one factor was the subordination of the freedom of the individual to what was thought to be the welfare of Church and State. Ability and energy were attracted to the service of Church and State rather than to economic or intellectual advance. In the old territory of the Netherlands the contrast could not be clearer: in the south (Belgium) Catholic triumph and economic and intellectual stagnation, to the north Dutch Protestant energy. But those are not the only criteria by which this movement deserves to be judged in a history of Christianity, for in the eyes of the Catholic reformers the cause of the Catholic religion was the cause of Christ: to accept or reject it had consequences for eternity. In 1555 Ignatius Loyola wrote a memorandum of advice to accompany a missionary to the heretics in Ethiopia. He recommended that the affection of the Ethiopian king should be gained 'by any honest means' but he should then be warned 'that there is no hope of being saved outside the Catholic Church and that in order to be saved it is necessary to believe what it defines for faith and morals'. The alternative to salvation, hell, was described in the Roman Catechism of 1566: 'inextinguishable fire . . . with every form of suffering'.

This Reformation, like the others, brought a new intensity of personal spirituality accompanied by a new activism and inspired by a new concentration on Christ himself. The new methods of printing and of administration enabled ideas believed to be authoritative to be disseminated and discussed through books, pamphlets, catechisms and conferences. The bishop or the parish priest became a serious preacher and the clergy attempted more strenuously to adjust the minds and morals of the laity to what was preached.

A Catholic church still could not be mistaken for a Calvinist temple. It had images calling for reverence; it had the 'reserved sacrament' calling for adoration; if of any size, it had chapels with their own altars where a number of priests could each 'say Mass' each day. The Mass was still mostly in Latin; when the bread and wine were 'consecrated' by the priest as a 'sacrifice', the words were said quietly or silently and the laity were impressed by their sacredness. Whatever else changed, Catholics wanted the Mass to remain in all its atmosphere of mystery, with all its treasure of memories. But there were now some significant similarities between the Catholic church ordered around the Mass and the Protestant church ordered around the pulpit. A Catholic church could now exhibit the new importance of the laity, for it could be designed or reordered so that the whole congregation could see the main altar and approach the rails in front of it for a communion more frequent than had been the medieval custom; the most devout laity began to communicate weekly. The pulpit would be often prominent and sometimes ornate and the man in it would (hopefully) be the eloquent local pastor, a man they knew. The enclosed boxes where sins were confessed (much more often than in the Middle Ages) were not only instruments of social control by the clergy: they testified to the extent of a sense of guilt in the presence of God. They enabled priest and penitent to talk face to face through a grille. There the priest could become a 'spiritual director' consulted regularly or at least the preacher of a private and short sermon to a penitent whose ears were probably more open in this intimate setting than they were while half-listening to the generalities propounded at greater length in the pulpit.

So this renewal may be called a Reformation, whatever may be the objections of Protestants or Catholics against being grouped together in this way. Yet it is equally true that this Reformation was definitely Catholic and papal, with a clarity due largely to the unexpected achievements of the council of Trent.

Catholic Vitality

Some thirty bishops, mostly Italian, assembled in Trent with their advisers in 1545. They did not know whether the pope, Paul III, really wanted them to meet. Papal fears that a council would insist on concessions to the Lutherans, or to the Catholic monarchs or to the bishops themselves, had largely accounted for the delays which had contributed to the spread of the 'heresy'. There had been talk of a council since the 1520s, plans since 1536 and an announcement of a meeting since 1542. Pope Paul did not look like a reformer. He lived like a Renaissance prince, as may still be observed in the rooms which he had decorated in the fortress of Sant' Angelo; he was proud of his four children and made one of them the duke of Parma, leading to a bitter quarrel with Spanish-controlled Milan; he made two teenage grandsons cardinals. He had been persuaded to convene a council in the hope that it would reaffirm Catholic doctrine in answer to the heretics, yet the bishops who gathered were scarcely experts on Reformation theology. The emperor and the king of France fulfilled papal fears by sending ambassadors to demand changes in the Church, although they also raised conservative hopes by sending very few bishops who could vote. The Spanish Church held aloof: it was totally anti-Protestant but also totally under the control of its suspicious king. The council met in Trent, a city within the empire, but two years later it was moved by its papally appointed presidents away from the emperor's influence to Bologna in Italy, and was suspended in 1549. When it reassembled in Trent in 1551–52 it was repudiated by the French king. It was unable to extract any agreement from Protestant envoys and was again adjourned. The next pope had no intention of recalling it. But under another pope it did meet for a final session, in 1561–63, and with a wider membership—only to be dissolved in a hurry because its presidents feared that it might insist on discussing and damaging the papacy.

The scope of the reforms which the council managed to make was, of course, limited. It could not define the nature of the Church and made no arrangement for any future council: no council met for another two hundred years. The argument that bishops derived their jurisdiction from the pope was rejected, yet it was revealing that many rights of appeal to Rome remained and that the papacy could still dispense bishops and priests from their obligation to reside and perform the pastoral work to which they had been appointed. Bishops were to be associated more closely with parish priests in this pastoral work, yet nothing was done to stop bishops being very different indeed from poverty-stricken parish priests. The religious orders were urged to be holy but almost nothing was done to reform or merge them, or to give the bishops effective control over them: in the years to come many monasteries were to be thought too small or too corrupt to survive and the disputes between Dominicans, Franciscans and the new orders were to trouble the whole Catholic world. The bishops resisted Protestant pressures which it was thought would reduce the holiness of the Mass and the priesthood. Priests were not to marry; the Mass was not to be said in the local language; the laity were not to be given the cup (although the pope might allow exceptions). The council, however, could not reduce the powers over the Church which the lay rulers of nations exercised: governments continued to nominate many bishops and other clergy to their posts and to employ some of them in the state's service. Nor could the council end local rejection of the legal powers of popes and bishops: thus the *parlement* of Paris never formally enrolled Trent's decrees, the Spanish crown ignored them when they seemed to question its control of the life of the Church and Venice successfully defended its own courts against papal claims. In the eighteenth century the papacy's jurisdiction was to be restricted or ignored by most of Catholic Europe, whatever Trent had said.

However, the council's decrees redefined Catholicism as a working system—a system which was to be called 'Tridentine' from the Latin name for the city. The doctrinal authority of the Church was derived from Scripture (whose contents, defined by the Church, included the Jewish books called 'Apocrypha' by Protestants) together with unwritten traditions inherited by the Church from the apostles. The Vulgate translation of the Bible could be trusted although the council did not prohibit either the revision of its Latin or translation from the Hebrew and Greek into modern languages. Lutheran interpretations of 'justification' by divine grace received through faith in Christ's 'alien' righteousness 'imputed' to sinners were condemned and the medieval doctrine that Christ's righteousness was 'imparted' to saints-in-the-making was reaffirmed, although it remained possible for some Catholic theologians to remain severely Augustinian in their rejection of human merits. It was declared that Christ instituted all the seven sacraments of the medieval Church, the effects of which do not depend on the individual's faith; they confer God's grace 'upon those who do not place obstacles in its path'. It was also re-emphasized that the substances of the body and blood (together) replace the substances of the bread and wine in the Mass. Marriage was now definitely a sacrament of the Church, ending only with death if both valid and consummated but demanding for its validity the presence of a priest and other witnesses and excluding the informal partnerships or the forms of 'engagement' which had previously allowed sexual intercourse outside the sacred bonds of marriage.

An important change was the decree ordering bishops and parish priests to reside and to toil. Trent thus restored the position of the bishop as the pastor and reformer—although its decrees that every parish must be visited every year, and that all the clergy of the diocese must gather for an annual synod, were not always to be treated as realistic. It also changed the whole look of the priesthood, which was not to be bestowed on any man under the age of 25. It hoped that every diocese would establish a seminary to train priests. There were still complaints that too many men were ordained without real vocations or proper training, but the new activism of bishops did mean that priests were examined before being given responsibility for a parish, were under more pressure to be celibate in practice and were in general expected to be more professional: the custom developed of always wearing black cassocks in public. And above all Trent changed the character of the papacy.

The papal bureaucracy was reorganized in order to reflect this new character: it was now to function in 'congregations' under cardinals, most of whom must reside in Rome although a few working elsewhere (usually for monarchs) could receive the honour. The powers of archbishops were reduced but for more than half a century the papacy became once more the centre of reforming vigour. Pius IV promptly accepted all Trent's decrees and he and his successors set themselves to apply them. 'Nuncios' were appointed to deal with local rulers and with bishops, who were also summoned to Rome to report and to be instructed. All bishops and other church leaders had to make a new 'profession of faith' and all parish priests were expected to base their teaching on a new catechism. The Mass and the lesser 'offices' to be said by all priests every day were revised, as was the list of church festivals. A new ('Gregorian') calendar was followed by Catholic Europe from 1582. The Vulgate translation of the Bible into Latin was revised and an 'index' of books forbidden to Catholics was published and sternly updated, although its local effectiveness was far from complete. The papacy's exercise of its right to dispense from the normal operation of the Church's laws was reduced, as was the staff needed, and the laws themselves were revised comprehensively. Indulgences were kept but were no longer to be preached in sales campaigns.

Inevitably there were criticisms, hesitations and serious problems. Paul Sarpi, a Venetian priest, wrote a history of the council published in London, attacking the bishops for surrendering their ancient rights to the papacy. Cardinal Robert Bellarmine defended papal claims but hesitated over the popes' role in politics, denying that they had the clear right to depose princes except when grave spiritual issues were involved: consequently he pleased neither monarchs nor popes and was not declared a saint until 1930 although he was the leading defender of Tridentine Catholicism against the Protestants. There were financial problems: although the papal states could be exploited and loans could be obtained from bankers who used the papal connection to attract Italy's savings, it was not cheap to build or maintain the Rome of the Catholic Reformation. And some popes aroused more than hesitations. Paul IV was hated in Rome because of his cruel use of the Inquisition and was so foolish as to enter into a ruinous war against Spain. Pius V, who executed two of his predecessor's nephews, alienated Catholic monarchs almost as much as most of the English when he claimed the right to depose Elizabeth I.

But these difficulties were not fatal. When 1600 was celebrated as another 'jubilee' year pilgrims to Rome saw a city transformed since 1500 and entering a period of further glorification. In 1622 a new 'congregation' was created and given large resources to supervise the propagation of the faith. *Propaganda* concerned itself not only with the eastern churches, and not only with the Catholic minorities in Protestant Europe, but also with the missions which were converting the 'Indians' of South America and Asians in numbers which no Protestant had imagined as remotely possible—partly because it seemed unlikely that God had predestined so many to heaven. And in the same year Gregory XV presided over a spectacular ceremony. Four of the great figures of the Catholic Reformation were canonized as saints, so that the faithful could invoke their prayers in heaven and follow their examples on earth: Teresa of Avila and Philip Neri, Ignatius Loyola and Francis Xavier.

Charles Borromeo had already been canonized, in 1610. He was as influential as any of these saints of 1622, for he was the model of the bishops who translated the decrees of Trent into local reality by self-dicipline and strenuous pastoral work—energizing the clergy, visiting the parishes, insisting on accurate records of increased activities, rebuking the laity, founding colleges, schools and hospitals, caring for the poor and confronting any who dared oppose a mission so clearly apostolic. He owed his position to the fact that he was a nephew of Paul IV: now as in the past, popes made nephews cardinals because they could trust them. But he owed his influence to his spiritual stature and to an all-consuming passion for the orthodox reform of the Church demonstrated in his labours as archbishop of Milan from his early twenties to his exhausted death in his mid-forties. His nephew Frederico was a later archbishop of Milan with much the same character, for almost forty years from 1595.

A New Mission

Teresa of Avila, who preferred to be called Teresa of Jesus, and her disciple John of the Cross were the greatest mystics of sixteenth-century Spain. Their sanctity included an indisputable orthodoxy and thus they escaped the worst wrath of the Inquisition, the organization which arrested the country's most senior bishop on charges of heresy. Lesser Christians who claimed to be 'illuminated' by their own religious experience, the *Alumbrados*, did not escape the fate of that archbishop. The Inquisition had by now almost exhausted the possibilities of heresy-hunting among former Jews and Muslims but even in this period of relaxation, when it was on the whole popular, it examined 49,000 cases between 1540 and 1700, burning almost eight hundred people alive and about as many in effigy because it could not get hold of them. But the main opposition to Teresa and John came from within their own Carmelite order. They led the 'discalced' (barefoot) branch and urged others to share their own austerity, to the fury of those who were somewhat more relaxed in self-denial. John of the Cross was imprisoned for fourteen years.

The two saints symbolized the Catholic Reformation because they combined mysticism and activism.

Teresa was probably 21 when she took her vows as a Carmelite nun and the step probably seemed natural because she came from a family of twelve all devout and all eager. As children she and her brother planned to beg their way to Morocco and there become martyrs in order to go to heaven; then they played at being hermits. But her body announced by many illnesses that a nun's life was not ideal for her. There were symptoms of hysteria, eased when she gave up praying. She blamed herself for worldliness and wickedness. She found release from distress (although not from illness) when at the age of forty she was reading Augustine's account of his conversion. Now prayer became for her 'the prayer of quiet' followed by 'the prayer of union'. As she wrote about her raptures in order to prove that they were not inspired by the Devil (as some priests she had consulted had thought more than possible), she was able to show that they had been given, not sought—all of them: the visions, the voices, the levitations which were so embarrassing in public. She compared her spiritual life with watering a garden: first the hard labour of drawing a little water from a deep well, then the discovery of water nearer the surface, then the gift of water from a spring, then rain. She drew other images from Spain: God is His Majesty the emperor, Christ is the Great Captain, the God-defended soul is a castle with seven walls. And like a soldier she exercised in her later years the ability to campaign, fighting and organizing so that the Carmelites should abandon everything which stood between them and the heaven she had seen.

John of the Cross also impressed Spaniards who admired toughness. There must be a 'night of the senses', he taught, followed by a 'dark night of the soul'. But what attracted most about these two was their common promise that ecstasy, union with the divine, was possible. Teresa wrote about a spiritual marriage, John about the soul as a log of wood, thrown on the fire to make a 'flame of love' in the night.

In comparison Protestant teachers seemed to be earth-bound and Protestant laity seemed to be summoned to *bourgeois* respectability, comfort and commerce. But Catholic spiritual teachers were also able to reach those who did not aspire to the heights of the mystics. They did so with an emphasis different from Luther's on faith, Calvin's on discipline or the Inquisition's on terror: they stressed love. In 1544 Philip Neri experienced an ecstatic union with Christ which encouraged him in his vocation to help and instruct the poor of Rome. Over the next half-century his gentleness made an impact on the city which almost balanced the Inquisition's. From his many friendships with men and boys sprang an 'oratory', a community of priests which combined prayer with gaiety and culture including music; from it came the tradition of the *oratorio*, with the words sacred but the singing rather more informal than in church.

In 1611 an oratory was founded in Paris by Cardinal Pierre de Bérulle, whose spiritual teaching endeavoured to put Christ at the centre of French Catholicism as Copernicus had put the sun at the centre of the new picture of the universe (and the comparison was his). De Bérulle also introduced the Carmelites to France. His immense influence on the clergy included Francis de Sales, who reached the laity. It was the vocation of Francis to counter Calvinism by a mission to the French teaching that a sane and healthy life of prayer and charity could be lived calmly amid the duties of the world. He had been the nominal bishop of Geneva since 1602 and his attractive *Introduction to the Devout Life* was published in 1609. 'Charity', he wrote, 'is a spiritual fire and when it bursts into flame it is called devotion.' His own spirituality deepened as was shown in 1616 by his *Treatise on the Love of God*, originating in guidance to a community of women founded by his saintly friend Jeanne Frances de Chantal. But although there was this degree of development in his teaching, love was still his theme, for he never forgot his experience while a student. For six weeks he had taken to heart Calvin's insistence that most are predestined to hell and had placed himself in that majority. The torment had ended when he recited a simple prayer: 'Remember, O most loving Virgin Mary, that no one ever turned to you and was left forsaken.'

New religious orders sprang up in Italy and spread, with a devout dedication but also a new focus on the needs of the laity. The Capuchins developed the Franciscan tradition by adopting a style mid-way between the rigorism of the Observants and the laxity of the Conventuals. They shook off their association with the Lutherans and as agents of the Catholic Reformation their numbers grew rapidly. The Theatines were a small order of priests able to support themselves in poverty without begging because they came from rich families; the order turned out to be a nursery for reforming bishops. The Ursulines were another order, originally of unmarried women living in their family homes but going out in order to teach young girls. They became more organized and cloistered, and founded schools in many countries. And in France Vincent de Paul was beginning his work in the 1620s. Whereas de Bérulle's impact had been on the clergy and the educated laity, Vincent de Paul acted out of compassion for the people. He had been for a period enslaved by Arabs and on his return to France devoted himself to the welfare of the prisoners who rowed the galleys—at a time when French Calvinist pastors were expected to devote themselves to controversial theology. Then he founded the Lazarist missions to the rural poor and recruited women who were not rich for charitable work. It was the origin of the Daughters of Charity, the Grey Sisters, who over the years broke through the bishops' insistence that holy women ought to be cloistered or confined to domestic duties.

Among these new orders by far the most important was the boldly named Society of Jesus. In 1521, the year when Luther finally defied pope and emperor, a young Spanish nobleman, Ignatius (in Spanish Iñigo de Lopez), was at home in the castle of Loyola, recovering from wounds received as he had begun the life of a soldier. In his boredom he read devout books from the Middle Ages, was specially impressed by a Life of Christ by Ludolf of Saxony, and began to desire to become a saint like Dominic or Francis. When sufficiently mobile he went on pilgrimage to Montserrat, where he hung up his sword before the image of Mary and exchanged the clothes of a knight for those of a pilgrim before entering a battle with doubts. For years he pursued the fantasy that as a pilgrim in the Holy Land he could convert Muslims but gradually his vocation became clearer and more realistic. Having been arrested twice by the Spanish Inquisition because he seemed an ignorant enthusiast, he set himself to learn Latin (being mocked by the schoolboys on the same benches) and then to learn theology during seven years in the Paris which Calvin had just left. There in 1534, in a chapel on the hill of Montmartre, he took vows together with companions including Francis

Xavier; it was a tiny group drawn by the magnetism of his adventurous faith. Already he had worked out the 'exercises' which were the secret of his own spiritual power.

In 1548 these *Spiritual Exercises* were published. The book was meant not for readers but for spiritual directors who would use it to guide a 'retreat' lasting four weeks or longer. It was plainly the work not of a theologian or scholar but of a man who wanted to record how his own soul had been reshaped so that he might be a soldier of Christ. It barely mentioned the Holy Spirit, for as a Spanish Catholic Ignatius was determined to avoid any taint of heresy. The exercises included the daily and rigorous 'examination of conscience' but no exceptional physical austerities. The sense of sin was intensified but only as a prelude, for one purpose of the 'examination' was to detect signs of progress in the soul thanks to God's grace. The senses, the affections and the powers of the imagination, the intellect and the will were not to be denied, but all were to be brought into Christian obedience by the discipline of concentrated, precise and prolonged meditation on the life of Christ. Time need not be spent on the elaborate 'choir offices' of the monasteries but this enrolment under the 'standard of the cross' was utterly essential. There should be no Lutheran denial of the importance of the will, but the whole direction of the will must be changed 'to the greater glory of God'. And after these preparatory exercises came the life: a life of heroism seeking perfection through obedience, of adventurous activity, fighting and not heeding the wounds, finding God in all things. The mood was very different from what Thomas à Kempis had thought would be the result of the imitation of Christ.

The pope formally authorized the new order in 1540. The vows to be taken by the fully trained Jesuits included a promise of obedience to any papal command to undertake a mission, and the obedience to be given to the general of the order was expected to be like a corpse's, or a stick's, willingness to be moved. Those two provisions have sometimes been understood as making all Jesuits mere instruments of the pope's or the general's will in every detail, and in the years to come they were to contribute to a sinister reputation. Certainly they formed part of a submission to the Church avoiding all criticism, and in the *Spiritual Exercises* may be read a rule to 'believe that what seems to us white is black if that should be the decision of the hierarchical Church'. But the Jesuits' commitment was only to carry out the pope's strategy and to accept their own general's orders about tactics; and one motive was to be free of control by any bishop inferior to the pope. There could be tension in Rome between the pope and the general (who was elected for life) and the activity of Jesuits in situations far from Rome was far from being corpse-like. When Ignatius died in 1556 there were about a thousand of these men whose rigorous training had not killed their powers of initiative. One of them was Peter Canisius, a preacher and writer of tireless energy who went through central Europe as an apostle of the Catholic Reformation, everywhere insisting on a new spiritual and theological discipline, everywhere making it understandable and attractive.

Gradually the main thrust of the Jesuits' work had become clear: it was to be educational. By 1750 some fifteen thousand Jesuits were to be teaching in more than eight hundred colleges and seminaries. At first Ignatius had seen only that recruits to the Society of Jesus—in his vision, a small band of mobile missionaries—must be trained thoroughly but a few other young men were admitted for a general education. A network of colleges and schools grew up, quite often turning pupils into Jesuits but also slowly raising the educational standards of all Catholic Europe. The council of Trent had ordered every diocese to found a seminary to train priests but these had not been easy to finance or to staff; they were often too small and although they often admitted boys aged twelve attendance before ordination had not been made compulsory. The Jesuits took the lead among the religious orders which rescued this ill-conceived system, including colleges in Rome to prepare sons of the aristocracy for their futures as bishops. But there were also fee-paying boarding colleges for the sons of the gentry many of whom became influential in lay life, and for the less privileged there were many free secondary schools. Against all his original dreams, Ignatius Loyola had founded the best educational system yet seen in Europe and had greatly strengthened the Catholic Church by offering parents, including Protestants, an education for their sons.

The great philosopher René Descartes, who spent eight years in a Jesuit college, was a very exceptional pupil. Looking back, he wrote: 'The only profit I seemed to have gained from trying to become educated was to have discovered progressively my own ignorance.' But Descartes listed the subjects which he had encountered as a schoolboy: Latin and Greek, 'fables' and history, poetry and mathematics, ethics and theology (whose 'revealed truths are beyond our understanding'), and an introduction to philosophy, law, medicine and the sciences. Jesuits were no-nonsense teachers, with a standard curriculum and strict discipline, but their involvement in education brought about a development which is surprising if one considers the austerity of the *Spiritual Exercises*. The main complaints came from Protestants who disapproved of features of school life which the young could enjoy (competitions and theatricals were encouraged) and from Catholics who attacked the leniency of the advice given as the pupils began a lifelong habit of the regular confession of sins to an understanding priest.

A sophisticated body of Jesuit teaching about the ethical questions raised by particular cases ('casuistry') was accompanied by generous doctrine which regarded behaviour as probably acceptable because one 'doctor' or teacher of the Church could be found to approve it although most others condemned it ('probabilism'). The suspicion which had surrounded the earlier advice given to penitents or half-penitents by the medieval friars was now intensified (with the friars in the leadership of the hostile), particularly in connection with the medieval question whether the taking of interest by businessmen could ever be condoned. Already in the seventeenth century the word 'Jesuit' was beginning to mean someone weaving a web of unhealthy influence among the powerful, a devious and sinister man tolerant of moral compromises for the sake of religious victories.

The educational activity of the Jesuits (and also of their rivals the Oratorians) suggests a temptation to think of the Catholic Reformation as producing a Catholic Renaissance. The temptation has to be resisted, for the Jesuits avoided, and the Inquisition suppressed, the intellectually disturbing tendencies of 'humanism'. The notorious case of Galileo displayed the higher clergy's hostility not to science as such (circles of scientists were allowed to do good work quietly in Florence and Venice) but to the disobedience involved in taking science beyond investigations which did no harm to religion. The order had been issued not to spread discussion about scientific observations by Copernicus and others which seemed to contradict Scripture. Galileo had disobeyed. So a conforming Catholic who had spent a life in the honest use of the microscope (which he invented) and the telescope was made to recant, and to promise silence, by the threat of torture. The scandal of 1633 has never been forgotten and in 1981 the Vatican admitted that an error of judgement had been made. Almost as notorious were the cases of the two Dominican friars Giordano Bruno and Campanella, the one burned in Rome in 1600, the other imprisoned for 27 years, because their excitement over the Copernican vision of the central sun had led them into theological indiscretions. The books of Copernicus and Galileo were officially forbidden to Catholics until 1835. And history punished this denial of intellectual freedom, for the discouragement of independent thought about experimental science played a part in the cultural and economic decline of countries predominantly Catholic.

However, the greater control of lay life by the more organized clergy also led to a reduction in those elements of late medieval popular religion which could be called superstitious, magical or pagan. Much evidence suggests that in many places medieval beliefs ended in the nineteenth century at the earliest, but certainly the appearance of Catholic religion was changed, often in a direction closer to the New Testament. Veronese's sensuous picture of a luxurious banquet in a palace, commissioned as a painting of the Last Supper, was rechristened *The Feast in the House of Levi* (Luke 5:29) when the artist's attention was drawn to the displeasure of the Inquisition. Bishops now did their best to stop medieval practices in which merriment could get out of hand: parties in church, carnivals supposed to get paganism out of the system before Lent and crude festivities in honour of local saints. The laity were urged, although often in vain, to pray for spiritual rather than material blessings. Unusual images, new relics, new saints, new miracles all had to be approved by the bishop. There were attempts to make fraternities surviving from the Middle Ages more fervently religious under a priest's direction and new, exclusively religious, 'sodalities' and 'retreats' were organized. While dramatic processions through the streets continued, imaginative efforts were made to bring popular religion into church. Specially made cribs began to dramatize the nativity of Christ and the candlelit adoration of the 'blessed sacrament' gathered parishioners in relays over forty hours at least once a year. Devotion to the Virgin Mary was developed by the increased use of the 'rosary' in prayer and by the spreading celebration of her immaculate conception and her physical assumption into heavenly glory—and also by the cult of her husband Joseph, to encourage the men. The Catholicism of which bishops approved was becoming both more standardized and more dramatic in order that the individual might be converted to a faith both more regulated and more intense.

Artists or architects as different as El Greco and Velazquez, Murillo and Rubens, Borromini and Bernini, provided the glories but even when talents as great as theirs were not employed the Catholic Reformation exposed the cultural poverty of Protestantism. Ignatius would have been surprised, and probably scandalized, had he seen his sumptuous tomb in the church of Il Gesù in Rome, not far from the bare little room from which he had directed the Society of Jesus, but he might have grown to forgive the expensive pomp of that church: it was an advertisement for the cause to which his life had been totally dedicated. The style which the nineteenth century was to call Baroque has seemed in the twentieth too theatrical, but its direct appeal to emotions was its whole point. A church was a theatre where the sacred drama of the Mass was performed, where audiences in heaven and on earth applauded, where the courage of Ignatius in the wars against Protestantism and heathendom could be celebrated like a Roman emperor's triumph, where the spiritual marriage of Teresa with her Lord could be sculpted by Bernini as being (as has been commented) like the climax of sex, where art honouring the unmarried clergy and nuns could also be sentimental about the pink, fat cherubs. And just as captivating art developed from the more austere beginnings of the Catholic Reformation, so did music. The council of Trent declared that music in church must be nothing more than a plain accompaniment to the authorized words, but such puritanism could not suppress the Catholic love of music. The beauty of plain chant, counter-point or polyphony developed into the glorious happiness of eighteenth-century music for the Mass, Palestrina through Monteverdi into Haydn and Mozart.

This Catholic Reformation coincided with the early years of the Spanish and Portuguese colonial empires. For the peoples who were conquered and enslaved the results were disastrous, as they ultimately were for the Spanish and Portuguese themselves. But as a small redeeming feature the new experience of colonialism resulted in a new emphasis on human rights in theory. Pope Paul III pronounced that 'the Indians are truly human' and therefore entitled to be baptized. The most courageous of those who drew the conclusion that 'Indians' ought to be treated humanely was Bartolomé de Las Casas, a Dominican missionary and bishop who had accepted the exploitation tamely for some years before he was driven by conscience to protest in speech and print. He still accepted the right of the pope to bestow the 'kingdoms of the infidels' on the best available Christian monarchs, but he did not accept the use of violence: it was 'contrary to the sweetness of Jesus Christ' and made the Christians' God seem 'the most cruel, unjust and pitiless god of all'. He now preached the fundamental equality of all human beings, government with the consent of the governed and 'respect for those who err in good faith'. He seemed sentimental, was accused of hysteria by the white sheep in his flock, and was well in advance of his time; yet in 1542 the Spanish government did issue laws attempting to curb the exploitation and there were more philosophical arguments in favour of human rights put forward within Spain, particularly in the university of Salamanca. Juan de Mariana defended the rights of subjects to rebel against tyrants (but this was in the context of Catholic resistance to Henry of Navarre, then a 'heretic'). Domingo de Soto and Francesco de Suarez worked out a theory of national and international law as an authority higher than any government.

Suarez also developed what became widely held Catholic theory about the freedom of the will to do good: God gives his saving grace to those whose good works he foresees. And the reaction of Ignatius Loyola to the Protestants' talk about faith and predestination became typical of Catholic teachers: faith is required and predestination to heaven is true, but neither doctrine should be presented in such a way as to suggest to simple minds that they could safely neglect good behaviour guided by the priest and fed by the Mass—or in such a way as to suggest to the clergy that they could safely neglect their own duty to seek converts.

Across the Oceans

The most astonishing part of the early history of the Jesuits was their leadership in the expansion of the Catholic Church to, and even beyond, the frontiers of the colonial empires. In 1571 the Turkish fleet was destroyed in the battle of Lepanto and with it sank a great load of fear which had kept Catholics on the defensive. In 1539 Mercator's first map showed that the world did not consist of three continents with Jerusalem as the centre, surrounded by an unexplored ocean and full of mythological creatures. Catholic missionaries were now courageously willing to meet the peoples of the world that was real and to cross the vast gulfs between the cultures of these peoples and their own culture of the Catholic Reformation.

In Asia missionaries from Europe encountered civilizations which technically were at least as advanced and which regarded themselves as spiritually superior. So Jesuits trained by a combination of medieval theology with the *Spiritual Exercises* had to bring their minds as well as their bodies to the great strangeness of India, China and Japan. They regarded these peoples as pagans bound for hell, yet they also found much to admire and much which they had to accept if they were to get a hearing, so that the spiritual encounter was no easier than the task of learning new languages. They accepted the need to impose the Inquisition in India but they also exposed themselves to great dangers and hardships, both physical and mental. They could not be other than European but also could not approve of other Europeans who were often arrogant and debauched plunderers. They had to deal with the 'Syrian' Orthodox already in India, with rival Catholic missionaries who attacked their methods and eventually with hostile Protestants, and always in the background were European governments which regarded them either as nuisances or as their own agents. Their courage was extraordinary both in its vision and in its perseverance.

Francis Xavier, one of Ignatius' earliest and closest companions, landed in the Portuguese trading post of Goa in South India in 1542. Before his death ten years later, on an island within sight of the coast of China, he had gone through Sri Lanka and the Indonesian islands to Japan. He knew only a few words of the local languages. It was at first his practice to baptize as many as possible and it seems probable that most of the new Christians accepted the ceremony not because they believed in Christianity or knew much about it but because they hoped that some of the magic which had brought the Portuguese so dramatically to Asia would touch and protect them. In Japan where he spent two and a half years before his death in 1552 (he was then planning to move on to China), the numbers were smaller but their conversion meant more—as was to be seen in the acceptance by Christians of tortures and exquisitely cruel deaths when persecution began. But always one factor must have been the very strange sight of this preacher from afar, barefoot, ragged, sleepless after nights of prayer, unafraid. His message might seem an arrogant intrusion into Asia; his life spoke differently.

There were some non-religious reasons why a Christian mission was able to take root in Japan. A few European traders were tolerated there since the Chinese did not allow the Japanese (then despised for their poverty) to trade directly with them. A few of the lords who controlled the country in the absence of a strong monarch took a liking to the Spanish missionaries, as did the missionaries to the Japanese: they admired each other for being brave, however poor. But the Jesuits had to finance their mission by taking part in the trade and before long the Japanese began to interpret this as involvement in European plots to seize wealth and power. The Tokugawa dictatorship became determined and able to get rid of traders, missionaries and converts alike: Japan would be kept pure in isolation. The cross had already been found offensive in the context of the Buddhist reverence for tranquillity and now obstinate Christians were crucified or subjected to other executions with conspicuous cruelty, from 1614. A brief rebellion by Christian peasants was crushed with the massacre of about 35,000.

Other experiments by Jesuits planted 'the standard of the cross' in non-Christian cultures with more thoughtfulness than had marked Francis Xavier, a pioneer in a hurry to save souls from hell. Alessandro Valignano, who supervised the Jesuit mission in the east from 1577, believed in a gentler approach from the headquarters on the island of Macao.

Matteo Ricci therefore entered China in more than the physical sense. In 1583 his reputation as a scholar led to an invitation to settle in the country. By 1601 he was able to secure a base among the courtiers within the 'Forbidden City' in Peking (Beijing), being able not only to claim 'a sound knowledge of astronomy, geography, geometry and arithmetic' but also a respectable knowledge of the Mandarin language and the Confucian classics. He did not fit into the Chinese picture of all westerners as barbarians: he dressed in the silk robes of a Mandarin wise man and wrote a treatise on friendship in the best Confucian style. The Jesuits' subsequent mission achieved a success different from their history in Japan, where the Buddhists had seemed to them simply heathen. They were not unorthodox in their Catholicism but in order to communicate with the sophisticated culture around them they presented Jesus as a wise man like Confucius, the Christians' God as the 'Lord of Heaven' and the Christian message as a teaching about how to be virtuous with the help of heaven. It was a message aimed at the elite and some of the elite responded, so that in 1692 Christianity was officially declared a tolerated religion. The approach had its dangers, however. There were complaints to Rome about the veneration of Confucius and ancestors; Franciscan and Dominican missionaries who arrived complained that the gospel ought to be preached to the poor; those of the poor who were willing to be baptized often did not turn out to be as virtuous as had been promised.

In 1605 Roberto de Nobili began a long mission with the same strategy but this time among the higher-caste Hindus of Madurai in South India. He dressed like a Brahmin priest, learned the Sanskrit and Tamil languages, wrote books and discussed the Hindu Scriptures. Although he hoped that other missionaries would identify with, and work among, the lower castes, his whole acceptance of the Hindu culture including the rigid caste system was the subject of complaints to Rome. Did not the Old Testament command the end of idolatry and the New Testament the end of social divisions? But for the time being this small experiment, more dangerous than Ricci's, escaped censure.

In 1609 another Jesuit, Marcel de Lorenziana, was entrusted with a task on the fringe of the Spanish empire in Latin America. The Guarani tribesmen trying to preserve their traditional way of life in what was to become Paraguay had to be saved from being infected, corrupted and exploited by European settlers beyond the reach of European laws. It became the Jesuit policy, accepted for the time being by the colonial authorities, to protect the Guarani in 'reductions' (about thirty townships) keeping as many of their customs as were compatible with their conversion to Catholicism and with the Jesuits' benevolent supervision. The large experiment succeeded, with different reactions among other Europeans: some rejoiced that at last the dream of a Paradise in the New World corresponded with reality, others readily believed rumours that the Jesuits were themselves exploiting the Guarani, others were angry that mere 'Indians' were being protected.

In 1625 Jean de Brébeuf began to apply the Jesuits' friendly approach to the conversion of the Huron tribesmen who were in contact with French settlers in what was to become Quebec. The Hurons, like the Guaranis, suffered from European diseases and exploitation and it was again the missionaries' policy to make them a Christian community, protected but not deprived of their traditions. Catholic teaching was expressed in their own language and idioms. But their traditional enemies, the nomadic Iroquois who had obtained guns through an alliance with the English and the Dutch to the south, drove the Hurons out of the territory where they had been settling and killed the missionaries, first testing their manhood by torture. In 1649 Brébeuf so endured his tortures that when death had come to his rescue his captors ate his heart, hoping to receive a share of his courage.

By the courage needed to take their faith into these far-off countries and cultures the Jesuits demonstrated the character of Catholicism as being what its name suggested, 'universal'. Never before had the Catholic Church spread to such an extent from its Mediterranean origins, but once the little, slow and very uncomfortable ships of this age could cross the oceans Catholic missionaries used them and once they had begun to understand societies far distant from Europe some of these missionaries did not insist on European clothes for body or mind. Protestant churches were also represented but on a much smaller scale and almost entirely among European traders and settlers, with nothing like the same risk-taking mission to the world. Columbus had calculated that the end of the world would come in 1656; instead, by then a new Catholic world had been created.

During this Catholic Reformation, scarcely anyone expected that the next age would bring far greater challenges to Christianity and in particular to the Catholic Church.

7

ese ese esea

In the Modern Age

The Enlightenment and Religion

IN the 1780s Immanuel Kant, who has a good claim to be called the greatest modern philosopher, looked back over a movement of thought during the previous 150 years, the 'Enlightenment' (*Aufklärung*). To give it a motto he used two words from the Roman poet Horace, *sapere aude*. To him they meant: dare to find it out by the evidence of your senses or by scientific knowledge, dare to think it out by well-reasoned philosophy, dare to judge for yourself by your conscience. And as he saw, what had given the movement its greatest impact was the challenge to the beliefs of Christians which no Reformation had changed. The effects were visible in his own routine (when he was obliged to go to church with other professors, at the church door he would leave the procession) but they were also substantial in the minds and lives of contemporaries less intellectually eminent. To be 'enlightened' was to refuse to be content with the submissive acceptance of religious orthodoxy and church-dictated morality which had commonly been expected from those who wished to be ordained, or to be counted as true believers, among Protestants and Catholics alike, with penalties for defiance in the form of excommunication on earth and purgatory or hell in eternity.

In the 1680s there had been a controversy between writers in Paris, the Ancients and the Moderns. It had made the word 'modern' more familiar but had not touched many hearts. But now some well-known thinkers whose opinions could not be dismissed, and some of their readers who were serious about such matters, questioned or denied what Europe had officially believed for more than a thousand years. It could now be implied or asserted that since all truth and goodness come from God, newly discovered truths and newly respected standards of justice and benevolence could supplement or correct the Bible and the Church—and the individual could be the judge, the very attitude which in previous ages had aroused horror as 'heresy', a word derived from the Greek for 'choice'. As we have seen, there had been individuals and a measure of individualism in earlier periods, but in the main Christianity in the shape that was familiar had been viewed as an object somewhat like the sun shining in the sky, objectively there. The disagreements between the Reformations had been chiefly about how to gain the benefits of the sunshine. Now there began the modern tendency to regard religion as a matter of opinion, as 'subjective', and essentially as a private affair. This profound change has been called 'the turn to the subject'.

Theologians could discuss the new mood of subjectivism which might amount to scepticism and could exaggerate its thoroughness. In 1736 Joseph Butler introduced his masterpiece of English theology, *The Analogy of Religion, Natural and Revealed, to the Constitution and Course of Nature*. He wrote sardonically: 'It is come to be taken for granted by many persons that Christianity is not so much as a subject of enquiry, but that it is now at length discovered to be fictitious. And accordingly they treat it as if in the present age this were an agreed point among all people of discernment, and nothing remained but to set it up as a principal subject of mirth and ridicule, as it were by way of reprisal for its having so long interrupted the pleasures of the world.' In 1799 Friedrich Schleiermacher's *On Religion: Speeches to its Cultured Despisers* began: 'It may be an unexpected and even a marvellous undertaking that anyone should still dare to demand from the very people that have raised themselves above the mob, and are saturated with the wisdom of the centuries, attention for a subject so entirely neglected by them.'

Some other famous works encouraged this contempt or neglect. In the 1690s Pierre Bayle's *Dictionnaire Historique et Critique*, and later the great French *Encyclopédie* (in 37 volumes by 1780), demonstrated the falsity of many legends, and the wickedness of many cruelties, to be found in the Christian past. At the same time such works made accessible a treasure house of new knowledge, historical, technical and scientific. Even before he began to compile his dictionary Bayle had been deprived of his professorship in Calvinist Rotterdam and in 1759 Catholics were papally forbidden to consult the encyclopaedia; but such censures could not halt the spread of the new knowledge or extinguish the influence of the critical spirit and the prestige of usefulness.

Edward Gibbon's many volumes commemorating *The Decline and Fall of the Roman Empire* all began when he heard 'barefoot friars' singing Vespers one evening in the autumn of 1767 in the church on the site of the Roman Capitol. He remembered also a brief period when he had been a Roman Catholic himself: he had been an unhappy young man, cured by a stay in

Protestant Switzerland. He now conceived a magnificently mournful project as a lament over the 'triumph of barbarism and religion'—a triumph which, he trusted, was now ending. A very different theme might have struck him had he been musing amid the ruins of the Colosseum, that vast monument to the 'games' of Roman imperial sadism, but he was a man of the Enlightenment and the Enlightenment tended to blind eighteenth-century people to any light which might have arrived with Orthodoxy or Catholicism.

However, it should not be thought that the Enlightenment had cut all connections with Christianity. Gibbon was an industrious researcher and a stylist with a tone which belonged to his own age and his own personality, but he relied heavily on earlier historical work by scholars among the clergy, even including some colleagues of those 'barefoot friars' in Rome; and his reliance on such predecessors was typical of the Enlightenment's relationship with the Christian tradition.

Despite the gloom expressed in their introductions, the books which Butler and Schleiermacher wrote in order to commend religion to 'people of discernment' who were 'saturated' with wisdom were well received by that limited public. When Butler wrote in the 1730s much talk was heard in England about 'the Church in danger', and Schleiermacher's book was part of the Europe-wide reaction to the violent dechristianization in revolutionary France sixty years later. Real as the dangers and disasters were, the strength of the Christian religion was still very considerable. In the seventeenth century the various Reformations of the sixteenth bore fruit in a richness of spirituality and of religious activity. The eighteenth century brought a reaction against religious controversies, persecutions and wars, in particular against the horrors of the Thirty Years' War, but in this Age of Reason church life was largely maintained in the old styles, or even intensified when hearts were touched, and there was no complete separation between the Enlightenment and the candle-lit churches.

The bishops of Protestant England or Catholic France are not easy to defend. Usually appointed because of their connections with the government or the aristocracy, they could express liberal (the English word was 'Latitudinarian') theological views uncongenial to most of the faithful, and often they performed their ecclesiastical duties with an energy less than the ideals of the Reformations. But these bishops could be positive in their conviction that Christianity deserved to be separated from superstition, ignorance and intolerance; some of the clergy, particularly in France, were 'enlightened' scholars; and the more ordinary priests and preachers were often still engaged in the battles of the Reformations against the magical paganism which lingered in the countryside. The spread of 'enlightened' ideas among the German Protestant clergy, and the wish to spread them further among any who would listen, were sufficiently strong to make conservative Lutherans and Calvinists greatly alarmed. And three musicians of genius represented much of the lay elite, Catholic or Protestant, by being both 'enlightened' and in their own ways Christian. Mozart was glad to escape from employment by the prince-archbishop of Salzburg and to enter a world of new delight, following the magic flute and finding in Freemasonry an alternative to the Church, but he set the Mass to his music sixteen times. Often the music had a suitable setting in the exuberant joy of the architecture in the Late Baroque churches but in his unfinished last Mass he voiced very seriously, searingly and sublimely his faith in the God-given glory of life on the brink of death. A twentieth-century Protestant theologian, Karl Barth, was to say that Mozart's is the music preferred by the angels. Handel's first but unprofitable love was for operas in the Italian style far removed from his Lutheran background and his oratorios with Old Testament themes came as near to being opera as he dared; but in three weeks in 1741 he composed *Messiah*, drawing on his more secular music to create for many millions in many generations a moving experience of Christ. And the music of Beethoven, a rare churchgoer but the composer of perhaps the greatest Mass music, reached depths beyond even Handel's reach, depths of suffering and joy which were (and are) religious.

Most people in Europe then went to church, at least to be baptized, married or buried. They believed either in a church's God or in 'Nature's God' and in public, and specially on paper when they could write, they approved of 'virtue'—and it was not virtue unconnected with belief in God. 'Enlightened' philosophers were themselves often worried when they contemplated the possibility that the churches, unable to answer the new criticisms, might in the course of time lose even the nominal allegiance of the people. What would happen if the servants overheard, and believed, the talk of some of their betters at the dinner tables, treating what the clergy said in the pulpits as 'a principal subject of mirth and ridicule'? If duties were no longer thought to be divine commands, would any duties still be acknowledged? If there was to be no hope of heaven, would any worthy meaning still be found in life before death? In 1793 Kant, who certainly believed in the reality of evil, was driven by these concerns to publish his *Religion within the Limits of Reason Alone*. He argued that while 'pure reason' cannot reach things-in-themselves, let alone the infinite and eternal God, and cannot suggest the proper 'ends' of Man's spiritual and moral nature, yet 'practical reason' comes to the rescue. It concerns the decisions which we have to make if we are to live worthily. It teaches that God is needed, for the God-given freedom of the human will is needed if truly moral decisions are to be made, if the 'categorical imperative' dictated by the conscience is to be obeyed whatever the risk or cost. And God's gift of immortality is needed if good choices in ethics are to be rewarded worthily and attractively. Papers left behind at his death in 1804 suggest that after 1793 he moved further from the Lutheran orthodoxy of his boyhood, but if he did so he published no other major discussion of religion. He had seen the danger—and it was not only a danger to his own position as a professor paid by a state which did not want its loyal subjects' religious feelings to be disturbed. Introducing the second edition of his *Critique of Pure Reason*, he claimed that while he had destroyed the simple certainties claimed for metaphysical 'knowledge' including the knowledge of God, he had made room for 'faith'.

Summing up a collection of studies of the Enlightenment which he edited in 1981, Roy Porter wrote that 'throughout the eighteenth century all *Aufklärer* of all nations revered English government, society and opinions as the pure crystal of Enlightenment' and that 'Enlightenment goals—like criticism, sensibility and faith in progress—throve in England within piety'. He also noted that 'few French *philosophes* and hardly any German, Italian, Swiss or Scottish thinkers were determinists, materialists or atheists'. In the same volume Norman Hamson defined this 'piety' of the Enlightenment by summing up its most important beliefs as three: Nature is a self-regulating system of laws, Man should study himself as a part of Nature, and Nature and Man are both 'the creation of a beneficent Providence'.

But it does not seem enough to say merely that there were traces of Christianity left in this Age of Reason, the Enlightenment.

In some significant ways it was similar to the earlier Reformations and may even be counted as a Reformation itself, an overdue Reformation which was the real end of the Middle Ages. The 'enlightened' may be said to have resembled the earlier Protestants when they protested against lies and censorship, against violence and injustice, and against privilege not earned by usefulness, even when such practices were defended by the highest ecclesiastical authorities. They often wished to recover the pure essence of genuinely Christian faith—and so they had no patience with the bitter theological controversies which had developed both between and within the ranks of the Lutherans and the Calvinists. And they wanted a religion more truly universal than the European Catholicism of that age. In the long correspondence between Bishop Bossuet and Baron Leibniz in the 1680s and 1690s there was a competition in largeness. The bishop argued that Providence had controlled all previous history so that the glory of the Catholic Church was the climax: nothing more was needed. But Leibniz claimed that a wider Church was needed, embracing new truths revealed through the recent Reformation, through the new knowledge and thought, even through the cultures of newly discovered continents. His slogan was *ecclesia semper reformanda*, 'the Church always needs a Reformation'.

The future was to agree with Leibniz very largely. It was not to be satisfied with a Reformation which merely sought to restore the remote past, whether in the Erasmian or in the Zwinglian style. Nor was it to understand faith precisely as in the Lutheran account of 'justification' as distinct from 'sanctification'. Nor was it to accept that Calvin had perfectly understood either the New Testament's vision of the Church or its vision of the will of God for humanity. Nor was it to think it right that the cause of God should be identified so completely with the cause of a city or a nation as many Protestants believed in the course of the violent history of the sixteenth and seventeenth centuries. Nor was it to believe that the Catholic Reformation ought to be the final shape of Catholicism.

During the age of the Enlightenment many people who wished to be counted as Christians began to ask what 'Nature' when observed actually said about the Creator—and what Scripture when examined actually said about Christ. They began to separate the man they saw as the Jesus of the gospels from the Christ of the churches and to ask what the churches would have to say, were they to repeat what was now perceived to be the simple and reasonable teaching of their understandable Lord. *Ecrasez l'infâme*: with that motto, Voltaire declared war in the 1760s on many aspects of the Catholicism around him, but in the future many Catholics would come to think that at least some of his attacks had been justified. And that great Protestant Kant, although awakened from the 'dogmatic slumbers' of his Lutheran youth, proclaimed what he thought was the true God, to be found not in the sermons of that time but in 'the starry heavens above me and the moral law within me', two things which 'fill the mind with ever-increasing wonder and awe'. That exactly echoed Psalm 19 and what Kant meant by the 'moral law' did not seem to be a million miles away from the Bible: 'Act only on that maxim through which you can at the same time will that it should become a universal law' and 'act in such a way that you always treat humanity, whether in your own person or in the person of another, never simply as a means but always at the same time as an end'.

Some of the 'enlightened' attacked the religion of the churches for the very reason that many of the clergy attacked the religion of the peasants: it seemed to be superstition. One reason was that much in the Bible seemed to be (in the word which Bishop Butler used) 'fictitious', yet most of the clergy treated it all as the Word of God dictated to the men whose names were traditionally associated with its books. In 1675 the Swiss Reformed churches issued a 'consensus' about the authority of Scripture which reasserted a position to be found in many other official declarations: in this position, the submission to Scripture was uncomplicated. But three years later a French Oratorian priest, Richard Simon, was the first churchman to commend the soundly historical study of the Hebrew Scriptures by demonstrating in a published book that Moses could not have written their first five books. He then turned his attention to the New Testament. Although a devout Catholic he experienced such isolation that he burned his many unpublished papers before his death.

Almost a century after Simon's pioneering book a German Protestant professor, Johann Semler, published a plea for the 'free investigation' of the Bible with some suggestions as a tentative beginning. But then Gotthold Lessing, a librarian serving the duke of Brunswick, published fragments of a vast manuscript left behind by Hermann Reimarus, a local professor. In his own isolation that scholar had uncovered what he believed to be the true story of Jesus. Sadly Jesus, while teaching much that was permanently true because rational and moral, had been too much of a Jew, deceived by the current enthusiasm for the kingdom of God and expecting its imminent arrival. When he and his dream had died he was said to be resurrected, but only by fraudulent apostles who founded their own kind of religion. The publication of these fragments, beginning in 1774, was enough to bring down on Lessing's head the wrath of Semler, of churchmen and of the duke; publication was discontinued; the nervousness of those few who wanted the free investigation of the Bible became paralysing. The result was that some honest thinkers said openly that the history in the Bible could never teach a religion which would stand up to investigation by reason: the truth of the stories in it was too uncertain. Influentially, Lessing taught that any truths in history were merely 'accidental'. 'Since no historical truth can be demonstrated', he wrote, 'history cannot be used to demonstrate anything else.' A 'nasty big ditch' separated history from 'the necessary truths of reason'. He was not being irreligious. For him, one of the necessary truths was that 'the final reason of things must be found in a necessary substance' which is 'what we call God'. The 'detail of changes' has this source. But in the final analysis, the changes reported in traditions about history such as the Bible are irrelevant to a reasonable religion.

A series of books published in England explored the possibility of finding in Scripture some simple truths about God which were not contrary to 'the necessary truths of reason'. Lord Herbert of Cherbury was the English equivalent of Leibniz. In a book published in 1624 (but safely in Latin) he listed five true ideas in religion, inspired by 'the breath of the divine spirit immediately felt': God exists, he ought to be worshipped, virtue is the chief part of worship, there ought to be repentance for vices and crimes, and there are rewards and punishments after death. (But Lord Herbert's brother George was an Anglican priest and a tenderly devotional poet, covering much more than those ideas.) Thirteen years later William Chillingworth published *The Religion of Protestants*, which he limited to 'fundamental truths' taught plainly by the Bible and by 'the Bible only'. During the English civil wars Benjamin Whichcote pleaded that 'universal charity is a thing final in religion' and his own religious position combined Lord Herbert's rationalism with Chillingworth's biblicism. 'To go against reason is to go against God', he maintained, but he accepted as reasonable the simple truths which the Bible taught. What interested him was that these truths could be combined with the philosophy of Plato, which he regarded as the summit of human reasoning. But could they be combined with the new science which relied on observation and experiment?

In a treatise in Latin published in 1687 on *The Mathematical Principles of Natural Philosophy* Isaac Newton confidently presented gravity as the chief of the forces which kept the planets in their courses around the sun and determined many natural movements on this planet. He was equally convinced about the power of God: 'This Being governs all things, not as a Soul of the World, but as Lord of the Universe . . . supreme over all, eternal, infinite, absolutely perfect.' He declared that both Nature and the Bible had taught him to believe in this 'Lord of the Universe'. With a unified vision he believed in the Bible's miracles and also in future interventions by God as predicted in the Bible: such events within the ordered universe seemed akin to what he believed to be divine adjustments needed because the workings of gravity in Nature were occasionally inadequate. People might be sceptical about these old-fashioned parts of Newton's great system, but at least many could accept his general reconciliation of science with a reasonable belief in the existence of the 'Lord of the Universe'.

One of his many admirers, John Locke, published in 1689 an *Essay Concerning Human Understanding*. He denied that any ideas are present in the mind at birth. He also denied that the human mind can have true ideas about the character of God without assistance. Most propositions which are reliable, he wrote, are those 'whose truth we can discover by examining and tracing those ideas we have from sensation and reflection, and by natural deduction find to be true or probable'. Other propositions should be believed if judged by the reason to come 'from God in some extraordinary way of communication'. Since many ideas then in dispute between Christians did not fall into either category, Locke urged toleration. But he did not extend toleration to atheists, who seemed to him arrogant fools since 'we more certainly know that there is a God, than there is anything else without us'. Moreover, the folly of atheism destroys a society. Locke's cautiously anonymous book on *The Reasonableness of Christianity as Delivered in the Scriptures* limited the essential Christian faith to the belief that God has sent his Son as the Messiah in order to teach a 'true and complete morality' in 'plain propositions' and to offer the forgiveness of sins to those who give themselves up 'to be his subjects'. This was not a comprehensive theology but 'our business here is not to know all things, but those which concern our conduct'. Thus God had been wise to limit the contents of his 'extraordinary way of communication': the truths which he had revealed in this way were few but they were adequate and they were 'not contrary to reason'.

Newton and Locke differed from two earlier thinkers about religion, Descartes and Spinoza.

René Descartes, the French mathematician and philosopher whose insistence on 'doubt' as the only way to reliable science was to be his most enduring contribution, based his religious thought on the claim that some ideas are not subject to doubting. They are 'innate', lodged in the mind at birth—the claim which Locke demolished. To him as to Locke, the existence of God 'who is all-powerful and by whom I was created and made as I am' is at least as certain as any proposition in geometry, but for him this is not because such a belief is always reached by an adult who reasons properly. It is because the existence of such a God is a 'clear and distinct' idea present in the child's mind before it begins its search for other ideas also true because also 'clear and distinct'. 'I have known with certainty only my own existence and God's', he wrote. 'Just as I cannot think that I exist without existing myself, so I cannot conceive of God without existence' (as Anselm had said long ago). But what if in fact a child needs to be taught about God? Would it then be reasonable to say that God's existence may be known by 'all who will give it careful thought'—known by 'the natural light of the mind'? Would it then be intellectually respectable to share with Descartes the belief that the sovereignty of the adult's reasoning, reaching 'clear and distinct truths' through the method of 'doubt', ought to leave untouched 'the religion into which God was good enough to have me instructed from childhood'? We can see why the faith of Locke was welcomed when he taught that an adult belief in the existence of God was 'the most obvious truth which reason discovers' and that the acceptance of the truths taught by Jesus also passed the test of being reasonable.

Baruch Spinoza, although he owed much to Descartes, was essentially a Jewish mystic who had abandoned the Jewish belief in the Lord of the Universe partly because he was a pioneer (and Richard Simon's teacher) in modern biblical studies. As he investigated the Scriptures for himself, as he explored the world for himself and formed his own conclusions about it, the religion of his childhood was eclipsed by a cloud of doubt. Accordingly he had to earn his living by the use of his hands and most of what he wrote was published only after his death in 1677. He concluded, however, that 'God or Nature' deserves worship, for absolutely everything that exists or occurs, whether or not it is 'good' according to human opinion, is an expression of the divine substance. 'God or Nature' has no love for us or interest in us; it cannot 'save'; miracles are out of the question; but this austere religion to be known by 'natural illumination' seemed to him to be the only possible survivor for an educated mind as modern science began, while the Scriptures which ordinary folk still needed must be understood as teaching the same truth less clearly. We can see why the faith of Newton, the greatest scientist yet seen, in the power of the Lord of the Universe was easier for minds accustomed to Christianity to accept—but Spinoza's religion of 'God or Nature' (pantheism) did not go away and in the years to come it would often be simplified to mean a worship of Nature as divine without Spinoza's continuing interaction with his Jewish religious heritage.

It was significant, and in the long run an advantage to Christianity, that Voltaire did not popularize the religious views either of Descartes or of Spinoza, for he was often regarded as the Enlightenment's principal spokesman. He shared and spread the faith in the Lord of the Universe which Newton and Locke seemed to have justified. There was a serious bottom to his quip that if God did not exist it would be necessary to invent him. He rejected the atheism of some of those who were otherwise close to him (including Diderot the joint editor of the *Encyclopédie*). Once on a mountaintop at dawn he astonished his companion by prostrating himself before the Creator of such majestic beauty—adding, however, that he did not extend his worship to the Son or the Mother. He had not found it easy to hold on to a faith even with this restriction. His mind had received the full intellectual impact of the earthquake which destroyed the centre of Lisbon on All Saints Day in 1755. He wrote his best book, *Candide*, in order to link that natural disaster with many other evils suffered by humanity, inflicted either by nature or by humanity itself—and he wrote it in order to demolish the optimism of Leibniz, who had maintained against Newton that the creation which already existed was 'the best of all possible worlds'. He never reconciled the existence of God with the existence of evil but continued to think both to be real. Indeed, he added a chapel to his house at Ferney having demolished the old parish church. Basically his belief in the Creator seems to have been the answer to the question which Leibniz had asked: 'Why are there entities at all, and not nothing?'

Neither Newton nor Locke, nor their publicist Voltaire, nor Leibniz could accept what was presented as the Trinity. The old formulations had begun to seem meaningless but no one was clear about what to put in their place and even discussion was full of risks. To be called a 'Socinian' might be a personal disaster: it did not mean merely an interest in developing the theology of Fausto Sozzini who had died in Poland in 1604 maintaining—as he claimed, on the basis of Scripture—that Christ possessed the *divinitas* of his function as Saviour although not the *deitas* of eternal divinity. John Milton had written a treatise in Latin on *Christian Doctrine* which had explored the question afresh with a conclusion like Sozzini's. He had begun it in the 1650s but it was not published until 1825. In 1712 Samuel Clarke published his *Scripture-Doctrine of the Trinity* in which he demonstrated that the Bible was not trinitarian in the sense of the later councils of the Church, but he had to promise to write no more on that dangerous subject. Now hesitations or denials were reinforced by the Enlightenment's conviction that the mind of Man cannot penetrate the life of God in eternity. Newton, for all his pride in his science and his theology, famously compared himself with a child playing on the seashore before the great ocean of truth. Locke wrote about the limits, as well as the growing powers, of human understanding. Fontanelle, who achieved much as a promoter and popularizer of science in France, remarked to a friend as they looked up at the night sky that humanity had two characteristics, inquiring minds and short sight.

Thus humility was an ingredient in the Enlightenment's scepticism about much of the theology of the past. And in this period Christians produced a few examples of theology done within the limits of reasonableness and humility.

Bishop Joseph Butler's *Analogy of Religion* was impressive because it had both those characteristics, answering without naming John Toland's cocksure book of 1696 (*Christianity not Mysterious*), and Matthew Tindal's of 1730 (*Christianity as Old as Creation: or The Gospel a Republication of the Religion of Nature*). This reasonable bishop demonstrated by his constant tone as much as by his actual arguments that a truly religious mind always has to deal with mysteries. 'Natural' religion can, he thought, persuade a reasoner that there is an 'intelligent Author of nature' and that 'this little scene of human life' has 'a reference, of some sort or other, to a much larger plan of things'—but everything else in religion, 'natural' or 'revealed', depends on our decisions about 'probability', humbly considering 'all the evidence taken together'. His tone was very different from that of another English theologian, William Paley, who as the eighteenth century became the nineteenth was still claiming that the new knowledge of nature had made it all the more obvious that the universe was designed by an almighty and benevolent God, as it was obvious that a watch had been made by a watchmaker. That kind of confidence made an impact but the impact was not to last. What lasted was Bishop Butler's feeling for the mystery surrounding human life.

Some Effects of Enlightenment

When 'enlightened' thinkers about morality began to pay less attention to the will of God as interpreted by the churches, and more to 'natural rights' or to calculations about 'pleasure' or 'utility' for 'the greatest number', many Christians raised the alarm: surely any rights were derived from the grace of God not from Nature, and surely the pursuit of happiness ought not to be the main aim of life before death? But the Enlightenment could reply that when it argued that morality should be humane it did not imply that morality should be weak.

In 1761 the son of a Huguenot manufacturer in Toulouse was found hanged in his father's shop. At first the father concealed the fact of suicide, because he knew that a suicide's corpse would be dragged naked through the streets before being hanged. The authorities decided that the father had done the hanging himself, for fear that the son was about to become a Catholic. They executed him by breaking him on a wheel. Voltaire heard of the case and at the age of 68 threw himself into the vindication of justice, to the astonishment of many. He ended his published protest with a prayer to God that the day might come when Christians might exercise towards each other elementary justice and even charity. Five years later a young French-man was executed for laughing at a religious procession. Pleas for mercy came from the local bishop, the papal nuncio and the lawyers' *Parlement*, but the law took its course. In fact the whole penal code of the eighteenth century, with frequent executions for theft, was barbaric.

Its stronger sense of justice was an ingredient in the Enlightenment's rejection of the classic doctrines about Adam's 'original' sin and Christ's 'atoning' sacrifice. In the new light it seemed clear that no good God would doom most of his children to unending tortures because of a sin once committed by one man, or demand the mental and physical agony of the innocent Christ before forgiving the guilty or only the 'elect' among the guilty. What had been taught by François Turretin, the admired professor of theology in Geneva from 1648 to 1687, now seemed repulsive: with great assurance he had expounded the theory that the Father first decided on the few he intended to save whatever their merits and then decided to send the Son in order that he might be crucified as a satisfactory substitute for them and for them alone. Nor did it seem good enough to teach that a man's hard work was God's just punishment of Adam's sin, or that the daughters of Eve were punished by being made to desire their husbands and to give birth in pain. A religion based on such doctrines seemed as morally wrong, as much in need of reform, as the penal code of this eighteenth Christian century.

Doctrines which could now seem unreasonable and even immoral remained in the churches' official documents, whether Catholic or Prot-estant. But the Enlightenment did not reckon that because doctrines were orthodox in the eyes of the Church they must be true. It appealed instead to the verdict of 'humanity'. Lessing could pronounce after a long search for the truths of religion: 'It is enough to hold to Christian love, what happens to the Christian religion does not matter.' In his greatest play it is Nathan the suffering Jew who is the wisest and best because the most humane.

By 'humanity' the Enlightenment did not mean to advocate any total democracy, for these intellectuals reckoned that most people were too ill-educated to have opinions worth considering. Voltaire and Diderot preferred to put their trust in an 'enlightened' monarch's despotism, although Voltaire's time at the Prussian court of Frederick the Great ended in disaster and Diderot thought it wise to confine himself to correspondence with Catherine the Great. But by 'humanity' a reference was intended to something big in space and time. This was an age when Europe eagerly read travellers' reports or inventions about the newly discovered world, from the surprisingly civilized Turks to the innocent and inviting maidens of Tahiti, and also many histories about a past which was larger and stranger than had ever been imagined. A sense of the development in history was beginning, although the philosophers who first expounded it (the Catholic Vico in Italy and the Lutheran Herder in Germany) were pioneers and not widely known. It seemed that Europeans had something to learn from the 'noble', or at least virile, savages who roamed the North American plains, or from the ancient Egyptians; most of all, perhaps, from the wise men of China. Montesquieu's *Spirit of the Laws* (1748) began the intellectual adventure of comparing the laws and customs of one people with those of another, often to the discredit of his own France. He showed that the newly understood differences in humanity's circumstances—in climate, for example, or in the size of the country, or in religion—made the critical comparison necessary, always with the aim of assisting the progress of 'civilization' through the application of 'reason' to a wider range of 'knowledge'. The allegation that the 'enlightened' were middle-class European men who merely admired each other was to be made in the future, but it was largely unfair.

It was often also to be alleged that the Enlightenment ignored the emotions when it attempted to be 'reasonable'. That, too, was an unfair attack. The 'enlightened' were not utterly detached from the realities of human life. This age began the influence of Jean-Jacques Rousseau which was to increase during the later age of Romanticism. He was as subjective— indeed, as irrational—as any Romantic could desire. He left behind him *Confessions* which by their candid self-absorption helped to set the fashion for extreme individualism; he also prepared the way for revolutionary terrorism by offering the political theory that although society had been established by a contract between individuals 'born free' that 'social contract' now obliged them to obey the 'general will' which was entitled to 'force men to be free'; he used a cultivated style in order to argue that humanity had been corrupted by the improvement of the arts and the sciences; in his novel *Emile* (1762) he propounded a perfect course of education (with a pupil–teacher ratio of one to one) although he had dumped his own children in an orphanage; and this advocate of total honesty presented (also in *Emile*) as his hero in religion a 'Savoyard vicar' who remained a Catholic priest although his beliefs deviated largely from the Church's. Yet he seems to have been honest in his response to the gospels. 'I recognize the divine spirit in them: it is as immediate as can be. There are no men between the proof and me.' His own feelings made him a kind of Christian and a 'Deist' with a belief in God, as the universe's 'First Cause'.

A more weighty rejection of rationalist over-confidence was a central thrust in the philosophy of David Hume. This philosopher was no friend of religious orthodoxy, as his early essay on miracles made plain: a miracle is simply 'a violation of the laws of nature' and it never happens. But he was determined to remain on good terms with the ministers of the Church of Scotland who shared with him the intellectual life of Edinburgh. He therefore delayed the publication of his *Dialogues concerning Natural Religion* until after his calmly atheistic death in 1776. In that conversation Philo, who represents Hume's own views, disagrees with the happily traditional Christian (Clea) but devotes more energy to contradicting Cleanthes, the Deist exponent of the belief that the existence of the Creator is obvious. We do not really understand the causes of everyday events: how, then, can we know what finally causes everything? If we like to call the First Cause 'God', is that more than a matter of 'habit, caprice or inclination'? If we like to think of God as the Creator, what evidence is there that he was competent if he wished to create a world we could call good? Religion must have originated in emotions very different from the reasonings of the Deists and the only truly reasonable verdict on 'the whole' which is 'a riddle, an enigma, an inexplicable mystery' is 'doubt, uncertainty, suspense of judgement'. But Hume also denied the belief that morality can be based on unemotional reasoning. In real life, he taught, we have to make decisions amid intellectual uncertainty and reason is, and ought to be, 'the slave of our passions'. This acknowledgement of the role of the emotions was all the more substantial because his own life was a model of calm benevolence.

The kind of reasonableness about which the 'enlightened' could begin to agree may be seen in the field then called Political Economy. It had been the teaching of the medieval Church and of many Protestant preachers that every article for sale had its just price and every worker his just wage. In practice these principles had often resulted in the restriction of trade and the control of prices by privileged groups of producers, or at the least in the discouragement of free enterprise. It had been the teaching of the more modern and secular 'mercantilists' that the possession of wealth in coins should be the supreme objective of governments, to be achieved by enlarging the territory under a nation's control, by excluding foreign competition in trade and by taxation. An example was the system under which the British empire operated in the eighteenth century. The North American colonies were defended from the French because that was in the interests of Britain and 'taxation without representation' seemed natural: of course they should not be represented in Parliament but of course they ought to pay for their defence. Although encouraged to trade with the British West Indies, they were discouraged or forbidden if they wished to trade with foreign nations. Manufactured goods must be imported from Britain only. The Royal Navy, which relied heavily on North America in building its own ships, policed this system under which Navigation Acts claimed the monopoly in merchant shipping for British vessels, for example in the slave trade. The 'physiocrats' accepted this mercantilist philosophy as a whole but stressed the production of food as a nation's chief wealth. However, in the year of Hume's death his friend Adam Smith published his *Enquiry into the Nature and Causes of the Wealth of Nations*.

Truly 'enlightened' and truly radical, Smith attacked all restraints on free trade, on the prices it found profitable or on the wages it found necessary if a profit was to be made. Free trade and uncontrolled bargaining for wages, with the minimum of government and taxation, would serve all the nations best: more goods would be available, the prices charged for them would come down, in real terms all would benefit. Smith also wrote a book on the 'moral sentiments' needed to maintain honest trade and civilized life, but his main belief was that if individuals pursued their selfish interests with a reasonable degree of co-operation it would be for the ultimate benefit of everyone, as if by the working of an 'invisible hand'. And Britain was to benefit massively by adopting free trade in 1846, earlier than its continental neighbours. The future was to produce social problems of which Adam Smith was blissfully unaware, as the state refused to intervene in the workings of a market always competitive and often brutal. Nevertheless, the free trade which Smith advocated generated the wealth of nations until it was generally abandoned in the 1930s and it may be judged that the Christians who supported it were not entirely wicked.

When pondering the prospects of humanity as it became more reasonable, the 'enlightened' believed in 'progress'. By this they did not mean that a continuous progress could be guaranteed. Voltaire was among the 'enlightened' who could be eloquent about their misfortune to live in an age of decline. Diderot declared that the human heart remained partly a sanctuary and partly a sewer and he feared that the sewer was about to overflow. Kant acknowledged that the Enlightenment had not made an 'enlightened age' and that if the kingdom of God was ever to be established on earth, built with the 'warped wood' of human nature, it must be by the action of God— which, according to Kant's religion, did not make it very likely. The most eloquent plea that humanity was capable of reaching perfection was made by the mathematician and aristocrat Condorcet: his book was written as terror was unleashed by the French Revolution in the names of reason and liberty, and he wrote it while in hiding before his suicide. But the 'enlightened' were not entirely incorrect to believe that some progress was possible if humanity applied reason to its tasks. In Europe there was observable progress in the seventeenth century; Francis Bacon's advocacy of experimental science was followed, however slowly, by the application of science to tasks which in Asia (for example) were still left to muscle-power. That century also knew problems—a little ice age in the climate, a long succession of poor harvests, continuing disease and poverty, governments which did little or nothing to improve the wealth of nations. One problem could be overpopulation, meaning that it became too expensive to buy land: this was a factor in the decision of some of the English to face the hardships of migration to America, although the hardships were such that religion was needed as the main incentive. In the eighteenth century population growth resumed more substantially (it seems to have doubled in Europe, 1500–1800) and there was more food. The *Encyclopédie* listed cultural and technical developments which were going some way to improve the human situation deplored in *Candide*. If people would dare to find things out, to think things out, to judge for themselves, to use the minds given to them by the Creator, to seek justice, to be humane, to be reasonable without ignoring the emotions, some progress was possible.

Two Responses

Locke and Butler cleared some of the ground that needed to be cleared: they insisted that the 'reasonable' and essential truths of Christianity were fewer than had been thought and that none of them apart from belief in the Creator could be reached as a certainty by the unaided use of reason. But before Schleiermacher began to teach in Germany as the nineteenth century began, no major European theologian answered constructively the full challenge of the Enlightenment. It was left to two laymen to produce the most pertinent thoughts.

This tiny group did not include Immanuel Kant, despite his eminence in philosophy. His 'religion within the limits of reason alone' has not convinced sceptics—not even when it has been explained that the reason involved is 'practical', not 'pure'. Sceptics have said, as David Hume said: of course many people have the idea that God exists but that is no proof that he does; of course we are impressed by the grandeur and orderliness of the universe but many other features are difficult to reconcile with belief that a good God made it all; of course we are impressed by our own consciences but that moral sense may have arisen from sources not including God; of course we hope that we are free and immortal but we may not be able to escape from our circumstances and our deaths. And Kant's 'religion within the limits of reason alone' has not usually satisfied people who are at any depth religiously minded. In their experience religion has not been solely a deduction from reasoning. Hopefully it has been reasonable, contemplating the starry heavens and the imperatives of the conscience, but it has not stayed within the bounds of reason. It has been the response of a heart, of a life, to a mystery, a revelation, given in public or personal history. Many people, events, writings or objects may be the medium of this revelation which points to what transcends what is easy to understand; many different communities may make the revelation possible or support it when it is believed to have occurred; but usually religion has been a response to some kind of revelation. It has produced the kind of faith which is the whole person in response, influencing all of that individual and (in a diluted or corrupt form) the whole of a society. So religion has stood on its own ground. We can glimpse this ground if we look at the work of two seventeenth-century authors: the Dutch lawyer Huig van Groot, usually called by the Latin name Hugo Grotius, and the French scientist Blaise Pascal.

Grotius had been sentenced to prison for life because he had supported the Arminians against the stricter Calvinists. Having escaped from prison by hiding in a box thought to hold books, he lived mostly in Paris and there published his own writings, among them *The Truth of the Christian Religion*. This religion, he maintained, is essentially simple. It proclaims the power of the Creator, now being confirmed as the orderliness of the creation is more fully revealed to the beginnings of science; and it repeats the teachings of Christ, who told his disciples to order their lives around a trust in this power. Most other doctrines are optional but not the resurrection of Christ: that is the great exception to God's general policy of setting an example of adherence to the Law of Nature. By making that exception, Grotius separated himself from the Deists: his God is active, his Nature leaves room for revelation.

Another book, tackling the biggest scandal in the behaviour of Christians, was on *The Law of War and Peace* (1625). After only a few years of the Thirty Years' War, which directly or indirectly was to cause the deaths of about a third of the population of central Europe, Grotius urged the nations to obey the God-given Law of Nature even if they disagreed about the definition of 'God'; to arrange their affairs without violence; and if they had to go to war, to restrict its disasters to those truly needed to re-establish peace with justice. In 1642, when the great 'religious' war ruining Germany was not yet over, he issued an appeal to Catholics, Lutherans and Calvinists to unite, or at the very least to tolerate each other. In the same year, when civil war was breaking out in England and everyone used biblical arguments, he published his thoughts about the Bible. In answer to the churches which continued to insist that the Scriptures had been dictated by the Holy Spirit Grotius urged the acceptance of sound criticism of them as literature and history, while in answer to the radicals who made the individual's interpretation of the Scriptures the only authority for Christians he advocated respect for the churches' traditions as the vehicles by which the Bible's message had reached successive generations. Grotius could be denounced by Christians who regarded themselves as orthodox because he tried to appeal to moral laws which he believed to be written in all human hearts and to be valid whatever version of religion might be held. People, he thought, knew that they ought not to kill each other; ought not to divide themselves from each other; ought to accept facts reached by reason while also accepting the duty of courtesy to heritages. All these would be obligations 'even if God were not given' as the centre of human life. But to him, God was the centre.

Blaise Pascal, the other layman who outlined an interpretation of Christianity relevant to the Enlightenment, was a Catholic.

Although an outstanding mathematician and scientist who devised the first computer, he was more passionate than Grotius—as passionate in his concern for religious truth as he was in his youthful enthusiasm for calculations and experiments. But for many years he also took part in the social life of smart Paris, an experience which gave him the ability to sum up shrewd observations of human nature pithily as if in intimate conversation. The turning point in the solitary self-questioning of Descartes came when during one winter in Germany 'I spent the whole day shut up in a room heated by an enclosed stove where I had complete leisure', but the turning point for Pascal (who thought that Descartes 'would like to do without God' but did not dare) was very different. It came one night in November 1654, when he had a mystical experience of 'fire'. He understood it as an encounter with the God of Abraham, Isaac and Jacob, 'not the God of the philosophers and scientists'. It gave him 'certitude, emotion, joy, peace'. He kept a written memory of the event for the remainder of his life. He died in 1662 while not yet forty, leaving behind only *Pensées*, thoughts towards his projected defence of a biblical and Catholic faith, a faith which was very much more than conformity to an institution.

He was to be ridiculed by Voltaire because he disbelieved in the power of reason, believed in miracles and was not critical of the Bible. But he was deeply serious about the question of the truth of belief in God, leaving technical theology to others, and had he lived a hundred years later it seems probable that he would have been more critical. (The *Pensées* include remarks that 'the pope hates and fears the learned, who do not submit to him at will', that 'the history of the Church ought properly to be called the history of truth' and that 'the Church is in an excellent state when it is maintained by God alone'.) He observed that 'there are few true Christians, even as regards faith. There are many who believe but it is because of superstition. There are many who do not believe but it is because of wickedness. Few are between the two.' So most people are like condemned criminals who play cards shortly before being hanged. Deserted as he was in Gethsemane and on Calvary, 'Jesus will be in agony until the end of the world'.

Pascal knew from conversations that scepticism, even atheism, was becoming an alternative to Christianity, partly in reaction to the 'religious' wars, and he felt its power. To him it was by no means obvious that the existence of the Creator can be known by the unaided light of reason. The universe is orderly—but is also now known to be extremely large; indeed, 'the whole visible world is only an impossible atom in the ample bosom of nature'. 'The eternal silence of these infinite spaces frightens me.' An adjacent note explains that famous confession: 'When I consider the short duration of my life, swallowed up in eternity before and after, the little space which I fill or can see, engulfed in the infinite immensity of spaces which I do not know and which do not know me, I am frightened, astonished at being here rather than there ... Who has put me here?' What seemed certain to Descartes seemed very strange to Pascal. 'It is incomprehensible that God should exist, and it is incomprehensible that he should not exist; that the soul should be joined to the body, and that we should have no soul.' He imagined a believer protesting to him: 'Do you not say yourself that the heavens and the birds prove God?' and 'Does not your religion say so?' His answer to both questions was no.

He abandoned the claims which had occupied many minds in many centuries, saying bluntly that even if God's existence could be proved 'faith is different from proof; proof is human, faith is a gift from God'. He acknowledged that in religion as in other spheres we often have to learn from other people what seems to be the truth, while noting also that 'truth on this side of the Pyrenees is error on the other'. But in the last analysis, religious truth was for him a gift which the individual receives through faith, through the 'reasons' which come from the depths of the self. His own faith, reached and held with difficulty, arose out of intense thought about a profound paradox: the greatness and littleness, the glory and misery, of Man. Many a tree will outlive a human being, but 'a tree does not know that it is miserable'. In his account of 'misery' there is, however, little mention of the physical suffering and social injustice which troubled Voltaire and Grotius as they have troubled so many others who have been told that God is both good and almighty. Pascal the introspective concentrated on the dissatisfaction of Man without God, soon bored if alone in a room, soon bored if seeking pleasure with others, plunging therefore into more humiliating pleasures, made for eternity but ignoring it. Even when we attempt to conquer our natural vices we are morally corrupt: Pascal was an Augustinian to the extent of believing that 'we are born guilty'. We are not guided by reason in our most important decisions: 'all our reasoning reduces itself to feeling' and 'the heart has its reasons which reason does not know' (other Augustinian touches). Yet the reasons of the heart may turn us in the right direction, finding with Augustine that 'the Christian faith proceeds mainly to establish these two facts, the corruption of nature and redemption by Jesus Christ'. These facts are, however, revealed only to those who have already been chosen by God—as if God were saying to them: 'You would not seek me if you had not found me.'

The religion which Pascal wished to commend to the heart, and through that to the mind, was not intended to be unreasonable, for 'if one shocks the principles of reason, our religion will be absurd and ridiculous'. To this great intellectual, another word for the 'heart' was the 'intelligence'. But neither was this religion the mere contemplation of the non-controversial Author of Nature 'within the limits of reason alone'. It was a surrendered disciple's love of Christ. 'Jesus Christ did nothing but teach people that they loved themselves too much; that they were slaves, blind, sick, wretched and sinners; that he must deliver them, enlighten, bless and heal them; that this would be effected by hating self and following him through suffering and the death on the cross.' So 'the God of Christians is a God of love and comfort, a God who fills the souls and hearts of those he possesses, a God who makes them conscious of their inward wretchedness and his infinite mercy . . . who makes them incapable of any end other than himself'. In a plea very different from Kant's motto about the courage to judge for yourself, and very different from Bishop Butler's calm talk about probability, Pascal urged: everyone must decide. As a mathematician he was interested in gambling and he drew images from the social life of Paris and from the new, risky voyages. 'You must wager. It is not optional. You are embarked . . . If you win, you win all.' But even in this central challenge to the Enlightenment he struck a note which could never have been heard in a medieval or Reformation sermon. It was the admission of the possibility that God does not exist, that death is not survived. His response to that possibility was to say that if there is no God you will never know; if death is the end, a Christian life is still the best; if you lose, 'you lose nothing'.

We have now to see why the group to which Pascal belonged, the Jansenists, was condemned by Church and State.

Church and State before the Revolution

As the twentieth Christian century closes almost every Christian is 'enlightened' in this sense: it is thought wrong for any state to force anyone to subscribe to a religious belief. It is taken for granted that a state has no business to interfere in an individual's freedom to believe or not to believe, to worship or not to worship, and the 'freedom of religion' which the churches have learned to allow to their critics is enshrined in constitutions even when the regime is Communist. It is commonly agreed that enforced belief is likely to be insincere and therefore worthless religiously, while the church which encourages the use of the law and the police for such a purpose is discredited. It is assumed that all religious beliefs, however precious or outrageous they may seem, ought to be left to stand or fall on their own merits. It is hoped by believers that, if so left, the true beliefs will stand persuasively—although it is also often agreed that religious truth does not benefit by being defined in elaborate theological systems.

During the eighteenth century these ideas began to be born. Although (as we have noted) most people still went to church the non-churchgoers who had existed in earlier ages—men who could be discovered in the tavern on a Sunday morning, women who did not fit into the social life—were now joined by more numerous abstainers in the towns and in some villages where neither priest nor landlord applied pressure. Churchgoing was beginning to be a habit which could be dropped without inviting punishment by public opinion or by the government. In that limited sense Europe was on the eve of 'secularization'.

But across eighteenth-century Europe the vast majority of those going to church went to a church which the state supported exclusively and the complete toleration of Christians by all other Christians seemed a fanciful idea. It seemed obvious that a people ought to be united in loyalty to a religion as well as to a government. It was one of a government's most important duties to do what it could to support both unities. In return the favoured church would, it was hoped, make good use of its more or less complete control of education and charitable work and of its influence on the state (for example, by bishops sometimes heading the French government or in the House of Lords in Westminster). To sceptics it seemed obvious that although what a church taught might be nonsense what a church did was, on the whole, useful or could be made so. To almost all believers it seemed obvious that it was to everyone's advantage that the true religion should be encouraged by every means possible including support by the state, for the true religion was the passport to heaven. It was assumed that no subject or citizen should be given any encouragement to ruin his or her immortal soul by adhering to a wrong religion, any more than physical suicide should be encouraged. Thus kings swore solemn oaths at their coronations to uphold the true religion, the magistrates of many a city or county acknowledged a duty to keep the place clean of heresy as well as of crime, and villagers did not need to be told why their parish church was so prominent. For essentially political reasons it might be necessary to tolerate the peaceful, and preferably hidden, devotions of a specified religious minority, but a minority could hope that it would one day become the majority, expecting the magistrate to penalize ungodliness.

Such was the position still held by most of Europe about Church and State: their alliance seemed essential to both. When Catholicism was imposed on Central and South America the popes allowed the Spanish and Portuguese kings to appoint to all offices in the Church, to dispose of all tithes collected in the parishes and to censor all communications from Rome to the New World and all the decisions of church councils held within it—all in exchange for the promise to make and keep these vast territories firmly and exclusively Catholic. When dealing with Calvinist Scotland, where the efforts of the monarchy to impose bishops had to be abandoned in 1689, the Parliament in Westminster was able (in 1712) to restore the rights of lay patrons to appoint parish ministers. Rich laymen could be trusted far more than bishops—trusted to keep Scotland a Protestant people.

The damage inflicted on religion by the combination of religious intolerance with state control may be seen in the history of the *ancien régime* in France, in the eighteenth century Europe's largest nation. The combined forces of Church and State seemed irresistible in a largely churchgoing society where no religious alternative to the officially defined Catholicism was permitted and in an apparently stable society where no political alternative to monarchism seemed conceivable. Some survivals from the eighteenth century in Rome belong to the same world as Louis XIV's Versailles; they include lavish monuments to undistinguished popes. But in the reality of that age *roi* and *loi* took precedence over *foi*, since the king decreed the law and controlled the faith. A bishop might be the king's prime minister but he knew his place: he was the king's servant. The papacy had ceased to be the initiating centre of creative reform and was no longer even the effective protector of the clergy; on the contrary it endorsed, or acquiesced in, actions initiated by the royal government which gravely weakened French Christianity.

This damage to the official religion was done at a time when popular religion—'magic' or 'superstition' in the eyes of the 'enlightened'—was being weakened by the continuing pressure of the Catholic Reformation. The peasants who constituted the bulk of the population were finding that the clergy were increasingly hostile to many of the practices which had survived since the Middle Ages and earlier paganism, using Christianity to provide material for rituals intended to increase fertility, to ward off physical dangers and to celebrate the unity of a neighbourhood. Often by warnings about the eternal punishments which awaited 'superstition' which the Church had not authorized, often by contempt for ignorance and sometimes by charm, the clergy now attempted to preach a religion which concentrated on the spiritual and moral life of the individual. Many of the devout responded, so that its twentieth-century historian, Henri Brémond, called the spirituality of the seventeenth-century French teachers of prayer and behaviour 'the golden age of our religious history'. Such teaching was marked by 'devout humanism', by the concentration on God but also by a sensitivity to the human nature of the devout. However, it had its weakness as well as its strength, as may be seen in the teaching of Jean-Pierre de Caussade, a Jesuit who died in 1751. His only published book was a disciple's exposition of the conservative theology of Bishop Bossuet, but after his death talks were edited which he had given to nuns.

These talks became the book known and loved in English as *Self-Abandonment to the Divine Providence*. De Caussade belongs to the tradition which by practice finds the presence of God in the situation and the soul, the one requirement being a patient humility. He repeats the saints' call to renounce and to suffer for the sake of the vision of God—a vision possible amid circumstances which may seem entirely hostile, a vision so overwhelming that it makes any sacrifice of worldly pleasures seem slight. The weakness of this teaching, however, is that it is addressed to the devout rather than to more earthy people who have to do the work of the world. By encouraging a passive acceptance of circumstances and of authority it can obscure those elements in Christianity which are revolutionary, being hunger and thirst for the kingdom of God which has not yet come. At its weakest this 'abandonment' of self-will may mean little more than prostration before throne and altar in a religion of total submission. And such a religion was indeed the atmosphere in the seminaries where boys and young men were turned into conventional and obedient priests.

One damaging action was the royal government's near-destruction of French Protestantism. This removed the possibility that many French people who objected to their official Church would find an alternative church resembling the English churches which were 'nonconformist' but Bible-based, robustly lay in their ethos but not without spirituality.

As we have seen, the wars of religion could not be ended in France until the Protestants were recognized as virtually a state within the Catholic state—but a state without a clear frontier. As the Catholic Reformation brought strength to the French Church the privileges granted to the Huguenots were increasingly resented and increasingly precarious. Their attempts to reassert their rights by force were answered by superior force and ended with the fall of La Rochelle in 1628. Their numbers then dwindled and they supported the monarchy which seemed the only basis of any remaining hope of toleration but five years after the beginning of his personal rule in 1661 Louis XIV officially listed the ways in which the state and the

Catholic clergy could apply pressure and persecution on these 'heretics' and in 1685 the edict of Nantes was formally revoked. One result was the exodus of many thousands of France's most skilled and enterprising workers, strengthening the economies of Holland, Britain and other hospitable countries. Another result was that Frenchmen who wished to be Christian without conforming to the Catholic Church and without leaving France had to accept a life little short of martyrdom. The laws were enforced less rigorously during the eighteenth century but they remained laws until the 1780s.

To other Protestants this persecution seemed to be one more loathsome example of Catholicism in action, but in fact Innocent XI, while approving the revocation, three years later deplored the cruelties. It was also the case that another cruel persecution, this time directed against the Jansenists, was inspired mainly not by Rome but by the conviction of the French government that these were crypto-Protestants presenting another threat to the ideology of the centralized state. What got the Jansenists into trouble was not their belief that salvation depended entirely on the free decisions of God: it was their belief that they were free to think so, whatever human authorities said.

In 1643 Urban VIII was persuaded to censure five propositions said to be part of an exposition of Augustinian theology by Cornelius Jansen, bishop of Ypres until his recent death. He agreed to the French report partly because Augustine of Hippo's emphasis on God's irresistible grace saving the predestined few had always threatened the practical workings of Catholicism, where sinners were exhorted to improve their lives by improving their church attendance and morality, of course with God's grace. Jansen's beliefs that Christ had died only for the elect, and that even for them faith without works was inadequate, hinted at the elitism which was also to mark the Jansenists, who (for example) held that for most people the habit of frequent communion would encourage moral laxity. Even so, the public condemnation of the scholarly, austere and vast book narrowed the room in the Church which the council of Trent had deliberately left to those who still believed the gospel according to Augustine. Many French (and other) Christians who were deeply serious in practising austerity for themselves, and in challenging others to decide to join them, were now branded as 'Jansenists' and heretics. Among the nuns of Port-Royal near Paris, which was the Jansenists' spiritual centre, was Blaise Pascal's sister. His own *Letters to a Provincial*, a masterpiece of witty scorn, were unfair to the Jesuits who were attacked as being too lax when counselling penitents, but at least it ought to have been clear that he did not intend to be a lax Catholic himself. The Jansenists were Augustinians within Catholicism (like Augustine) and they showed it in their usual reply to the papal censure: they agreed that the five condemned propositions were false but maintained that they were not accurately quoted from Jansen's book. However, another pope censured this reply as evasive and another required all the French clergy to accept without any qualification what had become an irreversible condemnation. Eventually the buildings and even the graves of Port-Royal were demolished by the government.

That was not the end of this union of Church and State in the demolition of theology thought to be dangerous. In 1699 Innocent XII censured 23 propositions drawn from a devotional book about the saints by François Fénelon, the archbishop of Cambrai who was an outstanding preacher and spiritual director, very active in charitable works and in efforts to convert Protestants. This time the heresy detected was Quietism, a movement to encourage the humble 'prayer of quiet' and the selfless 'prayer of union' (as Teresa of Avila and John of the Cross had done, and as Jean-Pierre de Caussade was to do, but without all their safeguards). Quietism had been discredited by a Spanish priest, Molinos, who had been a much admired director of nuns and other souls in Rome. His teaching about the need to annihilate all human thoughts and wishes, even the hope of heaven or the fear of hell, in the journey to union with God had been taken by some followers, and perhaps also by him in private, to mean that there was no lasting purpose in communion with Christ or in participation in the Church's prayers. He was also accused of teaching that there was no point in being chaste. He had spent the last dozen years of his life in a papal prison, confessing everything but in effect denying his accusers' charges by his saintly patience. One of this enigmatic teacher's admirers was a French widow, Jeanne Guyon, who wrote popular books about the need for self-forgetful-ness; as her critics alleged, gushingly and heretically. (She taught that the soul at prayer ought to resemble the babe at the breast.) Fénelon was, however, a man very different from such Quietists. He accepted the rebuke and kept quiet. Historians have suspected that his real mistake had been to defend Madame Guyon against Louis XIV's favourite bishop, Bossuet, and to criticize the monarch's policy of aggressive wars. He had written a novel which was a portrait of an ideal king. It was not a portrait of Louis.

Another move which damaged the vitality of French religion was made when another pope, Clement XI, took another step at the behest of Louis XIV. In 1713 he agreed to condemn 101 propositions extracted from a devotional book, *Moral Reflections on the New Testament*, by an Oratorian priest, Pasquier Quesnel. He alleged that they expressed Jansenist opinions, but most of them echoed saints of the authority of Paul and Augustine and among the propositions censured were seven which urged that all Christians, including women, should study the Scriptures. Clement was a partisan of the French king. (He had made his most important decision when he had backed

Louis XIV's grandson Philip as heir to the kingdom of Spain in opposition to a Habsburg duke.) What was really at stake was not the wisdom of Quesnel but the Church's role in support of royal power in France. This was demonstrated when the monarchy approved a ruling that the Church's sacraments should be refused to dying Catholics unwilling to confess their sins to a priest who accepted the condemnation of 1713. The lawyers in the *Parlement* of Paris protested and eventually, in 1757, all public discussion of the matter was prohibited. Fortunately, Quesnel's *Reflections* continued to feed the spiritual lives of many Catholics.

One reason why king and pope were anxious to collaborate in the detection and suppression of heresy was that they wished for no false impression to be given by the fact that they were for a long time in dispute about royal power over the Church.

Louis XIV was convinced not only that he understood Christianity better than any Jansenist or Quietist, but also that he had the right to appoint all the bishops and abbots in his kingdom and to receive the revenues while the posts were vacant. This opinion did not seem so convincing in Rome but a weapon in the royal armoury was the threat to do what Henry VIII had done in England. In 1664, on hearing that some unruly papal troops had trespassed into his embassy in Rome, Louis occupied the papal territory of Avignon, threatened to invade the papal states in Italy and compelled the pope to erect a monument apologizing for his soldiers' guilt. In 1682 all the French bishops were compelled by their king to accept 'articles' agreed by representatives of the clergy in an obedient assembly. These resolutions asserted the 'Gallican' position: the rights of the French crown over the Church accepted by the papacy back in 1516 are inviolate and popes have no authority over kings in temporal affairs or over councils in ecclesiastical affairs. Such warning shots were heard in Rome. Eleven years later Louis and another pope were reconciled but in practice Louis had won the battle, in preparation for a great victory under his successor. And this time the defeated enemy was to be the Society of Jesus, which had recently won its battle against the Jansenists thanks to the state's support.

In 1764 the French government expelled the Jesuits despite a public, and as he hoped permanent, protest by the pope. One of the first acts of the next pope (a Franciscan, Clement XIV) was to assure Louis XV of his support and in 1773 he decreed the complete dissolution of the Society of Jesus, worldwide, without conducting any full investigation or commanding the reform of any abuses which such an investigation might have uncovered. The Jesuit general did not resist but nevertheless was imprisoned. A boatload of Jesuits who were now refugees was refused permission to land in a succession of Mediterranean ports. Clement had been elected precisely in order that he might abandon the Jesuits to their fate. In theory the ambassadors of the Catholic powers were not supposed to influence a papal election but in practice they did, as in this case, and an important custom acknowledged their influence: France, Spain or Austria could veto the cardinals' choice even when this had been reached by the required majority of two-thirds.

The initiative in the suppression of the Jesuits was not taken by the French government alone. It was popular, inside and outside France. No proper account was taken of the potential in the missionary work which the Jesuits had already done, in North America for example. Quebec had been founded as a trading post by Samuel de Champlain in 1608 and had become a royal colony in 1663. A great bishop trained by the Jesuits (Laval) had energized church life from 1659 to 1688, but the insistence of later government-appointed bishops in Quebec that the Jesuits should be prevented from offering any threat to their authority had been one of the factors in the decline of missionary spirit in the transatlantic 'New France'. Even larger was the problem of the insistence of the fur traders on selling alcohol which corrupted the 'Indians'. In 1682 the vast territory of Louisiana had been claimed for France: it stretched from the Great Lakes to New Orleans (founded in 1718). Jesuits could have been encouraged to inspire the conversion of the 'Indians' and settlement by the French; a French Jesuit, Jacques Marquette, had accompanied the first European explorers of the Mississippi river in 1673, eager to discover possibilities for missionary work whatever the cost. But Louis XIV, preoccupied with comparatively petty territorial ambitions in Europe, had been unable to imagine a French Catholic empire in the new world, and his successors had not corrected his sense of priorities. For the future of Roman Catholicism in the USA it was indeed fortunate that a American gentlemen belonging to a family of leading republicans was available to work very successfully as the new republic's first Catholic bishop, from 1790 to 1815. Before 1773 John Carroll had been a Jesuit.

The suppression of the Jesuits worldwide began when they were accused of encouraging resistance to the transfer from Spanish to Portuguese sovereignty of some of the 'Indians' whom they were protecting in Paraguay. In Portugal an unconnected attempt to assassinate the king was used as an opportunity to expel all Jesuits from that country in 1759. France followed that example, using the pretext of the refusal of its own Jesuits to pay large debts incurred by colleagues while trading in the Caribbean. (One of the reasons why the Society of Jesus was often vulnerable to its enemies was its need to finance some of its missionary work by commerce.) Spain soon followed. But the basic reason for the French government's move was resentment at the Jesuit control of higher education and at the general strength of the Society's influence in a state meant to be under royal 'absolutism' meaning despotism. And although there was some popular sympathy as the Jesuits became refugees, most people seem to have thought that their day was over. Their colleges had become somewhat old-fashioned; their successes had aroused the jealousies of bishops, parish priests and other religious orders; they were said to whisper wickedness into the ears of the powerful—the very people who now took effective action against them. But there were no plans and no finances available for a new apparatus of missions, colleges and schools; there did not exist any network of Catholic intellectuals with anything like the same armoury of resources and dedication; and the papacy's supine willingness to sacrifice these loyal agents indicated how far the leadership which had done so much for the Catholic Reformation had sunk.

One defect in these condemnations of sincere Christians was a failure to listen to their own explanations of their teachings and practices. Before their abolition without trial the Jesuits had already experienced this failure when decisions had been reached in Rome to wreck their missions in China and India. Here, however, the complaints which the papacy heeded had not come from any local government: on the contrary, the Chinese emperor and ruling class admired and actively supported the Jesuits and in India there had been no difficulties of the kind experienced in Paraguay. The Jesuits had been attacked by their fellow missionaries, the Franciscans and Dominicans.

They were in trouble because they had tolerated the insistence of their converts from the higher classes on continuing to venerate tablets representing their ancestors. This ancient custom represented a Chinese culture which the Jesuits accepted—without, they claimed, betraying Christianity. By this strategy they had attracted some to be thoroughly Chinese Catholics and they had good reason to hope for many more. A Chinese emperor of the new Manchu dynasty, who had already declared Christianity to be a recognized and tolerated religion, took the further trouble to assure the papacy that these rites expressed veneration for ancestors including Confucius but no worship of idols. But other Catholic clergy, preoccupied by the battles against the cruder beliefs of the lower classes, denounced the Jesuits as encouragers of idolatry and as preachers who did not teach clearly that all dead pagans were everlastingly tormented in hell. Pascal, too, alleged that the Jesuit missionaries did nothing but compromise. In 1645 one pope warned the Jesuits against encouraging idolatry; in 1656 another agreed that they might allow rites which did not involve it; in 1704 and again in 1715 another condemned them; in 1742 another cancelled all exemptions from this ruling, a little later extending the ban to end the acceptance of Hindu customs in South India. The reaction in China was disastrous. While a few Jesuits were allowed to remain for the sake of their scientific work, and local governors could overlook the existence of more obscure Christians, most of the missionaries were expelled. In 1724 Christianity was declared illegal and there was persecution.

In their own eyes, and in the eyes of many Catholics, the popes were discharging their sacred duty to safeguard the unchanging faith entrusted to the Church, but their abandonment of the Jesuits was not the only sign that they had ceased to be the confident leaders of the Catholic Reformation. The papacy also abandoned the Poles when their country was carved up by Russia, Prussia and Austria in the 1770s (until 1919). Two-thirds of the population were now Roman Catholic and many remained patriotic although there was no longer a Polish nation on the map. Yet the papacy was not a source of much encouragement when the Russian persecution was the main factor in the movement of most of the 'Uniates' out of communion with Rome into submission to Orthodoxy, or when Prussian pressure supported Protestantism, or when the Austrian government supervised the Catholic Church; and any risings against the occupying powers (as in 1832) were denounced in Rome as rebellions against divinely appointed authorities.

In 1763 a German bishop, Johann von Hontheim, writing as 'Fabrionus' in the futile hope of concealing his identity, published a book *On the State of the Church* which combined many compliments to the pope as the successor of Peter with denials that he was infallible as a teacher or absolute in his power as the Church's governor. This position was very close to the Gallicanism still powerful in France, and it ended with an appeal to princes to lead national councils in reforming the Church should the popes continue to fail. This plump bishop was no Luther and was persuaded to recant (ambiguously), but his was not the last signal that a conservative papacy was losing control. In 1786 the clergy of the diocese of Pistoia in Tuscany, meeting in synod under their 'enlightened' bishop whose appointment had been secured by their 'enlightened' grand duke, passed many resolutions which suggested clearly enough which reforms ought to be pursued. Popular devotions ought to be guarded against superstition and missions in the parishes against emotionalism. Lay people ought to be encouraged to communicate at every Mass and to read the Bible (with Quesnel's book as the recommended guide). Monasteries ought to be placed under the bishops and reduced in numbers. Legends and festivals honouring the saints ought to be scrutinized.

One timorous bishop in Germany or one diocese in Italy which had no wish to revolt could not do much to change the Catholic Church, but for half a century, 1740–90, the power remaining to the emperors, based on Austria, was in the hands of Maria Theresa and Joseph II. Their attitudes were very different from those of Ferdinand II the hero of the Catholic Reformation or Leopold I, emperor 1657–1705, who had been trained as a priest and often acted like one; for they were more or less 'enlightened'.

Maria Theresa persecuted Protestants but under her the state supervised the Church's finances and reduced its role in education. The clergy were now taxed like other men, forbidden to charge for their services and compelled to read government edicts from their pulpits. Under Joseph a third of the monasteries were closed, partly in order to supply the finance for new dioceses, parishes, schools and hospitals. Diocesan seminaries were merged into larger colleges where the clergy were to receive a more modern as well as a more biblical education (an experiment which was soon ended). Marriage was made a civil contract; pilgrimages and processions were controlled and statues of the Virgin were no longer to be dressed like dolls. The emperor was to censor any communication with the pope. There was talk of further reforms: the Mass in German, married priests ... It seemed as if a new Protestant Reformation was about to be started, even if only in an English Tudor shape under a reforming monarch. Pius VI, a pope who in his reign since 1775 had been almost as ineffective as Leo X had been in Luther's day, travelled as a suppliant to Vienna in 1782. He found the people affectionate but the emperor politely obstinate. In the eighteenth-century alliance between Church and State the Church was not the senior partner in the crisis.

The French Revolution

Seven years later the storm broke in France. For some time many people had been complaining about the *ancien régime*, although this was the richest country in Europe: there had been no constitution or national assembly, the inflation and the indirect taxes had been too high, trade had been handicapped. And more recently the harvests had been ruined by the weather. Such complaints were supported by many of the clergy. Most of the senior clergy were complacent sons of the nobility, but some were different. Most of the sixty thousand parish priests certainly were different, not exactly on fire with faith but often sharing the poverty of their people in a time of distress. Although the bishops had failed to support the efforts of the government before the Revolution to rescue the national finances from bankruptcy, there was a moment of hope in June 1789. By a narrow majority the clergy elected to the Estates-General for its first meeting since 1614 decided to join the non-noble, lay Third Estate to form a National Assembly. It seemed possible that these parliamentarians would further unite to reform the nation without violence, according to principles both Christian and 'enlightened'.

Thunderous rhetoric and the roar of the mob in Paris then translated the Enlightenment into the Revolution and lightning struck. In July the Bastille prison was opened; in August all feudal laws were repealed and the system of tithes which had financed the parish priests was abolished; in November all the lands of the Church, amounting to perhaps a tenth of the soil and the buildings of France, were confiscated. Three months later laws were passed against the religious orders and in July 1790 a 'civil constitution' for the Church was decreed without consultation with the pope or the bishops. Parish priests were to be salaried instead of receiving tithes and churches would be maintained, the poor assisted and schools funded. But the clergy were not to hold public office, bishops were to be elected by the departments into which France was now divided, parish priests were to be elected locally (the bishops being in effect their chairmen), there were to be fewer dioceses and no cathedral canons, the papacy was to be honoured but powerless and Catholics were to have no political or legal privileges above others. When an oath of allegiance to the state under these arrangements was demanded the pope refused permission but about half of the clergy disobeyed him and hoped to rebuild. Then Pius VI went further: he denounced the 'liberty, equality, fraternity' of the Revolution as 'words empty of meaning' and made clear his sympathy with Austria, whose emperor postponed all thoughts of church reform and declared war on republican France.

In the reign of terror which began in September 1792 king and queen, bishops and priests, were among the thousands killed as traitors. A year later dechristianization began, first with altars of the Fatherland and the cult of Reason and Liberty, then at Robespierre's initiative with the non-Christian worship of the Supreme Being, then with the new religion of Theophilanthropy. A new calendar was dated not from the birth of Christ but from 1792 and Sunday was no longer to be special. Clergy, instead of being salaried, had to forsake the priesthood or to be persecuted if they remained at their posts. Many fled into exile or joined the counter-revolutionary peasants' revolt whose badge was the Sacred Heart of Jesus.

The pope did not escape the storm. In 1796–97 General Napoleon Bonaparte expelled the Austrians from Italy and with the help of local risings took over most of the papal states. Pius secured a temporary stay of execution by surrendering that territory. In 1798, however, French troops entered Rome, where a French-style republic was proclaimed and, on the whole, accepted by the Romans. The pope was taken by force from the city and was followed by the cardinals. In Paris the 'Directory' which was still nominally in control of Bonaparte called Pius 'the last pope' and it seemed possible that he was indeed the last of the line when he died in French captivity, in August 1799. Next March the cardinals met in Venice, now part of Austria, to elect a successor. In their bewilderment they could not agree whether or not the next pope should be expected to recognize these sudden republics.

In the end they elected Pius VII, a Benedictine monk ready to accept the new reality which for him was to include five years as a prisoner. The Austrians refused to produce the money needed, so there was no coronation. Yet there were forces at work which would give the Christian Church a future longer than the Napoleonic empire's. It was possible for the force of the cry for 'freedom' to result not in the overthrow of the Church but in new vitality for many churches.

The Birth of Religious Freedom

Politically the French revolutionaries were greatly encouraged by the success of the American rebellion against Britain, but religious history was very different on the two sides of the Atlantic. In the 1730s the Catholic Church had seemed to be firmly established in the mighty and 'Most Christian' kingdom of France, by tradition called 'the eldest daughter of the Church', while in the small British colonies in North America church life was much in need of awakening. A hundred years later Alexis de Tocqueville's *Democracy in America* reported a new phenomenon. In France the Revolution had severely damaged the Church, so that Religion and Republic seemed to be sworn enemies, yet surprising numbers of the now independent Americans were convinced that a vigorous faith was compatible with the pursuit of happiness in freedom. Indeed, they now reckoned that religion was 'indispensable to the maintenance of republican institutions'.

This contrast was, he saw, largely due to the fact that in the United States of America governments smiled on many churches and religion was voluntary: churches were established not by laws but in hearts. When the constitution of the United States was ratified in 1787 any religious test as a qualification for an 'office or public trust' was prohibited but five of the states continued to support the clergy out of taxes. Not until 1833 did Massachusetts end all such support and taxpayers' money assisted colleges and schools controlled by Protestant churches well into the nineteenth century. But the first amendment to the constitution, ratified in 1791, provided that 'the Congress shall make no law respecting an establishment of religion or prohibiting the free exercise thereof'. To that extent 'Church' and 'State' were to be separate although neither was mentioned—and to that extent, the Americans had achieved a religious revolution.

In Europe the position of Christians who dissented from the official religion improved gradually, but life was as difficult for any Protestants in Spain as it was for any Catholics in Scandinavia or Ireland and the improvement granted was mainly because governments saw less need to worry about threats to national security. Any belief in religious liberty as a principle had less influence. It was only in the 1960s that the Second Vatican Council unambiguously blessed this belief; previously official Catholic teaching had not favoured 'Americanism' as a model for Church–State relations. In Quebec the Catholic Church claimed the exclusive right to run French-speaking schools until 1964. For long, Anglican bishops in the rest of Canada objected not to the principle of a church being dominant in a society but to the fact that in Quebec this church was not Anglican. History had meant that Holland had no strong central government and no church with a large majority; consequently the Calvinist ministers could not compel the people to listen to their sermons and were not allowed to sit on the local councils. But as their treatment of 'heretics' within their own ranks showed, the Dutch clergy were not tolerant by conviction. England was often admired by the 'enlightened' for its Toleration Act of 1690, for the end of the licensing of publications and for John Locke's *Letters on Toleration*. But only Protestants who believed in the Trinity were tolerated.

Governments moved towards the principle of toleration when they saw that religious dissent did not necessarily involve political disloyalty. When Frederick William inherited a mixture of Lutherans, Calvinists and Catholics with the lands of Brandenburg and Prussia in 1640 he was shrewd enough to see that tolerating them all would serve his political ambitions and his successors in the Hohenzollern dynasty maintained this policy. When Frederick the Great, who was nominally Lutheran but in fact a sceptic, conquered Silesia in 1742 he felt safe in absorbing and tolerating half a million Polish Catholics. Half a century later the Habsburg emperor Joseph II thought it safe to repeal the penal laws against the Protestants because he no longer feared their threat to the unity of his sprawling empire and Louis XVI repealed similar laws in France because any remaining Protestants had been thoroughly tamed by persecution. In England it was felt safe to repeal in 1828 the Test Act of 1673 which required all holders of public offices to receive communion in the Church of England, and although Protestant Dissenters were still under other disabilities and the cry of 'No Popery!' was still heard it was also considered safe to allow Roman Catholics to own land and to maintain churches and schools. The richer Catholics in Ireland were allowed to vote for the Irish Parliament and when Ireland had been united to Britain in theory, almost thirty years later it was seen to be necessary to allow Catholics to sit in the Westminster Parliament. To be sure, there were exceptions to this tendency to relax security. In 1731 the prince-archbishop of Salzburg drove Protestants out of his territory and in 1755 the British governor of Nova Scotia expelled most of the Catholic Acadians. But these actions were quite widely criticized, for in fact the Protestants did not threaten the archbishop or the Acadians the governor. The British were thought, and proved, to be wiser when in their Quebec Act of 1774 they assured Catholics of a secure place under their rule. They were rewarded by the loyalty of the French-Canadians during the American War of Independence and the later war with the USA in 1812. Indeed, in Canada the Catholics trusted the British more than they trusted the Americans.

How, then, did Americans whose families had come mostly from England reach the conviction that 'the Congress shall make no law respecting an establishment of religion'? In Europe the idea of a church as a voluntary society, put forward by the enthusiasts on the left wing of the Protestant Reformations, had been opposed and crushed by everyone with theological or political power and 'toleration' had only been granted when dissenters were reassuringly weak. But in America churches became strong in freedom. Why? To find the answer we have to go back into English history.

From England to America

The Elizabethan government's belief that everyone born in England should belong to the Church of England had been defended as vigorously as possible, by laws as well as by books—like the belief that the monarch should effectively govern the Church. Elizabeth I's successor James I, the first in the Stuart dynasty to rule England, had fancied himself as a Calvinist theologian but had been as determined as Elizabeth that bishops should remain in place, enforcing the use of the Book of Common Prayer. The consciences of other Calvinists (the 'Puritans') objected on the ground that certain ceremonies were not decreed by Scripture, but it was enough for King James that he had issued decrees by his God-given power. Indeed, in his time the distinctive doctrine of the Church of England became 'the divine right of kings' to rule, with bishops as agents of the royal 'Supreme Governor'. Under his son Charles I this church developed its religious identity: the king and the more important clergy were now 'Arminians' in the sense that they were more positive towards the world than were the strict Calvinists, and more interested in the beauty and traditional ritual of their churches. But much still depended on this Established Church's identification with the Stuart dynasty and when that monarchy was violently overthrown by Parliamentarians largely Puritan in religion in the 1640s, the Church of England had the unexpected experience of being persecuted (mildly). Its Supreme Governor was beheaded.

The experience of the Parliamentarians was now equally unexpected. There is much to be said for R. H. Tawney's understanding of the outcome, that Puritanism 'was the true English Reformation and it is from its struggle against the old order that the England which is unmistakably modern emerges'. But when the victorious Oliver Cromwell became Lord Protector he depended not on any parliament but on the army. Under Puritan rule a new Established Church arose, with a Westminster Confession (agreed in Westminster Abbey in 1646) which became the main standard of Calvinist orthodoxy in the English-speaking world and a parish system modelled on the (Presbyterian) Church of Scotland. However, the 1640s and 1650s saw also a ferment of sects voicing religious and social aspirations of those previously dispossessed: the Diggers, the Levellers, the Ranters, the Quakers and others. These were unprecedented in the radicalism of their demands for equality under God and in their insistence on direct communication with God. But since they had to live under a continuing state, to communicate with the men in power who had no wish for a social revolution, and to try to convince a people who were mostly conservative, most of their fireworks fell to the ground.

The exception was the movement which was to be called 'Quakers' by indignant magistrates but was more properly called the Society of Friends. Their most significant beliefs could survive when their industrious integrity made them prosperous—beliefs in the guidance of the Spirit in silence, in the ability of uneducated men and women to express that guidance and to find the truth of Christ, in the presence of truth to be met in every living person, in the need to 'walk in the Light', in the need for peace, in no need for churches ('steeple houses'). Their first leader, George Fox, was one of the most remarkable religious leaders in a century and a country crowded with religious leaders.

Not long after Oliver Cromwell's death the dissolute and cynical son of Charles I was restored to the throne, bringing back with him the Church of England and most of the old social order in a reaction against Puritanism. The Church of England restored in the 1660s was, however, somewhat different from the church for which Charles I had been 'martyred'. Its continuing enthusiasm for the monarchy concealed for a time the fact that a partly new and independent identity had been found by its leaders when in exile or living obscurely: it was now firmer in rejecting both Roman Catholicism and Puritanism and rejoicing in its own heritage of ordered worship, moderate theology and a steady relationship with the bulk of the nation. This 'Anglicanism' (although the word was not in use before the nineteenth century) enabled it to survive when Charles II became a pensioner of Louis XIV and a Catholic when dying; when his brother James II was indiscreetly keen to encourage his fellow Catholics while Louis was persecuting Protestants; and when James's daughter Mary and her husband William of Orange, both securely Protestant, had to be summoned from Holland to occupy (together) a throne declared vacant by Parliament. What the Established Church should do about the Protestant Dissenters surviving from the Cromwellian era was another of its problems. 'Indulgence' towards the Dissenters seemed to threaten the existence of the Anglican state and their ill-treatment was successfully demanded by a Parliament full of triumphant Cavaliers, but persecution could not eliminate them. In a nation under William and Mary, and at war with France, it was necessary for Protestants to unite or at least to live in peace. It proved impossible to include them in a Church of England which had bishops in control and Catholic elements in its Prayer Book, so they had to be tolerated.

After these dramas the eighteenth century was a time of quiet security for a Protestant England. Even the small Catholic minority was in practice allowed to worship. People could concentrate on improved agriculture, on commerce, on wars against France and on the conquest of an empire in North America, the Caribbean and India. But the sea-power of England did not result in any power, or ardent wish, to impose the Church of England's system on colonies overseas. Instead, English ships had transported across the Atlantic families eager to build new lives for themselves by their own initiative and hard work.

The share of English-speakers in the European settlement of North America was to prove one of the most momentous facts in the history of the world. The English language was to be spoken not only in that continent, from sea to sea, but also by a powerful minority in every modern country. And partly because no English government made a sustained attempt to impose an official religion, the English language was to speak in the main of enterprise and argument, of creativity rather than conformity. All this was to be different from the influence of Spain and France in North America. These governments wanted to see a New Spain and a New France made in the image of the old but they did not send many settlers; Spain with its empire in Central and South America already had plenty of land, like France. Nor did people who dissented from the Catholic Church go; the Inquisition deterred them from Spanish territory and any Huguenot refugees from France went to Protestant colonies when Spaniards had destroyed their own little colony founded in Florida in 1560. The result was that by 1800 there were three times more people of European origin in North America than in South—and most of them were of English stock.

The first permanent Spanish settlement on the coast of Florida, in 1565, was named after St Augustine and a hundred years later some forty missionary priests were at work around it, but despite its importance alongside the sea route from the Caribbean and its flowery name Florida did not then attract European settlers. By 1708 the missions had all been closed, mainly by British military action, and many of their converts had been taken to the Carolinas as slaves. Missions (mainly Franciscan as in Florida) probed north from Mexico, producing North America's first martyr in 1542. They made converts but no large numbers of settlers appeared until that arid land had been seized by the Americans in the 1840s. The French sold western Louisiana, stretching to the Rocky Mountains from the Mississippi and complete with New Orleans, to the Spanish in 1762 and surrendered the land to the east to the British next year. When the Americans had won their independence from the British they bought the Spanish west in 1803. Spanish missions were more successful in California, as place names on the Pacific coast still testify: San Francisco, Santa Cruz, Santa Barbara, Los Angeles, San Diego . . . But even there Catholicism was not strong enough to make much of an impression on the nominally Protestant gold-diggers and other immigrants in the nineteenth century. The ethos of the young USA was to be Protestant and the Protestants were to be varied.

In the early years of the English colony of Virginia much was said about a missionary purpose, the conversion of the 'Indians', and the first act of the first permanent settlers, in 1607, was to receive Holy Communion in a Church of England service. Until the 1740s church attendance was compulsory, at least in theory. But the large riverside parishes were not noted for the vigour of their church life. After much initial suffering the settlers found a way to prosper: they imported 'Negroes' from Africa (the first in 1619, on a ship called *Jesus*) to grow tobacco for export, and after a time they turned these 'indentured servants' into slaves. They continued to prefer a Church of England service to any other, but there was little enthusiasm for it. An important factor was that North America had no bishop sent by the Church of England until Charles Inglis began his work in Canada in 1786: the authorities did not see how a bishop of the Church of England could function outside England and the colonists did not want one to interfere. Thus even where the Church of England became 'established' in some American colonies the pattern of church life expressed what Locke said ought to be seen as the real truth about all church life: that the Christian Church was a 'voluntary society'. The basic unit of church life was not a diocese under a bishop appointed by the state, or a geographical parish, but a congregation financed and governed by itself. In Virginia the 'trustees' of a church, all laymen, hired the priest or decided that they could not afford one.

However, thousands of definite Puritans took the opportunity to escape from England before their victory under Cromwell and after their defeat, and it may have been no accident that the 'Pilgrim Fathers' landed far to the north of the Virginia where the king intended them to settle. The two most famous voyages, in 1620 and 1630, began 'the New England Way' in Plymouth, around Massachusetts Bay and up the Connecticut valley; and what a Puritan preacher, John Robinson, had told those who were to sail in the *Mayflower* became true, that the Lord had indeed 'more light and truth to break forth from his Holy Word'. Famous priest-poets who stayed in

England shared some of the excitement: George Herbert wrote that religion was 'ready to pass' to America and John Donne, who compared the settlers in Virginia with the apostles, more privately compared a woman's body with America the 'new-found-land'. At first the only large new light came to New England with the strengthening of the idea of the covenant, owing much to the 'practical divinity' of two English Puritans, William Perkins and his pupil William Ames: God makes a trustworthy covenant with individuals predestined to be saved, but he also makes one with a whole community, a godly commonwealth pledged to obey his laws, and the people in it make a covenant to form a compact 'civil society' based on praying families and honest traders. To all such God promises prosperity. 'We are entered into covenant with him', said John Winthrop in his sermon at sea aboard the *Arabella* in 1630, '. . . that the Lord our God may bless us in the land whither we go to possess it.' And some prosperity did come to these Puritans who so bravely crossed a very large ocean in a very small ship and landed in what was well called the 'howling wilderness'. They endured much suffering and never moved very far from the ocean. 'We came hither', Cotton Mather recalled in the 1690s, 'because we would have our posterity settled under the pure and full dispensation of the gospel, defended by rulers that should be ourselves.'

But in history the most significant change from English and European traditions came in the very period when the Puritans lamented decline, for the sense of being a new Chosen People, a light to other nations, survived the inevitable end of an austere and exclusive regime. The New England 'town' had been a village, a collection of log cabins around a 'meeting house' with its Bible-hearing, its psalm-singing and its plain but argued and long sermon each 'Sabbath'. The right to vote had been restricted to men who were full members of the congregation and full membership had been confined to the 'visible saints' who could give a convincing account of their experience of conversion. There had been no distraction from the routine of worship and work and it had been quite easy to banish an individual such as Anne Hutchinson, who claimed that God inspired her to preach to other women 'by the voice of his own spirit to my soul'. In the 1690s that pure community was being diluted from many strange sources. In the process a theology which had included many elements reminiscent of Augustine had to abandon for ever that saint's intolerance. The new 'light and truth' discovered in America was to include Christianity's support of freedom.

One rare feature of the English migration to North America was that whole families went: men, women and children. But the less committed children of the Pilgrim Fathers had their own children who, it had to be agreed, could be baptized according to a 'half-way covenant' although never to be admitted to Holy Communion unless demonstrably converted.

Gradually other foundations of the Puritan regime crumbled. After 1661 no more Quakers were hanged on Boston Common and after 1662 no more 'witches' in Salem Village. In 1691 it had to be agreed, even in Massachusetts, that the right to vote depended on property ownership and not on church membership. Before this the little colony of Rhode Island had been founded as a refuge for people with a whole variety of religious opinions held as firmly and as individually as those of the courageously eccentric founder, Roger Williams. Another little colony, Maryland, was founded in 1634 with the approval of an English monarchy keen to get rid of Catholics and it was willing to approve an Act of Toleration in 1649 legislating for the principle that Catholics would neither persecute nor be persecuted. When a Dutch trading post had been changed by the British into New York in 1664, Calvinist churches had to be tolerated and when the governor reported on which church most of the settlers attended in 1687, he had to say 'none at all'. In 1681 Charles II granted to William Penn an extensive territory between New England and Maryland; he had been unable to sell it although it turned out to be some of the best farming land in the world. Penn had succeeded George Fox as the leader of the Quakers. It was hoped to get rid of these troublemakers across the Atlantic and it was agreed that from the beginning Pennsylvania would tolerate Christians of many churches. It was to welcome Baptists from Wales and Ireland, Presbyterians from Ulster and Lutherans from Germany.

The generally accepted theory, however, still assumed that a state, or a union of states, needed a generally agreed religion and that a people needed strong guidance by the state if there was not to be religious anarchy. In the southern colonies in America the Church of England became established and privileged by law—not only in Virginia but also in Maryland (in 1702), in the Carolinas and in Georgia. And in the 1780s the Puritans' struggle to build a godly commonwealth had not been forgotten: it had been changed. While a minority of Americans wanted the colonies to remain under British rule and had no strong wish to alter the ecclesiastical arrangements, almost all the republicans who were more able to influence events wanted their new nation to be godly in a new sense. They had gradually accepted a diversity in religious belief and allegiance. Indeed, they had come to think that freedom, rather than purity, was to be America's example to other peoples. Their faith in it was such that Edmund Burke (who sympathized with them) could speak of the transatlantic flourishing of 'the dissidence of Dissent and the Protestantism of the Protestant religion'. So their rebellion against the British government could be seen as a war of good against evil and preachers could develop the idea of spiritual liberation from sin into the patriot's fight for political liberty. Tom Paine, who in 1799 was to hail the arrival of *The Age of Reason*, proclaimed that 'the cause of America is, in a great measure, the cause of all Mankind'. But 'the cause of America', a preacher announced, 'is the cause of Christ'. The evidence suggested that at this stage most Americans did not greatly care what preachers did say, but this could be said.

The power of the belief that 'all men are created equal' was such that some of the 3.25 million white inhabitants of the new republic found themselves thinking about the rights of about 750,000 black slaves, although not thinking to any great effect. George Washington freed his own slaves in his will. Thomas Jefferson could not see what action could be taken but wrote in this connection: 'I tremble for my country when I reflect that God is just.' The importation of slaves was declared illegal in 1808 and a campaign began to send some back to Africa in freedom. But not many were emancipated and those who went to Liberia under the auspices of the Colonization Society did not find that they had entered Paradise.

It was easier to decide that liberty must mean that America's new federal republic would not grant privileges to any one of the churches. At this time the churches were not strong; in the ex-colonies taken as a whole less than a tenth of the adults enrolled in full membership although church attendance was wider. In particular the Church of England, the most 'established' church, was unpopular because so many of its clergy had been Loyalists opposing independence and had led an exodus to Canada. One reason why the Americans had not yet become a Bible-reading people was that no Bible in English could be printed in those colonies, the publication of the Authorized (or King James) Version being a monopoly of printers in England. And even had the churches been stronger, the individual states were accustomed to so many different ways of giving official support that it would have been very difficult to get agreement for one federal way. So Virginia's Act for Establishing Religious Freedom showed the way and it was settled by the first amendment to the constitution that there should be no religious 'establishment' at the federal level. But in addition to the taxpayers' money which could still be sent to the churches more quietly (as already noted), that decision taken in 1791 left untouched an atmosphere in which a Protestant ethos not tied to any particular denomination or dogma could become the soul of America. Prayers were offered on official occasions, the keeping of Sunday and of special days of prayer was officially encouraged, references to the guiding hand of God and to the imagery of the Bible were frequent in the orations of statesmen. Washington, Adams, Jefferson and Madison, the presidents who had the most influence on the constitution and early years of the USA, were nominal Anglicans who had an 'enlightened' rather than a biblical view of God but like Voltaire they believed in 'Nature's God'. They did not rely on the clergy to give them moral instruction but they advocated and practised 'virtue'. They could not accept all stories about miracles but they gave thanks for the wonderful progress of America in liberty, virtue and civilization. Jefferson, although privately scornful about 'Christianity', thought the 'philosophy of Jesus' sufficiently important for him to compile an edited version of the gospels for the benefit of simple folk.

The more educated of the new nation's preachers passed through colleges such as Harvard, Princeton and Yale. They imbibed theology from teachers such as James Witherspoon, the only clergyman (a Presbyterian) who signed the Declaration of Independence. This was a 'common sense' theology which comfortably combined the acceptance of much of the Enlightenment with a moderately (even mildly) Calvinist form of Christianity. It was imported mainly from Scotland, where teachers of the assurance of Francis Hutcheson and Thomas Reid had not been greatly shaken by the courteous and cautious scepticism of their neighbour David Hume. Around them was a Scotland which had been made into a nation by the religion and morality of the Protestant Reformation. Knowledge and philosophy had developed but had only added to this sound basis. Now in America the story had been repeated, obviously under the hand of a 'favouring Providence'.

The Religion of the Heart

But actually Christianity did not depend on this claim that it was common sense. The main reason why it was able to revive in Europe after the shock of the French Revolution was that it became more personal, more heartfelt, and the main reason why it was able to flourish in the USA after the separation of Church and State was that while still under colonial government many of the Americans had come into contact with the 'Great Awakening' (so called in a book of 1841). The churches deprived of 'establishment' in the USA might have dwindled in influence, as most of the 'enlightened' expected. Instead, they fully shared the American energy in making their liberty their opportunity. The government was weak; they would be strong. These Awakenings (for there were a number) aroused 'enthusiasm' to the alarm both of the sceptical and of the sober, but through them many Americans experienced for themselves the 'new birth' which resulted in personal faith and church membership. Common sense theology remained an ingredient in the rich mixture that was to make up the religious history of the USA but it was not to be the main force. That was to be a Protestantism found in the people's hearts and in the people's churches.

The most famous preacher in the Awakenings was George Whitefield. Although a Calvinist ordained in the Church of England, in his appeals for a 'new birth' he did not insist on the adoption of any particular theology or denomination and his spectacular tours of the colonies, beginning in 1739, converted many thousands by a simple, Bible-based message about sin and salvation, preached in the open air, from the heart and not from a manuscript. The 'religious affections' aroused, although sometimes producing waves of self-disgust or hysterical joy, were defended by America's first great theologian, Jonathan Edwards, another Calvinist. They were derived, he said, 'from immediate divine influences' if they inspired 'virtue'. In 1749 Edwards was expelled by his own congregation in Massachusetts when (like the original Puritans) he attempted to restrict communion to people who could testify to their conversion, but he ministered quietly to another congregation for nine more years and wrote books of high quality. He insisted on God's choice of those who are to believe and be saved, leaving the rest as 'sinners in the hands of an angry God'. Apart from that 'election' no one can reasonably have any ultimate hope. What, then, is the freedom of the will? The answer of Edwards was that the freedom does not amount to much; from Locke he had learned the limits of human understanding and from the Bible he drew the lesson that in the making of human decisions limits are imposed by the power of the 'motives'. So the hearts of the 'elect' must respond to the unmerited grace of God. Then their 'motives' will be changed through their 'affections' and they will show how many God has in fact chosen as recruits for heaven. He now expected from the American revival 'something vastly great' in the history of a sinful world. He pondered the possibility that the kingdom of God might be established on earth—on American earth—before the Second Coming of the Saviour.

Jonathan Edwards argued thus for a mixture of the philosophy of the Enlightenment with the 'new light' of the Awakenings. Some distinguished Americans who did not share his interests could applaud at least the enthusiasm and the energy of this creative movement. A very non-theological president of the USA, John Adams, called the enthusiasm which had been awakened a 'noble infirmity' which could be used for noble purposes. Although he thought Calvinism a 'doctrine of devils' Benjamin Franklin admired George Whitefield's power as an orator: it matched his own as a journalist and perhaps it stirred some favourable memories of a Puritan childhood. In later years many historians have judged that the Great Awakenings, renewed before and after Whitefield's death in 1770, were of central importance in America's history. They were the first national movement, preparing for the revolutionary enthusiasm for political independence. They showed that some Americans not attracted by the historic churches had in their hearts needs which religion could supply—and had in their minds enough echoes of the traditional Christian language to be able to understand what the awakeners were saying. People needed a religion more than they had thought, because they needed a faith in their own dignity or potential. They were for the most part rural pioneers, often lonely, and needed the fellowship which a revivalist meeting or a regular congregation could provide. Above all, because their lives were usually hard they needed a God who was on their side: a God who awakened memories of the most prestigious side of European life, but also a God who awakened their own hopes, for time as well as for eternity.

'Let the Church be planted!' was the vigorous motto of Henry Muhlenberg, the Lutheran pastor who arrived in 1742 to minister to the recent flood of German immigrants. And the churches did now take root in American soil—but in an American way. The Awakenings showed that there would be a response if preachers were not aloof, if the churches joined America before asking Americans to join them. Most of the preachers who went to the people still preached about hell, but did not insist on the size of the inheritance of hell-bent sinfulness from Adam. It became usual to stress vigorously that the individual had both a liberty and a duty to respond to, and to co-operate with, the freely available grace of God. Thus preachers appealed to the aspirations of a people who looked beyond their toils, struggles and setbacks with a sense that under God great things were possible, for themselves and for their new country. It was not primarily a political message about America: the same message was preached in Nova Scotia by Henry Alline during nine influential years after his conversion in 1775 and politically Nova Scotia joined Canada not the USA. But this message about a second birth through conversion to Christ became part of the story of the birth of the USA.

In Europe the climate of opinion never became so sunny, but the kind of appeal which Whitefield made to sinners was made by preachers in a variety of churches. In Italy Alphonsus Liguori influenced many by writings which exuberantly commended the devotional practices of the Catholic Reformation, for example in *Visits to the Blessed Sacrament and the Blessed Virgin*. He founded the Redemptorist order to evangelize and do charitable work among the poor and, having been a brilliant lawyer before ordination, powerfully resisted Jansenist attempts to make the Church's moral demands more rigorous. His solution to their controversies with the Jesuits was to say that in moral problems the laxer course was no sin if authorities allowing it were at least equally balanced with those condemning it. His mission to present a Catholicism attractive to the hearts of sinners was strengthened by the growing popularity of the cult of the 'sacred heart' of Jesus himself, originating in visions which a French nun experienced in the 1670s. This was incorporated into the Church's official calendar in 1765. Another emotional and popular cult spread in the eighteenth century from Franciscan churches: following the way of suffering to the cross and the tomb of Jesus with penitential devotions helped by fourteen pictures or carvings. Less dramatically, this was an age when a simple piety was combined with a simple education by new religious orders founded in France to instruct ordinary priests (the Sulpicians and the Eudists) and ordinary children (the Christian Brothers or Salesians).

In Protestant Europe there were strong revivals of religious emotion among the Lutherans of Scandinavia and the Calvinists of Scotland, but it was in Germany and England that the religion of the heart was most conspicuous. In those countries the churches established by governments were strongholds of a religion that was cool, whether they concentrated on Lutheran or Calvinist conservatism as in Germany (where orthodoxy had been developed into a system by theologians of stature such as Johann Gerhard) or on an unexciting code of moral duties as in England. That is understandable as a reaction against the religious enthusiasms which had encouraged civil wars to do so much damage in the seventeenth century, but the hearts of the people were mostly untouched. Lutherans spoke about the need for faith in Christ, but believers or half-believers were ready to be shown how to live close to him since the life was what mattered. Calvinists spoke about predestination in eternity, but people wanted to be told about the divine Spirit able to transform them now. The Church of England taught a rational morality, but people needed something more if they were to be freed from the coarse lives which they actually led. In response to such needs movements arose for which the word 'Evangelical' became more appropriate than 'Protestant'. The Protestant protested against medieval Catholicism. The Evangelical believes and spreads the gospel of salvation in the modern age.

In Germany Johann Arndt, who died just before the outbreak of the Thirty Years' War, issued pleas for 'true Christianity', by which he meant not controversial theology but piety and sanctification: these pleas were, of course, controversial. The disasters of that war, and his own sufferings, were the background to the moving hymns of Paul Gerhardt; for example, he based on the medieval Bernard a hymn which was a meditation on the wounded and sacred head of the dying Saviour. And as the seventeenth century ended Gottfried Arnold begged Christians to move from controversies into heartfelt piety. His was the first history of the Church to find some truths in all heresies and it was deeply resented.

A book of 1675, *Pia Desideria* by the Lutheran pastor Philip Jacob Spener, was consistently gloomy about the situation in Church and State. But Spener took it for granted that at least some of the laity had experienced 'rebirth' when converted to Christ and wanted to gather for Bible study and prayer outside the public worship: such was the pious desire in their hearts. He showed how such 'colleges of piety' might be formed—and they were formed, in large numbers, transcending the class divisions, watering the arid soil of theological arguments. Moreover, he influenced August Francke, a scholar who had a genius for organization. As a professor Francke became the dominant influence in the new Prussian university of Halle, which became the spiritual headquarters of 'Pietism' as a definite movement. He began a publishing house from which devotional books poured, and a school for destitute orphans which was so efficient that children of the rich were sent to learn there before a separate school was founded for them. Young Germans educated in such institutions or influenced by Pietist pastors went on to transform Lutheranism—not without meeting resistance from those who preferred other sides of Luther's legacy: the stability in society, the love of ordered worship, the intellectual interests, the enjoyment of the normal pleasures of life. What characterized the Pietists was the 'enthusiasm' which to its critics became a term of abuse. In 1710 the world's first Bible Society began to distribute Scriptures cheaply. An urgent sense of mission drove some of these Protestants to look for the first time beyond Europe, and Germans and Danes went as missionaries to Sri Lanka, South India and North America.

One of the pupils in Halle became Count Nikolaus von Zinzendorf, who founded a pious community when Protestant refugees from Moravia settled on his estate at Herrnhut in Saxony. Particularly in the years when he was exiled at the demand of conservative Lutherans, he travelled in many parts of Europe and North America, everywhere pleading that Christians should together enter 'into' the Saviour. He was not afraid of being a dictatorial aristocrat, of being lushly sentimental, of being innovative (every month there was a 'love-feast' and a 'watch-night'), of encouraging physical contact (his followers kissed each other and washed each other's feet). Above all, he was not afraid of pioneering evangelism: he encouraged disciples to preach in places from Greenland to South Africa (and David Zeisberger to be the first really effective Protestant missionary among the 'Indians' of North America, labouring for more than sixty years from 1748). He was made a bishop of the exiled Czech Brethren, the 'Moravians', but his message about the heart given to Christ transcended all divisions between the churches.

So did the contrapuntal music of Johann Sebastian Bach, organist and choirmaster in Leipzig for 27 years from 1723. He drew on the Lutheran tradition of the chorale to voice a penitent believer's response to the gospel with a profoundly heartfelt faith in the crucified and risen Christ. His cantatas interpreted sermons; his Christmas Oratorio was a celebration, his Passion music a tender meditation, more moving than any sermon. All this music was composed at speed for performance in church and although for a time after Bach's death in 1750 it seemed to be forgotten, after two centuries and a half it still communicates what was most real in Pietism, the religion of the heart.

Baptists and Methodists

Part of the English equivalent to German Pietism was associated with the firm repudiation of the practice of infant baptism which Zwingli, Luther and Calvin had all defended. In 1582, in the safety of Holland, Robert Browne published a little *Treatise of Reformation without Tarrying for Any* and ten years later Francis Johnson became pastor of a little congregation of 'Separatists' in London. When in exile in Amsterdam in 1609 John Smyth baptized himself as the logic of Separatism. When those who became known as 'Baptists' rejected the 'Christenings' of babies who could not respond with their hearts to the Saviour they rejected much else in the Christian past. They could not escape divisions in their own small churches: Arminians disagreed with strictly Calvinist or 'Particular' Baptists. Nor could they avoid persecution by the alarmed authorities. But they persevered in their spiritual journeys and in sharing their experience with other folk not interested in theology. The Baptist Missionary Society formed in 1792 began the Protestant missionary movement from England to India and the east (although there had already been Danish missionaries). However, among all Baptists the best communicator was John Bunyan, who wrote the first version of *The Pilgrim's Progress* in gaol in 1676. When free he had been a salesman peddling his simple wares around English villages. He now used the doubts, temptations and tribulations of common life, and the directness of common speech, to communicate the spiritual reality of the Christian's often lonely struggles on the long and hard road from the City of Destruction to the Celestial City. His was a religion in the open air and in the human heart. He wrote much more, but it was *The Pilgrim's Progress* which endured together with the story of his younger years, *Grace Abounding to the Chief of Sinners*. In terms which lodged in the imagination and the memory it showed the unsophisticated individual how to get rid of a burden of sin and how to be guided by the Bible to a death which would be a glory with all the trumpets sounding.

Although in England the Baptists declined in the first half of the eighteenth century, in the second half they began an expansion which ended only after 1900. In America Baptists from England and Wales formed their first congregation in 1639, in Rhode Island. They had more than a hundred congregations by 1740 and gained more than any other group from the Great Awakening, specially in the expanding southern colonies where even the Blacks enslaved to the Whites could hear a gospel about God's grace. (Previously slaveholders had resisted the possibility of conversion and baptism for 'Negroes' because it might unsettle them, but before the end of the 1770s the first permanent black congregation was formed.) The message was spread by eloquent full-time missionaries such as Shubal Stearns, but chiefly by farmer-preachers, as close to their rough audiences as Bunyan had been. And although the 'Particular' or 'Hard Shell' (Calvinist) tradition remained strong among the American Baptists, in the course of expansion the more popular 'General' or 'Free Will' (Arminian) alternative gathered strength. Personal conviction was still the preacher's aim and 'Are you saved?' was the key question, but now it often meant: 'Will you decide to be saved? If so, you will be accepted.' It was also in America that the Baptists reduced the separateness of one congregation from another: if it was to be planned and sustained, evangelism required the unity of a denomination.

In America, however, as in England the Baptists were not so well organized as the Methodists, a denomination which was directly influenced by German Pietism.

John Wesley was an Oxford scholar who remained a scholar throughout his life. He had gone to Georgia in order to convert Americans, but the lesson which he had learned had been that he needed to be converted. Inherited from his domineering parents, his had been a religion of orthodoxy and morality rather than joy and love; his father had been a dogmatic Anglican priest prone to quarrel with those around him, his mother had been determined to instruct her many children and also the parishioners during the father's frequent absences. In Oxford he had been prominent in a Holy Club of the like-minded, one of many religious societies formed to promote piety as the seventeenth century became the eighteenth. In one such society in London one evening in May 1738 this troubled priest heard one of Zinzendorf's Moravian missionaries expounding Luther's commentary on Paul's letter to the Romans. 'I felt my heart strangely warmed . . . I felt I did trust in Christ.' It was the emotional crisis, the 'new birth' to which preachers such as Whitefield or Zinzendorf, or many lesser Pietists or Evangelicals, acted as midwives. The image of God as the angry Father condemning sinners who broke the moral law was now in the background: more prominent in the believer's heart was the image of Christ as the Saviour who had himself borne the punishment deserved and could be trusted to complete the good work in the lives of those who responded. The at-one-ment to which the believer responded was still interpreted as it had been in Calvinism's Heidelberg Catechism (1563): 'I belong body and soul, in life and in death, not to myself but to my faithful Saviour, Jesus Christ, who at the cost of his own blood has fully paid for all my sins.' But the interpretation was in the convert's 'warmed' heart, not merely in the sermon addressed to the mind. As John Wesley put it, 'the Spirit of God immediately and directly witnesses to my spirit that I am a child of God'. And to Whitefield's dismay he rejected the Augustinian and Calvinist doctrine of the 'total depravity' and doom of all humanity apart from the few predestined to heaven. Everyone needs to be born again as he had been, but the Spirit of

God, he taught, can reach any open heart and can so transform the life of that converted individual that 'Christian perfection' (meaning freedom from wilful sin) becomes attainable. Thus the English tradition of Arminian theology which in the previous century had supported the Stuart monarchy and cultured humanism now turned to the people in ardent evangelism.

His was one of the most effective missions in Christian history—and it was needed, for in England non-Anglican churches, Catholic or Protestant, had been reduced to small numbers and the Church of England established by the state had been weakened by the terms of its establishment. Its bishops were appointed by politicians with little regard to the requirements of pastoral leadership; some of its clergy were country gentlemen rather than priests or preachers; others were miserably paid and usually despised; many who attended its worship were there because the 'squire' who employed and housed them in the village insisted on it; in many parts of the north of England, and in Cornwall, the Established Church made few efforts to reach the people; and in the places where factories were beginning the Industrial Revolution, and in London, a class was forming which for the first time since the conversion of the Anglo-Saxons had little or no contact with organized religion. There was a better side to the Church of England: in it could be found dutiful piety and help for the poor. But only about a tenth of the population seems to have received the sacrament when Holy Communion was 'celebrated', usually four times a year.

Until his death in 1791 John Wesley travelled up and down and across England on horseback, praying often, reading when he could. He was tireless in order to preach in churches or the open air and in order to found and supervise 'societies' and 'classes'. These groups were somewhat like the Holy Club of the Oxford days but he was now more realistic about human nature. People, he now saw, needed mutual support and friendly criticism ('watching over one another in love') year after year, but they also needed to experience forgiveness and joy as he had done and to be assured that the goals of 'Christian perfection' and heaven were attainable. As a teacher and organizer he combined the talents of the Pietists Spener and Francke and although Methodist societies and congregations did not have a musician of Bach's genius (indeed, the nineteenth-century introduction of organs caused a major controversy) they did have John's brother Charles, who wrote more than seven thousand hymns. The most famous of these was full of joy over the arrival of what had been lacking before the heart-warming of 1738, 'Love divine, all loves excelling'.

German Pietism formed its own religious societies but never its own denomination. In contrast, so far from believing that each society or congregation should be responsible only to itself John Wesley never hesitated to control the 'connexion' he had founded. In many ways he was a son of the Church of England, where during his lifetime the Evangelical movement began to preach much the same message as Methodism ('scriptural holiness') but in loyalty to the Prayer Book and to the organization in parishes. He was indebted to many spiritual teachers including Puritans and the saints of the Roman Church, and he recommended 'the Catholic spirit' to his own followers, but he owed most to his own Anglican church. He loved its public prayers (he taught a high doctrine of the Eucharist) and its tradition of private devotions. He was greatly influenced by William Law's *Serious Call to a Devout and Holy Life* (1728) and by the earlier writings of Jeremy Taylor on *Holy Living* and *Holy Dying* and of an anonymous exponent of *The Whole Duty of Man* in the 1650s. For many years he insisted that Methodist activities should not clash with the times of the services in the parish churches and should not include Holy Communion. But he was a pragmatist in his determination to preach the gospel in other priests' parishes ('the world is my parish') and to follow up his preaching; from 1743 he would not preach in any place where he could not also organize. When bishops or parish priests did not welcome him, as they often did not, he would preach without their permission; when Methodists wanted their own services of Holy Communion he finally allowed them and when they found some of the psalms of the Book of Common Prayer not Christian he deleted them; when not enough of his fellow priests were willing to take care of them, he appointed and controlled a large network of lay preachers including women; when the Americans needed more ministers to be pastors and evangelists, he 'set apart' or ordained them (beginning in 1784). In his last years he assured his followers that 'the best of all, God is with us' and despite all his hesitations about being the founder of a separate denomination he made the legal arrangements for a conference of a hundred preachers which would inherit his control of all the chapels and societies (also in 1784). And Methodism did not die although after his death it splintered for many years into 'connexions' under preachers as assured as he had been, and as determined to make as many new Christians as possible without waiting for the approval of the authorities.

Like Luther and Calvin, Wesley did not reach those at the bottom of the pile in society but enabled many others to develop a new sense of their own potential within the new religious associations and the new religious assurance. Methodism appealed particularly to people who were not now dependent on a landlord: to independent farmers, to people who did work later to be regarded as industrial but in their own cottages, to the men working in the small mines. It taught them virtues such as honesty, thrift and temperance which helped them to prosper financially. Wesley urged them not to be nervous about well-earned success ('gain all you can, save all you can, give all you can') and he was himself stoutly conservative in politics. He condemned the rebellion of the American colonies and more influentially he set his face against any overthrow of the social order in England, warning Methodist preachers that 'you have nothing to do but save souls'. Such conservatism in politics was to be one of the factors dividing English Methodism after his death; the divisions were not to be healed before 1932. His life therefore bore witness to the tension between Church and Democracy.

He was also a conservative in religion. Being interested in the scientific and medical progress connected with the Enlightenment, he made it his business to communicate some of the new knowledge to 'the people called Methodists'—but (of course) without showing or encouraging any religious scepticism. When the two greatest men in the Church of England in that age met, they failed to understand each other because one was an apostle and the other was a philosophical bishop: Joseph Butler warned against 'enthusiasm', against 'pretending to extraordinary gifts and revelations of the Holy Ghost' ('a very horrid thing'), but John Wesley remembered the conversation with scorn. He was at heart so little a man of the Enlightenment that he constantly believed that the weather was adjusted to his work as an evangelist. The itinerant preachers whom he authorized as 'helpers' were even closer to their hearers' traditional beliefs in the supernatural. His life therefore also bore witness to the tension between religion and science, but that did not trouble him. His description of studying the Bible became famous. 'I sit down alone: only God is here. In his presence I open, I read his book; for this end, to find the way to heaven.'

He lived in a different world from David Hume, who was worried by the spread of this religion of the heart. In 1756 Hume lamented to a correspondent that the English seemed to be 'relapsing fast into the deepest Stupidity, Christianity and Ignorance'. He was prophetic in this alarm. John Wesley left behind him about 57,000 Methodists in England. By 1850 these were about half a million and in America Methodism, with more than a million, was the largest of all the churches.

A Heartfelt Catholicism

Eventually a modern form of European Christianity was born, on the defensive in a civilization it had not made but free to practise the religion of the heart.

In some ways it was a return to the beginnings of Christianity itself, to the minority status before Byzantine Orthodoxy and medieval Catholicism had shaped and dominated societies, but now the churches were in a world very different from the world of ancient paganism. They were again given an opportunity to shape empires and nations but soon they were discredited by their identification with a nominally Christian social order which increasing numbers rejected as unjust, oppressive and exploitative. Moreover, their official beliefs were discredited by their identification with pre-scientific dogmas thought to be incompatible with a true understanding of humanity's situation and possibilities. By the twentieth year of its twentieth century Christianity faced hostility, suspicion or indifference as great as in the early centuries, and one of its problems was that it was far more uncertain and divided than the Church of the Fathers had been. Any strong expression of Christianity was sure to be rejected by many other Christians.

Modern Christianity was uncertain and divided because it emerged out of different reactions to the Enlightenment, the French Revolution and the Napoleonic empire. Christians could not ignore the effects of those great events. More people than ever before did dare to judge for themselves; did hope that humanity using reason would achieve progress; did see religion more as faith which was voluntary and optional, personal and private, than as the assured moral foundation of a united state; did look more into their own beating hearts and less into an unchanging tradition. And in Church and State many remnants of medieval feudalism were no more. Liberty was talked about and in religion as in politics it could mean the anti-authoritarian attitudes which were now called 'liberal'. That word need mean no more than an approval of liberty but 'liberty!' had been the cry of the French Revolution and the first use in English of 'liberal' as the opposite of 'conservative' has been traced to 1801.

There was also a reaction against the arrogance of those who used 'liberty' as they defined it to demolish a whole world in order to build on the ruins a new world according to an improved pattern which might deny freedom to anyone who disagreed. Edmund Burke's *Reflections on the Revolution in France* were eloquent in this reaction as early as 1790. He pleaded for a slower, gentler development, conserving what had been good in the past, respecting the rights of individuals as well as the Rights of Man, cherishing what was beautiful as well as what was immediately useful. In the eyes of many the appeal of Burke's conservatism seemed to be increased by the arrogance of Tom Paine's replies to it in the 1790s, *The Age of Reason* and *The Rights of Man*—for if reason led to the chaos and terror of the French Revolution, and if the Rights of Man produced the reaction of Napoleonic imperialism, did not people have a right to keep their souls alive by going back to the past's images and perhaps to its beliefs? Already in the eighteenth century there had been a superficial fashion for a 'Gothic' playfulness. Now the 'Gothic revival' in architecture, like the 'Romantic' movement in literature, belonged to a seriously worried age. Many who disliked what they saw in the novelties turned to a conservative religion not ashamed to be partly medieval—and the chief beneficiary was, of course, a Catholicism centred on Rome.

The first essential was for the papacy to come to terms with the new France. Pius VII was a man of prayer, not totally wedded to the cause of the restoration of the privileges which the senior clergy of France had enjoyed under the *ancien régime*. He entrusted negotiations to a shrewdly pragmatic cardinal, Ercole Consalvi, who consequently incurred the enmity of the ultra-conservative *zelanti* who were before long to recapture the papacy. In France considerable numbers of the clergy dissented from the agreement, protesting that the papacy had yielded either too much or too little. But an agreement was possible because Napoleon's seizure of power had ended the chaos of the revolution. This 'First Consul' whose only real belief was in his own destiny knew that many of the French remained Catholics and he consoled himself with the reflection that 'society is impossible without inequality, inequality intolerable without a code of morality and a code of morality unacceptable without religion'. His objection was not to religion as such but to the clergy being powerful. The French term *sécularisation* was used to describe the changes which he forced on the German territories which he conquered: at this stage it meant that bishops would continue their religious roles but must no longer rule as princes.

For the sake of the agreement the papacy made major concessions, increased when it had to accept later regulations imposed unilaterally. Bishops were to be nominated to the papacy by the government and men who had accepted the Civil Constitution in 1790 were to be eligible; the estates of the Church were to remain in the hands of their lay owners; new parishes were not to be formed without the state's permission; the clergy were to be loyal to the state, paid by it, and forbidden to hold a national council without its permission; all marriages were to be solemnized by the *maire* even if the priest was later involved; the Roman Catholic religion was recognized as the faith of the majority of the people but not as the religion of the state. And the papacy could not protest effectively when later the Napoleonic empire tightened its grip on Catholic life while also practising toleration towards the Protestants. But the concordat (treaty) agreed by the pope and Napoleon in 1801 was the legal framework for the survival and recovery of the French Church, although the strength of its position before the 1790s was never recovered.

The concordat also turned out to be the death sentence for the Gallicanism which had previously united most French Catholics in excluding the papacy from any decisive say in their affairs. This development was, of course, contrary to Napoleon's intention. He crowned himself emperor in Paris in 1804, although the pope was in attendance. But the medieval system by which bishops and parish priests were 'beneficed', each with substantial rights and traditional sources of income, was ended for ever; the state nominated the bishops, the bishops appointed the priests and all were salaried by the state. Contrary to Napoleon's plan, the clergy and faithful did not accept the state as the source of their spiritual identity under these new arrangements. They looked to Rome. Thus Chateaubriand's sentimental book of 1802, advertising Christianity as the best available source of spirituality and ethics, was to be followed by Joseph de Maistre's book of 1819 celebrating the papacy as this religion's only sure foundation, and in 1817 the pope was able to veto a new arrangement which would have restored some Gallican 'liberties' after the restoration of the Bourbon monarchy. Under these monarchs the religion which the state supported energetically was a religion defined in Rome, and when the Bourbons fell in 1830 and the new king (Louis Philippe) distanced his *bourgeois* state from the Church the position of the papacy in the hearts of the faithful was only strengthened.

But the papacy was itself vulnerable because of its position in Italy.

Pius VII became Napoleon's prisoner in 1809 not because he caused trouble in France but because he resisted the absorption of Rome and the papal states into the Napoleonic empire despite the offer of a large salary. In 1814 he returned to Rome as a hero and the papal states in Italy enjoyed a brief period of moderately good government under Consalvi. After his death the earlier conditions of incompetence combined with intolerance returned and became intolerable in the eyes of most of the inhabitants and most of the rest of Europe. In 1846 a pope was elected who seemed to be a modernizer, Pius IX, and was greeted with enthusiasm. But after granting some reforms he made it clear that he would not support Italian nationalism by joining any campaign to expel the Austrians and would not sacrifice his own sovereignty by allowing a modern, constitutional state to make Rome its capital. Revolutionary violence erupted again in 1848, in Rome as in Paris: his prime minister was murdered, he was forced to flee, his heart was permanently hardened against 'liberalism' in any shape. In Paris Louis-Napoleon emerged as president (later as emperor) and thanks to his troops papal rule was restored in Rome. In the 1860s, however, almost all of Italy agreed to form one nation, leaving papal Rome isolated. In 1870 the protecting French garrison was withdrawn from Rome and a referendum of the citizens influenced by the presence of Italian troops ended the centuries when the bishop of Rome had been a king among, and over, other kings.

The pope who was now the 'prisoner of the Vatican' forbade Catholics to take any part in the political life of Italy and this prohibition remained in place until 1919. The new nation suffered grievously from this conflict between Church and State, but for the papacy itself the end of its 'temporal' power in 1870 was far from being the disaster prophesied.

Pius IX was the first modern pope not in the sense of having any modern ideas but in the sense of being the first to appeal deliberately to the Catholic public by a warm charm combined with an insistence on the infallibility of a pope's most solemn teaching about faith or morals. Under him Roman (an adjective increasingly appropriate) Catholicism enthusiastically taught and practised the religion of the heart. In 1854 he bestowed a new blessing on heartfelt devotion to Mary by the formal declaration of her 'immaculate conception' beginning her freedom from sin. In 1856 he made the Sacred Heart of Jesus a festival to be observed everywhere and three years before his death in 1878 he consecrated the whole world to that heart. In 1864 he further exercised his authority by attaching a 'syllabus of errors' to the positive teaching given in the 'encyclical' *Quanta cura*. He had been finally provoked by manifestations of 'liberalism' by Frenchmen: amid much applause Charles Montalembert had advocated the separation of Church and State (at a Catholic congress in Belgium, where governments unsympathetic to the Church were in power until 1884) and Ernest Renan had published a hugely popular biography of Jesus full of praise of him as a man and a moralist but empty of any belief that he had been in any way supernatural. In general terms Pius now hit out against liberty of religion and of the press, and against rationalism and socialism, concluding with a robust condemnation of any who dared to think that 'the Roman pontiff can, and ought to, reconcile himself to, and reach agreement with, progress, liberalism and modern civilization'. The Catholic religion of the heart was now firmly in opposition to the modernity of the mind, and it was clearly intended to lead to the submission of a whole society to the truths which this religion of the heart embraced; one of the propositions rejected was that 'every man is free to embrace and profess the religion which he will have deemed true according to the light of reason'. But since the pope had spoken without going into details it could be—and was—maintained that his words did not apply directly to any particular situation, intellectual or political.

The syllabus of 1864 has become embarrassing or notorious but it deserves to be understood in its context. Pius IX was at heart a pastor and he knew the hearts of Catholics who were dismayed, as he was, that the controlling position of the Church and the divine status of the Saviour seemed to be crumbling under blows struck year after year by 'modern civilization'; a very firm reaction seemed to be vital. Pius was also profoundly shocked that fellow Italians who were (of course) Catholics in some sense—Mazzini the idealist nationalist, Garibaldi the romantic guerrilla who was a legend in his lifetime, Cavour the coldly calculating politician—should fail to see that papal Rome, which needed revenues from the papal states, was Italy's chief glory and the Eternal City to which all Catholic hearts should turn. This was also a time when the statesmen controlling the policies of Protestant countries seemed to think ethics irrelevant in politics, just as Machiavelli had said ought to be the case: such were Lord Palmerston in Britain and, in charge of affairs in Prussia 1862–90, Bismarck. But we should note other facts about the age to which Pius belonged. Priests and nuns were better trained and more professionally dedicated than ever before and they formed a large army at his command, with power although without guns. The laity might be more critical of his political attitudes (most Italians certainly were), but many of them agreed with him in religion.

This conservatism still dominated the Church in South America and, far to the north, in Quebec, whose system showed what France might have been without the Enlightenment or the Revolution. In Europe Catholicism was at its most conservative in Spain, partly because the middle class there was small. It aroused the hostility of the Spanish Liberals, and within the ranks of the Liberals of the more determined Progressives, during the many nineteenth-century tensions and conflicts between Church and State. After the overthrow of the absolutist monarchy in 1834 church property was confiscated and religious orders were expelled. In the concordat of 1851 the Church had to accept impoverishment but the state now paid the small stipends of the parish priests and the priests' poverty was ultimately to their advantage: they were close to the people in the poverty-stricken countryside (but less so in the south than in the more churchgoing north). Spanish Catholicism also forged alliances with other elements who disliked the centralizing Liberal governments and their mainly urban support; so the Church moved closer to the aristocracy and to the Basque and Catalan separatists. By the late 1860s it had become clear that there was to be no radical dechristianization in Spain as there had been in France. This remained the situation for another seventy years, although anticlericalism certainly was a large element in the psychology of Spain, as of Italy, in response to the Church's antiliberalism.

The international strength of the religious position of Pius IX was also shown when he summoned a council of bishops to the Vatican in 1869. This First Vatican Council repeated the insistence of Trent that the Catholic faith in its entirety was based on the revelation by God in Scripture and Tradition, but it had no time to go into details. Its only other achievement was to add to the inheritance, as Trent had not done, by a doctrine about the papacy. It declared this doctrine to be part of the Catholic truth from which no one can deviate without harm to 'faith and salvation'. It taught that 'the pastors and faithful of every rite and rank' should submit to the jurisdiction of the bishop of Rome in 'matters which concern the discipline and leadership of the Church spread throughout the earth'. And on 18 July 1870, only three months before the Italian army's occupation of Rome, the council agreed that if the bishop of Rome speaks *ex cathedra* (very solemnly, 'from his throne') and decides 'that a doctrine of faith or morals is to be maintained by the whole Church', then 'he possesses that infallibility with which the divine Redeemer willed to see his Church equipped' and his definitions are 'unalterable and not based on the assent of the Church'.

It is improbable that this doctrine would have been accepted by any council of the Church in the west before the nineteenth century, and certain that any eastern council would have been horrified by such a proposal. At the time there was opposition or hesitation, mainly expressed by Germans and Americans among the bishops for they feared the worsening of relationships with Protestants. The two leading Catholic historians, Ignaz von Döllinger and Lord Acton, were hostile on scholarly grounds, and the former was in the end excommunicated. But some sixty bishops who thought the definition 'inopportune' left before the final decision, when only two voted against it; and all later submitted. This victory was eased by the defeat of enthusiasts who had wanted all future papal pronouncements to be declared infallible and in the event only one doctrine was to be clearly in that category, the doctrine of the Assumption of Mary proclaimed in 1950. The main factor in 1870 was loyalty to the papacy, and in particular to Pius IX: it seemed that to call for unquestioning loyalty to a man who personified the Church which had been promised 'the Spirit of truth' as its perpetual guide was the only alternative to the confusion of the modern age. Hearts went out to him with feelings in which sympathy as he lost political power was mingled with a new veneration for his role in religion.

Catholicism as Development

The only Catholic theologian of this period who was to remain famous, John Henry Newman, was often unhappy about some features of that version of the religion of the heart, but he never thought that he should reverse his conversion from the Church of England in 1845: then his own heart had made a decision, for good. When he was made a cardinal in 1879 he declared that 'for fifty years I have resisted to the best of my powers the spirit of liberalism in religion', meaning by 'liberalism' the right of each individual to make revealed religion 'say just what strikes his fancy'. Now that it was on the way to becoming the religion of a minority Christianity was being more sharply defined, and being defined by Christians not by governments; and for most Christians who took their religion seriously that meant that it must be the response of the total person to an authoritative revelation. But it became the teaching of Newman that the response could develop.

Like John Wesley he did not find enough 'scriptural holiness' in the church which had baptized and ordained him. Indeed, he did not find 'the Church' fully in it. It was not enough to be an establishment in which the semi-religious, half-holy English could be English; 'the Church' must be seen, and loved sacrificially, as a sacred and ancient society with its own structures of faith and life. This vision led Newman into brave decisions although also, in his Anglican period, into a conservatism which could be thought indefensible. In 1833 his friend John Keble preached in Oxford against a plan by the government to introduce an element of rationality into the finances of the over-endowed Anglican clergy in Ireland, a country consisting largely of Roman Catholic peasants. Newman edited a series of *Tracts for the Times*, the first of which proclaimed that Anglican priests must depend no longer on their social status but on their descent from the apostles through the bishops who had ordained them. Later the 'Tractarians' of this 'Oxford Movement' showed no enthusiasm when other governments began to rationalize the finances of the Church of England in the interests of the poorer clergy labouring in the towns, and even to reduce its privileges in England's two ancient universities. But finally, after much heart-searching, Newman decided that he must abandon the Church of England altogether. This was the logic of his personality. 'The whole man moves', he reflected; 'paper logic is but the record of it.'

He said that since childhood the existence of God had been as obvious to him as his own existence; for him as for Descartes, it was the existence of the world that might be doubted. But he could not avoid being aware of the challenges to the traditional Christian faith; his own brother Francis was a well-known atheist. In 1870 he was to complete his *Grammar of Assent* as his final effort to describe the processes by which 'real assent' and 'certitude' were reached in an age of many doubts and denials. Faith, he argued, cannot be proved to be true, but it is more than a matter of opinion. It is a person deciding to take action, knowing that there are alternatives but having a 'practical certainty' that this action is the right course for this person; and Christian faith is the decision to accept a revelation given in history as the inspiration of action.

As the 1830s became the 1840s what preoccupied him was the question of the nature of the continuity of Christian faith in that age with the 'revealed religion' of the first apostles and the Fathers of the early centuries. He came to see that the Roman church had been a rock amid these ancient controversies and he wanted to take his stand on such a rock in the nineteenth century. But he also saw that it had become inadequate to repeat the traditional Anglican claim that the Church ought to teach the religion of the Scriptures and the Fathers without any addition or subtraction. That now seemed a mere 'paper religion', not alive in hearts, not arousing action. The book which justified his conversion was his *Essay on Development*, with the theme that 'to live is to grow' but not to depart from 'the essential idea'. Protestantism had departed but there is, Newman argued, sufficient continuity between the apostles, the Fathers and the popes. Elsewhere at this time interest in church history was increasing: in Paris in 1844 Jacques Migne, a parish priest turned theological publisher, launched a series of editions of the Greek and Latin Fathers which eventually grew to 379 volumes. And some were drawing the conclusion that Christianity was able and entitled to develop. At any rate, 'development' was an idea whose time had come. In Germany Herder and Hegel propounded whole philosophies of history and Johann Möhler, a church historian, produced a theological interpretation of his studies somewhat like Newman's. In America Philip Schaff's *What is Church History?* (1846) was subtitled 'A Vindication of the Idea of Historical Development'. Schaff shocked Protestants by arguing that Luther was the 'full ripe fruit' of 'all the better tendencies' of the Middle Ages. He remained in the Reformed tradition but could contemplate the possibility of further development.

For many years this emphasis that Christianity could develop legitimately did not greatly appeal to the Roman Catholic authorities. While defending the Church's right not to be restricted to the clear words of Scripture, they also maintained that they were teaching truths which had been present in the Church from the beginning even if not fully understood and not explicitly written down. But gradually many came to agree that Catholicism must indeed develop, so that the question was whether the development which had produced the triumph of Pius IX in the First Vatican Council was final. It is clear that Newman, for all his loyalty to the church of his conversion, saw dangers in the possibility that with or without the agreement of the bishops a pope might now go ahead without the proper acknowledgement of Catholicism's other sources of authority. He taught that although the Bible does not contain the whole of Christianity truly Christian and Catholic development must have that origin: 'Revelation is the initial and essential idea of Christianity.' His other emphasis was on the supremacy of the conscience. From this followed the need of the pope and the bishops to 'consult the faithful' even in matters of doctrine, only consulting but not suppressing discussion: any truly Christian and Catholic faith must satisfy the consciences of the people of the Church. He once wrote that if he had to propose a toast after a dinner it would be to 'Conscience' before 'The Pope'. In 1870 the First Vatican Council decreed that the pope had no such need to consult, but in the 1960s, when Pope John XXIII had decided on a massive consultation, the Second Vatican Council was to be called 'Newman's Council'. It was to show that Catholicism could indeed develop—and do so in directions which he would have welcomed.

But although he spent much of his life in an industrial city (Birmingham) Newman did not fully confront the challenge which we shall now consider: a challenge which claimed that the religion of the heart, whether Protestant or Catholic, whether 'liberal' or based on divine revelation, was always and everywhere like every other kind of religion, for it was a drug to keep people from demanding what was rightly theirs.

Opium for the People?

In the nineteenth century Europe's churches slowly moved away from the blind acceptance of the divine right of kings to govern badly and to exclude most of their subjects from any say about government. The Holy Roman empire could not be restored after its abolition by Napoleon in 1806. The new German Confederation was presided over by the Austrian emperor, the new Customs Union was planned by the Prussian king, and neither emperor nor king was a democrat; but there were stirrings of talk about the German people. In alarm about the possible spread of democracy Alexander I, whose own despotic government of Russia was no real model to anyone, initiated the Holy Alliance after the defeat of Napoleon at Waterloo. In the name of the Holy Trinity and claiming to be in conformity with Holy Scripture, this treaty united the Christian sovereigns of Europe as a club to replace the French revolutionaries' fraternity: all the sovereigns were 'members of a single Christian nation'. The implication was that they would come to each other's assistance. But the pope refused to sign since some of the sovereigns were Orthodox or Protestant. So did the government of Britain, a country now more interested in worldwide free trade and eventually (for that reason mainly) a sponsor of the rebellion in Latin America against the colonialism of Spain and Portugal. When the other Catholic sovereigns failed to uphold the reactionary regimes in France and Spain, or to prevent the Italians from throwing out their Austrian rulers, they in effect endorsed the opinion uttered by the British minister Castlereagh at the time of the Holy Alliance: it was 'a piece of sublime mysticism and nonsense'.

The stirrings of democracy in this period after the Napoleonic wars arose out of the economic distress which, paradoxically, arose out of the fact that more food and better medicine meant the growth of the population between 1750 and 1850. There was threefold growth in Britain, where the problem of overpopulation in the countryside was increased by the introduction of greater efficiency, and even of some machinery, into agriculture. Large numbers of people for whom the alternative was starvation, or the utter humiliation of dependence on the cold charity of the time for the poor, had to accept the harsh conditions of employment in the new factories. Capitalism now began to flourish with plentiful 'hands' for the productive machines. Large profits were made which could be used partly for the comfort of the privileged families but mainly for investment in the new enterprises. The process was most noticeable in England, the world's first industrial nation and the first to be united by railways. After the 'Hungry Forties' the new wealth was to trickle down, spreading prosperity. But in the meanwhile, for the workers on low wages and for those who could not find any work, the conditions of life were such that Karl Marx and his collaborator Friedrich Engels (a Manchester businessman) expected a revolution. The attitudes of successive governments did not help. Attempts by the workers to combine were suppressed with a vigour which was not matched when great distress was caused in the 1840s by a famine in Ireland (virtually an English colony). Indeed, such action as there was by the government added to the distress. And that was no accident, for it was the philosophy of the governing class that no government had the duty or the right to intervene in social problems. The acceptance of the iron 'laws of economics' as part of the law of God by many of the clergy explains why Engels thought, wrongly, that the English working class was so alienated at this stage that it had very little or no religious belief of any kind.

In this crisis for society the voices which carried furthest often came from outside the churches. In 1848 Karl Marx's *Communist Manifesto*, published in London, attacked the churches' talk about heaven. To him it was 'opium' to keep the workers subdued as horses were kept quiet in that age. In France Auguste Comte announced that 'positivism' avoiding all speculation had now replaced theology and metaphysics. He was, however, the prophet of a new religion, 'the religion of Humanity', which had many imaginative aids to devoutness (with science but without God): it was well described as Catholicism without Christianity. Saint-Simon was both the founder of socialism and the apostle of a 'New Christianity' which had as its most urgent mission help for the poor. But many in the churches were as troubled as these secularizers about the sufferings of the victims of the economic changes, and some Christians spoke out.

F. D. Maurice was the son of a father who could not believe in the Trinity and a Calvinist mother who could not believe that she had been predestined to heaven. One of his sisters became a Baptist; the others were Evangelicals within the Church of England. That experience of religious divisions in a family helped him to find his central message as an Anglican priest: unity. His book on *The Kingdom of Christ* offered a vision of 'signs' in the Church—the Scriptures, the sacraments, the creeds, the ordained ministry—which all pointed to Christ as the King of all and to God as the Father of all. He was convinced that belonging to a family or a nation was meant to be an education in belonging to humanity, all loved by God. He broke with the Tractarians of Newman's Anglican days by maintaining that baptism is not a new birth; it declares that a child has always been a child of God. He broke with Calvinists and Evangelicals by denying not only that some human beings are predestined to hell but also that the punishment of sinners in hell is 'everlasting'. (He did not deny hell as an 'eternal' possibility, only that its punishments would last for a very, very long time.) The basic error of the frightened conservatives was, he wrote, 'offering to "the spirit of the present age" the spirit of the former age, instead of the ever-loving and active Spirit of God'. He believed (he claimed) in God's 'revelation' as much as any conservative, but was sure that God had revealed himself to 'a creature formed to know him and to be like him'.

All that passionate theology about human dignity lay behind Maurice's share in a little group not afraid to be called 'Christian Socialists'. While other middle-class people were simply hostile to the demands of the 'People's Charter' and to the Chartists threatening London in 1848 Maurice and his friends saw this as an opportunity for sympathetic Christian leadership. He never advocated socialism in the sense which Marx was to give to that ambiguous word: his answer to economic problems was the formation of small producers' co-operatives, not a very practical answer. But he put his own energy into the Working Men's College as an example of education for the people. Nor did he advocate 'democracy' if it meant rule by the uneducated. But his was a voice crying that in the kingdom of Christ there must be social justice, that already in human nature collaboration is more basic than competition. And idealism of that sort, although usually without the theology, inspired a host of efforts to improve the conditions of life for the people. In the countryside clergy gave a lead. In the cities the Young Men's Christian Association drew many thousands to its hostels and activities; it was begun in London in 1844 and became a worldwide movement.

In Scotland a great churchman, Thomas Chalmers, had wide interests and a strong Evangelical faith. A professor, preacher and author, he was controlled by a vision of the Church of Scotland as the spiritually powerful church of the nation, meeting the material as well as the spiritual needs of the whole people, and he worked this vision out in a Glasgow parish. But he insisted that the ministers leading parishes should be appointed from within the local church, not by the richer and less Evangelical lay patrons as decreed by the state, and in 1843 he influenced the 'Disruption', the departure of almost half the Established Church's clergy to form the Free Church which enjoyed such popular support that it had covered Scotland with its own churches before his death in 1847. The story was repeated in Canada, and in the Netherlands a similar division in the Reformed Church was to occur in 1886.

In Protestant Germany the Inner Mission launched by Johann Heinrich Wichern in 1848 took action and did some thinking about social problems but was always nervous about involvement in politics. Support for the government's efforts was acceptable, but 'Social Christianity' was thought to be out of place in the pulpit and in the 1890s Kaiser Wilhelm found it easy to frighten off such preachers as had temporarily strayed into territory reserved for governments. The Inner Mission concentrated on supporting a large network of institutions, agencies and individual workers dedicated to helping the victims of the grim social problems. Specially notable was the work of the Lutheran deaconesses begun by the pastor of a village church, Theodor Fliedner, in 1836. It had links with England: one inspiration behind it was the example of the Quaker Englishwoman Elizabeth Fry who visited and changed previously inhumane prisons, and it was in the deaconesses' centre in Kaiserwerth that Florence Nightingale first observed modern nursing before her own work as a great reformer. In Catholic Germany a prophet arose and became bishop of Mainz, Wilhelm Ketteler; and he encouraged the growth of activities and associations of Catholics in the world of work. These Lutheran and Catholic pioneers who faced suspicion or hostility in their churches have not escaped other criticism: charity can seem to be, as Marx said, 'holy water' thrown at problems which remain because the economic basis of the unjust society remains, and a church-related association can be held to be unhealthily clergy-dominated and timidly opposed to the necessary war between the classes. But at least moves were made by some brave Christians, in some cases at the cost of personal tragedy.

In France Félicité de Lamennais and a group of ardent disciples pleaded for the Church to identify itself with the struggling people, not the *bourgeois* state. They urged as the first steps the end of state control over the Church and the establishment of the freedoms of conscience (including the non-Catholic conscience) and of association (including workers' unions). The motto of their utopian paper *L'Avenir* was 'God and Liberty', but the combination of the words shocked Gregory XVI, who condemned Lamennais in 1832. In earlier years Lamennais had written with passion against individual judgements in matters of religion and in favour of the pope's authority, so that for a time the pope's sentence seemed a kind of death, but since he could now speak as an individual he remained active in politics and religious thought for another twenty years—without much effect. Amid the violence in Paris in 1848, when Louis Philippe lost his throne and the archbishop his life, disciples of Lamennais tried to start a movement to begin a 'new era'. But the day of 'Social Catholicism' in France was slow to dawn.

The Birth of Modern Theology

In all these small movements of protest, outside and inside the churches, lay the beginnings of the 'social gospel' which was one day to be regarded as an integral part of Christianity. But because Christianity is a religious rather than a political movement, the most significant part of its modernization was the attempt to answer modern questions about God and about Jesus.

The pioneers were Protestants whose answers were of the 'liberal' kind which Newman denounced. In 1819 an American theologian, William Channing, was in the midst of what was to be a ministry of almost forty years in Boston, which had become a stronghold of 'enlightened' Unitarianism. He preached a sermon on 'Unitarian Christianity' which concisely, even crudely, summed up some of the challenges which more conservative believers had to consider, however reluctantly. He announced that God is One, not three beings; that he is morally perfect (therefore Calvinism should not be admired); that he does not change because of the crucifixion of Jesus (therefore traditional doctrines of the atonement should be revised); that virtue arises from Man's own moral nature, not from God's irresistible force; and that it implies no discredit to Jesus to say that he was a man distinct from God. Basing true religion squarely on reason as Kant did, Channing was bolder than Kant in his denials of orthodoxy. But the fate of Unitarianism, which became a small middle-class denomination, was to show that there was substance in the reply of Christians such as Pascal and Newman: religion is based on feelings which go deeper than reasonableness and decency, and for Christians it concentrates on the revelation of God in Christ. Liberal Protestantism was going to need to take account of this reaction although it was never going to satisfy its critics who saw no alternative to the uncomplicated authority of the Bible or the Church.

In the eleven months before his death in 1855, Søren Kierkegaard's journalism reached a new intensity as it attacked the memory of a local Lutheran bishop who had represented the tradition that a 'Folk Church' must include many people with less than fully Christian beliefs or lives in order to establish 'Christendom'. The best exponent of this idea was another Dane, N. F. S. Grundtvig, whose theology resembled that of F. D. Maurice. Because Kierkegaard wrote in Danish he was scarcely known outside that country before the next century; because this layman wrote rhetorically and turbulently rather than systematically (indeed, he hated all systems), he was not a major theologian; and because all his writing sprang out of his own unhappy life he has never appealed to those whose more relaxed experiences have not led to the 'existential' approach to religion which Kierkegaard admitted was intellectually 'absurd'. But precisely in those characteristics lay his ultimately fertile contribution. For him Christ, the 'God–Man', was the challenger, addressing each individual with a command to take the 'leap of faith' and to enter a radically new life. This Christ steps directly out of the gospels, causing offence and 'fear and trembling', and 'the fact that the eternal once came into existence in time is the paradox by which all are to be tested'. Either we say yes to a new creation or we say no, and our yes must be said with 'the most passionate inwardness'. But after this explosion Kierkegaard left it to others to reflect more calmly on what might be the contents of a faith so formed.

In Germany in 1852 J. C. K. von Hofmann began the publication of a Christ-centred theology which was rejected by most conservative Lutherans but which inaugurated the treatment of the Bible not as a book without errors but as the record of 'salvation history'. In this presentation the death of Christ was not needed as the substitutionary payment of the penalty for humanity's sin, but the life of Christ with the cross as its climax was needed in order to restore the relationship between God and Man. And three years previously, in America, Horace Bushnell's *God in Christ* had articulated theologically what had already become a frequent theme for American preachers: in their relationship what needs to be changed is not God's attitude but Man's. Christ's work is this: 'He does produce an impression in our minds of the essential sanctity of God's law and character.' Bushnell's other books expounded what he meant by 'an impression'. In *Christian Nurture* he emphasized the slow but sure influence of the home which conveyed that impression, in contrast with the dramatic emotionalism of the revivalist preachers pleading for conversions. Elsewhere he stressed that Christian doctrine necessarily had a poetic, not scientific, character and that it ought to find God in the natural as well as the supernatural. These were correctives to the emotional preaching of hard and narrow doctrines, but Bushnell came to see that he himself needed correction: he had been too cheerful.

In Scotland in 1856 John McLeod Campbell published a solid book on *The Nature of the Atonement and Its Relation to the Remission of Sins and Eternal Life*. His theology had grown out of his pastoral experience in the ministry of the Church of Scotland, from which he had been expelled in 1831. There had been very little argument when the General Assembly expelled him: he had failed to preach a doctrine on which almost all Calvinists and other Christians were then agreed, that the Son died in order to satisfy the Father's just demand for punishment. As he had listened to his parishioners he had formed the impression that they did not love the Father because they did not believe that the Father loved them. In his book he systematically attacked the idea that Christ was a substitute for the guilty in a divine law-court: he was, and is, the revelation of God's loving wish to forgive sins and to bestow eternal life. Already in 1830 one sentence had been enough for Campbell to be condemned as a heretic: 'God loves every child of Adam with a love the measure of which is to be seen in the agonies of Christ.'

Many Christians (not only Calvinists) adhered to the older doctrine, explaining that when the Son bore the Father's just punishment—just, because the sins of the world deserved it—this was the Father's own

413

provision to deal with human sinfulness. In that way it manifested the Father's love. And those who were not satisfied with this explanation could still see the need to take seriously Campbell's words about 'the agonies of Christ'. Those agonies, he thought, were Christ's 'perfect Amen to the judgement of God on the sin of Man' because they showed how much holy love must suffer in a sinful world and how much this costs the Father as well as the Son. That became the theme of *Lectures on the Moral Government of God* by another American theologian, Nathaniel Taylor: God governs by ending the power of sin through suffering. And towards the end of the civil war in America Horace Bushnell published a book on *The Vicarious Sacrifice* which showed how his own theology had deepened. The war had left 600,000 dead. All had suffered in what they believed was a good cause; all America had been moved; peace was now possible. A new meaning had been given to St Paul's words, 'without the shedding of blood there can be no at-one-ment'. And Bushnell dared to say that the 'agonies of Christ' made visible the suffering of the Father himself because of the evil in the world: 'There is a cross in God before the wood is seen on the hill.'

The chief figure in the modernization of Christian thought was, however, an earlier theologian, Friedrich Schleiermacher. He decisively influenced Bushnell, for example. In his German background he had strong support. His father, an army chaplain, sent him to absorb permanent impressions in a boarding school run by the Moravian Pietists. Newman, who knew little about Schleiermacher because he could not read German, was right to guess that his was 'an attempt of the intellect to delineate, philosophize and justify that religion, so called, of the heart and feelings'.

As a young man Schleiermacher was close to the Romantic movement whose German giants were Herder and Schelling, Goethe and Beethoven, but which also included great English poets who moved from enthusiasm for Revolution through enthusiasm for Nature to a more biblical faith. Such were Wordsworth and Coleridge. True religion, the latter maintained, is about truth: 'He who begins by loving Christianity better than truth will proceed by loving his own sect or church better than Christianity and end by loving himself best of all.' But what is truth? In religion it is not what is left after the individual's self-doubt, as Descartes had thought when advocating a religion which was very much a matter of thinking. Nor is it the conclusion of humanity's capacity for 'practical' reasoning, as Kant had taught. It is spiritual truth, reached by intuition and best expressed in images not propositions, revealed supremely in the Bible which 'finds me'. Do not try to prove it by arguments: 'make a man feel the want of it' and 'try it!' Coleridge was greatly indebted to Germans, particularly Friedrich Schelling, for such insights: indeed, often his words repeated theirs.

In Germany this was the time of *Sturm und Drang*, a movement calling for the heroic individual's courage amid modern 'storm and stress'. And it was the hour of nationalism, calling for heroes to lead modern nations. In Berlin Schleiermacher was the colleague of Hegel, who like him propounded a comprehensive philosophy which included support for Prussian patriotism. Hegel despised the theologian, remarking that his insistence on 'absolute dependence' on God suggested that the perfect Christian would be a dog, but there were some intellectual connections between the two professors. For Hegel, the 'Absolute Spirit' expresses itself in nature and history, particularly in the progress of the human spirit for which the 'absolute religion' is Christianity. Christianity has offered the best 'representations' of spiritual truths, but the modern age demands something yet more spiritual. Philosophy should provide it, showing that crucifixion really means the death of what is not infinite and resurrection means the ascent of Man to the Absolute.

Glad to be a part of the outburst of Prussian patriotism after the shock of the defeat by Napoleon at Jena in 1806, Schleiermacher spread his own message about a reborn nation from his pulpit while also being a leader in the foundation of Berlin University and in the meetings of the Berlin Academy of Sciences. He also coincided with the merger of Prussia's Calvinists and Lutherans by royal command in 1817: he was an enthusiast for that bit of modernization too. And with his gift for friendship he was popular. There was in his adulthood none of the uneasiness of Newman's whole life. He went further than Maurice in advocating the redistribution of wealth by taxation and the payment of benefits to the poor as of right, but not even such radicalism made him unpopular with his middle-class audience.

Like Hegel, later German thinkers such as Feuerbach and Marx were to denounce the whole idea of religion as dependence on God. Conservative Christians have, however, often accused Schleiermacher of reducing theology to anthropology, abandoning a close attention to the Word of God in order to talk about what Emil Brunner was to attack as 'mysticism' and what Karl Barth was to scorn as 'Christian pious self-awareness'. Others who have acknowledged his reverence for the Infinite and the Redeemer have nevertheless thought his theology too optimistic. He said little about the challenge which the large-scale existence of evil poses to faith in God's goodness. He made much of Jesus as 'Redeemer' but having never been there said little about the prison of life without redemption. His lectures on the life of Jesus were the first ever given in a university (in 1817), but he never faced the historical questions which were to preoccupy his successors: 'the ideal must have been completely historical in him', he declared, and he relied on John's gospel as 'the narrative of an eyewitness'. Nor did he deal very carefully with the traditional doctrines about Jesus as God the Son, born of a virgin amid angel-song, manifesting his divine control over devils and nature, dying as a substitutionary sacrifice to the Father, raised physically from death to heaven, founding the authoritative Church, due to return to earth as Judge in glory. (He told his students that probably Jesus was revived after apparent death, only to die a few weeks later.) Like Hegel he praised the old doctrines as old 'pictures'—praise which the conservatives did not applaud. While in these ways he has been regarded as too smooth, there also has been the complaint that his exposition of *The Christian Faith*, published in its first German edition in 1821–22, has a style less readable than that of Calvin's *Institutes*, with which it claims and deserves comparison. (It was not translated into English until 1928.) But when all that has been said, he may still be called the father of modern theology and may even be admired for not being entirely clear about the being and purposes of God.

In 1787, when he was not yet twenty years old, he had to confess in a letter to his indignant father that he could no longer believe that 'he who called himself the Son of Man was the true, eternal God' or 'that his death was a substitutionary atonement'. But that brave confession is mainly of interest as illustrating his lifelong honesty. He found sufficient faith to become a Calvinist or 'Reformed' minister in keeping with his family's tradition and to attempt to re-form the beliefs of the sixteenth century. This reformation was radical, for he shared the Enlightenment's rejection of the Calvinist idea of the predestination of the majority to hell as he shared its suspicion of the Lutheran emphasis on faith as an intensely emotional experience of escape from hell. He shared, too, its insistence on the freedom of inquiry: his *Christmas Eve* (1806) took the form of a dialogue about the incarnation when contributions could be made in a domestic setting from the standpoints of unquestioning joy or near-total scepticism. But he was not fully 'enlightened' in Kant's sense, for he did not identify true religion with Reason or Morality. Nor did he look to a world invisible but somehow more real, although he translated the works of Plato. For him religion is a 'feeling' (the inadequate translation of the German *Gefühl*) about the world around us. It is a 'consciousness' of the deepest reality of the world, and all religious sentiments and statements arise out of this consciousness.

'What the pious contemplate', he wrote, is 'the universal existence of all finite things' while knowing that they also are merely finite, doomed to die, so that in reaction 'true religion is a sense and taste for the Infinite'. Everyone must be 'definitely active in some one department of life'—but should also allow himself or herself to be passively 'affected by the Infinite'. Partly because he was persuaded by attacks on his earlier sympathy with Spinoza ('the Universe was his only and everlasting love'), he developed as his central theme the understanding of religion as awareness of the transcendent God— 'the consciousness of being absolutely dependent or, which is the same thing, of being in relation with God'. At its most intense, the spirit of religion dissolves 'the whole soul in the immediate feeling of the Infinite and Eternal'. But religious experience is the experience of the normal, finding the Infinite and Eternal not in a First Cause distant from us or in miracles interfering with nature but in 'all that lives and moves, in all growth and change, in all doing and suffering'. To lack this religious feeling is to be less than fully human. Possibly some of the cultured despisers lacked it, and Schleiermacher put Anselm's warning on the title page of *The Christian Faith*: 'No one will understand unless he has experienced.' But he could scarcely believe in the existence of such people. He respected the non-Christian religions as the social expressions of this feeling within the constraints of history in different lands, but he was sure that Christianity was the best religion. It is distinguished from other monotheistic religions 'by the fact that in it everything is related to the redemption accomplished by Jesus of Nazareth'.

When Schleiermacher said that, he intended to separate himself from various heresies of the past, listed in *The Christian Faith*. To him the essence of orthodoxy is that the Redeemer is both fully divine and fully human and that redemption is both necessary and possible. He used a German word usually translated as 'redemption' but better understood as 'deliverance' without any necessary connection with the idea of the payment of a price. What delivers is the 'consciousness of God' in Jesus, complete 'in each historical moment of his experience'. That is unique, for 'no more perfect form of the God-consciousness is put before the human race' and Christian faith rightly 'knows no other way to a pure conception of the ideal other than an ever-deepening understanding of Christ'. And that is divine, for 'to ascribe to Christ an absolutely powerful God-consciousness, and to attribute to him an existence of God in him, are exactly the same thing'. That much can be said although 'we have no formula for the being of God in itself as distinct from the being of God in the world'. The God-consciousness of Jesus was of course influenced by the human environment to which he belonged, but his 'unique spiritual content' can be explained only by taking account of 'the creative and divine act' of 'the universal source of spiritual life'. In particular 'he must have been free from everything by which the rise of sin in the individual is conditioned'. Because Jesus is in these senses unique and divine, 'the whole development and maintenance of Christian piety must always proceed from vital fellowship with Christ'—and the whole maintenance and development of theology also, for 'Christian doctrines are accounts of the Christian religious affections set forth in speech'.

As Schleiermacher summed up his understanding of the at-one-ment between God and Man, 'the Redeemer lifts the believers into the fellowship of his unclouded blessedness and that is his reconciling activity'. Jesus does this by the whole course of his life and death, not by his death alone; he does it not by appeasing the Father's wrath but by showing the Father's 'sympathy with misery'; and after his death he is spiritually present in the Church, the fellowship where 'God-consciousness' leads to the knowledge that sins are forgiven. In response to the existence of multitudes outside this fellowship, Schleiermacher remained enough of a Calvinist to say that their unbelief is the will of God—but he added, as Calvin did not, that after death their 'God-consciousness' may be awakened and may bring with it what in his *Speeches* he called the only 'religious' kind of immortality: 'to be one with the Infinite'.

He warned the people to whom he preached not to expect miracles. We may express our wishes to our Father: 'Christ did it.' But we must learn from the Christ of Gethsemane that prayer is more importantly the adjustment of our wishes to God's will. Our 'absolute dependence' then becomes dependence on God working through the world as it is, not on any occasional interventions by him.

Another great figure arose in German Protestant theology: Albrecht Ritschl. The kingdom of God about which he spoke was full of goodness but (critics said) not sufficiently dependent on God.

As a young man Ritschl was more influenced by the all-encompassing philosophy of Hegel than by the theology of Schleiermacher. When he worked on church history he was one of those who applied the pattern laid down by Hegel for all history: thesis, antithesis, synthesis. The thesis had been Jewish Christianity, the antithesis the Gentile Christianity of Paul, the synthesis the Catholicism of the ancient Church which now needed replacement. But during the 1850s he became bored with these attempts to fit all history into a neat pattern and more interested in the reconstruction of Bible-based doctrine for the modern age.

He, too, concentrated on the 'completely spiritual and ethical religion' established by Jesus. He, too, was a patriot full of optimism about the future of Germany; in his lifetime the German empire was formed under Prussian leadership after the defeat of Austria and France in 1866–70 and Germany overtook Britain in the wealth generated by the new industries. He, too, as he sought a message for Germany was not concerned to defend any system of doctrine inherited from the past, believing that Jesus himself had not taught systematically, being interested chiefly in behaviour. The Germany which Ritschl knew was of course excited by its new unity, wealth and power, but its philosophers spoke much of moral values. 'Philosophy', wrote Wilhelm Windeband, 'can live only as the science of values which are universally valid.' There could still be attempts to make ethics a 'science' but this Germany was the background to the *German Requiem* of Brahms, where immortality for the souls of the righteous is affirmed on the basis of Scripture.

What, then, was the right message for a Christian theologian? Like Schleier-macher, Ritschl believed that we cannot know what God 'is in himself'—only how he loves us. And he, too, did not believe that the death of Jesus had been necessary to reconcile the Father to us. In the 1870s his three volumes on *Justification and Reconciliation* explored but criticized the imagery of the law-court and ended up with the imagery of family life, with the Father eager to forgive his children: 'The ground of justification is the benevolent, gracious, merciful purpose of God to vouchsafe to the sinful the privilege of access to himself.'

However, there were significant differences. He had none of Schleier-macher's gratitude to Pietism. His long history of that religion of the heart was hostile; it had been a 'monkish method of self-abasement'. He would have nothing to do with 'mysticism'; the mysticism of Catholicism only added to his hostility to that tradition. He was not in favour of 'absolute dependence' on an Infinite revealed through nature to the whole of humanity. On the contrary, 'In every religion what is sought, with the help of the superhuman spiritual power reverenced by Man, is a solution of the contradiction in which Man finds himself: he is both a part of the natural world and a spiritual personality claiming to rule nature'. In Christianity this tendency in all religions 'finds its perfect consummation'; he knew more than Schleiermacher did about non-Christian religions but respected them less. In Christianity, the best of all the religions, is shown 'the independence of the human spirit over against nature'. 'The divine will creates the world with spiritual life as its final end' and spiritual life ends in 'the attainment of eternal life'. The world is not to be despised, but 'the individual is worth more than the whole world'.

Although 'beyond all doubt Jesus was conscious of a new and hitherto unknown relation to God, and said so to his disciples', his chief purpose according to Ritschl was 'to bring his disciples into the same attitude to the world as his own, and to the same estimate of themselves, that under these conditions he might enlist them in the world-wide mission of the Kingdom of God'. When Christians agree to be enlisted they decide to make 'value-judgements' about God, Jesus (who 'had the value of God') and the world; they now believe in the origin of Jesus 'from above, out of God'. Such value-judgements are very different from scientific knowledge which is 'impartial knowledge gained by observation', but so far from apologizing for being non-scientific Ritschl affirmed that 'the Christian ideal of life, and no other, satisfies the claims of the human spirit to a general knowledge of things', leading to 'peace of mind, inward satisfaction and comfort', the 'new dominion over the world through confidence in God's universal provi-dence', and the 'elevation above the world in the Kingdom of God which accords with our true destiny'.

Writing in the 1950s, Karl Barth was to find this theology sinister. He alleged that Ritschl had taught that Jesus merely assisted his followers to 'live according to reason in the best sense' by increasing their sense of their own worth, the help of God being merely 'valued' in their own judgements. Ritschl was to Barth no more than 'the very epitome of the national-liberal German *bourgeois* in the age of Bismarck' and was not unconnected with the evil desire of Germans to build a kingdom (*Reich*) which would dominate the world. But Ritschl deserves better than that: such criticism may be applied justly to a popular 'liberal' religion which was virtually reduced to morality, but Ritschl himself was a major theologian and he deserves to be judged by his actual teaching, which referred at great length to the Bible and to the history of Christian doctrine, and by his influence on his leading disciples. One (Kaplan) taught that 'the consummation of our faith in revelation is the belief that God himself, through Jesus Christ, has interfered in human history and offers himself to us for fellowship with him'. Another (Herrmann) taught that 'the inner life of Jesus makes an impression on the soul', so that 'we find in God nothing but Christ'. And the influence of Ritschl was by no means confined to the support of Bismarck. In the USA it provided the main theological support for the 'social gospel' which had a considered theology while it attacked the cruelties of unfettered capitalism. In Canada the high moral tone of much of the society owed something to the teaching of a great Ritschlian, John Watson, a fervent believer in God through Christ.

One criticism of Ritschl which does seem fair is that, being very much a theologian, he found it difficult to communicate with a wide public. That criticism could not be made about another disciple, Adolf von Harnack, although Harnack was even more learned as an historian of doctrine. In the winter of 1899–1900 he delivered a series of extempore lectures, taken down by a student and published in English as *What is Christianity?* (and in many other languages). With his deep learning he believed that Christian history 'presents eternal truth in historically changing forms' but must always be corrected by a return to the original message of Jesus. This concerned a 'calm, simple and fearless' religion of the heart: God is our Father, Jesus is 'the way to the Father', now the soul may be 'so ennobled that it can and does unite with him', the fact that we are all God's children as he declares is 'at once a gift and a task'. That pure gospel was corrupted by theologians who made too much use of Greek and Gnostic ideas, and then more powerfully by Byzantine Orthodoxy and medieval Catholicism as oppressive dogmatic systems, and Luther and Calvin remained too medieval; but now we can know the Christianity of Christ, the simple faith in 'God the Father and the infinite value of the human soul'. To that faith he summoned his enthusiastic young audience in Berlin as the twentieth Christian century began. Many of them were to die in the war of 1914–18.

The Shock of Evolution

Even before the great wars of the twentieth century had killed the belief that Germany was leading Europe into a joyful recovery of God's fatherhood and Man's dignity and therefore brotherhood, thoughtful Europeans had been disturbed—and in many instances, profoundly distressed—by questions which the liberal Protestants did not fully confront. Does contemplation of the real world produce a feeling of 'absolute dependence' on a God who is so good and so powerful as to be the God and Father of Jesus Christ? Does it even justify belief in such a God? And was Jesus essentially a teacher of truths congenial to the Enlightenment or to these liberal Protestants?

In the nineteenth century the picture of the world suggested by the progress of science gradually became much more alarming. Whether or not they were still Christians in one sense or another, increasingly scientists saw it as their duty to observe, experiment and deduce without reference to religious doctrines. When the astronomer Laplace was asked by Napoleon where God came into his system, he replied that he had no need of 'that hypothesis' (as Napoleon had no need of prayer when fighting a battle). And increasingly what scientists discovered made it harder to treat the Bible as a book dictated by God and therefore as at least equal to 'Nature' in the revelation of truth. This crisis of faith was most public in Victorian England, where the Christian religion—whether 'reasonable' or the 'religion of the heart'—had often come to mean an absolute dependence on the Bible.

In the first half of the century the challenge was posed for open-minded Englishmen by the new science of geology, involving much amateurish fascination with rocks and fossils but ordered into a coherent system by Charles Lyell's *Principles* (1831). The implications of this science for the literal truth of the myths about the world's creation in Genesis were resisted valiantly by conservative believers: perhaps God had put the fossils in the rocks in order to test faith? But the implications became irresistible. It had already been learned that the earth was in orbit round the sun despite the Old Testament's picture of the sky as a curtain full of lights stretched above a flat earth. Now it was revealed by science that the earth had existed for a period far longer than was suggested by the Old Testament's chronology, usually said to teach a creation in 4004 BC. The estimate of the age of the universe that eventually emerged allowed for between ten and fifteen thousand million years. Nineteenth-century science also demonstrated that the earth's development had been by a uniform, natural process, not by the separate acts decided on by the Creator. And with the discovery of patiently creative time by geology went the discovery of space by astronomy. People who accepted that advancing science had to adjust themselves emotionally to the picture of this planet first as a pebble and then as a pinprick in a universe which, in so far as its width could be grasped, had to be measured by the years taken for light to travel at an unimaginably rapid speed. The picture that eventually emerged was of a universe wide by at least ten thousand million of those years—and expanding.

Inevitably the discoveries of the staggering immensities of time and space raised a philosophical or religious question which could not be answered by the scientists' researches: what is the status of Man? Pascal's answer could still be given: Man is a creature who thinks as the stars do not and is the best witness to the existence of the stars' Creator who thinks. Like almost all his contemporaries Lyell insisted on that uniqueness of the mind or spirit of Man and was therefore not religiously discouraged by finding out that Man's environment was so much older than had been believed. But in the second half of the nineteenth century new science was widely understood to correct all the traditional Christian doctrines about Man. The geologists had now persuaded many of the truth of a history of the earth covering long ages, although few yet guessed that the figure of at least 4,500 million years would be reached. Now biologists demolished the literal truth of the picture in Genesis of the Creator making by a brief act each species in a fixed form, with Adam and Eve as the crowning glory, made godlike because infused with the spirit breathed by God. At the same time they destroyed the picture of Man suggested by the philosophy of (for example) Descartes, a picture in which there were two distinct entities, the thinking mind with its innate awareness of God and the material, machine-like body. What the uncountable years had produced was an animal.

In 1859 Charles Darwin published *The Origin of Species by Means of Natural Selection*. It was not a long book but he had been preparing it for twenty years as he reflected on, and developed, previous observation and research. Twelve years later he published *The Descent of Man*. Neither in science nor in religion was it completely new or disturbing to argue that much as a human child grows from the parents' egg and seed so each living species had evolved from earlier forms of life. During the first half of the nineteenth century England had produced a considerable number of scientists or clergymen who struggled with considerable success to reconcile scientific truth as then known with a liberal version of Christianity. While still standing within that tradition Darwin reflected at the end of *The Origin*: 'There is a grandeur in this view of life, with its several powers, having been originally breathed into a few forms or into one; and that, whilst this planet has gone cycling on according to the fixed law of gravity, from so simple a beginning endless forms most beautiful and most wonderful have been, and are being, evolved.' But the sensationally new element in *The Origin* was the power of the detailed argument that the 'endless forms' of life had all been the result of 'natural selection'. This idea struck Darwin as he read a warning by a scholarly clergyman, Thomas Malthus, against the overpopulation of England. He now saw that evolution (a fact which had been guessed at previously) had come about through adaptations which in a given environment had increased the chances of surviving and breeding. In the struggle for life, food and mates, many less adapted, weaker species had perished. Those still alive were proofs not that God resembled a watchmaker whose superlative skill any sensible person must acknowledge but that nature was a battlefield where many corpses were buried. Man had himself evolved like every other victorious survival from the long, grim struggle. Man was 'higher' than other species among the animals, but not nearly so high as the religions and philosophies of the world had believed.

What Darwin had discovered did not seem to him to demolish Christianity completely, although it did mean that the Fall of Adam and Eve from blessed perfection must be a myth like the Flood covering the whole sinful earth. 'Science', he wrote, 'has nothing to do with Christ, except in so far as the habit of scientific research makes a man cautious in admitting evidence.' By the word 'Christ' he referred to a religious and moral tradition which he valued to the end: his wife was a devout believer, many of his friends were churchgoers, he was himself a Christian in his morals, and while young he had at first accepted the plan to make him a clergyman. (Indeed, in his student days he had unthinkingly accepted the Bible as literally true.) But his own frequent illnesses may have been in part the nervous expression of a fear of the spiritual results of his scientific work. With some regret he acknowledged that he grew less sensitive to things which science could not handle but his habit of caution in 'admitting evidence' gradually extended to great difficulty in believing that the human mind, 'developed from a mind as low as that possessed by the lowest animal', should 'be trusted when it draws such grand conclusions' about God.

He was no philosopher but his honesty made him question the validity of Kant's appeal to the 'moral law within' as a reliable witness to the existence of the divine law-giver. Man's moral sense could have been developed from what Darwin observed in other animals: a sense of what was needed by offspring and by the group as a whole. The evolution of ethics based on religious belief would then have needed only the development of language, and in particular of talk about gods or God to many generations of children. In that case, the proper basis for morality might be what was already advocated by the 'utilitarian' philosophers: thought about what made for the greatest happiness of the greatest number, as the only right constraint on the individual's pursuit of happiness.

Some leading Christians (including Asa Gray the distinguished American botanist) urged the acceptance of the picture of one species being transmuted to another instead of being created separately by the intervening hand of God. To them it still seemed possible to believe in the Creator and John Fiske's phrase 'evolution is God's way of doing things' spread. But for many years the more normal Christian reaction on both sides of the Atlantic was to leap to the defence of the Bible and to believe that in this defence of the God of Holy Scripture (or, rather, of Genesis, as only one of the biblical pictures of the creation) lay the only chance of defending the dignity of Man. At a meeting in Oxford in 1860 the local bishop asked whether a scientist claimed descent from an ape through his grandfather or his grandmother. Thomas Huxley, who was to devote his talents and energies to popularizing Darwinism, then replied to the effect that he would prefer to be descended from an ape rather than from a man who used his great gifts to obscure the truth. Yet the reaction which the over-eloquent bishop voiced was not so flippant as he foolishly made it appear. In America a conservative theologian, Charles Hodge, saw that the 'natural selection' of species struggling with each other for survival was the key idea and in *What is Darwinism?* (1874) he pronounced the theory to be incompatible with traditional beliefs in a Creator both omnipotent and benevolent. At the same time preachers in close touch with the American poor, particularly black preachers, were passionate against what seemed to be Darwinian applause for the victory of the strong. To deny that the human race is descended from Adam and Eve contradicts the Word of God—and denies fundamental human equality.

It was basically no joke when Disraeli, the leader of the Conservative party in England, orated in 1864: 'The question is this, Is man an ape or an angel?' For there was a serious and well-founded dismay at the new vision of Man, never perfect in the past, never capable of rising above the battles of the hungry animals, never entitled to draw 'grand conclusions' from what could be known. The new belief in the evolution of Man could be so interpreted that it supported optimism about what could be achieved by the 'fittest' who had already survived by being superior: in England a semi-philosopher, Herbert Spencer, propounded that comforting interpretation of 'Social Darwinism' and in America liberal middle-class preachers baptized it. But Darwin's science could also be used to support the belief that the end of the 'survival of the fittest' justified the means: ruthless competition between ambitious individuals, between businesses expanding or going under, between nations conquering or conquered, between races superior or enslaved. In 1889 H. S. Chamberlain wrote an evolutionist and racist book on *The Foundations of the Nineteenth Century*. In the next century it was to be admired by those of the Nazis who read books.

Thomas Huxley, in character a Victorian gentleman, was to conclude that 'the ethical progress of society depends not in imitating the cosmic process, still less in running away from it, but in combating it'. Those who were less confident of humanity's ability, or inclination, to contradict the law of the jungle saw with horror the death of the Man of old, the Man of faith, the Man whom Tennyson remembered:

> Who trusted God was love indeed
> And love Creation's final law,
> Tho' Nature, red in tooth and claw
> With ravine, shriek'd against his creed.

The religious dismay could increase when scientists began to understand more. Researching by the study of plants in his monastic garden in the 1860s, an Austrian abbot (Gregor Mendel) began to learn how physical characteristics are inherited genetically. His theory became more widely known and more exactly developed, and it led to the conclusion that although some changes (mutations) in the genes turn out to be favourable most are detrimental to the chances of survival and all are 'random' (unrelated to needs). Further scientific advances reduced—in the opinion of many, to vanishing point—any gap between matter and life or between brain and mind. Gone were the days when Descartes could argue that matter and mind were so distinct that God was needed to hold them together. (Descartes had believed that the connection was in a gland in the brain.) Thus was built up a picture of Man which in the twentieth century was to be accepted by many as unfortunately true. In this picture there has been less emphasis on the advantages gained by a species, or by individuals in it, through the devoted care of parents or membership of a protective group, but Man has taken his place fully among the animals, with no freedom except in relatively trivial matters since the necessities of physical survival are supreme; with no immortality at all since in the continuum of matter-life the more complex forms become all the more vulnerable to the death of brain-mind; with no fundamental dignity, since the evolution of the human form of matter-life and brain-mind has been from first to last the product of random mutations— or in other words of sheer chance. The purpose of life as understood in biology is to survive and multiply, and there has often seemed to be no other great purpose in the short lives of human animals.

And even when the perennial human habit of being optimistic or at least light-hearted worked against these gloomy conclusions, there remained the question of whether any reliance was to be placed on any reports about the supernatural. Perhaps science did not dictate any beliefs at all about the status of Man, but to many it seemed to say that all effects had causes excluding the supernatural. It seemed to promise that one day all these causes would be understood and meanwhile it seemed to forbid all attempts to invoke the supernatural in aid or explanation. Even an instinctively religious poet such as Tennyson could therefore 'falter where I firmly trod':

> I stretch lame hands of faith, and grope
> And gather dust and chaff, and call
> To what I feel is Lord of all,
> And faintly trust the larger hope.

The Death of God?

In Victorian England the anxiety to save the morality and the beauty inherited from the Christian tradition amid the wreckage inflicted by modern knowledge received eloquent expression in the poetry and prose of an unorthodox lay theologian, Matthew Arnold. As the tide ebbed from the shingles of Dover beach he heard the 'long, withdrawing roar' of the 'sea of faith'. He tried to hear instead the more welcome music of righteousness and love in a culture marked by 'sweet reasonableness'. He was no optimist: he dreaded the arrival of 'anarchy' if the mob gained control, he despised the dead orthodoxy and the 'Philistine' superficiality of most of the church life of his time, he did not think science or socialism a substitute for the old power of religion. But he could still hope. While his poetry was (like Tennyson's) essentially melancholic or nostalgic, when he wrote prose his tone could become more jaunty and more preachy. There was still 'the eternal, not ourselves, that makes for righteousness'. Perhaps an undogmatic religion could survive as a sense of the great mystery, as a love of the great tradition, as 'morality touched by emotion'? Perhaps that was what Jesus and Paul had meant to teach? Perhaps poets were the new teachers?

Some American thinkers were similarly convinced that the old forms of religious belief were in retreat in the age of science, but their message was far from pessimism. Ralph Waldo Emerson was descended from a long line of New England clergymen and was for a short time a Unitarian pastor himself, but he resigned in 1832 to become for half a century the most influential exponent of Transcendentalism, denouncing 'historical Christianity' because 'it dwells with noxious exaggeration about the person of Jesus' but affirming an elevated spirituality which, he thought, should replace it. 'The simplest person who in his integrity worships God', he taught, 'becomes God.' He meant by 'God' much what Spinoza had meant, for 'all things proceed out of the same spirit and all things conspire with it'. His mysticism transcended any low view of humanity but his God did not transcend Nature. And his cheerful message could be popularized among those many Americans who had no patience with the depression and nostalgia in the poetry of Tennyson or Arnold. The future seemed to be theirs to make; they insisted on making it with the aid of the faith that their own ideals and hopes were in harmony with the universe; and they proved able to produce semi-secular preachers who coarsened the message of the thinkers. Thus the Transcendentalist philosophy was to lead long after Emerson's death to the immense success of Ralph Waldo Trine's *In Tune with the Infinite*, a book of 1897 subtitled *Fullness of Peace, Power and Plenty*. However, peace, power and plenty were not to be infinite, not even in the USA.

Some of the themes underlying this optimistic reconstruction of religion could be expressed by distinguished academics. In America and Britain the philosophical movement called 'idealism' flourished for a period at the turn of the nineteenth and twentieth centuries. It agreed with the scientists that nature is a continuum without sharp breaks but it argued that the lowest should be understood in terms of the highest. The highest is Man's mental, moral and spiritual equipment and endeavour. The person who is so much more than a body reaches out to the Mind which is the deepest reality in all that exists, to the Reality behind all 'appearances', to the 'Absolute' (whether or not the Absolute is in any real sense personal). But the philosophers almost always held themselves aloof from the churches, which to them still lived in a pre-scientific world of naive mythology. Their lofty teaching about minds and the divine Mind was also above the heads of the public—and in the twentieth century it would be regarded by increasing numbers in a new generation of philosophers as rhetorical nonsense. G. E. Moore published his 'refutation of idealism' in 1903 and Bertrand Russell expounded a world-view: 'that Man is the product of causes which had no prevision of what they were achieving; that his opinions, his growth, his hopes and fears, his loves and beliefs are but the outcome of accidental collisions of atoms . . . destined to extinction in the vast death of the solar system—all these things, if not quite beyond dispute, are yet so nearly certain, that no philosophy which rejects them can hope to stand.' While the human condition was seen in this light, Moore argued that certain things remained obviously 'good': 'personal affection and the appreciation of what is beautiful in Art and Nature'.

Some of the Germans were, like Russell, thorough and eloquent in their rejection of the Christians' supernatural God—and of all vague or flimsy substitutes for him. In 1841 Ludwig Feuerbach expressed what he considered to be *The Essence of Christianity* (the title given to the English translation by George Eliot). He argued that Christianity is 'the perfect religion' because among religious believers Christians have the best ideas about what it ought to mean to be human. But all religious believers are mistaken. Every idea about God is merely the projection into the supernatural of what is in truth natural, into the non-existent divine of what is human. To say that God is 'good' is really to say that Man ought to be good. And the unreality involved in all religion was for Feuerbach more than a harmless mistake: it distracts Man from his human tasks.

Later in the 1840s Karl Marx developed the attack. The descendant of many rabbis, himself interested in the New Testament as a baptized schoolboy, he had lost interest in the question of the existence of God because 'for Germany the criticism of religion is in the main complete', but was sure that 'criticism of religion is the premise of all criticism'. He respected religion only as 'the heart of a heartless world, the cry of the oppressed creature'. What mattered was 'to change the world' by ending the social conditions which had made religion attractive as a consolation or protest. The criticism of society must lead to the revolution and the revolution must end all 'alienation'.

Marx's ideas about how the world should be changed were not likely to appeal to many members of the upper and middle classes, but from 1868 onwards the philosophy of 'monism' was propounded to the educated by Ernst Haeckel, incorporating Darwinian science but not necessarily involving politics. Haeckel's best-seller, translated into English as *The Riddle of the Universe*, appeared to solve the riddle by pointing out that everything has a material cause. All Kant's talk about the conscience, and Hegel's talk about the spirit, ought to be reduced in the final analysis to that unromantically solid reality. And for those who found even 'monism' too like a metaphysical theory about everything, there was the 'positivism' taught by Ernst Mach: the facts observed by science are the only truths which are accessible. Middle-class people might feel or hope that love within the family, or a love of literature, music and the arts, or a love of nature, disclosed truths which lay beyond the scope of science. They might welcome the invitations to a higher life which they heard from preachers when they went to church— for many, although not all, still did go to church. But in practice there was also in nineteenth-century middle-class life an acceptance of hard realism: science-based industry is what makes the new earthly hopes possible, competition is the law of life if these hopes are to be fulfilled, in that competition what is most admirable is financial or military strength. And when this was accepted as the tough reality of life in the time between a man's leaving home and his return in the evening, there was some willingness to be told that the ultimate reality in the universe was 'Nature, red in tooth and claw'.

Christians not persuaded by any of these new philosophies ending in atheism might have restated their faith in a way which reached the public.

They might have shown that a purified faith in the reality and goodness of God could still be held, although no longer as a calmly assumed certainty. They might have communicated more powerfully a sense of wonder about the evolution of life with all its mental and spiritual potential. The miracle of 'life's endless forms most beautiful and most wonderful' could remain after all the demolition of fanciful stories and ignorant explanations. And the awe which is the basic religious instinct could have been deepened as science went on to reveal the methods by which the uncountably many forms of life had evolved through unimaginably many years, struggles and failures—methods involving both the iron laws of physical necessity and a large element of (apparent?) chance, but producing a staggering amount both of beauty and of success. Such things were said, as when Charles Kingsley expressed his early reaction to Darwin: 'Now they have got rid of an interfering God—a master-magician as I call it—they have to choose between the absolute empire of accident and a living, immanent, ever-working God.' But few had this insight.

Many of the Christians who became aware of these questions were thrown on the defensive and responded negatively. As science made it more difficult, if not impossible, to retain the old ways of explaining the world and expressing belief in its Creator, the new lack of certainty was not seen as a reminder of the Creator-Father's willingness to allow a great variety in belief or unbelief about himself and his work. It was seen instead as a stimulus to make larger and louder claims that since the preferred authority (the Bible or the Church) cannot err, unbelief or a new belief is a stupid sin. When evolution was accepted as an unavoidable fact it was often not with the ugly Darwinian addition of 'natural selection'; or the 'theory' of evolution could be totally rejected, together with most of the rest of modernity. As the sea of faith retreated from the modern world, it could still make waves—which, however, did not drown most people's doubts.

And so in 1882 Friedrich Nietzsche recorded what seemed to be the logic of modernity in Europe. He was angry about the effects of the Christian message that those with the 'will to power' should be humble, and he was fearful about the rise of mindless democracy which would for ever frustrate those who were fit to exercise power. He hoped that 'Superman' would emerge and that 'our whole European morality' inherited from the Christian centuries would be changed. In some moods he thought this outcome inevitable and he was joyful. But first it must be accepted that the Christians' God who had ruled Europe for centuries had now joined the pagan gods—and 'Nature's God' had joined him. For worse or for better, history had begun again. He put the decisive words of alarm into the mouth of a 'madman' and he was to go mad himself when he paid the price for his full acceptance and expression of what many others were beginning to think was the reality: 'God is dead! God remains dead! And we have killed him! The holiest and mightiest that the world has hitherto possessed has bled to death under our knife!'

Jesus and History

If conscience and virtue, spirit and God-consciousness, were to remain words of truth for intelligent and honest people in the modern age, among those who had inherited Christianity a great deal depended on an estimate of the value of Jesus as the supreme revealer of humanity and divinity. But in the early years of the twentieth century Jesus was being dethroned. He was being placed at a level less than supreme among the great figures of the non-Christian religions and judged in comparison with the modern carriers of lights brighter and more dazzling than the Enlightenment.

While it was still difficult for Christians to respect their nearest neighbours, the Jews and the Muslims, new light seemed to come from the history of religion in the rest of the world. It came from the religions of the east, now being studied as never before. Hindu, Buddhist and Confucian Scriptures became available in translation and their peaceful wisdom, without too much emphasis on God, impressed in comparison with a Christianity which had become over-familiar and entangled in the restless problems of theology and of 'Christian' societies. Emile Durkheim, the founder of modern sociology, specialized in the study of 'the elementary forms of the religious life' (the title of his famous book of 1912), but he suggested that his conclusions applied to the 'higher' religions also. When people worship—when Australian aborigines chant and dance around their clan's totem, for example, or when a beast sacrificed to a god is consumed by those assembled around the altar—in reality the group celebrates and affirms its 'moral unity' (usually in a hierarchy) by honouring this shared symbol as sacred. A contemporary anthropologist, James Frazer, brought together in *The Golden Bough* a much wider range of religious myths and rituals from all over the world (although he did not travel physically) and urged his many readers to remain superior to this curious material. He certainly did, since for him all religious beliefs were in essence attempts to manipulate nature by magic with the aid of the spirits of the dead or of imaginary gods. Socially religion may still have its uses; intellectually it is contemptible. In 1917 a Lutheran theologian, Rudolf Otto, influenced by travels around the world, published a study which was to be translated into English as *The Idea of the Holy*. To him religion was neither merely social nor merely magical; nor was it mainly ethical. It originated in a feeling of awe and dread in the presence of objects or people regarded as 'numinous', as being overpowering in their very strange spiritual energy. Here religion is vindicated but is neither rational nor moral; the mystery is 'tremendous and fascinating' but this is religion within the limits of mystery alone. And in therapy and writing which continued up to his death in 1939 Sigmund Freud attempted to penetrate this mystery by psychoanalysis. To him the 'holy' is concentrated in the image of God as a Father and this image is part of the memory of the human father in childhood. The morality taught by religion is also part of the heritage left by the parental and other early influences. It can support civilization by its restraints but it can also be poisonously neurotic—and often is. In any case all religion rests on an illusion.

Whether or not these conclusions were thought to discredit religion totally (about that writers and readers might disagree), Christianity was being classified among other phenomena. All could be investigated without assuming that high claims made for them were true. After careful research Ernst Troeltsch persuaded many that Christianity was not the 'absolute religion' as Hegel had claimed, not even the 'perfect religion' in the sense of being indisputably the best. He remained a Christian, but this was perhaps because he was a European: as he was to put it in 1923, 'we cannot live without a religion, yet the only religion we can endure is Christianity, for Christianity has grown up with us and has become a part of our very being'. Christianity was 'a manifestation of the Divine Life itself'—but so, for non-Europeans, were other religions. He wrote a thousand pages about the social teachings of the Christian churches and sects, demonstrating their great variety, and as eloquent as anything he wrote was his decision to become a professor of history, no longer of theology, in Berlin in 1915. However, he remained convinced that Christianity had one unique feature: although akin to other religions in many ways, although exhibiting many developments in its history as it encountered societies and compromised with them, yet it was always distinguishable by being related to the Jesus who had lived in history.

Who, then, had Jesus been in historical reality?

This question was asked in a time when a number of Protestant scholars in Germany were studying the Bible without much regard to traditional doctrines but with pleasure in being reassured that at least some of its contents corresponded with the nineteenth century's elevated insights into the moral and spiritual life of Man and God. Thus Julius Wellhausen, the first scholar to unravel the strands gathered in the Bible's first five books, expounded in addition to his arguments about probable facts in the history of that literature a general thesis: that the history of ancient Israel was a history of God's progressive self-revelation, climaxing not in Law or Temple but in Prophecy with its proclamation of God as One and Holy, demanding righteousness. The Old Testament was not the only part of the Christian Bible which could be approached by this scholarly movement: as we have

431

seen, the historically minded Ritschl derived liberal Protestantism from the New Testament.

But in three books published in German between 1901 and 1911, Albert Schweitzer protested. He claimed that Jesus, fully believing that he was the Messiah, had announced that what many hoped for was very soon going to occur: God would miraculously bring to the earth his all-transforming kingdom. When Jesus was dead and that kingdom did not come, Paul began the mysticism about life 'in Christ', and the high doctrines about Christ in eternity, which John's gospel and the Orthodox and Catholic traditions developed. But in the stark original message of Jesus, people had not been invited to become devout or righteous: 'there is for Jesus no ethic of the kingdom of God.' Those predestined by God to belong to his kingdom 'are called to it and show themselves to be called to it'. The parables teach not the growth of the kingdom but its character as God's mysterious action. The apostles are called to be associated with Jesus as rulers in this kingdom, not to spread the teaching of Jesus after his death.

A 'new direction' was given to the life of Jesus when the kingdom failed to appear as quickly as he had promised in Galilee. Finally he went to Jerusalem 'solely in order to die'—or, rather, to suffer, convinced that his suffering would be accepted as a substitute for the tribulations expected to mark the Last Time and would therefore bring about the End. He was convinced that very soon after dying he would be 'supernaturally removed and transformed' and totally vindicated as part of the End (in Greek, the *Parousia*). The agony of his death was increased by the failure of its aim to secure the rapid end of the world and 'the whole history of "Christianity" down to the present day ... is based on the delay of the *Parousia*'. Schweitzer's eloquence showed that he was moved by this reconstruction of a long-buried history. 'The Son of Man lays hold of the wheel of the world to set it moving on that last revolution which was to bring ordinary history to a close. It refuses to turn, and he throws himself upon it. Then it does turn; and crushes him ... The wheel rolls onward, and the mangled body of the one immeasurably great Man, who was strong enough to think of himself as the spiritual ruler of mankind and to bend history to his purpose, is hanging upon it still.'

Yet 'that is his victory and his reign', for Jesus rose from the dead in some sense. Although 'the historical Jesus will be to our time a stranger and enigma', more important is the truth that 'the abiding and eternal in Jesus is absolutely independent of historical knowledge and can only be understood by contact with this spirit which is still at work in the world ... The very strangeness and unconditionedness in which he stands before us makes it easier for individuals to find their own personal standpoint in regard to him ... He comes to us as One unknown, without a name, as of old, by the lake-side, he came to those men who knew him not. He speaks to us the same word: "Follow thou me!" and sets us to the tasks which he has to fulfil for our time. He commands. And to those who obey him . . . he will reveal . . . who he is.'

The middle of Schweitzer's three books was translated into English as *The Quest of the Historical Jesus*. The German title indicated more dully that it was a study of what he had inherited: a series of quests by German scholars 'from Reimarus to Wrede'.

He admired both the courage and the truthfulness of Reimarus who had died in 1768 with his vast manuscript still a secret. That pioneer had grasped the point that the message of Jesus was 'eschatological', to do with the End, and in 1892 Johannes Weiss had made the point again in a little book which Schweitzer accepted and elaborated. In 1835–36 David Friedrich Strauss had shown a courage even greater than that of Reimarus by publishing while still a young man the first biography of Jesus which deserved to be called modern. He concluded that the gospels had been compiled in the second century and were in many places specimens of mythology. In England many were shocked when the novelist George Eliot translated the book. In far-off New England most of his fellow Unitarians were dismayed when Theodore Parker drew from it the conclusion that it should not matter to Christianity if Christ had never existed. Surprised and battered by the hostile reception, and denied an academic career, Strauss temporarily withdrew some of his conclusions but went on to publish a history of the main Christian doctrines, showing how each had begun vaguely, had been refined philosophically and had been destroyed by modern knowledge and thought. And in 1872, soon after Bismarck's triumphs over Austria, Bavaria and France, his book on *The Old Faith and the New* insisted that the new religion needed must exclude all belief in a personal, active God and in an authoritative, risen Jesus; but he was more positive about his faith in the newly resurrected Germany. Since the pioneering courage of Reimarus and Strauss serious study had continued. It had produced solid reasons for thinking that the New Testament's gospels all belonged to the first century, Mark's being the earliest and John's the least historical. Efforts to penetrate through that mixture of history and myth had also continued. Schweitzer could be contemptuous of them (Renan's *Life of Jesus* was 'perfumed with sentimentality') but took more seriously the work of Wilhelm Wrede, then recent. Wrede had not believed that Jesus thought of himself as the Messiah and had not been sure what Jesus really did think or say: historical Christianity, the cult of Jesus as Messiah, had been begun after his death.

Schweitzer's own theory had the great merit of insisting that the historical Jesus was different from the unalarming preacher presented by the Liberal Protestant theologians of the nineteenth century. But it depended on assuming that many passages in the gospels were accurate reporting untouched by any editorial hand and on disowning others (such as the calls for God-consciousness and righteousness) which do not conveniently fit the theory; on claiming to be able to find the secret of Jesus, 'a stranger and an enigma', 'One unknown', as no one else had done before; and on trying to persuade readers that the Jesus who was constantly and credibly presented in the gospels as a man who prayed that the Father's will should be done really thought of himself as the Superman of Nietzsche's hopes, as 'the spiritual ruler of mankind', able to 'bend history to his purpose'. It was then (as before and later) possible for a Jew to think of his death as a martyrdom without believing that after it God would have no alternative to the immediate and complete establishment of his kingdom, but no less than the Liberal Protestants this interpreter of Jesus was influenced by the atmosphere of his time when many hoped to 'bend history' to their own will.

Schweitzer's conclusion stated dramatically that since the kingdom did not come in the way hoped for in some of the recorded sayings of Jesus, Christians need not—indeed, cannot—be guided in their lives by the gospels. Yet the gospels were compiled by men who knew that early hopes had been disappointed—and were, nevertheless, evangelists for a faith in a Lord who (they believed to the point of martyrdom) deserved total allegiance. And so Schweitzer's conclusion raised the question: how Christian is it to follow 'One unknown' from a 'personal standpoint' which is 'absolutely independent of historical knowledge'? His own long and heroic life (he died in 1965) supplies two answers. One is that he indeed followed Jesus by imitating his self-sacrifice. Schweitzer, a man of many talents, sacrificed much in order to be a doctor in tropical Africa: he was a saint. The other answer is that his mature beliefs did not obviously owe a great deal to Jesus.

Having correctly demonstrated that the teaching of Jesus concerned the dawn of the kingdom of God on earth, he threw away that key to an interpretation of Jesus' message to the modern world. In his maturity he never revised his conclusions about the historical Jesus but he did powerfully expound a philosophy of 'reverence for life'. This philosophy arose partly out of his study of Asian religions but more out of his own life and work in his hospital in the African jungle. Human life is essentially tragic and therefore the world ought to be 'negated', yet human beings and all that lives still ought to be treated with 'active love'. A biographer (James Brabazon) has summed up what Schweitzer in the end made of the historically remote One who had commanded him to 'follow'. 'It was precisely because the end of the world was so near, because God was so near, that his ethics were the purest ever preached. There was no need to compromise any more . . . With his limitations as a man Jesus had no choice but to follow the highest that he saw. It was a mirage. With its disappearance

434

his spirit is freed, to be applied anew to all other situations and civilizations.'
But the twentieth century has produced not only strong revivals of non-
Christian religions and moralities but also many post-Christian sceptics who
have been unable to see why as they tackle the challenges of their time they
should follow a man who about two thousand years ago spoke about a
mirage, the illusion of water in the desert of human existence.

The End of Jesus?

The Roman Catholic Church's leadership saw that this disaster might be the
outcome of the debate and responded by forbidding any serious consideration
of the questions.

In 1907 Pius X condemned a long series of propositions associated (at least
in his mind) with the 'modernist' movement. Three years later an anti-
modernist oath was required from all who held teaching positions in the
Church or sought ordination to the priesthood. A 'council of vigilance' was
established in every diocese and a secret society reported to the Vatican
about any modernists who had escaped public exposure. The official position
was clear: the Bible was 'free from every error' and there could be no
opposition between it and the Church's dogmas which so far from changing
'from one meaning to another' stated 'absolute and immutable truth'.

The placing of the Bible in the context of historical reality had been
inaugurated for Catholics by the foundation of the École Biblique in
Jerusalem in the 1890s, but it was now subjected to severe censorship. The
idea that Catholic doctrine had developed in the past provided the theme
for Louis Duchesne's history of the early Church but in 1912 Catholics were
forbidden to read his three volumes. German textbooks of quality suffered
the same fate. The result was that for about half a century almost all Catholic
scholars were cautious in avoiding territory which if explored might lead
them into accusations of heresy. In biblical studies the Old Testament
seemed safer than the New, although even there the watchfulness of the
very conservative Biblical Commission was a deterrent; in church history
praise for the Fathers or for later saints seemed safer than grappling with
questions about the merits of developments; in philosophy it seemed wisest
to accept Leo XIII's instruction in 1879 to learn from the perennial wisdom
of Thomas Aquinas. 'Neo-Thomism' eventually produced a number of
philosophers deserving respect who varied in the degree to which they
merely echoed Aquinas. Their achievement was to develop the insistence
that Christian philosophy seeks the knowledge of what really exists and in
particular the adoration of the real God, 'He who is'. In principle this
philosophical 'realism' could lead to the frank acceptance of all truths, but in

this period most Catholic theologians were not willing to question doctrines which had scarcely changed since the death of Aquinas back in 1274. The propositions set out in textbooks and lectures at an intellectual level lower than that of the philosophers did not equip the clergy to deal with the questions of a generation not prepared to accept a faith simply because it was taught dogmatically. In Italy, for example, there was in this period no shortage of small seminaries where parish priests were supposed to be trained from boyhood, but the anti-modernist measures reduced the number of competent theologians teaching the older students. There were no theologians at all in the state's universities after 1872 or in the Catholic University which emerged in the 1920s. Even in maturity parish priests (and Italy still had 67,000 of them in 1911) were not allowed to write a letter to a newspaper without their bishop's permission. Thus the Catholic Church's continuing strength in its religious life was not matched in its thinking.

The danger of this gap between the Church and the contemporary mind was shown by the books of two priests, Alfred Loisy and George Tyrrell. Neither was a major theologian, but both started with the intention of combining heartfelt loyalty to the Catholic spiritual tradition with an honest reckoning with the German Protestant scholarship which had been communicated in French since the foundation of the *Revue Germanique* in 1858 and which even the English were beginning to discover. Their aim now was 'to substitute the religious for the dogmatic spirit', as Loisy put it. And they had the courage to speak in public.

Loisy was happy to lecture on the Bible in the Institut Catholique in Paris until dismissed in 1893 and until after 1907 he was reluctant to make public the extent of his departure from official Catholic doctrine. In response to a French Protestant thinker (Auguste Sabatier) who had rejected all 'religions of authority' in favour of 'the religion of the spirit', he urged that Christianity must be more than a feeling; it must arise from a revelation and it must result in a command. In response to Harnack he maintained that Christianity was more than a timeless truth about God as Father and about humanity as a spiritual brotherhood of individuals not needing any church: the gospel, understood and obeyed, must produce a distinct community which must carry it to others. But he alarmed the Catholic authorities because in order to feel able to defend the Church he felt compelled to adjust some of its doctrines to modern insights and discoveries. God's revelation, he now said, had not been in clear propositions demanding 'assent'; the truths in it had been expressed in terms of a particular society or psychology; miracles had not been proofs of the truths but 'signs' supporting what believers believed; the Church's doctrines and practices had developed extensively rather than perfectly. The Church should not merely repeat what had been taught by Jesus and the apostles, for they had believed that the kingdom of God would be established miraculously and rapidly. 'Jesus foretold the Kingdom, but it was the Church that came ... enlarging the form of the Gospel.' So Loisy wrote, holding at that stage that the Church had been right to enlarge the original message. However, the church to which he belonged interpreted that defence as an attack.

Tyrrell's books were more passionate and more destructive. From the usual reliance on Aquinas this Anglo-Irish Jesuit moved to an emphasis that all theology could talk about God only by 'analogy' with earthly things, that even if theology were thus limited Jesus and the apostles had never 'declared' it, that the 'medievalism' lingering in the Catholic Church's theology and organization should be allowed to die. Christianity found itself 'at the cross roads' and needed to turn resolutely away from outmoded doctrines and practices if it was to take the road leading to truth and life. As he contemplated the new century, he was moved by the end of the story of the transfiguration of Jesus, when the cloud of glory had gone together with the great men of the past and the disciples saw only their Lord.

Both unusual thinkers were excommunicated. In 1909 Tyrrell had to be buried in an Anglican churchyard and before his death in 1940 Loisy moved to a position far removed from the Catholic Church: the historical Jesus is unknowable and the early Church was influenced more by pagan religions than by its own memories. It remained possible for Catholic intellectuals suspected of modernism to remain more or less within the Church, with the conviction that religious experience is a reality more important than the words of any theology or philosophy and more significant than any scientific or historical fact or uncertainty. Thus in England Baron von Hügel (who was much more than a baron) appealed to the evidence of the saints' mysticism. In France Maurice Blondel defended the 'action' of faith ('to think of God is an action') as making possible the experience of 'the personality of Christ and the Church which prolongs it'. In Spain Miguel de Unamuno similarly defended the decision to believe because it leads to a higher, richer life ('life is the criterion of truth'). But, said Unamuno, reason cannot firmly support that decision, not even to the extent of confirming belief in God, in eternal life after death and in the ultimate value of human suffering—and that is the tragedy of life.

Authority in Catholicism, and the loyalty of Catholics to that authority, still prohibited any more thorough and independent participation in intellectual life and when a 'new theology' began to emerge in the France of the 1930s and 1940s it was condemned by the encyclical *Humani Generis* in 1950. Pius XII did not give the names of the culprits, but measures were taken against the leading French theologians of the time and warnings were given against the trends in science, philosophy and historical studies. In the same year the pope proclaimed a new dogma as being 'based on Sacred

Scripture' and warned that anyone calling it into doubt should 'know that he has fallen away completely from the divine and Catholic faith'. It was the dogma that the Blessed Virgin Mary had been 'assumed body and soul' into heaven. Yet the New Testament was silent about Mary's death and, as we have seen, the belief that she had been exempted from a normal death had not become general in east and west before the ninth century. Making that belief compulsory for Catholics in 1950 was a deliberate signal that the Church could know more than the historians, as it could know more than the scientists.

The degree to which Protestants were involved in modern thought should not be exaggerated although Liberal Protestants in Germany had brought about this modernist crisis in Catholicism. In Germany itself the pressure of the government on the universities and Protestant churches was great and the government preferred to secure the appointment of safe conservatives, not trouble-makers. In Britain most theologians were conservative by German standards and the main currents in church life did not flow out of any intellectual passion: the mild liberalism of the contributors to the book *Lux Mundi* (1889) shocked many men who led the pastoral work of the Church of England and the liberalism which he detected among his fellow Baptists aroused the active wrath of that denomination's most prominent preacher, Charles Spurgeon. To many Protestants as to many Catholics, an impression was being conveyed that modern thought and church life were incompatible activities.

It could have been stated more confidently and more widely to modern Europeans that it positively helped faith to see the life of Jesus in terms of activity within knowable history, not in the terms of Greek philosophy— and to see the death of Jesus in terms of active, self-sacrificial love, not in the setting of a heavenly law court presided over by an angry Judge who demanded the punishment of the guilty human race. Whatever truth might still be found in the old language about the Holy Trinity, at least the unique activity of divine love in Jesus, the great rescue from evil, might be celebrated vigorously and it could be added that the message of the historical Jesus about the dawn of the kingdom of God had been partially fulfilled in the course of a history which, as it continued, admittedly was largely disappointing. Such constructive things about Jesus and the kingdom of God were said; but they were not often said with the spiritual power and intellectual thoroughness which had belonged to the older doctrines and still did belong to them in the hearts and minds of conservative Christians. Many 'liberal' Christians were at least in danger of reducing Christianity to the further improvement of morality in a civilization which God had blessed and which then seemed to be on top of the world. Almost all preachers taught more than that; the great theologians certainly did; but much of the public did not hear the more religious side of the message. This was to be demonstrated in 1914 when much of that civilization was split into two halves in a great war with each other, and in each half there was an undiscriminating enthusiasm in the churches for a national cause which was identified with the cause of God. All European theology, conservative or liberal, was to be shaken to its foundations.

Already in the 1880s the weaknesses of the churches in Europe were becoming apparent. The numbers of regular churchgoers and of the ordained in the most modern countries—in Britain, France and Germany—were beginning to be seriously out of keeping with the growth in the population. The leaders of thought and politics were now for the most part openly distanced from the Christian tradition and colleges and schools were spreading their scepticism. And even a Christian scholar of Schweitzer's intellectual and moral stature was saying that the teaching of Jesus was in no sense a gospel for 'our time'. Europe still appeared to be Christian in many of its habits but for many thinkers it was as if Nietzsche's 'madman' announcing the death of God had been accompanied by another messenger saying persuasively: 'Jesus is dead! Christ is not risen! And we have seen that he is no longer important! The Messiah of the martyrs, the Lord of the saints, the Saviour of the sinful, the Son of Man who was God wearing human flesh like a robe, has been buried by history!'

Europe's Secularization

The English word 'secular' has had a history which says much about Europe's history as a whole. It comes from classical Latin, where *saecularis* meant no more than 'belonging to a considerable period'. It passed through medieval Latin, where it meant that a clergyman was not a monk or friar living under a rule. He was therefore not a 'regular': in a way, a 'secular' priest belonged to an age of the world. After the Reformations 'secular' tended to be used negatively, to mean 'worldly'. Then it could be used more positively, to refer to a transfer from control by the clergy to something more modern. And in the nineteenth century 'secularism' began to be used, to advocate the exclusion of the clergy from teaching and public life. In the twentieth century 'secularization' has often seemed to be an irresistible process which is inseparable from modernity, banishing religion from serious consideration.

If we try to see a pattern in the life of Europe's churches in the period 1870–1950 (apart from the Orthodox) we do not find that usually the decisive factor in secularization was a failure to answer the intellectual challenges. Science or history could be decisive for the more educated, and for others cruder attacks on the Bible spread the impression that it was not

439

'true', but the working class, rural or urban, was not dechristianized mainly by the thoughts of professional thinkers and a profound consideration of the theological debate was not what caused growing numbers in the middle and upper classes to cease to identify themselves with the churches. In a realistic history of Christianity it has to be said that Schleiermacher's or Harnack's influence in Berlin mattered less than these facts: for many years of the nineteenth century there were too few churches and clergy; there were too many feuds occupying conservatives and liberals in the churches at the expense of evangelism; there were too many gaps between urban and industrial life and the churches; there were too many reasons for the workers' attitude that the clergy were in league with the bosses who were exploiting them. Such were the non-academic influences which by the 1880s had made it possible to call Berlin 'the most irreligious city in the world'.

The churches of Europe were divided more obviously than ever before. To the divisions inherited from the age of the Reformations were added modern factors. The government no longer decided the people's religion; the population no longer found it difficult to form and express a great variety of opinions; denominations old or new were more active in competition; after the Enlightenment and the rise of science Christians disputed more loudly and more confusingly about whether the right message to be preached to a newly critical audience was conservative or liberal, fundamentalist or modernist. Christianity had become blatantly a household divided against itself.

This divided religion confronted an age when many governments of countries where throne and altar had been allied became thoroughly hostile. In France, after laws which established a secular system of education (1850–86) the Napoleonic concordat between Church and State was terminated in 1905 and church schools were denied any state subsidy until the 1950s. Portugal and Spain were under anticlerical governments for considerable periods of the nineteenth century. Portugal had such a government for sixteen years from 1910 and in 1931–39 the Spanish republican government encouraged or tolerated the killing of some seven thousand bishops, priests or religious and the destruction of many churches. In Italy the papacy did not reach agreement with the national government until 1929, when it had to accept the Fascists' control of the country. In Germany Bismarck's anti-Catholic *Kulturkampf* in the 1870s was a half-hearted rehearsal for the Nazis' attacks on the churches begun soon after their seizure of power in 1933. Before the end of the 1940s almost the whole of eastern Europe had fallen under Communist rule, which launched a persecution more thorough than the Nazis'.

More quietly other agencies were taking over from the churches what had always been their most popular activities: the education of youth and the care of the sick, the elderly and the destitute. In Scandinavia, for example, the pastor of the parish was no longer responsible for its material welfare— only for the births, marriages and deaths of people who mostly found no need to hear him preach. Other forms of recreation were becoming available: organized sport and paid holidays; much easier travel by the railway, the bicycle or the motor car; entertainment and information through the cheaper newspapers, the wireless and the cinema; escapism or realism through novels. And many voices were being raised against 'respectability' as being life-denying (Ibsen's voice, for example, against Scandinavian middle-class conservatism or the voices of Wells and Shaw in post-Victorian England). There was an open rejection of the churches' teaching that sexual activity ought to be confined to marriage and that within marriage the wife must obey the husband. Chastity had never been Europe's favourite occupation and now the spread of contraceptives was making sex safer and even more enticing. More people were getting married formally but divorce was beginning to be accepted as a way of ending a relationship often one-sided but previously thought to be indissoluble. Upsetting old patterns of subordination, jobs for women outside the home and the fields were gradually accompanied by votes for women in democratic elections. The pattern of life for women was being widened from the old triangle: kitchen, children, church.

Men were now influenced less by sermons than by the mass media, less by visits to a church in order to confess sins than by visits elsewhere to drink, smoke and gossip. In many a French village the *cabaret* was now the centre; on many a street in England the 'pub' attracted the public while the church depended on the older women.

And men could be sociable without using a church if they wanted something more than a drink. Governments gradually made trade unions legal after 1870 and these enlisted masses of the less skilled workers. In Germany the Social Democratic Party which was under Marxist influence offered a vision of a world without capitalism. In Britain socialism was defined and backed by the congress of the trade unions in 1894 as 'the nationalization of the land and of the whole means of production, distribution and exchange'. It was a utopian dream but in many countries socialism and the unions which advocated it could offer an exciting creed and a serious fellowship as an alternative to the churches and chapels which in Britain had trained many of the unions' early leaders. Clergy who in earlier centuries had done something to slow the progress of capitalism by their attacks on usury and greed now found themselves denounced as the stooges of the capitalists. In some countries this tension between 'socialism' and 'religion' could produce ferocious violence against the clergy and their buildings, as it did in Barcelona in 1909 or in much of the rest of Spain in the 1930s. And for the upper working class or the middle classes, the churches were not needed to provide sociability any more than socialism was. In traditionally Catholic countries Freemasonry supplied social occasions, romantic rituals and mutual help replacing the Church; and the conversation at table did not praise the clergy.

In the countryside there was now less need of the churches' traditions to provide means for the practice of magic. As we have seen, the clergy had usually been hostile to the essentially pagan use of Christianity to invoke supernatural help against the dangers and disasters of rural life—but the magic had gone on. It was now being replaced by modernity ('artificial fertilizers make atheists') and the images and rituals provided by the churches seemed to have lost their usefulness. In many areas there was also a decline in such prosperity as the countryside had known, because of imports of cheaper food from overseas, or because farming now used less labour, or simply because of overpopulation (for the population of Europe quadrupled during the nineteenth century). Although those who had money could also have the habit of churchgoing, embittered labourers could be hostile towards the 'snobbish' and 'useless' clergy. Many migrated unwillingly to America. Others moved to the industrial towns and cities of Europe.

In these urban places of human habitation (it might be too generous to call them communities) numbers grew and, with them, the difficulties for churches still predominantly conservative and rural in their ethos. The new buildings provided at challenging expense might be used for worship by the middle classes, particularly in the more elegant suburbs where people were anxious to keep up traditions about family life in conditions as near as possible to the countryside. In the overcrowded poorer quarters of the city or in the grim suburbs churches, if available, might be visited by people needing charity which was distributed or wanting to have their children taught (or at least kept quiet) on Sundays. But the institutions of religion meant little to most of the 'proletariat' (the Marxist term), the 'hands' (as they were called by the capitalists who owned the machines). Life in the slums or the working-class suburbs such as the 'Red Belt' around Paris did not inspire the worship of Nature's God and did not provide much scope for pagan magic. Almost everything in daily experience had been made, it seemed, not by God but by Man.

The resulting humanism might have been at least as proud as the humanism of the Renaissance or the Enlightenment. But from the 1880s onwards it was not, for the artist, musician or writer of 'modernism' had to try to interpret a world of disorder where the spirit of Man could shriek or probe but not control. So the aesthetic life of Europe, when it was not simply nostalgic for the safer world of the past or envious of the simpler world of the 'primitives' of other continents, could be introspective, esoteric, experimental or surrealistic, seeming 'nonsense' to the person in the street and 'decadence' to the person who preferred to remember what Europe had been. The *fin de siècle* mood might be in part a mere rebellion against the dying century, and more basically a rejection of Renaissance optimism and the Enlightenment's rationalism, but if so the next century brought solid reasons for despair.

Many millions of men were conscripted into armies to fight the two great wars of the twentieth century. The armies' chaplains could not help noticing that if it was no longer believed that religious charms could stop bullets, not much religious belief was left. The clergy at home provided prayers for victory or at least for peace, and comfort for mourners, but in the end the wars did not strengthen the Christian faith for most Europeans, because the brutal realities seemed to be beyond control by the God whom the churches were thought to have preached. More than the churches' routine was disturbed, although that disturbance had its damaging effects. The confidence in life—an assurance which religion had both expressed and nourished, going deeper than intellectual doubts or denials—was wrecked for many.

The nineteenth century, although on the whole for Europe an age of peace after 1815, developed a militarism surprising in the strength of its influence. Wars seemed to be successful; at little cost they had conquered large empires overseas for Britain and France and had made Germany an empire in Europe alongside the Austro-Hungarian empire of the Habsburgs. Even churches now marched 'onward' as Christian soldiers. In Britain the efforts led by William Booth, a former Methodist minister, and his wife Catherine, another eloquent preacher, to bring the gospel to the dregs of society achieved success only when in 1878 they changed their 'Christian Mission' into the 'Salvation Army', soon complete with ranks, uniforms and brass bands, with 'citadels' not churches. Through strict discipline, aggressive evangelism and a willingness to enter forbidding territory it now spread from London into many countries. Another successful movement, the Boy Scouts and Girl Guides, under another partnership, Robert and Olave Baden-Powell, was inspired by a war in South Africa. Across Europe large numbers of young men were now surprisingly willing to be conscripted into armies and mobilized for war, and willing even to volunteer; the new bureaucracies were able to organize them, the new industries to supply them with weapons, and the new railways to transport them; the public celebrated their loyalty to monarchies and national ideals; and rivalries between the great powers were bound to provide reasons why they should be sent to fight a war expected to be short and exciting, not much more than a charge by the cavalry followed by the infantry's triumphant march.

Alliances in Europe formed for defensive purposes could easily spark a conflagration. France feared another German attack; Britain feared

Germany's naval and colonial expansion; Russia feared the loss of its position in Eastern Europe. France and Britain therefore struck bargains in their empire-building in Africa and concluded an *entente cordiale* in 1904, and Russia adhered to it three years later. Germany had allied with the Habsburg empire in 1897 because already at that stage it had felt surrounded by enemies. It was thought-provoking that the first world war was waged between these five great powers, all claiming to be defensive, all with a record as centres of Christian civilization much stressed in their imperialism. And in those countries no section of civilian society was more militantly patriotic than the churches. The churches on both sides helped to make it a 'holy' war although in fact the fuse for it was lit when on 28 July 1914 the Austro-Hungarian government declared war against Serbia, rejecting a Serbian offer to negotiate after the Habsburg archduke's murder in Sarajevo. The short-term aim seems to have been to add Serbia to the Habsburg empire, but by 4 August Germany had joined its ally's war and Russia had mobilized its army. Germany had then declared war against Russia and France. Britain now declared it against Germany after the violation of Belgium's neutrality, thought necessary by the German general staff if France was to be invaded. The outcome was to surprise the monarchs and statesmen who had known Europe at peace (the Habsburg emperor had reigned since 1848). In effect the European civilization did its best to commit suicide.

In the second world war the churches were both more aware of the moral dilemmas and more entitled to say that it was morally necessary to use force to stop Hitler. Karl Barth, who could take an independent view as a theologian living in Switzerland, regarded the first of the world wars as a tragedy but the second as a crusade. However, some facts provoked thought, then or later.

The great folly of the Versailles Treaty after the 'war to end war' left another great war waiting to happen. The victors humiliated a nation which acknowledged defeat but not guilt and retained most of its numbers and skills. Heavy 'reparations' demanded by France added to the economic problems when the Weimar republic ought to have been supported for the sake of peace. The collapse of the currency in 1923–24 ruined the salaried class and after a period when recovery was beginning the effects of the collapse of the American economy in 1929–34 bankrupted Germany. Agitators had their chance; since 1920 one of them, Adolf Hitler, had been a leader of the small National Socialist Party formed out of the even smaller Workers' Party. A scapegoat was now needed for the nation's accumulating disasters. The class that had entered and lost the war was still too respectable to serve in this role (a general, Hindenburg, was the country's president); Germany's enemies who had lost the peace were for the time being too distant; but the Jews were conspicuously available and vulnerable within

Germany. So the scene was set for Hitler as the messianic leader, the *Führer*: it was a background of despair.

It is not completely surprising that so many Germans, including Catholics and Protestants, were swept into the enthusiasm which welcomed the national revival under Hitler, caused partly by Nazi policies including the propaganda which restored a people's pride and the rearmament which helped to cure unemployment.

It is not utterly amazing that countries strongly Catholic, and partly for that reason accustomed to strong authorities, were either allied to Hitler or neutral during the war: Italy, Spain, Portugal and Ireland. Most Austrians welcomed their incorporation into the great *Reich* and after the defeat of France many of the French collaborated with their conquerors, particularly but not exclusively under the Vichy regime in the south. Hitler's 'National Socialism' could be excused, if not admired, as part of a worldwide move to increase the powers of national governments in the face of the economic crises: democracy had a lower priority. Nor is it a mystery why before 1939 British and French statesmen persuaded themselves that agreements could be reached, and would be kept, if Hitler was appeased: they dreaded any repetition of the first world war. And the thought was murmured, if not loudly voiced, that at least the Nazis were not Communists. So Hitler was allowed to take over the previously demilitarized Rhineland and, later, Austria and Czechoslovakia, and the German army which could have dethroned that ranting ex-corporal was impressed by his successes.

When it was at last seen that the sheer evil of Nazism must be fought, those who defended 'Christian values' were not always handicapped by Christian morality as they waged modern war. They had to ally with Stalin, a monster not much (if at all) better than Hitler. They felt that they had to destroy large areas of cities in order to break the enemy's morale: the Royal Air Force flew from Britain to devastate some forty German cities. And they felt that they had to demand the enemy's 'unconditional' surrender, a demand which prolonged the war at a very great cost in death and destruction. From this acceptance of total war the acquisition, and the actual or threatened use, of nuclear weapons was not a big step.

Probably more than thirty million Europeans were killed during the two world wars, or died of their direct consequences including the influenza epidemic at the end of the 1910s. In 1918 some, and in 1945 much, of the continent was in ruins. Twice, therefore, Europe became a beggar needing food and essential materials, although in the 1940s (as not in the 1920s) the USA was generous and wise enough to meet some of the immediate needs. And during those great wars some religious beliefs previously important were wounded mortally. When Germany went to war in 1914 its church bells rang out. Before the end of that war many of them had been taken away, to provide the metal needed to increase the slaughter. And in a sense the church bells would never ring again in Europe. No longer was it to be believed so easily that God was completely in control of events, that he had inspired the leaders of Church and State, that he had blessed the division of Europe into nations waving bloodstained flags, that it was in accordance with his will that officers of one class should lead men of another into death.

Violence could be used and praised in causes other than nationalism. It could achieve the victory of the working class or at least of the men who considered themselves the best spokesmen for that class and its best instructors. In 1908 a French engineer, Georges Sorel, published *Reflections on Violence*. He urged social engineering through a general strike by trade unions to seize power, inspired by appropriate 'myths' but not handicapped by any Christian sentiments. Five years previously, in London, the *Bolsheviki* (majority) had persuaded a small meeting of refugees in London that their new Russian Social Democratic Party should have a membership restricted to militants; their majority was two, their leader was known as Lenin. And within forty years of the appearance of Sorel's book the myths of Marxist-Leninism, reinforced by the Red Army and by lesser instruments of violence, had taken over almost the whole of eastern Europe. Violence was to remain essential, as the crushing of the East German, Hungarian and Czech revolts demonstrated. However, another cause of the Communists' temporary triumph was that nationalism, which had emerged from the violence of the first world war as Europe's dominant creed, was now a discredited myth; yet the chaos was such in the 1940s that a strong state seemed more necessary than ever. The pre-war ruling class was now dead or ruined and workers could feel that Communism would be better, or no worse, than the social order which between the wars had conserved poverty and unemployment: so there was some acceptance of the building of a strong state on the basis of Marxist internationalism. The Communists were quick to begin persecutions of religion, another 'ideology' which now seemed ready for burial, and there was some agreement that the churches, whether or not they deserved persecution, did not belong to the future. Many people in the west shared this feeling in the 1940s. In Italy and France the Communists received about a quarter of the vote in elections and were strong (and full of further ambition) in the trade union movement. It seemed possible that in such countries the Communist creed might gather enough adherents to win victory.

One belief that had been encouraged or tolerated by the churches did, however, display its power in the 1940s: European Jewry was almost completely exterminated in the Nazis' 'final solution'. 'Righteous Gentiles' including some bishops did save tens of thousands of Jews, but their efforts were small in comparison with the fact of six million murders, a colossal and cold-blooded crime which would have been impossible without a general indifference to the fate of the victims. The Holocaust became European Christianity's most terrible source of guilt—of course, not because the murderers were pious or because church leaders had been entirely silent about the laws and actions of the Nazis over the years, but because of the undeniable record of anti-Semitism in the churches' teaching over the centuries. Not only ignorant peasants or monks but also eminent theologians and spiritual teachers had attacked the Jews as the 'killers of Christ', as a people now abandoned by God, a race deserving not its envied wealth but revenge for plots and acts against innocent Christians. Not only had the Jews of Rome been forced to live in a ghetto until popes no longer governed that city; not only had Luther allowed himself to shoot inflammatory words at this easy target; but almost everywhere in Europe Jews had been made to seem strange, sinister and repulsive. A long road of disgraceful preaching was one of the paths across the centuries which led to the Nazis' death camps and in the end not Judaism but Christianity was discredited.

Europe had become for a time the economic and cultural centre of the world and considerable numbers of missionaries took the opportunity to spread Christianity as they understood it. They brought considerable benefits to the people (as we shall soon see in this book) but their mission was linked with the expansion of an economic system which was centred on Europe and North America and often based on exploitation. It was also a fact that Christian evangelists, however purely spiritual might be their motives, however critical they were of exploitation, were protected by having the same white skins as the colonial governors. Their association with the colonial system turned out to be one more problem or scandal as that system began to disintegrate; when in India, for example, the Europeans no longer had the will to rule and certainly lacked the means. The 1950s arrived with the leadership of churches in Asia and Africa still largely, and very danger-ously, in white hands. By that stage, however, many Europeans had begun to think that in comparison with themselves the 'natives' who had once been patronized as 'primitive' or 'heathen' had in fact been innocent, for in the corpse-strewn mud of the trenches in the 1910s, or in the bombed ruins of famous cities in the 1940s, Europe could be seen to be near death, physically but also morally. A depressed countryside, dehumanizing con-ditions in the industrial towns, wars which destroyed winners as well as losers, exploitative empires which fell as quickly as they had arisen, anti-Christian persecutions under totalitarian dictatorships of the Right or the Left, the massification of ill-treatment of the Jews—these features of European history, 1870–1950, encouraged no one to believe that this continent had much to teach.

We cannot be surprised that the basic pattern in the European churches' history in this period was one of failure. Their revival, however vigorous, was inadequate. Their courage, however admirable, ended in a defiance of the prevailing trends. For many Europeans some belief in God as Father (or Grandfather) and in Jesus as a teacher of purity and kindness survived, together with the customs of baptizing babies, marriage in church and the religious funeral (the 'rites of passage' at the turning points of life), but that kind of post-Christian attachment to a decaying tradition did not involve faithful membership of a Christian community. Instead it often belonged to the same compartment of the mind as a belief in the power of Fate or the stars. The countryside was changed, the cities populated, the wars fought to a finish, the empires acquired and dismantled, the tyrannies within Europe accepted or rejected, without much regard to the churches. Churches are not much mentioned in the general histories of the period.

If we think that the churches did not entirely deserve to be ignored, we have to be careful in making this comment. Our plea has to be that there were exceptions to the tendency to retreat into irrelevance. In Europe there were many variations between nation and nation, between church and church, between people and people and between time and time; and although the general pattern over the continent was one of inadequate revival in the face of secularization, some of these variations showed the European churches' defiant vitality.

Europe's Churches

The vitality of the churches in the period 1870–1960 was markedly less in Europe than in North America, but the explanation seems to be not that the European churches were pathetically feeble but that the challenges to them were tougher.

When similar challenges surfaced in the America of the 1960s, the historic churches suffered. Before 1960 it was in Europe that the main intellectual battles were fought, the phenomenon of a large urban society based on industry arose, the imperial nationalisms developed modern warfare and many people lost faith in all of the old conventions. Yet we need not conclude that the European peoples became essentially irreligious, for when they crossed the Atlantic they often became more keen on supporting European-style churches and being supported by them. The poor, tired, huddled masses 'yearning to breathe free' were the 'wretched refuse' of Europe (in the words of the poem inscribed on the base of the Statue of Liberty in New York in 1886)—but many of them also liked to breathe the atmosphere of a church. Between 1800 and 1950 almost forty million Europeans migrated to the USA and this was one of the reasons why voluntary church membership as a proportion of the total American population increased almost continuously in that period. After 1870 the Irish, Germans, Italians and Poles made the Roman Catholic Church, already the most numerous religious body in the USA, the most strikingly successful; Catholic numbers grew before 1910 from three and a half to fifteen millions. In the same period immigration from Germany and Scandinavia multiplied the Lutheran numbers fivefold. It is not surprising that the American author of a *History of Christianity* (K. S. Latourette in 1953) called the nineteenth century 'The Great Century', with 'growing repudiation paralleled by abounding vitality and unprecedented expansion'.

Even amid Europe's problems the vitality of the churches was more significant than is granted by a number of historians or sociologists who find the subject of the survival of Christianity distasteful. In Hugh McLeod's fair-minded summary, 'as large numbers were alienated from the official churches religion ceased to provide a focus of social unity, but it became instead a major basis for the distinctive identity of specific communities, classes, factions in a divided society. Many people found their loyalty to their churches intensified in the process', so that paradoxically 'the nineteenth century was both the archetypal period of secularization and a great age of religious revival'. And the same pattern continued into the first half of the twentieth century, although usually without the semi-theatrical excitements of the earlier revivalism (which was often under American influence). That is a cool sociological observation, but we can also observe that as a religion became more private this change did not necessarily mean that it was confined to sentimentality about relatively insignificant areas of life. It could be so personal that it generated a power at the centre of a personality. In a period which was for many a time of many disasters, people could prefer to continue to derive their value from the old-fashioned churches. Others could find their way back—it might be, after a long and painful journey through a waste land—to a religious faith which might be old-fashioned. The churches might have a new appeal as places of escape from the world around them, but it could also be thought that where secular education had failed the salvation offered by the churches could change human hearts and save society from the abyss. And a faith based on the rock-like authority of the Church or the Bible could seem to possess extra advantages in an age which gradually fell under the dominance of authoritarian movements in politics which by being thoroughly evil turned out to be thoroughly destructive.

In this atmosphere of reaction against tendencies which groups or individuals could deeply dislike, there certainly was a religious revival. Old churches were repaired and 'restored' to beauty and many tens of thousands of new churches were built. These churches which by their architecture were reminders of a non-modern dimension to life were made more lively by new hymns, new forms of ritual and spoken worship, and a new vigour in preaching. Confident and famous preachers could be called princes of the pulpit, almost on an American scale. There were great bishops and heroic priests. New activities united the faithful and could be organized more easily thanks to the new railways and postal services. Gas and electricity made evening activities possible. Women were organized, and young people; even men. First cheap printing and then radio brought forth a new quantity of religious talk outside the pulpits. Education spread, often with a religious content, particularly in the very successful Sunday school movement. New charitable work responded to distress and new missionary work to unbelief. There was a new conviction that Christianity ought to inspire behaviour in the world of work and ought to be applied to politics, whether or not this called for specifically Christian trade unions and political parties. It was an age of enterprise in religion no less than in business; an age when the churches marshalled their forces and fought back.

A good deal of solid history was summed up in Hugh McLeod's words that many Europeans 'found their loyalty to their churches intensified', and there was in practice (if not in theological theory) a new definition of what was meant by 'churches'. The contrast drawn by Ernst Troeltsch between 'churches' and 'sects' had already become old-fashioned when he finished his history (stopping in the eighteenth century) in 1912, for the 'church' which operated as a religious society more or less co-extensive with the state, and more or less under the state's control, was being replaced in many European countries by a voluntary body, a 'denomination'. This organization depended on its members' commitment and did all that it could to strengthen and enlarge membership by building up its own network of congregations and associations. And it increasingly became the case that a denomination could not afford to wait for the like-minded to gather in a group which must be small because exclusive, seeking greater purity in doctrine and discipleship. Denominations sought not purity but expansion. To be sure, some Christians could be thoroughly sectarian because spiritually elitist; such were the Exclusive Brethren in England, who found even the Plymouth Brethren with whom they had been united too inclusive. But usually a small congregation chose to belong to a denomination, the development of the English Congregationalists being fairly typical: congregations which had been 'gathered' from a neighbourhood and had insisted on their independence now formed a national 'union' which was termed a 'Free Church' and which was moving into unity with the highly organized Presbyterians. Troeltsch's definition of a 'sect' began: 'lay Christianity, personal achievement in religion and ethics, the radical fellowship of love . . .' But that was how all the Protestant denominations now saw themselves, without being national and therefore state-controlled but also without being exclusive and therefore sectarian.

In Scandinavia, for example, on the surface little changed in the life of the Lutheran national churches. They were still able to count on the membership of almost the whole population and on support through taxes, accepting in return a large amount of control by the state and a decreasing amount of churchgoing. But beneath the surface could be seen signs of denomination-alism: the formation of councils representing the congregations and the growth of dissenting Free Churches. In Scotland, too, the national church seemed secure, specially since most members of the Free Church were willing to return to the Church of Scotland in 1929. But it, too, was becoming a denomination: in the course of the reunion it explicitly renounced state control and increasingly had to react both to the rise of Roman Catholicism (largely through Irish immigration) and to the general decline in churchgoing.

However, the extent of that decline in Europe before 1950 should not be exaggerated. Across Europe Catholics attended Mass in remarkable numbers and for most of those who did not, or who had never been Catholics, what can be called dismissively 'religiosity' or 'superstition', or a 'respectability' based on a form of Christian morality, was not extinct. Two facts may be cited: strange facts, but they belong to a mass of evidence about this continuity with the past. In 1917, while a great war was at its worst, three Portuguese children in Fatima claimed to have seen the Virgin Mary six times: she had told them 'I am the Immaculate Conception' and that they should say their prayers. Very large numbers showed by pilgrimages or otherwise that they believed the children. When a census of the Germans was taken by the Nazi government in 1940, all but 5 per cent professed to be Christians in some sense. In many of the nations which were then the enemies of those Germans a census would probably have produced much the same result, which as Germany's post-war history was to show was not completely without significance. And it was an advantage to Christianity when people alienated from the national churches which the states estab-lished were able to turn to denominations resting on popular support such as Methodism in England, which had approximately doubled in size during the nineteenth century. Moreover, although the Protestantism which could be called fundamentalism was virtually ignored by most Christians in Europe as well as by the secularized, it survived with a strength sufficient to be linked with the later Evangelical revival.

In this period the churches were still heavily involved in the whole life of the community. The countryside was in decline, or at least was changing to the disadvantage of labourers, but many country folk still held to country ways which mixed Christianity with paganism. In the early stages of the industrial revolution work in homes or small factories was the norm and old rural attitudes could more or less continue. Even in the great cities which expanded around the new industries religious loyalties or habits could be retained from rural days and could identify communities as villages or towns within the cities, even without the physical separation of a ghetto. Thus workers moving to jobs in the Ruhr or the Rhineland might keep Catholic or Protestant affiliations and because of immigration Geneva, the city of Calvin, acquired a large Catholic element. In the sixteenth century Calvinism had given an identity to many of the Dutch in the northern provinces of the Netherlands; now that the southern provinces had become Belgium, many industrial workers in that new nation were willing to join Catholic associations and even to go to church. The clergy sympathized with them—and it was also a factor that they wished to show that they were Belgians, not Dutch. But among the Dutch, after 1875 society was organized into 'pillars' defined by loyalties to rival churches and complete with separate educational systems, newspapers and trade unions. Until the 1960s the Catholics formed the most solid pillar but no Catholic leader matched the stature of Abraham Kuyper, a Protestant who founded a university and a political party, edited a newspaper and became prime minister.

In terms of most regular support the most successful denomination in Europe (speaking sociologically) was the Roman Catholic Church; and much of its story can be told in terms of the personalities of the five popes of outstanding ability who governed it in the hundred years after the death of Pius IX in 1878.

The Popes' Church

Leo XIII was shrewder than his predecessor and for that reason had been kept out of Rome as bishop of Perugia after brilliant early years in the Roman colleges. Now aged 68, he was as orthodox as Pius IX but saw that the Church must expand its interests to some extent. He made that the policy for the quarter of a century still left to him. He did what he could to reach agreement with the governments both of Germany and of France. He pleased scientists by establishing an observatory to survey the stars from the Vatican and historians by opening up the Vatican's archives to all researchers; and he acknowledged the existence of new worlds on this nineteenth-century planet. In his encyclical *Rerum Novarum* (1891), while defending private property against the socialists and attacking any idea of a war between classes, he upheld the right of a trade union to seek a just wage, enough for a man to raise a family: in comparison with previous papal announcements, it was a move to the Left. In other encyclicals, while pronouncing Anglican ordinations to be 'utterly null and absolutely void' he urged 'separated' Christians to return to the true Church. And while warning American Catholics not to 'desire a church in America different from that which is in the rest of the world' and not to believe that the Church 'ought to adapt herself somewhat and show some indulgence to modern popular theories and methods', he was energetic in organizing the world-wide expansion of a Rome-centred Catholicism. He established regular hierarchies of bishops in Scotland, North Africa, India and Japan and appointed many bishops to new dioceses (28 in the USA).

In 1903 it was expected that he would be followed in every sense by his Secretary of State (Rampolla) but the emperor of Austria made known his opposition to the choice of a man who was somewhat liberal. The candidate who satisfied that emperor, Pius X, was in many ways a replica of Pius IX and he appointed an even more conservative bishop as Secretary of State, the Spaniard Merry del Val. Over eleven years these two men not only conducted the anti-modernist crusade already mentioned but strengthened the organization and spiritual life of Catholicism as a distinct, disciplined community. The Church's laws and central bureaucracy were reformed; the Gregorian chant was restored as the model of church music after a more operatic period; frequent, even daily, communion was encouraged. This stern pope condemned marriages with Protestants unless there was a binding promise to bring any children up as Catholics. He ended attempts in France to come to terms with the hostile government or with the workers' protests against the harsh conditions in industry. He also ended the co-ordination of the Catholic associations in Italy by the *Opera dei congressi*, fearing a move towards the dreaded socialism. In his view the Church's only duty was to stand firm under its divinely appointed leadership—to stand firm and all would be well. The process to acknowledge him as a saint was completed in 1954.

The reign of Benedict XV, who had been Cardinal Rampolla's chief assistant, was overshadowed, but also given a great opportunity, by the first world war. This pope could only plead for peace against the increasing horror of the war, urging in vain both a German withdrawal from neutral Belgium and the maintenance of neutrality by Italy and the USA. His own neutrality irritated all the belligerents and specially the French but it finally raised the Holy See above the status of an Italian principality which needed to take part in the deadly game of political alliances. Benedict was also constructive as he ended two previous papal policies: the ban on Catholic participation in the politics of the Italian nation and the stern heresy-hunt against modernist theology.

His two successors were scholars equipped with the iron wills which they needed: Pius XI (1922–39) and his Secretary of State who became Pius XII

(1939–58). They pursued a consistent policy. An agreement (a 'concordat') about the rights of the Church must be reached with any willing government. Any condemnation of a government should be conveyed privately unless an emergency made the risk of a public attack worthwhile. Pressure on society as a whole should be mainly through Catholic Action, defined as the subordinate participation by the laity in the apostolic mission of the bishops. In a dangerous world the spiritual life and geographical expansion of the faithful Church must have the priority. Every two years the Church's true strength was demonstrated in an international Eucharistic Congress.

In pursuance of this policy Pius XI solved the 'Roman question' in 1929 by making sacrifices. The Popular party of Catholics, founded ten years previously, was abandoned and its leader, Luigi Sturzo, was exiled. When the Fascists under Mussolini then showed their determination to control the whole of the national life, Catholic associations were regrouped as Catholic Action and restricted to definitely religious activities. In exchange the Church was allowed privileges in the schools and in the marriage law and the Vatican became a tiny state with international contacts.

Much the same attitude was taken to Hitler's rise to power in 1933. The German bishops had previously condemned the Nazis' violence and crude racism, but now a concordat secured (it was hoped) the Church's status in law at the price of encouraging the support of almost all the Catholic third of the population for the nation's renewal under the Nazi banners. The Centre party, which had represented Catholic interests since 1871 and had been very influential in the Weimar republic, was sacrificed, although in elections to the Reichstag the Nazis had won only 288 out of 648 seats. The Nazis soon outwitted and outlawed their remaining rivals, the Social Democrats. When they began their systematic persecution of the Jews in 1938 few Catholics (and few Protestants) raised any loud objection.

In Spain the parties of the Right won only 132 seats in the election of 1936, as compared with the Left's 267, but very foolishly the legitimate government allowed or encouraged violence against the Church, which still had the religious loyalty of many of the people. The senior clergy therefore blessed the rebellion by the army and the Falangists. After the victory of General Franco's 'crusade' with indispensable help from Mussolini and Hitler, the Church rapidly agreed with his regime although a formal concordat was not settled until 1953. Much was sacrificed: the Falangists did not behave like saints. But in return for loyalty to this version of Fascism any tendencies to 'Communism' or 'immorality', Protestantism or atheism, were suppressed very firmly. National Catholicism was the official theology and Franco suppressed any dissent in the Church, as in the public.

These working arrangements with totalitarian regimes had a certain integrity. Piux XI published an indignant rebuke of the Nazis in 1937 and before he died in 1939 was about to deliver a public denunciation of the Italian Fascists. But his motto was 'Christ's peace in Christ's kingdom'. What he implied by that was seen in his pleas that managers and workers should become partners in face of the terrifying economic problems; that a Catholic school should prepare every Catholic child for the difficulties of modern life; that in face of every temptation 'the family that prays together stays together' (as another current slogan promised). His policy was seen also in his insistence that as the Church expanded outside Europe 'native' priests must be ordained to 'govern' it. However, this pope forbade Catholics to share worship or to take part in theological dialogues with other Christians. When the Anglican bishops changed their minds and approved some use of contraceptives in 1930, in Rome the ban was reaffirmed. The Catholic Church was for Pius the only true Church of Christ and its discipline, reaching into the marriage bed, was needed all the more in a world full of confusion and danger. His teaching about society included the influential principle of subsidiarity: 'It is contrary to justice to claim for the higher and wider community what the smaller and subordinate can achieve to a good end.' But he did not believe that it was right to delegate power in the Church.

In effect Pius XII had the same policy. As a diplomat he had been the principal agent in the making of concordats with Nazi Germany and other countries intended to secure the network of Catholic churches, associations and schools; and when war broke out again he continued Benedict's policy of neutrality accompanied by active charitable work. A great, and often debated, moral question about this policy is whether he ought to have spoken out more explicitly against the Nazis' barbarism towards the Jews. It seems probable that his predecessor was preparing to do so when death overtook him, but the new pope was conscious of the danger that the barbarism would be fully unleashed in fury against Catholics while it continued unabated against Jews. He did much to protect Jews where he felt able (in Rome, for example); he was compassionate as well as diplomatic, and he was no coward, since for a time the Nazis occupied Rome and could have occupied the Vatican. It is also a question whether he ought to have denounced more openly the Nazi policy of sending troublesome priests to the concentration camps. But no fair verdict can be reached without noting that Pius believed that Communism was at least as great an enemy as Nazism and that he accepted the probability of a Nazi triumph until 1941, when with great folly Japan declared war by sinking a large part of the American Pacific fleet and in loyalty to his treaty with Japan Hitler more formally declared war on the USA. His mind had been shaped in years when many people in western Europe, including almost everyone in the Vatican, had been somewhat consoled for the evil deeds of Hitler by the thought that Stalin was worse.

After that unexpected turning point he was uneasy (to say the least) about the presence of Stalin in the anti-Nazi alliance, formed when by a further act of great folly Hitler broke his recent treaty with his fellow dictator by invading Russia. At any rate this pope believed that in addition to his frequent calls for peace his greatest contribution was to teach about the Bible and the Church, a voice from eternity and a door into eternity whatever the military or political prospects. He issued wartime and later encyclicals about the Bible as the Word of God, allowing Catholics a somewhat greater freedom in use of historical scholarship, and about the Catholic Church as the Body of Christ. He encouraged translations of the Latin for use by the laity and allowed Mass in the evening to make corporate worship more accessible, relaxing the previous rule about fasting before communion. During the Mass the Bible readings could be in the local language. In these still restricted ways he blessed the 'liturgical' renewal which had begun many years previously in Benedictine abbeys—in Solesmes in France and Maria Laach in Germany.

After the war he talked to innumerable groups of pilgrims about the moral principles which ought to guide their daily work and he used radio broadcasts to reach a much wider audience. His main political interest was now in spiritual resistance to Communism, believing that in eastern Europe neither atheism nor Russian rule would be permanent, and his wholehearted sympathy was with the archbishops who accepted imprisonment or worse: Beran in Czechoslovakia, Mindszenty in Hungary, Stepinac in Croatia, Wyszynski in Poland. In Italy he excommunicated anyone willing to help the Communists. As he grew older he never seemed to need to consult anyone or to need any collaborator; he refused to appoint a Secretary of State. But it was reported that visions assured him of divine approval of his inflexible faith and benevolent dictatorship. In particular it was said that his policy was influenced by his belief that when the Virgin Mary had appeared in Fatima in 1917 she had promised that Russia, then about to be taken over by Communism, would be converted back to Christ in answer to prayer. In 1942 he consecrated a war-torn world to her 'immaculate heart' and in 1950, in his most solemn act, he proclaimed the dogma that she had been 'assumed' into the glory of heaven. The story about the influence of Fatima may have been no more than a rumour, but it says much about him that the rumour spread.

He was uneasy in his relationships with the laymen who led the Christian Democratic parties in these post-war years, regretting that they needed to compromise by allying with parties of the Left. Yet both Pius XI and Pius XII did what they thought right to protect and strengthen Catholicism in an evil time, and so conserved a strength which was now to show itself in ways they had not expected, in country after country.

Catholics in Modern Europe

Centuries of division under foreign rulers and of stagnation under a reactionary Church had placed immense difficulties in the way of the ambition of the Italian state to become modern. In the south the countryside remained almost medieval and it seemed that the only solution to its problems was massive emigration to the USA and Argentina. In the north industrialization was slow and harsh. Resources were lacking for entry into the competition for colonial empires, although Italy tried. Alliances seemed necessary with other European nations but the alliances with France in the first world war and with Germany in the second both proved disastrous. The turning to the 'action' promised by Mussolini ('Believe! Obey! Fight!') ended in humiliation and anarchy. Even when the post-war reconstruction by successive coalition governments dominated by the Christian Democrats included great economic progress in the north, problems remained. In comparison with other countries the Italians did not yet constitute a nation. The Mafia controlled much local life by violence and corruption. The control of much local government by the Communists was more beneficial, but violent anarchists of the Left made their presence felt. There was a general avoidance of paying taxes to 'the thieves in Rome'. And many of the politicians were thieves, not least those who were meant to distribute large subsidies from the north to the south.

As a result of all this, Italy was scarcely an advertisement for the teachings about society coming from a Vatican which was widely blamed for its own long contribution to the difficulty of uniting Italians. Nor did history make Italy (or Rome itself) a model to the world in Catholic life. When millions of Italian immigrants crossed the Atlantic they shocked the Americans by seeming in general irreligious and immoral and it took all the vitality of American church life to change them. But it is also significant that Americans objected to the noisy exuberance of the immigrants' celebration of the festivals of saints familiar in Italian villages. Catholicism was by far the largest continuing factor in such identity as Italians possessed, and in some ways the society established by the Christian Democrats as the 1940s ended has remained morally impressive—more impressive than the politicians altogether desired. It persuaded the Communists to become the Democratic Party of the Left, rejecting the path of violence which had been taken by the Red Brigades in the 1970s. It also persuaded the Christian Democrats to become the Popular party when they had been crushed in the election of 1994. When they re-entered a coalition government in 1996 it was in alliance with the ex-Communists and in the hope that they were being forgiven for the many cases of corruption proved against them. And at the cost of their own lives police and lawyers fought the Mafia.

Before Napoleon ended the Holy Roman empire and the regime of the prince-bishops it was assumed that the power of the Catholic Church in Germany rested on the power of Catholic princes. In fact the changes which began the nineteenth century began also a new closeness between the clergy and the Catholic laity, with a new liveliness in German Catholic theology. The effects were demonstrated when in 1871 Bismarck took advantage of criticisms of the First Vatican Council to launch his *Kulturkampf* or patriotic campaign against a church said to be controlled by a dictatorial pope and by the sinister Jesuits. Actually what aroused his wrath was the clergy's sympathy with the complaints of lay Catholics about the dictatorial Prussian state, which discriminated against them. All the clergy were made to take a special oath of loyalty to the state; their function as registrars of births, marriages and deaths was ended; all religious orders except those caring for the sick were dissolved; all subsidies of the Church by the state ceased. But from 1880 onwards all this legislation was dismantled. The masters of the new German empire saw that instead of making martyrs and arousing demonstrations and pilgrimages it would be shrewder to rely on the Catholics' patriotism to support their policies even if these involved great wars—and their hope was for the most part fulfilled in 1914 and 1939. The Catholic religion of the heart could not be ended by any *Kulturkampf*. Indeed, it survived Hitler and it survived its compromises with Hitler.

The western half of Germany was not occupied by the Red Army in 1945 although it was devastated and full of refugees. Half its population belonged in some sense to the Catholic Church which was the country's strongest surviving organization. The opportunity was seized to expand church life (with the financial help which the state collected from all who did not opt out) and to contribute substantially to the reconstruction of the nation when this was allowed and subsidized by the victorious allies.

Despite the conservatism of many churchmen, the contribution was made in a spirit of co-operation with the Protestants: the Christian Democrats in political power deliberately included them, as did the Christian Social Union of Bavaria. The background of Konrad Adenauer, the dominant politician, was the Rhineland, where Catholicism was more 'open' in spirit than it was in Bavaria. And the agreed ideology of the new nation—an ideology as definite as Communism, and taught as part of religious education in all schools—was co-operation between the classes in a democracy. The relationship between the two main political parties illustrated and strengthened this basic consensus: the Social Democrats, supported by many Protestants, differed from the Christian Democrats about the extent and the right purposes of public expenditure, but did not differ radically. Previously the official Catholic teaching had not blessed democracy and therefore its talk of co-operation had been used by the Fascists to endorse the 'corporate state' where employers and workers co-operated under the direction of a strong government which favoured the employers. Now the co-operation formed part of a drive to make Germany strong industrially in the context of a renunciation of war (and even defensive rearmament as part of membership of NATO was to be highly controversial). The power of the state was also weakened by a division into regions: this was the 'Federal Republic'. Germany, it was hoped with deep feeling, would show the world not that 'might is right' but that democracy brings prosperity. There was an economic miracle—but also a psychological miracle.

In France the Third Republic's hostility to the Catholic clergy presented a challenge far more serious than Bismarck's brief *Kulturkampf*. The 'empire' of Louis Napoleon which favoured the Church had ended in defeat by Prussia. The violence of the Commune in Paris, which shot the archbishop and some fifty priests, led to a reaction but most of the Catholics were frozen in nostalgia for the monarchy until that incompetently led cause was defeated finally in the election of 1876. The most effective political expression of the Catholic Right was to be Action Française, led by Charles Maurras from 1899. He, however, was not Catholic in religious belief or in social philosophy and eventually, in 1929, Catholics were forbidden by Pius XI to support a movement which was by now virtually Fascist. A great bishop who saw the need for reconciliation with the republic was Cardinal Lavigerie, but he was active mainly as the leader of French missionary work in Africa. This work was connected with the spread of the French colonial empire and thus with the French army, whose officer class was full of conservative Catholics.

In the 1890s the army was exposed as having perpetrated a gross injustice against an alleged spy, the Jewish Captain Dreyfus, in a sensation which once again demonstrated the bitter hostility between the 'two Frances'. Thus the twentieth century opened with the total separation between Church and State (1905): the religious orders were expelled, subsidies to the Church were ended, church buildings had to be leased from the state by 'cultural associations' which Catholics refused to join. Yet this was not the end of Catholic history in France. The Church found ways of working unofficially under this system and of manifesting its patriotism when war came: the clergy and the religious orders were willing to be conscripted and some 4,500 were killed in action. After that war the atmosphere so far improved that diplomatic relations were resumed between the republic and the Vatican and Catholics were allowed to legalize their use of the churches. In 1923 the state allowed the return of the Jesuits.

More significant than any legal arrangement was the rebirth of French Catholic life. The days were gone when aristocratic bishops resisted control by Rome: now most of the bishops came from the peasant class, as did most of the still numerous priests. The *curé* (for forty years) of the remote village of Ars, Jean-Baptiste Marie Vianney, became famous for his holy simplicity. So did Thérèse Martin, the saintly young nun of Lisieux (one of five sisters who became nuns), and Charles de Foucauld, the hermit praying until killed in North Africa. Young women saw visions of the Virgin, most famously at Lourdes in 1858. Numbers in the religious orders grew, particularly in the orders of women active in educational or charitable work. Churchgoing was still weak in a band of regions which stretched from the south west through central France to the north east, but a popular religion arose which was not based on pagan magic or on the fear that hell might punish any who disobeyed the clergy of the Catholic Reformation: the new spirit was declared in love for Jesus (often the Jesus of the Sacred Heart), for his mother (revealing herself to the devoutly simple) and for Mother Church (specially as seen in the good works of the 'sisters'). And this certainly sentimental revival of popular Catholicism was accompanied by a tough intellectual revival. The novelist Mauriac attacked *bourgeois* superficiality; in a great novel Bernanos presented the discovery of 'grace everywhere' by a country priest who seemed to stand alone; in modern art Rouault depicted the suffering Christ; part of her *Story of a Soul* suppressed at the time of that book's first appearance but published many years after her death showed that Thérèse Martin had not been the mindless 'little flower' of her popular image. The intelligent *bourgeois* who in the nineteenth century had usually been anticlerical were now less so. A movement of 'Young Christian Workers' trained them not to be obedient but to 'see, judge, act'. In the 1930s France was so divided between Right and Left that a civil war might have broken out and produced a Fascist victory with a Catholic colouring as in Italy, Germany or Spain, but the anti-Fascist element was more vocal here than elsewhere, with lay Catholic spokesmen of the stature of Maritain and Mounier.

In the 1940s the rival strength of a Catholicism definitely of the Right was seen in the Vichy regime which came to terms with the Nazis, but in the end the Catholic statesman who won was Charles de Gaulle—and although he made no secret of his characteristically stubborn religion he became the greatest figure in the Fourth and Fifth Republics, which had lost interest in the battle between State and Church. In the post-war years the Church felt free to concentrate on a mission to a nation which by now was in large part not so much hostile to Catholicism as out of touch with it: no less than Africa was France a *pays de mission*. Catholic scholars made an unexpectedly sympathetic approach to what Henri de Lubac's book called *The Drama of Atheist Humanism* in order to appreciate the radical seriousness behind some of the modern rejection of the old images of God. Some Catholic priests took manual jobs, and took part in the agitations of ordinary trade unions alongside Communists, in order to get close to the alienated working class. In the 1950s Pius XII condemned these open-minded scholars and the courageous worker-priests, but in less dramatic forms the mission to France continued. In 1984 when politicians seemed to be about to reduce the state's support of church schools, protesters' demonstrations warned them against reviving the old struggle.

In Ireland rebellion against the British had never been entirely blessed by the bishops, who had wisely concentrated on a policy with a far greater chance of success: building up the parish churches (with their schools) as symbols and centres of the Irish culture. Paul Cullen, Archbishop of Dublin 1850–78, was the leader of this victory. When independence was won after the civil war in the 1920s the 'free state' made it very clear that its legislation would reflect the fact that Catholicism was the faith of the majority of the people. This cultural identity was made firm in the constitution of the republic in 1937. Yet from the 1960s the old style of Catholicism became modernized, to the extent that in the 1990s divorces and some abortions were allowed as they already had been in the other Catholic countries of Europe. The work of the Catholic Church among the Irish migrating to Britain (in a small flood in order to escape famine in the 1840s) has been another illustration of the truth of Hugh McLeod's observation that a church may provide the basis for the distinctive identity of a specific community. The centre of the exiled Irish often became the church with its school, built by 'the pennies of the poor'. A regular system of bishops could be erected (in England in 1850); the bishops could lead the parish priests in hard pastoral work; even the monks had to be busy in parishes and schools. Gradually English attitudes became friendly—and remained on the whole friendly even when violence erupted again in Ireland's north-east corner, Ulster, using Catholic and Protestant labels. In England the conversions of prominent writers strengthened the standing of the Catholic community, which also kept a working-class membership more successfully than any other British church. Its values were undeniably democratic and in the 1990s it was to have about as many at regular worship as did the still state-established Church of England.

Ireland has not been the only example of a European nation asserting its cultural identity through Catholic churchgoing. Other examples include Lithuania, Slovakia, Croatia, Poland and Spain. In Poland as in Ireland the papacy had not encouraged rebellions, but when the frontiers existing before the partition of 1793 were restored (approximately) in 1919, and the Communists were repulsed from Warsaw, the Catholic element in the population, already two-thirds, began to grow. It so increased that when the nation was again destroyed twenty years later the Church was able to be the great symbol of Polish nationhood and spirituality during twenty years of persecution by Nazis and Communists.

Protestants in Modern Europe

It is even harder to sum up the story of Europe's Protestants in Europe, 1870–1950. They had no popes or other undisputed leaders. They were divided more sharply than the Catholics into conservatives and liberals. Their churchgoing, being more clearly optional, was less impressive statistically. Their situations varied between the great national churches of England, Scotland and Scandinavia (which were, however, decreasingly attended by their nations) and the faithful few gathered in a chapel. Yet over much of this period the activity of the Protestants bore some comparison with the Catholic Church.

Indeed, in the Church of England the most vocal movement stressed that Anglicanism was Catholic. Many (not all) of these Anglo-Catholics modelled on Roman standards their worship, doctrine and practices including the centrality of the Mass and an emphasis on the confession of sins to a priest. Such 'ritualism' produced many tensions in a nation still essentially Protestant. It took time for this church to admit that its Book of Common Prayer needed revision and enrichment and twice in the 1920s the House of Commons vetoed the church's proposals. Less controversial was the work done by Anglo-Catholic priests in poor parishes. But this 'High Church' movement remained somewhat exotic even when there were no strong 'No Popery!' feelings against it—as there often were.

The form of religion which did much more to shape the national character resulted from the influence of the Evangelical movement. This had made progress within the Church of England along lines parallel with the advance of Methodism. Its appeal was always and simply to the Bible: Anglican Evangelicals collaborated with other Protestants in the formation of the British and Foreign Bible Society in 1804 and the distribution of the printed Scriptures to a people becoming more literate was matched by preaching which the scornful could call 'Bible-thumping'. The theology of these Evangelicals was in important ways Calvinist, but usually without Calvinism's emphasis on the predestination of few to be saved: what was sought was the conversion and salvation of many, or at least their rescue from material misery or unchristian behaviour, and the kingdom of God on earth seemed a real possibility. Evangelicals battled for temperance in a nation of drunkards and for pity in a nation dedicated to profit. Two of its great figures were laymen active in Parliament. William Wilberforce was more than anyone else the leader of the agitation which so far as Britain was concerned ended first the slave trade (1808) and then slavery (1833) despite the large profits which those iniquities had brought to some of the British. Then Lord Shaftesbury successfully campaigned for Factory Acts which did something to improve working conditions within Britain, and he was one of the Evangelicals involved in a multitude of other philanthropic crusades. The results visible by 1870 were described by a general (not ecclesiastical) historian, Robert Ensor: 'No one will ever understand Victorian England who does not appreciate that among highly civilized countries . . . it was one of the most religious that the world has known. Moreover its particular type of Christianity laid a peculiarly direct emphasis on conduct; for, though it recognized both grace and faith as essential to salvation, it was in practice also very largely a doctrine of salvation by works. This type . . . may be called, using the term in its broad sense, Evangelicalism.' And alongside these Anglo-Catholics and Evangelicals were many Anglicans whose theology, where it existed, was 'Broad Church' and whose interpretation of the Bible and of Christianity gave almost all the emphasis to morality.

Whether under High Church, Evangelical or Broad Church leadership the Church of England attempted to become again what its name suggested, but its internal divisions were not its only problem. The Protestant Nonconformists—Methodists, Baptists and Congregationalists—recruited so vigorously that by 1900 they had become almost equal in numbers to the communicants at Easter in the parish churches (the best test of active or semi-active Anglican membership). Their message could be as Evangelical as anything preached in the parish church, or more so—or, as life and faith became less intense, it could become 'Broad' or 'Liberal' theology. Their appeal was to the lower ranges of the middle classes and the upper range of the working class; their worship was less formal; although the sermon was the centre, their activities included much fellowship or entertainment; their support went to the Liberal party which emerged in the 1850s, governed for a number of years and won its last electoral triumph in 1906. They sought the disestablishment of the Church of England and against a continuous resistance achieved a large reduction in the Anglican privileges including the disestablishment of the semi-colonial dioceses in Ireland and Wales. But even less than the Church of England were they able to expand at a rate which equalled the growth in population. They could not afford to run a network of schools, so that they preferred the state's own system set up in 1870. They objected to state subsidies for the many church schools—in vain. They could not provide attractions to rival those developing outside the churches. Their worship was not centred on that unique corporate act, the Eucharist. If their message was not Evangelical in a conservative and revivalist sense, people might not be sufficiently attracted by the prospect of hymns with sermons or prayers by the minister; and if they were conservatively Evangelical, so were many Anglican churches. They could not supply leadership for the Liberal party: its greatest peacetime leader (Gladstone) was a committed Anglican and its wartime prime minister (Lloyd George) was cynically insincere as he collected votes from the 'Nonconformist conscience'. And the war of 1914 exposed that conscience's lack of a coherent political philosophy. Its preachers, previously almost all pacifists, almost all became patriots almost overnight. After that war the story of the 'Free Churches' (now so called) was a story of almost continuous numerical decline.

The decline of the Church of England was real (in a larger population the number of its clergy halved, 1900–90) but was masked by its continuing connection with the state and with millions of baptized half-members. For most of the period 1870–1945 it could be called 'the Conservative party at prayer'. Before the second world war England was the centre of an empire which covered a quarter of the land-surface of the globe and ruled a quarter of its inhabitants; and throughout the colonial system the governors tended to be Anglicans willing to go to church although often the missionaries who were closer to the 'natives' kept their distance from the government. During the war an exceptionally able and popular archbishop, William Temple, was at the centre of the national spirit—a determination to continue a fight which did not appear to have many military chances and an optimism about the moral content of post-war reconstruction. Temple sympathized with the Labour party, then still socialist in its aspirations, but his teaching was much more than political. A philosopher able to write confidently about *Nature, Man and God* in 1934, he was also a devotional writer whose Christ-centred religion was able to survive the shocks of the 1940s. And although it was not to have another leader of his stature after his death in 1944 a diminished Church of England proved able to survive both the end of this empire and the decline of Christian Socialist idealism. When Labour repeated its electoral triumph of 1945 in 1997, its leader was a Christian without socialism.

As we have noted, German Protestantism was closely bound up with the German national cause which seemed set to dominate Europe after the victories over Austria and France in 1866–70. In 1878 the Evangelical Church Council prohibited any preaching against decisions by the government: the answers to social discontent made by Bismarck's legislation combining welfare with discipline ought to be enough. Protestants might be conservatives or liberals in theology but all were patriots. A profound crisis was therefore created by the Bismarckian empire's total defeat in 1918. During the Weimar Republic and under Hitler the Protestants had the unwelcome experience of being marginalized in comparison with the days before 1914. And in the 1940s the Protestants who were very much the majority in East Germany, at least nominally, went straight from the Nazi regime to persecution by the Communists.

It became essential to find new ground on which Protestantism could stand and this turned out to be the old ground of the Bible, however greatly interpretations of it might differ. In the 1920s Paul Tillich and others tried to find a new basis for a defeated, impoverished and demoralized nation in 'Religious Socialism' but this movement never attracted the Lutheran conservatives and foundered when National Socialism (Nazism) presented itself as a panacea. There was an inter-war revival in the study of Luther himself: it bore fruit not only in a reappraisal of that giant of the past but also in two influential books by Swedish Lutheran bishops, Anders Nygren and Gustaf Aulén, the one distinguishing between divine and human loves, the other reviving the interpretation of the Atonement as Christ's victory over demonic evil. But in the realm of politics this 'Luther renaissance' mainly served to show that the great Reformer had seen the state as God's 'ordinance' alongside a church of believers.

Pride in Luther as a great German was thought to justify the response of the 'German Christians' to the advent of a national saviour, Hitler. His publicized programme included 'positive Christianity' and the response of *Hosanna* was led by the Reichsbischof Müller, a former army chaplain and an ardent Nazi. The state's decree that Christians of Jewish descent must not be allowed to mix with 'Aryans' in the congregation of believers was quite widely accepted as part of the purification of national life and for the time being Hitler gave the impression of being a German Christian himself. The soul of German Protestantism was then saved by the 'Emergency League' which rallied a third of the clergy and by the Barmen Declaration of the synod of the 'Confessing Church' in 1934, beginning: 'Jesus Christ, as witnessed to us in Holy Scripture, is the one Word of God which we have to hear, trust and obey in life and in death.' The Church should not be guided by 'the ideological or political views which happen to have the upper hand at the moment'. It was intended to give such leadership to Protestants where possible and to form rival administrations in any churches still controlled by the German Christians. The Nazis, however, drove the Confessing Church underground, imprisoning its chief spokesman, Martin Niemöller, and exiling its chief theologian, Karl Barth. It was clearly their intention, after the total victory which they expected, to pursue the policy which Martin Bormann phrased in a moment of honesty in 1941: 'The influence of the churches must be completely eliminated.' Meanwhile Hitler, worried or bored by the controversies, abandoned his patronage of the German Christians. He also modified his plan for widespread euthanasia after mainly Catholic protests. His real attitude to the churches may be expressed in one word, contempt, but had their opposition been more general and more threatening their treatment by the Nazis would, no doubt, have been even tougher than it was when the honeymoon of 1933 was over. Protestants were in fact divided. Most were essentially patriotic although uneasy. Some kept alive the spirit of the Barmen Declaration, although at great personal risk or cost. Some of the most respected opponents of the Nazis, including the theologian Dietrich Bonhoeffer and some even in the higher ranks of the armed forces, now felt driven by conscience into planning the assassination of the tyrant in the hope that peace could then be negotiated. The allies at war with them refused to negotiate in any way which offered hope to any Germans; under the Nazis' systematic tyranny no revolution could be planned; the murder plot failed; the conspirators were hanged.

After the war the Evangelical Church in Germany (combining Lutheran, Calvinist and United churches) refused to be led by radicals such as Niemöller. The emergency had not permanently buried the differences between the radicals, the conservatives and the moderates and it was found that the future would not be so 'religionless' or churchless as Bonhoeffer had expected while in a Nazi prison. Not even the brave confession of guilt which the Council of the Evangelical Church made public in Stuttgart in October 1945 healed the wounds. Most Protestants (in this, like most Catholics) were right to regret that they had not 'borne testimony with greater courage, prayed more conscientiously, believed more joyously and loved more ardently' but many Germans believed that the confession went too far along the road of humiliation and repentance. People in other countries might feel that it did not go far enough. Yet the courage of Christians who had resisted the Nazis, and had paid the price, had been greater than the courage of any other section of German society; university professors, for example, had been far less bold. That record of courage now entitled Protestants to stand alongside Catholics in building a new nation. For example, from 1949 their annual *Kirchentag* was a very large gathering of people eager to hear about, and to discuss, the Bible, Germany and a range of other subjects. 'This is the end', said Bonhoeffer as he was taken from other prisoners to be hanged; 'for me, the beginning of life.' And for Germany.

Signs of Hope

After the first world war there was an outburst of internationalist and pacifist idealism in the churches. Its focus was in the Geneva-based League of Nations, which turned out to be largely ineffective. The cruel truth seems to be that this idealism assisted the coming of a new war because a theoretical policy of disarmament was not enforced and left the field open to aggressors: the nations which belonged to the League (as the most powerful of them, the USA, did not) allowed the Nazis to march into the demilitarized

Rhineland and the Japanese into Manchuria. After the second world war Christians were among the Europeans resolved to be more practical about unity. During that war people of all nations, including some Germans, had been united in resisting the Nazis: that was the origin of the 'United Nations', now to be more strongly organized than the old League. Catholics and Protestants had resisted—and, although they were not supposed to say the Lord's Prayer together, had been shot shoulder to shoulder. Now it was seen that the atomic bombs which had in fact been dropped by Americans on Japanese could have been developed in time for use in Europe, and it was also seen that nuclear weapons stored in Europe could not be disinvented. There could be no escape from the moral obligation laid on Europeans to build 'Europe' and therefore peace, and to build Christian unity as an example to the world. The futile dreams of many past prophets must come true.

In 1949 the Council of Europe began to function as a meeting place for the discussion of social and cultural issues. Next year it issued the European Convention on Human Rights, a document which was more than words for it became the basis on which appeals could be made by aggrieved individuals against governments which would have to listen humbly to decisions by an international commission or, in major cases, by a court of judges. 'Human rights' constituted a social philosophy which Christians and non-believers could endorse in opposition to Communism as well as Fascism, and Christians could produce their own reasons for believing that individuals, however humble, had such rights. Moreover, it was thought to be a human right to be protected against sickness, harsh employment, unemployment and the worst problems of old age; and there governments must act. But the Council of Europe had few powers or resources and it was seen—at least by some, excluding insular Britain, neutral Scandinavia, eastern Europe and the southern countries still under Fascism—that the peoples needed an economic organization which would have political consequences.

The Coal and Steel Community was therefore formed in 1952 in order to make sure that France and Germany, now recovering, would never have the means to wage modern war against each other. In Rome in 1957 that experiment developed into the European Economic Community covering six nations. In cold reality this was an agreement to allow French agriculture to export to its neighbours in return for free trade (within this 'common market') which would benefit the German and Italian industries, but the new community was an unprecedented form of association explicitly designed to 'lay the foundations of an ever-closer union among the peoples of Europe' by offering stability and prosperity. Its founders included men whose connections with the churches were few or none, most prominently the French bureaucrat Jean Monnet. But they also included thoughtful

Catholic politicians of the new sort: Schumann of France, Adenauer of Germany, de Gasperi of Italy, with Belgians delighted that Brussels was to be the seat of the new administration which might one day grow into the government of the United States of Europe. The new start, initially opposed by socialists, would have been impossible without the Christian Democrats.

In Amsterdam in 1948 the World Council of Churches was inaugurated. It is significant that the setting was not an American city: many Americans encouraged the council but its central problems were perceived as lying in Europe. Its first general secretary was a Dutchman, Wilhelm Visser 't Hooft, and most of his collaborators were Europeans. The council did not include any Roman Catholics but some members of that church were more sympathetic than the popes with the progress of this 'ecumenical' movement.

Its history went back to the World Missionary Conference in Edinburgh in 1910. That conference had chiefly been aware of the problems or scandals caused by the lack of unity between Protestant missionaries in non-Christian countries where the disputes between the sixteenth-century Reformations were largely irrelevant. 'Give us friends', one of the few Asians present had pleaded—and the chief act of friendship which the new churches needed was, they said, more agreement about the simple gospel in the Europe from which too many of the missionaries arrived with too much theological baggage. This plea for unity was favoured by American Protestants who were accustomed to collaboration in good causes such as 'foreign missions' without much regard to denominational divisions, but the presence in Edinburgh of a few Anglicans who did not regard themselves as simply Protestant had been a reminder that Christian unity, if it ever proved possible, ought to include the Catholic or Orthodox majority of Christians, whose churches regarded Protestant missions as divisive intrusions. And instead of ending in a cloud of words, this conference had set up a 'continuing committee' which developed into the International Missionary Council.

The great war had come and had demonstrated not only the need for the missionaries of one nation to care for the missionaries and converts of another (for example, the British and the French took over territories where Germans had been at work) but also the need for a more united and powerful approach to social problems such as war itself. During the war the Swedish archbishop Nathan Söderblom had pleaded for peace from his neutral base. After 1918 he had been the key figure in the 'Life and Work' movement which had attempted to mobilize Christian support for the ideals of the League of Nations, for 'the need of the world is so burning that we cannot bear to wait for the fulfilment of the great hope of a reunited Christianity'. In the 1930s this activist movement had begun to merge with the more scholarly 'Faith and Order' movement initiated by Anglicans in the USA who, believing that their denomination was a 'bridge church' between

Catholics, Orthodox and Protestants, hoped that Christians would not remain so divided and ignorant of each other as they then were. An international conference of Anglican bishops in 1920 had appealed for Christian unity, reviving the vision seen in Edinburgh ten years before. There had been few practical results, but at least in the 1920s representatives of the Lutheran and Reformed churches of the world had begun to meet as 'federations' and in 1927 the first World Conference on Faith and Order had met in Lausanne. When further conferences met in 1937 what was now seen increasingly as the single ecumenical movement had acquired the unofficial slogan 'Let the Church be the Church!', meaning that the world's crisis must be met by the churches' united message and visible example. It would be wrong, even suicidal, to be content with an isolated existence as a denomination not interested in evangelism or in the problems of society. The advent of Hitler had added an urgency to a movement which otherwise might have got stuck in the traditional disagreements.

In wartime, 'the World Council of Churches in process of formation' had done what it could to maintain communications. Hopes of reunion had been encouraged by the formation of the united Church of South India in 1947 (although it did not include Roman Catholics). Now the council had been formed and those sent by their churches to support it had announced that 'we intend to stay together'. It was a time of renewed confidence, specially in the Student Christian Movement which in many countries was bringing students together from different denominations; the visions and friendships of students could be remembered when they became church leaders. But what was now meant by 'together' was far from clear. No convincing model of unity between the churches was available: the Orthodox who had begun to participate had ideas very different from those of the Protestants, and the Roman Catholic Church held aloof. Protestant denominations co-operated in many causes (specially in America), but if the goal of that co-operation was seen as 'federation' through 'intercommunion' (as it often was in America) many would say that this was an inadequate understanding of Christian unity as demanded in the New Testament and in the non-Protestant churches' traditions. Nor was it clear how much doctrinal agreement was necessary before this fuller unity was reached, if co-operation was not enough. For example, what did it mean to agree that the World Council was to be 'a fellowship of Churches which accept our Lord Jesus Christ as God and Saviour'? Many in the churches were more interested in practical questions than in theology and the slogan 'doctrine divides, service unites' described their approach, but that was not the position of the Orthodox or of the conservative Protestants; nor, of course, of the Roman Catholic Church. And now fresh divisions between the nations, affecting the churches, appeared as some forty years of 'cold war' began. In Amsterdam in

1948 the American politician John Foster Dulles spoke (and two years later the council's 'central committee' was to take sides against Communist aggression in Korea). But Josef Hromadka, a Czech theologian who had returned from America to live under a Communist regime, spoke differently. And so did Karl Barth, who was beginning to make clear his view that there was no contrast between good and evil in the tension between capitalist and Communist superpowers. But for those churches whose representatives had resolved to 'stay together' a voyage had begun with the admission that neither the reality of the world's political divisions nor the reality of the life of the divided denominations should satisfy Christians. There was hope.

The Renewal of Theology

Many of those Europeans who were at all aware of the work of Christian theologians thought that the only part of it which made sense was the investigation of the Bible and of the history of the Church using methods which were as scientific as possible. The mood which rejected 'metaphysics' as meaningless had a focus in the Vienna circle of philosophers who were 'logical positivists'. Between 1924 and 1936 (when the Nazis dispersed them) they taught that meaningful statements must represent reality, so they must be about logic itself, mathematics or empirical facts unless their purpose is to advise the 'performance' of some behaviour rather than to convey information. No room could be found for 'God talk' which could never be 'verified' as being objectively true and could never be 'falsified' in the opinion of believers. Books which spread this message included the *Tractatus Logico-Philosophicus* of Ludwig Wittgenstein (1921) and the more militant *Language, Truth and Logic* by A. J. Ayer (1936). Both Wittgenstein and Ayer later regarded the narrowness of this understanding of language as wrong, but they never showed much respect for traditional theology.

Yet during the first half of the twentieth century theologians as creative as any in the past suggested that the faith of the future would replace the image of the Church as a self-satisfied institution demanding submission to authority and respectability. It would be a faith in a God greater than the universe, yet within it and able to reach the anxieties and failures of the individual. These theologians reflected the dark unhappiness of their age and could look dated when the sun began to shine. And they did not produce a doctrinal system about which all could be expected to agree; each had his own style. But this was precisely because theirs was an age of disintegration and crisis. Each thinker responded by seeing with a new intensity some aspect of the Christian tradition. What emerged was a common character: a religion of the critical mind but also of the broken heart, a hope arising from a grave, a faith (meaning essentially a trust, as Paul and Luther had meant) resulting from an encounter. Thus Emil Brunner was a representative theologian when he taught that for Christians 'revealed' truth was 'encountered' truth, truth revealed by the impact of God in Christ. However, there could be different encounters.

In the world of Catholic theology, nervous because of the Church's own crusade against modernism and still anxious because of the anti-Christian movements in the world, some voices with promise were heard. In France there was Jean Daniélou with the message that the Bible reveals through images not polished doctrines and Yves Congar showing that reform and reunion, with a far greater emphasis on the laity, would be possible without abandoning the living tradition of Catholic faith. In Germany, there was Karl Adam with his vision of Catholicism as nothing less than 'Christ making himself real in his Church'; Bernhard Häring with the proposal to make the criterion of the Church's 'moral theology' love not law, the Saviour's grace not the Judge's demands; and Romano Guardini with an approach to unbelievers not through 'apologetics' defending pre-defined doctrines inflexibly but through a 'fundamental theology' dealing with the currently common questions coupled with a fresh presentation of the 'spirit of the liturgy'. But the most important Catholic voice suggesting a new theology, Teilhard de Chardin's, was silenced by his Jesuit superiors on orders from the Vatican.

Teilhard had formed his spirituality through two loves, for the Catholic Church and for the creation, for Christ in the flesh and the consecrated bread and for the Father in all the beauty of nature; and for him, the two loves were one. These loves made him ultimately optimistic despite the suffering in his life. Even as a stretcher-bearer carrying mangled bodies in the first world war he saw God at work in evolution: the crisis of civilization must end in progress. He became an expert on the early history of Man, discovered fossils and speculated about the glory in which the history would end. His theology, undeniably poetic rather than coldly systematic, seemed deficient because it did not start with Adam's sin or end with the Judge's condemnations; he was forbidden to make his heresies public and banished from the intellectual life of Paris to China. But in China he continued to think and to write. His unpublished manuscripts, particularly *The Phenomenon of Man*, now lay like a time-bomb waiting to explode when he could no longer be silenced, after his death in New York as Easter Day began in 1955.

A thinker whose style was more Protestant and more abstract, the Englishman A. N. Whitehead, developed essentially similar themes into 'process philosophy'. Before going to America (like Teilhard) he had collaborated in work on the foundations of mathematical logic with Bertrand Russell, the author of *Why I Am Not a Christian*, and he knew well why so many intellectuals now shared Russell's certainty that Christianity deserved no respect. His own world was the world revealed by science: not 'substances' invisibly underlying reality as in the philosophy of Aquinas or Descartes but an indivisible mixture of the material and the mental (as for Teilhard). But with many setbacks this world moves towards the scarcely imaginable perfection we may call 'God' (again, as for Teilhard). Meanwhile God is not the omnipotent king of most of the Christian tradition. He is involved in the necessary suffering of his creation which is not yet perfect (he is 'the great companion, the fellow-sufferer who understands'); like a parent he will be enriched 'consequently' as the creation reaches its fulfilment; and somewhat like a leader in a democracy, he 'persuades' it towards its destiny. This 'process' theology was to be developed, particularly in the USA, into a sophisticated and comprehensive account of what the word 'God' could mean in the age of science.

Teilhard and Whitehead (with their disciples) were attacked vigorously by the secular-minded. They were also criticized for blurring the distinction between God and the world, but they were not pantheists as Spinoza had been with his 'God or Nature'. Both pointed to modern ways of glimpsing the perfection of eternity within a visibly imperfect world. Whitehead held that 'the fact of the religious vision, with its persistent expansion, is our one ground for optimism' because it is 'the vision of something which stands beyond, behind, and within, the passing flux of immediate things; something which is real, and yet waiting to be realized; something which is a remote possibility, and yet the greatest of present facts; something where possession is the final good, and yet is beyond all reach'. Teilhard was always the priest, wanting to show modern people how to be both devout and scientific, and in practical terms 'how to be as Christian as possible while being more human than anyone else'.

If such theology seemed to make God too human and too weak, that tendency was corrected by Paul Tillich who was exiled from Germany to teach in America after the Nazis' victory. What survived from his years in the Weimar Republic was his ability to deploy a Marxist analysis on the failures of the *bourgeois* civilization and to use his knowledge of art to illustrate spiritual emptiness. He took with him the message that the 'ultimate concern' of humanity is properly the religious quest for meaning in existence. Through him, thoughtful Americans came into contact with an agony and a search very different from what was usually regarded as 'religion'. They glimpsed the depths of the European experience of the possibility that existence has no meaning—and they met what he called an 'answering' theology.

To Tillich the inner meaning of religion is the encounter with the God who is no mascot of a tribe, no magician producing miracles for his favourites, no object among objects or person among persons, but 'Being itself', distinguishable from everything that merely exists but also the 'ground' of all that does exist. Here an old mystical tradition about the 'God beyond God' was brought into contact with the modern protest against the superficiality of all dogmatic formulations—and into contact with the profound fears of the modern age as 'anxiety' was experienced in the Europe of the great wars. For Tillich the main result of the religious encounter with 'Being' is not the ecstasy of the famous mystics but a much less high-soaring emotion: the insight that despair and death need not provide the final truths. He found in Jesus what he called the 'New Being' although he was not greatly interested in the historical Jesus of Nazareth, and in the 'New Being' he found victory over the 'demonic' evil in the human mind although he was not at all interested in the old theory that the cross had achieved victory over personal devils who had gained control over the world since the Fall of Adam. His *Systematic Theology*, in three volumes which eventually appeared between 1951 and 1963, presented the great 'symbols' of traditional Christianity as the answers to the questions of an age when the very foundations of confidence had been shaken: can we know anything humanly important, can we see beyond finite lives which appear to be guilty, doomed to die and ultimately meaningless, can we transcend the ignoble ambiguity which spoils even our best thoughts and actions, can we heal our alienation from our fellows and even from our selves, can we find a meaning in all the tragedy of history? His sermons were powerful and when printed even popular, and although he was far from being a joyful saint what he wrote and what was reported about him touched many who shared his own dislike of feeble conventions. He communicated to many, through his own continuing anxiety which he did not hide, what he called 'the courage to be', the courage 'rooted in the God who appears when God has disappeared in the anxiety of doubt'.

Karl Barth, then a young pastor in Switzerland, was shocked to the depths when 93 of the Protestant scholars whom he had admired as his teachers in Germany supported the war in 1914. (Harnack compared the German invasion of neutral Belgium with Jesus breaching the old commandment to rest on the Sabbath.) He now wanted a gospel stronger than the mild form of Christian humanism and socialism which he had been preaching to his industrial parishioners. He found it in 'the strange world of the Bible', in particular in Paul's letter to the Romans: God is the Wholly Other 'revealed as Lord' and Man is the ignorant sinner who needs salvation. That was, he said, the bell-rope which he clutched in his village church to save himself from falling as his teachers had fallen. Gradually the bell of alarm was heard far and wide, specially when it was mingled with strong words taken from the traditional theology which Barth began to study with fascination when unexpectedly made a professor. He began to move towards a position where he could define his own task, and the proper task of all theologians, in these terms: 'the theological discipline of dogmatics is the Christian Church's scientific self-examination with respect to the contents of its distinctive speech about God.'

The new sound was heard in his public onslaught on Harnack alleging a betrayal of the Christian gospel; in reply the bewildered Harnack accused him of betraying the tradition of modern German culture. (It was like the dialogue of the deaf between Luther and Erasmus.) The new sound was heard no less clearly in Barth's own decisions to revise his commentary on Romans and to abandon a project to write *Christian Dogmatics* after publishing the first volume in 1927: he was determined to rid his theology of all attempts to find diplomatic 'points of contact' with 'natural theology'. In 1932 he began to publish his *Church Dogmatics*, incomplete when he died in 1968 but by then running to some nine thousand pages.

He did not begin by seeking to commend a defence of 'religion' to its 'cultured despisers'. He began by proclaiming the sovereignty of God, the necessity of God's self-revelation, the reality of the Holy Trinity as Speaker, Word and Response, and the supremacy of Holy Scripture; and in contrast he attacked human 'religion'. He made comparatively minor revisions in traditional doctrines. He was not a fundamentalist, for while insisting on obedience to the 'Word of God' he did not insist on details not essential to the Bible's message: 'What counts is that the Bible speaks and is heard.' But in the phrase of Anselm (on whom he wrote an admiring book), Christian theology is 'faith seeking understanding'—and for him, as for Anselm, true faith is contentment to receive the gift of God's revelation without prying into hidden mysteries. Jesus Christ is no mere historical figure (more or less strange) or ethical teacher (more or less trite): 'Under this name God himself became Man.' Christian ethics is not a morality which seems rational to the individual's conscience or to enlightened humanity as a whole: it is the acknowledgement of creatureliness, of sin whose essence is pride, of the commands uttered in Scripture. 'Knowledge of God is obedience to God'— an obedience always 'compelled to be a prayer of thanksgiving, penitence and intercession'. And because infants cannot decide and promise to be obedient as Christian disciples, infants ought not to be baptized.

As the *Dogmatics* progressed, however, Barth made another turn: he gave increasing emphasis to the thought that the 'Wholly Other' is now 'with us', that 'in Jesus Christ God becomes Man, the fellow-man of all men'. For him God is still 'the One who loves in freedom' but the love now matters at least as much as the freedom: 'God has espoused the world's cause, has not left the world to itself but has aided and saved it, preserves and rules it and conducts it to its salvation.' Barth even distressed some of his more austere disciples by writing about *The Humanity of God*. He expounded with a loving emphasis the divine decision to become human in the shape of Jesus Christ, a decision made long before Christ's birth; for him, the whole of the creation was mere background, made for the sake of the 'covenant' with humanity. But for him Christian hope should never be based on the comfortable belief that since God has become human, Man can become divine without too much difficulty. Instead, Barth got back behind Calvin and Augustine to Paul himself, developing a theme which had already appeared elsewhere in the revision of Calvinism. On the cross 'God submitted himself to the law of creation by which the contradiction of the Creator can be accompanied only by loss and destruction'. There 'he took upon himself the rejection which Man had deserved' and tasted himself 'the damnation, death and hell which ought to have been the position of fallen Man'. As a result there is 'reconciliation', for the God who 'elected' to share and bear the doom of his human creatures has also 'elected' to save not the chosen few but all without exception if they are willing to respond. 'God's deity', he said in a lecture in 1956 which summed up his mature teaching, 'is his freedom to be in and for himself but also with and for us, to assert but also to sacrifice himself, to be wholly exalted but also completely humble, not only almighty but also almighty in mercy, not only Lord but also servant, not only Judge but also himself the judged, not only Man's eternal King but also his brother in time.'

Barth also grew somewhat less hostile to the human element in theology, granting that there could be reflection on the biblical revelation which used 'analogy', the comparison of the divine with the human, but always he insisted that the possibility of thinking or acting faithfully in relation to God rests on the self-revelation and the essentially miraculous action by God who takes the initiative. It is only by God's grace that language about God can be adequate enough to refer to his reality, as it is only through salvation by God that the human creature is liberated to love God and other creatures. When his colleague Emil Brunner cautiously hoped that some revelation of God might be found outside Christ, he replied: *Nein!* He always stuck to this passionate denial. Thus he gave an intellectual backbone to European Protestants resisting the claims of the Nazis. The 'neo-orthodoxy' in which he was the leading figure also had a great influence on Christian thought in the English-speaking world, sweeping away the sentimentality of liberalism. He has often been ranked as the greatest theologian to appear since Thomas Aquinas.

But there remained the question: how could modern people hear and believe that the Christian gospel about God offered good news about their personal existence? Basically, like Aquinas Barth took the truth of that gospel for granted and urged Christians to receive it as God's gift—but what if people were sceptical, what if they were unwilling to go to school in the

475

world of the Bible, what if they were unwilling to be instructed by the Fathers and Reformers of vanished ages? In his Nazi prison Dietrich Bonhoeffer pondered this question day after day, night after night, and was able to record fragmentary thoughts in letters published after his execution in 1945. Himself a man being punished for his involvement in plots against Hitler, his vision was of a suffering God: 'only a suffering God can help.' He was utterly devoted to Christ and during the war he wrote an academic book about Christian ethics where the theme was the acknowledgement of the lordship of Christ over the whole of life. His heart was in the Church: his first book (in 1927) had been about 'Christ existing as a community'. And he was insistent on the cost of discipleship: 'when Christ calls someone, he bids him come and die', for in Christ God calls the disciples to share his own suffering. But having worked and suffered alongside good and brave people whose morality was not so thoroughly Christian, he came to agree to some extent with the thought of the Enlightenment: humanity is no longer childish, Man has 'come of age'. A saint who loved the Bible and the hymns, he wrestled with the question: how to speak about faith in a 'religionless' world? Would there have to be a long period of silence with lives and deaths as the only communication? Or would it be possible to say in words 'who is Christ for us today'? Like Barth's theology, Bonhoeffer's was often to be misunderstood as pessimism about the future of Christianity. In fact the 'religion' which he thought was doomed was the 'religion' which Barth also attacked: a religion which was in the last analysis little more than the self-congratulation of a nation or a culture, a religion which fed on the weakness and gullibility of the individual, a religion which erected dogmas and institutions with little reference to the truths declared by the God who had become human, suffering flesh.

An answer to Bonhoeffer came, also in wartime Germany, from a New Testament scholar, Rudolf Bultmann. He always claimed that his answer had been grasped before the war through his wrestlings with the problems in his academic specialism, but like many other theologians in earlier or later periods he was a child of his age and therefore able to be heard by it. His *Jesus and the Word* (1926) stressed that Jesus proclaimed the reality and rule of God, not a moral philosophy and not 'religion'. He first expressed a gospel for the modern age clearly when asked for help by former pupils now serving as chaplains in Hitler's armies. After the war he preached it with power amid the ruins left by Hitler, although with almost no reference to politics or to economic realities. The New Testament, he taught, is full of myths and miracles, supremely the mythical miracle of the descent of the Saviour through a virgin's womb into the dark world in order to offer his death as the necessary sacrifice, to rise from his tomb in the same body and to return in the clouds as the Judge. None of that, Bultmann said very bluntly, can be believed by modern people. What they can believe, because they have had the experience, is that reliance on the things of the earth makes for anxiety and dread, for these things may be destroyed violently (as was happening around Bultmann) or will decay and vanish in death (as is the universal lot of mortal humanity). This 'existential situation' was analysed at depth in the existentialist philosophy of Martin Heidegger, who was Bultmann's fellow professor in Marburg, but it was felt in simpler terms by millions of non-philosophers in a period when so much of the old Europe went up in flames. For a time, therefore, Bultmann's use of Heidegger's jargon was more or less intelligible to many whose interests were not academic—and he made use of it with a message very different from that of the philosopher, who publicly urged the academic community to trust Hitler. The essential command of Jesus, he said, is to trust God and therefore to be 'open' to the future. That, he taught, is what the first-century idea of the kingdom of God means nineteen hundred years later. The person who trusts is delivered from every anxiety into faith and so into 'faithful' or 'authentic' existence, whatever may be the material losses. The true resurrection is the rise of faith, of 'being-towards-God', in the hearts of those who understand this meaning of the teaching and the crucifixion of Jesus.

Bultmann's conclusion to his prolonged study of the New Testament, and to his profound awareness of the spiritual situation of many of his contemporaries, provoked an intense discussion among Europeans and North Americans interested in religious questions. Much of the discussion was critical. It proved possible to make a long list of what he seemed to have ignored: much of the teaching of Jesus, much of the experience of Christians, most of the ordinary concerns of humanity. When he concentrated on a desperate need for a new 'self-understanding' he seemed to have ignored the traditional claim of Christianity to offer a sufficient understanding of the real God, the ocean in which all self-concern is washed away; and it seemed to be a disastrous defect in his theology that the resurrection of Jesus was no longer a mighty act of God in history. 'Faith in the resurrection', he taught, 'is really the same thing as faith in the saving efficacy of the cross.' The 'historical problem'—the question whether it occurred—is 'scarcely relevant to Christian belief' because 'if the event of Easter Day is in any sense an historical event additional to the event of the cross, it is nothing else than the rise of faith in the risen Lord' and only this 'rise of the Easter faith' is 'the act of God in which the redemptive event of the cross is completed'. To many critics this interpretation seemed to leave Jesus as a tragic figure, defeated by evil, until the belief arose in his followers that in the deepest reality his renunciation of all that was not 'authentic' had been the true victory, to be imitated in their own 'self-understanding'.

But those who deplored Bultmann's reduction of the gospel of the triumph of God to 'self-understanding' would have done justice to him if they had remembered one fact about his influence. His was an age of basic despair in Europe and his message could speak to it about faith. He was a preacher who believed that 'Christ meets us in the preaching as one crucified and risen'. In his Gifford Lectures in 1955 he answered his critics by reiterating what he had said during and immediately after the war. The 'decision of faith' brings a 'new understanding of myself as free from myself by the grace of God'. This 'new self' is now 'grounded in the grace of God' and free for the love which 'consists in unreservedly being for one's neighbour'. In some important ways Bultmann was the Luther of the twentieth century.

It may seem strange to end this chapter with Bultmann, a theologian often bitterly attacked or cheerfully ignored. In the modern age it has seemed that a new division has been deeper than the split between Catholics and Protestants, for traditionalists (whether simple or sophisticated) and 'liberals' or 'modernists' can appear to belong to different religions. Each side has accused the other of being blind to truth and of creating a great danger to Christianity's survival. At the end of the twentieth century the outcome seems to be that a tension or conflict of this undeniably troublesome nature has to be accepted as an unavoidable part of the reality of contemporary Christianity. Yet deeper even than this controversy has been the wish of both sides to identify themselves as Christians, disciples of the Lord from Nazareth, and as many modernizers have had some conservative feelings, so large numbers of Christians inclined to be conservative have felt something of the force of modern questions. Thus there has been a kind of unity: these Christians, although disagreeing on many matters, have all wished to preserve what was really essential and life-giving in their heritage but have lived after the Enlightenment, that turning point when people were summoned and enabled to think for themselves. And if we ask whether a heartfelt religion is compatible with a refusal to be controlled by old authorities, we can leave Europe behind and turn to the history of the churches in the Americas, Africa and Asia, for in those continents Christianity has once again been renewed.

8

⁊⁊⁊⁊

The Americas

The American Way

THE population of the USA grew and grew. It doubled 1790–1815, more than trebled 1815–60, doubled again before 1890 and kept on growing with the result that restrictions were imposed on immigration in the 1920s. After that it still kept on growing, by births or by immigration both legal and illegal, to about 260 million in the 1990s. All generalizations about the USA can be countered by pointing to exceptions, but it seems sufficiently right to say that about 400,000 places of Christian worship open in the 1990s had a common character: democratic rather than clergy-dominated, energetic rather than coldly orthodox, emotional rather than intellectual, moral rather than ritualistic, cheerful rather than Augustinian. In trying to analyse their history it often seems right to use statistics, for here Christians have admired and worked for quantifiable successes: conversions made, congregations gathered, buildings financed, missions and charities launched ambitiously. From the Pilgrim Fathers onwards Americans have hoped that the kingdom of God might appear and have been willing to help build it on their own soil. For many years there was little debate about the nation's identity apart from the great, terrible question whether it was right to own slaves as the economic basis of that identity, for the dominant culture was white, Anglo-Saxon and Protestant. Then, when the problem about slavery had been answered by a war, Protestantism split into movements whose disagreements could be militant, the Catholic Church became the largest of the denominations, the faiths and communities of non-Christians secured a fuller recognition and many Americans managed to avoid any close contact with organized religion. But still the favourite hymns often suggested that the faith itself had taken an American shape in reliance on a divine power working to make human life healthy and human thought positive. The simpler hopes about the kingdom of God coming to American earth might

479

or might not survive, and might or might not be reduced to the faith that American moral values and technical know-how were an unbeatable combination, but as the twenty-first century began to dawn two beliefs were usually taken for granted in the USA: that most of the history of the nation lies in the future, and that most of it will be good. Nowhere else in the world was there such optimism—and nowhere else in the world were there such reasons to be hopeful.

The national character could have become what it has been alleged to be by bitter critics in other continents: crudely materialistic, coarsely ignorant, ruthlessly competitive, with violence a large fact of life (and death) before it becomes daily entertainment. And certainly North America has turned out to be a tough place. The Pilgrim Fathers found it so. In the early years of independence the characters of the first four presidents harmonized with the belief that gentlemen could reason, even argue, together in freedom without destroying the basic conventions (including the ownership of slaves) which made them comfortable. But that social philosophy of the Enlightenment could not survive the changes in social conditions. The get-rich gospel for democracy of Andrew Jackson prevailed; the growing millions went on cart or by railroad to their manifest destiny in the often wild west; the slaves were freed; cities arose and scraped the sky; the 'imperial republic' had to make the world safe for exports and investments. What could tame these Americans so determined to achieve success? They could eventually agree about the individual's right to a large amount of freedom; they could also agree that justice requires equal opportunities for all to be successful; but what kind of life should the successful individual want, and what kind of society was needed in order that the poor might have real opportunities? To these awkwardly difficult questions the main answers came from religion. Within a constitution produced by the Enlightenment and an economy powered by capitalism, the churches provided a surprising amount of the nation's identity and made that identity surprisingly a matter of morality with a religious input. What might have been merely crude individualism became this faith in Kennedy's inaugural address as president: 'human rights come not from the generosity of the state but from the hand of God.' Almost all Americans could be expected to applaud not only the affirmation of human rights but also a reference to their divine source, a touch of theology about which most Europeans would hesitate.

Under this 'hand of God' American optimism proved able to survive great disillusionments. After the gathering of the millions into the churches came the disasters of the civil war and of the subsequent victory of white racism in a less formal shape. After the 'gilded age' when further progress seemed to have no limit came the great failures: peace could not be made after 1918, the lingering Puritanism represented by the legal prohibition of alcohol could not be maintained, the economy which had fed the optimism went into deep depression. After the New Deal and the triumphant crusades in Europe and the Pacific came the bitter defeat in Vietnam, 'doing your own thing' in the 1960s, the almost-civil-war over the black people's rights, Kennedy's own assassination. In the end the melting pot in which so many millions had been made into good Americans lost much of its power to melt and the USA became undeniably a pluralist society, so nervous about interference by the government in this pluralism that worship was stopped in the schools. But a more private commitment continued to support flourishing churches and after the ending of their more ambitious visions most Americans still had something better than a dream: a belief that more or less any problem carries a solution with it. Their internal divisions and their criticisms of their own performance were accompanied by the forward-looking energy which was their greatest asset as a nation and which helped them to win their bloodless victory over the Soviet Union at the end of the 1980s. The USA was more hopeful than people were who saw Communism in action: that was one big difference. And partly because a strong element of religious belief strengthened this hopefulness, it could survive disasters: that was another contrast with the people who experienced Communism's terminal sickness.

In the seventeenth and eighteenth Christian centuries white North America was culturally very close to Europe and in this history, which up to now has been Eurocentric, mention has already been made of some events and personalities in this transatlantic offshoot. But the crowded life of these peoples and churches in the USA between the 1790s and the 1990s deserves to be thought about as one story, of an importance second to none in the story of Christianity.

The Way Begins

The gaining of independence by rebellion left the citizens of the USA very conscious of their nationality. They believed that 'governments derive their just powers from the consent of the governed' and now they had consented to what they had achieved. No other people in the world had this experience at this time. The Americans were, however, also very conscious of their rights as individuals (they attached a Bill of Rights to their constitution); mostly absorbed in daily work or politics, not religion; and very suspicious about the role of the historic churches in this 'new order of the ages'.

The Church of England in America, for example, was tainted with loyalism to the Crown and now had to become thoroughly American (although the Church of England in Canada continued to be called by that name until 1955). No longer established by colonial governments, the

Anglicans had to face life as a minority, decreasing by 1850 to well under a twentieth of the churchgoers. And it was not easy to settle into an American identity. After rebuffs in London a bishop was consecrated for American work by the bishops of the small Anglican church in Scotland and eventually an Anglo-Catholic emphasis on bishops, priests and sacraments reached the USA; but account had to be taken of a more characteristically American element, Protestant and lay, and the bishops of what was now the 'Episcopal Church' had to agree that they should be elected with few powers and that clergy and laity should sit side by side as 'deputies' also elected democratically to the church's General Convention. The Methodists who in America had already forgotten John Wesley's Anglican identity now had to persuade their fellow Americans to forget his opposition to their independence: for them as for the Episcopal Church, virtually a new start was necessary and they declared their independence from British control in 1784. The first General Assembly of the Presbyterians met a little later, being more cautious. The Catholics were of course conservative about their faith and about the right ordering of their international church; yet in America, as not in Europe, the clergy depended on the laity. As trustees of the church buildings for which they had paid, the richer laity could defy the authority of any bishop. Provincial councils formally resolved that tension in the bishops' favour but other problems came with increasing numbers. Irish and Germans, Poles and Italians, had been very different in Europe. They remained different in an America where most people believed them to be not American enough: they owed allegiance to the pope who was a foreign monarch, they were poor because lazy. In the 1850s 'nativist' movements such as the Order of the Star-spangled Banner arose to resist this Catholic invasion.

In New England, with Boston as the centre, Unitarian preachers persuaded some fellow citizens that a new nation deserved a new start in religion through a radically simplified form of Christianity. Most affirmed the human supremacy of Christ while denying his divinity; a few went further in democratizing religion. There were also Universalists who concentrated exclusively on love for all as Christ's message, rejecting the long tradition which had assigned most of the human race to hell.

Other Americans affirmed the centrality of Father, Son and Spirit but not the importance of church history. Alexander Campbell's advice was to 'open the New Testament as if no mortal man had seen it before'. Those who took this advice called themselves simply 'Christians' or 'Disciples' or 'the Churches of Christ' but these different names were to reflect vigorous disagreements as Campbell's own intrepretation of what he read was developed. One disagreement was about the morality which the New Testament taught. Was it a quite calm morality as in Early Catholicism—or intense 'holiness' after the dramatic event of being filled with the 'power of the

Spirit'? In 1837 the wife of a New York physician and the mother of children who had died young, Phoebe Palmer, experienced a strange power as her sister had already done, and together they led the 'Tuesday meeting for the promotion of holiness'. In that meeting and others like it there was some ecstatic speaking in 'tongues' but there was not yet the Pentecostal movement's insistence on that experience: these were the beginnings of the 'holiness' churches which in the next century were to be different from those which were fully Pentecostal. Meanwhile Phoebe Palmer's charm was such that there was no outrage when she wrote a book about her conviction that a Spirit-filled woman was entitled to 'prophesy' as in the days of the Bible.

When they opened the New Testament the Adventists concentrated on another part: the promise that the kingdom of God would come completely and soon. William Miller predicted the advent of the kingdom in the 1840s, a decade which came and went. Nevertheless the movement survived and much of it became identified also with the belief that the promised kingdom had been postponed because the churches worshipped on Sunday instead of on the seventh day of the week as laid down in the never-repealed Ten Commandments. For other Americans consolation for the non-arrival of the kingdom on earth was found in a sense of the reality of invisible spirits. A large number of spiritualist groups began in the 1840s when a young woman in New York state claimed that she had successfully rebuked a poltergeist troubling her family.

The Mormons were the most spectacular of all these Christian or semi-Christian movements in American religious independence. Every stage in their early history was extraordinary by European standards. In 1827 Joseph Smith, a farm boy in a village in New York state whose hobby was magic, saw golden plates inscribed with 'Reformed Egyptian' writing. Before they disappeared they enabled him to translate their language into an English which was equally remarkable because reminiscent of the Authorized (King James) Version of the Bible. Here was a history of the earliest inhabitants of North America. His book not only satisfied popular curiosity about that history; it also provided the Scripture of a new church, the Church of Jesus Christ of Latter-day Saints. After persecution a group inspired by his claims moved to Illinois, where the founder proved himself to be an enterprising leader of a visionary community but was murdered. Another leader arose, with still more extraordinary gifts: Brigham Young. Like Moses of old he led his people through the wilderness. He took them to the edge of the Salt Lake far in the west and there (in 1847) he founded the community which was to become the state of Utah, with his famous exclamation 'This is the land!' After irrigation the land was to support millions in comfort. There was a snag: Mormonism included a plan to multiply children by reviving the practice of polygamy as authorized in the

Hebrew Scriptures. This last practice was too eccentric even for American public opinion, with the result that Utah was not incorporated into the Union before 1896, when formal polygamy had been abandoned. In the twentieth century the Mormons were to become models of respectable prosperity.

These cheerfully innovating American movements have aroused the interest of many historians. But more significant in American history was the adaptation to American conditions of denominations which had originated in England. By 1850 Methodist and Baptist congregations included more than a third of all church members in the USA.

Methodism had the initial advantage because it launched the better organized campaign. Not for nothing did Francis Asbury, its first leader, call himself a bishop in defiance of John Wesley's wishes; and not for nothing was he as tireless as Wesley in journeys, sermons, personal evangelism and ability in managing congregations and their preachers, both itinerant and local. Methodism used the talents of ministers who did not aspire to be gentlemen and the energies of enthusiastic laity. It placed them in the strong fellowship of a local 'society' but linked them to a stabilizing central body.

The Baptists also relied on local preachers and enthusiastic congregations but appealed to people who had no wish for much more by way of organization. Some Baptists even objected to a national missionary society and more objected when gatherings wider than the local church seemed to be removing the 'landmarks' of truly biblical religion.

Both Methodists and Baptists evangelized among the 'Negroes' in the southern states. They had to try to communicate in English since no African language survived to any considerable extent. Converts were allowed to worship in congregations led by white 'boss preachers' but were usually confined to the segregated area called the 'Nigger benches' in church. The preachers exhorted them to be obedient to their masters and to work from dawn to dusk except on Sundays—and the masters hoped to stop the slaves from organizing their own churches which might become centres of rebellion (although many other measures made a rebellion virtually impossible). However, the slaveholders could not prevent the message of the Bible from spreading in a form which to them was undesirable. Usually the slaves were not allowed to learn to read but the great biblical promises and stories of deliverance, once heard, could be transmitted by Christians of their own race to black ears and suffering hearts. The Bible inspired the 'spirituals', songs for work in the fields or for prayer-meetings in the huts where this music of freedom was often sung very softly in order to escape detection. These songs were almost always sad, not militant, but they voiced a unity, they avoided total despair and their longing for heaven was in part a coded reference to the dream of a better life before death. In the northern states

Blacks were allowed rather more freedom, mainly because their smaller numbers were less threatening to the Whites. A major white denomination even permitted the ordination of a black minister in 1785, Lemuel Haynes. His credentials were impeccable; he had fought against the British and was now a conservative Calvinist eager to serve Congregational churches in New England. Nine years later another black clergyman, Absalom Jones, became the minister of an Episcopal congregation in Philadelphia. His friend Richard Allen organized the first black denomination, the African Methodist Episcopal Church, in 1814; later he was elected president of the first national organization for Blacks. Even in tolerant Philadelphia, even among Methodists, he had been humiliated by racism, but American law, which recognized very few rights of black against white, did acknowledge the right of free men to own property and in this case the law defended the right of Allen's little congregation to have its own chapel.

Presbyterians and Congregationalists saw the opportunities for evangelism among Whites and agreed on a 'plan of union' to help the mission, but the plan collapsed: the Presbyterians were like the Methodists in believing that the local congregation should not have the final say in church life. While being more fervent than the Congregationalists in preaching 'God's plan of salvation', they too had their internal divisions; the 'Christian Reformed Church', for example, insisted that others were not fully entitled to use those three proud words. The Lutherans were also divided, partly on ethnic grounds and partly because of controversies between conservatives and liberals. On the conservative right was the Missouri Synod formed under the leadership of Carl Walther in 1847; cynics said that it was trying to set up 'Zion on the Mississippi'. On the liberal left was 'American Lutheranism' led by Samuel Schmucker. But their main, common problem was simple: the shortage of Lutherans in America before the immigration of the 1870s. So the churches with the most direct inheritances from the great Reformers of the sixteenth century derived less benefit than might have been expected from the Protestant peopling of North America.

It is not in the least surprising that the relatively small efforts made to convert 'Indians' met with little success. The black slaves had been deprived so far as possible of access to African religions, and of their tribal names and cultures, and had often suffered the destruction of family life as children or adults were sold to other slaveholders, but the 'Indians' were not wanted as slaves: they were not thought suitable for hard physical labour. They could not be robbed of their knowledge of their own religious traditions and they remained members of tribes and families even when in degradation. They had to leave their traditional territories, however, when the Whites wanted them: after the discovery of some gold the Cherokees, although thought 'civilized', were driven out of Georgia. Other 'Indians' lost their tribal lands when a third of Mexico was transferred to the USA in 1848. One of the things about the white man which they could never understand was the ruthless determination to own land as private property; another was the insistence that those who were not landowners should work for money. But they could resist by not being willing to understand the white man's religion which accompanied the spread of diseases and alcoholism and the slaughter of buffaloes. In the nineteenth century they were confined to 'reservations' and, it was hoped, elevated by the sincere attentions of Christian missionaries. In 1890 came their last big massacre, mostly of women and children, at Wounded Knee, and after that they had to admit defeat. From the 1920s they were American citizens and from the 1960s they could be called 'Native Americans' by Whites who now often respected their traditions; a Native American Church emerged. But they never had the strength to match the story of the Blacks who could be respected as 'African Americans'. They lived like exiles in the continent which had been theirs.

Far easier was the preaching of a message of personal salvation to the Whites who were making great material advances but experiencing their own psychological problems. In this evangelism the formation and teaching of a regular congregation was the main weapon; accordingly a great preacher, Lyman Beecher, urged Protestant churches to put more and more effort into this expansion in his *Plea for the West* (1835). But the emphasis on the provision of churches (by 1860 the USA contained almost forty thousand of them) was supplemented by meetings for revivalism. The first famous one was the 'camp meeting' at Cane Ridge in Kentucky in 1801. Many later meetings, usually gathered by Methodists or Baptists, included scenes of enthusiasm merging into hysteria, the effect of excitement coming after months of silence, of heaven being offered after years close to the earth. Somewhat more sedate were the 'new measures' introduced by revivalists such as Charles Finney. What was most visible there was not hysteria but organization. Meetings were held whether or not the local churches invited the visitors. The offer of salvation to all was proclaimed by a predictable sermon and by carefully planned hymns and the 'anxious bench' (how much the name reveals about the Americans of this period!) started a new tradition, the personal counselling of potential converts.

Americans who could not be converted by attendance at a church or a revivalist meeting could be helped or improved by charitable activities sponsored by the ever-active churches in the absence of effective action by a government. Outstanding among the human angels were the Sisters of Charity of the Catholic Church founded by Elizabeth Seton, who in 1975 became the first citizen of the USA to be an official saint. But inevitably Protestants were more numerous in these activities, creating what came to be called their 'benevolent empire'. Their societies were nation-wide and interdenominational. They supported schools, colleges and hospitals; they reformed prisons and attacked brothels; and in defiance of the brewers they urged temperance or the taking of the 'pledge' of total abstinence. They advocated peace between all nations and also a cause which cost them more dearly: the abolition of slavery in the USA.

The northern states found that they could prosper without slaveholding and, state by state, they made it illegal. One motive was to safeguard the wages of white workers. In contrast, the southern states depended on what was tactfully called a 'peculiar' institution. The production of cotton had become increasingly profitable: new machinery could process it and new customers wanted to wear it. But new land needed to be used for this production and at least four million slaves were needed to do the work. Attempts to arouse slave rebellions—Nat Turner's in Virginia, John Brown's at Harper's Ferry—seemed to fly in the face of the reality that there was no alternative to the system. Another factor was that the North wanted to protect its new industries against foreign competition while the South wanted free trade in order to sell its cotton to foreign customers.

On these economic foundations two different cultures, almost two nations, had been built. The northerners cherished the virtues of the Puritans, or at least the virtue of dedicated, disciplined and ambitious work, and they saw the railroads opening up in the west a land with no final frontier short of the ocean, an 'empty' land where work could win success with no limit. But in the South life for the successful Whites was in its way more gracious, and certainly more leisured, relying on slave labour to work the fields and to staff the mansions. In the North the ideal was that a mother should nurse children and train them in the ways of respectability and industry; in the South, that a mother with the right skin should entrust her children to the care of loyal servants. A southern lady, if religious, could be active in charitable works and sincere in a piety which was marked by more introspective guilt than was to be expected in the North. If not religious, she could display the wealth of her husband by being beautiful and idle.

Both the North and the South could appeal to the Bible. When white northerners read 'the good book' they now found in it what the slaves had already found: many praises of freedom and many calls to set God's people free. Anti-slavery seemed, as in the hymn, 'some great cause, God's new Messiah'. The call came as in another hymn of this time: 'Stand up, stand up for Jesus!' But in the South the Whites read the same Bible. They found in the New Testament clear instructions to accept slavery and in the Old Testament the emphatic approval of the enslavement of a people made inferior by God. A basic text was Genesis 9:25, recording that the children of Ham had been cursed by Noah, indignant after being seen drunk and naked. Many of the slaveholders in the South, being more respectable than

Noah, went to church. Particularly in recent years when they had been irritated by accusations that slavery was unchristian, they had encouraged Blacks to believe, to be baptized and to worship. They liked to think that life for the 'Niggers' they knew or half-knew was no worse than the 'wage slavery' practised by the 'Yankees' in the North.

Two sets of values were thus in conflict and almost inevitably the tension ended in the division of denominations. In 1845 the Methodists split on the question whether a bishop could hold slaves and the Baptists on the question whether a missionary could. And almost inevitably there was a civil war.

As often happens, the immediate causes of war were smaller than the real issues: there was a long dispute about the terms on which new states in the west might be admitted to the Union. But Abraham Lincoln, elected president in 1860 as the candidate of the new Republican party, told Mrs Stowe that her novel *Uncle Tom's Cabin* (1852) had caused the war. The daughter of a famous preacher, the wife of a professor who studied the Old Testament prophets, she burned with a northerner's indignation about slavery and as people read her moving story the old American dream about the coming of the glory of the Lord began to lead 'jubilant feet' into battle. Actually the war was started in the South, which broke away from the Union and fired the first shots in 1861. On both sides, in Lee's army as in Grant's, hymns arose. On both sides the victims of war were comforted in the name of the Saviour and assured that they had made sacrifices in an obviously just cause. 'In God we trust' first appeared on the Union's paper currency in 1865. But both sides so trusted.

It was the first modern war and it was won by the economic power of the North, which could prevent the export of cotton and send troops and supplies south by rail despite the large losses in battle. But the deaths of so many soldiers were not the only tragedy. The most fatal bullet was the one which killed Lincoln on Good Friday in 1865. Although he had attended a Presbyterian church while president, for most of his life he had belonged to no church—and for almost all his life he both hated slavery and did not see how it could be ended except by the slow process of persuasion. His emancipation proclamation of 1862 would have been inconceivable before the war. In the last years of his life he had felt the suffering of the combatants and the bereaved, and with his Bible in his hand had tried to discern the purposes of God above the smoke of battle and the clouds of pulpit-rhetoric. His famous speeches showed that he had concluded that the war was God's punishment of all for the long toleration of slavery and ought to be followed by compassion for all. He had given a new stature to Christian statesmanship.

But after his death and the North's triumph came the compulsory 'reconstruction' of the South. Ex-slaves were now told to work for wages and new amendments to the constitution of the restored Union sought to provide for their rights as citizens and voters. That was the theory. The reality was that the North soon got bored with the problems of the South while in defeat the southern Whites were embittered and the economy, which included almost no industry or competitive agriculture, went into decline. Pests ravaged cotton; other countries produced it; debts grew. Wages were low and many Whites almost as poor as the Blacks. By new laws restricting freedom, by loud-mouthed intimidation and by unpunished violence the 'Niggers' were deterred from getting so 'uppity' that they might claim their civil rights, register as voters, get equal education or own land. For almost a hundred years white racism succeeded in these aims and was often accompanied by a passionately defensive faith in the faultless Bible.

The Way Continues

In the 1860s five-sixths of the American population were still rural. In the South when Booker Washington led a campaign to improve the lot of his fellow Blacks he was to concentrate on the need for training for agricultural tasks within a system which, like it or not, had to be accepted. But the South could not provide enough jobs for a black population which almost doubled between 1860 and 1900. Gradually Blacks moved north, a third of them by 1910, about half by 1965. And gradually they began to organize politically: in 1909 the National Association for the Advancement of Colored People had small beginnings around W. E. B. Du Bois, who was to end up as a Communist. But their main organization was religious and by 1910 about half of them belonged to Black-led churches.

One fact about them was also true about the Whites: their churches were their most important institutions. In the Union which had been nominally reunited most politicians were conservative, ineffective and in one sense or another corrupt. There was little ideological difference between the parties: to a large extent politics was a competition for the power to give or sell favours when in office. In what Mark Twain called the 'gilded age' the great men were the great capitalists such as Rockefeller and Carnegie, who had not grown rich by being soft. And some intellectual influences from an increasingly secular Europe spread the gospel of science, science being interpreted as teaching the survival of the fittest and the effective absence of God. In 1895 a leading educationalist, A. D. White, published his *History of the Warfare of Science with Theology*: in his eyes the war had been a long battle of light against darkness. This new philosophy influenced the new universities, colleges and schools which were taking the education of the people over from their church-related predecessors whose concentration had been on the Bible as the guide to morality; and popularizers such as Robert

Ingersoll spread the message of scientific atheism. But while large areas of the life and thought of the modern USA were becoming secularized, it was still the case that the American religion worked like an active volcano, frequently pouring out lava at various degrees of heat.

In the business world it was still proper to be connected with churches and charities; Rockefeller and Carnegie were both large-scale benefactors and Carnegie was the author of *The Gospel of Wealth*. In the more old-fashioned and prestigious universities professors, including philosophers, often expressed a nostalgia for the certainties of faith. Producing evidence that religious experiences had happened and had made some people 'healthy-minded', and believing that in the last analysis what was 'true' was what worked, William James defended the 'will to believe'. George Santayana, who despised James, said that some of his nostalgic colleagues were clergymen without a church; but he was one himself, dissatisfied with his own five volumes on *The Life of Reason*. And in this period there were actual clergymen who could draw crowds to hear an intellectually respectable, modernist gospel; the unemotional David Swing had that success every Sunday in Chicago's Central Music Hall.

In the historic churches there was often a warm faith, expressed in new hymns such as 'Blessed assurance! Jesus is mine!' By 1890 4.5 million Methodists and 3.7 million Baptists had at least some of this assurance. Sunday schools were teaching this faith to millions of children—with lessons uniform across many denominations, described by one historian as the Protestant equivalent of the Mass in Latin. And this was the period when the Catholic Church became firmly rooted in American soil: between 1860 and 1900 the number of its priests grew sixfold to twelve thousand. The success of its adaptation to the American way of life resulted in protests from its own higher, European authorities. Many of its laity were content to use the free public schools although they hoped that Catholic teaching would be allowed, but in 1884 they were instructed by their bishops to attach a Catholic school to every church. Some bishops continued to urge a full participation in the other normal activities of Americans; they included Cardinal Gibbons and Archbishop John Ireland. A new religious order, the Paulists, was founded by a very American priest, Isaac Hecker, who had not forgotten his own pre-Catholic past. German priests ministering to homesick immigrants were horrified by such English-speaking laxity (as many American Catholics were shocked to see the German Catholics' persistent consumption of beer). It was in response to complaints in Europe about a biography in French praising Hecker that Pope Leo XIII published his warning against 'American-ism' in 1895. The Church in America, he wrote, 'would bring forth more abundant fruits if, in addition to liberty, she enjoyed the favour of the laws and the patronage of public authority' and 'unless forced by necessity to do otherwise, Catholics ought to prefer to associate with Catholics'. But neither side wanted a split. American Catholics avoided heresy; their leaders assured the Vatican that they had never met 'Americanism' and the Vatican shrewdly avoided any heresy-hunt to prove them wrong.

There were fewer hesitations about being American in the religion preached in Chicago and in many other places by Dwight Moody. He linked a simple and conservative gospel with a folksy style, and the sentimental songs of Ira Sankey with admirable social work. He was particularly successful among young men exposed to the dangers of city or university, for whom the lifeboat rescuing in strong seas provided the appropriate image. Some revivalism was vulgarized and commercialized like much of the rest of American life, for example by Billy Sunday, formerly a famous professional on the baseball field. But Sunday's message stirred by its simplicity and Moody's preaching could touch critical audiences, often by recalling memories of a more innocent childhood.

For many Americans, however, the religion of the Sunday school, of the Catholic church or of Moody's lifeboat was not exciting or forward-looking enough. They asked for a version of Christianity which would respond with high drama to the feeling that despite all the factors suggesting otherwise the USA was witnessing the dawn of a truly golden age.

It had to be an age of health. In 1863 Eleen White experienced a trance in which she received divine instructions: she and all who would listen to her must avoid alcohol, tobacco, meat, sex and doctors. One of her converts had the surname of Kellogg. But a more formidable woman, Mary Baker Eddy, organized and publicized a more substantial movement with a brilliant name: Christian Science. After half a century of unhappiness and ill health she was cured—and not by ordinary medicine, as she explained very effectively. In 1875 she published an almost scriptural text book, *Science and Health*; she frequently revised it; she defeated or ignored many attacks; in many senses of the word she was powerful; and in a long life (she lived until 1910) she affiliated many grateful congregations to the 'First Church of Christ, Scientist', in Boston. Her message was that since God is All, the only Being, matter and all its attendant diseases are 'mortal illusions'; and to believe this is to be healed.

Other Americans expressed their vision of a dawning new age by renewing the traditional hope of Christ's 'Second Coming', often connected with the prophecy in Revelation 20:1-6 that the resurrected martyrs would be seated on thrones and 'reign with Christ' for a thousand years before the final Judgement. Charles Russell formed the Zion's Watch Tower Society in 1884 and announced that 'millions now living will never die'. When he had died J. F. Rutherford, an organizer as superbly energetic as Mary Baker Eddy, took over the leadership of a rapidly growing international movement which in the 1930s took the name 'Jehovah's Witnesses', partly in order to indicate an increasing distance from traditional Christianity. In contrast, a movement of 'dispensationalists' claimed to be very firmly based on the Christian Bible, in particular on the Schofield Reference Bible, a best-seller from 1909. Interpreting biblical prophecies, this Bible-with-commentary predicted that after six earlier 'dispensations' God would soon establish his own kingdom on earth, the thousand-year reign of Christ. This 'millenarian' excitement was to flow into twentieth-century fundamentalism—and into a movement which depended less on printed words, more on the Spirit.

In 1901 a young white woman in Topeka, Kansas, experienced the inrush of the power of the Holy Spirit and spoke in strange 'tongues'. Agnes Ozman had made Luke's account of the birthday of the apostolic Church on the day of Pentecost seem up to date in the new century. Five years later a whole group, mixed in race and gender but led by a black preacher (William Seymour), had the same experience first in a little wooden bungalow and then in a humble mission-house in Azusa Street, Los Angeles. The modern Pentecostal movement had been born. It was a time when many Christians in many countries were hoping and praying for an 'outpouring' of the Spirit and for the visible return of the Saviour; for example, there was a dramatic revival in Wales in 1904–05. But the events in Los Angeles defined the character of a movement which spread with astonishing rapidity through the USA and the world, without a head office or historic shrine (the Azusa Street mission-house was demolished), without a comprehensive theology, without an elaborately trained clergy, without connections with governments or the rich, without any weapon other than enthusiasm.

The central idea was that after 'water-baptism' there ought to be another crisis, 'Spirit-baptism', as an unmistakable event bestowing spiritual power. The result would be 'holiness' (more technically 'sanctification') and some believed that only this result was guaranteed. But it became the most characteristic Pentecostal belief that the gift of the Spirit was always, or almost always, accompanied by the gift of 'signs' as for the apostles on the day of Pentecost. The speaking of foreign languages which had not been learned was reported but rare, and the reports were perhaps influenced by the desire to repeat exactly what the Acts of the Apostles said about Pentecost. But if this *xenolalia* was disputable the emotional release in ecstatic joy using speech but no normal words (*glossolalia*) was what was usually called 'tongue-speaking' and it was—as it has remained—unquestionably frequent. By 1915 five American churches which were to enrol millions were 'Spirit-filled': the Church of the Nazarene, the Church of God in Christ, the Church of God based on Cleveland, Tennessee, the Pentecostal Holiness Church and the newest, the Assemblies of God, which was to be the largest. The divisions were due partly to differences about how a church should be organized (should it have a bishop or a presbytery or be entirely democratic?) but the main factor was that it was a movement spread from person to person by the infection of enthusiasm. The rise of Pentecostalism was the ultimate logic of the American development of the people's church based on the religion of the heart.

All of these (and other) Pentecostal churches had a similar style. They appealed mainly to people whose earthly security was smallest. Through the emotional crisis and the enlistment into an intense fellowship there was therapy. People who went through these experiences no longer felt completely trapped in poverty and ill-health, subordination and frustration. They expected miracles, particularly miracles of healing but also the greater miracle of the Second Coming which these miracles were expected to foreshadow. That reflected a social situation as well as religious faith, for in the USA there was in these years a strange combination of miserable poverty through low wages or unemployment with the hopes associated with the turn of the centuries: thus people could feel both trapped for the time being and able to imagine a radically better future, which for the poor would be the new city and the new earth of the Revelation of John. Another social factor was the relationship with the existing culture of the Blacks, who provided many of American Pentecostalism's first recruits. In the African-American tradition from the slave-fields onwards there had been the heartfelt religion, the compulsion to worship and to proclaim after a vision, the excitement and the use of the body, the informal preaching and the faith-healing, if not actual tongue-speaking. And there had been the thrilling music. It was not a complete coincidence that the early years of Pentecostalism were also the early years of the blues and of jazz, when musicians and their participating audiences expressed emotions too deep for spoken words. The division between the races brought division between the Pentecostal churches; segregation often had to be accepted in those years. But sometimes this new movement provided the added joy which black Christians had if hugged by Whites, in a reconciliation which seemed almost as miraculous as the Second Coming.

The Pentecostal movement breathed the air of millenarian excitement but did not directly tackle the problems of social injustice at this stage. This was in contrast with Black-led churches which combined a 'Bible-believing' gospel with a loud protest against the treatment which Blacks received, and it suggests that most of those who responded to the early Pentecostal preachers were not greatly interested in wider ambitions for 'social uplift'. But other groups had the self-confidence needed to be articulate in their protests, or the social status needed to hope for influential access to the positions of power in society. So the age of the Social Gospel began. In earlier years famous preachers such as Henry Ward Beecher and Phillips

Brooks had indeed preached about social problems and had inspired much charitable giving and work, but they had never attacked the comfortable theory held by many in their congregations that being poor was the result of sinful habits. Now the determination to right wrongs was more systematic.

A response which in the end seemed to be obviously Christian was provided by the 'rescue' work of the Salvation Army under Catherine Booth, a leader as great as her famous parents. But was the 'rescue' enough? Trade unions were only now becoming strong (too many immigrants had wanted any jobs going), but two widely noticed books drew the attention of many who had little or no first-hand knowledge of the conditions of life and work in factory and slum; and they demanded political action. In 1879 *Progress and Poverty* came from Henry George who dared to be a socialist in New York, and in 1890 *How the Other Half Lives* came from a Danish immigrant who aimed to influence America's powerful half. William Jennings Bryan, a Protestant conservative in his religion who was three times the Democrats' candidate for the presidency, avoided socialism but asked: 'Would you crucify humanity on a cross of gold?' Less rhetorically but after harsh experience as a Baptist minister in the district of New York known as Hell's Kitchen, the books of Walter Rauschenbusch argued for a 'Social Gospel', a hope of 'transforming the life on earth into the harmony of heaven', the alternative being 'the deluge'.

The Evangelical Alliance spread from Britain in the 1860s and concentrated on the encouragement of Protestant evangelism in the new cities, but in 1896 Josiah Strong left its leadership in order to concentrate on 'social questions' and 'social service'. Many less prominent Christians were now sure that evangelism addressed to the individual with the offer of heaven after death was not enough. Out of this concern grew in 1908 an organization which was small but represented many Protestants, the Federal Council of Churches. It adopted a 'social creed'. The demands were cautious—'the highest wage that industry can afford', a 'gradual and reasonable' reduction in the hours of work, the 'regulation of the conditions of toil for women', 'conciliation' in industrial disputes. But the creed also envisaged the general 'abatement of poverty' and even 'equal rights and complete justice for all men in all stations of life'. (One day women would be explicitly included.) And the inaugural meeting of this council heard a speech which saw its formation as a momentous step in the 'speedy Christian advance toward World Conquest'. Ten years before, the USA had defeated the Spanish navy. The Philippines in the Pacific and Cuba and Puerto Rico in the Caribbean were now 'protected' and one of the reasons given to justify this American form of imperialism was that the inhabitants would benefit from their experience of American religion and morality. In economics the production of the USA trebled between 1900 and 1914 and its commercial exports now needed an 'open door'—into China, for example, using the Panama Canal which was opened in 1914 after forcibly detaching Panama from Colombia. It seemed logical to hope that the world would welcome Americans who pushed through the open door with spiritual as well as material goods.

It began to be thought that since the mission to this growing nation had achieved so much, a similar success might attend a mission to all nations. Already American evangelists had gone to work in other countries—not only Moody and Sankey who made their names by their meetings in British cities but much earlier pioneers such as Adoniram Judson, the Baptist who had sailed in 1812 to begin nearly forty years of work in Burma. But now far greater things seemed possible. In 1900 John R. Mott, a Methodist layman who was prominent in the Young Men's Christian Association (as Moody had been), published a book advocating *The Evangelization of the World in This Generation*. By this he did not necessarily mean the world's conversion, but after seeing the response to the YMCA he had the vision—sufficiently ambitious in itself—of 'giving to all men an adequate opportunity of knowing Jesus Christ as their Saviour and becoming his real disciples'. And thousands of students responded to the call to dedicate their lives as missionaries; another book by Mott called the colleges from which these students came *Strategic Points in the World's Conquest*. The leading Protestant journal changed its name to *The Christian Century*.

In this period when innocence was accompanied by ignorance the possibility that other religions might be successful in resisting conquest by Christianity did not seem to be a real problem. But a question was raised within the USA, an awkward question: what was meant by 'evangelization', or indeed by 'Christian'? Pragmatic missionary leaders such as Mott did what they could to unite conservatives with liberals in the new crusade, but there was a rebellion.

In the 1910s businessmen paid for the free distribution of millions of copies of twelve booklets on *The Fundamentals*. Ninety essays defended the 'inerrancy' of the Bible and the need to accept straightforwardly Christ's virgin birth, his miracles, his death as a sacrifice satisfying the Father's just wrath against the sins of the world, and his physical resurrection and second coming. From this protest came 'fundamentalism', a term of the 1920s to describe a movement cruder than the conservative scholarship in *The Fundamentals*. In 1925 the trial of a young teacher for spreading the theory of evolution against the laws of the state of Tennessee aroused the mirth of much of the nation, particularly since the attack on Darwin was led in court by William Jennings Bryan. An old man who was soon to die, an orator rather than a scholar, Bryan believed with utter sincerity that the application of the 'evolution theory' to the 'American way of life' would mean the end of his social creed, summed up in his motto 'every man a king'. How could a descendant of an ape be a king?

It was easy to regard the fundamentalists as bigots, particularly when their favourite New Testament scholar, J. Gresham Machen, wrote a book to prove that 'modern liberalism not only is a different religion from Christianity, but belongs to a totally different class of religions'. Machen was so exclusive that he left Princeton Seminary where he had taught to found his own seminary, and he then founded the Orthodox Presbyterian Church. The American Council of Christian Churches was formed by men not nervous about being called fundamentalists and not willing to be polluted by belonging to any historic church. (But Machen differed from them, too.) To such Christians neither liberalism nor Catholicism was fully Christian: in a world full of strong and ugly facts the Christian message should be simply the confident proclamation of the strong and saving facts clearly contained in the Bible, the inspired revelation which needs no Liberal Protestant scholar or Roman Catholic bishop to explain it. Another very conservative theologian, Charles Hodge, taught that in any generation reading the Bible means 'encountering the very words, thoughts and intentions of God himself'. Two versions of Christianity seemed to be at war, precisely as Machen had said, and in 1922 Harry Emerson Fosdick, America's best known liberal preacher, asked with an anger shared by many: *Shall the Fundamentalists Win?* Rockefeller money built for Fosdick a large church in New York which would be truly modern, but even that church had Gothic architecture. Other men's money supported fundamentalism.

One of the beliefs regarded as fundamental was that Christ would return physically to end the wickedness of the world. Once again the hope that he would come soon was disappointed—but the long isolation of the USA from the world's troubles did end.

Despite the enthusiasm for the quick defeat of Spain in 1898, Americans showed no such willingness to get involved in the war begun by Europeans in 1914. Much talk about a spiritual 'World Conquest' had been based on a belief in the self-evident superiority of an 'Anglo-Saxon race' which included Germans and the idea of Anglo-Saxons destroying each other seemed insane. In 1915 William Jennings Bryan resigned as Secretary of State because his Christian conscience would not allow him to stay near a president who might not avoid entanglement in the 'foreign war'. Next year the president, Woodrow Wilson, a preacher's highly moral son who was by temperament a professor if not a preacher, won re-election with the promise to stay out of the Europeans' battles. But in 1917 he led the nation into the war.

The immediate cause was the launching of a German submarine offensive, a development even more hostile to American shipping than the objectionable British naval blockade of Germans had been. A German intrigue with

Mexico, offering the recovery of land seized by the USA, was even more stupid. But the loudly repeated promise which stirred American idealism was that this war would 'end all war' making the world 'safe for democracy'. So the American churches became almost entirely, and almost hysterically, patriotic; a history of their response is entitled *Preachers Present Arms*. Billy Sunday, for example, now suggested that God was punishing Germany for criticizing the Bible.

When the American intervention had made sure of the German defeat, the League of Nations was created with Wilson as its principal father, almost as a new Messiah. The map of much of Europe was redrawn in accordance with another American ideal, 'national self-determination'. But in order to achieve this settlement among the wily European politicians, the well-meaning president had to be absent from the American capital for six months. His absence was an error. On his return, full of hopeful words but dead tired, what he had achieved was wrecked. The Senate, responding to the national desire to return to isolation from the world's troubles but also scenting an opportunity to win a tactical political victory over a president who refused to negotiate, vetoed American membership of the League. There were protests on behalf of the churches but public opinion did not demand the reversal of this disaster for the hopes of a permanent peace.

The Inter-Church World Movement was started in order to raise millions of dollars for good works in the post-war world. It soon collapsed and had to ask the churches to pay off its debts (which they did). One cause of the collapse was that the movement had sponsored a report into the strike by steel workers who sought a reduction in their twelve-hour working day. The rich men on whom the churches now relied for large benefactions responded that shorter hours of work would ruin them financially and the workers morally. Anyway, the churches were far more interested in 'Prohibition'—the prohibition, first by the individual states and then by the federal government, of the sale or manufacture of alcoholic drink.

It was in many ways a repetition of the anti-slavery crusade. Women had played a leading role in the abolition of slavery and Frances Willard, formerly a Methodist schoolteacher, had led the strongly moral campaign for Prohibition, incidentally advocating votes for women and other social reforms. The Anti-Saloon League, campaigning on the single issue and enlisting anyone eager for that fight, fired the last shots. But probably the battle could not have been won had the League not been able to draw on the reactions which went wider and deeper—the reactions of women responsible for families against feckless men, of rural against urban America, of 'hundred per cent Americans' against foreigners with drinking habits. And the Anti-Saloon League paid a tribute to the churches' influence in arousing this crusade against alcohol. In an official publication it could be read: 'It is not the province of a political party to inaugurate or assume the guardianship of moral forces. That belongs to the Church.'

Victory over the men in the saloons was postponed until after the war in Europe but then the appropriate amendments to the constitution came into effect: women could vote, men could not 'drink', there was no mention of social reforms. It was the high point of the influence of a slightly modernized Puritanism and it was a disaster. Many men refused to stop drinking and the flourishing illegal trade was an important factor in the growth of organized crime before the amendment was repealed in 1933. And many Americans now identified the message of the Protestant churches with Prohibition. When Al Smith campaigned for the presidency in 1928 many Protestants opposed him because he was 'wet' (against Prohibition) as a part of being Catholic. They were not so interested in the fact that he voiced questions about the capitalist system. So many Americans asked what the 'dry' churches were really teaching to the half of the nation's children which went to the Sunday schools. In his *Preface to Morals* (1929) Walter Lippmann observed that to be impressive a religion must be full of 'myths'—and that the myths of the American churches no longer impressed. And his book was published only a few months before an event which blew away many myths.

As President Harding declared at their outset, the 1920s were intended to be in the USA a time of 'normalcy' needing no 'nostrums'. This was now the world's leading industrial nation: why not enjoy it? And for many Americans life in the 1920s was pleasant: isolation from the woes of the world, expanding commerce, the emancipation of women wearing lipstick, the pursuit of happiness through cigarettes and (illegal) cocktails, the Ford automobiles, the movies, jazz and public dancing. One Protestant preacher was so businesslike that he preached the same sermon six thousand times and expanded it into a best-seller: it was called *Acres of Diamonds*. Another best-seller (by Bruce Barton) praised Jesus as a man who knew how to translate 'a great spiritual conception into terms of practical self-concern'. The only danger seemed to be that too many immigrants might arrive to spoil the feast: so in 1921–24 laws were enacted to stop the 'yellow peril' of a human flood swelling across the Pacific and the other peril of hungry people crossing the Atlantic. But the power which spread the table for this American feast was a capitalism which was in fact far from secure, particularly since all the presidents after Wilson were futile. A crash of the overstretched financial centre had been narrowly averted during the economic recession of 1907 (when the saviour had been the leading banker, Pierpont Morgan). In October 1929 came the Wall Street Crash. An avalanche was started by investors selling shares. They were fearful that they had overreached themselves in excessively optimistic speculation—and the panic brought real ruin. We have already noticed the great damage inflicted on Europe, where the Depression was the background to the rise of Hitler. Even in the USA the Depression became so bad that it seemed to prohibit hope.

Farmers, already facing the problem that a Europe beginning to revive after the war no longer needed to import so much food, were bankrupted by the further contraction of trade. Manufacturers followed as international trade was wrecked still more by countries trying to protect themselves by raising tariffs. Five thousand American banks closed their doors. Millions of Americans lost their jobs. In 1932 the Federal Council of Churches adopted a new 'social creed': the crisis was so grave that free enterprise was no longer enough and the government must act. Three years later a report sponsored by the National Catholic Welfare Conference broke with the tradition that American Catholics separated religion from politics: it called for *Organized Social Justice*.

The Way to What?

Having virtually asked for it, most of the leadership of the American churches supported the New Deal with a new president, Franklin Delano Roosevelt. It put America 'back to work' by turning the money of taxpayers into wages for the unemployed. Roosevelt was also supported by the churches' leadership when he led the USA to victory in the second world war, incidentally presiding over a wartime reorganization and expansion of the economy which doubled the gross national product and finally ended the Depression. But the churches did not consist entirely of leaders. Many of their members offered no welcome to the 'socialism' which they detected in the New Deal's great expansion of initiatives by the federal government in a trend not to be reversed before the 1980s. Churchpeople could feel that their 'benevolences' to charities adequately discharged their duties to the poor, although they could admire saints such as Dorothy Day, who opened 'houses of hospitality' for the unemployed and made the *Catholic Worker* a paper of protest. Most of church life, Catholic or Protestant, continued in 'normalcy': most statistics neither rose nor fell, most preachers avoided politics. And just as it was understandable that a church should be an oasis for churchgoers during the Depression, so it was understandable that in a world of violence the gospel should mean peace. Many churchgoers were thorough pacifists. Most were isolationists, supporting the Neutrality Acts when war broke out in Europe. Only when Japan and Germany had declared war on the USA did almost everyone in the churches support a crusade.

Roosevelt rivalled Lincoln as the greatest of all the presidents and the Episcopal Church could rightly take pride in his connection with it (the finest result of its connection with the 'old wealth' of the east coast's states), but we see his achievement in context only when we remember that he faced much domestic opposition or hesitation. He probably could not have confronted it so well had the agonizing affliction of polio not made him both a cripple and a hero. A man who in his early years had been a playboy with ambition became, in the best sense of the word, a crusader in his wheelchair. Because he had conquered a disability which would have made a lesser man retire from active life, he was able to tell his fellow Americans that as they endured the Depression, and as they fought and died in a war against the two most frightening military powers on earth, they had nothing to fear but fear itself.

When Roosevelt's crusades had ended in a triumph which was moral as well as physical, the presidency of the victorious general, Eisenhower (1953–61), was the enjoyable time for a boom in the churches as well as in the nation. The boom was relished all the more because in the same period eastern Europe and China fell under Communist control and one of the reasons why almost three-quarters of all Americans now claimed membership of a religious body was that the alternative could easily seem to be disgracefully and dangerously 'unamerican'. As many as half of them did go to church quite frequently, without any compulsion other than the pressure of public opinion. The boom brought the greatest benefit to churches which preached the 'old-time' religion or to individual preachers who urged 'positive thinking' and promised 'peace of mind', but it also approximately doubled the strength of the churches which offered less mental peace: there was plenty of boom available to all. As Eisenhower unforgettably observed, 'Our Government makes no sense unless it is founded on a deeply felt religious faith—and I don't care what it is'.

This boom in organized religion did not last any more than the boom of the disorganized economy of the 1920s had lasted, and the 1960s brought statistical depression and psychological confusion to those churches which were historic without being fortresses defended against change. The mood of 1954 had added the words 'under God' to the words 'one nation' in the pledge of allegiance taken by new citizens and repeated by others; and over many years the judgements of the Supreme Court had affirmed the tradition that while Church and State were separate the Americans were 'a Christian people' (1931) or at least 'a religious people' (1952). But now legal decisions accumulated with the implication that America was the home of so many beliefs or unbeliefs that it was wrong for the state to assist any particular religion, let alone any particular church. In the early 1960s compulsory prayers and Bible lessons in the public schools were pronounced unconstitutional. It could be said that the nation was no longer 'under God'.

These were the years when many of the young 'dropped out' with the newly available chemical drugs or 'dropped in' to make love with the newly available contraceptives. Pop music festivals dramatized the protests against the conventions of the older generations in morals, politics, business, education and personal appearance. In filmed encounters 'hippies' with 'flower power' made their protests against the indignant (and sometimes armed) but bewildered representatives of order and respectability. 'Sit-ins' could give the heads of universities tremors of panic or heart attacks. In many ways this protest movement was very North American: it could afford to be idealistic, renouncing the money which could be earned quite easily in the 'rat race', and it was religious in its enthusiasm about the arrival of a new age. This New Age was usually connected with astrology by being celebrated as the Age of Aquarius, but there was a 'Jesus movement' whose bearded young men looked very like pictures of Jesus of Nazareth and whose belief in 'love' as the answer had at least some connections with his teaching. The new shape of American religion also had a connection with the worship of the spirits of Nature by the Native Americans previously despised as Red Indians, or with the prayers or meditations of the immigrants against whom the Oriental Exclusion Act of 1924 had been directed. A widely noticed cover of *Time* magazine asked 'Is God Dead?' It referred to the God of European Christendom (as Nietzsche had done). And that question arose not only out of the 'alternative' culture of the young and disaffected but also out of the radical questions now being asked in public by a group of Christian theologians. One of them, Harvey Cox, hailed the advent of *The Secular City* with an evangelist's enthusiasm: here at last was the city of freedom, the City of Man, and he thanked God.

The euphoria faded: Cox, for example, wrote later books equally enthusiastic about the quest for a spirituality which would be authentic and strong in a world which needed it. The world looked ugly again because it seemed to be ruled by violence. The assassinations of John F. Kennedy and Martin Luther King ended their heart-lifting speeches, but it remained a constitutional right of American citizens to 'bear arms' and it remained their moral right to watch violence on TV every evening. The threat of a violence sufficient to destroy a civilization seemed to be necessary to deter the expansion of Communism. As dismaying to the sensitive conscience, young or old, was the entanglement of the USA in the Vietnam war, escalated by the bombing of North Vietnam in 1965—a war which cost 56,000 American lives and which could not be won. The war in Korea in 1948–51 had ended in a stalemate after dreams of throwing the Communists out of the whole country; now, this other Asian war was bound to end in terrible losses and in America's humiliation. And by now many Americans could not regard it as a crusade although it had been supported by almost all politicians and by many church leaders before the horrors became too great and the protests too loud. The national crisis of self-confidence was so deep that many, seeing what was happening on 'spaceship Earth', could see little point in being able to walk on the moon very expensively.

Would the crusading of the Roosevelt years and the celebration of victory in the Eisenhower years now be completely forgotten? Now that Americans were sharing something of the European mood of disaster and guilt, would God 'die' in the USA as in Europe?

The answer was that the strength of the Americans' vitality, powered by their unique religious tradition, reasserted itself along with the strength of their unique economy. Their astonishing resources, spiritual and psychological as well as natural, were not exhausted after a mere two hundred years of independence. They would overcome.

In their national life they overcame their uncertainties by establishing a new consensus, symbolized by the tendency in their elections: if the president was of the one party, the Congress ought to be controlled by the other. Most Americans did not want high taxes; when high government borrowing pushed interest rates too high, it was often felt that the answer was to reduce the government's expenditure on welfare for the poor, hoping that the growth of the economy would gradually take care of poverty. So the New Deal never led to the Great Society of President Johnson's rhetoric. But most Americans also did not want the extension of the radical individualism of the 1960s. For example, they were unwilling to enshrine equal rights for women in an amendment to the constitution. Indeed, there was much talk that the 'moral majority' wanted an end to more or less everything that survived of the 1960s, although that kind of radicalism also failed to command an adequate majority: there was no amendment outlawing abortion.

One reason for the churches' recovery was that the ongoing history of the USA demonstrated the truth of the words of Hugh McLeod already noted as a comment on the earlier history of religion in modern Europe: 'Religion ceased to provide a focus of social unity but it became instead a major basis for the distinctive identity of specific communities.'

There were problems, of course. The growth of church membership accompanying the growth of the American population can be partially explained by the desire of immigrants to find, or make, a social centre where people from the same 'old country' could be met, the mother-tongue could be spoken, the ideals and customs of 'home' could be revived. To this cure for homesickness was later added the attraction of homely churches as people migrated further to the western frontier and to the industrial city. But after the 1920s the churches had to seek recruits in a country where city life had become familiar, perhaps even comfortable: in the 1920s more than half of the population lived in cities and by the 1950s about two-thirds lived in 'metropolitan urban areas'. And in the 1920s legal immigration had been greatly reduced. The largest group now came across the Mexican border or from the Caribbean, often without the green card entitling them to work and often using the Spanish language as a sign that they had no intention of being thrown into the melting pot. Some of these Hispanics found spiritual homes in Catholic, Pentecostal or other fellowships but many did not behave like 'good Americans' and were not good churchgoers.

In contrast, African Americans still often regarded their church as the focus of their identity. It was no accident that Martin Luther King, elected president of the Southern Christian Leadership Conference in 1957, was a Baptist preacher who expressed the dream of freedom in biblical imagery. Behind him were father, grandfather and great-grandfather, all Baptist preachers. Around him were many thousands of contemporaries who preached in his style although without reaching his level of power with words. They had kept their people's hopes alive when the end of slavery had not meant the end of contemptuous exploitation. In King's later years there were many indications that the leadership in the political struggle was passing from those who felt and thought and spoke in Christian terms to those who turned to Islam as being less western or to a tougher style of confrontation as being more productive than 'non-violence'. After King's death the drama of that struggle died down but the change did not restore the prominence of preachers. For many Blacks life now became a struggle towards middle-class status through education and a job—and they had to struggle in a society where drugs were more plentiful than jobs. For others life was bringing up children without a husband—children who might well lack an ambition as well as a father. The community now had less motivation to spend a lot of time under a pulpit. But the churches still had their faithful, numbered in millions, and even when the heroic days of Martin Luther King had begun to seem about as remote as the days of slavery most of the black citizens of the USA could not forget how their whole story had been bound up with the story of those churches.

The advance of African Americans over many obstacles was largely their own achievement, but it was helped by the troubled consciences of many in the white majority. After the war in which black soldiers had served with loyalty and courage orders were issued to end racial segregation in the armed forces and the civil service. Desegregation in the public schools seemed the logical next step and in 1957 Eisenhower used the presence of troops to impose it on the Whites of Little Rock in Arkansas. Three years later the 'freedom rides' of volunteers used moral force to stop segregation in transport and in restaurants in the South. Many racially mixed demonstrations followed in favour of desegregation; the most effective in politics urged Blacks to register as voters. In all these struggles church-related, white-skinned Christians were prominent and it did something to redeem the past.

Another section of the American people which gained from the churches' overdue support was the half consisting of women. In the early life of the churches the share taken by women had of course always been more than half, and in the USA this fact which is obvious in almost the whole of Christian history had been specially significant because the tradition of dominance by the male clergy had not been so strong as in other countries. But even in the USA the formal leadership of the historic churches had been almost completely male and one result had been the number of women leading movements of which these churches disapproved.

Now the Protestant churches resolved to ordain women, or to recruit and ordain more of them, and although the Orthodox and Catholic authorities condemned the step many individual Catholics were sure that it was right and would be followed sooner or later. It says much about the developing USA that while it had been slow to end slavery it gave the world a lead in this matter. However, part of the world's difficulty in accepting such leadership was the fact that the USA was far in advance in the whole 'women's movement'. It was here that it was seen to be hypocrisy to believe in equality without also believing that women should be given equal opportunities—or to believe in humanity without being sensitive to the use of 'men' to mean 'all'. And it was here that Christians first saw that the subordination of women which is a feature of most of the Bible and the Church's tradition results from the adoption of the norms of the surrounding culture, not from obedience to the Creator of all.

There was opposition within the USA and within its churches—a reaction which should remind us that conservatives, who in the American situation often expressed their social attitudes in religious terms, formed another group which felt obliged to raise its voice. Numerous Americans felt alienated from what others regarded as progress and they now added a new intensity of defiance when the nation's direction seemed to be leading away from what they held dear. In this case they defended 'family values' and their defence had substance. Conservative churches were often places where husbands, if within earshot, were told to respect their wives, not to run after other women and not to waste the family's income which they must earn by hard work; where children were given security, taught morality and shown access to the treasurehouse of the Bible; and where women were given opportunities to make friends and to organize events. The other side of the coin was also real: conservative churches could be suffocating and conservative homes could be prisons. But older Americans could remember a country which was in many ways less stressful—and not only the old could see loss as well as gain in 'progress'.

Denominations (or groups within denominations) which opened themselves more liberally to the contemporary culture had the experience of seeing many of their younger members use their open door as an exit, choosing either to be more completely secular or to be more completely secure amid all the modern confusions. Conservative churches also suffered losses as youth rebelled but on the whole they had a firmer grip on the hearts of adolescents. It was also relevant that these churches tended to be based (sociologically speaking) among the less affluent and the less educated; in the USA in the south or the midwest rather than the north or the east. Over many years these large sections could regard modernity as a threat because they did not fully belong to it. Even when people prospered economically (as in the New South symbolized by Dallas) they could retain an attachment to the 'old-time religion'. And even in the White House presidents could rely on the power of this religious conservatism: Jimmy Carter, the Democrat elected in 1976, was himself a 'born again' Evangelical southerner and Ronald Reagan, elected in 1980, while personally of less clear beliefs, depended on the strong religious element in the conservative wing of the Republican party as it moved away from the cynicism which had been incarnate in President Nixon. After Reagan's retirement the Christian Coalition under the evangelist Pat Robertson tried to capture the party's leadership. It failed because most Americans had become more sophisticated both in politics and in religion, but its strength was such that it could try.

After the second world war a more sophisticated account was offered of the Bible's trustworthiness as the basis of the faith of 'Neo-Evangelicals'. A fortnightly magazine, Christianity Today, was launched in 1956 and soon gained a circulation larger than that of its liberal rival, The Christian Century. It could review books of respectable quality by Evangelical scholars or communicators and it could record many activities taking the movement far outside the sphere of academic debate—for example, the evangelistic crusades of Billy Graham. From a background of simple fundamentalism Graham emerged in 1945 as a charismatic speaker on behalf of the 'Youth for Christ' movement. For his crusade in New York in 1957 he sought the collaboration of any church willing to co-operate and he went on to national celebrity as the leading spokesman of the 1950s' combination of patriotism with a simple and conservative religion and morality. In the 1990s he was still the same man, burningly sincere and untainted by scandal although also the master of an efficient organization for huge meetings and of a very large and very modern network of broadcasting and journalism. Audiences in many countries heard his insistence on what 'the Bible says' and his appeals to 'come forward' in commitment to Christ. By the 1990s a small army of evangelists had arisen. Some were content with meetings aiming to resemble those conducted by Graham, but others (including some who did not stress the Bible's message) used the new instrument of television to the full. The preachers of the 'Electronic Church' attracted audiences of millions—but also needed them to pay for time on TV. The easiest source of financial support was not a critical audience of non-believers: it was a far less sceptical section of the public which welcomed not only an opportunity to worship without leaving home but also a message of encouragement mixed with glamour. Some of the preachers abused the trust placed in them, by financial or sexual impropriety, and did so in a way which was as spectacular as their TV shows. Others, however, did the age-old job of pastors.

The stricter conservatives fought hard for what they believed. In 1976 Harold Lindsell urged no surrender in *The Battle for the Bible*. A Gallup poll taken shortly after this reported that about 40 per cent of all Americans believed that 'the Bible is the Word of God and is not mistaken in its statements and teachings' and in the 1980s Lindsell's own denomination, the Southern Baptists, made clear its agreement with his position by its elections to leadership. Such conservatism was rewarded: by 1990 the Southern Baptists had a membership of about fifteen million, having grown by almost a third since 1965, while in the same period the more liberal Methodists had lost 1.5 million. And conservatives had their agenda for society, with the focus on the defence of the family: against abortion, against the hiring of explicit homosexuals as teachers in school, in favour of prayers in school and, if such prayers were still to be ruled unconstitutional, in favour of the private foundation of definitely Christian schools. But talk about a conservative triumph was questionable. Millions of American Christians stuck to their liberalism, arguing vigorously that truth and justice were at stake. Others belonged to churches which were conservative but not in the fundamentalist style—to conservatively Lutheran or Reformed churches, for example, or to Pentecostal or 'holiness' churches which stressed spiritual experience not an intellectual position about written statements in the Bible. And there were other signals. When the National Association of Evangelicals was formed in 1942 it affirmed the Bible as 'infallible' but was based more broadly than the strictly fundamentalist and separatist American Council of Christian Churches. In the 1980s a survey of leading Evangelical colleges showed that at least half of the students, and more than half the teachers, were not fundamentalists. They agreed with the position that 'the Bible is not mistaken in its teachings but not always to be taken literally in its statements concerning matters of science, historical reporting, etc.' With this more relaxed attitude to biblical criticism went a wider interest in the issues confronting society without at all denying the importance of the defence of the family. In 1973 the Chicago Declaration of Evangelical Social Concern drew attention to the plight of the poor and to the destruction of the natural environment. Ten years later a book by Bernard Ramm announced that most Evangelicals were living and thinking *After Fundamentalism*.

At any rate it was incontrovertible that the USA had become less

Protestant in its statistics—and that its Catholic Church had become almost as varied as the Evangelicals.

During the Second Vatican Council the main contribution of the North American bishops was their successful advocacy of the principle of religious liberty. In that sense the 'Americanism' previously denounced had triumphed and it seemed reasonable to hope that the American Catholic Church could take over the moral leadership of its nation after this full recognition of the right of others to dissent. In 1990 it could claim a baptized membership of 58.5 million with 53,000 priests and its bishops had issued statements full of the prophetic courage which previously had been thought Protestant. In 1971 they had called for an end to the Vietnam war. In 1983 they had declared that the use, or threatened use, of nuclear weapons against civilian targets was morally unacceptable and that the policy of nuclear 'deterrence' was tolerable only if it led to determined negotiations for arms control and disarmament. In 1986 they had demanded 'economic justice for all' as a principle and had applied that principle to current issues: unemployment should be put at the top of the political agenda and more aid should be given to America's own poor and to much poorer nations. But the bishops had their problems, illustrated by the abandonment of a project for another 'pastoral letter', this time on the position of women.

Priests, sisters and laity were often now behaving in what had previously been the Protestant habit of 'private judgement'. Catholic institutions suffered. In the period 1965–85 about ten thousand priests left the active ministry (about a fifth of the total number); the number of men preparing for the priesthood dropped by three-quarters; the number of sisters fell from 180,000 to 100,000 and many of those remaining relaxed their communities' rules; thousands of Catholic schools closed; attendance at Mass declined sharply. A change in the character of American Catholicism was to be seen also in what many polls reported: most Catholics disagreed with the pope. They believed that the control of births by contraceptives was ethical, that priests should be allowed to marry, that people who married again after divorce should be admitted to the sacraments. There was also strong support for the ordination of women to the priesthood, particularly since during the shortage of priests women as well as laymen were being active in the leadership of worship and teaching. Interest was still strong in Catholic spirituality but the days when Fulton J. Sheen had attracted very large audiences for his broadcasts popularizing the authorized Catholic doctrines were no more. Two of the most influential spiritual teachers were very different from Sheen: a monk, Thomas Merton, developed a great sympathy with Asian spirituality and a friar, Matthew Fox, taught 'creation spirituality', stressing the sacredness of the creation and the essential goodness of human nature, 'original blessing' not 'original sin'. From 1967 onwards many

Catholics became 'charismatics' in a modified version of the enthusiasm of the Pentecostal churches. In the 1990s it seems that these tensions will have to be resolved before a more united Catholic Church can function as the nation's moral guide.

Equally dramatic was the statistical decline in the activities of all the Canadian churches. The liberty proclaimed by the Second Vatican Council took the crowds out of the churches in Quebec and Protestantism, too, suffered numerically in the 1960s. In 1925, after prolonged negotiations, most of that country's Methodists, Presbyterians and Congregationalists came together to form the United Church of Canada and there was excited talk that the country, then called a 'dominion' within the British empire, would become 'Christ's dominion'. But the Anglicans, who were almost as numerous, stayed separate—and so, over the years, did increasing numbers of other Canadians, with no clear religious belief at all. The religious history of Canada had always been affected by its southern neighbour; in more senses than one, the transcontinental frontier could not be defended. But church life in Canada, like that people as a whole, had always been more sedate and more deferential to authority. In the 1960s which brought a new cultural revolution across the undefended border, the people saw that the old authorities had lost control and in the next thirty years none of the historic churches showed any signs of recovering dominance.

However, before we briefly consider 'postmodern' religion (Chapter 10) we may concentrate on a single development in the USA: the historic Protestant churches' changed attitude to social and personal problems. One reason for doing so is that much of the history can be summed up as a story about two brothers, both professors of Christian ethics: Reinhold and H. Richard Niebuhr.

They were the most prominent exponents of 'neo-orthodoxy' in the USA. Like Karl Barth in Europe, they treated both the Bible and the Church with great seriousness in response to a new mood of 'crisis'. Their whole tone was different from the gentle *Faith of Modernism*, in which Shailer Mathews had commended to the public of 1924 the belief that Christ is 'the revelation in human experience of God effecting salvation'. Even more did their neo-orthodoxy differ from John Dewey's *A Common Faith* (1934), where the word 'God' was used in support of the American way of life but with a content difficult to discern. But unlike Barth, the Niebuhrs entered deeply into the problems involved in relating the Word of God and the Church of Christ to the world of sinners. In 1935 Richard co-authored a manifesto of neo-orthodoxy called *The Church against the World*, but being 'against' the world's evils did not mean being aloof from the world's dilemmas. The Niebuhrian emphasis on the transcendence of God had to be combined with a sensitivity to America's inescapable involvement in some developments which very harshly challenged the old moral simplicity. It seemed impossible to defeat the Nazis and the Japanese without the use of horrific force—or to defeat the Soviet Union in the 'cold war' without the nuclear arms race. This race, it seemed, had to keep the peace by using threats for which the word 'terror' was an understatement and had to win the victory by expenditure so colossal that it ruined the Soviet economy and brought about the dissolution of Soviet Communism. But what had this to do with the biblical teaching about peace? Then came the 1960s when many Americans, particularly the young, rejected the old morality which had guided personal relationships, particularly in the sphere of sexuality: contraceptives seemed to make sex 'safe' even for the unmarried, homosexual practices seemed to be 'natural' for some, divorces and even abortions could be the lesser of two evils. But what had this to do with the biblical teaching about holiness? What now, in real life, was American Christianity?

The problem of how to relate the ideals of love and of holiness to the realities of life in a 'fallen' world dominated Reinhold Niebuhr's thinking. He began by sharing the pleasant belief of multitudes of American Christians: love ought to solve social as well as personal problems. But he gradually came to see that the Sermon on the Mount cannot be applied directly to the dilemmas which cannot be avoided in the swampy plains of life, for as a matter of fact love does not, and cannot, direct the aspirations and activities of societies. All societies are immoral because they serve the corporate self-interest: that group comes first whatever may be the ideals of those who join it. By itself love cannot reconcile the tensions and conflicts which must arise between groups and nations. Therefore 'reconciliation' or 'peace' should not be the only aim: before real peace becomes possible there must be justice. To Niebuhr this approach was not merely realism about inter-group relations. It was realism about *The Nature and Destiny of Man*, the title of the Gifford Lectures which he delivered during the outbreak of the second world war. He analysed sin as essentially the result of the human situation of insecurity, being the choice for pride or lust against obedience to God. On this analysis, naturally the individual sins—but how much more does the society!

As a young pastor in Detroit Reinhold Niebuhr became convinced that a strike was a necessary and legitimate weapon to use against bosses such as Henry Ford. As a professor in New York he became, however reluctantly, sure that it was right to go to war against Germany and Japan—and to go to war in order to win. Later he defended the possession of nuclear weapons as a deterrent against Soviet aggression, understanding foreign policy as the balancing of one nation's interests against another. He saw the goal of politics as the establishment of justice in a perpetually imperfect world where all groups and nations are, to a greater or lesser extent, even more immoral than the individual. He was sympathetic with the politicians who often have to make decisions not between good and evil but between shades of grey. It is not sensible to expect them to create Utopia—not sensible and not biblical. 'History', he taught, 'moves towards the realization of the Kingdom, but yet the judgement of God is upon every new realization.' He applied that insight to the history of his own country, writing a book about *The Irony of American History* with the theme that a nation far from noble in its reality could yet serve noble purposes. And for Reinhold Niebuhr and those influenced by him the place for ethics in politics lay in the middle between the ideals and the practicalities. There, in the middle, some moral 'axioms' can guide the formation of practical policies, haunted by the ideals; there the 'impossibilities' of perfection can be made possible although never completely. In Christian faith a vision reaches 'beyond tragedy' to a realm where humbled people are ready to forgive the sins of others. They are willing because they are sensitive to the dangers in any feeling of moral superiority; because they know that God alone is equipped to be the final judge.

Many American Christians have experienced, as Reinhold Niebuhr did, the loss of moral simplicity—and they have felt the loss in their personal lives as well as in their responsibilities as citizens. The ideals of holiness remain; the Bible teaches them, the Church's great tradition witnesses to them, the hymns sing of them; Christians pray for the strength to live up to them—but in many situations those ideals cannot be applied without any complication. For example, because this drug is so often misused it may be the ideal to avoid all consumption of alcohol, but even on the Religious Right it has become inconceivable that a democratic state should re-enact the law of Prohibition. Nor does it follow that no Christian should ever 'touch a drop'. Nor is it possible to lay down a more informal law about what is the right limit for every individual who is not an addicted alcoholic. The substantial changes in traditional moral attitudes to 'drink' have been matched by relaxations (public or private) in attitudes to sexual behaviour, to divorce and to Sunday observance although many conservatives have struggled to maintain the old standards and the intensity of convictions against abortion shows that there are limits. That seems to be the state of uncertainty in the debate at the end of the 1990s.

Richard Niebuhr's interests were more strictly theological than his brother's. He concentrated on the Bible, on the Church and on the Bible's message which ought to unite the churches. That emphasis was typical of most of the 'neo-orthodox' and it helped progress in the reconciliation and reunion of the American denominations. The most significant phenomenon was the great improvement in Catholic–Protestant relationships in the turbulent 1960s, but even while the idea of Catholic–Protestant reunion seemed fanciful, thoughtful Protestants in the historic churches began to explore the idea of the One Church of the One Christ: it seemed better than what had become the reality of Protestantism: a multitude of splinters which often splintered again.

Within the Lutheran tradition some of the splits which had resulted in the formation in the 1860s of the General Council in opposition to the General Synod were healed in the 1960s. The American Lutheran Church emerged, with only the Lutheran Church in America (more liberal) and the Missouri Synod (more conservative) separate from it; and in 1988 the first two of these churches united as the Evangelical Lutheran Church in America, five million strong. In 1939 most Methodists (north and south) united and their union was broadened in 1968; in 1990 it numbered almost nine million, with a further three million in African Methodist churches. In 1957 Reformed and Congregational churches (but not all of them) came together as the United Church of Christ. That was a promising name and in 1960 Eugene Carson Blake, a Presbyterian leader whose own splintered tradition was becoming the Presbyterian Church (USA) and who was to serve as the second General Secretary of the World Council of Churches, proposed negotiations for a union of a number of major Protestant denominations. In 1976 a *Plan of Union* was published, proposing that congregations of different traditions should continue to meet for worship (preferably eucharistic) but that their ministers should form teams in order to share resources and that these ministers should themselves be co-ordinated by bishops. In 1984 a more modest proposal was made for a 'covenant' of co-operation between local churches. These ideas aroused little interest among ordinary Americans but at least they showed that the old atmosphere of blatant rivalry between denominations had changed.

Richard Niebuhr's first book was published in the year of the Wall Street Crash, on *The Social Sources of Denominationalism*. It was a cool analysis of the non-religious factors which had helped to make the American churches strong in their expanding society. He saw that reality but he also knew the dreams: another book was about hopes for *The Kingdom of God in America*. After that he wrote with learning and perception about the history of Christian thought, seen as changing relationships between 'Christ' and 'culture'. He still urged on Americans the need to know their past: to see their churches developing from Puritanism to pluralism, welcoming them as 'disinherited' immigrants, teaching them to believe and to behave, going with them to the west and to the cities, staying with them in their disillusionments. He celebrated much in that history. But as he wrestled in order to get at the meaning of it all, he was sure that the comfortable 'Christ of culture' should never satisfy Christians. Nor did he advocate 'Christ against culture' or 'Christ above culture', for 'culture' is humanity alive and thinking as a society and the true Christ can never be against or above humanity. What he looked for was 'Christ transforming culture', changing it by being within it but also transcendent. In 1941 he published a book on *The Meaning of Revelation*, arguing that the 'inner meaning' is what illuminates 'the story of our life' by telling the story of God's life in Christ: that shows 'what God thinks of us'. His last major statement, as the 1960s began, was his book called *Radical Monotheism and Western Culture*. He maintained that for 'radical monotheism' the 'value centre' is no 'closed society' but the 'One beyond all the many'. So he urged Americans not to make an idol of anything in their own society. All their history—their denominations, their whole culture—had been only the beginning of their transformation into a free society more open to the disturbing demands of the One.

The Tragedy of Latin America

When the Spanish and Portuguese invaded Latin America during the sixteenth Christian century, they did not know what they were doing. They called the native inhabitants 'Indians' and continued to do so even when Amerigo Vespucci had demonstrated that this continent was not Asia. They said that they were looking for easily available gold, preferably in the land of El Dorado, the man ceremonially covered with gold dust: they did not understand that wealth would have to be created by men covered with sweat. (Already the farmers in this fertile region had cultivated maize, the potato, cocoa, tobacco and rubber—wealth unknown in other continents.) They said that they were looking for souls to save from hell, but a contemptuous commentary on the methods they thought necessary was provided by the 'Indian' who refused to be baptized before being burned as a rebel, such was his fear that he might meet Christians in heaven. Sheer bewilderment seems to have been caused by these men with strange skins, arriving in strange ships, riding on strange horses and firing from strange guns. Even the aristocrats who had governed the Aztec and Inca civilizations were at a loss. They were told that the strangers wanted large quantities of gold, but they themselves used the little quantities which they knew existed for ornament: they could not understand why gold coins were so urgently needed in Europe. They saw that the invaders carried the apparatus of their religion with them, but they could not understand what the religion was; said to be about God's love, it was communicated by atrocities. In theory, before the Spaniards fired on the Indians they were supposed to read out a document offering to spare them and their women and children if they surrendered and accepted the Catholic faith. But it does not appear that a translation was thought necessary and even the European custom of reading from writing was something unknown in these civilizations.

The native population, which may have been as large as seventy million, perished apart from about 3.5 million. They were massacred. They died after exposure to European diseases such as smallpox. They died after overwork as conscripts in unfamiliar tasks such as mining. They died in despair after the ruin of their ancient culture, imperial or tribal; their traditional places of worship were destroyed and the townships into which many of them were herded were called *doctrinas*, for there Catholic doctrine could be taught and it included the teaching of submission. Over the years most of them became labourers on lands granted by the Crown in Spain or Portugal to the Whites. This was under the system of the *encomienda* which in theory insisted that the white settlers should take good care of the Indians allocated to them, including their Christian instruction. The system worked out so differently from this ideal of trusteeship that the authorities tried to end it, but in practice the harsh relationship of master with semi-slave remained. Millions of actual slaves were shipped from Africa in a system which ended only towards the end of the nineteenth Christian century. They were thought more suitable than the 'Indians' for labour in the sugar fields along the long coast of Brazil, although raiding parties could still enslave tribesmen captured in the interior. The captives were usually baptized before being sent on their terrible voyage but slaveholders were nervous about the consequences should they become Christians in any real sense. Priests who were both successful and discreet in instruction could be rewarded by gifts of their own slaves. There were also large numbers of *mestizos*, disliked by Whites and Indians alike because brief couplings had produced offspring of mixed race.

Within a hundred years of the start of the invasion the continent seemed to proclaim the Church's triumph. Baroque churches were often prominent in their central sites and lavish in their visual aids to devotion. There were many houses of religious orders and institutions of education and charity. The Indians were subject to discipline: priests could summon them to confess their sins and pay tithes by using the government's roll of taxpayers and the penalty for disobedience could be a flogging and the excommunication which withheld the Church's sympathy when dying or dead. In 1572 the last Inca of Peru was both baptized and executed: it seemed that 'idolatry' had surrendered. After 1569 the Inquisition kept watch over the orthodoxy of the Whites and even attempted to keep an eye on their morals. At any rate the continent was kept free of pollution by Protestantism.

But the triumph was shallow. Long distances often separated the churches and the vast interior was scarcely penetrated. Until the nineteenth century most of the priests were white and almost all the bishops were *peninsulares*, men born in Spain or Portugal. For many years few of the Indians were permitted to communicate at Mass said in Latin: the white wafers were for the white people who understood Christianity. When allowed, Indians usually communicated only at Easter. And although they had to accept new buildings and rites, new names for divinity and new places for pilgrimage, they could not be compelled to accept new interpretations of religious habits. The cult of Catholic saints could be practised in ways which did not obliterate old beliefs in semi-divine spirits. Nor were the Whites born or settled in Latin America, the *criollos*, devoted to the clergy, one reason being that the churches were also the banks: priests were themselves rich land-owners and set the terms of loans to lay landowners in trouble.

The conquerors of this continent imprisoned their descendants in attitudes very different from the psychology normal in North America. The militant culture of Spain and Portugal had been shaped by the long wars against the Moors, so that the most admired virtue was courage; and now courage had conquered a whole continent rapidly. The religion which supported this society was Catholicism, the higher clergy being well endowed but also kept quiet by being placed completely under the Crown's control. In the new world this control was even stricter than in Europe, so that the pope had virtually no jurisdiction. From the creation of a diocese to the appointment of an assistant in a remote church, every decision was subject to the wishes of the state. The whole official life of the Church thus established expressed or implied approval of those who had achieved the *conquista* on both sides of the Atlantic, and in the colonies as in Spain or Portugal the ruling class consisted of government officials or landlords who were always ready to suppress a revolt but otherwise lived with as much flamboyance as was possible. Honour was paid to *caudillismo* for the powerful and to *machismo* for all men. These words of praise referred to a masculine authoritarianism in which ranking was achieved by numbering servants and clients, spending was far more important than investment and life was good for the strong man.

For many years the main object of the colonial system was to ship some gold and much silver across the Atlantic. This wealth created inflation; most of it was consumed in the wars waged to defend or extend the Habsburg dominions which sprawled over Europe; very little of it was used to develop the economy in ways which would outlast this flow of treasure. By the end of the seventeenth century the supplies from the mines of Latin America had dried up and Spain and Portugal had settled into their declines. In the eighteenth century the ministers of the new Bourbon monarchies conducted a sustained attempt to make the colonies more profitable. Taxes were increased and controls tightened. Protests and risings showed the response of the Indians and Jesuits, and parish priests were punished for their sympathy with this resistance. The white colonists also protested, but more mildly, against the trading privileges of Cadiz and Lisbon and the appointment of *peninsulares* to the best positions in the government. In the early years of the nineteenth century the colonial regime collapsed, partly because of local rebellions led by the glamorous 'liberators' but mainly because Napoleon had invaded Spain and Portugal. Even then, the monarchy which was compelled to leave Portugal established itself in Brazil and survived until the 1880s.

After political independence the initiative lay with those members of the white elite who had the intelligence to dissociate themselves from the corpse of the colonial system. These 'liberals' turned for inspiration to Britain, France and the USA and could adhere to Auguste Comte's religiously flavoured philosophy of positivism as being more modern (and less expensive) than the religion of the clergy. The mentality of the people remained very different: they believed in the Virgin and the Christ, in the saints who worked miracles for neighbourhoods under their patronage and in spirits inherited from the 'Indian' past or from Africa. As an institution the Church was in disarray. The poorer clergy had actively supported independence; in Mexico Miguel Hidalgo had paid for his leadership of the cause with his life. When independence was achieved many saw no point in remaining priests, so closely had the Church been tied to the colonial system. Almost all the bishops remained tied to it and had to leave. Until after 1825 the popes refused to appoint successors. The new governments, having failed to secure a continuation of the colonial period's entire subordination of Church to State, struggled for their complete separation in a long process which ended in Chile's decision in 1925. Often the treatment of the Church was far from liberal. Its lands were confiscated, its buildings seized, its schools closed, its processions banned.

The conflict came to a climax in Mexico. It was not ended when a Catholic (indeed, a Habsburg) prince was persuaded to try his luck as an emperor: he was executed. After a revolution in 1857 Mexico was declared to be no longer an exclusively Catholic nation. From 1878 to 1911 it was ruled by a conservative dictator more successful than that emperor, Porfirio Díaz, who delayed the crisis. But then for some thirty years the philosophy of the *Reforma* movement included the belief that Mexico ought not to be Catholic at all. In the 1920s the battle between Church and State intensified to the long-postponed climax. The bishops used the weapon of a prohibition of public access to the sacraments. Many peasants used more lethal weapons, rebelling as *Cristeros* in the name of Christ the King. Those who were not killed were persuaded by the bishops to lay down their arms but many were then shot. So were many priests and nuns.

From the 1850s the Church made a recovery over much of Latin America, but only through closer links with Europe. Bishops were now trained and appointed by Rome and many of the priests and of the ideas were European. Large subsidies were provided by Catholics in Europe and North America to replace the wealth which had been confiscated and the money was allocated by the Vatican. When in 1899 the bishops held their first 'plenary' council, it met in Rome. Its decrees inaugurated or strengthened what was for Latin America a new kind of Catholicism depending on the Mass and the priests, not on the lay confraternities which had honoured the festivals of patron saints or on the mothers who had taught their own versions of the Faith. Communion at Mass after the confession of sins to a priest was placed at the centre of religious life and marriage in church (followed by the education of a large family in a church school) at the centre of society's life. Inevitably this reformation was never fully effective in changing the medieval character of popular Catholicism and the strategy of relying on priests from Europe was risky. Europe was not going to be able to supply them in any considerable numbers after the 1960s. Even if the supply had been entirely reliable, there would have been a great danger in the creation of an image of the official Church which was not authentically Latin American.

From the 1850s there was an economic advance: Europe's growing population resulted in migration and its demands for food and raw materials resulted in investment in this continent as a source of supply. Such development brought prosperity to landowners and cattle-farmers; by 1914 Argentina was among the world's dozen richest countries. But the Indians endured further suffering as their traditional lands were seized for the new herds of cattle or for agriculture using the virgin soil. Then the victims were 'civilized' in centres which were almost concentration camps, with culture-destroying programmes in which the Church participated, believing it to be evangelism (as in North America). Moreover, the limited modernization of South America meant that more babies survived infancy and economic hopes attracted more immigrants. The population, some fifty million in 1880, had approximately doubled by 1930. The people's wealth had not doubled.

Throughout the twentieth century the top tenth of the population has enjoyed considerably more than a third of the region's total income. If conservative, the elites have often regarded their privileges as rights bestowed by God, have wanted the Church to be strong for the sake of the social stability that would suit them, and have been supported by many of the bishops. If liberal, the elites have often remained anticlerical. (In 1895 a liberal general who had triumphed in the latest revolution staged a ceremony to undo the consecration of Ecuador to the Sacred Heart of Jesus, and relations between Church and State remained bad until 1937.) Liberals and bishops have, however, often agreed on what became known as Christian Democracy: wider and cleaner elections, civil rights for all, land or welfare for the poor, within a tamed capitalist system. But the harsh economic problems have often overcome any consensus that might be reached about desirable objectives. One major problem has been the *hacienda*, the large semi-feudal estate where the landowner often provides the seed and the implements in exchange for a large share of any income. Many attempts have been made to redistribute the land but the plots given to the peasants have often been too small, there has been too little access to seeds, machinery and credit, and productivity has not been much improved. The most profitable estates have grown tropical crops for export to the USA or Europe but have often been owned by foreign-based companies and have often displaced the peasants with their traditional lifestyles. The most profitable crops of all, this time under local ownership, have supplied the US market for narcotics. Trade between the continent's own twenty countries has been at too low a level. So in many countries the social tension problems have erupted into violence despite reconciling attempts such as Christian Democracy. For example, Colombia had a civil war (1948–56) which left about 160,000 dead and in the next forty years violence associated mainly with the production of drugs claimed many lives.

Millions have sought to escape from poverty by moving to the cities, in the end turning Mexico City and São Paulo into the world's largest urban areas. Rapid industrialization has been the policy of all governments which have felt able to attempt it—partly with the aim of creating jobs for these millions now in the slums, partly in hope of escape from the effects of fluctuations in the world markets for crops and raw materials, partly in order to spend less foreign currency on imported manufactures. But here, too, there have been great difficulties. For many years free enterprise involving risk did not suit the rich in Latin America, who preferred to invest their wealth more safely abroad. Capital therefore had to come either from governments relying on taxes or from foreign investors who would demand a high rate of profit. The second source was the largest and by 1970 almost half of Brazilian industry was under foreign ownership. In earlier stages of modernization capital had come from Britain (specially in Argentina), but now the USA was indispensable. This dependence was deeply resented, specially since the richer neighbour could carry in Latin America what Theodore Roosevelt had complacently called a 'big stick', but there seemed to be no alternative. And as jobs did not appear, as taxes rose and as the penalties of dependence on investments by foreigners became more and more obvious, another factor was introduced. In the 1920s the poor Whites, the Indians, the Blacks and the *mestizos* all entered the political process, at least on its margins as voters. Now governments intent on industrialization would have to woo the impatient people by pacifying gestures—or intimidate discontent by terror.

Populist regimes tried to be popular, at least in the towns, without disturbing the class system at all drastically. Power was seized by men such as Vargas in Brazil (1930) and Perón in Argentina (1943) and for a time the populist propaganda worked. The Church's leadership supported such regimes and was supported in its turn. But in the end discontent grew, the bishops voiced it and the army deposed those two dictators.

The solution to the economic problems in an age of democracy now appeared to be military rule promoting 'development' but ignoring or suppressing the discontent. Such regimes of 'national security' began in Brazil in 1964 and spread over most of the continent over twenty or more years. A military coup in Argentina overthrew the elected government in 1976 and caused tens of thousands of its critics to 'disappear' before it fell in 1983. But under populist and military regimes alike, the economic crisis deepened. Money was printed to finance development but inflation rose to fantastic levels, as did counter-inflationary interest rates. Wages were pegged to prices (encouraging inflation) but savings melted away and where it could capital fled abroad for safety. More money was borrowed from foreign banks but as development lagged and interest rates rose it became clear that the loans could not be funded: as major countries defaulted on their repayments in 1982, it seemed possible that the international banking system would be among the victims. And all the pain was not ending the people's poverty.

Often a revolution seemed preferable to such 'development'. From 1959 Cuba under Castro began to inspire many hopes and conferences of 'Christians for Socialism' linked these hopes with the continent's religion. The infamous Somoza regime in Nicaragua was overthrown by the Sandinistas whose government included three priests in senior positions. But the idealistic, often Christian, Socialism or Marxism of the revolutionaries did not turn out to be the answer as the 1980s became the 1990s.

Che Guevara arrived in Bolivia from Cuba, intending to stir up the peasants to rise in revolution, but was handed over by some of them to the army which shot him in 1967. In the 1980s the economy of Cuba collapsed when the Soviet Union could no longer subsidize it and the USA continued its blockade. The Sandinistas were voted out of power in 1990; US backing for the counter-revolutionaries was a factor but observers agreed that the main reason was that the electorate was weary of the civil war, whoever might hope to win. Ten forcible involvements by the USA in Nicaraguan politics dated back to 1853 and it was widely hoped that this would be the last. There was a wide, although often reluctant, recognition of the need to accept a massive US investment in the peaceful development of the whole continent's economy. The foreign banks' loans were written off or recycled and foreign capital flowed back. Latin America's own rich, sensing more security, began to invest in local businesses. Industries which had been state-run and inefficient began to hope for profits not subsidies. Mexico concluded a free trade agreement with the USA and Brazil with Argentina. From Argentina to Mexico there was an interlocking system of governments accepted by the people as legitimate and human rights had become the creed professed by Left and Right. It was a revolution, although not of the kind expected. Both Communism and Fascism seemed to have been sent to the history books in disgrace.

Colossal problems remain as the twentieth century ends, however. All over the 'developing' world the sad experience has been that prosperity never floods down to the poor and takes many years even to trickle down—and at the end of the 1980s the Economic Council of experts had indicated the task by estimating that Latin America contained 183 million 'poor' people and 88 million who were 'extremely poor'. In the 1990s, when the population was about 450 million, the 'extremely poor' became twice as many, Mexico plunged into yet another economic crisis and only in Argentina was the average daily intake of calories adequate for nourishment. It is far from obvious that the new politics should be thought permanent and it has been calculated that 253 constitutions have been tried since independence in the 1820s. In 1997 a small group of guerrillas took much of the local Establishment hostage when it thought it had gathered for a party in the Japanese embassy in Lima, demonstrating that the Peruvian government had been optimistic in announcing the repression of terrorism.

Simón Bolívar, the greatest hero of independence, died on his way to exile in 1830 observing that trying to govern (but he said 'to serve the revolution') was like trying to plough the sea. In an age of much more democracy and much more poverty, the sea is still rough.

The Liberation of Latin America

From the fact that the natural resources of Latin America have always been at least as great as those of North America (with a more congenial climate) it seems to follow that the difference in the histories of the two continents is due to the difference in their social systems, in the development of their human resources. And since Latin America's churches have been no less prominent than North America's, it seems to follow that their history has been responsible for much of the continent's tragedy and that their twentieth-century renewal constitutes a hope for the future. As we consider this renewal we may note that an English sociologist, David Martin, commented in 1990 on the tendency of some of his colleagues to predict that the secularization of Europe will be repeated everywhere. 'But maybe Europe does not provide the universal model', he wrote, 'and maybe Europe only illustrates what happens when social change occurs in states where religion has been tied to governments and to old elites. In the United States that tie was broken and religion floated free of the particular entanglement of status and power. Perhaps what is happening in South America is a complicated dance in which both Catholicism and Protestantism are floating free . . .'

But as David Martin also comments, in Latin America this dance of liberation is no easy exercise. It is controversial even to say that a living religion ought to be more than personal and to plead for the confession and correction of 'social sin'.

In this continent the history of the use of religion as opium for the people is longer than the history of any of the modern nations, longer even than the history of three centuries when the Catholic Church was the religious aspect of Hispanic colonialism. The Aztec emperors and the Incas whose empire stretched along the west coast compelled the tribes they conquered to take part in the imperial cults, for example by supplying the victims of the large-scale sacrifices in the magnificent temples. In exchange for this worship the gods would, it was believed, support the empire as well as the universe. It is not surprising that the Spanish conquerors owed much of their triumph to support from the people at the receiving end of this religious system. But religion could also be used for oppression in the communities which supplied the victims to the temples, for the tribe's elders would enforce conformity to religious traditions as the essential support for cultural unity. Often these traditions included the eating of enemies' bodies as a religious act. So the alliance between official religion and political power was a controlling fact in Latin America long before the Europeans knew that this continent existed.

It has, however, never been accurate to explain the role of religion without reference to the conviction of large numbers of people that the supernatural is a reality. That belief has been strong in the whole history of Latin America. It was strong before the colonial period and strong during it. Under the rule of Spain and Portugal (in their own ways intensely religious countries) religious symbols were the forms of genuine faith: people prayed for supernatural help amid their suffering. In modern times those symbols have often been criticized because they reconciled people to that suffering and so made them 'passive'. Such critics have failed to suggest what practical alternative there was to the conquered being 'passive'. Devotion was poured out to the Virgin because while on earth she had been poor—indeed, a poor woman—and now in her glory she was both willing and able to help, psychologically if not by miracles. That was the faith within which she appeared as la Morenita, the Brown Lady, to a peasant, Juan Diego, in a vision in 1531 on Tepayac hill in Mexico, where an Aztec goddess had been worshipped. The image of her son in the crib at Christmas, or on the cross during Holy Week and Good Friday, was more popular than anything connected with Easter because the people loved to think of God himself as knowing how it feels to be weak. Such a God might give them the strength they needed to endure. And in modern times the churches have been so prominent as the vehicles of protest against personal misery or social injustice partly because, as many people have believed, they have had an advantage denied to all the political parties: they have offered the religious strength needed for the struggle. The usual question of the people has been whether the God who is preached can somehow help their poverty, not whether he exists. And although many in the middle classes have become secular, it seems that their attitude is more often anticlerical than atheistic. As was the case with the liberals early in the nineteenth century, the main wish is to see the privileges of the clergy diminished, not God dead. In the twentieth century Latin America has produced a galaxy of novelists. The world they have described is filled with the spiritual and the supernatural.

It is because religion has so often been used to legitimize the men with status and power, yet has drawn on the strength of popular belief in the supernatural, that the role of the churches in the liberation of Latin America presents the problems which are acute in the 1990s.

Impartial observers often reckon that only about a tenth of the population attends a Catholic church with any regularity and that the most vivid religious experience is available to the minority (possibly another tenth of the total) which belongs to a Pentecostal church. The Pentecostals' growth has amazed observers since a couple of Swedes who spoke in 'tongues' were expelled from a Baptist congregation in Mexico and a small 'holiness' church in Chile split from Methodism early in the twentieth century, but it becomes rather less surprising if we consider its context: the ancient, still widely diffused, belief in the power of supernatural spirits or at the minimum in the power of human spirits over the material world. The Umbanda spiritualist movement has drawn on this reservoir of belief, communing with the dead. So have many movements which have made an exciting brew out of the mixture of a religious sect with revolutionary politics: one example was the *Reforma* which for a time intoxicated Mexico. Much of Latin American Marxism has been of this spiritual character, to the dismay of Marxist materialists elsewhere. But the Pentecostal churches have been at least as successful as any earlier phenomenon in the history of Latin American spiritism.

An explanation which takes account of religious needs and beliefs is necessary when believers say that their lives have been changed by 'seizure by the Spirit' and 'spiritual' or 'divine' healing. Being able to make such claims confidently is indeed a mark of membership of the Pentecostal group, but another mark is eagerness to spread the word in person-to-person evangelism and what is then offered is a spiritual rebirth. The message is not the secular promise of revolution or of personal advancement; as a matter of fact, an escape from poverty remains difficult whatever may be the benefits

521

of becoming a reliable member of a group, of learning to read (in order to read the Bible), of not spending money on alcohol and tobacco and in general of having more energy and drive. The most accurate analysis seems to be that the religious promise of the Pentecostals is attractive to people who remain eager to experience 'spirit' although not actively involved in the Catholic Church's official religion.

Such people say with conviction that they need a stronger religion in order to lead a more satisfactory life—or in order to be able to survive in desperate poverty. And here they find such a religion. Catholicism has been most attractive when providing the occasional *fiesta*; now a Pentecostal service may be experienced as a little festival, although festivity cannot be guaranteed. Here the offer of religious experience appeals to people as they are. Here the leadership is strong because the worshippers are accustomed to control by landlords or bosses, yet the leaders usually do not come from a superior class and depend for their success not on inherited money but on popularity. Here the group offers emotional security, yet it is a group with a voluntary membership. Here the sermons are spoken with enthusiasm, not read from a manuscript, and they tell stories about life instead of entering into arguments based on books. Music stirs emotions and bodies because it is made with gusto by instruments which the people already love: guitars, tambourines, drums. The people are expected to add their voices of assent to sermons and prayers. There may be 'happy clapping' and shouting, and there may be greater excitements: the dramas of 'tongue-speaking' in ecstasy, of the expulsion of demons in exorcisms, of physical cures by the 'laying on of hands' or by anointing. And in the background there will be prayer and fasting in the expectation of miracles. The supernatural—or, sceptics would say, what is believed to be that—is felt.

All this is more exciting than the sober, reasoned worship offered by the historic Protestant denominations, where even the ordered drama of the Mass is lacking, and it is not surprising that since the 1950s these churches have grown much less than the Pentecostals. They have sponsored some missionary work among 'Indians' but have usually preferred their improved relationship with the Catholic Church to aggressive evangelism among nominal Catholics. The question has been raised: 'Is Latin America turning Protestant?'—meaning in practice 'Pentecostal?' The correct answer seems to be 'no'. The growth of the non-Catholics has been impressive, specially in the large countries of Brazil and Mexico, in Chile and in two small nations, Nicaragua and Guatemala, and it is estimated that in Brazil there are more Pentecostal pastors than Catholic priests. But the centuries of Catholic religiosity (rather than orthodoxy) are not going to be ended within a few years. It seems more probable that the Pentecostal movement will change its own character under the pressure of Latin American realities. At present it shows by many signs that it originated in the USA. It is therefore open to the attacks which Catholic bishops periodically make against the 'intrusion' or 'aggression' of 'foreign sects'. It is also liable to be thought strange by ordinary folk: converts hold themselves aloof from local forms of sociability such as drinking. It can be said that they have been brainwashed by dictatorial pastors and not allowed to speak, or even think, for themselves except in outbursts of religious emotion detached from daily problems.

It may also be questioned whether the present style of the Pentecostal movement will retain even its present degree of popularity. If the economy improves, it is going to demand and produce more education and more middle-class values. There are educated, prospering Pentecostal believers but the style of worship just described seems unlikely to appeal to large numbers in the middle classes: the history of Methodism shows how the preferred style changes, as does the history of the Pentecostal churches in the USA and 'house churches' for the middle classes in Europe. In the most comprehensive account of *The Pentecostals* yet published, Walter Hollenweger (a former pastor) has observed that often 'by the second generation, if not sooner, the methods used to overcome deprivation are subjected to a critical examination, and the drug which serves to overcome the feeling of deprivation, and not the actual deprivation itself, is rejected . . . Secondary education becomes more important than the baptism of the Spirit and ethical rigorism is relaxed. But none of this is possible until the first generation has succeeded, with the aid of the drug, in rising out of the misery which crippled it.' And there is an alternative possibility: if the economy fails drastically in the battle to sustain the population growth, 'revolution' will return as the cry; yet so far most Pentecostals have distanced themselves from politics as a 'dirty business'. If Marxism returns then Pentecostalism will be attacked as opium for the people: the charge will be that it was the 'drug' which failed to change history because it failed to change economic realities.

It therefore seems possible that most of the future of Protestantism in Latin America will be Evangelical rather than specifically Pentecostal—as was suggested by an event in Switzerland in 1974. An International Congress on World Evangelization met in Lausanne. Many of its sponsors expected it to concentrate on methods of 'church growth', recommending a more or less Pentecostal style using North American methods, but instead it concentrated on the question of the contents of the message. Thoughtful Evangelicals persuaded most of those present to agree to a 'covenant' which was not crudely fundamentalist and two scholars from Latin America, René Padilla and Samuel Escobar, linked person-to-person evangelism with a much wider movement, 'Man's search for freedom, justice and fulfilment'. In the end the Lausanne Covenant declared that 'the message of salvation implies also a message of judgement upon every form of alienation, oppression and discrimination'. However, the next congress of this kind, in Manila in 1989, was less thoughtful, more closely resembling a North American 'convention' designed to strengthen the motivation of salesmen.

Whatever may be the Protestants' future, the Catholic Church seems bound to remain the Latin American church which is largest both in numbers and influence. But for Catholics as for Protestants there are great uncertainties.

Early in the 1930s Cardinal Leme made the erection of a gigantic statue of Christ on Mount Corcovado overlooking Rio de Janeiro the showpiece of a vigorous programme to influence Brazil in the style recommended by the popes: Catholic Action moving towards 'a new Christendom'. Other achievements included Catholic organizations for students, workers and voters and triumphalist Eucharistic Congresses. Catholic teaching was given in the state's schools, the clergy were given subsidies and favours, divorce was not allowed. In return the Church offered no opposition when Brazil became a one-party state. But this apparently successful cardinal died in 1942 without having reached anything like a final answer to the question of the practical meaning of these grand ideas in relation to the continuing and growing poverty of the people.

In Brazil in the 1960s the emphasis in church life changed to a reliance on *comunidades de base*, where lay women and men, mostly poor, met to discuss and improve the conditions of their daily lives. In these small groups guidance came from the Bible, seldom from a priest. Often for the first time in their lives, people could speak up with some hope that a complaint might result in an action—and often for the first time, they could relate the sacred stories and images of Christianity to action to improve the conditions they experienced, not by petitioning for comfort or for miracles but by praying for strength to act together and effectively. As they related the stories of the gospels to their daily problems they met for themselves a Christ who had known how it felt to be a labourer unemployed for most of the day or a woman frantic because she had lost a coin, and they saw the Mother of God as the mother of a family in a village. They could be aroused from the helplessness of centuries. For them the most respected bishop was Helder Câmara, archbishop of Recife and an outspoken advocate of the needs and rights of the poor, who rose very early in the morning to pray and then risked his life all day since many men who had guns desired only his silence. Although almost all other bishops were more conventional, they were influenced against sheer conservatism by the Second Vatican Council, which had opened many eyes: although none took a leading part in the debates, many testified that they had been moved by the council's emphasis on the dignity of the laity, reinforced by the teaching of Pope John XXIII about the rights of the poor. The climax came in 1980 and in the small, poverty-stricken state of El Salvador, then one of the many countries under a brutal military regime. Its archbishop, Oscar Romero, had been a conventional ecclesiastic before his appointment but he had drawn so close to the poor that he publicly urged soldiers not to shoot them when ordered. He was shot while 'saying' Mass in a cancer hospital, and became a martyr revered throughout the continent and often elsewhere. Two other bishops and many priests and nuns were among the Christians murdered because in this time of terror they defended the poor—who noticed.

In their conference in Medellín in 1968 the bishops, or enough of them to be representative, denounced not only 'foreign neo-colonialism' but also 'a situation of injustice which can be called one of institutionalized violence'. This should 'not be acceptable to anyone with any degree of awareness of human rights'. Undeterred, these bishops felt that they stood 'on the threshold of a new age in history for our continent, an age full of yearnings for complete emancipation, for liberation from all servitude ... In this painful period of gestation we see the signs of a new civilization.' It may be said that in the flesh of the new martyrs Christ now marched with a message of hope down from the mountain-top into the slums of Rio.

Almost as impressive was the intellectual backing given to this new form of popular Catholicism by the group who became known and admired (in many countries) as the 'liberation' theologians. They revived a tradition. In 1524 twelve Franciscan missionaries began their work in Mexico ('New Spain'). They could make contacts with the Council for the Indies established in the same year in Old Spain and they used their religious status to make many protests on behalf of the Indians, with results at least in legislation (particularly in 1542) although of course not in the transformation of cruelty on the ground.

In 1971 A Theology of Liberation by a Peruvian priest, Gustavo Gutiérrez, called for a new exodus from slavery. This was a theology more dynamic and more disturbing than the sixteenth-century appeal to 'natural law'—an unchanging law which did not question the low status of the poor although it could be used, and was used very bravely, to condemn the deepest indignities inflicted on the poor. Gutiérrez went back to the Bible, in particular to the Bible's proclamations of new acts of God in the history of a people often oppressed, ancient Israel. He denounced 'all and every dualism' including the dualisms of rich and poor, religion and politics. He saw 'only one history', the history in which God intervenes to liberate his people with nothing less than heaven on earth as the goal. Two years previously Rubem Alves, a Brazilian Protestant, had published A Theology of Human Hope. He had argued such hope could, and should, grow even in a country which in daily life offered little hope to the majority of its population, but being an intellectual rather than an evangelist he had not communicated passion:

indeed, in a later book he was to denounce the Pentecostal pastors for practising their own kind of oppression and exploitation among the gullible poor. A passionate identification with the poor animated the more single-minded prophecy by Gutiérrez. Later books in his style increased the force of this theological renewal by concentrating not on Moses but on Jesus himself. The Christians' Lord was celebrated as the proclaimer of nothing less than government by God on earth (here José Miguez Bonino precisely echoed the gospel of Jesus of Nazareth); as the announcer of total freedom for all, not merely of souls purified after death or for one class or race on earth (Leonardo Boff); as the crucified Messiah who on the hard road to freedom shows the invincible power of the love which suffers (Jon Sobrino); as the Living One whose triumph shows that the good receive an unearned victory and the evil an undeserved forgiveness (Juan Luis Segundo). In the 1990s the publications of these theologians and their younger successors began to show how many areas of life and thought could be made freshly fertile after this approach—and the example given by the six Jesuits who were murdered in 1989 as 'subversive' teachers in El Salvador has not been forgotten: they sacrificed their lives as seed falling into the ground and apparently dying.

A constant theme of liberation theology has been the insistence of involvement in *praxis*, in the life of the community which suffers and struggles: only such closeness to 'the wretched of the earth' can give the theologian integrity. As Sobrino has put it, to look at Latin America through Christian eyes is to see a 'crucified people'—and to wish to take them down from their cross: only if that wish is determined has a Christian a right to speak about Christ's own cross. Another theme, frequent though not universal, has been the need to make not only the 'preferential option for the poor' advocated by the Latin American bishops in their conference at Puebla in 1979 but also an option for 'socialism'. And these two themes have opened the liberation theologians to criticism which up to a point they have accepted (as Gutiérrez showed in the preface to a reissue of his pioneering book in 1988).

They have been criticized because they have seemed intellectuals not at ease in the highly emotional kinds of religion which have been common among the poor. They have written in a style which derives not only from their experiences of Christ and Latin America but also from the international language of theology at the academic level. Those who judge them from their books, rather than from their involvement in pastoral and social work and in the down-to-earth discussions of the *comunidades de base*, can therefore accuse them of being in practice aloof from the people whose cause they espouse. More likely to trouble them is the question whether they agree that the Catholic theologian's duty is to study loyally, and expound enthusiastically, what is taught by the *magisterium* (the bishops headed by the pope); and the Vatican has noted their reserve with displeasure. Certainly they have demonstrated very fully their intention to draw from the Christian tradition living truths which can help the poor now, as when in *Trinity and Society* (1988) Leonardo Boff wrote about the relationships within the Trinity as the best model for a human society with no dictator, but that book pleased neither the secularized who think the Trinity nonsense nor the apostles of market economics who think socialism nonsense.

Many critics have attacked the handling of economics and politics. Some have protested that theologians ought not to touch such worldly subjects and that priests should not take sides in any war between classes, but it has been fairly easy to reply that Christian thinkers should not ignore the acute poverty in an unjust society and that Christian pastors ought not to be distant from the exploited poor. Harder to answer has been the criticism that despite the best of intentions these theologians have not been sufficiently discriminating in their support of the poor and therefore of 'socialism'. They can be said not to have been realistic about the contributions made by the poor to their own problems, about the likelihood of inefficiency and corruption in a country where power is concentrated in the hands of politicians and those they appoint, and about the need to belong to an international economic system and to attract foreign investment. But 'liberation' theologians have replied that they are not so blinkered as has been alleged. Gutiérrez, for example, has written not only about *The Power of the Poor in History* but also about the impotence of Job as he confronts the timeless problem of suffering. Other theologians have discussed economics with some subtlety while never being happy with what are regarded as the immoral compromises of the 'Christian realism' of Reinhold Niebuhr, whose influence in the USA has counted against his reputation in Latin America.

The critics most able to worry the theologians are those in positions of authority in the Catholic Church. The 'instruction' issued by the Vatican in 1986 gave general support to them and to the *comunidades* behind them, whereas an 'instruction' in 1984 had been severely critical; but of course everything depended on how warnings or blessings (or mixtures of the two) were to be interpreted. In fact the Vatican secured the appointments of bishops, and of officers in the conferences of the bishops and of the superiors of the religious orders, who would be safely cautious and in many cases stoutly conservative. Although Gutiérrez escaped censure, Leonardo Boff was 'investigated' and silenced in such a manner that he felt compelled to leave the priesthood. When Pope John Paul II visited the continent he made many calls, beyond doubt sincere, for justice for the poor, but he also repeatedly admonished the clergy not to engage in 'politics' and not to encourage the growth of a 'popular' Church at the expense of the bishops' authority. Most of those who heard him, whether or not they welcomed this, concluded that at heart he wanted a renewal of the approach of the 1930s—a 'new evangelization' under the bishops' control rather than the 'new civilization' glimpsed by another, more radical, set of bishops in the time of the martyrs.

But in the 1990s it is improbable that this turbulent continent will ever again accept 'evangelization' if that means in practice instruction from the senior clergy. Politicians now wish to keep their distance from bishops while not refusing their support; parishioners avoid control by priests while being glad enough to see a reduced number of them in the background. The experience of Chile seems to teach a lesson. There the Christian Democrats' government of 1964–70 was openly supported by the bishops, with a blessing which in an earlier period would have been decisive; but it had to yield to regimes of the Left and Right, to the Marxist Allende and the Fascist Pinochet, because these offered stronger (although incompatible) cures for the malaise of the economy, and during these years the bishops were spectators and critics. The Christian Democrats needed to form a coalition, retaining Pinochet as head of the army, in order to recover the presidency in 1990 with an economic policy which, it is hoped, would last longer because based on more of a consensus, and Chile's bishops did not provide the power behind this shared throne. In Mexico the bishops' attempt to stop the use of contraceptives resulted in 1974 in the provision of a free supply being made the constitutional right of every citizen. And in the 1990s the refusal of marriage to priests has been a large factor in reducing the ratio of priests to Catholics. In the countries of Latin America it is now on average one to more than seven thousand and most of the priests are old. In the continent where more than half the world's Catholics live the bishops do not have enough agents to govern the Church effectively.

The *comunidades de base* which have been an instrument or inspiration of much renewal appear to have an uncertain future. Will an experiment originally announced and applauded as a 'new way of being Church' become a sideshow in Latin America (as, in the 1990s, it still is in Africa or India)? Will the *comunidades* settle down into the quieter life of a network of church societies (as they have largely done in the Philippines)? Will they continue to concentrate on social problems, in the neighbourhood or the nation, although the novelty has worn off and talk about 'revolution' has died down? Or will they discuss the problems of 'being Church' with a thoroughness which may well lead to conflicts with conservative bishops? Will they insist that the administration of the sacraments should no longer be confined to the parish churches? Will they evolve their own determined leadership, replacing guidance by priests or 'pastoral workers' authorized by the clergy? Will this leadership include many more women, who are already the majority in membership? And will the bishops become less conservative, not wishing to cease to be the pastors of a people on the move? All that is certain is that there will be change and that it will not be controlled by the clergy.

In the Caribbean region the basic problem has been the same: a truly local church has yet to be born. Here the historic churches are more popular than in Latin America, partly because they provided education after the emancipation of the slaves. Even before the end of slavery slaves saw it implied in the Christian gospel—and so did some preachers, of whom the bravest was a Baptist, William Knibb, who began to stir up Jamaica in 1825. But this is a region of small islands which prefer their independence to any prospect of economic progress through federation and it is a region where the fragmentation of the Church into European-looking denominations bequeathed by the colonial past seems to be irreversible. Poverty seems incurable, caused partly by competition from Latin America, but if people try to escape from it to Britain or the USA they find either closed doors or racial prejudice. The religion which reaches the poor most effectively comes from the Pentecostal churches. An alternative response, particularly in Jamaica, is the Rastafarian movement which with the aid of cannabis-smoking escapes to an imaginary Africa; Ras Tafari (meaning 'the Might of the Trinity') was the name of the Ethiopian emperor Haile Selassie before his coronation. His death at the hands of revolutionaries has not ended the attractiveness of his image, black and proud. At least this is a reminder that since the slaves arrived the Caribbean has belonged to Africa as much as it does to Latin America.

9
caocaocaoca

Global Christianity

Beginnings in Africa

WELL into the nineteenth Christian century most of Africa was viewed from outside as 'the dark continent', the breeding ground of diseases which quickly killed strangers and the battlefield of inter-tribal wars which produced slaves stronger in body than in mind. It appeared to be a cesspool of 'barbarism' and 'superstition' where 'Negroes' lacked elementary morality and either had no religion at all or else worshipped devils. As Europeans proceeded to 'discover' it, to trade with it, to settle in parts of it and to make colonies of almost all of it, the continent was still said to be inhabited by a 'race' which was 'primitive', or at least 'lower'. It seemed natural and right to exploit Africa for the benefit of Europe, although when feeling generous Europeans agreed that Africans deserved to be 'protected' and even educated while being ruled in preparation for the remote day when they might be judged to have progressed so far that they could be granted independence. Meanwhile Christian missionaries gathered their comparatively few converts into 'mission stations' or 'Christian villages'. When numbers grew they attempted to retain control because of the danger that, left to themselves, these untrustworthy people would relapse into 'heathenism'. It seemed likely that Africans were always going to regard Christianity as the white man's religion; and indeed, many attitudes or activities left the impression that a convert's mind must leave Africa, as surely as a slave's body had been compelled to leave it in earlier centuries.

The years after 1950 have brought a strong reminder of how resistant to Christianity the whole of Africa used to look, for Islam has seemed to be impregnable across the north of the continent. It revived and expanded during the nineteenth Christian century, spread (as Christianity was spread) by commerce and conquest as well as by evangelism but owing part of its success to the acceptance of African customs which the missionaries of the churches attacked and attempted to prohibit. All that was essential was that everyone should worship one God and acknowledge Muhammad as the supreme Prophet. This meant the painful renunciation of 'idols' but Africans were already disturbed in their religion and already had long traditions about the Creator and about prophets. Although Islam's prohibition of alcohol was awkward, it allowed polygamy after the example of the Prophet. Although Arab slave traders were hated by their victims, Muslim preachers did not have a skin colour and a culture very different from the Africans and therefore Friday prayers in the mosque could be experienced as an act of brotherhood. And although Mecca was a long way off a pilgrimage to its great shrine from, say, Nigeria was not impossible. It is easy to understand why in comparison with the Muslims the Christian evangelists, who despised so much and demanded so much, did not seem very likely to appeal.

However, in the second half of the twentieth Christian century the reality has been transformed. The churches south of the Sahara have been far more vigorous than the churches of Europe and even more popular than the churches of the USA. Although statistics about Africa and about Christians are always uncertain, it seems probable that the number of Christians increased from little more than five million in 1900 to about 23 million in 1950. It grew to about a hundred million by 1970, it approximately doubled by 1985, and it has kept growing by births or conversions. Basing itself on recorded baptisms, the Vatican reckoned that some two million Catholics in Africa in 1900 had grown to about 100 million in the 1990s. In 1957 a collection of essays was published in Paris explaining the possibility that one day there might be a truly African church life and theology within loyalty to Catholicism; it was called, very modestly, *Des Prêtres Noirs s'interrogent* ('some black priests ask themselves questions'). Within the next half-century many of those priests' questions had been answered in an explosion of African Christian vitality. In 1994 African drumming and dancing in St Peter's, Rome, marked a synod of Catholic bishops drawn from most parts of the continent. The meeting was mainly a celebration although again some questions were heard. This religious revolution has often, and rightly, been compared in importance with the conversion of Europe to Christianity—a conversion which took much longer. It has opened up the prospect of Christianity being dominated no longer by a Europe often said to be post-Christian, or by a USA often disliked by people outside its territory, but by the Church of the 'Two-Thirds World', with the churches of Africa in the lead alongside the more problematic churches of Latin America.

How did that transformation occur?

The ancient Church which had flourished in North Africa—the Church of Tertullian and Cyprian, Antony and Athanasius, Cyril and Augustine—fell under Muslim rule and therefore into extinction or retreat. We have already noted the sad history of the Christians of Egypt and Nubia. In the *Maghrib* (Arabic for 'west') Carthage surrendered in 698. By the year 1000 the Christians had dwindled to a remnant. In the 1170s most were ordered to choose between conversion and death and agreed to be converted. And although the conquests and persecutions by Islam were decisive, it seems that other factors contributed to this death of a proud tradition. While in Egypt a greater unity helped the Christians to survive, in the Maghrib there were divisions; while in Egypt a monastery in the desert was an oasis of continuous prayer and a training ground for bishops, this source of strength was absent in the west; and while in Egypt the Scriptures were translated into Coptic, there was no Bible in the language of the Berbers of the interior in the west. Romanized Africa spoke Latin usually although the older language (Punic) survived. It looked across the Mediterranean and ignored the possibility that its religion might spread to the south.

As we have noted, from the fourth century a church originating in Egypt survived in the Abyssinian highlands. But the only further evangelism done was, it seems, the conversion of tribes conquered by this little Christian kingdom. When the frontiers of the much larger modern state of Ethiopia were drawn, only about half the population had become Christian and the neighbouring states of Eritrea and Somalia were firmly Muslim. And the Ethiopian Church was not entirely innocent of the charges against it levelled by the Marxists who took over the government in 1974. It owned vast estates which it administered badly. It did little for the education of the people or of its own clergy. It was controlled by the monarchy and aristocracy. It was content to be isolated.

But in its isolation Ethiopian Christianity had developed a strength which the Marxists had underestimated, as the Italians had done when they had conquered the country (brutally) in the 1930s. The ideology which preserved Ethiopianism under the Amharic kings was expressed in a myth that the Queen of Sheba (in modern Arabia) had married King Solomon and that their son, Menelik, had taken the Ark of the Covenant with him when he established an African kingdom based on Aksum as a new Zion. Until 1929 there was only one bishop, the *abuna* who was a monk usually of advanced years and unable to speak the local language. He was sent by the patriarch of Alexandria in order to keep alive the (mainly true) story of how the country had been converted from Egypt. The first *abuna* born in Ethiopia was consecrated in 1950. The Ethiopian Christians adhered to the Monophysite understanding of Christ and argued about its implications between themselves with scarcely any reference to the rest of Christendom. They celebrated their own saints, went on pilgrimage to holy places, and had their own customs such as frequent fasts, mass ordinations and immersions in rivers which could look like a repetition of baptism during the festival of Epiphany.

They kept the Eucharist in their old language (Ge'ez) at the centre of their worship but out of reverence for its holiness few would receive the bread and wine. Out of reverence for the Scriptures they observed the Jewish food laws and the Jewish Sabbath as well as the Christian Sunday. Whether or not many of the first converts in this religion had been Jews, the practices of these isolated Christians now treasured these oddities—much as the customs of the local Falasha Jews (whom they persecuted) were very unlike rabbinic Judaism elsewhere. Other customs of the Ethiopian Christians were markedly African: the circumcision of young women as well as men, the allowance of polygamy, the drumming and dancing in worship. They also had the African respect for holy people, in their case for the monks who kept alive a strongly Christian life of devotion. In the sixteenth and seventeenth centuries zealous Catholics hoped to convert these 'heretics' to obedience to Rome, which meant baptizing and ordaining afresh, but it became clear that what the Ethiopians wanted from European visitors was not changes: it was guns. A king who accepted Catholicism and tried to impose it on his subjects had to abdicate. Later Protestant missionaries arrived full of hope that a church so obviously 'decadent' would welcome reform, but what was wanted from them was schools. In the nineteenth century the kingdom recovered its confidence and strength and defeated an Italian invasion. A vital part of this recovery was a revival in the Ethiopian Church, reasserting its traditions.

As news about that victory in 1896 reached the rest of Africa it added to the interest already being taken in a church undeniably both ancient and African. Orthodox Christians who joined the Ethiopians in a formal relationship with a patriarch of Alexandria were few but Ethiopia's example exercised some influence on the spread of customs more congenial to Africans than to the missionaries. In South Africa a former Methodist minister founded an 'Ethiopian Church' in 1892 and more cautiously an 'Order of Ethiopia' was begun within the Anglican Church eight years later. The history of Africa's 'independent' churches—of what has been called the African Reformation—had begun.

That nineteenth-century influence was not the earliest example of the power of Ethiopia over the imagination of Christians. It is possible that reports or rumours about it were the origin of a widespread and persistent legend that the devout and rich kingdom of 'Prester John' existed somewhere beyond the territory of Islam. In the Middle Ages many Christians believed that contact with the land of Prester John would be a prize worth great sacrifices: such was the thinking of Columbus. Prester John was a priest-king often located in Asia (perhaps because of the Nestorians), but the legend about him also encouraged European adventurers to explore the coasts of Africa.

The Portuguese explorers found gold, ivory and slaves, with supplies for ships sailing to or from Asia. In particular the slave trade encouraged African chiefs to sell neighbours, criminals or other unfortunates to the Portuguese and their Protestant competitors who in turn could produce manufactures, guns or alcohol. About ten million human beings were shipped across the Atlantic as slaves and about half a million died during the voyage. Iniquity on that scale caused misery beyond calculation and much evidence suggests that the areas affected were destabilized and demoralized. A pope condemned the inhumanity of the trade in 1686, but to little or no effect. Another hundred years were to pass before the condemnation of the trade in England by Methodists and Anglican Evangelicals had gathered substantial strength, and in the end the first Europeans to abolish slavery itself were the 'godless' French revolutionaries. The Portuguese carried on the slave trade even when a pope had clarified its prohibition in 1834 and the British navy had stationed a squadron to stop it. They paid more attention to the teaching of Pius IX, who in 1868 declared that slavery was contrary neither to Nature not to Scripture.

It is not surprising that Portuguese religious influence was almost completely restricted to the circles which derived profit from this unappealing arrival of Europe, near the forts along the west coast, in the Niger delta, in the little coastal kingdom of Congo, in the colony of Angola to the south, on the east coast in Mozambique, up the Zambezi river and as far north as Fort Jesus in Mombasa. Although many children were evidence that white men had needed black women, Portugal's own population was too small to produce a strong force of missionary priests and there was a great reluctance to ordain Africans. Local rulers were baptized as a sign of alliance with the Portuguese, but less subservient rulers replaced them; some humbler Africans followed their example, but at no depth. In Congo the first Christian king was baptized by the Portuguese in 1471 and the last was beheaded by them in 1665. When in the twentieth century a more determined effort was made to create colonies both obedient and Christian, the policy of the Portuguese government was approved by a concordat with the Vatican in 1940. The policy was to give large privileges to the Catholic Church and to control it through state-salaried bishops. Non-Portuguese priests were for the first time allowed to work in these African colonies, but some of those who went withdrew in protest against the cruelty of the methods used to maintain colonial rule. As a result the independence movements which won their victory in 1975 were inspired by Marxism. Many years of civil war followed, ruining both Angola and Mozambique.

The Dutch Protestants who intruded into what the Portuguese regarded as their sphere of influence and profit had approximately the same religious effects although on a smaller scale. Unexpectedly the future belonged to the British, who in 1795 secured the extreme south as the Cape Colony on the way to India, taking it over from the Dutch. An Englishman, William Carey, inspired the tiny beginnings of the Baptist Missionary Society in 1792. A Baptist pastor who earned his living as a village cobbler, he wrote a pamphlet on *The Obligation of Christians to Use Means for the Conversion of the Heathen*, refuting all the many leaders of life and thought in the Protestant churches who had left such a project to the Lord himself. His initiative was followed by the (Nonconformist) London Missionary Society and by the (Anglican) Church Missionary Society within that decade, although in 1796 the General Assembly of the Church of Scotland largely agreed with the verdict that 'to spread abroad the knowledge of the Gospel among the barbarous and heathen nations seems to be highly preposterous in so far as it anticipates, nay reverses, the order of nature'. This negative attitude was shared by most Lutherans; not many questioned the anti-missionary ruling of the theologians of Wittenberg in 1652. The contrast with the worldwide vision of Catholicism was striking.

If the idea of a missionary crossing oceans and probably dying of a tropical disease seemed preposterous to these Protestants in Europe, the invasion seemed deeply offensive to almost all the 'barbarous and heathen' Africans. Despite what most of the missionaries thought most Africans were deeply moral and religious, to the extent of not separating religion from daily life. But the religion they accepted was the tradition of a whole people, handed down by venerated ancestors. Naturally these traditions were in detail as various as the eight hundred peoples (a fact which must always be remembered when generalizing), but it seems safe to say that a great deal in them had no parallel in the missionaries' Christianity, specially if the missionaries were Protestants.

African traditions were unwritten; Protestants depended on the Bible. African worship was dramatic; Protestants sat and listened apart from the singing of strange hymns. African religions had no organization wider than the customs of a particular people; even for Protestants, the Church was an elaborate organization based in Europe. Africans affirmed life; it appeared that Protestant morality condemned most of the joys of life, implying much when it attacked beer-drinking and told men to cover their legs and women their breasts. Africans thought much about their past; Protestants claimed that all the dead ancestors of Africa were in hell and that the Lord Jesus would soon return to earth as Judge. Africans thought much about spirits with the power to harm; Protestants claimed either that they were demons or that they did not exist. Africans had no systematic theology; Protestants had a great deal and it seemed to be complete nonsense. And in twentieth-century Africa those evangelists who repeat the nineteenth-century Protestants' message are very often condemned as naive or worse by Christians and others alike. But at least this may be said: if the Protestants of this early period had not believed in their message with all their hearts and souls, they would not have gone to Africa to spread it—and the history of Africa would not have been better.

Many of the early missionaries were less alarming than their message, being more skilled at practical jobs than at preaching. Thus Robert Moffat, formerly a gardener, established a base at Kuruman in the heart of South Africa and translated the Bible, but accurately said that he would leave behind him 'fewer Christians than fruit trees'. His son-in-law, David Livingstone, had worked in a factory as a child before qualifying as a doctor. He abandoned the routine work of a missionary (in which he had less success than his father-in-law Moffat) in order to become an explorer, hoping that the making of a scientific map would eventually contribute to the making of 'the kingdom of Christ'. Johannes van der Kemp, a tough army officer and doctor who arrived in the Cape Colony in 1799, was the real founder of the Christian mission in South Africa because he proved himself to be the friend of the Africans. He married one; he sheltered refugees from the expansion of the new Zulu kingdom; he denounced the settlers of Dutch origin (the Afrikaners) for enslaving 'Hottentots'. Partly because of continuing pressure from missionaries, the British government insisted on the abolition of slavery. Many Afrikaners so objected that in 1838 they undertook the 'great trek' from the Cape to the north. From their wagons they looked at a land which seemed empty apart from a few people with black skins and primitive minds. In their Bibles they found that the Lord had given them this land. More than 150 years were to pass before they were firmly corrected.

The Mission in Africa

Already in those early years of the Christian mission there were glimpses of good results. Ntsikana, a prophet of the Xhosa people, spoke words which were to be sung across Christian Africa: God hunts for souls, he is the blanket under which many can take refuge, tribes can be united like two herds of cattle, 'a great hunting horn has sounded'. And Africans taught by the missionaries modernized. The plough driven by oxen and men began to replace the hoe used by women; guns procured meat and the fields grew new crops, vegetables and fruits; irrigation was more reliable than rainmaking by kings; babies lived longer and adults lived better, some of them with the ability to read and write. Languages were put into writing so that the Bible might be translated and the 'customs of the natives' were studied and written about so that some might be respected and some abolished in the light provided by the Bible. The translations were often clumsy and the anthropology was often unprofessional; in particular, accounts of African religion were spoiled by prejudice against 'heathenism' as later accounts were to be spoiled by a secular prejudice against 'magic'. But before the missionaries attempted these tasks, what was known in Africa was what was spoken about in a neighbourhood. And quite often it was the missionaries who showed Africans what European manufactured goods were and how to use them, and when these evangelists were welcomed by African chiefs it could be in the hope that traders would follow. The chiefs expected to be able to control mere traders, since they controlled everyone else in sight.

David Livingstone came to think commerce with Europe to be God's will for Africa because he hoped that as it developed it would destroy the incentive to sell slaves to the Arabs. He died in an African village in 1873, still exploring the interior of the continent for the sake of 'commerce and Christianity', still being the friend of Africans without converting them, still hoping for great things. His African servants paid him a truly great tribute: they buried his heart in Africa but carried his body to the coast for burial among his own people. Many Europeans then took up the mission and some founded 'Livingstonia'. Anglicans went inland from bases in Zanzibar and Mombasa. Catholics joined in what became something of a rush to evangelize before other missionaries arrived.

Five years before Livingstone's death Charles Lavigerie, the recently appointed archbishop of Algiers, had founded the society of priests and lay brothers vowed to missionary lives which became known as the White Fathers; it was soon joined by the White Sisters. Already the challenge of Africa had led to the dedication of smaller new religious orders, but the Franciscans, Dominicans and Jesuits who had done so much for the Americas had been lacking here. Although Gregory XVI had appointed three bishops as 'vicars apostolic' in the 1830s, none had been an outstanding personality. Now in the 1860s Lavigerie was, like Livingstone, a great dreamer. He wanted a French empire with a *mission civilisatrice* extending from Algiers into Tunisia, across to the Atlantic and into the tropics. He wanted a spiritual army of well-trained and patient evangelists, even suggesting that priests should be allowed to marry and to use the local language in the Mass. And although the empire was to melt away and these suggestions were premature, some of his dream came true. In 1890 an international conference agreed to suppress slavery. By the 1960s there were in Africa 35,000 Catholic priests, nuns or lay brothers.

This new missionary impulse sharpened the question of the role of Africans in the total mission, a question which went back to the earlier days when the focus of Christian hopes had been in West Africa. Most conversions were effected not by foreign missionaries but by local evangelists such as Philip Quaque who had founded the Methodist Church in Ghana before his death in 1816. Freed slaves based in Sierra Leone and Liberia could be effective. Off the east coast, white missionaries won few converts in Madagascar but enough to alarm Queen Ranavalona, who in response conducted a persecution cruel even by African standards during her long reign (1828–61). At the end of that great ordeal missionaries returned, to find that the number of Christians had grown during their absence. In London Henry Venn, general secretary of the Church Missionary Society for 31 years from 1841, urged that the aim should be the foundation of churches which would not need foreign supervision or aid. Yet in other places African Christians could be criticized because they disappointed the white missionaries by a failure to get results. Thus the 'native pastorate' which took over in Sierra Leone in 1860 was soon the target of criticism and the consecration in 1864 of Samuel Crowther in Canterbury Cathedral as the bishop to lead Anglican work around the river Niger was followed by an unhappy history. There seemed to be a great opportunity: he was an ex-slave, now saintly and dignified; he had been born a Yoruba and the Yoruba empire had recently collapsed; he could lead into this gap a team of evangelists recruited from other ex-slaves in Sierra Leone. But he had to wait for fourteen years before a steamer arrived for the mission's use on the river and then it had to earn its keep by trading. He could not get the results hoped for and before he died in 1891 his associates had been dismissed for incompetence or worse on the recommendation of keen young missionaries fresh from England. No other African was to be made an Anglican bishop before 1951. In Nigeria many converts were to be made by the *aladura* churches which were not controlled by missionaries. In the south of the country to which the Anglican mission retreated, the most effective evangelist was an African, Garrick Sokari Braide, who was regarded by the British as a troublemaker.

It was in the African tradition that a spirit-possessed prophet (a man or a woman) might banish the evil spirit causing illness or inspire a group to take some new action. On occasion such guidance could have tragic consequences amid the general unsettlement of the continent: in the 1850s the Xhosa people felt guided to slaughter about 400,000 of their cattle because two girls announced that the spirits of ancestors had promised that if this was done the dead would be raised to life as a mighty army. About 40,000 of the Xhosas then starved to death. The Xhosas had previously put up a resistance to the white settlers who wanted their land; now the Whites could move in. But at the beginning of the twentieth century the African tradition connected with the Pentecostal movement in the USA and elsewhere and one result was the formation by prophets of 'Zionist' churches among the Xhosas and other tribes in South Africa. They used this name because they were influenced by enthusiastic accounts of Zion City, a centre of 'divine healing' near Chicago. In these new groups Africans could have the Pentecostal experience without interference by white missionaries and often there was a 'Zion' to which the distressed went. That was the character of the Church of the Nazarites which Isaiah Shembe set up for his fellow Zulus in 1913.

William Wadé Harris was a striking example of the African Christian prophet and in the 1990s there is still a flourishing Harrist Church. Formerly a teacher, when about fifty years old he preached from late in 1913 to early in 1915. He had been jailed in Liberia after involvement in a little movement which had hoped that misrule by the 'Creoles' descended from American slaves might be replaced by incorporation into the British empire. In prison he had a dream: an archangel commissioned him as a prophet. After release he appeared in the neighbouring French colony, the Ivory Coast, with a long white beard and a long white robe. In his right hand was a tall cross but he carried also a Bible in English and a bowl which he used for the baptism of about a hundred thousand converts. He told them to trust the power of the Bible although they could not read it, to burn their pagan fetishes, to enrol in a church and to await the imminent kingdom of God. He told them also about the Ten Commandments but pointed out that these included no law about putting away extra wives. He avoided politics but the French colonial authorities soon beat him up and sent him back to Liberia and obscurity. They shared the belief of the British that missionaries ought to have a proper training, should see that any converts were well instructed before baptism, and should not admit them to communion if in accordance with African custom they had more than a single partner. In short, African Christians should burn not only their fetishes but also most of their old ideas.

In the million square miles around the tributaries of the Congo river the traditions of the tribes included many practices which Europeans called 'beastliness' (including cannibalism) but because the area was rich in minerals and rubber the Belgian king was not deterred from making it his personal estate from 1885 to 1908. When he found that it was not as profitable as he hoped, his agents encouraged work by practices which could also be called beastly and after many protests by missionaries and others 'the Congo' became a colony of the Belgian state. The government now arranged privileges and subsidies for Catholic missionaries but also allowed Protestants to work. About ten thousand missionaries poured into the colony; one of them was a Baptist who one day blessed a child in the village of Nkamba.

The incident was not forgotten in the family and when the child grew up the memory contributed, with visions, to his conviction that he was called to be a prophet. In March 1921 he began his public work. He preached; he healed; he announced that the kingdom of God was near. The excitement interrupted work for the European employers and in June the prophet was arrested. He escaped from prison but soon gave himself up. A petition from the white missionaries saved him from execution but he was flogged and sentenced to imprisonment for life. He died in prison in 1951. After his death his sons led a church which was recognized by the government in 1959 and welcomed into the World Council of Churches eleven years later. By the 1990s it had a membership of between six and eight million and had become increasingly orthodox. Its morals had always been strict (it did not accept polygamy) but it had been reluctant to adopt the Eucharist, regarded as magic performed by white priests using bread and wine which in Africa were luxuries, and initially the founder had been spoken of in terms usually reserved for Christ. Now the Church used baptism and the Eucharist, studied the Bible and could not be contradicted when it revered Simon Kimbangu as a saint.

In prison he had been quiet and cheerful and Africa knew that the spiritual message could be spread without any aggressive words. Young Africans spread it without preaching in Uganda in the 1890s. When the explorer Henry Stanley (who had won fame by making contact with David Livingstone when that great man was thought to be lost) reported that Uganda was ripe for conversion, missionaries made haste. French White Fathers brought Catholicism and Anglicans and others brought their own messages. At the same time Arab traders spread the teachings of Islam. The young Mwanga who was *kabaka* (king) became alarmed that in the talkative confusion he was going to lose his absolute power and when an Anglican bishop entered the kingdom he had him murdered. (Another bishop had become a martyr attempting to prove that the Zambezi could be 'God's highway' into the more southern region of Africa, as Livingstone had promised.) Mwanga was equally infuriated when young men attached to his court as pages refused to join him in the homosexual practices to which he had been introduced by the Arabs. He had them burned alive, beginning with Charles Lwanga, a Catholic. Their courage in their agonies led to thousands of conversions to their faith. This in turn led the Muslims to seize power and the Catholics and Protestants to form little armies for a triangular civil war. The British stepped in and established a pacifying 'protectorate' which favoured the Anglicans although Catholic missionaries also evangelized, now coming from Britain rather than France.

In 1884–85 the Congress of Berlin arranged the division of Africa between the European powers. It was inspired by Bismarck's determination that the new German empire should not be left out of the scramble for colonies but at least it postponed war between the Europeans and it included an agreement to encourage missionaries of every sort, partly because this was a cheap way of getting European-style hospitals and schools. A period followed when the missionaries had a status of assured paternalism very different from the dangers faced in earlier years. They arrived by steamship and train and for East Africa could use the Suez Canal opened in 1869; they used quinine to avoid malaria and vaccinations against smallpox; they had at least something in common with the men who ruled the land. Africans were now more eager to be cured, to be taught and to be told about the religion which seemed to have been behind the Whites' conquest of the continent—although sharp eyes could detect some evidence that not all Europeans were devout and that European Christianity was going through disturbances almost as great as the revolutions in African thinking.

Probably most missionaries accepted the truth of the Bible without probing, as they accepted the superiority of European civilization in general terms. But there were exceptions. John William Colenso had been a distinguished mathematician before becoming a missionary bishop among the Zulus. When asked whether the numbers and other facts in the Old Testament were all accurate, he could not reply with a simple 'yes'. Later he got into further trouble by defending the Zulus against other white men who were trying to acquire their land and against other missionaries who were trying to stamp out their tradition of polygamy, and he had to break with his fellow Anglicans. However, that uneasily thoughtful bishop was not typical and he made few converts.

Most Africans, when they had access to the Bible, were not interested in criticisms of its accuracy. They were fascinated to find how similar was the biblical world to their own, with purifying sacrifices, instructive dreams, important ancestors, the family with a large and extended membership, many wives for patriarchs and kings, disasters through curses, healing through spiritual power, dancing in joyful worship (did not King David 'dance before the Lord'?) and many miracles after prayer. If the missionaries told them that such African traditions had been superstition or at least not civilized, they could point to the Bible which they were told was the final authority. Yet they often welcomed the scientific medicine which had arrived along with the Bible, for leprosy, yaws and other ancient terrors could now be treated, and they welcomed the reading and writing, with a touch of science, which seemed to be the white man's magic.

It is not surprising that these encounters between biblical or African tradition and European modernity produced some confusion in the minds both of the missionaries and of the Africans. Very few people on either side saw even the beginnings of answers to the profound questions involved, although in Paris in the 1930s a group of African and Caribbean intellectuals led by Léopold Senghor defended the dignity of négritude in culture. Far more often it was agreed simply that the medicine and the education which Africa owed to the missionaries were needed urgently and that philosophy was less urgent. And even this was not agreed by all. Some missionaries and some Africans protested that they would have nothing to do with the mental disturbance caused by the hospital and the school. Some Europeans and even

Africans more quietly believed that the modern forces represented by the hospital and the school would one day demolish all religion.

Such was the encounter of mentalities when the European powers began their sudden scramble for colonies in Africa in the late 1880s—and the muddle was much the same when the Europeans began their equally sudden dismantling of their empires in the late 1950s.

The Cross in Africa

In colonial times before the 1950s there were African rebellions—in Nigeria, Rhodesia, Natal, Mozambique, Madagascar and two German colonies—but not many. One of the most ominous risings occurred in Kenya in 1952–54, when decolonization was not far off. The basic objection of the Mau Mau movement was to the acquisition of large areas of good land by white settlers: land was already getting scarce. Some Christians shared or supported that grievance, but others were horrified when the rebels used violence and forced fellow Africans to take grim oaths of loyalty, drinking blood after sacrifices; and some Christians who refused to take such oaths were martyred.

Usually the pent-up feelings of Africans were expressed without violence, for example by joining the growth of the 'independent' churches. These were usually founded by a prophet after an unhappy experience of Protestantism; one such was John Maranke who objected to the racism of the Dutch Reformed Church and founded the deliberately named Apostolic Church in 1932. In the 1960s a rarity emerged: an independent church formed by ex-Catholics in Kenya, the Maria Legio. The usual question was: the European Protestants protested against the Catholics, so why should Africans not protest against white Protestants? Thus the 'Church of Christ in Africa' broke away from the Anglicans in Kenya and Alice Lenshina inspired the Lumpa Church in Zambia (which to the fury of the Zambian government refused to pay taxes). These churches differed from each other, of course: some went much further than others in restoring African customs which almost all the missionaries condemned. The point, however, was that in these churches all the decisions were made by Africans. The need for such self-expression by ecclesiastical rebellion was somewhat reduced when mission-funded churches came under African leadership and it became more proper to call the 'independent' churches 'African-instituted' since all were now more or less independent. But the need did not disappear. The historic churches still looked to Rome or to the European or American centres of Protestantism and were still organized in a more-or-less European style, the cost of which was a factor in their continuing dependence on money from overseas. It was uncertain how they would react to the accelerating pace of political independence.

In the long run what counted in Kenya was the announcement of the English duke who was responsible for the British colonial empire that 'the interests of the African natives must be paramount'. That was in 1923. Elsewhere the former colonies of the German empire were handed over to the victorious European powers under 'mandates' from the League of Nations which implied a temporary trusteeship. And all over Africa European rule had to go, however strong might be the Europeans' belief that the time was not ripe. In 1956 Britain and France were humiliated when they tried to occupy the Suez Canal (taking advantage of a war between Israel and Egypt). Virtually, that was the end. By the end of the 1950s it seemed to most people clear that Africans were going to be the masters in their own continent—even in Madagascar and Algeria where the French tried to preserve their presence as rulers or settlers by ruthless force, even in Southern Rhodesia where the white settlers tried to preserve their privileges by declaring their own form of independence, even in South Africa where the victory of the Nationalists in the all-white election of 1948 began the racist regime of apartheid in defiance of the world. Africa was going to be self-governing—and, south of the Sahara, largely Christian.

The 1960s were the decade when the missionaries of the historic churches were more plentiful than ever but they now included many thousands of nuns and other women who were easy to love and church leaders who thoroughly acknowledged the need to hand over to Africans. It was only in Southern Rhodesia and South Africa that significant white church leaders could be found who did not feel the blowing of the wind of change. And the 1960s were the decade when a great harvest of new members was reaped. A church in touch with the modern world but rapidly being placed under local leadership was immensely attractive and two of the best known of the new political leaders, the Catholic Julius Nyerere and the Protestant Kenneth Kaunda, said openly and often that their statesmanship was inspired by their churchmanship. Nyerere's Arusha Declaration aroused admiration all over Africa, and all over the world, by its vision of a Tanzania where the leaders would be free of corruption and pride and the peasants would prosper in co-operatives. Gradually the missionaries' schools and hospitals were taken over by governments, but they had made a contribution illustrated by the number of members of the new elites who owed their chances in life, and at least some of their values, to mission schools. This contribution was now renewed by the churches' participation in many projects for Africa's development funded from overseas.

That new alliance of Church and State did not last. The numbers of missionaries with liberal views dwindled precisely because such women and men believed that the churches ought to be Africanized from village to headquarters. They were replaced by Pentecostal and other evangelists from the USA and elsewhere, enthusiasts who saw a need and an opportunity to gather Spirit-filled congregations of converted individuals but less need to be interested in cultural, economic or political problems; Kenya, for example, became a Babel of Bible-preachers from overseas. The growth of the African-led independent churches resumed in many areas; their involvement in the political independence movements had been small and the new governments did not encourage them, but in the new nations, disturbed by innumerable changes, prophets and healers attracted groups which could survive and increase. Two radical theologians emerging in the 1980s had Catholic backgrounds but were in rebellion: when Eboussi Boulaga, formerly a Jesuit, advocated a 'Christianity without fetishes' his plea included the end of middle-class fetishes imported from Europe and when Okomfo Damuah, formerly a priest, founded the Afrikania movement he excluded Christianity as taught in Rome. A Catholic archbishop, Emmanuel Milingo, attracted a large following because he encouraged beliefs in authoritative guidance through dreams and in healing through miracles after prayer and fasting; he was deprived of his position but the beliefs could not be suppressed, partly because they were prominent in the New Testament. When Protestant leaders gathered for the All-Africa Conference of Churches they were excited by a call for a 'moratorium' on 'external assistance in money and personnel'; the call did not end needs or requests for such assistance, but it indicated that the years when European-style churches would happily collaborate with European-style governments were coming to an end.

The main reason why the relationship between Church and State became less comfortable was, however, that the political leadership changed.

Political independence did not end the fact that Africa depended on Europe or the USA as the market for its products and as the supplier of capital and technology, manufactures and media. In the 1970s prices for African products fell disastrously and the costs of imports rose. In the 1980s rates of interest on loans also rose. So did Africa's population—and food production declined. In that real world elected leaders could not fulfil the promises with which they had been elected, but it was also relevant that the leaders and the elites around them were often personally corrupt and politically disastrous, neglecting the improvement of agriculture. Military regimes took over and turned out to be worse; as Latin America also found, a senior rank in the armed forces was no guarantee of skill in economics.

The Organization of African Unity assembled rulers who were able to agree only that the frontiers inherited from colonialism should be respected. Kwame Nkrumah dreamed of a United States of Africa, and Léopold Senghor of a Federal Republic in French-speaking Africa, but the realities were very different. When governments attempted to tighten their grip on their own nations the results could be disastrous civil wars. In Nigeria the Igbos attempted to establish their own state of Biafra and in Sudan the south rebelled at much greater length against the government in the north. In both those wars religion was involved, for the governments concerned were mostly or entirely Muslim, many of the Igbos were Catholics and many of the southern Sudanese were Catholics or Protestants. In the French-speaking states south of the Sahara there were rebellions against regimes whose extreme but bankrupt arrogance would have been comic had it not been tragic; while in Somalia the absence of a government made a cruel civil war the normal situation. First in Burundi, then in Rwanda, large massacres resulted from the hatred between Hutus and Tutsis, condemned by history to live together in some of Africa's loveliest land—and condemned by the power of evil to perpetrate atrocities which some clergy and even nuns either joined in or condoned. In earlier years these countries had been regarded as models to all Africa of 'evangelization' and 'revival'. As coup followed coup and killing avenged killing, and as disillusionment led to despair, Africa seemed to be slipping into chaos and savagery. In 1996 it was reported that cannibalism was a feature of the fighting between factions in Liberia.

In these very grim conditions the new leaders of Africa's churches rose to a moral height seldom seen in church history. In country after country they dared to speak out. They attacked rich countries for their indifference to Africa's plight although their own churches might need assistance from the rich—and they attacked their own governments. In Zaire, for example, Mobutu emerged as the strong man needed to stop the chaos after the sudden collapse of the Belgian colonial rule (leaving behind hundreds of missionaries dead and only a few highly educated Africans alive) but he was a corrupt dictator determined to silence criticism until his fall in 1997. Cardinal Malula now became the nation's other strong man, with a different strength. In Uganda a Muslim soldier, Idi Amin, was another dictator, even more brutal. Benedicto Kiwanuka, a leading Catholic layman who was the Chief Justice, and Janani Luwum, the Anglican archbishop, dared to stand up to him and became two of the thousands who were murdered. In South Africa church leaders and theologians, black and white, denounced a different kind of tyranny, apartheid, and were punished. Denis Hurley the Catholic archbishop of Durban and Michael Scott and Trevor Huddleston (two Anglican priests) were among the missionaries whose protests echoed around the world. In the end the pressure of the conscience of worldwide Christianity reached the Dutch Reformed Church which had previously supported the racist structure of the society with the pretext that it meant 'separate development' without injustice. With Beyers Naudé as their pioneer Dutch Reformed spiritual leaders than faced the wrath of church members who moved far more slowly. Here as in Southern Rhodesia before it became Zimbabwe, prophets who defended the rights of the majority of a country's inhabitants were accused by many in the white minority which clung to its privileges of treachery to 'Christian civilization'.

There have been political miracles, partly because brave Christians have been involved in politics. As the 1980s ended only three African states were genuine democracies but during the 1990s there were in most countries at least the beginnings of a change. In South Africa, instead of the bloodbath widely expected Nelson Mandela led the government of a multi-ethnic and multi-party democracy and Desmond Tutu the Anglican archbishop of Cape Town symbolized what the churches had contributed to this outcome. He had protested against apartheid, weeping over the violence, struggling to keep alive the vision of the 'rainbow people of God' when on every side people seemed to be overwhelmed by hatred and fear; and now he was appointed as the chairman of a commission to bring 'truth and reconciliation' out of the suffering.

If an attempt is made in the 1990s to discern the real situation of the African churches, praise for their leadership in the rescue of the states must not be allowed to conceal the fact that on the ground African Christianity is now largely out of control.

That is plainly true of the churches which were founded precisely in order to escape control by missionaries—and it is also true of many splinter-groups which have begun in rebellions against the founders of such churches or their appointed heirs. The 'independent' or 'African-instituted' churches have continued to be in flux, some becoming 'respectable', others becoming more defiantly 'African'; some growing into large memberships, others declining or vanishing. But it is highly improbable that this mighty river in African Christianity will disappear. And the authorities of the historic churches cannot even control the millions who remain more or less faithful. In Africa as in Latin America the shortage of priests has meant that on the ground Catholicism has often become the Church without the Mass. Protestant churches are also short of clergy. For Catholics and Protestants alike the possibility of giving instruction through church schools is much reduced, because most children go to the government's schools. So in practice rural Christianity largely depends on the village catechist or other lay assistant. This person is likely to be both devout and moral—but in his or her own way. It is far from unknown for the catechist to be excluded from communion when a visit by the priest makes a Mass possible, because of domestic arrangements not authorized by the Church. And what may be true about the catechist is certain to be true about other members of the congregation, often about most of them. Although the custom of polygamy is slowly dying out (because women object to it as humiliating and men no longer find it so attractive in practice) it is not dead, and converted men who are not willing to send away a second wife (often because they do not want her to lose all security) are still often excommunicated.

In African cities the situation in the 1990s is too new for any prediction to be sensible. It will be understandable if Africa's religious traditions, Christian or other, are overwhelmed by the new facts of urban life which intensify the new problems of village life—for the many, the poverty, the breakdowns in relationships, the mind-destroying drugs, the life-destroying horrors of AIDS; for the few, the intoxication of proud modernity. It will also be understandable if Africa's religious traditions are condemned as 'backward' by educated, prospering Africans but survive as folklore preserved for the entertainment of camera-ready tourists. And it will be understandable if Africa's religious traditions prove strong but flexible enough to create a new expression of Christianity within the new world of the city, whether for the poor or for the sophisticated. These traditions have already been strong but flexible enough to create much that is new within the Africa which no church leadership can now control.

The African Christ

A variety of Christianity has been born which is as African as the soil. Its intellectual expression, which has been substantial, may be called a theological miracle. Inevitably the African Christians who have performed the necessary intellectual task on the basis of the new spiritual reality have not been unanimous: some have been far more nervous than others about developments which can seem to be departures from the Bible or from the Catholic tradition. And inevitably publications by theologians have had a limited influence. They have been written in English or French in a continent where only about half the Christians can read and much less than half can afford to buy books. But some agreements seem to have been reached—and they are not only agreements between writers. African Christianity is lived.

Although the rejection of colonialism has sometimes brought with it a tendency to be romantic about the religion which the missionaries encountered, most African Christians seem to know perfectly well that there was a dark side. There is now a joy which was not known so fully in the centuries when the Creator was thought to be too remote and mysterious for either love or intimate prayer to be appropriate. There is now less of a readiness to believe that disease or disaster is the result of God's wrath, or the result of the displeasure of ancestors, or the result of sorcery arranged by evil neighbours. There is less fear of evil spirits and less reliance on the magic which claimed that the recitation of a spell would force good spirits to get to work. Less use is made of sacrifices; it is seen that what interests God is how a person lives. There is less cruelty towards those who deviate from customs still believed to be commanded by ancestors. There is more respect for human beings as such, including respect for women who are no longer segregated, despised and exploited to the degree that was frequent in the past. A light has shone which was not there before the Christian gospel was communicated by missionaries who shared it, often sacrificing themselves, and by lives and words which were African.

But not everything in the life of Black Africa before the arrival of Christianity was dark. The traditions of most African peoples included a belief in the Supreme Being—the 'One who has no equal', the 'One who fills all things', the 'One who is there'. And this common tradition helped the belief that with this origin human life is good enough to be lived, despite all its evils. There were suicides among the newly enslaved but not many once the Africans got used to the exile, the humiliation and the harshness. Amid continuing evils in recent years an essentially religious acceptance of life has been a source of African courage, patience and forgiveness. When Christianity came it found a word for 'God' in many African languages and often declared that the One who was already acknowledged could now be worshipped as holy and loved as fatherly. It is significant that the South African hymn written by a Methodist teacher which begins 'God bless Africa' has been so widely accepted. To sing that God can 'bless' is to say that God is One and is in a living and benevolent relationship with humanity.

Because the Creator was thought to be in the background but spirits, good or bad, were thought to be closer to daily human concerns, African traditional religion was often denounced or dismissed by Christians as mere 'animism' worshipping 'idols'. But a far more positive interpretation is possible and naturally it appeals to Christians proud to be African. According to this interpretation it was believed that ancestors who are remembered can be spiritually present, in blessing, in warning or in punishment, and that people who are now alive physically have a spiritual nature which can join the ancestors after death. It was also believed that the whole of nature is infused with this supernatural spirit, which was personified as 'spirits' in order to be pictured. This further belief could result in a fear of aspects of nature, but it also resulted in the constant feeling that nature is sacred.

African traditional religion can therefore be interpreted as a sense of communion between the living and the 'dead', between humanity and nature—a sense that received daily reinforcement from the experience of belonging to a family, a village and a tribe. Being a European philosopher, Descartes wanted the individual to begin from the position that 'I think, therefore I am' but as John Mbiti has observed, the fundamental African position is one of belonging: 'I am because we are.' In the European

Christian tradition many monastic saints taught contempt for the world, in particular for sexuality, and many Protestants taught the need to make a lonely pilgrimage from worldliness and also from Catholicism. Such ideas were brought to Africa in the books of Thomas à Kempis and John Bunyan and in the attitudes of many missionaries who were more or less saintly in one or other of these styles. But the isolation advocated has seldom made a deep appeal to Africans who need to 'belong'. Europeans or Americans of a more worldly disposition have often judged the success of a human life by the amount of possessions accumulated before death ends all enjoyment. But most Africans have placed a higher value on what cannot be purchased: the humble, grateful acceptance of the gift of life. A good life has meant the birth and rearing of children, the communion with the divine and the ancestors, the harmony with everyone and everything in the familiar neighbourhood. And life, thus valued, has been affirmed in the face of famine, conflict, disease and death. That spiritual heritage could itself be affirmed as Africa's Old Testament.

Recently there has been much discussion of some parts of church life where the customs of western Christianity can be shown to be poor in comparison with African traditions which can be linked with the traditions of ancient Israel.

The marriage service seems to be impoverished when little notice is taken of the families behind the partners. In Africa marriage has been regarded as an alliance between the families which arranged it or consented to it and the 'bridewealth' paid by the bridegroom has compensated her family for the loss of the bride's services. Normal sexuality has been regarded as important but always in subordination to a strong family life built on this sexual foundation. (Sadly, the family life has depended partly on the willingness of wives to forgive their husbands' infidelities, and male promiscuity has spread the enormous tragedy of AIDS.) Africans have rejoiced over the births of children and held them in loving discipline. Families have also looked after the sick and the old without aid from any other institution, and grandparents have been expected to be as active as possible in the life and work of the home. Obviously conditions are different for modern-minded families, in Africa as elsewhere. But Africa's strong traditions about family life contain elements which could enrich both the west and Africa's own future.

Western churches almost always have some ceremony accompanied by instruction in response to the crisis of adolescence: baptism for churches which do not baptize infants, confirmation for others, and more modern practices such as classes in school and youth camps. But no response yet developed by the west is as powerful as the African tradition of initiating young people by dramatic rites and by the systematic explanation of the lifestyle expected of responsible adults. African religious beliefs have been communicated as part of that elaborate process which takes the transition to adulthood with great seriousness. It is of course not being suggested that modern education should be abandoned; Africa is hungry for it. The suggestion made by many is that something can be learned by the west, and renewed in Africa, if modern youth is to be spared the immensely destructive results of the neglect of education encouraging maturity in emotional and social life.

Western churches have been actively interested in healing and their missions earned gratitude all over Africa because they introduced modern medicine. In recent years the west has also been interested in 'holistic' medicine, the healing of a whole body and of a whole lifestyle, and many churches have developed a 'healing ministry'. But it has often been felt that there is still something to be learned from the African religious emphasis on healing. Traditionally Africa has been sure that to be healthily human is to be a harmony of body and spirit in harmony with one's whole environment; and traditionally Africa has prayed for that.

And many in Africa (as elsewhere) think the Eucharist is impoverished if only the death of Christ is remembered, as has been the main tendency in the churches of the west. African traditions were brought into the Mass in an order for that celebration issued by the Catholic bishops in Zaire in 1975 (and similar experiments have been made elsewhere). Before the service both the saints of the Church and the ancestors of the congregation are invoked ('be with us') and any strangers present are named and applauded. The priest and his assistants are also named; as they enter they are dressed colourfully (in Africa a sign of vitality) and they dance. During joyous chants the people also dance and clap; extempore songs interpret the biblical readings; fragrant materials are burnt on a small fire; bread and wine are offered to 'you, the Sun which we cannot gaze on' with gratitude for 'all things', lovingly described in some detail. It is a celebration of the united, healthy creation; it is both biblical and African. But even so, some questions remain: for example, is it essential to use bread and wine where they are unfamiliar?

While recovering what may be called Africa's Old Testament, it has also proved possible to find 'African faces of Jesus' which are not essentially different from the faces to be found in the New Testament. In recent African theology these faces have included: Jesus the Black, with reference not so much to his skin colour (although Jesus of Nazareth was not white) as to his identification with the poor and darkly coloured majority of humanity; Jesus the Great Ancestor (in Milingo's words 'all that our ancestors have and more'), who is close both to the Creator and to those who pray on earth; Jesus the Elder Brother, who initiates those who would be close to him and belong to him; Jesus the Healer, whose touch can reach the depths of a personality and have physical consequences although instructively he accepted death in agony for himself; Jesus the Chief, although not a chief who wins military battles; Jesus the Head of the Great Family, although not of a family restricted to one place; Jesus the Liberator of Women, who sets a revolutionary example in their treatment; Jesus the Prophet, in a style close to Moses or Elijah but also to Harris or Kimbangu; Jesus the Priest who offers his own life as a sacrifice; Jesus the Suffering Servant, who within the hard experience of a human life does the will of the Father to the end.

Many African Christians have been fascinated by two figures in the New Testament. One is Simon of Cyrene: the only person who actually carried the cross of Jesus was an African. The other man is a man whose name has been lost but who was baptized on his way back from Jerusalem to his work at the court of an African queen. He had attracted the attention of a Christian missionary because in his carriage he had been reading aloud a passage from the Hebrew Scriptures—a passage about Israel, about Jesus, about Africa:

> He was led like a sheep to the slaughter,
> like a lamb dumb before the shearers.
> Without protection, without justice, he was taken,
> and who gave a thought to his fate?

Of all the continents Africa has known the most suffering and so is best placed to see the divine compassion, to hear the crucified Word of God.

In China

More than half of the world's population lives in Asia, with more than a sixth in China and almost as many in India, but at the end of the twentieth Christian century it is usually reckoned that Asians who identify themselves as Christians are less than 3 per cent of the total. And the challenge confronting the churches will grow: Asia's population is expected to increase between 1990 and 2010 by a thousand million.

Of course Asia deserves more than the treatment which can be offered now. More than a million Christians live in Taiwan, for example, and no snapshot of their life can be comprehensive. Many belong to 'independent' churches on this offshore island whose political independence cannot be established formally without risking the unthinkable: war between the USA, whose influence is everywhere, and China which regards this as a province in rebellion. Those who belong to the historic churches reflect the island's own complicated history. The original inhabitants were 'animists' in their 'primitive' religion but many of their descendants are now Presbyterians. There have been waves of colonialism: first the Dutch, then immigration from the Chinese mainland, then Japanese occupation from 1895, finally the arrival in 1946 of exiles under Chiang Kai-shek, a group which nursed the fantasy that it was still the legitimate government of all China. The result of all this has been tensions between 'early comers' and 'late comers', between poor and rich and between conservatives and those who are determined to see Taiwan as modern as, say, Singapore. Over everyone hangs uncertainty about the island's future. And what is China's future?

That second question hangs over all of Asia's future, for in the 1990s the population of China is more than 1,200 million. More than two-thirds live in the countryside. Almost all avoid dangerous politics.

About 30 million people may be Christian but precise numbers are not obtainable. The officially recognized Protestant body, the China Christian Council, is in touch with 'registered' congregations said to number about ten million and the Catholic Patriotic Association adds another 3.5 million, but it is well known that many Protestants and some Catholics do not relate to these two bodies which they regard as tools of Communism. If we ask whether the future will bring growth, history gives no clue. There is no precedent for the present situation in the country as a whole, which combines a lack of public criticism of the official ideology with the actual end of Communist idealism and puritanism, at least in the cities—and which unites the acceptance of Marxist economic theory with realities which are very different: the return of much of the land to family farming, the wide spread of small, private businesses, the large-scale growth of a middle class with western-style ambitions, a vigorous drive to modernize the industries with an eye on international trade. The future of religion is uncertain because the whole of the future is uncertain. And a clear lesson is taught by the history of the churches: it is disastrous to associate Christianity with aggression by 'foreign devils'. Any good future for the Church in China will be wrecked if foreigners interfere.

We have already noted how the Nestorian, Franciscan and Jesuit missions to China ended. All were initially addressed to China's rulers; all depended on the patronage of those rulers; all collapsed when that support was withdrawn. They included serious efforts to adapt Christianity to Chinese ways of life and thought but fellow Christians including popes condemned these experiments as a betrayal of the gospel and they made little impact on the people. After a disgusted emperor's edict in 1721 the Church in China became a persecuted minority but it seems that when the nineteenth century began about a quarter of a million Catholics were living in the empire without attracting much attention.

In 1807 Robert Morrison was sponsored by the London Missionary Society in an attempt to add a Protestant influence. He lived quietly in Guangzhou (Canton) and was fortunate enough to find help from two Catholics while he worked on a translation of the Bible printed in 1819. It was clumsy as it struggled with problems but it was a heroic beginning to a

Bible-based evangelism and it was accompanied by a dictionary. The difficulty of communication was shown by the absence of any agreed word for 'God'. Morrison's work began the tradition that Protestants and Catholics used different words—a custom which strengthened the impression that these were two different religions. The Catholic word for God has been *Tien-zhu*, 'Lord of Heaven'; *Shang-di*, 'Supreme God', was favoured by the Jesuits but had been condemned in 1704 as meaning 'Sovereign Emperor'. Most Protestants have favoured *Shen*, 'Spirit', and their religion has been called *Jidujiao*, the 'religion of Jesus' as distinguished from the Catholic 'religion of the Lord of Heaven'. And amid such problems there was a development which made it easy to regard Christianity as opium for the Chinese.

In 1839–42 the British waged war on the empire in order to force it to trade—and one commercial prospect which attracted them was the size of this market for the opium produced in or around India. Although the Chinese government wisely prohibited it, opium was the one import which Chinese customers wanted on a large scale. At the end of a disgraceful war the empire had to surrender the island of Hong Kong and to concede extensive privileges to foreign merchants in four other 'treaty ports'; the number was later trebled. From these ports Christian missionaries less tactful than the Jesuits or Morrison attempted to penetrate inland and when they met hostility from people who had never seen a foreigner before they appealed for protection to the consuls in the treaty ports. In these ports the European quarters were 'extra-territorial' since Chinese law was not valid, and converts of the missionaries were often regarded by other Chinese as also 'extra-territorial'. Spiritually they had abandoned their country, the 'Middle Kingdom', to Chinese eyes the centre of the earth.

Another tragedy followed the Tai-ping ('Great Peace') rebellion in the 1850s. The first rebels quoted the Bible, practised baptism and worshipped God under a name used by some Christians. They also rejected control by the missionaries, denounced the 'unequal treaties' with foreigners and defended Chinese customs such as polygamy. The original core of 'God-worshippers' was joined by millions of peasants more interested in attacks on landlords and very willing to perpetrate massacres. In 1864 the movement was defeated in great bloodshed by the army of the Manchu empire. The soldier in charge of the defence of Shanghai was Charles Gordon, then a young English mercenary but later to become a famous Evangelical and a hero when he was killed in Africa (defending Khartoum against other 'fanatics', in that case Muslims). Had the Tai-ping rebels won, it is conceivable that China might have developed its own form of Christianity a century before it did. Their first leader, Hong Xiu-quan, had received instruction from a Baptist missionary. But this was before he styled himself 'the younger brother of Jesus Christ'.

In the 1860s the French empire under Louis-Napoleon began to claim the right to protect all Catholic missionaries in China; they were issued with French passports whether they wanted them or not. And the missionaries exercised their right to dominate over the descendants of the Catholics who had survived persecution. Catholic numbers increased to 720,000 by 1900 but retribution for this foreign sponsorship of China's largest church came in that year. Urged on by the dowager empress, rebels whom uncomprehending foreigners called 'Boxers' killed about thirty thousand Christians including missionaries; the cry was that 'hairy men' preaching Christ were the agents of foreign powers. The cry was understandable at a time when Africa was being colonized in some association with the missionaries, the British empire in India was being justified as necessary for the 'religious and moral improvement' of the Indians and the French were ruling Indo-China having come to the defence of Catholics there. Also understandable was the general reaction to the China Inland Mission led by an Englishman, Hudson Taylor. This mission, started in 1853, was in many ways imaginative as well as courageous: Taylor insisted that the evangelists should be drawn from a variety of denominations, should live very simply, should dress as Chinese and should not be controlled by a committee in London. But he preached a narrowly Protestant message, made no secret of his motive which was to save as many as possible of the heathen from hell, and paid little attention to the need to build a fully Chinese Church and to found schools. Simply announcing that one God existed and had been full of wrath, that a Saviour both divine and human had paid the penalty for the sins of the world in far-off Jerusalem, and that he had risen from the grave to be the Lord of all, could be regarded as not the easiest way in which to communicate the gospel to the Chinese, a people who for many centuries had been taught that anyone who did not have the good fortune to be born in China was a barbarian. Yet this Evangelical was a saint, like Francis Xavier.

What requires some explanation is why the missionary-led churches in China continued to attract converts when the European powers had suppressed the Boxer movement, had killed, burned and looted in Beijing (Peking), and had imposed an immense fine as compensation for the massacre of Christians. (Hudson Taylor refused to accept any of this money.) One explanation is that many of the Chinese saw that the Manchu empire was disintegrating. The Protestant churches, whose main numerical strength lay in the south-eastern provinces, were uniquely placed to provide the western-style education needed to sustain the republic which would follow. (After 1905 the civil service was no longer recruited by examination in the Confucian classics.) The Catholic Church was less involved in educational work at the college level but its growth, mainly northern and rural, was helped by its policy of establishing Catholic villages: land was bought for a church and a small school and it was expected that the priests and sisters would attract peasants to move under the church's shelter in troubled times. Although great hostility to foreigners remained, it began to seem reassuringly improbable that the European colonial powers or the USA would treat China as India and Africa had been treated: advantageous trade would satisfy them, here as in Latin America.

For these reasons the activities of the new Anti-Christian League did not prevent the growth of hopes that China would increasingly accept Christianity. The first president of the republic established in 1911–12, Sun Yat-sen, was a Christian and one of his successors, Chiang Kai-shek, was baptized as a Methodist in 1930 after four years in power. A book of 1922 bore the undiplomatic title *The Christian Occupation of China* but in the same year a National Christian Council was formed, providing a platform for some Chinese complaints about the 'denominationalism' brought in by foreigners. Two years later the first Chinese Catholic Council assembled some fifty bishops who more cautiously wanted church life to be more thoroughly Chinese. In 1926 six Chinese priests were made bishops. But in reality foreign missionaries and foreign money seemed indispensable to the 'occupation'. In 1930 the China Inland Mission had a thousand missionaries in China. It did not belong to the National Council and it was certainly not Catholic, but it did believe that its gospel would bear much fruit. Some Protestants united to form the 'Church of Christ in China'.

Optimism was mocked by history. In 1927 the Communist party which had been formed as a tiny group six years previously became the bitter enemy of the Kuomintang party led by Chiang. Ten years later the Japanese invaded, causing devastation, chaos and the development of the Communists as a disciplined fighting force. Their ruthlessly determined leader, Mao Tse-tung, led a subsequently famous 'long march' to a position where he could secure the armed party's total independence and build up its appeal to a wide range of people, from intellectuals to peasants, who saw in it China's only remaining hope. The Kuomintang had become obviously corrupt and in the public mind was identified with the interests of foreigners and businessmen. In contrast the Communists were inspired by a kind of puritanism in their own lives and by an undeniably patriotic will to change China. So in 1949 Communism achieved here the revolution which was denied to it in Latin America and Africa.

What followed showed how great an opportunity had been lost by the Christians in the race to renew the country. The Maoist version of Marxism became almost a religion: it changed the thinking of the people by its images, scriptures, slogans, hymns, congregational meetings and youth movements. It combined stern moral instruction with promises of a glory to be reached through patient suffering. The new rulers published a constitution promising religious freedom but in practice were utterly determined to end both China's own 'feudal superstition' and also all foreign influence on the Chinese activities of the great religions such as Christianity. By the end of 1951 all foreign missionaries had either left the country or been imprisoned. Most of the Protestants left voluntarily, but the Catholics were under the Vatican's orders and these orders were disastrous. Missionaries were ordered to stay; then they and their flocks were ordered to withhold any recognition from the new government.

At the time of the Communist victory Protestant numbers were about one million with perhaps 600,000 enquirers on the fringes. When their 'Three-Self Patriotic Movement' was allowed to hold its first national conference in 1954 it could claim that about 400,000 had signed a petition in its support. Its aim was 'self-support, self-government and self-propagation'—which was scarcely heretical, for Henry Venn of the Church Missionary Society had made this his vision for the Church in Africa a hundred years previously. It was, indeed, the logical development of the old National Christian Council with its background in the YMCA. Inspiration in the early stages came from a YMCA man, in English Y. T. Wu, who had always been a radical; later it was led by an Anglican bishop, known in the west as K. H. Ting. It made no attempt to suppress denominational traditions in the congregations linked with it but such organization as it developed was to be called 'post-denominational'. It could be further developed into what was virtually a new and very large denomination when more freedom was allowed in the 1980s. In its early days the slogan was simple: 'love country, love church.' So was the creed: commitment to Christ. And so was the social policy: collaboration with the government in the 'United Front', building a socialist society with strong idealism and no interference from anyone outside China. In practice this meant close contacts between the leaders of the movement and the Communist leadership, which used it to spread ideas and decisions in the congregations. That could be—and was— criticized as a betrayal of Christianity but in the 1980s there was to be a greater distance between the movement and the government; for example, Ting openly supported the students who demonstrated in favour of democracy. The policy of Ting and his colleagues during the even more dangerous years before the 1980s may be compared with the policy of the Russian Orthodox bishops under Communism.

The simplicity of 'love country, love church' was very different from the atmosphere of controversy within the Protestant movement before 1949. In those years many had been attracted to baptism by its connection with personal 'progress' and social 'reform'; the simplicity could be like the spirit of those who now collaborated with the Communists. But some sophisticated thinkers had begun to relate Christianity to China's cultural heritage and social problems, most notably T. C. Chao. They were to have no known successors during the rest of the twentieth century and Chao became first a Barthian and then an agnostic. Many foreign missionaries never thought such involvements necessary; here they resembled the leaders of the independent churches which rejected their control from the 1920s onwards. A deeply personal, Bible-based discipleship which could be called fundamentalism formed the religion of 'Watchman' Nee whose followers were called the 'Little Flock' but became numerous. The True Jesus Church and the Jesus Family were Pentecostal churches and John Sung was a famous revivalist. Certainly the impatience with dialogues seeking reconciliation with China's religions can be understood. Confucius and his disciple Mencius (to use their Latin names) had been vague about *Tien* (Heaven) although emphatic about loyalty to family ties and earthly rulers. Buddhism and Taoism had taught detachment and serenity and certainly had been detached from any doctrine about God: one famous saying was that 'the Tao that can be spoken about is not the eternal Tao'. Apart from agreement about basic morality it was not easy to see the connections with Christianity. The earlier optimism of the Jesuits seemed to these biblically minded Protestants sheer sentimentality. Nor was it easy to respect the occultism and magic of much popular religion.

Thus the Protestant Christians in China before 1949 had been deeply divided. Now the 'liberation' under the Communists transformed that debate but new divisions appeared. The old religions were weaker than ever; the missionaries were gone; the Chinese Protestants were on their own. Some ceased to identify themselves as Christians. Others withdrew more deeply into the Bible and such Evangelicals, who could be martyred if not hidden from the authorities, had no respect for the Protestants who unheroically collaborated with the government. But to many who remained Christians collaboration seemed right as well as expedient, for socialism could be interpreted as the fulfilment of all that was best in China's past. Confucius and other sages had taught that a 'mandate from heaven' was bestowed on an emperor who would govern justly; that could now be held to apply to Mao. Buddhism and Taoism had preached the conquest of egotism; Communism, too, fought against selfishness. Many Christians had been among those struggling to build a better society in an age of revolutions; it could be said that now God was using a government which had the power to solve the social problems after too much talk. Did not a Hebrew prophet hail a Persian conqueror (Cyrus) as God's 'anointed' agent?

In practice, however, the position of Christianity in Maoist China was far more dangerous than the leaders of the collaborating movement could admit in public at the time. Most of the churches were closed. In the early 1950s many meetings for 'thought reform' became brutal: the denunciations, often by Christians, of the missionaries and their Chinese stooges could be followed by executions or by imprisonment which included physical hardships (often with torture) and 'brain-washing'. 'Watchman' Nee, for example, spent many years in jail, as did Catholic bishops. In particular the three million Catholic laity suffered. Many had indeed been under the influence of foreign missionaries with conservative teaching; now their piety and their patriotism were in conflict inside their consciences. And since the Vatican refused to allow Catholics to co-operate with it, and did not recognize that it had taken over from the regime now exiled to Taiwan, the government became determined that the Catholics should be split. Those who chose to remain loyal to the pope were imprisoned or driven underground but in 1957 a Patriotic Association of Chinese Catholics was formed under Pi Shu-shi, the archbishop of Mukden. It proceeded to make bishops and priests without reference to Rome (they were allowed, or forced, to marry) and it was denounced by Pius XII. Both groups of Catholics were cut off from the changes inaugurated by the Second Vatican Council and it seems probable that despite their own problems the Protestants now began to outnumber them.

In the attempt in 1959–61 to take a 'great leap forward' in the economy and to crush 'anti-nationalists' full-time pastors were conscripted to work in the fields and in the last ten years of Mao's life, which ended in 1976, the government's hostility to religion was open: the 'cultural revolution' closed almost every religious building in the land and attacked any religious person who came to the notice of the Red Guards. But it was not only Christianity that suffered during those terrible years. The over-ambitious 'great leap' moved the economy backwards. The 'cultural revolution' killed or reduced to distress a whole generation of the educated on whom any recovery would have depended. Millions of the Chinese people died—and one of the casualties was the myth of Mao the infallible 'Great Helmsman'.

As in the Roman Empire or in the Soviet Union, persecution did not break the Christian minority or totally destroy its credibility in the eyes of the people. Although unable to use church buildings or to be public about their religion, millions of Christians kept their commitment to Christ and were when necessary willing to be witnesses in suffering. In the 1980s it could be seen that Chinese Christianity had survived this, its greatest test. Now thousands of churches were reopened and new ones built, elderly Christians worshipped in them with great feeling and new members were recruited; the distribution of Bibles and of some Christian publications was allowed; some international contacts were resumed cautiously. The Three-Self Patriotic Movement was kept in being but many Protestants objected to its close links with the Communists and instead of using the churches affiliated to it continued to meet in their own homes and to evangelize among neighbours, in a style either Pentecostal or conservatively Evangelical. A China Christian Council was therefore created as an organization parallel with the movement and under much the same leadership; it undertook some of the tasks in church life in the hope of including some of the dissident Protestants.

The Catholic Patriotic Association was also allowed to be active in the open. The Vatican, however, still refused to come to terms with the Chinese government, which cracked down on citizens who recognized this 'foreign power'. The main problem for Catholics has become the shortage of priests but the acceptance in the 1990s of most of the changes made elsewhere in the 1960s offers a promise for the future.

Some Marxist intellectuals, in China as elsewhere, have now begun to admit that religion deserves to be taken seriously as a phenomenon which can be ended neither by persecution nor by 'socialist' developments in society. But in the 1990s little can be taken for granted. Although Deng Xiaoping's reforms from 1978 encouraged private enterprise and international contacts in support of it, giving China the world's fastest growing economy and opening up the prospect of many more contacts, under a regime which has forcibly made known its refusal to allow free speech it would be foolish for the 'religious', 'registered' nor not, to venture into controversial politics. The massacres of protesters demanding 'democracy' in Tiananmen Square in Beijing in 1989 shot away any illusions: like most of the urban economy, thought was to be controlled by 'central planning'. Attitudes were also made clear as guidance was issued about the current interpretation of the 1982 constitution. The Communist party was still committed to the propagation of atheism 'resolutely' but was willing to tolerate 'normal' religion and the use of religious buildings as 'the private affair of individual citizens'. Religious meetings in private houses were to be prohibited but 'not vigorously'. Obviously this left the local Religious Affairs Bureaux with the power to interpret what is 'normal' and in 1996 a new campaign against 'unregistered' activities, mainly non-Christian but including house churches, was ordered by a central government which seemed to be worried about stability even before Deng Xiaoping's death in the following year.

In Japan

Christianity has also remained a small minority in the life of a people as clever and as proud as the Chinese—the Japanese. And the main reason seems to be that Japanese Christians have never made a really determined effort to develop a Japanese Church after the persecution which almost entirely destroyed the brave beginnings made by the Jesuits (as related in Chapter 6).

Under the Tokugawa shoguns who were the effective rulers for more than 250 years from 1603 Japan was a feudal society dedicated to the traditional military virtues. The various sects of Buddhism were favoured but also tightly controlled like the rest of society; Zen meditation appealed mainly to the warrior class. It was designed to replace the reasoning and questioning mind by 'illumination' (*satori*), the entry into *Mu*, usually translated as Nothingness but also said to mean Somethingness, the two ideas being ultimately identical like 'good' and 'evil'. Zen was liberated from any connection with the Buddhist Scriptures as from all other propositions in words, but was as much a form of self-discipline as was any of the martial arts in physical exercise and despite its sprituality was originally somewhat political. An essential part of the Tokugawa ideology was that the country under this iron regime should be isolated from any disturbing foreign influence.

Under the direct rule of the Meiji dynasty from 1868 'modernization' was then pursued, but essentially this meant the use of foreign inventions in order to strengthen a prolonged attempt to establish the country's dominance over East Asia, from Manchuria to Indonesia. The heart of this attempt was the cult of the divine emperor associated with *Shinto* ('the way of the gods') and *Nihonkyo*, a celebration of the sacred land and of its divinely blessed history. When American ships anchored off these coasts in the 1850s the insult to Japanese pride was eventually swallowed because the government wanted some trade with the west and some contact with modern knowledge and technology.

Very reluctantly it was admitted that contact with Christianity would have to be a part of the price. Since 1614 this 'foreign' religion had been prohibited on pain of death and regularly the whole population had been ordered to trample on pictures of Christ and Mary. Not until 1873 were the laws under which Christians had been persecuted fully repealed, but missionaries did not wait for that day before they entered the land where Catholicism had once flourished. To his amazement a French Catholic priest who nervously began work in Nagasaki found that about ten thousand Catholics made themselves known and joined the restored church although they had to endure some fresh persecution. Other Catholics had also survived in an underground existence but had developed so many unorthodox elements in their religion that they refused to accept the newly arrived clergy and eventually became Buddhists.

Japanese converted by Protestant missionaries formed a 'Church of Christ in Japan' in the 1870s but it remained small. The missionaries' main achievement was to found colleges which grew into modern universities, with accompanying schools; these, however, served only an urban elite and within that elite the education was more popular than the religion. A later attempt to begin a thoroughly Japanese version of Christianity was the 'Non-church' (*Mukyokai*) movement founded by Kanzo Uchimura; in practice, however, this consisted of groups to study the Bible. These groups sat cross-legged on the floor in the Japanese style but they lacked the appeal of the traditional shrines and ceremonies. Another attempt was the 'Kingdom of God' movement founded by Toyohiko Kagawa, combining work in the slums with its literary output; this, however, depended on Kagawa's strong and saintly personality. The illegitimate son of a nobleman, he went to live in the worst slums of Kobe at the age of 21, five years after his baptism, almost losing his eyesight and his life. That experience led not only to a study of *The Psychology of the Poor* and to the writing of novels but also to a lifetime of creative involvement in trade union activity in town and countryside alike. Long before his death in 1960 he had become revered and loved internationally, but what he had lived to see in Japan disappointed his highest hopes.

In the 1990s only about one million Japanese are baptized members of the historic churches, in a population of about 125 million. The United Church of Christ (*Kyodan*) is the largest Protestant denomination but its formation was ordered by the government in 1940 in order to offer united support for Japan's war effort and for this reason many Protestants refused to join: they included Kagawa, a consistent pacifist, and the Anglicans, Lutherans and Baptists. Since the war this church has taken the lead in public penitence for that support of a war of aggression but the problems in its relationship with post-war Japan exploded into the controversy about its participation in the 1970 World Fair in Osaka. Few could object to the actual contents of the Christian pavilion in that exhibition but many did protest successfully against Christian involvement in an event designed to celebrate material success. Under the challenge of these dilemmas the *Kyodan* has needed a strong Japanese theology, but this has not appeared: the dominant intellectual influence has been European, mainly the theology of Karl Barth. By the 1990s the Catholic Church—more acceptable in a country with a long tradition in art and ritual—had become the largest of all Japanese churches, with about 400,000 baptized members, and it was beginning to show the localizing effects of the use of Japanese rather than Latin in the Mass. But it, too, still lacks a Japanese theology. A Japanese-American scholar (Joseph Mitsuo Kitagawa) has spoken of 'boxing in Japanese Christians into sect-type communities' and has discerned the main hope for the future not in the churches' official leadership but in a group of widely read novelists active since the war, led by Shusaku Endo. These novelists have explored the spiritual situation from a viewpoint both more definitely Christian than the usual attitude of equivalent writers elsewhere in the world and more definitely Japanese than their own church leadership, whether Protestant or Catholic. They have been courageously honest and their common emphasis has been on the challenge of the crucified Jesus to a society obsessed first by military power and then by economic prosperity.

After the trauma of devastation and defeat in 1945 what Kagawa had advocated became reality to some extent: the emperor renounced his divinity, the new constitution renounced war for ever, nine years of modern education were made compulsory for all, trade unions were recognized, the great industrial firms became more paternalistic, the farmers were given land and subsidized. But these changes were possible only because of the result of the war which Kagawa had abhorred and in their turn they resulted in the application of a military discipline to industrial development. The change of heart was limited. Since the war Japanese Christians have had many reasons to criticize continuing support for the nationalism of Shinto and the increased materialism of a consumerist society. These protests have centred on complaints about excessive honours paid to the 'heroic war dead' and inadequate laws against industrial pollution. But the leaders of politics have been aware of the size of the church leaders' constituency.

It is easy to conclude that the Christian minority in Japan is destined to remain tiny. But it seems to be significant that in recent years the annual sale of Bibles has always been more than a million (with the Protestants and Catholics combining to produce a common version in 1987) and that at least the ethical teaching of the Bible has been widely respected. The general celebration of Christmas obviously owes much to commercialism but the central image of Mother and Child appeals in contrast with the old image of the divine emperor. Many weddings have a Christian flavour. It also seems to be hopeful that Japanese Christianity has not been linked with the military involvement of the USA in Asia. Inevitably the Japanese have been aware that a 'Christian' country dropped the atomic bombs which ended the Pacific war. Not many responded to that crisis in the profoundly Christian style of the two theologians Kazoh Kitamori and Kosuke Koyama, who saw God as the Judge who condemns all militarism but also as the Father who suffers when his children have to pay the price for their choice of violence. In their teaching God is in these two ways 'passionate' and Koyama spoke of Christ as needing to be 'broken' in order to heal the wounds of a 'broken' world. This vision of God went beyond anything offered by Buddhism or by Shinto (although both theologians praised the Buddhist teaching against greed) and it has been applied to the post-war situation.

For all the huge success of the post-war industries, there is anxiety in Japan—and not only because its economy is fragile (the country has few natural resources and its rising sun may be eclipsed as other Asian economies develop). There is much self-critical talk of a spiritual emptiness. This vacuum has been filled partially by a large number of new religious movements, the largest of which is *Sokka Gakkai* (the Value Creating Society), a modernized form of Buddhism. The Spirit of Jesus Church, said to have as many members as the Catholic Church, is usually classified as 'new' or at least as 'independent' since it rejects European theology and practices. The older churches regard it as heretical but it seems that for them, too, the crucial question is whether Japanese Christianity can take a more united and more local shape which will be able to reach the society as a whole. Such a transformation could respond to a spiritual crisis which may deepen, for there are signs that the new generation is far from satisfied with what has replaced militarism and is not finding an alternative either in Shinto which belongs to the past or in the Buddhism which has discouraged the positive attitude to the world which is at the core of modernity. Japan, like China, may be searching for values more worthy of a great people.

Across the Pacific

The potential for Christianity which has not yet been fulfilled in China or Japan may be seen in South Korea. There the churches have not seemed so foreign, whether or not they belong to the historic denominations, and one of the reasons is that the colonial occupation by the Japanese challenged the Christians to identify themselves more thoroughly with their own nation. (The same process took place wherever the Japanese empire extended in the 1940s: when left without missionaries many Christians renewed their faith.) About a fifth of the population of South Korea registered as Christian in the 1991 census and religious movements which have flourished since their foundation in the 1950s have incorporated Christian elements—most notably, the Unification and Olive Tree Churches.

The small beginnings of Catholicism in the Korean empire were started by eighteenth-century contacts with Chinese Catholics and resulted in cruel and continuing persecution. There might have been a reaction almost as harsh against the converts to Presbyterian and Methodist missions which were allowed in after the 1882 treaty with the USA, but the Bible was now translated into the language of the people and the climate was altered by the Japanese conquest which resulted in the incorporation of Korea into that empire from 1910 to 1945. Christians became undeniably patriotic because under a colonial regime which was severe they took a leading part in resistance, even in the 1919 rebellion. They did so at great personal cost but Christianity now became Korean. After the collapse of the Japanese empire both Communists and Americans appeared as liberators but the tension between the two resulted in the country's division and in the war of 1950–53.

In the north Communism was very thorough, more or less obliterating religion, but in the south an American-style capitalism was rapidly and ruthlessly developed, with an anti-Communist ideology even stronger than in the USA. In both halves it seemed that the old Korea, for which sentimental names were 'the hermit kingdom' and 'the land of the morning calm', had been modernized out of existence. But in the south, where many refugees including Christians arrived from the north hungry for work and for emotional food, religion has boomed along with the economy. The traditional religion of the people ('animism') has survived and Buddhism has been active but the chief gainers have been the churches which are associated with the modern world without the handicap of a link with western power perceived as hostile. South Korea's churches have been widely popular because the religion which they teach seems to be compatible both with being progressive and with being patriotic.

Those which have prospered most obviously have been those which have promised personal prosperity with happiness and health; the leading example is the Yoido Full Gospel Church under Paul Yonggi Cho. Here large numbers assemble for enthusiastic worship in the Pentecostal style on a Sunday but members are also expected to attend small weekly meetings for the discussion of their own lives in relation to the Bible. The response is similar to the response to Pentecostalism in Latin America. But another form of Korean Christianity, powerful in a different way, is akin to Latin America's liberation theology. For economic development has produced not only 'progress' but also miserable poverty and drab surroundings for the workers and families who have been sucked into the new industries or into unemployment and who fiercely resent the luxury and consumption of the elites. Their lives are all part of what is called *han*, the unvindicated agony of the poor over the centuries. Many Christians, particularly students, have concentrated on protests on behalf of the *minjung* (oppressed), have been treated brutally and have contributed to the overthrow of and subsequent exposure of presidents and governments more or less Fascist and corrupt. It will be surprising if in the future Korean Christianity, vigorous amid modernity whether in the Pentecostal or in the liberationist style, does not experience further growth. These Christians certainly know how to organize and how to make an impact on the public, whether in the 'Here's Life' campaign which attracted large numbers to the Pentecostal churches in the early 1980s or in the student demonstrations which discredited the presidents. And already Korean missionaries have begun to fan out into Asia.

A close resemblance to the Catholicism of Latin America may be seen in the Philippines, where on paper the Christians make up nine-tenths of the population. These islands were 'discovered' by Magellan in 1521 and after the arrival of colonists from Mexico most of the bewildered inhabitants had been baptized by 1600. Here as in Latin America popular Catholicism was, however, largely an affair of saints and festivals, of the Virgin's compassion and Christ's suffering. This outpost of the Spanish empire was an ecclesiastical province which the Vatican did not entrust into the care of Filipino bishops until 1905. The crisis came with two rebellions at the end of the nineteenth century. Here as in Latin America (again) political rebellion was led by liberals who were anticlerical because of the previous union between Church and State but many priests supported the revolutionary cause. It is uncertain how genuine was the reconciliation to the Church of the most famous rebel, José Rizal, shortly before he was executed. This political revolution ended in the USA taking over the colonial power. The religious revolution ended in the founding of the Philippine Independent Church among other new movements. This church, originally under the influence of unorthodox ideas, formed an alliance with the American Anglicans in 1961.

The fact that influence from the USA took such a direct form has resulted in a big difference from the Latin American character: still in the 1990s, half a century after independence, a Filipino is more likely to accept that ultimate power rests in *Yanqui* hands, that it takes a General MacArthur to throw out the Japanese, that English is the best language, that one's own people is somehow doomed to a destiny of superstition in religion, corruption in politics and inefficiency in business. Of course people are not always merely passive when offered an escape from this position of low self-esteem. The movement known as the 'Church of Christ', founded in 1914 by the larger-than-life Felix Manalo, teaches beliefs which seem to outsiders either heretical or preposterous, but it enjoys much support because it is unmistakably, defiantly, both Filipino and cheerful. The Catholic Church has enjoyed a new vitality since the formation of 'base communities' (as in Latin America) and the introduction of Filipino elements into some of the worship. Protestant and Pentecostal churches, although mostly originating in the USA, have also won converts by being positively Filipino.

In these circumstances it is all the more remarkable that recently there has been co-operation between Catholics and Protestants in the pursuit of justice and a new start for the nation. Under the leadership of Cardinal Sin this pressure by combined Christians was of central importance in the overthrow of the Marcos dictatorship in 1986; Marcos, president since 1965, had imposed martial law since 1972. His fall awakened hopes for the future— hopes not entirely destroyed by the subsequent demonstration that the event had changed the society's leadership but not its structure.

In the other islands of the Pacific national pride is stronger than it has been in the over-colonized Philippines and this confidence has found some of its expression in a flourishing church life. The early missionaries did not find a tropical paradise; they found an atmosphere of fear in which human sacrifices were offered to the gods, and a climate of war which could lead to cannibalism. In 1839 the Protestant pioneer John Williams was killed and eaten. But in Tahiti, for example, the approach of the London Missionary Society in the 1790s could have provided a model for much larger missions in Asia: Christians with no great claims about their own status learned the language, shared their practical skills and by a modest and peaceable manner showed a preferable way of life. Very carefully they instructed the most powerful chief before baptism, without disturbing his authority in the island. It is an eloquent fact that in the 1990s the Evangelical Church in Polynesia is still the largest denomination in this cluster of islands which has been under French rule since 1842, when it was imposed because Queen Pomare had expelled Catholic missionaries. Also eloquent is the acceptance of Christianity as the majority religion in Hawaii after the conversion of its queen, and in Tonga after the coronation of a Methodist king.

From 1871 courageous missionaries approached the tribes of Papua New Guinea for whom cannibalism was a sacred duty. An equally brave German missionary, Christian Keysser, later achieved the baptism of whole clans and tribes; after his expulsion in 1920 (by the Australians who had taken colonial rule over from the Germans) churches under local leadership supplemented by foreign missionaries who penetrated into the forbidding highlands continued the evangelism until in 1992 the government's estimate was that all but half a million of the four million population was Christian. Not all the islands of the South Pacific were Christianized peacefully: Vanuatu remembers two bishops, Catholic and Anglican, murdered because falsely associated with the sailors who kidnapped islanders for virtual slavery. But taken as a whole, Christianity has been more successful in this region than anywhere else in the twentieth-century world. Inevitably the problems of success have been experienced: as the churches which are now historic have lost their enthusiasm, revivalist movements have entered and have caused divisions. And there are the problems of disunity between the islands, as in the Caribbean. But it seems to be generally agreed that Christianity has greatly deepened the enjoyment of life in the islands. A theologian from Tonga (Sione Havea) has expressed this by saying that whereas twentieth-century European theology has responded to wars and other evils—evils reaching the ocean called Pacific during the Japanese–American war and when the French tested nuclear weapons—on these islands Christian theology could be 'a theology of celebration', giving thanks for Christ 'the Coconut of Life'.

Results have also been encouraging in Indonesia. After the expulsion of the Portuguese in 1605 the Dutch East India Company employed chaplains but excluded missionaries. In the 1820s the Dutch government began to exercise direct colonial rule and did allow Protestant missionary work (reluctantly also admitting some Catholics). The new mission was far from easy. The eastern islands remained stoutly Muslim but many Bataks in Sumatra were won over from 'animism' through a sensitive approach. More decisive, however, was the active share taken by Christians in the costly war of independence during the 1940s when the Dutch tried to return after the expulsion of the Japanese. The national government now gave large grants to the mosques but it assured the Christians of equal citizenship. Indeed, it favoured them by insisting that belief in 'one all-powerful God' was the first of the nation's basic principles and by reinforcing this law by systematic propaganda and by teaching in all the schools. In 1965 religious freedom was limited to religion so defined. The only legal alternative to Islam, Protestantism or Catholicism (for Christianity was thus divided) became 'Hindu-Buddhism' although in 1973 some new religions were also allowed. The churches could now attract not only 'animists' but also believers in one God who did not wish to be tied down to Islamic law. One motive in these arrangements was to outlaw the Communists, although it proved more effective to massacre them when they had bungled an attempt to seize power. But the system survived when Communism became less of a threat and the churches proved well able to take advantage of it. The Catholic Church grew, as did many Pentecostal or other independent groups, but the chief beneficiary was historic Protestantism, popular because of its educational work and effective in evangelism because of its use of local leadership and small groups. In the 1990s it is estimated that of the population of almost 200 million about twelve million are Protestants and half that number Catholics.

However, the rapid growth of the Indonesian churches in the 1960s could not be maintained at the same pace—and the circumstances which favoured it have remained unique.

After various contacts with Vietnam a seventeenth-century Jesuit, Alexander de Rhodes, began a mission based on Macao. He learned the language and respected the customs of a people which was strongly Buddhist. Local priests were ordained in 1668 to serve a church with about a quarter of a million members and Vietnamese were made bishops in 1833. However, the growth caused alarm and persecution resulted. Many Catholics witnessed to their faith as martyrs over half a century but precisely what had been feared by the local rulers now came to pass: in the 1880s the French established a protectorate, pleading that they had to defend the Church. For a time the colonial regime did bring benefits and by 1940 there were about 1.5 million Christians. But after the long war for independence (1946–54) most of the Christians fled from the Communists who had triumphed. As in Korea, they went to the south which was now under a nationalist-capitalist (and corrupt) regime protected by the USA. After an even longer and more destructive war (1955–74) the whole country was under Communist rule. The position of the Catholic Church was now precarious and Protestant numbers were small, but Christianity proved to be rooted deeply enough to survive and Catholics were so loyal to their tradition that the government was never able to arrange the formation of a Patriotic Church on the Chinese model. By the 1990s the Catholic Church had about five million members in a population of about 72 million. It is not going to disappear but if the Vietnamese wish to be religious (as many still do) the easier option is a revival of Buddhism. In Laos and Cambodia the Catholicism of the French colonial period has, it seems, been overwhelmed.

In other countries which have been Buddhist strongholds Christianity has found it hard to make an impact. That has been the case in Sri Lanka apart from churches which consist mainly of the Burghers descended from European colonists or of Tamils brought over from India by British tea-planters; in Thailand apart from Chinese or Vietnamese immigrants; and in Myanmar (formerly Burma) apart from the Karen and Shan peoples living in partial or complete rebellion on the borders. For similar reasons the Christian mission has made little impact on the Muslims in Malaya although more on the Chinese immigrants and on the 'animist' tribes of Sarawak and Sabah. On Muslims in Afghanistan and in central and western Asia the impact has been very small indeed. There have been many Christian converts in Singapore, where no other religion is secure amid all the western-style modernity, but in the great sub-continent of India this has not been the case.

Into India

The brief mission of Francis Xavier to India in the 1550s had a more sordid sequel. The Portuguese colonists in Goa were determined to destroy Hindu 'idolatry' and to impose their version of Catholicism on the 'St Thomas' or 'Syrian' Christians who had survived for many centuries if not from the time of the apostle. Up to a point they succeeded: Hindus under their rule were not allowed to practise their religion in public, the records of the St Thomas Christians were all destroyed. In 1559 their frightened clergy accepted the Catholic archbishop's authority, and after the failure of a revolt in 1653 two-thirds submitted again to the 'Latin rite'. But temples destroyed in one place could be rebuilt elsewhere; devotions banned in public could be maintained at home; and the St Thomas tradition, although shattered into fragments, was not forgotten. Having achieved this 'conversion' of the territory under their government or influence, the Portuguese left the archbishopric of Goa vacant for long periods and did what they could to prevent the appointment by the papacy in the 1830s of 'vicars apostolic' (not ordinary bishops) to lead the mission in the rest of India. Thus Goa never became the missionary base once intended. Local Catholics were divided, for the St Thomas Christians who had agreed to be Roman Catholics were prevented from using their 'Syrian' liturgy outside a limited area (the future state of Kerala). Their unhappiness about this restriction meant that evangelism by these Indians in India was handicapped until their tradition was fully respected in the twentieth century. The uncertainty of the Catholic mission was also expressed in continuing arguments about the right attitude to the inflexible division of society into castes. The ideal was a welcome for all to the Mass. But in practice was it permissible for higher and lower castes to enter a church by different doors and to be separated by a low wall while at worship? And should men of the despised castes be admitted to the priesthood? Not even the Vatican had clear answers to such questions. While Catholics concentrated on their own problems, the sub-continent's political future was in the more energetic but far from tender hands of the East India Company of the British.

The company was motivated by commerce. It owed its astounding ability to protect and expand commerce mainly to the opportunity created by the decay of the Mughal empire, to a lack of unity and military skill in the Indians who refused its bribes, and to its ability to pay other Indians to fight its rivals, the French. The Catholic community in the south of India had to be left to itself but when a few Protestant missionaries insisted on arriving (from 1706 onwards) they were restricted to the little Danish or British colonies around the forts which protected trade: a wider distribution might disturb trade.

There was a disturbance. A few schools and colleges offering a western-style education were founded and could be welcomed as useful to the children of some of the richer Hindu families—who intended to remain Hindu, although to one Englishman (T. B. Macaulay) the admirable intention of the education offered was 'to form a class of persons Indians in blood and colour but English in taste, in opinions, in morals and in intellect'. He said nothing about religion. But in 1830 a keen young missionary from Scotland, Alexander Duff, arrived in Calcutta. He saw the opportunity to add the Bible to this education and opened a school with five pupils. He and other teachers so impressed some of the young Hindus that conversions and baptisms resulted, to the fierce indignation of the families concerned. Always higher-caste Hindus who joined churches could find themselves cut off from all their natural ties and naturally their numbers were not large. Far wider, although less dramatic, was an influence on India which did not involve baptism—although India could influence the west.

Already in 1820 Ram Mohun Roy, the founder of the Brahmo Samaj movement, had published a selection of the teachings of Jesus as 'the best guide to happiness'. He became Alexander Duff's leading Indian ally without ceasing to be a Hindu. Later Hindu teachers gave high praise to Christ while denying the missionaries' claim which made him the world's only Saviour. One such guru was a mystic, Ramakrishna. His leading disciple, Vivek-ananda, who had been educated largely in Christian schools, founded the Ramakrishna Mission on Christmas Eve in 1886 in order to take to the world a form of Hinduism which honoured Christ as 'the Messenger' among other 'Great Ones'. Within India this mission paid the Christians the further compliment of starting schools, colleges and hospitals. However, the impact was somewhat different when Vivekananda's electrifying address to the World Parliament of Religions in Chicago in 1893 started a western movement. Americans and Europeans responded who were not interested in the Messenger whose message had become the over-familiar Christianity: they were fascinated by what was a novelty to them, the long and assured but attractively inclusive tradition of Indian spirituality. In its turn this western form of Hinduism aroused a Christian response: surely people in the west needed to learn wisdom from their own religious heritage, not from sources remote from their history? Thus the main Indian reaction to the missionaries' claims for Christianity had a parallel in the main western reaction to claims for Hindu superiority. The religions were influencing each other but neither was surrendering.

Among writers and readers of religious literature in India there was a considerable debate about the status of Christ. Keshub Candra Sen, for example, found a Hindu Trinity in the classic description of the One as including *sat, cit, ananda* (being, consciousness and bliss). He wrote of Christ's 'loyalty to God' but also of his nature as 'humanity pure and simple in which divinity dwells'. That was language which Vivekananda could use but such experiments in theology aroused much criticism, both from the Christian missionaries who thought them unorthodox and from the Hindu intellectuals who treated them as unconvincing camouflage for an essentially stupid Bible. Experiments which it was hoped would prove that a Hindu Christianity could be translated out of books into church life failed. And a hundred years after Alexander Duff's arrival it could be seen that his pioneering of education in the English tradition with some teaching of the Bible had had mixed consequences. Since the 1850s the colonial power had subsidized such schools and colleges and across India their numbers were considerable—but the price of this success was an emphasis on learning by rote for examinations, with the Bible still taught but not included in the examinations. The fire which had produced conversions was dying down.

More important numerically were two contrasting popular reactions to the disturbance caused by the missionaries' challenge. On the one hand,

Hindu indignation about baptisms, or about books by Indians which treated Christ with excessive reverence, gave rise to the Arya Samaj movement which from 1875 militantly defended India's Hindu heritage against the intruders from Europe (or from Islam). On the other hand, some whole villages or tribes began to seek baptism.

Such 'mass movements' were of people more or less outside the Hindu system: the new Christians belonged to the lowest castes, the 'untouchables' or Dalits ('broken') doomed by the Aryan conquests, or to the tribal peoples never absorbed by these conquests (the Adivasis). They were very seldom literate (as late as the 1930s only about a tenth of the whole population could read) but that was not the only reason why they had no interest in books about Christ for Hindus. They had experienced the Hindu caste system as oppression and when they gathered courage to think for themselves they detested it, particularly because they had themselves been hypnotized by the teaching that their acute poverty had been caused by their own *karma* (action) in a previous incarnation. They were also utterly hostile to landlords who might be Hindus or Muslims and who were turning lands previously belonging to the tribe into their private property. Thus they had their own powerful reasons to be attracted to the religion of the British conquerors: the Christians' Bible gave dignity to the poor, the missionaries' schools could lift people out of virtual slavery by education, the colonial rulers would (it was hoped) provide protection in an emergency, the missionaries could bring food. In the Chota Nagpur region in Assam 'mass movements' of this kind began after the failure of futile rebellions in the 1850s and in the south many baptisms rewarded the help given by Christians during the famines of the 1870s. In the 1920s many of the Telegu people to the north of Madras were not only baptized: they were baptized as Baptists. Like the experiments on the Hindu–Christian intellectual frontier, these movements were criticized: many Hindus protested that these desertions of India's religious heritage responded merely to the bait of material help and many Christians lamented that the interest taken in 'conversion' was not leading to any depth of orthodox faith.

The connection between the missionaries and the British authorities underwent several developments. In 1813 Christian (mainly Evangelical) pressure in Britain forced the East India Company to modify its previous policy of aloofness from religious questions. A new charter declared that the company was in India partly for the sake of the 'religious and moral improvement' of the people. Missionaries were made more welcome and some local customs which had horrified them were made illegal: widows were no longer to be burned on their husbands' funeral pyres and travellers were no longer to be murdered ritually by the 'thugs' as part of their religion. Gradually missionaries were allowed to spread over the country. In 1857–58 a crisis came with the 'Indian Mutiny', a premature war of independence confined to the north but marked by atrocities on both sides. As a result Queen Victoria was declared empress of India and the country was administered by a British-controlled civil service which, although deeply resented as being foreign and humiliating, was admitted to be honest and efficient. To some extent it was also impartial, although the British discouraged or wrecked local industries: it was their policy that Indians should buy British goods brought on British ships. Railways now crossed a sub-continent which lived in an uneasy peace and the government which sought 'progress' subsidized a network of schools and hospitals staffed by missionaries. Specially valuable was the effect on the status of women: Christian schools offered unprecedented education to girls and Christian women showed their new religion by being willing to work as nurses.

The only source of conversions which was numerically substantial was, however, the series of 'mass movements' by marginalized peoples: this was the main cause of the doubling of Protestant numbers between 1850 and 1900, to about 2.5 million. Catholic numbers also grew, to about 1.5 million, partly because in comparison with the Protestants that church was by now more comfortably at home in India and less associated with the colonial power. Bishops appointed by the papacy could now lead church life, the earlier physical division of Catholic churches according to caste disappeared and many of the converts came from the bottom of society. The many 'sisters' who arrived as missionaries were loved for their simple piety and good works.

It was impossible for the British to rule India for ever: their army of occupation was never large and at home public opinion did not support violence. In 1885 the Indian National Congress was founded (by an English Christian who was a retired civil servant) and the pressure to 'quit India' slowly began, to end in political independence in 1947. Some Indian Christians became prominent both in the early stages of this nationalist movement and in attempts to make Christianity more Indian. For example, the poet Narayan Tilak retold the story of Christ in lyrics of great beauty and tried to inspire a Christian movement, 'God's Durbar', where baptism would not be necessary. A former Sikh, Sadhu Sundar Singh, caught many imaginations: converted by a vision in his youth and thrown out of his home, he adopted the lifestyle of the holy men who were familiar as wanderers on India's roads, except that whenever he spoke about Christ he was obviously speaking about a close friend. He was lost to sight on his last journey, as a missionary to Tibet. Other Indian Christians, and missionaries who had come to love India, adapted the tradition of the *ashram* as a place for prayer and hospitality; in that privacy they could use some Hindu helps to worship and meditation. Indian clergy began to be outstanding as bishops and in other positions of leadership in the churches. The importance of Christians in the 'quit India' movement was limited: a small group anyway, they knew that they owed much to missionaries from Britain who were still influential. But their low profile in this agitation was not to prove fatal.

The Church of South India was inaugurated almost simultaneously with the birth of the independent nation, after thirty years of negotiation between the churches. It aroused worldwide interest among Christians because it was the first union in history between churches with bishops and churches without them, and within India it ended part of the scandal that Christians were not together although they preached about one Saviour who had total demands. However, the unity achieved by the Church of South India was far from complete. The new church was not joined by the Catholics, by the Baptists, by the Lutherans who preferred their international connections or by those Methodists who were related to the USA. Nor was it likely to receive a large new influx of Hindus, for the preparatory discussions had been almost entirely about the problem of reconciling the differences imported into India by the European missionaries, not about the Christian–Indian dialogue. In the 1970s 'united' churches with a somewhat broader basis were formed in North India and in the Islamic nations further to the north but these had smaller memberships.

The British empire ended without a fight and in the constitution which independent India adopted there were remarkable continuities with the colonial period. Although Pakistan had to go its own way amid massacres and huge migrations, in the rest of the country the states acknowledged a central government, so that India preserved a strong cultural identity and the princes ruling locally soon lost power. Although many predicted that the problems of secessionism, of poverty, of an often corrupt and factional political leadership and of a bloated and time-wasting bureaucracy would prove too great, this complex country remained the world's largest parliamentary democracy. The constitution guaranteed the rights of minorities—of the layers in society tactfully called 'scheduled' from which the bulk of the churches' membership came and of the churches themselves as religious fellowships. Although Hindu nationalism became the chief political alternative to rule by the increasingly corrupt Congress party, instead of becoming Hindustan India became a 'secular' state. A small minority wanted that to mean 'anti-religious' but (as the Communists discovered in perpetual opposition at the national level) the abolition of religion was as much a dream as the abolition of poverty. Nehru, India's first prime minister, was respected despite (rather than because of) the secular outlook which he owed to his western education and his most powerful successors depended for much of their electability on the family name of mother and son (Gandhi). The constitution of 1950 made India 'secular' (a word added in 1976) only in the sense that 'the state shall not discriminate against any citizen on grounds of religion'. After tense debates all citizens were promised the right 'freely to profess, practise and propagate religion'. The churches were therefore free to evangelize and to grow—and they did, but not to any large extent.

In the 1991 census professing Christians constituted only about 2.5 per cent of the population. Catholics now numbered about nine million. Most were conservative, proud of their connection with Rome and anxious about any concessions to Hinduism for the sake of 'inculturation' (as was proved in the cautious proceedings of the Church in India Seminar in Bangalore in 1969 and its even more cautious sequels). The Syrian Orthodox Church numbered about 1.5 million. About two million Protestants were to be found in the 'united' churches but about six million belonged to other churches, Evangelical or Pentecostal, which were at least as conservative as most of the Catholics. In total the Christians numbered about twenty million in a population of 844 million. More than half lived in the three southern states of Kerala, Tamil Nadu and Andhra Pradesh.

The overwhelming majority of these Christians was poor but B. R. Ambedkar, who had presided over the making of the constitution and had inspired much else in the life of independent India, took an action which was a commentary on Indian Christianity's image as a 'foreign' religion. He resigned from the cabinet in 1951 and urged the poor to follow him out of Hinduism. The religion which he recommended was Buddhism, because it was Asian. Within a few years about four million people had followed his example. And as their secretary's report to the Catholic bishops in 1991 observed, 'a large number of *Dalit* (poor) Catholics have left the Church for various reasons, including socio-economic benefits from the government': they no longer looked to the Church for such help in their material needs.

However, the influence of Christianity on India has been greater than is suggested by the strength of the Hindu resurgence or by the comparative smallness of the churches' baptized and faithful membership. Indians whose personal beliefs more or less coincide with those of the churches, but who are unwilling to make the break involved in being baptized, seem to be numerous. On a much larger scale Indians who remain loyal to the Hindu heritage may stress those elements in it which are believed to be compatible with the teaching of Jesus. Many have adopted the Liberal Protestant slogan 'the fatherhood of God and the brotherhood of Man' and their religion can rise to the passionate spirituality of the poetry of Rabindranath Tagore, to the equally spiritual philosophy of Sarvapillai Radhakrishnan who was president of India, and to practical work for what Gandhi called *Sarvodaya*, 'the welfare of all'. As a law student in London in 1889 Gandhi the *Mahatma* ('great soul') was 'delighted beyond measure' when he read the Sermon on the Mount for the first time. It inspired him until the day in 1948 when he was assassinated by a Hindu fanatic. If we ask why he died with the name of the Hindu god Rama on his lips, his written words about the Christian missionaries supply one answer. He blamed their link with colonialism: 'As a body, with honourable exceptions, they have actively supported a system which has impoverished, enervated and demoralised a people considered to be among the gentlest and most civilized on earth'. His ultimate loyalty was to the spiritual tradition of his own people, with the emphasis on where it agreed with the Sermon.

India is a country which religion has saturated like an unending monsoon, and the wealth of its own religious history must be the main reason why the western-style Christian churches, for long associated with foreigners' invasions, have found it so difficult to make converts. But Jesus has not gone unnoticed.

Is it possible for Christians to hope for more, in India or in the rest of Asia?

A New Asia

A new Asia is being born. In nation after nation the key question used to be asked by colonialism, but in the 1990s colonial empires are not remembered personally by most Asians. The struggle against poverty has become the central fact of life and thought and the response in most of Asia has been to want 'development'. By this is not meant the mere imitation of the USA or Europe. Great as are the practical difficulties involved, it is widely agreed that foreign-controlled businesses should not be allowed to operate except by agreement with national governments and that the drive to achieve economic growth—in other words, to feed and house the millions in conditions worthy of humanity—ought not to be so directed that it produces either ecological or cultural disaster. But it is also widely agreed that nations cannot afford to be isolated in the style of Myanmar (Burma) under military rule. With all due respect to Gandhi, it now makes sense to strengthen modern education and production and international information-flow, investment and trade. Already Japan, South Korea, Taiwan, Hong Kong and Singapore have modernized in that style. Most other nations are beginning to take the same road—which seems likely to mean a decline in the attractiveness of some more ancient paths.

When Gautama the Buddha opened the 'noble eightfold path' by which the individual most courageous in self-discipline could escape from a world which could not be changed, a world of suffering and sorrow (*dukka*), he did it by intensifying the Hindu vision of the world as *maya*. *Maya* does not mean that the world is completely an 'illusion' as in the usual English translation, but certainly suggests that fundamentally the world lacks reality, significance and capacity for improvement. And the other world-views of Asia, while differing profoundly from that Hindu–Buddhist vision, have not been visions of a better future. When China and Japan withdrew from the rest of the world into isolation they became intensely conservative. Other Asian peoples remained isolated from modernity in the 'animist' fear of offending gods or lesser spirits if any change was made in a society's customs or in the use of natural resources. And in Asia as elsewhere the call of Islam has been a call to obey a detailed law decreed in the past. Now all these world-views have become questionable. Most Asians do not want as the alternative all the coarse materialism or crude individualism which pollutes countries said to be 'developed'. On the contrary, Buddhist, Hindu and Islamic ideas have been presented confidently to the west, whether teaching the spirituality of meditation or advocating the moral cohesion of society. But increasingly Asians think that what is needed is a world-view which includes an understanding of the world as real, important and open to improvement. And where Asia thinks this, there is a new Asia.

A profoundly important part of modernization is the challenge to the traditional Hindu and Buddhist teachings about personality. As we have noted, the strength of the caste system has been bound up with the strength of the belief that a high or low status in society is in the last analysis just, because caused by greed or bad behaviour in a previous life on earth. Although the Buddha rejected many Hindu traditions including the caste system, he accepted and developed this belief in reincarnation. One aim of Buddhist meditation is to dissolve the assumption that 'I am': the ego of everyday experience, it is said, is a temporary conjunction of many sensations and many lives. But recently these beliefs, which have determined how countless millions of Asians have thought about the meaning of their lives, have become less convincing. Not only does the modern belief in human rights undermine the rigidity of the caste system: the modern belief that the unique person has these rights undermines the belief in the reincarnation of souls, for being a soul in another body would mean being another person. Modernity often leads to the belief that save for influences started before death nothing of the personality outlives the body, but it is also possible for modern people to believe that somehow the personality survives, particularly if there is also the belief that the eternal Creator loves the unique person to the extent of rescuing that person from the finality of death. And where the possibility of life after death is either denied altogether, or else is separated from the tradition about reincarnation, there is an Asia new in its spiritual depths—an Asia of persons now standing on the brink either of extinction or of eternity.

If a new Asia is being born, so is a new form of Christianity. Painful change is seen to be essential wherever the facts about church life are pondered. Missionaries were needed to found churches but churches have grown more rapidly when no longer controlled by missionaries and their growth has been severely handicapped when they have been controlled by ideas and practices foreign to their people. If these realities are acknowledged, and if further growth is really desired, there has to be heart-searching about whether all the imported ideas and practices have to be kept because they are parts of the 'everlasting gospel' which has to be preached to all the world. A leading Evangelical missiologist in the USA, Donald McGravan, has been influential as he has made the point that churches grow when they are not too unfamiliar, that people 'like to become Christians without crossing radical, linguistic or class barriers'. The statistics of church growth across history and around the world clearly support that argument. But the history of the churches in Asia has shown that it is not easy to agree about the lessons to be learned. If people considering Christianity ought not to be asked to cross more than the necessary minimum of the barriers mentioned by McGravan, what is that minimum? And how high should the barriers constituted by religious differences be? Christians give different answers, some conservative, others radical. As in previous crises in the history of Christianity, there is mental and spiritual suffering. Risks cannot be avoided; in 1987 M. M. Thomas, a respected Indian Christian thinker, wrote a book on *Risking Christ for Christ's Sake*. Mistakes are made and, with greater damage, there are new divisions.

The issues are complicated by the conservative loyalty felt by most Catholics to the conservative papacy. But even while they look towards Rome Catholics can be truly Asian more easily than the Christians in the historic Protestant churches, for in principle its essential character of universality makes it easier for Catholicism to embrace a surrounding culture and to beget a spirituality which is located in a people's hearts. Without any disloyalty to the Catholic Church's official doctrine the Federation of Asian Bishops' Conferences could insist in 1987 on an ideal: 'the daily practice of brotherhood, helpfulness, openheartedness and hospitality' in the service of 'whatever leads to unity, love, truth, justice and peace'. Without any departure from the Christian belief in God Catholic parish priests have known why Asians like colourful processions and the images of the Mother of God and of the saints in glory. If the use of non-biblical readings is thought to be too dangerous, the drama of the Mass can still be an Asian drama and private prayer can still be an Asian devotion. In many cities the church which most boldly announces by its architecture that it belongs to Asia is still the Catholic cathedral and Catholics have been patrons of Asian art which has made Asian emotions visual. In India the lead in advocating the controversial 'inculturation' has been taken not by Protestants but by Jesuits.

The debate also has to take account of the input of Protestant evangelists who are sure that what Asia needs is a clean break with its religious history so that it may be born again into an Evangelical or Pentecostal faith of a confidently western character, as in the days of the China Inland Mission. The approach of AD 2000 has encouraged many plans for missionary work of that character, mainly originating in the USA. But it seems unlikely that the impact of these new missionaries will be very large or long-lasting. India's determination to exclude them is almost as great as China's and where they are allowed to work their success in spreading a religion with no local roots is often either temporary or else confined to places or sections which are not typically Asian. The new Asia is less hostile to foreign influences than Asia was in the past but it usually demands that these influences should be adapted to Asian ways. What happens to churches or missions when they are not so adapted is clear in Japan. But what can happen when a religion takes root in the local soil is clear in the history of much of the rest of Asia: the Aryan gods were once strangers in India, Buddhism was once a Chinese intruder into Japan, Islam was once foreign to the islands of Indonesia.

As Christianity has begun to join those faiths in being thoroughly Asian, it has become more intensely aware of Asia's continuing poverty. In the days of leadership by missionaries often the largest part of the work was done through schools and colleges, hospitals and refuges for women, but inevitably many of the white-skinned evangelists seemed to local people to be rich in comparison with them; or if not rich, then culturally remote. More recently, as institutions have been handed over to governments, the emphasis has been on church-related development projects where the representatives of churches have been in the background. More dramatic has been the occasional impact of demonstrations against notoriously corrupt dictatorships, as in South Korea or the Philippines. But the main development has been that Christianity has seen a truth: most people in Asia have been, and are, not so much the sinners as the sinned against, the victims of economic and social systems, international and national, which have kept them in situations where it takes some heroism (which has not been lacking) to be fully human. Christianity has seen this truth partly because it has produced some outstanding leaders in serving society and in protests against abuses in society, but mainly because most Asian Christians are themselves poor, not needing a telescope to perceive the reality of malnutrition, dirt, disease and premature death.

However, it is appropriate that the emphasis in Asian Christianity has always been distinctly religious. One reason is that since Christians are a minority without much influence in politics, their usual instinct has been to stay out of trouble in order to secure or keep freedom to practise their religion. But being religious in Asia need not mean being escapist, for most of the continent, in addition to being poor, is religious. Aloysius Pieris, a Sri Lankan Jesuit, has repeatedly said that Christianity needs to be crucified on the cross of Asia's poverty but also baptized in the water of Asia's religiosity. That is not something which has been said so firmly about their own continent by the liberation theologians of Latin America. But what is implied when 'liberation' is given a profoundly spiritual content? Was Rufus Jones right to challenge the International Missionary Conference in Jerusalem in 1928 by saying 'We ask them to judge us, not by what we have as yet made of Christianity, but by that better and more perfect religion to which in the providence of God we believe our Master is leading us'?

Many Asian Christians have been reluctant to admit that the churches are not yet fit homes for Asia's spirituality. In their hearts they are loyal to the Christ they have accepted as Lord and Saviour, and often also loyal to the missionaries who told Asia about him; and they fear that what is recommended as 'inculturation' would in practice mean 'syncretism', a great betrayal. In 1932 an American 'laymen's inquiry' financed by Rockefeller published seven volumes called *Rethinking Missions*. The theme that developed from carefully collected facts was that missions understood in western terms had largely failed to reach Asia's peoples. At the time both missionaries and their converts were often indignant about the criticisms. In 1938, in preparation for another International Missionary Conference, Hendrik Kraemer published a more theological book which was a sustained plea for the integrity of *The Christian Message in a Non-Christian World*. Kraemer's basic experience had been as a missionary among the Muslims of Java and after the numerical failure of that work he was extremely suspicious of optimistic talk about 'points of contact'. To him the right message was John the Baptist's: 'Repent and be baptized!' That cry has always been heard and obeyed in the churches of Asia and it will always be what committed Christians most want to say to their neighbours. But Kraemer's later writing shows that he became increasingly sensitive to the defects of the historic churches, and in Asia there has begun to be more willingness among Christians for their faith to be (so to speak) immersed without drowning in the Yangtze as it flows through the land and history of China, or in the vast waters of the Pacific, or in the sacred Ganges which is the Mother of India. And those Asian Christians who have been willing to take this plunge have been so willing not merely in order to be polite but also in order to be faithful to the truth.

Asian Christian thinking has largely abandoned the expectation that Christianity, more or less in one of the shapes it had acquired in Europe or the USA, would soon cover the earth 'as the waters cover the sea'—or at least would be so presented to all the world's peoples that 'the evangelization of the world in this generation' would be possible. It was now widely accepted that for a long time to come Christianity is likely to remain one of Asia's smaller religions, partly because the churches have not yet fully discovered how to present Christ to the continent where he was born and died.

In Asia as in Africa, attitudes towards those who have not accepted Christ as Saviour before dying have changed. As we have noted more than once, the message of most of the missionaries, Catholic or Protestant, was that 'heathen' ancestors and neighbours were bound to go to the endless punishment of hell; and it says much for the attractiveness of much of the rest of their message that they made some converts. It also says much about the loyalty of Christians to Christ amid non-Christian societies that many have resisted attempts to modify this teaching. If they have heard about it they have been suspicious of Karl Rahner's suggestion that non-Christian religions and moral codes are the 'ordinary ways of salvation'. But in 1964 the Second Vatican Council expressed a change which seems to have been accepted by most Christians when it taught that the God revealed by Christ can be trusted not to 'deny the assistance necessary for salvation to those who, without any fault of theirs, have not yet arrived at an explicit knowledge of God, and who, not without God's grace, strive to lead a good life'. The council's teaching, matched by some Protestants, has been blamed for making the conversion of non-Christians no longer a rescue mission and therefore less urgent. But it makes the gospel more obviously good news for Asia and although it was clearly a blessing on a new development in the Christian tradition theological discussion has shown that it was not entirely new. Even the old doctrine that there can be 'no salvation outside Christ' or 'outside the Church' can, it seems, be kept—provided that 'Christ' is understood as the Word of God, creating 'all that came to be', the 'true light which enlightens everyone' (John 1:1–9), and provided that 'the Church' is seen as the company of all who do what they can to walk in that light.

Increasingly it has been seen that the Creator of the universe and of this planet has not confined the revelation of his reality to two thousand years of Christian history predominantly in Europe. There are passages in the Bible which can be quoted to suggest the conviction that every people on earth has had its Old Testament, its own way of receiving the Creator's revelation of his character by action or inspiration. That way has been no doubt imperfect, but the reception of revelation in ancient Israel or in Christianity's own history was never perfect. It is no doubt dangerous to say that any non-Hebrew religion is in some sense an Old Testament, for there may be a temptation to forget that the actual Hebrew Scriptures fiercely condemn various forms of idolatry, immorality and magic; yet it is possible for Christians to seek the spiritual gift of discernment and some simple conclusions seem to be emerging from the recent very extensive discussion of the relationships between Christianity and other faiths.

The first is that the revelation of God in Christ is unique, for as Archbishop Söderblom insisted 'Christian revelation has the shape of a man'. But the second conclusion is that this is not the only shape, for Christians do not have a monopoly of divinely revealed spiritual truth. It is often thought patronizing to call a non-Christian a 'naturally Christian soul' as Tertullian once did, or to call members of other faith-communities 'anonymous Christians' as Karl Rahner did more recently, for such people have their own insights as they receive the self-disclosure of God. (Committed Christians would object to being called natural Hindus or anonymous Buddhists.) These two conclusions, which on the surface contradict each other, can be reconciled by repeating the traditional saying that 'Christ is wholly God but not the whole of God'. Since John's gospel was written it has been a part of biblical Christianity to believe that the light of God which came to a burning focus in Jesus of Nazareth has also shone wherever there is humanity, in particular wherever there is darkness. It does not seem to matter very greatly whether this light is called the *Logos* or the 'cosmic Christ' or the Holy Spirit: what matters is that the light has never been overcome.

In this light we can see why in the recent inter-faith discussions it has turned out to be rather futile to debate in general terms whether the religions are all incompatible with each other or are all 'paths to the one mystery'. The truth seems to be that the religions include both great disagreements, as in a family quarrel, and great similarities, as in a family likeness. More exciting is the discovery that bridges of understanding can be built between the places where the faith-communities actually stand. It has also become clear that the next task is to make these bridges accessible to the millions who cannot take part in the high-level, pioneering dialogues between experts. That means making the atmosphere right and the ideas simple. The religion which persuades cannot be dogmatic; the religion which is heard cannot be aloof. As it has been put by Choan-Seng Song, a theologian from Taiwan who very impressively writes of Asia's sufferings and prayers in a language drawn from Asian life, convincing theology is 'the poetry of God in the prose of the people'.

It has often been found that beliefs which are debatable intellectually become more accessible to the majority who are not intellectuals if they are propounded humbly, in an atmosphere of love and patience, with the readiness to share a silence and to appreciate the strong points of other positions, and with an eagerness to receive as well as to give. Doctrines become more persuasive if they are put forward not as the results of logical arguments designed to knock down objections and to force an intellectual surrender, but as the fruits of experience and meditation accompanied by awe at the mystery which is revealed or half-revealed to an unworthy recipient. Such dialogues usually begin with the explicit or secret assumption that the other 'side' will be changed—but as they continue both partners find that they are changed and enriched, with or without a conversion. In the past Asian Christianity could be described as having three aspects, 'politics, trade and imperial expansion', and three weapons, 'the Bible, barrels of whisky and bullets' (the words are those of a leading Buddhist who died in 1933). But as has been said by a Jesuit who in the 1990s speaks for many thoughtful Asian Christians, Michael Amaladoss: 'Proclamation witnesses to God's mystery as it has been manifested to us; but dialogue reaches out to the mystery of God active in others.' Even more profound and concise was the statement by Amaladoss that 'religions do not save; God does'. In this context Christian evangelism is only a part of what has been called by many Christians recently 'the mission of God'.

If people are persuaded through contacts which are not too threatening that they have something more to learn about the mystery of salvation by God, they will also find that the religion which has seemed monolithic and static when viewed from a distance is in fact full of diversity and full of development. As the dialogue between the great religions begins it seems possible that all of them will develop further. At any rate, it seems worthwhile to attempt to sum up some of the conclusions of Christian thinking about the encounters between the faiths in the twentieth Christian century.

A Meeting of Faiths

In its southern (*Theravada*) form Buddhism often seems very remote from Christianity. It does not teach faith in God and the acceptance of salvation by him. To it 'rebirth' is not a promise but a threat, for it has desired liberation from the otherwise endless cycle of highly undesirable reincarnations. This liberation is to be achieved through the intense meditation which destroys ignorance, greed and hatred and brings enlightenment—and eventually extinction, for the desired end is *nirvana* where the self is 'blown out' like a candle in the dark. But not all Theravada Buddhists have insisted on atheism; the early Buddhist texts do not deny the existence of the Indian gods although they marginalize or mock them and much more recently some Buddhists being friendly have granted that belief in God may be useful as a stage on the path to nirvana. Possibly, then, in the right atmosphere, some may listen to the Christian's question: how useful?

Some five hundred years before the birth of Christ Gautama the *Buddha* (the Enlightened) rejected many prominent features in the religion which he saw around him, in addition to the caste system. He found no usefulness in the recital of petitions or the sacrifice of animals in order to win the favour of a legendary god or goddess. Nor did he admire the quest of the mystic for the union of the permanent soul with the ultimate reality, for the urgent reality was the suffering in life before death. He saw no real merit in the self-torturing of the hermits; the one necessity was that every individual should seek moral and spiritual improvement. His message was addressed not to the few—not to priests, mystics or extreme ascetics—but to anyone, irrespective of caste, wealth or education, who wanted enlightenment and would accept purification through the discipline of the mind. All the features which he attacked in the Hindu tradition can be found in Christian history also, but it can be pointed out that he could not discuss Christianity (which did not yet exist) and that Buddhists might learn something if they did explore it. Christians believe in the Creator who is great beyond the reach of any human imagination but whose chief characteristic, so far is humanity is concerned, is a boundless love for every person. That unique person is loved until death and beyond it. Before death she or he is given a share in the Creator's own character which is creative love; after death a share in the Creator's own life, a destiny very different from extinction. Ultimately the Buddha despaired of human life: to live is to be attached, to be attached is to desire and to desire is to suffer. Christianity is not so blind as to deny the reality of suffering and sorrow, dissatisfaction and impermanence in all mortal life, but its message is that in Christ God becomes visibly attached to the world, passionately desiring to share the suffering and through it to raise human existence higher than the Buddha thought possible.

It has often been said in reply that when Christians ask Buddhists to consider their faith they are asking for a surrender to ideas totally alien to the Buddhist tradition. But that is not the case. It is relevant that in its northern (*Mahayana*) form Buddhism has emphasized not only self-purifying medita-tion but also what Christians recognize as prayer. Since the 1890s dialogues in Japan (for example) have gradually built a bridge. Of course there have been criticisms. It is easy to say that Christians are incurably restless and spiritually shallow, as it is easy to say that the priests and monks of Mahayana Buddhism exploit the superstitious people, particularly by selling their prayers for the dead (like the priests of medieval Catholicism). But it has been proved that a conversation can be held.

Here is a development of the tradition which says 'I take refuge in the Buddha' and makes statues and relics of Gautama prominent. A saviour may now be pictured as a *Bodhisattva*, a purified human being (for example, the Indian prince Amitabha) who has postponed entry into nirvana in order to assist others out of compassion. The assistance is mainly on the path to nirvana but that ultimate state is often pictured as the Pure Land (rather than mere Emptiness) and it is believed that the way to it is indicated clearly in a Buddhist Scripture such as the *Lotus Sutra*. It is also believed that it is possible to receive material blessings such as health through prayer. (These are features of the most successful of the 'new religions' in modern Japan.) This *Mahayana* ('Great Vehicle') form of Buddhism may therefore be so seen as not far from its contemporary, Christianity. Beginnings have already been made in developing it into an eastern form of Christianity, seeing Christ as the Enlightened who leads into a nirvana where the mortal self is 'blown out' only in order to be resurrected into a glory—and who also leads into the fullness of human life before death. If it could gather strength, such a Buddhist Christianity would be different from trade and colonialism, whisky and bullets.

What may be called a Hindu Christianity has also begun to emerge. We have seen that it has had an extremely difficult birth, since Christianity is usually given a very restricted place in neo–Hinduism and most Indians are either simply for, or simply against, their nation's religious heritage. We need to note the observation by Aloysius Pieris: 'One wonders whether the Indian Christ of the nineteenth and early twentieth Christian centuries survives today outside the historical treatises that deal with that epoch.' Nevertheless a Hindu Christianity does still seem to be possible. 'Hinduism' does not exist as a system; it has no one creed, no one church. It is the harvest of the history of many thousands of communities over forty centuries and in the 1990s it is the religious life of four Indians in every five, with a further 100 million Hindus outside India.

Here are, it is estimated, about 330 million gods and goddesses. The divinities of the Aryans mix with the divinities of the Dravidians whom the Aryans conquered, and divinities who seem to personify forces in nature indifferent to human morality stand alongside others who seem to personify the highest aspirations of the human heart. Here a religious philosophy as sophisticated as anything in the intellectual history of the world (Sankara's philosophy, for example) comes out of a mystical contemplation of the grounds of all that exists. Yet the spiritual elite does not object when another philosophy (Ramanuja's, for example) defends the passionate faith which adores and petitions one of the divinities with 'names and forms' in the *bhakti* tradition. The story-telling is as dramatic, the art as physical, the dancing as spiritual, as can be wanted. Here is the conviction that the ultimate 'One without a second' (*Brahman*) is beyond all images or ideas and need not be worshipped by words or actions. Yet it is also believed that something of this ultimacy (*Atman*) is found in every human person ('Thou art That!')—despite a history of accepting the belief that gross inequality between the castes is justified religiously. A Hindu saying about God reveals much: *Neti, Neti*, 'not this, not that, nor both, nor neither'.

In such a comprehensive tradition there seems to be room for 'the Indian Christ' and many Hindus have said so. While they have criticized Christianity particularly for its association with western colonialism, they have found it more congenial than either Buddhism or Islam because the former seems to deny God's existence and the latter his nearness. (Buddhism was eventually driven out of India and under Muslim rulers Hindus refused all real contact. When in the fifteenth Christian century Nanak tried to combine Hindu and Muslim ideas he had to found a new religion, organized three hundred years later into the Sikhs with their own Scriptures and dress.) But if Christ is welcomed by Hindus, Christians naturally ask: on what terms?

In all its many varieties Christianity has always believed in the decisiveness of the revelation and action of God in Jesus. The Hindu tradition that comes nearest to this is devotion to Krishna, but there seems to be little connection between the playful or solemn stories told about Krishna, teachings ascribed to him and the fragmentary evidence about his first appearance in history as the chief of the Yadava clan. If it is to be true to itself, Christianity can never abandon what one of the most enterprising of recent Indian Christian thinkers, Judge Chenchiah, called the 'raw fact' of Christ. But if Hindus wish to examine that 'fact' more closely, there are bridges already built by Christians in India.

Christianity and Islam belong to one family: both religions believe in one Creator (Arab Christians call God *Allah*), both treat as authoritative Scriptures in which he has revealed himself, both meet every week to hear these Scriptures read and expounded, both honour the prophets of ancient Israel, Islam honours Jesus. But everyone knows that these brothers are divided by a family quarrel. Both religions have claimed to be exclusively 'the true religion' and their adherents have used law and force in support of that claim: empires and civilizations have been controlled 'in the name of God'. In 'Christian' societies Muslims have experienced strong prejudice, anti-Muslim crusades have been launched, Muslim 'backwardness' or 'fundamentalism' has been both despised and feared. In Islamic societies Christians have been put under many pressures including outright persecution and murder, and it has not been unknown for someone born a Muslim to be killed because, being persuaded by a non–Muslim religion, he has become an 'apostate'. But it is also a fact that in the twentieth century (as in some earlier periods) neighbourly contacts, scholarly publications and dialogues between spiritually minded believers have shown that it is possible to throw if not a bridge than a rope across the centuries of dislike or violence.

The most obviously urgent question has concerned the *sharia* as the detailed religious law meant to decide the legislation and the daily life of an Islamic state. This law has been developed extensively since the Prophet's lifetime but in principle Islam has felt from the beginning that it is more than

CHRISTIANITY: THE FIRST TWO THOUSAND YEARS

an ideal or a private religion: it is the divinely revealed way of life. Modern Christianity has been criticized for its retreat into idealism and privatization: thus it advocates the restriction of sexual activity to marriages between the mature who remain married for life but in 'Christian' societies Muslims observe sexual permissiveness and a high level of divorces. Moreover, in the 1990s bitter memories of the humiliation of Islam under western colonialism are still alive and to these feelings about the past have been added the great realities of poverty under an economic system dominated by non-Muslim countries, so that millions of the poor turn from despair under capitalism to the enforcement of Islam. But it is also possible to argue that the experience of Christians may be helpful to Muslims. Christians have found that attempts to enforce a detailed religious law have broken down. People who are not personally committed to accepting the law have in the end rejected it as oppression; situations and problems have arisen which are remote from those covered by the law; teachers who cannot be called unspiritual have persuaded devout believers that the Holy Scriptures were intended not as a code of law but as a summons to sanctity and love. And many Muslims have been moving towards the acceptance of a less politicized and less legalistic form of their own religious heritage. Probably they do not admire 'Christian' societies but to some extent they have shared the experience of the breakdown of religious law. They have become a minority in a non-Muslim society or they have become more sensitive to the position of non-Muslims in their own societies. They have been involved in movements never envisaged when the Quran or the *sharia* law was formed: the modern movement for the equality of women, for example, or the modern banking system which depends on the payment of interest, or the rise of nationalism meaning that the position of the caliph as the 'Commander of the Faithful' can never be restored. It has become possible to think that a new form of Islam is needed no less than a new form of Christianity.

But discussion about the role of religious law in a modern society, like other serious and respectful discussions between Muslims and Christians, ends up with the question about Jesus. If he is not a lawgiver, what is he?

The Quran includes 93 references to him and his mother is 'chosen above all other women'. He was the greatest of the prophets before Muhammad, preaching *islam* (submission to God). He was born miraculously and performed miracles. He was the Messiah and was taken into heaven. As the 'Word of Truth' and the 'Spirit of God', he will return to judge the world. Sufi poets have developed these tributes while remaining within the Muslim tradition and it has become customary for ordinary Muslims to say 'upon whom be peace!' if they mention his name. In the Quran his followers, the *Nasara*, are said to include 'men who are devoted to learning, have renounced the world and are not proud'. In other passages, however,

Muslims are warned against Christians. These warnings may well reflect the Prophet's contacts with particular groups at particular times, but it is a permanently important fact that he was the consistent enemy of idolatry. As such he commanded his own followers to contradict the 'infidels' who say that 'God is three' or that 'God is the Messiah the son of Mary'. And in the course of a dialogue without hostility it seems to be possible to ask Muslims to investigate whether Christians do always say that. Most Christian scholars now agree with the Quran that 'Jesus the son of Mary' never said 'worship me and my mother as gods in derogation of God'. He never claimed to be 'God'; he believed in the unity of God as strongly as did Muhammad and echoed the insistence that the only God must be loved totally. Church historians would now agree that the complex doctrine of the Trinity was never intended to deny either the unity of God or the humanity of Jesus: it was complex precisely in order not to make these denials. But Jesus lived, taught, acted, died and continued to act in such a way that his followers acclaimed him first as the Son or Word of God and then as God the Son or the Word, sending the Spirit and therefore love, joy, peace and spiritual power. Much in the history of Christian theology now appears to many Christians to have been 'corrupt' (which has been the Muslim accusation): although unintentionally, it has obscured both the unity of God which Jesus proclaimed and the ethics on which he concentrated to the neglect of theology. And much work has been done in the consequent restatement of doctrine, as we have seen on many pages of this book.

On this basis it does not seem impossible to accept the invitation in the Quran: 'O People of the Book! Let us come together with the agreement that we shall not serve anyone but God and that we shall associate none with God.' Christians may reply not that they merely 'associate' Jesus with God but that Jesus is the man in whose life the love of the Merciful and Compassionate reaches humanity, the man in whose physically and spiritually painful death the love of God enters the depths of human suffering, the man in whose victory over death the victory of God is guaranteed. If that faith is held, then God is seen to be more parent-like than most people (Christians as well as Muslims) find it easy to think—and it is seen that out of merciful, compassionate love God allows more freedom to ignore or oppose his will than most people who believe in his powerful existence find it easy to accept. And they may add that Muhammad (on whom be peace!) is the Prophet with a message about the one, holy God. His teaching was not unlike the messages of the Hebrew prophets which Jesus, a Jew teaching Jews, could assume to be the accepted truth. In the world of the 1990s almost two thousand million people see (however dimly) a unique relationship between Jesus of Nazareth and God the Father—and about one thousand million Muslims, inspired by God through the Prophet, worship God.

If that suggested outline of a consensus sounds extremely superficial, it may be recalled that the Second Vatican Council said: 'The plan of salvation includes those who acknowledge the Creator. Foremost among these are the Muslims, who, professing to hold the faith of Abraham, along with us adore the one, merciful God, who on the last day will judge humanity.'

10

⊷⊷⊷⊷

In the Postmodern Age

A Journey into the Future

THE journey of the Christians has been full of surprises. What was originally the Jesus movement among Jews had in it the potential to become *katholikos*, 'universal', in spirit and global in its outreach to continents beyond the early Christians' knowledge. The spiritual tradition which has produced saints and martyrs from its origins to the present day has proved able to survive persecutions by empires, and when the persecutions ended it has not ultimately depended on the patronage of the many Caesars who have tried to control it. Orthodox and Catholic civilizations rose and did not fall completely.

A living faith, a personal trust, in God through Christ has also proved able to survive the shocks inflicted in the early stages by modern knowledge and modern lifestyles. It has been learned that it is right for modern Christians to be among those who dare to find out how the world is by scientific investigation, to think out what is the meaning of real experience, and to consult their consciences when they decide what is right or wrong. The reformation or revolution effected by the Enlightenment cannot now be undone where it has happened and seems certain to spread wherever modernity is allowed to make its full impact. It has, however, been seen that better science can deepen awe and wonder in the contemplation of the many marvels which remain and it has emerged that the Bible, when treated 'critically' as literature and history, can still—at least to some—speak with a gospel ('good news') and a life-changing power.

It has turned out that a Bible-based religion can be strong within the acceptance of modern science, freedom and personal responsibility but that it needs to be the 'religion of the heart'. When it is heartfelt Christianity can experience such an inrush of the divine Spirit that a new dynamism enters the individual and the community, with a new assurance and joy. Lessons have been learned from the experiences of the people's churches in North America, established in hearts not by laws, and of the Christians in Latin America, hearing a call to serve the cause of liberation from every kind of oppression and poverty. As Christianity has spread worldwide new lessons have been learned from its ability to reach, to admire and to raise to new levels Africa's openness to the presence of God, China's struggle for justice in the community, the Buddhist's meditative tranquillity, the Hindu's sense of life's mysterious richness and the Muslim's submission to life's mighty but merciful Creator. The meeting of the faiths has only begun but its early rewards have added to the conviction that Christianity itself is an unfinished project.

In all these spiritual adventures which were not foreseen when Christianity began its journey, a new understanding of Jesus has been reached person by person, community by community, generation by generation. Experience has suggested that spiritual unity with him is itself a foretaste of the kingdom about which he spoke, for it is reconciliation with God as 'Father' and with the other human being as 'neighbour'. In very many difficult situations it has been experienced that he does reveal who he is to the humble and does give them a power which may not end their suffering but which will end their sense that life is either meaningless or totally doomed. And despite all the disasters which have killed easy optimism the wider influence of Jesus has been at least one factor in the progress which has been a reality.

In our journey through the centuries in this book we have observed some progress amid the tragedies. The time has come to see that there has been some progress in the twentieth Christian century—progress which Christians can interpret as a little part of the dawning of the kingdom of which Jesus spoke, or (if that interpretation seems excessive) as a little part of the work of the divine Spirit.

This has been a time of many local wars, civil or international, but also of many protests against the madness and the suffering, not only from those who have been bereaved, maimed, ruined or traumatized but also from viewers of television news. One cause of the wars has been poverty, for many of the world's peoples have had little of the hope of economic progress in unity which has persuaded most of the Europeans to be less mad and to suffer less. But this has also been a time when the gap between the majority of humankind and the nations called 'developed' or even 'advanced' has aroused a guilt or fear among the rich as well as an anger or desperation among the poor. At the same time the richer nations (and even India in its poverty) have developed the moral idea that the state ought to provide through the taxation of the privileged for the welfare of the children, the unemployed, the sick, the disabled and the old—a revolution in politics. 'Justice' has begun to mean not only equality before the law, and not only the fairness of 'equality of opportunity', but also positive discrimination by the tax-raising state in favour of those who are handicapped in the competition of life: 'social justice'. However, in a vision as new as the photographs from the moon, our planet has been seen as fragile and in great danger either from nuclear power (in military or civilian uses) or from the exhaustion or pollution of natural resources including land, water and air. Here is a moral cause in tension with the hope that ever-growing numbers of the poor may be fed, housed and employed, but it is no less moral than that hope. And in this period 'human rights' have begun to constitute the public philosophy which can be enforced legally. It is no small thing that they have prevailed against Nazism, Fascism, the worst forms of racism and (in most countries) Communism. Equal rights for women have been asserted over the whole field of modern life, with a determination and with practical effects which would have seemed impossible almost everywhere before the 1950s. These moral movements have not often been taken together: enthusiasts have often concentrated on a single issue. But it is possible to reckon that this has been an age of moral progress.

These moral movements have all been supported by the World Council of Churches, for example, and have also been affirmed powerfully by recent popes, although with more caution about entering into controversial details; and ordinary Christians have often taken what action they could. These causes can all be seen as thoroughly in accord with traditional teachings about peace and social justice, about the world as God's good creation and about humanity as God's children. But it is also a fact that the main agencies which have taken the lead, most conspicuously the United Nations, have been shared by people of many religions or none, for the convictions which have inspired belief, teaching and action are not the monopoly of any religious community. Moreover, in the churches there has been an uneasy awareness that in the past Christian leaders did not lead prophetically on these issues. Many statements could be quoted to the effect that war is righteous and glorious; that the poor would always be poor, the slaves always slaves and the vulnerable always vulnerable, and should be content; that Adam (Man) had been given an unrestricted dominion over nature; that, in contrast, the entitlements of most human beings were extremely restricted; and that Eve (woman) had been condemned by God to be subordinate. The attitudes of the past may be defended, or at least excused, by asking for some consideration of the conditions of the past, but the admission that these attitudes were taken in the past within the churches now helps Christians to understand the Marxist contempt for religion, and the knowledge that these attitudes have not been completely abandoned may encourage some sympathy with, for example, the recent insistence of some leading feminists that the women's movement ought to be 'post-Christian'. What seems fair is to say that the great new moral movements are bigger than the churches—as Christians would add, because they have been inspired by the God who does not depend on the churches. The churches have had to learn like everyone else and to take their places as contributors like everyone else, in societies where they do not find it easy to make their voices heard.

In earlier chapters something was said about the prospects of the Orthodox and of the many Christians who now live in countries which are relatively poor in the terms of economics. But what are the prospects of the Christians in societies which are materially richer than others?

Postmodern Religion

The term 'postmodern' began to be used quite widely in the 1970s, partly because of the disturbances of the 1960s. It was coined in the 1950s by Arnold Toynbee, an English historian who attempted to see a pattern in the rise and decline of many civilizations including that which lasted from the sixteenth to the twentieth Christian century. He sensed the arrival of a new age or at least of a new stage in modernity's decline, and it was his belief that religion would be of central importance in the transition from modernity to the future (as religions had been, he thought, the most important survivals of past civilizations). Later analysis of swiftly changing cultural phenomena has tended to emphasize that Toynbee was himself 'modern' in that he believed in large patterns. The poet W. B. Yeats seems to be a better prophet of the future in his much-quoted expectation of 'mere anarchy' now that 'things fall apart, the centre cannot hold'. In this context it seems foolish to attempt to make a system out of this movement, but a few words may be offered. Although the age has no 'centre' it has a style.

Postmodernism comes after modernity and uses it. It lives in an atmosphere of freedom which is modern. It assumes, or hopes for, a material standard of living higher than many people enjoyed in any pre-modern age and for this purpose it does not hesitate to make use of modern materials and modern technology, with modern science conveniently in the background. But in postmodern architecture oddities are added deliberately and in rock music what is amplified by modern means is often an outburst of raw feeling. Postmodern people may or may not be 'reasonable' in the sense of the Enlightenment but certainly they are unlikely to believe what the 'enlightened' Kant believed: that as there obviously is order in 'the starry heavens above me' so there obviously is a force in human hearts which dictates how people ought to behave, decreeing a moral law which turns out to be remarkably like the Bible. It is not that postmodern people have no morality, as is sometimes alleged by traditionalists: they would not be human if they had no sense at all of what they reckon to be honourable, fair or right. But they see that there are many moral codes in the real world around them and that many of these are very strange by the standards of Kant or the Bible. Not only do they now know that people who have never become Jewish, Christian or 'enlightened' may be quite strictly moral according to their own lights. In the postmodern societies themselves there is great confusion about what is right or wrong. So many of the landmarks which set the scene for morality (in theory if not in practice) seem to have gone: not only God the ultimate law-giver but also the assumptions which supported firmly defined roles for gender and class, respectable sex confined to lifelong marriage, stable employment, unquestioning attachment to neighbourhood and nation. The postmodern conscience knows that a war which would have destroyed 'developed' societies was averted by nuclear deterrence, by the threat of 'mutually assured destruction' (MAD); and usually it does not know what to think about that. Even where the difference between good and evil seems very clear, there is no confidence that the good will be chosen. The murder of six million Jews in the middle of Europe was achieved by a rationally functioning bureaucracy using industrial technology in the supposed interests of the race and nation to which Kant belonged. Kant acknowledged that 'radical evil' was an ingredient in human nature but he never expected that.

As humanity faces terrifying problems no civilization or race or philosophy is now dominant, since the northern, white American superpower is now widely hated and even despised. No political ideology has remained convincing as a panacea: not 'socialism' as defined by Marx and other authorities (the ownership, or at least the control, of the means of production, distribution and exchange, with a command over wages, prices and planned developments, giving power to the state or the local community on behalf of the people), not capitalism as advocated by the apostles of the market (reliance for economic progress on private enterprise and free trade, with competition and bargaining freed from bureaucracy's interference). Instead the electorate shops in a supermarket of ideas new or old which are believed to 'work' (the 'social market')—and when one political party seems to have failed to deliver the goods, it is dismissed somewhat as a channel is switched off by a bored televiewer. And the decline of the authoritative book is a part of this postmodern experience. The postmodern culture believes that no grand narrative with a climax corresponds with the realities of experience: even the structured novel of the nineteenth century is abandoned. Post-modernism 'deconstructs' any 'text'—any writing or series of images—in order to discover what is the vision, the 'construction of reality', which the author is trying to put across by his or her 'signs'. It finds in the text a variety of equally legitimate meanings which are available for the person who wishes to 'construct reality' by choosing a vision or seeing an 'horizon' which is not the author's. For example, a 'patriarchal' author may write about women in a spirit of patronage, or may make them marginal to his narrative, but his text is likely to provide enough 'signs' of a different character for a feminist reader to begin to do justice to the women. (This approach has been applied to stories in the Bible.) It is not necessary to claim that any one interpretation will be, finally and exclusively, 'the truth': there may be many opinions which seem truths to be read out of the same facts.

While there is considerable agreement (at least in theory) about moral issues in the public domain, condemning injustice and the wreck of the environment, in the field of personal morality often the only agreement seems to be that decisions must be personal unless they are about the obvious evils such as murder or cruelty. Often the whole emphasis is on the need for the individual to make a decision not between black and white but between shades of grey, between rival 'goods': the 'pro-choice' option in the debate about abortion is typical of postmodern morality, which can also include the 'pro-life' choice against abortion. Yet postmodernism is not unadulterated individualism. It sees that the individual is 'situated' in a community, preferably in one freely chosen such as a sexual partnership but also in the given community of a family, neighbourhood, peer group, class or nation. That community provides the spectacles through which life is seen and the 'language game' through which an attempt is made to describe life. There are many voices because there are many communities using many languages.

It often seems that in such a cultural climate there is no place for Christianity, which has always claimed to offer a vision of life which can be defended reasonably and which puts the story of Jesus at the centre of humanity's history. In particular there seems to be no place for the churches with their dogmas and persecutions. Don Cupitt has claimed that 'postmodern religion is religion that fully accepts that it is just human, being made of human signs'; so religion 'must now continually remake itself as art'. Is there any common ground between Christianity and a culture which can be so described?

There is, it seems, in the recognition that a personal decision influenced by a community is needed before a world-view becomes possible.

For many who regard themselves as Christians as their twenty-first century begins, the option may be made for a fairly loose attachment to historic Christianity, questioning many of its doctrines and ignoring most of its rituals. The connection may be so loose that the person who makes it may be called with justice a 'post-Christian'. This position will be influenced by a community other than a Christian congregation; by family, neighbours and friends, by loyalties to class or nation, or by the media. Conversations, even if casual, may convey some Christian values such as admiration for dogged hopefulness, for self-sacrificing love, for compassion or for the conquest of bitterness by forgiveness. In the foreground there is likely to be a commitment to at least one of the moral movements just described as attempts to improve or rescue the world. In the background there may well be a belief in Someone or Something, capable of being named as God and able to be served in these moral movements. But if not definitely 'dead', God will be absent from the foreground; behaviour will matter more than any religious belief. And if the churches are not actively rejected, at least there will be no acceptance in practice of the right of any church leader to 'tell me what to think'.

However, the decision may be made for a much closer involvement in an organized religious movement, even in a distinctively Christian community and in what has traditionally been called 'faith in Christ'. Then there will be an entry, which may or may not be completely conformist, into a community which may or may not teach the doctrines and the morality which were taught in the past. For inside the postmodern culture an individual may decide that he or she needs a traditionalist community or a new religious movement which can supply more spiritual strength than is available elsewhere. For personal reasons he or she may feel more despairing or dissatisfied, uprooted or lonely, self-critical or dependent than others, more in need of security during adolescence or of reassurance during old age, more worried about the children or about the state of society. It is not at all difficult to think that despite its great moral movements a postmodern society has moved away from the foundations of morality towards cruelty, vandalism, materialism, selfishness, crime, births out of wedlock, divorce and the diseases of sexual promiscuity and of drug addiction; that such a society's disintegration has proceeded too far; that there must be a return to 'virtue'; that now as in the pre-medieval Dark Ages religious communities are needed to teach the elementary truths as the basis on which civilization can be rebuilt and on which, while we await that day, we can live decent lives.

Many postmodern people feel that they cannot be religious in the sense that the churches seem to require: to become that would, they think, mean the sacrifice of their honesty about truth and the surrender of their consciences (for they do not agree that decisions made for them by others are true morality). But some of these people—or perhaps many—envy those who have found it right to belong to churches or to new movements at a deep level, for they observe in them a peace and strength of mind which they would like to have for themselves. Often the furthest they can get towards the churches' religion is to feel confronted by Good rather than by God and challenged to be virtuous rather than holy, or they may believe in 'God' but not in a 'personal' God; but they have reached a conviction that human life is a spiritual pilgrimage towards the integration of the personality and that personal integration comes through being saved from selfishness and materialism. And they are uneasily aware of the great difficulty which most individuals have in rising to moral heights without support from a community which joins that expedition. In the end they may find themselves in a church, even in a church which is defiantly conservative.

These generalizations about the place of religion in the postmodern age will now be tested by brief visits to places where the churches have faced formidable difficulties.

In Secular Societies

In eastern Europe for about 45 years they had to live under Communist regimes. An alternative to their religion was propagated by governments which had many weapons at their disposal. 'Socialist morality' based on 'scientific materialism' did battle against the churches' 'superstition'.

In this battle the governments had varying degrees of determination. Countries were different. In Albania after 1967 the attitude of the state was that religion had been abolished. In Czechoslovakia the state was intolerant because in Bohemia it could draw on a reservoir of popular hostility to the Catholic clergy as stooges of the Habsburg emperors and in Slovakia it inherited a situation in which many of the clergy were discredited because they had collaborated with the Nazis. In Hungary, too, the Catholic clergy could be accused of being the enemies of the people. But in East Germany the Catholics did what they could to stay out of trouble and many Protestants did what their consciences allowed to work with the regime, for example by taking part in state-sponsored ceremonies recommending citizenship rather than Christianity. Their collaboration could be supported with the idealism of Christian Socialism or might be motivated by the simple desire to get children into higher education. In Poland the government had to come to terms with the people's warmly emotional loyalty to the church which safeguarded their national identity. Religious education in the schools, and even the existence of a Catholic university, had to be allowed. But surveys which seem to be reliable showed that the general trend in eastern Europe in those years under Communism, 1945–89, was that churchgoing and assent to the old doctrines declined rather more sharply than in the west, and often for the same reasons as in the west: the doctrines seemed to be incredible in the light of modern science, the lifestyle advocated seemed to be out of touch with reality, people cheerfully took advantage of their freedom from the clergy's moral supervision. In the late 1980s the governments saw that their efforts were having this success and acknowledged that it was more profitable to enlist Christians in support of causes which were useful in a socialist society: there was no point in making them martyrs. But it was still made clear that Marxism was the official ideology and that it was a purifying atheism. When dialogues occurred between Marxist and Christian intellectuals the central subject was the possibility of separating from the discredited religion a new kind of Christian discipleship without 'superstition' and within a socialist society. The most respected exponent of this reconciliation of Marxism and Christianity was the Czech theologian Josef Hromadka, who led the Christian Peace Conference.

However, human nature did not change merely because there was an 'iron curtain' between east and west in Europe, or a wall dividing Berlin. Under Marxist regimes in eastern Europe as in the Soviet Union or China, the human questions about 'Good' were still asked even if the official ideology was that the basic question about God's existence had been answered negatively. Was it enough to say that the struggle of the proletariat, in whose name the privileged Communists ruled, was the source of morality? Was it morally acceptable to go along with the lying and the cynicism which were in fact features of daily life? Was the individual's freedom really a luxury? Was love between persons really of little importance? Was death totally the end? Was God's own death as total as was being taught? Only in the churches could firm, public and community-building answers to these questions be heard which were not Marxist. The European Values Study reported that in 1990, after all the propaganda, about a third of the East Germans still believed in God. Elsewhere the figure was higher.

It would not be realistic to say that the churches overthrew Communism. These governments had been installed by coups after the victories of the Red Army, the Red Army had crushed popular risings in Hungary in 1956 and in Czechoslovakia in 1968 (to the despair of idealistic socialists such as Hromadka), and these governments now ceased to be able to govern because the Soviet Union was no longer willing to hold down an empire by force. But it is a fact that when the overthrow of Communism did become a practical proposition church buildings were strong centres of an alternative philosophy and obvious assembly-points for demonstrations, most notably in Poland and East Germany but also elsewhere. And it is a further fact that when disillusionment followed the euphoria of 1989, resulting in the election of ex-Communists to power in more than one country, the churches were still available as sources of values which did not depend on the new creeds of capitalism and consumerism any more than they had depended on Marxism. The churches still offered the public an alternative. They lost adherents in Poland and they could not gain many in East Germany; they were now judged as churches, not as sponsors of anti-Communism. But they had survived to be parts of the postmodern age—as did churches on the other side of the world after experiencing a different kind of secularism, a kind which was itself vigorously anti-Communist.

In the ancient and medieval worlds there was speculation that a great southern land, *terra australis*, might exist to balance the three partially known continents of Europe, Africa and Asia, and the early Dutch and English explorers were not entirely surprised to discover that there was indeed a coastline. Other people, to be called at first 'Indians' and then 'Aborigines', had discovered the fact some 40,000 years previously and had crossed from the Indonesian islands to make a nomadic, hunter-gathering life for themselves in a continental island which remained largely empty. Settlement by Whites began in 1788 when the area which was to become the city of Sydney was used by the British as a cheap prison for convicts who had been spared the frequent hangings at home. This use of Australia as a dumping ground continued until the 1860s and it is not surprising that the first church erected by the Anglican prison chaplain, Richard Johnson, was promptly burned down by convicts whose desire was to escape from what remained of the English union of Church and State. Nor is it astonishing that colonial bishops sent out by the Church of England from 1836 onwards failed to secure the establishment of that colonial-looking church. In the 1870s the various colonies composed of ex-convicts, their descendants and new immigrants passed Secular Education Acts which ended subsidies to church schools. The intention was to prevent domination by the Church of England although this restriction also affected the other churches exported from England and the Catholic Church which ministered mainly to the Irish. The outcome was an Australia very different from European settlement in the Americas, with far less of Christian rhetoric or reality. Not many of the Australians were directly indebted to the books of the Enlightenment or of later phases in modernity, but theirs was a modern society.

For some time the churches performed a function similar to that which we have observed in Europe and the USA: they met the religious needs of those who wished to be respectable or were homesick. The Anglicans, for example, began a Bush Brotherhood which reached lonely Whites in the vast and inhospitable interior. In the cities where most Australians lived the Catholic Church was the soul of the Labour party. But this role of the churches as links with 'roots' (even with 'home') diminished as the ties loosened between Australia and Britain or Ireland. In the two world wars Australia sent troops who fought with courage on the side of the 'mother country' but both wars ended by discrediting the British connection. Australian lives were lost by mistakes of British commanders in the Mediterranean area; British battleships which might have defended Australia were sunk by the Japanese in the Pacific. Resentment against conscription to fight Britain's wars was followed by closer economic and cultural links with the USA. Particularly when a post-imperial Britain had joined the European Economic Community and was no longer an open market for Australian agricultural products, trade with Asia was seen to be a necessity. It involved the acceptance of Japanese rather than British investment and the abandonment of the 'White Australia' policy which had restricted immigration to those who could write in a European language, preferably English. In 1901 the Australian colonies had federated as a Commonwealth; in 1941 the new nation had secured a greater political independence (with 'dominion status' like Canada); towards the end of the twentieth century the nation is no longer a British colony in any sense and the day may not be distant when it becomes a republic located very firmly in developments around the Pacific.

If they are not fully secular most Australians are, it seems, religious in the sense of being aware of 'God or Nature'. They have a great feeling for the outdoors, not only as facilities for sport but also as the land to which the almost-divine sun sends both cheerful light and dangerous rays. Many have developed a sensitivity to an environment which earlier generations damaged by the introduction of sheep and rabbits, or by mining, and they have a new interest in the Aborigines who knew and loved the land for many thousands of years before the Whites almost exterminated them physically or culturally. The tradition of loyalty to 'mates' in the dangerous interior or in the egalitarian new towns has produced a sense (however light-hearted) of being equally human and equally Australian. And there is a religious element in all these attitudes: nature is somehow sacred and so is humanity, although most Australians do not like to say why. Some Australians have, however, identified themselves with one or other of the organized religious traditions. Some of these organizations represent Asian faiths for the wider variety of immigrants; some are churches in the Pentecostal style; some adhere to the Eurocentric heritages of the Anglicans, Catholics and Orthodox; but Methodists, Congregationalists and most Presbyterians, feeling it right to make a more or less new start in a new country, came together in the 'Uniting Church of Australia' in 1977. The country has begun to produce its own theology and its universities now acknowledge some value in religious studies. What it has not produced is a United Church able to reach the people. In this postmodern society the churches survive as a minority.

The history of Christianity in New Zealand is not unlike that story. Here the original inhabitants were the more 'developed' Maoris who arrived from Polynesia and the intruding British were settlers who acquired their land (after stout resistance) by treaties which were formal although unequal; these agreements were subsequently broken. American and Asian influences have so far been less strong than in Australia, Man has been less able to damage islands much smaller but more fertile and more beautiful, and the position of the churches is stronger. However, although relatively conservative New Zealand is in significant ways postmodern. The days when missionaries hoped for a nation of Christian Maoris without settlers are distant.

599

Reconciled Diversity?

Obviously the churches which have survived into the postmodern age, and in societies largely non-Christian, would have more influence if they could reach more agreement about the essentials of their message and more unity in their work. But how? The question became more difficult to answer when the World Council of Churches held its seventh 'assembly' in Australia's capital in 1991.

This large conference slightly revised the council's vision of unity between the churches. At New Delhi in 1961 it had called 'all in each place' to unite in 'a fully committed fellowship, holding one apostolic faith, preaching the one gospel, breaking the one bread, joining in common prayer and having a corporate life reaching out in witness and service to all'. At Uppsala in 1968 it had looked forward to a 'genuinely universal council' which could 'speak for all Christians'. At Nairobi in 1975 this hope had been modified into 'a conciliar fellowship of churches which are themselves truly united'. Now in Canberra it was agreed that 'diversities are integral to the life of communion'. There are, however, 'limits to diversity', for to be in 'full communion' the churches must be able to recognize in one another 'the one, holy, catholic and apostolic Church in its fullness'.

But the most interesting address to the assembly in Canberra was delivered by a theologian from Korea, Chung Hyun Kyung. She spoke after a traditional exposition of the unity of the Trinity as the model for Christian unity, read on behalf of an absent Orthodox patriarch. Her speech was about the renewing Holy Spirit. It was preceded by dancing by Aborigines and combined with an invocation of 'the spirits of the women, children and men killed by oppression'. She burned paper on which some of their names were written. Because of them, she said, 'we can feel, touch and taste the concrete, historical, bodily presence of the Holy Spirit in the midst' who might also be 'a feminine image of the Christ', bringing near 'the compassionate God who weeps with us'. Behind these words was the Korean tradition about the unhappy spirits of the dead who need to be set at rest because they can still cause unhappiness and disease; in Korea this is a feature of at least some spiritual healing among the Pentecostals. Also in the background was the *Mahayana* Buddhist tradition which includes a compassionate goddess. All this was very different from Karl Barth's address to the World Council's first assembly in 1949. So was Christ still in the foreground? Dr Chung had invited her audience to take off their shoes, in the Asian and Muslim gesture of reverence. But many in that audience were indignant about what seemed to be syncretism, the betrayal of the gospel by the inclusion of beliefs incompatible with it. The Orthodox representatives were vocal in their anger. The Catholics were less vocal, partly because there are in Asia some Catholics who would applaud Dr Chung's courage but mainly because in Canberra the Catholic Church was officially represented only by observers. The gap between her and the Orthodox was large but the gap between her and the Vatican was larger.

That dialogue, or the lack of it, seemed to show that if the 'life of communion' between Christians is ever to lead to 'full communion' it will be necessary to accept a very large amount of diversity, with more care and courtesy than was evident in Canberra in 1991. A model of 'reconciled diversity' as the ecumenical movement's goal was put forward by the Lutheran World Federation in the 1970s. As many now see things, it appears to be more realistic than any hope that the fullness of 'the one, holy, catholic and apostolic Church' will be recognized by other churches in any existing church and will lead to the reunion of all Christians in a single organization. But it seems to be possible, despite every discouragement, that if Christians listen to each other they will recognize Christ in each other and gradually learn from each other, thus growing towards a 'fullness' not yet visible. Indeed, that learning process already occurs as Christians meet and talk as friends in many neighbourhoods in the 1990s. It has been most famous in the ecumenical community in Taizé, in the French countryside near Switzerland. Founded by a few unusual Protestants in the 1940s, as a monastery it has attracted members from other Christian traditions and many thousands of visitors, specially young visitors. They go to its conferences and its worship from all over Europe and from other regions. They become quietly inspired.

It is not a mere coincidence that Taizé is a monastery, for much of the growth of 'reconciled diversity' has been in the experience of worship and private prayer. On the one hand it has been recognized that Christians have many ways of praying, different according to region, temperament and generation as well as according to denomination. That diversity is not obliterated in Taizé, although the music with simple words in Latin and various modern languages does much to unite. It is certainly not absent in the world's churches, where people who pray and reflect carefully still disagree as to whether infants should be baptized or about the connection between the Eucharist and the self-sacrifice of Christ on the cross. But the twentieth century has brought a considerable reconciliation between worshipping Christians whose habits and theories used to be much more different. Baptism is seen as highly important, as the incorporation into the Church as the Body of Christ and so into a new life 'in Christ'. The Eucharist is seen—and, more important, practised much more frequently—as a communion with Christ and each other, a mysterious drama in which Christ is present in spiritual reality. Striking agreements were registered within the World Council of Churches in a document finalized in Lima in 1982 on *Baptism, Eucharist and Ministry.*

Is it possible that more unity is growing through the acceptance of diversity combined with a common belief in the Christian essentials? Any realistic answer to that question must involve some consideration of the prospects in the Pentecostal and Evangelical movements which are mostly outside the World Council.

The part of a divided Christianity which has been expanding most rapidly in the postmodern age can be called Pentecostal if that word is taken to refer to an immense variety of groups which without any central organization depend on the renewing Spirit. Most of them would be as hostile as the Orthodox to Dr Chung's alleged 'syncretism' and she does not belong to a Pentecostal church, but traditions about the power of many spirits like those in her Korean background are also part of the history of many who become committed Christians through the Pentecostal style of worship.

The numerical success of these groups has been seen by many as both impressive and disturbing. They have grown while others have lagged behind or declined, but it has often been asked how many of the converts who will swell the proud statistics remain to develop a mature spirituality within this tradition. It is clear that many people get bored by the repetition of very simple themes in the sing-along songs and the story-telling sermons; or they prefer another pastor's or prophet's church; or they reject the dominant 'shepherding' which almost all pastors and prophets in this tradition think should accompany the informal spontaneity of the worship; or they begin to think that the informality is itself managed by the pastor as a dependable routine. As they seek to deepen their spiritual lives Pentecostal Christians may move into the older and richer traditions to be found in Orthodoxy, Catholicism or historic Protestantism. And as they become more educated they may ask awkward questions and not get satisfactory answers from their pastors. What seems to be happening is that this movement which was itself a rebellion against what seemed to be the lifeless formality of the historic churches has now experienced the rebellion of many individuals in its own ranks. The postmodern phrase is heard: 'I'm a bit of a heretic.'

In the Pentecostal tradition the authority of the Bible has usually been interpreted in a more or less fundamentalist way, taken for granted as correct. But modern or postmodern questions have arisen, here as in other traditions. The account of the experience at the Pentecost festival given in the Acts of the Apostles (2:1–13) refers to speaking in ordinary languages which have not been learned. This account has often been interpreted as a reversal of the curse of unintelligible languages inflicted to punish human pride in Genesis 11:1–9 (the story of the tower of Babel). The dramatic gift of the Holy Spirit has almost always been experienced by Pentecostals not in this form but as the ecstatic 'tongue-speaking' (*glossolalia*) discussed by Paul in his first letter to Corinth. Paul never suggests that he could communicate in a language he had not learned. What, then, is the significance of the story in Acts? Does it teach mainly that Christianity is international? And what is the importance of 'tongue-speaking' in ecstasy, not in foreign languages? Paul put it on record that he had this gift and that he fully accepted that some fellow Christians had it also. This acceptance does not surprise students of religion, for the 'animism' which we have often noticed in our own brief tour of the continents as the basic religion of a 'pagan' people often includes priest-doctors (nowadays classified as 'shamans') who seem to be in touch with spirits during ecstatic trances. But Paul firmly subordinated 'tongue-speaking' to the 'prophecy' which uses words which people can understand: 'I would rather speak five intelligible words, for the benefit of others as well as myself, than thousands of words in the language of ecstasy.' Indeed, he thought that 'tongue-speaking' could be an obstacle to evangelism: 'If some uninstructed persons or unbelievers should enter, will they not think you are mad?' And if Jesus had this gift, it was not thought worthwhile to say so in the New Testament. So it can be asked whether in its early history the Pentecostal movement got this gift out of proportion.

The expectation of the imminent coming of the kingdom of God has often been preached by Pentecostals as by others, yet Pentecostals have also planned and worked as if the future will be considerable for themselves and their churches. What, then, is the real meaning of this hope? Unity between races and classes has been hailed as a foretaste of the kingdom, yet Pentecostal churches have not always embodied that unity. Christ's blessings on the poor have often been treasured, but in recent years some prominent Pentecostal preachers have proclaimed a gospel of wealth, saying that Christian prayer can 'name it and claim it', while others have been on the far Right of politics. And what should be the position of women? The Pentecostal movement has often brought new power to women in their daily lives, and in the congregations women have often been in the majority and in the lead, giving 'testimonies', but they have usually not been allowed to preach. Is that understanding of the Bible's message now correct? And although Pentecostals have often condemned the historic churches as being without the Spirit, in the 1970s they had to come to terms with the fact that many members of those churches became 'charismatic', including Roman Catholics advised by Cardinal Suenens with papal authority. What, then, is the present status of these churches? Should Pentecostalism become fully part of the ecumenical movement?

The discussion of these questions in the Pentecostal churches is beginning to be open and discussion may be followed by development as this movement moves into its second unpredictable century. And there may be a parallel process in the Evangelical movement. There have often been tensions between the two movements, since for the Pentecostals the right emphasis has been on the experience of the present power of the Spirit, an experience fully open to the illiterate, while the more bookish Evangelicals have put the emphasis on the authority of the Scriptures as witness to the Saviour. For some time many Evangelicals were sceptical about the miracles of healing which were a feature of Pentecostalism: it was said that the time for miracles had ended when the Bible was completed. At the end of the twentieth century Evangelicals still say what the Protestants said in the sixteenth: salvation is given only by the grace of God, grace received through faith, grace proclaimed by the Scriptures. But the question is what that tradition means now, for the Evangelical movement, like the Pentecostal, includes many people who ask that postmodern question.

We have noted that American fundamentalism was a reaction against modernity but was expressed in terms which belonged to the modern tradition of attention to written propositions: therefore the fundamentalists insisted that all the propositions in Scripture were 'inerrant' or 'infallible'. There was also a reaction against the pluralism of a modern society. This took the form of insisting that only one Saviour 'saves' and that the way in which he saves is by offering himself as a substitutionary sacrifice in order to satisfy the wrath of the Father against sin. That, they said, is what must be believed if the biblically defined salvation is to be received. But increasingly in the Evangelical movement there has been a return to a vision older than modernity or the Protestant Reformation: a vision of human life, including Christian life, as an affair more emotional than intellectual, the emotions being fed by experiences which cannot be accounted for by an over-simplifying dogmatism. This culture-shift has brought to a head questions which are now discussed by Bible-based Evangelicals as well as the Spirit-dependent Pentecostals.

In his book *Evangelicalism and the Future of Christianity* (1994) Alister McGrath took a justifiable pride in the fact that this vigorous Christian movement has often been more successful than others in appealing to students and other young people but he bravely confessed to the reality of the 'dark side of Evangelicalism', identifying this as a dogmatism, the cult of personality and the unhealthy intensity (particularly about personal guilt) which can lead to 'burn out' rather than maturity. He showed another kind of courage when he set out 'six fundamental convictions' in comparison with which all other matters have tended to be regarded as 'matters of indifference' since 'responsible Evangelicalism has refused to legislate where Scripture is silent or where it offers a variety of approaches'. The six fundamental convictions are: '(1) the supreme authority of Scripture as a source of knowledge of God and a guide to Christian living; (2) the majesty of Jesus Christ both as an incarnate God and Lord and as the Saviour of sinful humanity; (3) the lordship of the Holy Spirit; (4) the need for personal conversion; (5) the priority of evangelism both for individual Christians and for the Church as a whole; and (6) the importance of the Christian community for spiritual nourishment, fellowship and growth.'

It seems probable that few believing Christians, Orthodox or Catholic, Protestant or Pentecostal, would refuse their assent to any of these convictions. The last four are an obvious necessity wherever believing Christians are in a minority, as is the case almost everywhere at the end of the twentieth century. The Catholic Church, for example, now officially teaches that its whole tradition has its source in Scripture, that Christ is the unique Saviour and that all should fully participate in the faith, worship and life of the Church. The 'lordship of the Holy Spirit' is also acknowledged wherever Christianity is seen not as a state-supported institution but as a spiritual movement dependent on what is believed to be spiritual contact with God; and this attitude is now almost universal. But discussion has shown that much turns on what is meant by the first two convictions. To what is the Christian community meant to point? To what is the Christian individual meant to be converted?

When interpreting 'the supreme authority of Scripture', is what is emphasized what Dr McGrath quotes with approval? The Evangelical leader James Packer is cited as 'rightly' agreeing with Calvin that 'God completely adapted his inspiring activity to the cast of mind, outlook, temperament, interests, literary habits and stylistic idiosyncrasies of each writer'. In a slightly later book, *A Passion for Truth*, Dr McGrath quotes with approval David Wells, 'one of Evangelicalism's most significant and respected exponents', as teaching that 'it is the task of theology to discover what God has said in and through Scripture and to clothe that in a conceptuality which is native to our age'. If Scripture is not dictated by God and if its message needs to be 're-contextualized in order that its content may be meshed with the cognitive assumptions and social patterns of our own time', as Dr Wells says, it seems that there may be more common ground than has been thought with the 'liberals' who have attempted to study the biblical writers in the context of their times and to communicate the biblical message in the context of our time—unless the word 'liberal' is identified with biblical studies which were unacceptable because unscholarly or with popular teaching which contradicts the Bible's central message. In the twenty-first century the growing number of Evangelical scholars and communicators, sharing a passion both for truth and for the relevant expression of truth, seems likely to exercise a leadership which will be welcomed by many Christians who in the past have equated Evangelicalism with fundamentalism.

By 'the majesty of Jesus Christ' as God, Lord and Saviour, is what is meant what the New Testament points to when it uses a variety of approaches? As we have seen, the bishops' councils in the Byzantine empire defined the incarnation of God in Christ in terms which were acceptable to most (although not to all) Christians in that period but which are not fully intelligible to any Christians in the modern and postmodern ages who have not made a special study of church history. In practice Evangelical preachers have seldom insisted on these definitions, or been very interested in them. Despite their suspicion of Paul Tillich as a 'liberal', probably most would be happy to praise Jesus with him for 'the undisrupted unity of the centre of his being with God'. Even the word 'Lord' does not have the resonance which it once had if a society is democratic. The word 'Saviour' is understood more readily, as when a statesman saves a country or a rescuer an individual. Christians who have experienced a deep sense both of a personal guilt and of a spiritual union with Christ will understand Alister McGrath when he says that 'the cross is the unique and perfect sacrifice which covers and shields us from the righteous anger of God against sin, reconciles to God and opens the way to the glorious freedom of the children of God'. It was Paul Tillich (no fundamentalist) who said that this understanding of the cross 'meets the burden of guilt and the impossibility of making up for what we have done' by declaring that the person who trusts in God's forgiveness has been accepted although unacceptable. But other people to whom the gospel must be communicated are nowadays more likely to ask whether God himself can be justified (or redeemed) in view of the suffering in his creation which he is said to control. Such people will be more interested in Dr McGrath's next sentence, which says that the death of Jesus 'established the full extent of God's love for us'.

In recent years Evangelicals have participated vigorously in attempts to express a Bible-based message in a conceptuality which is native to our age. In a age which has begun to appreciate the time and space taken by what may be called the patient Plan of God, the patience on the cross of the man who embodies that Plan can have a meaning both for an understanding of the evolving cosmos and for an encouragement of the suffering individual. When vast audiences watch athletes whose victories are hailed as being triumphs for the nation or city from which they come, it is not difficult to think of Jesus as being 'satisfactory' as the victor on behalf of a humanity which is feeble. When the great sacrifices made by people for each other are often reported and admired, and when animals lay down their lives daily for the sake of the food-chain on which humanity itself depends, it does not seem necessary to recall the sacrifice of a lamb in a temple unless such sacrifices are familiar. When liberation is a theme at which eyes light up, it does not seem necessary to recall talk about a ransom from slavery, let alone talk about a ransom paid to the Devil or to God. When the demonic power of evil in human life is known to all except the few who are complacent in their isolation, it does not seem necessary to repeat talk about the conquest of personal devils unless a belief in devils is a part of the mental world of those being addressed and needing liberation. Or if one or more of the traditional Evangelical doctrines must still be defended as essential, at least it is possible for many who regard themselves as Evangelicals to agree with the more general point that the living message of the Bible cannot be stated precisely, permanently and exhaustively in the old propositions. Thus even an Evangelical author with the prestige of Carl Henry proved unable to stabilize theology with his six volumes on *God, Revelation and Authority* (1976–83). Younger theologians (such as Donald Bloesch in the USA) have taken positions which would have shocked earlier Evangelicals.

What is necessary, many Christians now think, is the priority of evangelism by lives and living words—and for such evangelism to be effective, it is above all necessary that it should come out of personal experience and conviction. In his conclusion to a 1994 book of scholarly essays on *Evangelicalism*, David Wells gave a verdict which raised a question for the future. 'It is not that Evangelical beliefs about biblical inspiration, the necessity of regeneration, the divinity and substitutionary atonement of Christ, or his second coming, have been greatly modified. Rather these beliefs have simply moved from the psychological centre to its periphery. Once they were powerful; now they are not the moving forces in the Evangelical mind.'

Does that mean that the future of the Evangelicals will be a less distinct part of the future of Christianity? Does it mean that the Evangelicals will be fully part of an ecumenical movement which seeks not necessarily a new organization but 'the life of communion' between Christians who accept each other in a 'reconciled diversity'?

Postmodern Protestants

In the historic Protestant churches the diversity which still worries Pentecostals or Evangelicals obviously flourishes. Many of their members protest against changes in their heritage; many others protest against conservatism; and the question often seems to be whether there can be reconciliation within the churches, between groups whose convictions are so different. As the American Lutheran theologian George Lindbeck has written: 'The pressures of modernity push us all either towards updating the faith or else, in the case of traditionalists, towards immobility.' Would-be reconcilers have often proposed as the solution agreement about the essentials, but one question is: what are the essentials?

At the cost of causing distress to many of the churches' conservative members, the worship has been renewed by translation into language which is easier to understand but also richer because more poetic. New translations of the Bible have been welcomed. At the cost of causing even more offence, historic theological positions have been modified. At Lauenburg in 1973 theologians representing the Lutheran and Reformed (Calvinist) traditions reached a 'concord' by seeing that the division of those movements in the sixteenth-century Reformations had not been a division between right and wrong. On the one hand, Luther's orthodox heirs had been wrong to place such an emphasis on 'faith' that the importance of discipleship in the whole of life had been obscured; it is right to understand salvation by Christ as the salvation of the whole person. On the other hand, Calvin's orthodox heirs had been wrong to stress the limitation of God's offer of salvation to the predestined few; it is right to understand salvation as meant for all. And in the Anglican churches the sixteenth-century claim to be restoring the faith and order of the early centuries in protest against 'Popish' innovations was abandoned, at least implicitly. No action was taken against churchmen who embraced modernism and decisions were taken to ordain women to the priesthood: Anglicans could not now claim to be entirely conservative. Yet many merits have been seen in contemporary Roman Catholicism and theologians have found it possible to reach agreement about the Eucharist, about the priesthood which serves it and about the salvation which it proclaims. In the 1990s agreements are in place between Anglicans and Lutherans in the USA and Europe, recognizing that in all these churches the Word of God is preached authentically, the sacraments duly administered and the ordained ministry received as a gift of God; and a closer relationship with the Methodists seems possible.

But because these historic churches have contracted into minorities which are voluntary—because, sociologically speaking, they have become more like the Pentecostal and Evangelical groups—it has proved possible for them to neglect or dispute the need to restate their message in terms which would communicate outside their own ranks. Some of the songs, talks or publications which have been intended as fresh evangelism, and which certainly have communicated an attractive happiness and enthusiasm, have still included words which can mean little to a new generation. In some of the renewal of officially authorized worship there has been little concentration on the question of what newcomers might understand; the interest has been in using treasures drawn out of church history before the sixteenth century. Friendly dialogues between expert theologians may have buried many of the disputes of that century but there has been less agreement about a simple message which might reach the postmodern age, an age which knows that even the greatest Christians of the past belonged to a very different world. It was inevitable that a far-reaching debate should explode.

In the 1960s the English-speaking theological world was dominated by a radicalism which questioned or rejected the traditional images of God and Christ. A paperback entitled *Honest to God* by John Robinson (an Anglican bishop) presented these images in phrases which would make sure of their widespread rejection: God is not an old man in the sky who occasionally intervenes to stop his grandchildren on earth being too troublesome, Jesus is not God dressed up to look human as a father on earth dresses up to look like Father Christmas, prayer is not shopping for favours. But what was to be put in place of these images? The appeal was to the experience of God in the 'depths' of all life and the resulting theology could be called 'panen-theism': not the pantheism of Spinoza's 'God or Nature' or the theism of God's transcendence which might be aloofness but the belief that God is in everything: everything owes its existence to God's presence in that thing, yet God allows that thing to be distinct from the divine Being, to be a creature. The traditional images of God should be made less human (less 'anthropomorphic'); Christ should be seen as the 'Man for Others' whose love for others was a 'window into God'; prayer should be seen as a truly Christian approach to life and life itself should supply the 'secular meaning of the gospel'. These radicals were in their own style concerned for the gospel's communication by offering the vision of God as both genuinely ultimate and genuinely intimate, but the public was not persuaded that what they advocated resulted in a knowledge of the power which Christians call 'God'. The postmodern tendencies remained, with most people content to have no clear image of God but minorities happy to choose traditional images, perhaps because of their appeal to the imagination; and as the optimism of the 1960s faded some theologians moved beyond its degree of radicalism to say that God is not a reality, that Jesus taught his fellow-humans how to live without childish ideas about God, that what actually happens in prayer is meditation in order to calm and strengthen the mind and the will before living without any trust in God.

A reaction came from American theologians, in some distinguished cases teaching in Yale Divinity School. Hans Frei maintained that the heart of the Bible is a narrative which, whether or not it is completely accurate history and whether or not it may be analysed in completely adequate theories, inspires a community of faith. George Lindbeck argued that Christian doctrine is derived from the culture—from the life, the psychological structure and (using Wittgenstein's term) the 'language game'—of the Church or a part of it. Stanley Hauerwas interpreted Christian ethics as the teaching about behaviour given by a community with its own character. Here is 'postmodern' religion in a shape very different from that suggested by believers in the death of God: it is religion shaped by the experience of the impact of Christ on a distinct community which has the right to be itself and to speak with its own voice. But other theologians have commented that this approach to old questions does not entirely avoid the problems which lie in the old answers. Frei's emphasis on the 'narrative' avoided the treatment of the Bible as a source of propositions about God, the world and history, but it could not avoid the need to interpret the story in terms which seem reasonable. Lindbeck's understanding that doctrine 'regulates' the 'performance' of the members of a community avoided the treatment of theology as an intellectual attempt to probe the mysteries of eternity, an attempt which might end in hot air, but it could not avoid the need to demonstrate that doctrine corresponds with reality (at least up to a point) and not merely with the feelings of the community. The stress on the community's role in the teaching of ethics was realistic, but Hauerwas still had to face the problem of relating specifically Christian ethics to other codes of morality, particularly since very few Christians look exclusively to the Church for moral guidance. So the debate has continued. More importantly, no very clear or convincing reasons seem to have reached the public with explanations about why the message given by the Bible is true, why Christian doctrines make sense and why self-consciously Christian behaviour is admirable. So Paul's question to the tongue-speakers of his day may be addressed to the theologians who have concentrated on the Christian community in the postmodern world: 'If some uninstructed persons or unbelievers should enter, will they not think you are mad?'

The question may be asked even when a theologian has unquestionable intellectual power and integrity. Wolfhart Pannenberg has, like Barth, Bonhoeffer and Bultmann, responded to the challenge of theoretical atheism and practical materialism—in his case, in the shape of Marxism controlling the eastern half of his native Germany—but his response has been very different from theirs. With far more confidence than they showed (perhaps influenced by a development which Bonhoeffer could not predict: the strength of the West German hostility to Communism) he has affirmed a Christian's right to interpret the whole of reality and the whole of history in the light of the resurrection which manifests the union of Jesus of Nazareth with God the eternal and ultimately victorious Father.

In this Easter light the dim consciousness of God which is part of human nature can be seen as the beginning of God's self-revelation (Pannenberg has nothing of Karl Barth's scorn for the pride and folly of human 'religion') and the sign of victory given when the tomb of Jesus was found to be empty can be seen as guaranteeing the completion of the triumph and the disclosure (Pannenberg has nothing of Bultmann's scorn for 'myths' such as the story of the empty tomb). If this complex theology could be summed up in a few words, the words might be: revelation as history, promising a fuller revelation in the future. But it seems fair to regard it as a magnificent example of a Christian thinker strengthening the faith of intellectually equipped readers who are already persuaded. In the postmodern world that is a limited audience.

The most ambitious attempt to restate the Christian message for the postmodern age has come in eight books published by Jürgen Moltmann from 1964 onwards. A thinker who is equal to the best in the tradition of German Protestant theology, he stands in the neo-orthodox position of Karl Barth but also carries on the work of Paul Tillich, the work of answering current questions.

He is sure that the idea of including a whole people in a church (the *Volkskirche*) is dead although conservatives have prevented its burial, and he has no expectation that the non-Christian religions will die in the future that can be foreseen. In *The Church in the Power of the Spirit* he stated an alternative: a church without the baptism of infants and without a hierarchy of officers, alive in a spirit of discipleship and friendship and in a solidarity with society's rejects. Its character ought to be expressed in an open invitation to its repetition of the meals which Jesus had with 'sinners'. Its mission is 'Messianic' in that it seeks not its own numerical growth but a service to the coming kingdom of God. Moltmann admires the liberation theologians of Latin America although he has been criticized by them for not being specific enough in his politics, as he admires feminist theologians although criticized for still speaking about the divine in terms of the male.

He is postmodern in that he refuses to trust in reason leading to progress. He was shaped by the 1940s; when no longer a prisoner of war he returned to a Germany in physical and moral ruin. He has understood well the interpretation of the Holocaust which Elie Wiesel gave in his autobiographical novel *Night*. There a Jew has to look at a boy suffering the prolonged agony of hanging because his body is so light. A man behind asks: 'Where is God now?' His answer is: 'Here he is—he is hanging here on this gallows.' Wiesel meant what Nietzsche meant: the impotent God is dying or dead. Moltmann is deeply moved by the disillusionment at the heart of the modern age and courageously attempts to address the further questions, almost as disturbing, which have been asked by the postmoderns. He is profoundly aware of the crisis caused by the human mistreatment of nature. And he recognizes the difficulty of defending human rights while rulers still oppress peoples and men oppress women.

His answer has its focus in the crucifixion and resurrection of Jesus and the gift of the Spirit. *Theology of Hope*, the first book in this series, did not repeat Bultmann's translation of the 'myth' of the resurrection into Christian faith's understanding of the cross: to Moltmann the resurrection was an action by God after the crucifixion and it promised that God will overcome all the sin, suffering and death in human history. In later books it is said that the Easter promise was made to the whole of creation and not (as for Bultmann) solely to the individual who makes a decision to choose 'authentic existence'. In *The Crucified God* the concentration was on the time when Jesus hung on the gallows and died, and the meaning of the cross was explored through the cry 'My God, my God, why have you forsaken me?' The meaning was understood as the full entry of God the Son into the human condition of feeling the absence of God and the presence of failure and death. But the conclusion wrung out of that agony was that God is not dead but 'is love', for true love must be affected by how it is received and often rejected. The cross shows, too, what is hinted at in the rest of history: God does not dominate, for he prizes the freedom of his creation to respond to, or frustrate, his purposes: thus he leaves the Nazis free to perpetrate the unspeakable evil of the Holocaust. The resurrection is not a complete victory: Jesus Christ remains 'on the way' to that future and needs others to join him on the way. But the resurrection is God's promise that the End will be the victory of his love.

This fairly simple message would probably be accepted by most Christians as a legitimate attempt 'to discover what God has said in and through Scripture and to clothe that in a conceptuality which is native to our age'. But Moltmann has added ideas which have proved controversial.

He writes that on the cross God the Son was godless and godforsaken and that God the Father then suffered through grief; that the resurrection was the Father's protest against that condition of the world which the Son had had to endure; and that God the Spirit suffers when frustrated in the work of bringing nature to its destined perfection. These teachings are supported by his account of the Trinity. To him Father, Son and Spirit are three persons more or less in the modern sense of 'persons' and they are in a changing relationship where no one is 'monarch'. In particular the Spirit is for him fully a person, doing work which in traditional theology was thought to be the work of the Father as the Creator or of the Son as the *Logos*. Here he goes beyond most of the New Testament where the Spirit is often called the Spirit 'of God' or 'of Christ', communicating the teaching and life of Jesus like fire or wind, creating strength and fellowship but compared more easily with human power than with human personality. He criticizes theologians, from the Cappadocian Fathers to Karl Barth, who have insisted on the unity of God because the Father is the ultimate source of divinity and of divine activity ('Christian monotheism'). He pays little attention to recent theologians who have tried to recast the doctrine of the Trinity into language about 'holy Being' rather than 'persons' (as in John Macquarrie's suggestion of 'primordial, expressive and unitive Being'). Critics have complained that his own version of trinitarianism is bound to look like a belief in three gods (perhaps even as a belief in three people in trouble?) and that it is hard to see how on this basis dialogues either with atheists or with non-Christians are possible. The thought of these three divine persons as a democracy may attract but what seems to be missing is any adequate defence of the goodness of the Father. In this theology the Father seems somewhat aloof from the suffering which the Son and the Spirit have to undergo in a world which he had inexplicably allowed to become a disaster; in human terms he is not a great success as a father.

Critics have also complained that it is hard to see how dialogues can continue with scientists unless it is accepted more clearly that when the Christian hopes for the final glory it is not a hope that what is physical will then last for ever. In the Bible there are dreams of 'new heavens and a new earth' and in the ancient profession by faith of those baptized in Rome (the 'Apostles' Creed') there is belief in the 'resurrection of the flesh', but reflection had led many Christians to think that they are allowed not to take such expressions literally. Moltmann makes much of Paul's ecstatic vision of a glorified creation in Romans 8, but less of the sober reminder to the Corinthians that 'flesh and blood cannot inherit the kingdom of God', so that in eternity a new 'flesh' is needed which is not the 'flesh' of the present world. In what we know of the teaching of Jesus speculation about the material contents of the kingdom of God is conspicuous by its absence: the whole emphasis is on human beings being willing to do God's will. To many Christians who take the New Testament very seriously it has seemed possible to think that neither Jesus nor the creation was ever godforsaken; that Jesus embodied God's constant love for the distressed when he taught and healed and when he experienced human despair; and that the Spirit given after the resurrection has enabled the true disciples of Jesus to share his love for the Father and the 'neighbour'—and to share also his love of the natural world even though the wild flowers of Galilee may keep their beauty only briefly.

So the question is whether these ideas which may seem to be unnecessary difficulties in Moltmann's theology are really essential to the communication of the Christian message. Different answers are likely to be given to that question. And the diversity in Christianity towards the end of its twentieth century is even more plain in the controversies about a question which cannot be answered by diplomatic ambiguities. Should the Christian Church always be dominated by men and by traditions which stress the masculine characteristics of God? Part of the debate following Chung Hyun Kyung's speech in Canberra was about the right of a woman to lecture men. In the Protestant churches at least, an acceptance of that right has emerged since the 1950s. One of the most effective advocates of Christian feminism has been Jürgen Moltmann's wife and collaborator, Elisabeth Moltmann-

Wendel. An attempt will now be made (by one man) to sum up the discussion which the feminist protest has provoked in what looks like becoming a Reformation.

It is widely agreed that women are right to demand an end to their historic role as passive victims, for they are specially well qualified to see the most important tasks facing humanity as the twentieth century ends. Women are the ones who have suffered most from the poverty of most of the world's population. Women are treated almost as slaves or as ornaments, are beaten or put on the shelf, and have even fewer personal opportunities than men. Women know best how hard it is to sustain a family in dehumanizing conditions. Women are left to grieve after the violence. Even in 'developed' societies which in theory acknowledge the equality of women with men progress has been incomplete and real and comfortable equality remains a goal. Yet women often find it easier than men to have insight into the nature of human society and into the nature of Nature, for the role of women in caring for children, or their biological potential for that role, gives them the insight that insensitive dominance can lead to disaster. Human societies and the natural world are in reality systems which demand to be understood and handled with respect, care and where possible love. Women see more easily than most men do that the whole of creation deserves that attention and flourishes as its worth is affirmed—as is obviously true of young humans and as ought to be true of women themselves. This flourishing, this fulfilment of evolution after slowness and set-backs and great pains, may be compared with the most feminine of all experiences (tragically often viewed in the churches in the past as a pollution): giving birth. And when societies no longer depend on physical strength to get work done, women can find it easier to get, and do, the jobs which are needed outside the home: their brains and hands become more valuable than men's muscles. It seems probable that the twenty-first century will be the women's century.

It also seems probable that few believing Christians who are prepared to examine the conventions of male-dominated societies would now deny these facts or regard those conventions as acceptable. Christianity has inherited the basic belief of the Jews that when God 'created Man in his own image' he created 'male and female' and saw that this feature of his creation was 'very good', not only because it enabled the fulfilment of his command to 'be fruitful'. Thus 'male and female' was from the first the true norm. (The belief of Thomas Aquinas that a woman is a misbegotten man was imported into the biblical tradition from Aristotle.) The Hebrew prophets thought it right to compare God with a mother giving birth or a parent stooping down to lift up a child and the Hebrew Scriptures show that although women were usually subordinate in Israel as in almost every other premodern society there could be women showing a strong character (such as Sarah the wife of Abraham and Deborah the 'judge') and there could be mutual enchantment in love and in marriage (as in the Song of Songs). The strength of Judaism in the home where a woman is the key figure is shown by the ruling that whether or not a person is a Jew depends on whether the mother is.

As we have noted, a revolutionary estimate of women was apparent in the practice of Jesus and of the first Christians, before the acceptance of the patriarchy of the Roman empire. In the later history of the churches the position of women was definitely unequal, but exceptions have been observed: in Orthodoxy and Catholicism the large role of women in the religious communities, in the churches of the Reformation a more positive attitude to marriage, in the churches of the Protestant Left, particularly in the USA, some religious leadership by women no longer confined to the convent or the kitchen. (A *Women's Bible* was published in the USA in the 1890s.) Above all, the prominence of the mother of Jesus in Orthodox and Catholic piety has meant honouring some qualities usually regarded as feminine. Her response to the will of God with what a woman could provide made possible the humanity of Jesus and the character of her holiness has been seen by many millions through words in Luke's gospel: 'you too will be pierced to the heart' but 'the humble have been lifted high'. When Mary is called 'the new Eve' the veneration of her can do much to undo the damage done by the portrait of Eve in Genesis 2, where she is ambitious to acquire what she has no right to and uses her charms to trap her man into committing sin. Mary often remains for this piety the unique virgin-mother, even 'immaculate' and 'assumed' into heaven, but in her virtues she is a model which can be imitated. The gospels say that women including Mary were near the dying Jesus when the male disciples had fled and that 'some women of our company astounded us' because having gone to anoint the corpse they were the first to find the tomb of Jesus empty; and so they indicate who will constitute the majority of the close followers of Jesus throughout the history of Christianity. In the light of this tradition it can be predicted that great benefits will come to the churches which share in the wider movement of society towards full equality between the two halves of humanity.

Is it therefore necessary to reject completely the theology done by DWEMs (dead white European males)? Or is it necessary to accept the official rejection of women priests by the Orthodox and Catholic authorities? Both questions are hotly debated in the 1990s.

Some feminist theologians, most notably Mary Daly in the USA, have argued that the liberation of women will not be accomplished until Christianity has been either ended or mended. They seek the removal of every trace of the male dominance which has inflicted so much suffering and humiliation over the centuries; for example, 'sin' has been more or less identified with sex, the more sensual Eve being the temptress, or with pride when it would have been right for women to assert themselves against exploitation and cruelty. As the supreme symbol of liberation, it has been held to be necessary to move 'beyond God the Father'. But probably most Christian women, as well as men, fail to see this necessity. They do see the dangers in the central biblical images of God. To call him 'king' or 'judge' can easily suggest that he is deficient in patient love. To call him 'father' can suggest that he is tyrannical or remote. Since the eternal Creator cannot be male or female it may well correct false impressions when God is referred to as 'she' or 'mother' or 'friend' or 'lover', but most Christians also see that insisting on the exclusive use of such language would also carry dangers. It might appear to disown the foundation of Christianity by Jesus with the prayer of his life to 'Abba, Father' and to dismiss the two thousand years of Christianity using the old language; and it might seem to forget the reason why in the history of 'higher' religion male imagery for the supreme god has been preferred. When the great Mother Goddess is worshipped the emphasis is on the sheer fertility of nature and the worship, essentially an adjustment to the rhythms of nature, can become a cult of fertility (complete with orgies as in the Canaanite religion against which the Hebrew prophets urged war). The image of the king or judge at least suggests some distinction between the One who is 'holy, holy, holy' and a creation which does not entirely commend itself even to the human sense of morality. And even if that old issue seems irrelevant to the debate in the 1990s it can still be held important not to exaggerate the differences between the masculine and the feminine either in the idea of divinity or in the idea of humanity, for the 'feminine' can easily be defined so as to suggest weakness and sentimentality. That is, many think, wrong about the God who is pre-eminently powerful and rational—and it is wrong about the capacities of women. It seems possible to meet the valid demands of feminism by stressing that God is above gender and that being human is above the myths about the feminine and the masculine. Within the limits set by biology, neither women nor men should be compelled to renounce the strengths and the tasks said to be characteristic of what is unfortunately called the 'opposite sex'.

This debate about the character of God has sometimes got entangled with the debate about women priests, for it has been feared that the new thinking encouraged by feminism will end in heresy. When that conclusion (which seems to forget the women who have been devoutly orthodox in their millions) has been rejected, it can still be said that a woman cannot represent Christ in the Eucharist; to this the reply is that women saints have very often represented him in life. Or it can be said that since no woman was included among the first apostles, the 'apostolic' ministry of the bishops, with the priests and deacons ordained by them, must exclude women; to which it is replied that the original twelve included no Gentile although the Church was to become almost entirely Gentile. Or it can be said (it was said by Karl Barth) that the Bible forbids the 'headship' of women, ignoring the fact that many restrictions on women which are taken for granted in the Bible have been removed recently as belonging to a past culture which need not be accepted if the Bible's central message is to be accepted. But the basic difficulty for the Orthodox and Catholic authorities seems to be that nowhere in their churches in two thousand years have women been recognized as priests. That difficulty has been connected with the long hesitation over the ordination of women in other historic churches. In Europe the development was begun by Lutherans in Denmark in the 1940s but in Sweden it required an act of Parliament in 1958 and it took almost half a century before the Church of England agreed to it. In some parts of the world it still seems highly premature if not wrong in itself. This conservatism is surely understandable in the 1990s.

Similar arguments and difficulties have appeared in the debate about the position of homosexuals in the churches. In the Bible homosexual practices are utterly condemned (by Paul among others). But the debate has its focus in the question whether these passages in Scripture issue a commandment valid for all time or reflect a lack of knowledge. In the twentieth century most of the relevant scientists have agreed that homosexuality, the condition of between 5 and 10 per cent of humanity, is caused by a combination of genetic factors with the environment during early years, not by personal sin; therefore homosexuals are not perverts but feel according to their own nature. More disputably it is said that homosexuals have no moral obligation to refrain from the sexual acts which accord with their nature, since their frustration may damage their personalities. But it is understandable that many heterosexuals draw the line when invited to approve 'genital' activity expressing the homosexual condition, however great may be their charity towards individuals. That reaction arises from basic biological instincts—but has often been denounced as sheer prejudice. This debate, too, continues.

It has been a feature of the closing years of the twentieth century that disputes about sexuality have greatly troubled the Catholic Church in a period when its baptized membership has been larger than ever before.

Catholicism Enters the Future

The two most influential Catholic theologians in the last forty years of the twentieth century have deliberately avoided adding inessential doctrines.

Karl Rahner's aim was to show that the Catholic teachings which had already been defined could be interpreted so as to be helpful to his two audiences: Christians aware of the intellectual difficulties and pastors aware of the practical problems. Hans Küng's aim in reaching a larger public has been more radical: to simplify the message by returning to Jesus as the criterion of Christianity, by showing that doctrinal formulations of the past related to cultural situations ('paradigms') in the past, by denying that popes have been exempt from the human tendency to make mistakes and by working out ways of relating the message with fresh vigour to the issues which are important to the postmodern age.

Rahner's lectures on *Foundations of Christian Faith* which made a book in 1976 were his most substantial single work although essays which he called 'theological investigations' were published in many other volumes. To him the foundations were not the same as they were to Protestant or Catholic fundamentalists. For example, his interpretation of the dogmas about Mary were that she is 'not only the mother of Jesus in a biological sense' but also 'someone who has been redeemed radically' and that in death she reached 'the fulfilment of God's salvific act' redeeming her life. However, he did not stress arguments over the significance of particular texts in the Bible or in church history. His interest was in demonstrating that a sense of being confronted by God is at least implied in all human experiences of the transcendent: not only the conviction that one is a free person under a moral obligation to think and do what is right even under the threat of death with its 'invincible ambiguity'; not only the glimpse through a great love of 'an inexhaustible and indestructible mystery' stronger than death; but also the very awareness that the person who has this conviction and this glimpse is a mere creature, always living under the constraints of one's biological and social origins, never able to control either the beginning or the end of mortal life. Others could have selected other signs pointing to God; these were the signs most important to this Jesuit scholar, as humble as he was honest. And this restatement of the Catholic doctrine about the 'natural desire for the beatific vision of God' avoided any claim to be able to prove God's existence, as his restatement of specific Christian beliefs was at every point sensitive to modern or postmodern objections. And the same desire to communicate with the thinkers of an age very different from the times of Augustine or Aquinas was shown by two Catholic theologians in North America, Bernard Lonergan and David Tracy. They argued with great care that the intuitive knowledge of God ('insight') is not entirely unlike the basic forms of human knowledge of the world and that the expression of that knowledge by 'analogy' with the things of this world is not entirely unlike other uses of images in human language. Philosophical theology done at this level could never become popular, but at least it was done and done in an atmosphere different from the old dogmatism. Here God is the 'holy mystery' transcending human minds and words but never far from human hearts.

Rahner also discussed many specific doctrines and edited more than one encyclopaedia of theology. His account of the Three-in-One God argued that as a result of biblical and Christian experience three 'modes of God's presence' in his 'self-expression' are known—and are rightly believed to be 'modes of God's being' in an eternity which is a 'mode of spirit'. His account of the resurrection of Jesus granted its uniquely mysterious character within God's 'self-expression' but understood it as 'the irreversible beginning of the coming of God as the absolute future of the world and of history'—without detailed predictions. His account of the work of the Spirit was summed up as 'God given and received'. And as he spoke to fellow Catholics Rahner repeatedly showed that while he defended the belief that the Catholic Church was 'founded by Christ' he was not willing to attack other churches, or to defend as irreversible all the decisions of the Vatican, or to say that the historical Jesus had 'founded' the papacy or the priesthood in its present shape. Many questions were, he maintained, rightly 'disputed'; for example, the question of the possibility of women priests. The Mass could remain the centre of Catholic life without the insistence that the bread and wine are changed in their 'substance' by the priest's words. His vision of the local church had more in common with Moltmann's ideas than with the Vatican's.

Hans Küng has shared all Rahner's questioning but none of his caution. He has substituted for the dogma of the pope's infallibility proclaimed by the First Vatican Council the belief that the Church is 'maintained in the truth' so that what is received by it in the long run as its faith is truthful ('indefectibility'). This was a decisive step. In 1979 it resulted in the withdrawal by the Vatican of his right to teach as a Catholic theologian since 'he deviates from the complete truth of Catholic belief'. He remained a Catholic priest but a new post had to be created for him in the university of Tübingen. A new audience was also created by the publicity of his condemnation: his lectures and books have received attention and admiration in many countries. He has set himself the task of explaining what 'being a Christian' means in the postmodern age, tackling questions about the existence of God and the possibility of life after death and using a style much more down-to-earth than Rahner's. In earlier years he had shown well-informed sympathy with Protestants, particularly with Hegel's insistence on history and Barth's on faith, and now his sympathy, knowledge and influence crossed all divisions between churches. His interests also expanded to include detailed studies of the non-Christian religions with an approach similar to Rahner's although with a characteristically practical stress on the need to agree to meet the urgent moral challenges of the age. It was also characteristic of him that he offended non-Christians by his constant emphasis that Jesus is the best revelation of the Creator. But he did not lack energy for a conversation with the Vatican which was scarcely a dialogue: the authorities did their best to ignore him and he did not try very hard to conceal his dislike of the pope's policy and personality. In 1980, for example, he was among 130 German-speaking theologians who publicly demanded the recognition of Protestant clergy as valid ministers and the welcome of Protestant church members to communion in the Mass. They also demanded the allowance of artificial contraceptives, the admission to communion of forsaken partners who had remarried, and the ordination of married men and women to the priesthood. Many Catholics wanted such points to be raised as questions not answers but polls of public opinion showed that many others agreed with this rebel's blunt radicalism, specially in western Europe and the English-speaking world. Indeed, to many he seemed infallible.

Protestants have often wondered why a theologian such as Rahner remained committed to the Church as a Jesuit and why a rebel such as Küng has not become a new Luther. The answer lies in the loyalty which is still given to the living tradition of Catholicism. When we notice the rise of a genuinely 'answering' theology among scholars who consequently have been condemned or investigated with suspicion by the ecclesiastical authorities, we should not ignore the work of a 'kneeling' theologian such as Hans Urs von Balthasar. He was a traditionalist but no coward: he left the Jesuit order so that he might be free to found a new order for people earning a living in the ordinary ways, in co-operation with a mystic, Adrienne von Speyr, whose visions he interpreted. Partly because of these visions, one of his major themes became the willingness of God the Son to taste the full experience of human death and even to 'descend into hell'. But his main emphasis was shown by the title of his major work, *The Glory of the Lord*.

He did indeed seek to relate the Christian tradition to the human world, the world of suffering and death but also the whole vast world of religion and culture, believing that in every time and place the beauty of a thing discloses not only its own deepest reality but also something of its Creator. However, he resisted any tendency to minimize the uniqueness or supremacy of the revelation of the divine beauty given by the divine grace in Christ—as he resisted any tendency to restrict to Scripture the Church's witness to this revelation: he expounded the testimony of the saints and the thinkers. Humility was his plea, as when one studies a masterpiece of painting. One is interested in one's own experience of being changed and enriched, but more in understanding the painter's purpose and methods, and more still in contemplating the overwhelming beauty of what is painted.

It seems significant that in the Catholic world the most organized attempt to set up a church in opposition to the official leadership was made by an ultra-conservative group led by Michel Lefebvre, formerly a missionary bishop in French West Africa, who was excommunicated after his unlicensed ordination of other bishops sharing his convictions. He aroused some sympathy because many Catholics including von Balthasar felt that much that was beautiful and spiritually strong had been destroyed by, or after, the Second Vatican Council. But the larger numbers who rejected the official ban on contraceptives, or who had ceased to have any real belief in some other official doctrines, saw no need to establish a new denomination to propagate liberal views. Their protest could be made simply by staying away from Mass or by attending it with their own thoughts.

In a modern or postmodern society people who belong to a church, even people with a conservative temperament, have often tended to pick and choose as to what they will support and what they have supported with enthusiasm has often been friendship and its rituals. The religious community to which they belong influences their intellectual or moral decisions but in the last analysis these decisions remain their own: they, too, are postmodern. Thus they quietly interpret official doctrines so that these fit into what they think to be true and right (and, if possible, also beautiful) in their own hearts. To achieve this, they have no need to form a new organization.

The (Roman) Catholic Church provides the largest example of these tendencies. Most of the thousand million living people whom it has baptized have little regular contact with its clergy and many of those who do attend Mass frequently do so without being controlled in what they think or do except by their consciences. At work, or in bed with a partner, they behave as they decide, as they also do when they vote in elections or think theologically. But the sacraments of the Church remain important to them, partly because these are done rather than said. And intellectual support has been given to this widespread mood by the central conclusions of the thought of an immensely learned and voluminously productive New Testament scholar, Edward Schillebeeckx, who has called the Church 'the sacrament of our encounter with Christ' and Christ 'the sacrament of our encounter with God'. In his earlier writings, which depended on the theology of Thomas Aquinas, he was more inclined to treat the sacraments as material things conveying 'grace' and the Church as an institution, but it became his message that there must be a personal response to God in Christ, so that the Church of God must be 'the Church with a human face'. While never less than pastoral, he was also now never less than critical of institutionalism.

Between 1962 and 1965 the Second Vatican Council gave some encouragement to this mood. Some 2,500 bishops of the Catholic Church, advised by hundreds of theologians and other experts, met in Rome in the presence of almost a hundred 'delegate-observers' from other churches and others including some women who were 'auditors'. They were also watched and overheard by the media of the world as they debated in Latin. They changed the centuries-old tradition that 'error has no rights' by agreeing that the Church has no right to persecute; the acceptance of its doctrines must depend on belief in their truth. 'Nobody may be forced to act against his convictions, nor is anyone to be restrained from acting in accord with his conscience in religious matters, in private or public, alone or in association with others.' They altered the emphasis in the idea of the Church, which had been heavily hierarchical and legalistic: it was seen as the 'people of God' and it was said to be 'on pilgrimage', to be the 'sign' and 'instrument' of communion with God and of human unity. They declared that the *magisterium* (the teaching authority, in practice the pope and the bishops) 'serves the Word of God and is not above it' and that ultimately there is only one 'source of revelation', the Bible. They quoted Jerome: 'Ignorance of the Bible is ignorance of Christ.' They described the bishops as a 'college' presided over by the bishop of Rome and acting in harmony with him in the continuation of the mission of the first apostles. They restored the ordained ministry of the deacon as a life-long possibility for a married man (although not yet for a woman). They urged the laity to participate fully in the worship of the Church and in accordance with this call a new form of the Mass using the local language and allowing the wine to be given to the laity was soon issued. They wanted the Catholic Church to move both confidently and charitably into the modern world. They spoke of the world's workers with sympathy and allowed priests to do some manual work in order to get closer to the workers; they spoke of the Church of Christ as 'subsisting' in their church instead of making any more obviously exclusive claim; they addressed the non-Christian religions and the unbelievers with respect; they emphatically blessed the ecumenical movement for Christian unity and clearly taught that God can save people who do not belong to any church. And they issued no condemnations of heretics, not even of the Communists. The only new evil clearly condemned by them was indiscriminate nuclear warfare.

But they deliberately placed no restrictions on the power of the pope to govern the Catholic Church and it is right that the last words in this history should be about the four popes who belong to the era of Vatican II. The differences between these four will be a reminder that the personal factor will count for much in the future of this church, as it counted for much in the past.

Angelo Roncalli took the name of John XXIII because the John of the gospel was the apostle of love. He was loved as no other pope had been for many centuries. Born in the large family of a peasant farmer, deeply devout in the conservative Italian style, relaxed, open and optimistic, he radiated goodness and during his brief time as pope (1958–63) the world knew it.

He was almost 77 when he was elected: enough of the cardinals wanted this patriarch of Venice as a contrast with Pius XII but knew that with this temperament and at this age he would not lead a revolution. In the event he did not see through any major change. He was concerned about his own new diocese but could do little about Rome's secularity apart from visiting parishes, hospitals and prisoners. He saw the need to begin the revision of canon law but had no great personal interest in a project not completed until 1983. Within a few months he announced to the astonished and alarmed Vatican that he would summon an 'ecumenical' council. Since 1870 it had been thought that the power of the pope was now so great that no council would ever again be needed, but because this pope wanted it the council met—after a preparation which was confused because even Pope John was unclear about what it was intended to accomplish. In his opening address he asked it to state the faith in a new way but not with a new content. He made it obvious only that the *aggiornamento* (renewal) he wanted would be mainly spiritual, a renewal of hopeful love. He expressed too his longing for more Christian unity. In saying that much he spoke out of the experience of a lifetime: a prolonged study of the labours of Charles Borromeo as a bishop of the Catholic Reformation and 28 years in the papacy's diplomatic service, meeting Christians and other contemporaries of many different kinds in Bulgaria, Turkey and France. His chief personal statement was to be *Pacem in Terris*, an encyclical which switched Catholic interest to the poverty of the Third World and ended the axiom that no Marxist could do any good. But he needed others to organize the council.

Conservatives in the Vatican assumed that theirs would be the safe hands to which the unwelcome task could be entrusted. Had they prevailed, this council in the 1960s would have been very like the council which Pius XII had briefly considered holding in the 1940s. But their initiatives were rejected by the majority of the bishops as they got to know each other and the council was rescued from chaos by three cardinals with a vision of the future: the Belgian Suenens, the Austrian König and the Italian Lercaro. And behind the scenes was Cardinal Montini of Milan.

Giovanni Battista Montini, who became Paul VI, had served Pius XII as one of his two closest assistants from 1939 to 1954. He was not made pope before 1958 because Pius had made him an archbishop but had refused to make him a cardinal. His election when the good Pope John died was almost inevitable but was not quick because people who knew him well knew that unlike John he was both highly efficient and introspectively intense to the point of being tortured. During his long service in the Vatican he had privately dreamed of a much more 'open', and therefore modern, style for the papacy and in his early years he had shown great sympathy with anti-Fascist students as their chaplain. He was a well-read intellectual, influenced by the 'new theology' in France which Pius condemned, and he knew the need for the Church to change if it was to show Christ to the world; he had been shaken by the rise of Fascism, by the world war and then by the secularity of Milan. But he would never have embarked on a council had the decision been his. While wanting to reach the modern world he was at heart almost as conservative as Pius and was determined that the *aggiornamento* which the council launched would not mean the end of Catholic unity around the papacy.

His contributions during the council showed his character. He genuinely wanted the Church to be centred more on Christ and also wanted to make 'collegiality' effective. He sincerely believed in the awareness, dialogue and renewal which he advocated. Visits to the Holy Land, India and the United Nations headquarters signalled his desire for a new outreach. But other actions showed his caution. While agreeing that the mother of Jesus should be treated not separately but in the council's statement about the Church, he declared on his own authority that she was the 'Mother of the Church'; he made last-minute changes in the council's documents as part of his policy of not alienating the conservatives; he prevented discussion in the council of suggestions being made that married men might use contraceptives and even be ordained.

Later he developed Pope John's ideas. He ended the 'index' of forbidden books; he authorized theological dialogues with churches not yet 'joined in perfect communion'. In an encyclical of 1967 he announced that 'development is the new name for peace' in the Third World. He broke the stranglehold of old men less forward-looking than John when he made bishops submit their resignations at the age of 75 and cardinals cease to be the electors of popes at the age of 80. But when a commission reported in favour of a limited permission of artificial contraception, he agonized privately for two years and then made public his negative encyclical, *Humanae Vitae* (1968), which was widely attacked and even more widely ignored. After that humiliation he never wrote another encyclical and became more depressed and more conservative. In 1974 he was distressed because he had to dismiss Cardinal Mindzsenty from the archbishopric of Esztergom because in exile his attacks on the Communist government had continued and were making life difficult for the Hungarian Church. Two years later he had to deprive Archbishop Lefebvre, another obstinate man, of his right to exercise his priesthood, because he was setting up a splinter-church of other extreme conservatives. In the last year of his life he was further distressed by the Red Brigade terrorists' murder of the Italian prime minister, a Christian Democrat and a lifelong friend, and he had not been pleased when in 1974 almost two-thirds of the Italians had voted in favour of the state allowing divorce. (In 1981 they were to support making some abortions legal.) But he carried on into his eighties. He issued a truly magisterial statement of the theology behind evangelism and a brief *Credo of the People of God* stating the essentials as he saw them.

In 1978 the cardinals wanted a return to the happiness of Pope John and they elected another smiling patriarch of Venice—who, however, died within 33 days of beginning his work in a Vatican which was strange territory to him. Then they turned to the first non-Italian to be chosen since 1522, Karol Wojtyla who took the name of John Paul II. He has not seemed happy to live in Italy: every inch a Slav and a Pole, his youth had been spent under the Nazis and the Communists, his experience as a labourer had been one of the inspirations of his warm sympathy with the world's poor and his widening knowledge of the west had not increased his respect for its morals or its spiritual life. But he has been as hard-working, and as influential, as any among his 263 predecessors in the papacy: a man truly great. It helped that he had been in his youth an athlete, an actor and a poet. His physical stamina has enabled him to take long flights to great occasions and smaller meetings in most of the countries of the world, making the papacy more visible than ever before. His training as an actor has helped him to put across his message through his personality without ever losing dignity and his outstanding ability as a thinker and writer has made his teaching memorable in an unprecedented flood of encyclicals and lesser instructions. Above all, he has been a spiritual force. Everywhere he has been decisive and everywhere many have rejoiced. When he assembled Christian and non-Christian leaders in Assisi in 1986, to consider the worldwide threats to the natural environment of Man, he showed that a pope such as this has no rival as the moral leader of the world.

But he differed from Paul VI in policy as well as in personality and this made him a controversial figure. Paul had accepted the feeling of the majority of the bishops that the council's own documents, agreed with difficulty, were the nearest it was desirable to get to a full statement of the Church's current teaching; John Paul let it be known that he wanted to see a Universal Catechism and a long one was produced in 1992, incorporating the council's work but leaving little or no room for a variety of opinions. Paul had taken it for granted that a variety of men would rise to the top of the Catholic Church, so that the arguments in the council were unavoidable; John Paul often used the Vatican's right to appoint all the world's bishops in order to transfer power to a sound conservative, whatever the wishes of the diocese concerned. Paul had accepted the wish of the bishops to consult and act together on a national, regional or international basis, and to exercise some freedom in doing so, and he had given his Secretary of State (Jean Villot) responsibility for co-ordinating these fellow bishops; John Paul kept the important decisions in his own hands, made a conservative theologian, Joseph Ratzinger, his chief assistant and supported Ratzinger's denial that episcopal conferences had any theological status in the Church. Paul had warned other churches against proceeding to the ordination of women priests; John Paul declared 'that the Church has no authority whatsoever to confer priestly ordination on women and that this judgement is to be held definitively by all the Church's faithful'. Reluctantly Paul had allowed the international synod of bishops in 1971 to discuss whether married men might be ordained to the priesthood and had released many priests from their vows when they were resolved to wed (46,000 received this dispensation, 1963–83); John Paul reduced the flood to a trickle and forbade public discussion of the idea that the general ruling against marriage for priests might be relaxed. Paul had allowed the Jesuits and other religious orders to pursue their vocations in their own ways; John Paul appointed his own nominee to control the Jesuits when their innovating general (Arrupe) had a stroke and was equally firm with religious sisters who wished to dress like ordinary women. Paul had taken no firm steps to stop the spread of the practice of giving a 'general' absolution of sins after a congregation's general confession; John Paul refused to accept this as a substitute for the more painful private confession and took action against any prominent expression of the opinion that the use of contraception within marriage was no sin. Paul had loved the Latin Mass but had thought it his duty to end it; John Paul blessed its revival for congregations which preferred it. Paul had alarmed conservatives (and, it seems, himself) by apologies to other churches for any errors in the past; John Paul authorized the Congregation for the Doctrine of the Faith (the descendant of the Holy Office which had run the Inquisition) to regret that the agreements reached between the Catholic and Anglican theologians were unsatisfactory because they did not reproduce clearly enough the traditional Catholic faith about the Mass, the priesthood and papal authority. Paul had taken special trouble over reconciliation with the Orthodox; John Paul appointed bishops for Russia and despite sincere gestures of friendship appeared to have no intention of allowing papal authority to be reduced by an inch.

The difference between the two popes could be seen clearly in their attitudes to Spanish Catholicism.

Paul blessed the rebirth of Spain. During the last years of Franco (who died in 1975) his dictatorship with the accompanying 'National Catholicism' could seem secure, but the popular vote in 1936 for democracy and modernity had not been forgotten and many of the bishops, now encouraged by Rome in this, wisely moved away from their identification with the regime. In 1971 Enrique y Tarancón took over the leadership of the Spanish Church and, with it, the leadership of a quiet religious revolution. Within seven years Spain had become a democracy again, with a Socialist government, a constitutional monarchy and a constitution which declared cautiously that 'the public authority shall take the religious beliefs of Spanish society into account and shall in consequence maintain appropriate co-operation with the Catholic Church and other confessions'. Later legislation showed that this 'co-operation' did not extend to maintaining censorship or forbidding divorce and abortion—and no Catholic party emerged to fight the collapse of authoritarianism although the change produced a sharp decline in attendance at Mass and the increased industrial output included the production of eagerly studied pornography. Instead, the Church embarked with some success on a mission rather like the mission to France. The agreement of 1976 by which the government surrendered its centuries-old right to appoint bishops signalled that the mission was no longer to be identified with political power. And when the Socialist government drowned in an Italian-style sea of corruption and scandal in the 1990s, it was seen how much this mission was needed.

In contrast, John Paul did all he could to revive the medieval pilgrimages to the shrine of St James in Compostela and to encourage an organization, Opus Dei, which originated in circles in Spain with (at least) sympathy with the Franco regime. He exempted it from control by local bishops by giving it the unique status of a 'personal prelature' answerable only to himself and attempted to stop criticism of its founder, Escriva de Balaguer, by insisting that his had been the life of an 'exemplary priest' and by starting the process to declare him a saint. Because Opus Dei worked in secret and claimed total control over its members (who were not monks but worked mainly in the professions) its international outreach resulted in rumours which were probably exaggerated but its spirituality stressed conservative doctrine and its influence on society was beyond question distinctly conservative. In Italy another conservative organization which aimed to influence public life, *Comunione e Liberazione*, worked in a more public and democratic style. It, too, was favoured by the pope while the influence of the more broadly based Catholic Action declined and the Christian Democrats were pushed out of power by scandals similar to those which discredited the Socialists in Spain.

John Paul's impact has been strongest in his own country. His triumphantly popular return to Poland in 1979 encouraged the anti-Communist Solidarity movement; ten years later Solidarity formed the government. His thoroughly Polish psychology has also accounted for his impact on other countries, in its strength and weakness.

He has often stressed the need to base the life of a whole society on the Christian understanding of the dignity and freedom of the person, thus opposing the inhumanity of both Communism and capitalism. His first encyclical proclaimed his conviction that Christ had already redeemed every human person, who had only to accept that salvation, and in the 1990s he was still eloquent about the 'splendour of truth' in the Church's teaching about the sanctity of life. To him the necessary battles against the 'culture of death' include not only the protection of the unborn child against abortion but also the openness of the sexual act to the beginning of the glory of a new human life. But with the defence of humanism or personalism against all materialism has gone an equal emphasis on the necessary solidarity of a community in the acceptance of this interpretation of human dignity, preferably through the acceptance of the Catholic Church's moral authority. The acceptance must be free and he has endorsed democracy in the state more clearly than any previous pope. But partly in order that the Church may defend the dignity and freedom of the person, it must speak with one voice. In order to persuade people to accept the truth, imagination and energy are needed in the Church which must be as disciplined and confident as the Polish Church. He was clear about his position when he spoke to the council when he was only a cardinal in some tension with the senior Polish cardinal, Stefan Wyszynski, who was far more nervous about the outcome of the changes being authorized. 'It is not in question that the truth is already known to us', he said; 'the issue is how the world will find it for itself and make it known.' And there he has had to face problems, for his belief that the conscience of the free individual will witness to the 'splendour of truth' has not been supported by the actual behaviour of most people including most of the Catholics who have welcomed and applauded him around the world and most of his fellow Poles.

He has lived to see the Church's favoured politicians and proposals for legislation rejected by the majority of the Polish (as of the Italian) electorate. He has halted the movement for the ordination of women and of married men as priests (and of women as deacons) but he has experienced a face-to-face complaint by the elected leader of the Catholic sisters in the USA. He has also faced public protests against his policies by many German theologians in addition to his great critic, Hans Küng. He has been the leader of a 'pro-life' crusade but he has not been able to persuade Catholic politicians to go against the opinions of the electorate that the distribution of condoms will check the spread of AIDS and population growth, and that abortion may sometimes be the lesser of two evils. He has pleaded on behalf of the world's poor but in international conferences the Vatican has been supported only by conservative Islamic governments in saying that population growth need not be reduced by contraception. He has separated the official Church from the struggle between the classes in Latin America but he has not stopped the Latin American poor from belonging to a self-conscious and militant class. He has not silenced the questioning theologians: he has made the Church's official doctrine the same everywhere but his necessarily brief and formal visits to all the continents have not stopped theologians, or Africans or

Indians, from being true to their own formation in their thinking and praying. He has not given the government the reassurances needed before the Vatican can revive its relationship with the Catholic Church in China. In 1997 he authorized the excommunication of Tissa Balasuriya, a Catholic theologian in his seventies who has been respected internationally for his closeness to the poor in his own country and for his courageous insights as the church of which he has been a devout priest meets the religious heritage and the new ferment of hopes in Asia. This unquestionably dedicated and multi-talented pope, a leader of rare stature, has been determined to show that the priest is a man with a mission from God, a mission nobler than any other task in the world; yet his leadership, doing what he could to suppress questioning about doctrinal formulations and about the possibilities of married and women priests, has done much to make Catholicism on the ground in many places a church without a regular priest and therefore without the Mass and without a priest's direction.

Throughout he has been loyal to his own heritage, the Polish kind of Catholicism; this unites all the elements of his teaching which has ranged widely. He thinks of a church which has been strong in prayer; strong like an army with little dissent in its ranks; strong to be the soul of its nation, defending all that it knows as best in its nation's culture and values; strong to defend the dignity of the person against any imposed government or any ruthless profiteer. It may well be judged that any limitations in this outlook have been dwarfed by the resistance both to Communism and to consumerism but it remains to be seen what, if any, change of emphasis will be made by the next pope or the next council. This book has been a history of many changes in the Catholic Church, some of them rapid.

The twentieth Christian century is therefore ending in an atmosphere of basic uncertainty in the churches which have inherited the Protestant and Catholic Reformations. In both traditions the wish is strong to establish again a confidence based on a consensus about the authority of clear teaching, but it has proved impossible to end the influence of the Enlightenment's insistence on *sapere aude*: dare to judge for yourself. The Bible has been placed again at the centre of a church's life but the results of 'criticism' of its contents as history and literature have been accepted widely and so its authority has not been as clear as conservatives would wish. There has been a more keenly committed participation in the life of a gathered church, particularly in the Eucharist as a corporate act but often also in a Spirit-filled enthusiasm; yet individuals have often retained their rights to make their own decisions about faith and morals. In the postmodern age not only has it proved possible to choose to be an active member of a Christian church: clearly within the historic Protestant churches, but also among the Pentecostals and the Evangelicals, and even within Catholicism under a disciplinarian as pope, it has proved possible to choose for oneself what membership involves. However, it may be thought that the history of the papacy as the centre of Christian unity in truthful faith and charitable holiness has a great future ahead of it.

This uncertain conclusion to the history of Christianity's first two thousand years will seem depressing only to Christians who allow themselves to forget how many ways of being a Christian were tried in those years—and how many more years (two thousand million?) may lie ahead. Never has one way led to the agreement or permanence which was hoped for but never has the spirit of Christ been entirely absent or powerless where his disciples have gathered. Each group, large or small, has believed it was being loyal to the gospel; yet when that group has disappeared into history, somehow the news about Jesus Christ has remained good and his announcement of the dawn of government by the Father has received a fresh application to a different society. Even when an age is seen to be breaking up in fragments—in the death of the Judaism which Jesus knew, or the death of the Church of the martyrs in the Roman empire, or the death of Byzantine Orthodoxy, or the death of Rome's empire in the west, or the death of medieval Catholicism, or the end of the sixteenth-century Reformations, or the end of Europe as the centre of Christianity, or the end of 'enlightened' modernity, or the end of male supremacy—it is possible to detect new life coming out of the pain. So the end of the twentieth Christian century may be the beginning of a new Reformation which will be richly creative. Mark's gospel called the pain of a society's death the beginning of 'the birth-pangs of the new age'. In his farewell to his disciples before his death the Jesus of the fourth gospel says: 'A woman in labour is in pain because her time has come, but when the child is born she forgets the anguish in her joy . . . So it is with you: for the moment you are sad, but I shall see you again and then you will rejoice and no one shall rob you of your joy.'

℘℘℘℘

For Further Reading

These mostly recent books, almost all in the English language and scholarly but not too technical, are a selection in addition to the general histories mentioned in the Preface and the books mentioned in the text. Almost all provide valuable bibliographies, as does the *Oxford Dictionary of the Christian Church* edited by E. A. Livingstone (3rd edn 1997). A bibliography listing American publishers is in *Two Kingdoms: The Church and Culture through the Ages* by Robert Clouse, Richard Pierard and Edwin Yamauchi (1993).

1   Beginnings

It is understandable that John 21:25 supposed that the whole world could not contain the books that might be written about Jesus. My paperback on *The Real Jesus* (1992) tried to justify the even briefer interpretation offered here. More authoritative studies include E. P. Sanders, *Jesus and Judaism* (1985), *Judaism: Practice and Belief 63 BCE–66 CE* (1992) and *The Historical Figure of Jesus* (1993). Gerd Theissen, *The Shadow of the Galilean* (1987), was a reconstruction both vivid and scholarly. The background was also presented by Geza Vermes, *Jesus the Jew* (2nd edn 1994) and *The Religion of Jesus the Jew* (1993).

Christopher Rowland, *Christian Origins* (1985), and N. Thomas Wright, *The New Testament and the People of God* (1993) and *Jesus and the Victory of God* (1996), are excellent books by British scholars while W. G. Kümmel supplied magisterial guides in the German tradition in his *Theology of the New Testament* (1974) and *Introduction to the New Testament* (1975). New approaches were mapped in *Hearing the New Testament* edited by Joel Green (1995). Introductions to *Paul* include those by E. P. Sanders (1991) and C. K. Barrett (1994) and Jerome Murphy-O'Connor wrote a 'critical life' (1996). James D. G. Dunn assessed *Christology in the Making* (2nd edn 1989), *Unity and Diversity in the New Testament* (2nd edn 1990) and unity and diversity between Jews and Christians in *The Parting of the Ways* (1991). The social background was explored by Gerd Theissen's essays on *Social Reality and the Early Christians* (1993) and Philip Esler's on *The First Christians in Their Social Worlds* (1994). The position of women was explored by E. Schüssler Fiorenza, *In Memory of Her* (2nd edn 1996), and Luise Schottroff, *Lydia's Impatient Sisters* (1995). Paula Frederiksen traced the early development *From Jesus to Christ* (1988). Images in later Christian cultures were illuminated by Jaroslav Pelikan, *Jesus through the Centuries* (1985), and modern and postmodern images by William Hamilton, *A Quest for the Post-Historical Jesus* (1993). John Macquarrie, *Jesus Christ in Modern Thought* (1990), was more academic and the essays on *The Study of Spirituality* edited by Cheslyn Jones, Geoffrey Wainwright and Edward Yarnold (1986) illustrated the variety of devotional approaches across twenty centuries.

2   Early Christians

The best introduction remains Henry Chadwick's *The Early Church* (3rd edn 1993), although Norbert Brox's *History of the Early Church* (1995) is more sociological. Chadwick's volume in the *Oxford History of the Christian Church* is awaited. In 1997 the standard history to 600 is W. H. C. Frend, *The Rise of Christianity* (3rd edn 1985). A useful volume of non-technical essays was edited in his honour by Ian Hazlett, *Early Christianity* (2nd edn 1991). Frend's own studies include *The Donatist Church* (2nd edn 1971), *The Rise of the Monophysite Movement* (1972) and *The Archaeology of Early Christianity* (1996). F. van Meer and C. Mohrmann supplied an *Atlas of the Early Christian World* (2nd edn 1985).

Ray Pritz studied *Nazarene Jewish Christianity* (1988) and Robert Eisenman endeavoured to reconstruct the Church around *James the Brother of Jesus* (1997). Giovanni Filoramo wrote the latest good *History of Gnosticism* (1990) and Christine Trevett explored *Montanism* (1996). Gerd Lüdemann was sympathetic with *Heretics: The Other Side of Christianity* (1996). Wayne Meeks meditated instructively on *The Origins of Christian Morality* (1993), Eric Osborn on *The Emergence of Christian Theology in the Second Century* (1993) and Jaroslav Pelikan on *The Emergence of the Catholic Tradition* in theology (1971). Robert Grant studied *Irenaeus* (1997) and T. D. Barnes *Tertullian* (2nd edn 1985), *Constantine* (1982) and *Athanasius and Constantius* (1993). Henri Crouzel defended the memory of *Origen* in some detail (1989), R. Joseph Hoffmann reconstructed *Celsus on the True Doctrine* from Origen's quotations (1987) and Elizabeth Clark surveyed *The Origenist Controversy* (1992). E. R. Dodds, *Pagan and Christian in an Age of Anxiety* (1965), Ramsay MacMullen, *Christianizing the Roman Empire* (1984), and Robert Wilken, *Christians as the Romans Saw Them* (1984), were about areas not reached by theology. Averil Cameron, *Christianity and the Rhetoric of Empire* (1991), analysed the Church's apologetics and the sociological reasons why such rhetoric persuaded some. Deborah Sawyer studied *Women and Religion in the Early Christian Centuries* (1996). Samuel H. Moffett's *History of Christianity in Asia* (vol. I 1992) went to 1500. Guntram Koch introduced *Early Christian Art and Architecture* (1996). Documents to 387 were edited by J. Stevenson and W. H. C. Frend as *A New Eusebius* (1987).

3   Byzantine Orthodoxy

The best introductions are Timothy Ware, *The Orthodox Church* (2nd edn 1993), Jaroslav Pelikan's mainly theological *The Spirit of Eastern Christendom 600–1700*

(1974) and John Julius Norwich, *Byzantium* (3 vols, 1988–95), which concentrated very readably on the dramas in the capital. Less colourfully, Donald Nicol told the sad story of *The Last Centuries of Byzantium* (2 vols, 1993). J. F. Halam studied *Byzantium in the Seventh Century*, a turning point (1990). John Meyendorff's essays on *The Byzantine Legacy in the Orthodox Church* (1982) are valuable.

Expert surveys of the society include H. W. Hussig, *A History of Byzantine Civilization* (1971), and Cyril Mango, *Byzantium: The Empire of the New Rome* (1980). The art was introduced by John Beckwith, *Early Christian and Byzantine Art* (2nd edn 1979), and related to the society by Richard Cormack, *Writing in Gold* (1985). Joan Hussey wrote with authority about *The Orthodox Church in the Byzantine Empire* (1986) and Judith Herrin about east and west in *The Formation of Christendom* (1987). History was seen in an Orthodox perspective by John Meyendorff, *Imperial Unity and Christian Divisions: The Church 460–680* (1989), and Aristides Papadakis, *The Christian East and the Rise of the Papacy* (1994). Aziz S. Atiya's account of the non-Chalcedonian churches in his *History of Eastern Christianity* (1968) has not been replaced but Bat Ye'or recounted *The Decline of Eastern Christianity under Islam* (1996). Samuel Moffett covered Asia in the 1992 history already recommended and James Byrne provided a history of *Traditional Egyptian Christianity* (1996). Kenneth Cragg encountered *The Arab Christian* (1991).

Olivier Clément surveyed *The Roots of Christian Mysticism* (1993) and John Meyendorff introduced *Byzantine Theology* (2nd edn 1983). The controversy about Arius was analysed by Rowan Williams, *Arius* (1987), and R. P. C. Hanson, *The Search for the Christian Doctrine of God* (1988). Maurice Wiles treated the survival of Arianism as the *Archetypal Heresy* (1996). Robert Browning studied the pagan backlash in *The Emperor Julian* (1975) and Philip Rousseau the work of *Basil of Caesarea* (1994). Anthony Meredith celebrated the theological victory of *The Cappadocians* (1995) and Jaroslav Pelikan expounded their use of Platonic philosophy in *Christianity and Classical Culture* (1993). Other recent studies include Frances Young, *From Nicaea to Chalcedon* (1983) and *The Making of the Creeds* (1991), and Christopher Stead, *Philosophy in Christian Antiquity* (1994). J. N. D. Kelly's *Early Christian Doctrines* (5th edn 1977) and *Early Christian Creeds* (3rd edn 1972) have not been superseded. His biography of John Chrysostom, *Golden Mouth*, maintained his standard (1995). J. Stevenson and W. H. C. Frend edited documents about *Creeds, Councils and Controversies* (2nd edn 1989). Maurice Wiles and Mark Santer edited *Documents in Early Christian Thought* (1975).

4 Orthodoxy after Byzantium

The history of the Balkans and Russia to 1473 by Dimitri Obolensky, *The Byzantine Commonwealth* (1971), was supplemented by his essays on *Byzantium and the Slavs* (1993). Stephen Runciman, *The Great Church in Captivity* (1968), was about Orthodoxy under the Turks. The standard *History of Russia* is by Nicholas Riasanovsky (5th edn 1993). John Fennell wrote a fresh *History of the Russian Church to 1448* (1995) and Paul Bushkovitch covered 1500–1700 in *Religion and Society in Russia* (1992). Robert Crummey, *The Old Believers and the World of Antichrist* (1970), told that tragic story and Gregory Feezi studied, also with sadness, *The Parish Clergy in Nineteenth Century Russia* (1985). G. P. Fedotov edited *A Treasury of Russian Spirituality* (1950) and studied *The Russian Religious Mind* to 1550 (2 vols, 1946–66). Georges Florovsky presented more recent *Ways of Russian Theology* (2 vols, 1979–87) and Nicholas Zernov remembered *The Russian Religious Renaissance in the Twentieth Century* (1963). Most of his heroes were exiled in the Communist era, studied by John Anderson in *Religion, State and Politics in the Soviet Union and Successor States* (1995) and by Nathaniel Davies in *A Long Walk to Church* (1995). The later period was studied by Jane Ellis, *The Russian Orthodox Church: Triumphalism and Defensiveness* (1996).

Some of the spiritual depths were distilled by Vladimir Lossky, *The Mystical Theology of the Eastern Church* (1957), Nicholas Arseniev, *Russian Piety* (1964), and John Zizioulas, *Being as Communion* (1985). Gennadios Limouris edited *Orthodox Visions of Ecumenism* for the World Council of Churches (1994). Exploratory essays include those by John Meyendorff, *Catholicity and the Church* (1983) and *Rome, Constantinople, Moscow* (1996), John H. Erikson, *The Challenge of Our Past* (1991), and Vigen Guroian, *Ethics after Christendom* (1994). Constantine Tsirpanlis, *An Introduction to Eastern Patristic Thought and Orthodox Theology* (1991), was an ordered summary. Andrew Walker and Costa Carras edited *Living Orthodoxy in the Modern World* (1996).

5 Medieval Catholicism

The best guide to the so-called 'dark' ages is Peter Brown, whose books include the introductory *The World of Late Antiquity* (2nd edn 1989) and *The Rise of Western Christendom* (1996), the best biography of *Augustine of Hippo* (1967) and studies of *The Cult of the Saints* (1981), *Society and the Holy in Late Antiquity* (1982), *The Body and Society* (1988) and *Power and Persuasion in Late Antiquity* (1992). Judith Herrin, *The Formation of Christendom* (1987), is also illuminating. A short introduction to the thought of *Augustine* was achieved by Henry Chadwick (1986), who also edited the *Confessions* (1991), and John M. Rist's *Augustine* is the best of the comprehensive expositions (1994). Robert Markus analysed his political thought in *Saeculum* (2nd edn 1988) and the background in *The End of Ancient Christianity* (1990). Kim Power, *Veiled Desire* (1995), was about Augustine's attitudes to women. Neil McLynn wrote a fresh biography of *Ambrose of Milan* (1994) and J. N. D. Kelly's *Jerome* (1975) has kept its place.

We owe the best scholarly *Introduction to Celtic Christianity* to J. P. Mackey (1995). There is a wider scope in *The Celtic World* edited by Miranda Green (1995). Henry Chadwick presented *Boethius* (1981) and Carole Straw *Gregory the Great* (1988). The Franks were studied by J. M. Wallace-Hadrill in *The Barbarian West* (3rd edn 1977) and *The Frankish Church* (2nd edn 1983), and by Rosamund McKitterick in *The Frankish Kingdoms under the Carolingians* (1983). She edited essays on *Carolingian Culture* (1994).

The Oxford History of Medieval Europe was edited by George Holmes (1986). Other general introductions include Malcolm Barber, *The Two Cities: Medieval*

Europe 1050–1320 (1992), John M. Mundy, *Europe in the High Middle Ages* (2nd edn 1991), David Nicholas, *The Evolution of the Medieval World* (1992), and Steven Ozment, *The Age of Reform 1250–1550* (1980). Jacques Le Goff surveyed *Medieval Civilization* (1988) and edited essays on *The Medieval World* (1992). Georges Duby wrote *The Age of the Cathedrals* (1981) and edited *Revelations of the Medieval World* as vol. II of *A History of Private Life* (1988).

Medieval religion may be seen in rather more detail in Rosalind and Christopher Brooke, *Popular Religion in the Middle Ages 1000–1300* (1984), Caroline Bynum, *Jesus as Mother* (1982), C. M. D. Crowder, *Unity, Heresy and Reform 1378–1449* (1977), Bernard Hamilton, *The Medieval Inquisition* (1981) and *Religion in the Medieval West* (1986), C. H. Lawrence, *Medieval Monasticism* (2nd edn 1989) and *The Friars* (1994), Jean Leclercq, *The Love of Learning and the Desire for God* in the Benedictine tradition (3rd edn 1982), Jacques Le Goff, *The Birth of Purgatory* (1984), Bernard McGinn, *The Foundations of Mysticism* (1991) and *The Growth of Mysticism* (1994), Colin Morris, *The Papal Monarchy: The Western Church 1050–1250* (1989), Dennis Nineham, *Christianity Medieval and Modern* centred around AD 1000 (1993), Francis Oakley, *The Western Church in the Later Middle Ages* (1979), R. R. Post, *The Modern Devotion* about the late Middle Ages (1968), balancing Albert Hyma's enthusiastic *The Christian Renaissance* (2nd edn 1965), I. S. Robinson, *The Papacy 1073–1198* (1990), Miri Rubin, *Corpus Christi: The Eucharist in Late Medieval Culture* (1991), Beryl Smalley, *The Study of the Bible in the Middle Ages* (3rd edn 1983) which may be supplemented by G. R. Evans, *The Language and Logic of the Bible* (2 vols, 1984–85), Benedicta Ward, *Miracles and the Medieval World* (1982), and Christopher Wilson, *The Gothic Cathedral* (1990). Richard Barber inspected *The Knight and Chivalry* (2nd edn 1995). Magisterial studies by R. W. Southern include *The Making of the Middle Ages* (1953), *Medieval Humanism and Other Studies* (1970), *Western Society and the Church in the Middle Ages* (1970), *St Anselm: A Portrait in a Landscape* (1990) and *Scholastic Humanism and the Unification of Europe* (vol. I 1995). Also in the first class are studies by David Knowles of *The Monastic Order in England* which crosses to the European mainland (2nd edn 1963) and *The Evolution of Medieval Thought* (2nd edn 1970), although a more critical view was taken by Anthony Kenny, *The God of the Philosophers* (1979). J. N. D. Kelly, *The Oxford Dictionary of the Popes* (1986), sums up their whole history.

Also useful are Regis Armstrong, *St Francis of Assisi* (1994), A. D. Coggan, *The Medieval Universities* (1975), Sabrina Flanagan, *Hildegard of Bingen* (1989), Robert Forman, *Meister Eckhart* (1991), J. T. Muckle, *The Story of Abelard's Adversities* (1964), Helen Nicholson, *Templars, Hospitallers and Teutonic Knights* (1993), Iris Origo, *The Merchant of Prato* (1957), Jean Richard, *Louis IX* (1992), Jonathan Riley-Smith, *The Crusades* (1987), and Jane Sayers, *Innocent III* (1994). Jaroslav Pelikan's doctrinal history covered *The Growth of Medieval Theology 600–1300* (1978) and *Reformation in Church and Dogma 1300–1700* (1984) with the influence of Augustine as his central theme. The more widely ranging *History of Christian Philosophy in the Middle Ages* by Etienne Gilson (1955) has not been replaced although J. A. Weisheipl freshly presented the life of *Friar Thomas Aquino* (1974) and Brian Davies *The Thought of Thomas Aquinas* (1992). Alexander Murray studied *Reason and Society in the Middle Ages* (2nd edn 1986) and Gordon Leff *The Dissolution of the Medieval Outlook* (1976). For the dissenters see F. M. Bartos, *The Hussite Revolution* (1984), Norman Cohn, *The Pursuit of the Millennium* (2nd edn 1970), Anne Hudson, *The Premature Reformation* about Wyclif and the Lollards (1988), E. Le Roy Ladurie, *Montaillou* about Catholics and Cathars in a French village (1974), Malcolm Lambert, *Medieval Heresy* (2nd edn 1992), and R. I. Moore, *The Formation of a Persecuting Society* (1987). Also of value are Jeffrey Richard's more lurid story of *Sex, Dissidence and Damnation* (1991), the study by James Brundage of *Law, Sex and Society in Medieval Europe* (1995) and the essays on *Christendom and its Dissenters* edited by Scott Waugh and Peter Diehl (1996). Rachel Jacoff edited *The Cambridge Companion to Dante* (1993). Hugh Kennedy wrote with accurate sympathy about Islam to AD 1050 in *The Prophet and the Age of the Caliphates* (1986) and Albert Hourani achieved *A History of the Arab Peoples* (1991). Robin Briggs was as authoritative as is possible about *Witches and Neighbours* (1996).

The beautiful *Atlas of the Renaissance* edited by Chris Murray (1993) leads into the riches gathered by Denys Hay and John Law in *Italy in the Age of the Renaissance* (1989) and by John Hale in *The Civilization of the Renaissance in Europe* (1993). Roy Porter and Mikulas Teich edited essays on *The Renaissance in National Context* (1991). J. A. F. Thomson studied the relations of *Popes and Princes 1417–1517* (1980). Charles Trinkhaus explored Christian elements in Renaissance humanism in *In Our Image and Likeness* (2 vols. 1970) and edited with Heiko Oberman *The Pursuit of Holiness in Late Medieval and Renaissance Religion* (1974). There are studies of *Michelangelo* by George Bull (1995), *Machiavelli* by Quentin Skinner (1985) and *Thomas More* by Richard Marius (1985).

6 Reformations

When Pierre Chaunu edited valuable essays on *The Reformation* (1989) he guessed that 'a bibliography, even when scientifically selective, would include more than 100,000 titles from Europe and America' and since then the flood has not ceased, but we have some sound boats: *The Reformation 1520–59* edited by Geoffrey Elton (2nd edn 1990), Euan Cameron's *The European Reformation* (1991), Carter Lindberg's *The European Reformations* (1996), and the more theological account of *Reformation Thought* by Alister McGrath (2nd edn 1993). A. G. Dickens summarized the historians' own controversies in *The Reformation in Historical Thought* (1985) and those who prefer to go to the sources have the *Documents of the Reformation in Germany and Switzerland* edited by Pamela Johnson and Bob Scribner (1993).

The best recent English biographies of the key thinkers are A. G. Dickens and W. R. D. Jones, *Erasmus the Reformer* (1994), George Potter, *Zwingli* (1976), Heiko Oberman, *Luther* (1989), and Alister McGrath's *Life of John Calvin* (1990). These may be supplemented by R. J. Shoeck, *Erasmus of Europe* (1994), L. P. A. Jardine, *Erasmus, Man of Letters* (1994), W. P. Stephens, *Zwingli: An Introduction to His Thought* (1992), Heinrich Bornkamm, *Luther's World of Thought* (1958), Gerhard Ebeling, *Luther: An Introduction to His Thought* (1970), Bernhard Lohse's introduction to *Martin Luther* (1987), François Wendel's introduction to the theology of *Calvin*

(1963) and Harro Hopful, *The Christian Polity of John Calvin* (1982). Research into the effects on daily life was brought together by Gerald Strauss, *Luther's House of Learning* (1978), Stephen Ozment, *Protestants* (1993), and Bob Scribner, *For the Sake of Simple Folk* (2nd edn 1994). Menna Prestwich edited *International Calvinism 1541–1715* (1985) and later studies about Calvin's wider social influence include Henry Heller, *The Conquest of Poverty* (1985), and Ralph Hancock, *Calvin and the Foundations of Modern Politics* (1989). The left wing was studied by George Williams, *The Radical Reformation* (3rd edn 1992), Gordon Rupp, *Patterns of Reformation* (1969), and William Estep, *The Anabaptist Story* (3rd edn 1996). A. G. Dickens surveyed *The English Reformation* (2nd edn 1989) and Christopher Haigh *English Reformations* (1993). Eamon Duffy lamented *The Stripping of the Altars* in Tudor England (1992) but something revived: see Patrick Collinson, *The Religion of Protestants* (1983). I. B. Cowan presented *The Scottish Reformation* (1982), Mark Greengrass *The French Reformation* (1987) and Alastair Duke *Reformation and Revolt in the Netherlands* (1990), while Ole Peter Grill edited essays on *The Scandinavian Reformation* (1995).

Links with medieval thought were studied by Lewis Spitz, *The Religious Renaissance of the German Humanists* (1963), Steven Ozment, *The Age of Reform 1250–1550* (1980), and Alister McGrath, *The Intellectual Origins of the European Reformation* (1987). Keith Thomas explored the underworld of popular beliefs in England in *Religion and the Decline of Magic* (1971).

Steven Ozment edited *Reformation Europe: A Guide to Research* (1982). Recent scholarship was presented in five volumes of essays: *The Impact of Humanism in Western Europe* edited by Anthony Goodman and Angus MacKay (1990), *Religion and Society in Early Modern Europe* edited by Kaspar von Greyerz (1984), *The Early Reformation in Europe* edited by Andrew Pettegree (1992), *The Reformation in National Context* edited by Bob Scribner, Roy Porter and Mikulas Teich (1994) and *Calvinism in Europe* edited by Andrew Pettegree, Alastair Duke and Gillian Lewis (1994).

The best introduction to *The Counter-Reformation* is still that by A. G. Dickens (1968) but A. D. Wright's *The Counter-Reformation* (1982) supplemented it, with an extensive bibliography. Jean Delemeau's study of mainly French *Catholicism between Luther and Voltaire* (1977) and John Bossy's wider *Christianity in the West 1400–1700* (1985) concentrated on changes in popular religion. So did Max Forster, *The Counter-Reformation in the Villages* (1992). John O'Malley edited *Catholicism in Early Modern History: A Guide to Recent Research* (1988) and wrote about *The First Jesuits* (1992). H. O. Evernett, *The Spirit of the Counter-Reformation* (1968), still repays study. R. J. W. Evans threw light on *The Making of the Habsburg Monarchy 1550–1700* (1979). Tessa Bielecki introduced *Teresa of Avila* (1994) and Gustavo Gutiérrez studied *Las Casas* (1993). Henry Kamen, *Inquisition and Society in Spain* (1985), Hilary Smith, *Preaching in the Spanish Golden Age* (1978), and J. A. Fernandez-Santamaria, *Reason of State and Statecraft in Spanish Political Thought 1595–1640* (1983), help with the background. Good essays on saints of the Catholic Reformation are in *Christian Spirituality: Post-Reformation and Modern* edited by Louis Dupré and Don Saliers (1989). In *A Vision Betrayed* Andrew Ross told the story of the Jesuits in Japan and China (1994) and there was more detail in J. F. Mason, *The Japanese and the Jesuits* (1993). Jacques Gernet, *China and the Christian Impact* (1985), drew on Chinese sources and Charles Renard and Bonnie Oh edited *East Meets West: The Jesuits in China 1582–1773* (1988). Philip Caraman recounted the story of Paraguay in *The Lost Paradise* (1975) and T. S. Cummins studied *A Question of Rites* (1993). Owen Chadwick, *The Popes and European Revolution* (1981), surveyed the effects of the Catholic Reformation, particularly in Italy.

In addition to the histories of the USA recommended for Chapter 8, valuable studies of the earlier period include Harry Stout, *The New England Soul* (1986), David Lovejoy, *Religious Enthusiasm in the New World* (1985), Alan Heimert, *Religion and the American Mind* (1966), and Jon Butler, *Awash in a Sea of Faith* about popular religion (1990). Charles Stanford made the most of *The Religious Life of Thomas Jefferson* (1984).

7   In the Modern Age

The Enlightenment was surveyed in two volumes by Peter Gay (1966–69) and in one by Urich im Hof (1994), but the essays edited by Roy Porter and Mikulas Teich in *The Enlightenment in National Context* (1981) also shed light, as did the essays edited by W. J. Callahan and David Higgs on *Church and Society in Catholic Europe of the Eighteenth Century* (1979). There are good biographies of Locke by Maurice Cranston (1957), Newton by Richard Westfall (1983), Voltaire by Jean Orieux (1979), Rousseau by Jean Starobinski (1971) and Pascal by Francis Coleman under the title *Neither Angel nor Beast* (1986).

Robin Briggs studied the variety in the French Catholic Church, elitist or popular, in *Communities of Belief* (1989), Alexander Sedgwick *Jansenism in Seventeenth Century France* (1977) and Raymond Deville *The French School of Spirituality* (1994). The account by John McManners of *Religion and Society in Eighteenth Century France* is awaited and meanwhile we have the vivid detail in his *French Ecclesiastical Society under the Ancien Régime* (1960) and *Death and the Enlightenment* (1985). Norman Ravitch compared the English and French bishops in *Sword and Mitre* (1966). Gordon Rupp surveyed *Religion in England 1688–1791* (1986) and Owen Chadwick *The Popes and European Revolution* excluding France (1981). R. Po-Chia Hsia studied *Social Discipline in the Reformation 1550–1750* with emphasis on the clergy's battles against 'superstition' in central Europe (1995) and F. E. Stoeffler *The Rise of Evangelical Pietism* (1965) and *German Pietism in the Eighteenth Century* (1973). Muriel Fulbrook compared *Piety and Politics* in England and Germany (1983). For the USA see Chapter 8. Reichard Heitzenrater, *Wesley and the People Called Methodists* (1995), is the latest in a pile of good books about him. Good recent studies of the wider picture include William Doyle's *The Old European Order 1660–1800* (2nd edn 1992) and his *Oxford History of the French Revolution* (1989), which may be supplemented by Michel Vovelle, *The Revolution against the Church* (1991).

Claude Welch expounded *Protestant Thought in the Nineteenth Century* (2 vols, 1972–85) and Ninian Smart and others edited experts' essays on *Nineteenth Century Religious Thought in the West* (3 vols, 1985). Karl Barth, *From Rousseau to Ritschl* (1972), was one great theologian's critical view, but see Keith Clements, *Friedrich Schleiermacher* (2nd edn 1990), and James Richmond, *Ritschl: A Reappraisal* (1978).

Bernard Reardon studied *Religious Thought in the Victorian Age* (1980), French thought in *Liberalism and Tradition* (1975) and mostly German thought in *Religion in the Age of Romanticism* (1985). Alec Vidler's *Prophecy and Papacy* (1954) studied the tragedy of Lamennais. The best biography of Newman is by Ian Ker (1988) and Stephen Sykes compared him with Schleiermacher and others in *The Identity of Christianity* (1984). The best biography of Charles Darwin is by Janet Browne (vol. I 1995) and John Durant edited *Darwinism and Divinity* (1985). James Brabazon told the story of *Albert Schweitzer* (1975). Recent studies of Catholic Modernism include Gabriel Daly, *Transcendence and Immanence* (1980), and Ellen Leonard, *George Tyrrell and the Catholic Tradition* (1982). Owen Chadwick diagnosed *The Secularization of the European Mind in the Nineteenth Century* (1975) and S. S. Acquaviva *The Decline of the Sacred in Industrial Society* (1974). David Martin's *General Theory of Secularization* (1978) was illuminating. Steve Bruce, *Religion in the Modern World* (1996), was more secular. Daniel Dennett, *Darwin's Dangerous Idea* (1995), was an eloquent plea that this challenge to religion has never been answered.

In the absence of any equivalent in English, vol. XII of the *Histoire du Christianisme* (1990) is to be recommended. Edited by Jean-Marie Mayeur, it sums up studies of worldwide church life, Catholic and Protestant, 1914–58, in the main European languages. J. Derek Holmes, *The Papacy in the Modern World* (1981), introduced the history of Catholicism which was set out in more detail in vols IX and X of the *History of the Church* edited by Hubert Jedin and John Dolan (1981). The papacy's Italian environment was sketched by Roger Absolom, *Italy since 1800* (1995). A good introduction to *Religion and the People of Europe 1878–1970* (excluding thought) was provided in 1981 by Hugh McLeod, who also edited essays on *European Religion in the Age of the Great Cities 1830–1930* (1995). My *Leaders of the Church of England 1828–1944* (1971) and vol. III of my *Christian England* (2nd edn 1989) included many suggestions for further reading, but Owen Chadwick, *The Victorian Church* (2 vols. 1966–70), is indispensable. Hugh McLeod studied *Religion and Society in England 1850–1914* (1996) and Adrian Hastings, *A History of English Christianity 1920–1985* (1986), continued the story. A. D. Gilbert was more sceptical about the churches in *Religion and Society in Industrial England* (1976) and *The Making of Post-Christian Britain* (1980). Edward Norman, *Church and Society in England 1700–1970* (1976), thought leaders too responsive to changing fashions. Different conclusions about the significance of 'believing without belonging' were presented by two sociologists: Grace Davie, *Religion in Britain since 1945* (1994), and Steve Bruce, *Religion in Modern Britain* (1995). Callum Brown provided *A Social History of Religion in Scotland since 1730* (1987), Patrick Cornish analysed *The Irish Catholic Experience* (1985) and David Hempton covered *Religion and Political Culture in Britain and Ireland* (1996). Sheridan Gilley and W. J. Sheils edited *A History of Religion in Britain* (1994): essays going from pre-Roman times to the present were accompanied by a bibliography.

John McManners outlined *The French Revolution and the Church* (1969) and *Church and State in France 1870–1914* (1972). Ralph Gibson summed up French studies in *A Social History of French Catholicism 1789–1914* (1989). The background was surveyed by François Furst, *Revolutionary France 1770–1880* (1992), and Maurice

Agulhon, *The French Republic 1879–1992* (1993). W. J. Callahan studied *Church, Politics and Society in Spain 1750–1874* (1984) and Francis Lannum *Privilege, Persecution and Prophecy: The Catholic Church in Spain 1875–1975* (1987). Raymond Carr supplied a general history of *Spain 1808–1975* (2nd edn 1982). Nicholas Hope studied *German and Scandinavian Protestantism 1700–1914* (1995) and Jonathan Sperber *Popular Catholicism in Nineteenth Century Germany* (1984); illuminating detail is in David Blackbourn, *The Marpingen Visions* (1993). Klaus Scholder, *The Churches and the Third Reich* (2 vols, 1988), covered 1918–1934 as 'the time of illusions' and its end. Klemens von Klemperer investigated *German Resistance against Hitler* as the 'search for allies abroad' from 1938 (1992). Gordon Craig surveyed the history of *Germany 1866–1945* (2nd edn 1981).

The early years of the World Council of Churches were recounted in W. A. Visser 't Hooft, *Memoirs* (1973) and the council published in 1991 a *Dictionary of the Ecumenical Movement* which amounts to a history. John Macquarrie mapped the frontiers of philosophy and theology, 1900–1980, in *Twentieth-Century Religious Thought* (4th edn 1988). Some of the story was told in the biographies of Teilhard de Chardin by Mary and Ellen Lukas (1977), Paul Tillich by Wilhelm and Marion Pauck (1977), Karl Barth by Eberhard Busch (1975) and Dietrich Bonhoeffer by Eberhard Bethge (1970). Recent studies include George Hunsinger, *How to Read Karl Barth* (1991), and Gareth Jones, *Bultmann: Towards a Critical Theology* (1991).

8 The Americas

There is of course a wealth of literature on American Christianity. This Englishman has found the most helpful summaries to be Sydney Ahlstrom, *A Religious History of the American People* (1972), Robert Handy, *A History of the Churches in the United States and Canada* (1976) and Mark Noll's *History of Christianity* in the same nations (1992). More detailed studies include Robert Handy's account of Protestant hopes for *A Christian America* (2nd edn 1984), Donald Mathews, *Religion in the Old South* (1977), Albert Raboteau, *Slave Religion* (1978), William Wolf, *The Almost Chosen People* about Lincoln's religion (1973), Paul Carter, *The Spiritual Crisis of the Gilded Age* (1971), Ernest Sandeen, *The Roots of Fundamentalism* about millenarianism 1800–1930 (1970), George Marsden, *Fundamentalism and American Culture* (1980), James Hunter, *American Evangelicalism* (1983) and *Evangelicalism: The Coming Generation* (1987), Robert Anderson's account of Pentecostal origins in *The Vision of the Disinherited* (1979), William Hutchinson, *The Modernist Impulse in American Protestantism* (1976), Donald Meyer, *The Protestant Search for Political Realism 1919–41* (2nd edn 1988) and the essays edited by Donald Dayton and Robert Johnston on *The Variety of American Evangelicalism* (1991). Martin Marty surveyed *Modern American Religion since 1893* (3 vols. 1986–96) and Wuthnow Robert *The Restructuring of American Religion since 1945* (1988). Jay Dolan studied *The American Catholic Experience* (1985), Henry Bowden *American Indians and Christian Missions* (1981) and C. Eric Lincoln and Laurence Mamiyu *The Black Church in the African American Experience* (1990)—an experience which has produced James Cone, *A Black Theology of Liberation* (1970) and *For My People* (1984). Scholarly essays on *African-American*

Religion were edited by Timothy Fulop and Albert Raboteau (1977). Among many examples of American self-criticism *Habits of the Heart* by Robert Bellah and others (1985) was outstanding. Richard Fox wrote the best biography of *Reinhold Niebuhr* (1985).

A history of *The Church in Latin America 1492–1992* from the viewpoint of liberation theology was edited in 1992 by Enrique Dussel, who affirms that 'a complete re-reading of the history of Christianity is a task facing Christian historians in the Third World'. Other volumes in the series are announced: *The Church in Africa* edited by Ogbu Kalu and *The Church in Asia and the South Pacific* edited by Teotino de Souza. I referred to much Two-Thirds World theology and church-related thought in *The Futures of Christianity* (1987) and Leonardo Boff and Virgil Elizondo more expertly edited *Third World Theologies: Convergencies and Differences* (1988). *Voices from the Margin* were edited by R. S. Sugirtharajah (1991). David Barrett edited the unique *World Christian Encyclopaedia* (1981) and has updated his statistics each year in the *International Bulletin of Missionary Research*; even so, they are often considered too optimistic.

José Miguez Bonino explained why *Revolutionary Theology Comes of Age* in Latin America (1975), wrote *Towards a Christian Political Ethics* (1983) and edited *Faces of Jesus: Latin American Christologies* (1984). Rosino Gibellini edited *Frontiers of Theology in Latin America* (1980) and *The Liberation Theology Debate* (1987). Alfred Hennelly edited *Liberation Theology: A Documentary History* (1990). David Stoll asked *Is Latin America Turning Protestant?* (1990). David Martin's *Tongues of Fire* (1990) was a sociological study which preferred the 'explosion' of Protestantism, mainly Pentecostal, to liberation theology and Guillermo Cook edited essays on the mainly Protestant *New Face of the Church in Latin America* (1994). Rubem Alves criticized the Pentecostal preachers in *Protestantism and Repression* (1985) but John Burdick thought them more influential than the Catholics in *Looking for God in Brazil* (1993). Detailed historical studies include James Lockhart and Stuart Schwartz, *Early Latin America* (1983), J. Lloyd Mecham, *Church and State in Latin America* (2nd edn 1966), Robert Quirk, *The Mexican Revolution and the Catholic Church 1910–29* (1973), Jean Meyer, *The Cristero Rebellion* (1976), Kenneth Medhurst, *The Church and Labour in Colombia* (1982), and Scott Mainwaring, *The Catholic Church and Politics in Brazil 1916–85* (1986). Edwin Williamson surveyed the background in *The Penguin History of Latin America* (1992). Burton Sankeralli edited papers on *African Caribbean Religion and Christianity* (1996).

9   Global Christianity

Adrian Hastings supplied the first thorough history of *The Church in Africa 1450–1950* (1994), following his *History of African Christianity 1950–75* (1979) and his essays on *African Catholicism* (1989). Elizabeth Isicher was briefer but quoted many Africans in her *History of Christianity in Africa* (1995). *Africa: A Church History* by Bengt Sundkler and Christopher Steed is announced. Rosino Gibellini included a bibliography with the essays he edited on *Paths of African Theology* (1994) and Robert Schreiter edited *Faces of Jesus in Africa* (1991). Recent studies include Kwame

Bediako, *Christianity in Africa* (1995), Eboussi Boulaga, *Christianity without Fetishes* (1984), Jean-Marc Ela, *African Cry* (1986) and *My Faith as an African* (1988), Emmanuel Martey, *African Theology* (1993), John Mbiti, *African Religions and Philosophy* (2nd edn 1990), Musimbi Kanyoro, *The Will to Arise* on the position of women (1992), Lamin Sanneh, *Translating the Message* (1989) and Aylward Shorter, *The Church in the African City* (1991). Paul Gifford edited essays on *The Christian Church and the Democratization of Africa* (1995) and J. W. Hofmeyr a *History of the Church in South Africa* (vol. I 1994).

R. S. Sugirtharajah edited *Asian Faces of Jesus* (1993), Virginia Fabella and others *Asian Christian Spirituality* (1992) and Parig Digan *Churches in Contestation* about 'social protest' (1992). Aloysius Pieris wrote *An Asian Theology of Liberation* (1988). Murray Rubenstein studied *The Protestant Community in Modern Taiwan* (1991). The leading Asian theologian, Choan-Seng Song, is Taiwanese: his books include *Theology from the Womb of Asia* (1988) and *The Crucified People* (1991). Hans Küng and Julia Ching explored *Christianity and Chinese Religions* (1989). Ralph Covell presented Chinese history in *Confucius, the Buddha and Christ* (1986) and Paul Cohen the anti-foreign response in *China and Christianity* (1963). Paul Varg's account of *Missionaries, Chinese and Diplomats* from 1890 to 1952 (1958) is another classic. The developments within Communist China were studied objectively by Bob Whyte in *Unfinished Encounter* (1988), and by Alan Hunter and Kim-Kwong Chang in *Protestantism in Contemporary China* (1993). Tony Lambert, *The Resurrection of the Chinese Church* (1991), was more enthusiastic about the Evangelical house churches and Philip Wickeri, *Seeking the Common Ground* (1988), about the Three-Self Patriotic Movement. Richard Drummond supplied *A History of Christianity in Japan* (1971) and Kumazawa Yoshinobu and David Swain edited *Christianity in Japan 1971–90* (1991). James Philips commented on Church and society in *From the Rising Sun* (1981) and Robert Schildgen wrote a biography of Toyohiko Kagawa (1988). Joseph Kitagawa concentrated on the Japanese–US dialogue in *The Christian Tradition beyond Its European Captivity* (1992). Kosuke Koyama, *Mount Fuji and Mount Sinai* (1984), recounted a 'pilgrimage in theology'.

Allen Clark supplied *A History of the Church in Korea* (1971) and Hyun Younghak *Minjung Theology* (1983). T. Valentino Sitoy has begun *A History of Christianity in the Philippines* (1985–   ) and Eleazar Fernandez, *Toward a Theology of Struggle* (1994), was about the liberation of the Filipino people. Charles Forman is the historian of *The Island Churches of the South Pacific* (1982). Frank Cooley, *The Growing Seed* (1982), was about Indonesia. *A History of Christianity in India* is being written by India's church historians (7 vols, 1984–   ). Stephen Neill got to 1858 in his history with the same title (2 vols, 1984–85). Christian studies include M. M. Thomas, *The Acknowledged Christ of the Indian Renaissance* (2nd edn 1976), and R. H. S. Boyd, *An Introduction to Indian Christian Theology* (2nd edn 1975). *Readings in Indian Christian Theology* were edited by R. S. Sugirtharajah (1993). A non-Christian, Arun Shourie, reacted to *Missionaries in India* (1994) and an American scholar, Gerald Larson, studied *India's Agony over Religion* (1995).

Stephen Neill's *History of Christian Missions* was revised by Owen Chadwick (1986). The best introduction to *The World's Religions* is by Ninian Smart (1989) and the *Christian Systematic Theology in World Context* which he wrote with Steven Konstantine (1991) was illuminating. John Hick, *An Interpretation of Religion* (1989), was of special value in the inter-religious dialogues but see also Gavin d'Costa's *John Hick's Theology of Religions: A Critical Evaluation* (1987) and perhaps also my dialogue with him in *Tradition and Truth* (1989). The questions raised by Paul Knitter in *No Other Name?* (1985) were taken further by Stanley Samartha, *One Christ, Many Religions* (1991). Paul Griffiths edited *Christianity through Non-Christian Eyes* (1990). Considerations of Buddhism include John Cobb, *Beyond Dialogue* (1982), Aloysius Pieris, *Love Meets Wisdom* (1988), and Ninian Smart, *Buddhism and Christianity: Rivals and Allies* (1993). William Phipps compared *Muhammad and Jesus* as prophets (1996) and the many sympathetic treatments of Islam by Bishop Kenneth Cragg include at least one classic, *The Call of the Minaret* (2nd edn 1986).

10   In the Postmodern Age

Stephen Connor explored *Postmodernist Culture* (1989) and Zygmunt Bauman *Postmodern Ethics* (1994) but Alasdair MacIntyre, *After Virtue* (1981), and Iris Murdoch, *Metaphysics as a Guide to Morals* (1992), were among the philosophical protests against the distintegration of the traditional sense of the Good. Anthony Thisleton, *Interpreting God and the Postmodern Self* (1995), was a brave attempt. Owen Chadwick summed up the story of the victory of *The Christian Church in the Cold War* (1992) and my *Christians in a New Europe* (1990) recorded the resulting hopes. Trevor Beeson, *Discretion and Valour* (2nd edn 1982), recorded the churches' troubles in eastern Europe under Communism and Michael Cathcart usefully abridged *Manning Clark's History of Australia* (1993). A. W. Black edited essays on *Religion in Australia* (1991). Terence Tilley edited essays on *Postmodern Theologies* with a North American perspective (1995).

W. J. Hollenweger analysed the history of *The Pentecostals* (2nd edn 1972), Harvey Cox vividly reported the continuing developments in *Tongues of Fire* (1994) and Karla Poewe edited scholarly essays on *Charismatic Christianity in a Global Context* (1994). S. M. Burgess and G. B. McGee edited a *Dictionary of Pentecostal and Charismatic Movements* (1988). I edited *The Honest to God Debate* (1963). Studies of more hard-line Christians are included in the series on *Fundamentalisms Observed* being edited by Martin Marty and Scott Appleby (from 1991). In addition to the books referred to in the text, the historical studies of *Evangelicalism* edited by Mark Noll, David Bebbington and George Rawlyk (1994) are illuminating. Alister McGrath edited *The Blackwell Encyclopaedia of Modern Christian Thought* (1993) and wrote *Christian Theology: An Introduction* (1994). Donald Bloesch made an American 'call for unity and diversity' in *The Future of Evangelical Christianity* (1983).

A constructive interpretation of *Christian Feminist Theology* has been produced by Denise Carmody (1995) and by Mary Grey's more difficult *Redeeming the Dream* (1989). Ursula King edited essays on *Feminist Theology from the Third World* (1994) and *Religion and Gender* (1995). Rosemary Radford Ruether and Eleanor McLaughlin edited essays showing how many Christians have been *Women of Spirit* (1979) but Daphne Hampson reckoned that feminist theology must now be 'post-

Christian' in *Theology and Feminism* (1990). Carol Newsom and Sharon Ringe edited *The Women's Bible Commentary* (1992). David Bosch made the best presentation of recent missiology in *Transforming Mission* (1991), a fruit of the discussion related by Timothy Yeats in *Christian Mission in the Twentieth Century* (1994). James Phillips and Robert Cooke edited an international collection of essays moving *Toward the 21st Century in Christian Mission* (1993).

Useful essays on *Christian Theology: An Introduction to its Traditions and Tasks* were edited by Peter Hodgson and Robert King (1982) and on *The Modern Theologians* by David Ford (2nd edn 1996). Richard Bauckman studied *The Theology of Jürgen Moltmann* (1995). *The Trinitarian Faith* in its traditional form was defended by T. F. Torrance (1988) but criticized by another Edinburgh professor, James Mackey, in *The Christian Experience of God as Trinity* (1983), and by another learned patristic scholar, G. W. H. Lampe, in *God as Spirit* (2nd edn 1983). I conducted a dialogue with the Evangelical leader John Stott in *Essentials* (1988; US title *Evangelical Essentials*) and with some radical theologians in *Tradition and Truth* (1989).

Thomas Gannon edited a survey of *World Catholicism in Transition* (1988) and Adrian Hastings essays on *Modern Catholicism* (1991). Gene Burns approached *The Frontiers of Catholicism* mainly in the USA as a sociologist (1993). Much information and shrewd comment are conveyed by three biographies of popes: John XXIII and Paul VI by Peter Hebblethwaite (1984 and 1993) and John Paul II by Michael Walsh (1994). Thomas Reese explored *Inside the Vatican* (1996). My *What is Catholicism?* (1994) discussed *The Catechism of the Catholic Church* (1992) with suggestions for other reading, to which should be added Richard McBrien, *Catholicism* (3rd edn 1994). John Redford replied to my comments in *Catholicism: Hard Questions* (1996).

Index

Aachen 139
Abba 21, 616
Abbasids 13, 190–1, 285
Abel 173
Abelard 225, 237–9, 240, 300–1
Abgar 34, 58
Aborigines 597–600
abortion 56, 145, 217, 461, 502, 510, 594
Abraham 18, 20, 24
abuna 532
Acre 233
Action Française 459
Acton 405
Acts of Apostles 8–10, 16, 17, 21, 25, 602
Adam *see* Fall
Adam, K. 471
Adams 389, 391
Adenauer 458, 468
Adoptionists 64
Adventists 483
African Catholics 531, 533–4, 537, 539, 540–1, 544–7
African Christ 550–1
African churches 530–47; spirituality 547–51
African Independents 533, 538–40, 542, 544, 546
African Protestants 533, 534–8, 540–2, 544–7
African theology 547–51
Afrikaners 536
Afrikania 544
agape 25, 55
aggiornamento 623
Agnes 229
Aidan 176
AIDS 547, 549, 628
Ailly 256
Aksum 532
Alaska 87, 150
Albania 132, 596
Albigenses 207–8
Albrecht (archbishop) 298
Albrecht (duke) 322
Alcuin 189
Alexamenos 72

Alexander (pope) VI 275–6
Alexander (tsars) I 408; II 139; III 134, 227
Alexander and Rufus 16
Alexander Severus 50
Alexandria 34, 42, 52–3, 65–8, 93, 102, 104, 107, 112, 117, 126, 150, 532–3
Alexis (patriarch) 141
Alexius (emperor) 124, 201
Alfred 184, 191
Algeria 534, 537, 543
Ali 117, 285
All-Africa Conference of Churches 545
All Souls Day 220–1
Allen 485
Allende 528
Alline 392
Alumbrados 338
Alves 525
Amaladoss 582
Ambedkar 574
Amboise 254
Ambrose (patron) 66
Ambrose (saint) 120, 158–60, 174, 196, 288
American Council of Christian Churches 496, 506
American (North) colonial churches 363–5, 385–9
Americanism 452–3, 490–1, 507
Ames 387
Amiens 213
Amin 545
Amitabha 583
Amsterdam 316, 329, 468
Anabaptists 294, 313–14, 321, 324, 330
Anagni 209
Andhra Pradesh 574
Andrew 106
Angelico 278
angels 14, 29, 44, 68, 83, 169, 179, 246
Anglicans 148, 352, 384, 406, 452, 455, 468, 483–4, 499, 608
Anglo-Catholics 462, 482
Anglo-Saxons 177, 179, 185
Angola 534
Anima Christi 256

645

Anna 124
annates 204, 255
Anne (mother of BVM) 251
Anne (queen) 331
Anselm 160–1, 174, 235–41, 358, 417, 474
Anskar 191
Anti-Christian League 555
Antioch 2, 9, 64–5, 72, 76–7, 93, 124, 150, 194–5
Anti-Saloon League 497
Antony 63
Antwerp 329
Apocrypha 335
Apollinaris 106–7
Apollonius 59
Apollos 36
apophatic 83, 102, 261–2
Apostles 5, 15, 21, 25, 31, 33–6, 52–3, 147, 195, 432
Apostles' Creed 54–5, 613
Apostolic Church 542
Apostolic Tradition 54–5, 57
Aquinas see Thomas
Arabia 116–17, 385
Arabs 108, 116–18, 129, 187
Aramaic 2, 21
Aragon 193
Argentina 457, 516–19
Arians 105–6, 115, 159–60
Aristeides 55–6
Aristotle 235–7, 240–5, 247, 258, 297, 299, 322, 614
Arius 28, 97–8, 104
Armada 325
Armenia 114, 123, 207, 269
Arminians 315, 366, 383, 396–7
Arndt 393
Arnold, G. 393
Arnold, M. 426
Arnold of Brescia 238–9
Arrupe 626
art
    Byzantine empire 93
    Early Church 56
    Middle Ages 247
    modernism 442–3
    Renaissance 273–4, 278–9
Arthur (king) 202
Arthur (prince) 323
Articles of Religion 325
Arusha 543
Arya Samaj 571
Asbury 484
ashram 572
Asia 284, 346–8, 551–87
Assumption of BVM 95, 113, 122, 405, 437–8
Athanasian Creed 167
Athanasius 63, 84–5, 98–9, 101, 106
atheism 359, 368, 421–30, 470, 489–90, 521, 595
Athenagoras (patriarch) 147
Athenagoras (writer) 49, 67
Athos 86, 93
Atman 584
atonement 24, 78, 84, 175, 185, 236–7, 250, 297,

314, 361, 396, 412–14, 417–18, 438, 465, 475, 604–7, 611–12
Augsburg (city) 322
Augsburg, Peace of 326
Augsburg Confession 305–6, 323, 332
Augustine of Canterbury 185
Augustine of Hippo (life and thought) 160–75; (mentioned) 43, 59, 64, 103, 120, 180, 184–5, 218, 234, 237, 240–1, 243, 257, 259, 260, 267, 288, 297–8, 313, 338, 368–9, 373, 387
Augustinian orders 180, 227–8, 231, 240, 254, 262, 300–1
Aulén 465
Aurelian 60, 65
Australia 597–9
Austria 329, 331
Avars 130, 188
Ave Maria 251
Averroes 240–1
Avicenna 240–1
Avignon 127, 249, 268–70, 375
Awakenings 390–2
Ayer 470
Aztecs 512, 526
Azusa Street 492

Bach 394
Bacon, F. 365
Bacon, R. 231
Baghdad 123, 191
Balasuriya 629
Baldwin 125
Balearic islands 190, 192
Balthasar 260
Bangalore 574
baptism 7, 35, 54–6, 61–2, 78, 85, 104, 165, 217, 247, 293, 316, 395, 474
Baptism, Eucharist and Ministry 601–2
baptism of Jesus 42
Baptists 395–6, 438, 535; see also Dissent; Nonconformists; USA
Barcelona 441
Bardaisan 58
Barlaam 123
Barmen 465–6
Barnabas, Letter of 39
Barth (life and thought) 473–6; (mentioned) 353, 415, 420, 441, 444, 465, 470, 557, 561, 600, 610–1, 616, 619
Bartholomew 34
Barton 498
Basil (emperor) 130
Basil of Caesarea 84–5, 91, 99, 100
basilica 71
Basilides 42
Basle 271, 291
Bataks 567
Bavaria 186, 331, 458
Bayle 351
Beatrice 257, 259
Beauvais 213
Bec 235–6
Becket 199, 211
Beckwith 127

Bede 185–6
Beecher 486, 493
Beethoven 353, 414
Beghards 227
Beguines 226–7, 260
Beijing 347, 554, 559
Belgium 188, 333, 403, 452
Belgrade 554, 559
Benedict XV 453
Benedict of Aniane 223
Benedict of Nursia 180–2, 230–1
benedictions 12
benefices 216, 254
Berbers 129
Berdyaev 147
Berengar 197, 235
Berlin (city) 415, 440
Berlin Congress 540
Bernanos 460
Bernard 192, 203, 224–5, 235, 238, 393
Bernardino 255
Berne 294, 312
Bernini 344
Bérulle 339
Bessarion 275
Bethlehem 70
Beza 319
Bible
    in Middle Ages 248
    in Reformations 286–7
    see also canon of Scripture; Scriptural authority
Bible Societies 394, 462
Bill of Rights 481
Birmingham 407
bishops 31, 35–6, 51–4, 62–3, 86, 254–5, 317,
    335, 352
Bismarck 404, 420, 433, 458, 464
Black churches 395: see also African Independents;
    USA
Black Death 219, 265–6
Blake 511
Blandina 50
Bloesch 607
Blondel 437
Boccaccio 253
Bodhisattva 283, 583
Bodin 327
Boethius 182–4
Boff 526–7
Bogomils 43, 131
Bohemia 131, 267–8, 329–30
Bolívar 519
Bologna (city) 235, 257
Bologna concordat 277
Bonaventure 161, 232, 234–5
Bonhoeffer 466, 476, 610
Boniface see Willibrord
Boniface VIII 208–9, 269
Bonino 526
Book of Common Prayer 325, 383, 398, 462
Book of Kells 176
Booth 443, 494
Bora 304–5
Borgias 276, 279

Boris 134
Bormann 465
Borromeo 337–8, 623
Borromini 344
Bosnia 131–2
Bossuet 285, 354, 372, 374, 399
Boston 387, 412
Bostra 58
Botticelli 278
Boulaga 544
Bourges 310
Boxers 554
Boy Scouts 441
Brabazon 434
Brahman 584
Brahmo Samaj 569
Brahms 418
Braide 538
Bramante 276
Brazil 513, 515, 517–18, 522, 524
Brébeuf 348
Bremen 322
Brémond 372
Brethren of Common Life 263, 288
Bridget 269
Britain, Roman 58, 69, 160
British empire 385–8, 540, 543, 569–73
Broad Church 463
Brooks 494
Brothers of the Sword 192
Brown, J. 487
Brown, P. 68
Browne 395
Brunner 415, 471, 475
Bruno 343
Bryan 495–6
Bucer 311, 317, 324
Buddhists 110, 283–4, 347, 557, 560, 563, 574,
    582–4
Bulgakov 143, 147, 149
Bulgaria 130–2, 144–5, 626
Bullinger 294
Bultmann 75, 77, 476–8, 610, 611
Bunyan 395, 549
Burckhardt 273
Burgundians 186–7
Burgundy 264–5, 300
Burke 388, 400
Burma see Myanmar
Burundi 545
Bush Brotherhood 598
Bushnell 413–14
Butler 351–2, 360

Cabisilas 84
Caesarea 67
Caesarius 187
Caiaphas 4, 5
Cain 173
Cajetan 300
Calcutta 567
California 386
caliphs 117, 285, 586
Callistus 54

Calvin (life and thought) 309–19; (mentioned) 161, 246, 288, 355
Calvinists 320–32, 355, 361, 390–3, 396–7, 412–13, 416, 418, 462, 608; see also Barth
Câmara 524
Cambridge 235, 324
Campanella 343
Campbell, A. 482
Campbell, J. 413–14
Canaanite religion 616
Canada 348, 382–3, 386, 410, 481, 508
Canberra 600, 613
Cane Ridge 486
Canisius 342
canon law
  Catholic 200, 336–7, 622
  Orthodox 103–4, 120, 150
canon of Scripture 51, 76
Canossa 198
Canterbury 212
Canute 191
Cape Colony 534–5
capitalism 90, 233, 317, 408, 593
Cappadocian churches 93
Cappadocian Fathers 99–101, 120, 121, 612
Capuchins 301, 340
cardinals 200, 256, 336, 376, 624
Carey 535
Caribbean 529, 541
Carmelites 231, 338
Carnegie 489, 490
Carolinas 381, 388
Carroll 376
Carter 505
Carthage 11, 532
Carthusians 224, 262
Cassian 63
Castellio 313
castes 347–8, 569, 571, 576
Castiglione 279
Castile 193
Castlereagh 408
Castro 518
casuistry 342–3, 392
catacombs 56
Catechism of Catholic Church 154, 625
Cathars 43, 131, 207–8, 221, 266
cathedrals 212–15, 254
Catherine of Aragon 323
Catherine of Siena 263, 269, 270
Catherine the Great 137, 363
Catholic 27, 79, 153–8, 354, 436–7
Catholic Action 455
Catholic League 327
Catholic Patriotic Association 552, 559
Catholic Reformation 330–49
caudillismo 514
Caussade 372, 374
Cavour 403
Celestine V 208–9
Celsus 47, 59, 66, 603
Centre party 454
Cerinthus 77
Chadwick 171

Chalcedon 111–16
Chalmers 410
Chamberlain 424–5
Champlain 376
Channing 412
Chantal 339
chantries 354
Chao 557
Chardin 471
charismatic 508, 603
Charlemagne 119, 130, 180, 188, 190
Charles V (emperor) 277, 291, 300
Charles (kings) I 331, 383; II 331, 384; VII 276
Charles Martel 187
Charles of Anjou 126, 206
Chateaubriand 402
Chaucer 212
Chenchiah 585
Cherokees 485
Cherson 130, 134
Chiang Kai-shek 551, 555
'children's crusade' 125
Chile 521, 522, 528
Chillingworth 350
China 109–10, 347, 552–9
China Christian Council 552–9
China Inland Mission 554–5
China National Christian Council 535
Chora 127
Chota Nagpur 571
'Christ' 2
Christendom 156–7, 193, 211, 218
Christian Brothers 393
Christian Century 495, 505
Christian Coalition 505
Christian Democrats 457, 468, 516, 528
Christian Science 491
Christian Socialists 410, 596
Christian Social Union 458
'Christianity' 40
Christianity Today 505
'Christians' 1
Christians for Socialism 518
Christina 331
Christmas 16, 104, 158, 220, 229, 274, 344
Chung Hyun Kyung 600, 602, 613
'Church' 194
Church Missionary Society
Church of Christ (Philippines) 565
Church of Christ in Africa 542
Church of Christ in China 555
Church of Christ in Japan 560
Church of God (in USA) 492
Church of the East see Nestorians
Church of the Nazarene 492
Church of the Nazarites 539
Cicero 162
Circumcellions 71
circumcision 7, 10, 11
Cistercians 224–5, 228, 262
cities
  Byzantine 88
  Dark Ages 178
  Middle Ages 205, 210, 215–16, 233

Modern Age 442, 451-2, 501-2
Reformations 281-2, 295, 322
Civil Constitution 401
Civil War (USA) 414, 487-8
Clare 229
Clarke 359
Claudius 1
Clement I 21; IV 255; V 268-9; VI 249; VII
    324, 327; XI 374; XIV 375-6, 447
Clement, Letter of 35-8
Clement of Alexandria 21, 65-6
Clermont 201
Cloud of Unknowing 262
Clovis 186
Cluny 201-2, 221, 223-4, 239
Coal and Steel Community 467
Cochrane 171-2
codex 15
Colenso 541
Coleridge 414
Colet 288
collegia 31, 45
Cologne 196, 213
Colombia 517
colonialism
    medieval 193
    modern 447, 533-5, 540-1, 554, 571-2, 575
Colossians, Letter to 27-8
Columba 176
Columbanus 176
Columbus 193, 274, 349, 531
'common sense' theology 390
Commune (Paris) 459
Communism 81, 114, 139-46, 149, 280, 446,
    455-6, 470, 481, 555-9, 596-7, 610
Communist Manifesto 409
Comnenians 122
Compostela 179, 627
Comte 409, 515
comunidades de base 524-6, 528-9
Comunione e Liberazione 627
conciliar movement 270-1
concomitance 216
concordat 401
Condorcet 364
Confessing Church 465-6
confession 86, 197, 217-18, 248, 305, 334, 342,
    373-5, 626
confessors 62
confirmation 61, 179, 217, 302, 549
Confucius 347, 557
Congar 471
Congo 534, 539; *see also* Zaire
Congregationalists 450, 463-4, 485; *see also*
    Dissent; Nonconformity
congregations (Roman) 336-7
Conradin 206
Consalvi 401-2
Constance 270-2, 322
Constantine I 70-3, 87, 96-7, 102; IV 115; VII
    95; XI 87, 128
Constantinople 72, 87-8, 93, 106, 122, 125,
    127-8, 135-6, 184, 201

Constantinople, councils I 101, 106; II 115, III
    116; IV 119
Constantius 98-9, 129
Constitution of USA 381, 389, 500, 502
consubstantiation 294
Contarini 301
contraception 217, 441, 455, 501, 507, 528, 620,
    624, 626
Conventuals 232, 262
Copernicus 274, 343
Copts 112, 114, 178-9
Corinthians, Letters to 17, 22-6, 30, 174
Cosmas 109
Council of Europe 467
covenant theology 387
Cox 501
Cranmer 324-5
creation 20, 36-7, 85, 92, 165, 176, 214, 230, 431
cremation 179
Crete 190
Crimea 130
criollos 514
Cristeros 515
Croatia 130
Cromwell 383-4
Crowther 538
crucifixion 5, 18, 21, 25, 71-2; *see also* atonement
crusades 124-6, 192, 204-7, 209, 218-19, 222,
    276
Cuba 279, 494, 518
Cullen 461
cultural revolution (China) 558
Cupitt 594
curates 198
Cynics 23
Cyprian 62-3, 162, 288
Cyril of Alexandria 107, 112-15
Cyril of Balkans 131
Cyril of Jerusalem 98
Czech Brethren 268, 330, 394
Czechoslovakia 596-7

Dalits 571, 574
Dallas 505
Dalmatia 130
Damascus 21, 25, 150
Damasus 195-6
Damuah 544
Danes 191; *see also* Denmark
Dante 127, 209-10, 234, 257-60, 269
Daphni 93
Dark Ages in east 88; in west 177-8
Darwin 422-5
Datini 221-2
Daughters of Charity 340
David (saint) 176
David (king) 3, 21, 35, 541
Day 499
Dayly 615
de *see last name*
deaconesses 55, 411
deacons 30, 31, 35, 48, 52, 148
Decius 60
deconstruction 593

decretals 196
deification 84–5, 92, 260–1
Deists 363
Demetrius (of John's Letter) 34
Demetrius of Alexandria 53
Demetrius of Thessaloniki 93
Deng Xiaoping 559
Denis 213, 239
Denmark 191, 332–3, 394, 412, 617
denominations 450, 511
Depression 499–500
Descartes 342, 358, 367, 412, 422, 425, 548
Desert Fathers 63–4
Detroit 509
development of Christianity 37, 73–80, 154,
    156–7, 399–401, 431, 435, 478, 581, 589, 590,
    592, 629–30
devils 4, 44, 64, 68, 78, 92, 176, 178–9, 183, 188,
    246, 606–7
devotio moderna 263
Dewey 508
Diaspora 6, 11, 195
Diaz 515
Didache 35–7, 51
Didascalia 54
Diderot 359, 362, 364
diocese 53, 69
Diocletian 69, 72
Diognetus, Letter to 56
Dionysius Exiguus 95
Dionysius of Alexandria 60, 65, 97
Dionysius the Areopagite 83, 213, 239
Diotrephes 34
Dirtad 114
dispensationalists 492
Disraeli 424
Disruption 410
Dissent in England 384, 388
divorce 4, 86, 217, 304, 441, 507, 624
Docetism 53
Döllinger 405
Dominic 228, 234
Dominicans 233–4, 240, 347
'dominion' for Wyclif 267
Domitian 29
Donation of Constantine 187–8, 272
Donatists 71, 166–7, 174
Donne 386–7
Dort Synod 315–16
Dostoevsky 86, 137, 234
Doumergue 318
Dream of Rood 179
Dreyfus 459
Dryden 212
Du Bois 489
Duchesne 435
Duff 569
Dulles 477
Dunn 10
Duns see John Duns
Dura-Europos 58
Durkheim 430
Dutch Reformed Church 542, 545–6

Eadmer 197
Early Catholicism 26–31
East Germany 596–7
East India Company 569, 571
Easter 49, 54, 72, 85, 141, 148, 177, 195, 217
Ebeling 247
Ebionites 38
Eckhart 260–1, 263
Ecole Biblique 435
economics
    Africa 544
    Asia 575
    Byzantium 90
    Enlightenment 363–5
    Latin America 518–19
    Middle Ages 215–16, 265–6
    Modern Age 408, 442
    Reformations 332–3
    Renaissance 278
'ecumenical' 101, 121, 154
ecumenical movement 286, 306, 468–70
Eddy 491
Edessa 58, 124
Edict of Union 114
Edward VI 324
Edwards 191
Egypt 112–13, 117–18, 125
Einhard 180
Eisenhower 500, 503
El Dorado 512
El Greco 344
El Salvador 525–6
Elbe 192
elect 318
Elias 231
Elijah 8, 44
Eliot 427, 433
Elizabeth of England 324–6
Elizabeth of Hungary 229
Emerson 426–7
Emmaus 3
encomienda 513
Encyclopédie 351, 359, 365
Endo 561
Engels 409
England 176–7, 185, 210, 246, 265, 323–6, 371,
    382–5, 409, 461–4
England, Church of 318, 324–6, 382–6, 389, 393,
    397–8, 405–6, 462–4
Enlightenment 350–65, 399, 476, 589, 629
Ensor 463
enthusiasm 390–1, 394, 399
environment 591
Ephesians, Letter to 27, 32, 315
Ephesus 32, 52
Ephesus, councils 107, 111
Epicureans 23, 259
Epiphany 42
episcopacy see bishops
Erasmus (life and thought) 287–92; (mentioned)
    295–6, 301, 310, 315, 325
Erastus 322
Escriva de Balaguer 627
Essenes 6, 15

Establishment 287, 320–30, 370, 388–9, 598
Ethiopia 114, 129, 333, 532–3
Eucharist 21, 25, 35, 55–7, 61, 123, 152, 301, 540,
    550, 601–2, 629; *see also* Holy Communion;
    Liturgy; Lord's Supper; Mass
Eudists 193
Eugenius III 224; IV 271
Eugenius (usurper) 160
Eunice 30
Eunomius 99
Europe 190, 193, 215, 467
European Union 145, 467–8
European Values Study 597
Eusebius of Caesarea 10, 34, 38, 68–9, 74, 77, 96,
    98, 118, 133
Eusebius of Nicomedia 98
Eustathius 99
Evangelical Alliance 494
Evangelical Church in Polynesia 566
Evangelicals 393, 398, 462–4, 505–6, 523, 603–7
evolution 421–30, 614
Exclusive Brethren 450
excommunication 205, 311
existential 307, 412

Fabian 60
Fabrinus 278
faith 29, 47, 168–9, 297–8, 308–9, 316, 354, 368,
    406, 470–1, 589–600
Falangists 454
Fall 84, 166, 168–9, 237, 423
falling asleep of BVM 95, 122
False Decretals 188
family life 549
Farel 511
Fascism 457, 459
Fatimids 123
Febvre 272
Federal Council of Churches 494, 499
Felicitas 50
feminist theology 504, 591, 615–16
Fénelon 374
Ferdinand II 330–2
Ferrara/Florence, council 127–8, 175, 271
Ferrer 255
Feuerbach 415, 427–8
Ficino 274
Filioque 120–1, 123, 126–7, 135, 168
Finland 322
Finney 486
Fisher 324
Fiske 424
Flanders 265–6
Fliedner 411
Florence 127, 215, 233, 257, 260, 271, 277–8, 343
Florida 385
Florovsky 147
folk religion 156, 371–2
Fontenelle 364
Ford 509
forgery 27, 187–8
forgiveness 6, 54, 60, 70, 77–8, 86, 173–5, 177,
    194–5
Formula of Concord 307

Fosdick 496
Foucauld 460
Fox, G. 384
Fox, M. 507
France 187–8, 190, 210, 265–6, 326–8, 371–6,
    379, 382, 385–6, 400–2, 409, 436–8, 440, 446,
    459–61; *see also* French empire
Francis I 227, 313
Francis of Assisi 228–31
Franciscans 231–4, 243–4, 262, 269, 347, 385–6
Franco 454, 626
Franklin 391
Frazer 430
Frederick II 125, 205–7, 211, 240
Frederick Barbarossa 205–6
Frederick of Denmark 322–3
Frederick the Great 363, 384
Frederick the Pious 322
Frederick the Wise 300
Frederick William 382
freedom of religion 369–70, 381–3, 621
freedom of trade 364
freedom of will 291–4, 315, 392
Freemasonry 353, 442
Frei 609, 610
French empire 376, 385–6, 537, 543, 567, 569
French Revolution 364, 379–81, 400
Freud 431
friars 228–9
Frisians 186
Fry 411
Fuggers 298, 300
Fulbert 325
fundamentalists 424, 429, 435, 451, 495–6, 506,
    604; *see also* Scriptural authority

Gaius 181
Galatians, Letter to 9, 17, 21
Galen 47
Galerius 70
Galilee 4, 67
Galileo 343
Galla Placidia 94
Gallicanism 375, 378, 401–2
Gamaliel 5
Gandhi 573–5
Garibaldi 403
Gaul 34, 58, 69, 186
Gaulle 40
Gautama 283, 513–15, 582–3
Gelasius 196
General Baptists 396
Genesis 20, 161, 164–5, 421–2, 487
Geneva 311–19, 452
Genoa 90, 126
Gentiles 2, 7–9, 16, 77
George 494
Georgia 123, 388, 485
Gerhard 393
Gerhardt 393
German Theology 261
Germany 58, 186, 188–90, 210, 281–2, 295–309,
    313–14, 321–2, 331–2, 410, 411, 414–21,

443–6, 451, 458–9, 464–6, 476–8, 610–13, 617–20
Gerson 245
Gethsemane 14, 86
Ghana 537
Ghent 328
Ghibellines 205
Gibbon 45, 351–2
Gibbons 490
Giles 232
Gilson 173
Giotto 93
Girl Guides 447
gladiators 56, 104
Gladstone 464
Gleb 135
glossolalia see tongue-speaking
Gloucester 213
Gnostics 40–2, 68, 72, 76
Goa 346, 568–9
Goethe 414
Golden Legend 220
Gordon 553
gospels 14, 15
Gothic 212–15, 400, 496
Goths 60, 105, 159, 160
Gottschalk 160, 170
grace 247, 297
Graham 505
Grant 488
Gratian 159
Great Schism 270, 271
Greber 293
Greece 81, 143–5
Greenland 176
Gregorian calendar 336
Gregorian chant 453
Gregory IX 230; X 126; XI 269; XV 337; XVI 411, 537
Gregory of Nazianzus 84–5, 90, 99, 106
Gregory of Nyssa 83–4, 85, 92, 94, 100, 104, 152
Gregory of Rimini 161, 247
Gregory of Tours 187
Gregory Palamas 86–7
Gregory the Great 183–6, 218
Gregory the Illuminator 114
Groote 263
Grotius 366
Grundtvig 412
Guangzhou 552
Guarini 348
Guatemala 522
Guelfs 205
guilds 233
Guise 127
Guroian 150
Gutenberg 248
Gutiérrez 525–7

hacienda 516–17
Hadrian (emperor) 11
Hadrian (pope) 277
Haeckel 428
Hagia Sophia 88–9, 128

Haile Selassie 529
Halberstadt 298
Halle 393–4
Hamburg 322
han 564
Handel 353
Harald 191
Harding 498
Häring 471
Harnack 420–1, 436, 440, 473–4
Harris 539, 551
Harvard 390
Hasidim 284
Hauerwas 609, 610
Havea 566
Hawaii 566
Haydn 345
Haynes 485
Hebrew Bible 3, 6, 9, 29, 32, 39, 53, 59, 66–7, 614–15
Hebrews, gospel of 38
Hebrews, Letter to 27–8, 100, 194
Hecker 457, 490
Hegel 319, 415, 418, 619
Heidegger 477
Heidelberg 322
Heidelberg Catechism 322, 396
Helen 71
hell 17, 173–5, 258–9, 296, 339, 409, 410
Hellenists 8, 9, 24
Heloise 239
Henry (emperors) II 121; III 196; IV 198; VI 205; VII 210
Henry (English kings) II 199; III 322; V 271; VII 252; VIII 280, 323–4
Henry (French kings) II 326; III 327; IV 327–8
Henry, C. 607
Heraclius 115
Herberts 356, 387
Herder 362, 414
heresy 350, 351, 593–5, 602
Hermas 43–4, 52
Herods 5
Herrmann 420
Herrnhut 394
hesychasm 87, 122–3
Hidalgo 515
Hilary 99, 120, 314
Hillel 7
Hilton 262
Hincmar 160
Hindenberg 44
Hindus 283, 348, 377, 568–75, 584–5
Hippolytus 54–5, 57–8
Hitler 445, 454, 465–6
Hodge 424–5, 496
Hofmann 413
Hohenzollerns 322, 382
holiness churches 483, 492, 506
Holland see Netherlands
Hollenweger 523
Holocaust 593, 611, 612
Holy Alliance 408
Holy Club 396

Holy Communion 325, 397–8
Holy Roman empire 189, 190, 209, 210, 321, 331, 408, 458
Holy Spirit *see* Spirit
Holy Trinity *see* Trinity
Homer 6, 94
homoiousios 102
homoousios 64–5, 96–8, 101, 102
homosexuality 56, 204, 217, 617
Hong Kong 553
Hong Xiu-quan 553
Honorius 116
Honoratus 63
Hooker 326
Horus 67, 93
Horace 250
Hosius 98
host in Mass 175, 216–17, 220, 250
household ethics 30
Hromadka 470, 597
Hsianfu 109
Huddleston 545
Hügel 437
Huguenots 385
human rights 467, 480, 590–1, 611
Humanae Vitae 624
Humani Generis 437
humanism 27, 343, 361–2, 442
Humbert 123, 198
Hume 363, 365, 390, 399
Humiliati 227–8
humour (medieval) 220, 253
Hundred Years' War 265
Hungary 130, 132, 329, 330, 596–7
Hurley 545
Hurons 348
Hus 161, 267–8
Hutcheson 392
Hutchinson 387
Hütten 290
Huxley 424–5
hymns 19, 26, 32, 82, 159, 249, 479, 487, 490, 608
Hypatia 107
hypostasis 19, 100, 148, 168

Ibn Rushd 240–1
Ibn Sina 240–1
Ibsen 441
Iceland 176, 190, 322–3
icons 82, 93–4, 118–19
idealism 427
Igbos 545
Ignatius Loyola 288, 333, 337, 340, 344–5
Ignatius of Antioch 27, 33, 39, 40, 56
Illinois 483
Immaculate Conception 121–2, 251, 403, 451
Incas 512–13, 526
'Index' 336, 624
India 54, 108–9, 346, 394, 569–75, 578, 590, 594
individualism 258, 282–3, 367, 594
Indonesia 108, 285, 346, 566–7, 578
indulgences 209, 249, 252, 298–9, 337, 340
infallibility 198, 404–5, 619
inflation 514, 518

Infralapsarians 315
Ingersoll 490
Inglis 386
Ingolstadt 331
initiation in Africa 549–50
Inner Mission 410, 411
Innocent III 192, 205–8, 216, 228–9, 231; VI 269; VIII 246; XI 373; XII 374
inquisitions 156, 193, 208, 234, 256, 338, 385, 513
Inter-Church World Movement 497
interdicts 205, 208
inter-faith dialogues 581–7
International Missionary Conferences 579
International Missionary Council 468
investiture 198–9
Iona 176
Iran 110, 123, 285
Iraq 110, 123
Ireland 175–7, 254, 382, 406, 409, 461, 463
Irenaeus 15, 44–5, 53, 76, 79, 195, 288
Irene 119
Iroquois 348
Isaac the Syrian 85–6, 109
Islam 108–9, 116–17, 123–4, 149, 218, 261, 284–5, 503, 530–1, 585–8
Italy 105, 183–4, 205–6, 209, 210, 217, 273, 279, 321, 402, 436–7, 440, 446, 453–4, 457–8, 624, 627
Ivory Coast 539

Jackson 480
Jacob Baradai 113
Jacob of Edessa 113
Jacobites 113, 117–18
James (apostle) 179, 218
James (brother of Jesus) 5, 9, 10, 38, 113, 194
James, Letter of 6, 8, 194, 308
James I 329, 331, 383; II 331, 384
James, W. 490
Jansen 373
Jansenists 373–4
Japan 346–7, 559–63, 578, 583
Java 579
Jefferson 389, 390
Jehovah's Witnesses 491–2
Jena 415
Jerome 166, 170, 172, 288, 622
Jerusalem 5, 8–11, 16, 25, 93, 124–6, 150, 170, 194, 200, 202, 206–7, 222
Jesuits 340–3, 345–9, 375–8, 459, 526, 578, 626
Jesus Family 557
Jesus of Nazareth 1–8, 74–8, 432–5, 590
Jesus prayer 84
Jewish Christianity 5–13, 38–9
Jews 11, 13, 38–9, 46, 124, 139, 193, 444, 446–7, 455, 465, 533; *see also* Judaism
Joachim (father of BVM) 251
Joachim of Fiore 232, 259
Job 8, 183–4, 527
John V 89, 127; VIII 127–8; XXI 259; XXII 232, 244, 269; XXIII 622–3
John XXIII (antipope) 270
John, gospel of 2, 7, 10, 12, 17–21, 26–7, 30, 37, 41, 194, 501, 581, 630

John, Letters of 33, 194
John Chrysostom 86, 91, 95, 107, 289, 313
John Duns 243–5, 251
John Frederick 304
John of Damascus 119
John of Eck 301
John of Kronstadt 133
John of Monte Corvino 110
John of Plano Carpini 230
John of Sinai 86
John of the Cross 338–9, 374
Johnson, F. 395
Johnson, L. B. 502
Johnson, R. 598
Joinville 222–3
Jones, A. 485
Jones, R. 579
Joseph II 378, 382
Joseph of Arimathea 5, 203
Joseph of Nazareth 3, 344
Josephus 11–13
Judaism 3, 5–8, 11, 12, 29, 39, 44, 284, 533, 614
Judas the Galilean 5
Judas the traitor 4, 258
Jude, Letter of 29
Judson 495
Julia Domna 59
Julian (emperor) 74, 102–3, 106
Julian of Eclanum 170
Julian of Norwich 262
Julius II 276, 279, 290
Julius Africanus 58
Julius Caesar 258
justice
    Enlightenment 361
    Middle Ages 210, 237
    postmodern age 590, 591
justification 298, 305–7, 315, 335, 419, 607
Justin Martyr 14, 44–5, 52, 201
Justinian 88–9, 115, 120

Kagawa 561
Kant 350, 353–5, 364–6, 416, 423, 592–3
Kaplan 420
Karlstadt 301, 303
karma 571
katholikos 27, 589
Kaunda 543
Keble 406
Kellogg 491
Kemp 536
Kennedy 480–1, 501
Kenya 542–4
Kerala 569, 574
Kerensky 140
Kettler 411
Keysser 566
Khazars 129
Khomyakov 147
Khrushchev 141
Kierkegaard 412–13
Kiev 134, 136
Kimbangu 539–40, 551
King 501–3

Kingdom of God 3, 6, 13, 14, 16, 73, 75, 356, 419, 477, 479, 511, 603
Kingdom of God movement 561
Kingsley 429
Kirchentag 466
Kitagawa 561
Kitamori 562
Kiwanuka 545
Knibb 529
knights 201–4, 303
Knights of St John 204
Knights Templar 203–4
Knox 319, 320
König 623
Korea 470, 501, 563–4, 600
Korean war 501
Kosovo 132
Koyama 562
Kraemer 579
Krishna 585
Kublai 110
Kulturkampf 440, 458
Küng 617, 619, 620, 628
Kuomintang 55
Kuruman 536
Kuyper 452
Kyodan 561

Labour party 464, 598
Lactantius 69
Lamennais 411
Lanfranc 197, 235
Langton 208
Laodicea 32–3
Laon 214
Laplace 421
La Rochelle 328, 372
Las Casas 345
Lateran councils II 200; IV 216–18, 228; V 255, 262, 277
Lateran palace 71
Latin America 512–29
    Catholics in 512–21, 524–9
    Pentecostals in 521–4
    Protestants in 513, 522–4
    theologians in 525–9
Latourette 449
Lauenburg 608
Lausanne 469, 523
Laval 376
Lavigerie 459, 537
Law of Moses 6, 7, 9, 10, 13, 17
lay power in Reformations 281–2
Lazarists 340
League of Nations 466, 497
Lee 488
Lefebvre 620, 624
Lefèvre 310
Leibniz 354, 359
Leiden 328
Leme 524
Lenin 140
Lenshina 542
Lent 104, 181

Leo III (emperor) 119
Leo III (pope) 121, 189, 195; IX 196–7, 223; X 276–7, 290; XIII 435, 452–3
Leo the Armenian 119
Leo the Wise 91
Leonardo da Vinci 278–9
Leontyev 138
Leopold I 378
Lepanto 346
Lercaro 623
Lérins 63
Lessing 356, 361
liberals in theology 307, 352, 400, 403, 405 413–21, 433, 438–9, 478, 605, 628
liberation theology 525–7, 611
Liberia 389, 537, 539, 545
Licinius 70
Liège 226
Life and Work 468
Liguori 392
Limbo 259
Lindbeck 607, 609, 610
Lindisfarne 176
Lindsell 506
Lippmann 498
Lisbon 359
Lithuania 135, 192, 330, 461
Little Rock 503
Liturgy 82–6, 92, 146
Living Church movement 140
Livingstone 536–7, 540
Livonia 192
Lloyd George 464
Locke 357–60
Lodi 275
logical positivists 470
Logos 19–21, 42, 44, 65, 68, 97, 581
Lois 30
Loisy 436–7
Lollards 267
Lombards 105, 184, 187–8
London 136
London Missionary Society 535, 552, 566
Lonergan 618
Lord's Supper 293–4, 311, 316
Lorenziana 348
Loreto 251
Lossky 82–3, 147
Louis IX 222–3; XII 324; XIV 372, 374–5; XVI 380, 382
Louis-Napoleon 402, 459, 554
Louis Philippe 402, 411
Louisiana 376, 385
Lourdes 460
Loyola *see* Ignatius Loyola
Lubac 460
Lucaris 146
Lucian 47
Ludolf 340
Ludwig 369
Luke 3, 8, 9, 11, 14, 16, 17, 30, 37, 73, 615
Lumpa Church 542
Luther (life and thought) 290–309; (mentioned) 161, 246, 261, 318–19, 355, 396, 407, 465

Lutheran World Federation 601
Lutherans 306–7, 309, 320–4, 393–4, 410, 413, 478, 523, 535, 573, 601, 608, 617; *see also* USA
Luwum 545
Lux Mundi 438
Lwanga 540
Lyell 421–2
Lyon 50
Lyon, council of 312

Macao 347
MacArthur 565
Macaulay 569
Macedonian dynasty 122
McGrath 309, 604–6
McGravan 577
Mach 428
Machen 496
Machiavelli 279, 404–5
machismo 514
McLeod 449, 461, 502
Macquarrie 612
Macrina 94
Madagascar 538, 542–3
Madison 389
Madurai 348
Mafia 457–8
Magdeburg 191, 298
Magellan 554
Maghrib 532
magic (rural) 253, 371, 442
magisterium 154, 527, 622
Magna Carta 208
Magyars 130, 191
Mahayana 583–4, 600, 603
Maimonides 284
Maistre 402
Maitland 157
Malaya 568
Malthus 423
Malula 545
Manalo 565
Manchuria 467, 560
mandates 543
Mandela 546
Manfred 206
Manichees 42–3, 72
Manila 524
Mannerism 247
Mao Tse-tung 555, 557–8
Maoris 599
marana tha 21
Maranke 542
Marburg 229, 477
Marcian 111
Marcion 72
Marco Polo 110
Marcos 565
Marcus Aurelius 46, 49, 50, 58, 163
Maria Laach 456
Maria Legio 542
Maria Maggiore 107
Maria Theresa 378–9
Mariana 345

Marignano 593
Maritain 460
Mark 5, 10, 14, 15, 17, 37, 52, 179, 194, 250–1, 288, 344, 520, 524, 615, 618
Maronites 125
Marquette 376
marriage 39, 45, 58, 62, 64, 86, 146, 170, 171, 217, 274, 318, 336, 441, 549
Marsilio 210
Martin I 115; V 270
Martin, D. 519, 520
Martin of Tours 106, 186–7
martyrs 16, 32, 45, 48–50, 60, 62, 66, 159, 201
Marx 409, 411, 428
Mary I 325; II 331, 384
Mary (BVM) 10, 11, 95, 107, 113, 121–2, 154, 224–5, 344, 615, 618, 624; see also Assumption; Immaculate Conception
Mary of Magdala 2, 30, 179
Mary Queen of Scots 329
Maryland 388
Mass 153–5, 179, 180, 185, 197, 216–17, 249, 250, 266, 294, 302, 305, 333, 456, 513–14, 516, 577, 619, 622, 626
mass movements in India 571–2
Massachusetts 386–8, 391
Mather 387
Matthew 11, 13, 15, 17, 18, 34, 37, 39, 194–5
Matthews 508
Mau Mau 542
Mauriac 460
Maurice 409, 410, 415
Maurras 459
Maximilian 300
Maximilla 43
Maximus the Confessor 83–4, 115–16
maya 575–6
Mayflower 386
Mazzaloni 301
Mazzini 403
Mbiti 548
Mecca 116, 131, 218, 586–8
Medellín 525
Medicis 215, 276–9
Meiji 560
Melanchthon 305–9
Melkites 113
Melville 320
Mendel 423
Menelik 532
Mennonites 313–14
mercantilism 368
Mercator 346
Merovingians 187
Merton 507
Messiah 2, 3, 7, 8, 15, 23, 29
Meteora 93
Methodists 396–9, 451, 463, 523, 537, 608; see also Nonconformists; USA
Methodius 131
Meung 220
Mexico 385–6, 515, 518, 521, 522, 525, 528
Mexico City 517
Meyendorff 118, 147–9

Michael Palaeologus 9, 126
Michelangelo 215, 278–9
Middle Ages 156
Mieszko 191
Migne 407
Milan 158, 197, 213, 278, 338, 623
Milan, edict of 70
Milingo 544, 550
military service 23, 56, 197, 290
millenarian 492
Miller 483
Milton 283, 359
Milvian Bridge 70
Mindszenty 456, 624
minjung 564
Minucius Felix 46
miracle plays 248
miracles 166, 184, 220, 418, 476, 603–4
Mishnah 7
missionary impulse 345–6, 495, 512, 535–44, 577
Mistra 94
Mithraism 59
Mobutu 545
modernism 435, 442, 453, 508
modernity 318, 350, 351, 399, 400, 541, 589
Moffat 536
Mogila 146
Mohacs 329
Möhler 407
Molinos 374
Moltmann 610–13, 619
Moltmann-Wendel 613–14
Mombasa 534, 537
Monarchians 64, 371, 612
monasteries 63–4, 86, 91–2, 146, 176, 180–2, 223–5, 253–4, 262–3, 289, 334–5
Mongols 109, 110, 230
monism 428
Monnet 467
Monophysites 81, 87, 92, 111–15, 117, 118, 129–30, 148, 532
Monreale 93
Mont St Michel 179
Montaillou 221–2, 269
Montanists 43, 62, 72, 76
Monte Cassino 180, 198, 240, 262
Montesquieu 362
Monteverdi 345
Montfort 308
Montmartre 340
Montserrat 340
Moody 491
Moore 427
Moors 192–3
morality
    Enlightenment 360–3
    postmodern 592–5
morality plays 248
Moravia 131
Moravians 394, 396, 414
More 279, 280, 289, 324
Morgan 498
Mormons 483–4
Morrison 522

Morton 329
mortuary 253
Moscow 129, 135–6
Mott 495
Mounier 460
Mozambique 534, 542
Mozart 345, 352
Mughal empire 569
Muhammad 116–17, 190, 218, 585–7
Mühlberg 321
Muhlenberg 392
Müller 465
Münster 314
Müntzer 314
Murillo 344
Muslims *see* Islam
Mussolini 454, 457
Mwanga 540
Myanmar 495, 568, 575
mystery 83, 260–1, 360
mystery religions 23, 46, 50, 401

Nag Hammadi 40, 41
Nagasaki 560
Nairobi 600
Nanak 585
Nantes, edict of 328, 373
Naples 240, 241
Napoleon 380, 400, 401, 421
Natal 542
Nathan 361
National Association of Evangelicals 506
Native Americans 394
Naudé 545
Nazarenes 10, 12
Nazareth 2, 13
Nazis 307, 444–5, 465–6
Neander 314
Nee 557–8
Nehru 573
Neo-Thomism 245, 435
Neri 337, 339
Nero 1, 31
Nestorians 81, 87, 108–10, 117, 148, 533
Nestorius 107
Netherlands 188, 313, 315–16, 321, 328–9, 331,
    333, 410, 452
Nevsky 135
New Age 500–1
New Deal 499
New Delhi 600
New Orleans 150, 376, 386
New Testament 51, 76, 288
New York 150–1, 388
New Zealand 599
Newman 405–8, 414–18
Newton 357, 359, 365
Nicaea 9, 104–5, 158–9
Nicaragua 518, 522
Nicholas I (emperor) 137
Nicholas I (pope) 196
Nicholas of Cusa 256, 261–2, 271–2
Nicodemus 5
Nicopolis 265

Niebuhrs 508–12, 527
Niemöller 465–6
Nietzsche 429, 430, 611
Nigeria 531, 534, 538, 542, 545
Nightingale 411
Nihonkyo 560
Nikon 136
nirvana 582–4
Nisibis 108
Nixon 505
Nkamba 539
Nkrumah 544
Nobili 347–8
Noetus 64
Nominalism 244–5, 297
non-church movement 500, 501
Nonconformists 463–4
non-possessors 135
Normans 93, 191, 199, 202, 205
Northumbria 177
Norway 191, 322–3
Nova Scotia 382, 392
Novatian 60–1, 72
Novgorod 135
Noyon 310
Ntsikana 536
nuclear deterrence 445, 501, 507, 593
nuncios 336
nuns 95, 226, 339, 340, 507
Nygren 465

Obolensky 131
Observants 232, 262
Odes of Solomon 38–9
Olaf 191
Old Believers 136
Old Testament *see* Hebrew Bible
Olive Tree Church 563
Olov 190
Onesimus 33
Opium war 553
Opus Dei (prelature) 627
opus dei (worship) 181–2
Oratory of Divine Love 339
orders (religious) 91–2
Organization of African Unity 544
Oriental Exclusion Act 498, 501
Oriental Orthodox *see* Monophysites
Origen (life and thought) 66–8; (mentioned) 38,
    44, 59, 73, 76, 85, 96–7, 118, 287, 291
original sin 166, 168–9, 175, 237
Orleans 264, 310
Orosius 172
Osaka 561
Ostrogoths 105
Otto I 190, 191; III 188, 190
Otto, R. 430
Otto of Freising 160
ousia 100
Oxford 231, 235, 243, 288, 406
Ozman 492

Pachomius 63
Pacific spirituality 566

pacifism 201, 466, 499
Packer 605
Padilla 523
Padua 210
pagani 102
paganism in Roman empire 22–3, 40, 41, 58–9,
    66, 69, 102–4
Paine 388, 400
Palaeologi 126
Palatinate 222
Palmer 483
Palmerston 404
Pamphylia 32
Panama Canal 495
Pantaenus 34
pantheism 359
Panthera 47
Pantokrator 133
papacy 154, 179, 195–9, 204–11, 268, 272–7, 309,
    336–7, 401–6, 452–6, 622–9
Papias 15, 43
Papua New Guinea 566
parables 3, 6, 16, 21, 23, 35, 432
Paraguay 348, 376
Paris 136, 234–5, 264, 310, 340, 459
Parker 433
Parousia 8, 13, 14, 21, 74–5, 287, 391, 432, 603
Particular Baptists 395–6
Pascal 161, 367–9, 373, 422
passion plays 248
Passover 1, 5, 8
pastors in Calvinism 317
Patmos 32
patriarchs 91, 94, 113, 116, 120, 135, 143, 150,
    184
Patrick 175
Paul (life and thought) 21–31; (mentioned) 2, 9,
    10, 16, 36–7, 41, 51, 116, 150, 163, 174, 195,
    283, 288, 315
Paul III 334, 345; IV 325, 337; VI 147, 623–7
Paul, Vincent de 340
Paul of Samosata 64–5, 72, 102
Paulists 490
peace of God 202
peasants and Luther 303
Pelagius 169, 174
Pelikan 174
penance 54, 70, 77, 159, 177, 179, 197, 218, 237,
    247–9, 288
peninsulares 513–14
Penn 388
Pennsylvania 388
Pentecost 8, 602
Pentecostals 492–3, 506, 521–4, 599, 602–3
Pergamum 53
Perkins 387
Perpetua 50
Persian Church 108
persona 61, 100, 168
Peru 513, 519, 525
Peter (apostle) 2, 9, 16, 18, 36–7, 194–5
    writings attributed to 13, 22, 27, 284
Peter Lombard 153, 160
Peter the Great 136

Peter's, St (Rome) 71, 276, 299, 531
'Peter's Pence' 177
Petrarch 161, 260
Petris 322
Pharisees 5, 11–13, 22, 284
Philemon, Letter to 33
Philip II 321, 325, 328, 331
Philip Augustus 206
Philip of Hesse 294, 304
Philip the Arab 58, 60
Philip the Fair 203, 209–11
Philippians, Letter to 31
Philippines 494, 528, 564–5
Philo 6, 19
Philostratus 59
Phoebe 30
Photius 90, 94, 122, 131
physiocrats 364
physis 111
Pi Shu-shi 558
Pico della Mirandola 273–4
Pieris 579, 584
Piero della Francesca 278
Piers Plowman 255
Pietism 307, 394–6
Pilgrim Fathers 386–7
Pimen 141
Pinochet 528
Pionius 60
Pirenne 190
Pistoia 378
Pius II 275–6; III 277; IV 336; V 325, 337;
    VI 379, 380, 401–2; VIII 380; IX 402,
    404–5, 534; X 435, 453; XI 453–5; XII
    437, 453–5, 461, 558
Platonism 23, 44, 65, 67, 97, 163–5, 182–3, 242,
    280, 351, 357, 416
Plotinus 59, 165
pluralities 254–6
Plymouth Brethren 450
Pobedonostsev 139
Poitiers 187, 190
Poland 132, 135, 191–2, 219, 330, 378, 471, 596,
    627–9
Pole 301, 325
Polycarp 48, 52–3
polygamy 304, 531, 539, 540, 546–7
Pomare 566
Pompey 5
Pontian 58
Popular party 457
Porete 227
Porphyry 59, 103, 106
Port-Royal 373–4
Portugal 193, 346, 376, 440
Portuguese empire 193, 346, 512–15, 533–4,
    568–9
positivism 428
post-Christian 591, 594–5
postmodern 152, 592–5, 621, 629
Pothinus 50
Prague 213, 267
Prato 222
Praxeas 64

preaching 154, 249, 304, 317, 333, 450, 478
predestination 170, 173–5, 294, 298, 307, 315–16, 318, 608
Presbyterians 329, 463–4
presbyters 31, 36
Prester John 533
priests 154, 179, 197, 216–18, 241, 253, 267, 302, 316, 626, 628–9
Princeton 390
printing 248–9, 329
Prisca (in NT) 30
Prisca (Montanist) 43
Priscillian 106
probabilism 343
process theology 472
Procopius 89
progress in Enlightenment 590–1
Prohibition 497–8, 510
proof of God 236, 356–60
prophets in Early Church 31, 35–6
prosopon 100
Prosper 173
Protestant 281
provisions 255
Prussia 322, 382, 415, 418
Psellus 94
Puebla 526
Puerto Rico 494
Pulcheria 94
purgatory 86, 155, 170, 185, 220–1, 248, 258–9, 296
Puritans 326, 383, 386–8

Quakers 384, 387–8
Quaque 537
Quebec 348, 376, 382–3, 404, 508
Quesnel 374–5, 378
Quietism 374
Qumran 6
Quran 116, 218, 285

Rabelais 253
Radbertus 164
Radhakrishnan 574
Rahner 122, 580–1, 618–19
Ramakrishna 570
Ramanuja 584
Ramm 506
Rampolla 453
Ranavalona 538
ransom 29, 78, 606
Raphael 276
Rasputin 139
Rastafarians 529
Ratramnus 164
Rauschenbusch 494
Ravenna 93, 105, 187
Reagan 505
Reccared 120, 185
reconciled diversity 601
recusants 325
Redeemer 417
Redemptorists 292
Reforma 515, 521

Reformations 281–7, 320, 354–8
Reformed see Calvinists
regular 439
Reid 390
Reimarus 356, 433
Reims 196, 213, 235
reincarnation 41–2, 576
relics 159, 179, 217, 220, 299
Rembrandt 329
Remonstrants 315
Renaissance 272–80
Renan 403, 433
Requiem Masses 252, 254, 257
resistance for Calvinists 319
Resurrection of Jesus 2, 36, 62, 476–7, 610–12, 615
Rethinking Missions 570
Reuchlin 308
revelation 366, 407; see also Scriptural authority
Revelation, Book of 12, 27, 31, 37, 57, 492–3
reverence for life 434
revivalism 449–50
Rhineland 282, 452, 458, 467
Rhode Island 388, 395
Rhodes 203
Rhodes, A. de 567
Rhodesia 542, 543, 546
Ricci 347
Richard I 125, 206
Richelieu 332
righteousness of God 297
Rimini 187
Rio de Janeiro 524
rites of passage 252, 448
Ritschl 418–20, 432
Rizal 565
Robertson 505
Robespierre 380
Robinson (bishop) 608–9
Robinson (Puritan) 386
Roch 251
Rockefeller 489, 490
Roland 159, 203
Rolle 262
Rollo 191
Romance languages 189
romances 202–3
Romanesque 183, 214
Romania 130, 132
Romanovs 135
Romans, Letter to 13, 21, 174, 297, 308, 396, 473, 613
Romantic movement 400, 414
Rome (church) 16, 35–7, 53–4, 106, 121, 183–4, 195; see also papacy
Rome (city) 1, 181–2, 196, 204–5, 209, 238–9, 271, 275, 380, 402–3, 455, 622
Romulus 178
Roosevelt, F.D. 499, 500
Roosevelt, T. 517
rosary 251, 344
Roses, Wars of 265
Rotterdam 316, 351
Rouen 213

Rousseau 362–3
Roy 569
Rubens 344
Rublev 149
Ruhr 452
Russell 427, 471
Russian Church 133, 143, 147–50, 219
Rutherford 491
Ruysbroeck 263

Sabah 568
Sabatier 436
Sabbath 3, 4, 387
Sabellius 64
sacraments 62, 82, 153, 155, 165–7, 252, 293–4, 302, 316, 336, 602–3, 621
Sacred Heart 226, 380, 392, 403, 516
sacrifice 28, 78, 154, 175, 185, 237, 604, 606
St Petersburg 136, 138–9
Saint-Simon 409
St Thomas Christians 568–9
Sainte Chapelle 222
saints 154–5, 159, 217, 220, 251
Saladin 125, 206, 229
Salamanca 345
Salem 388
Salisbury 213
Salvation Army 443, 494
  in Asia 580
Salzburg 353, 382
San Francisco 150
sanctuary 200
Sandinistas 518
Sankaara 584
Santayana 490
São Paulo 517
Sarajevo 444
Sarawak 568
Sardinia 190
Sardis 33
Sarpi 337
Sassanian empire 108, 115
satisfaction 61, 236–7, 606
Saviour 23, 84–5, 112, 259, 394, 580, 604, 606
Savonarola 255–6, 273, 276
Savoy 311, 312
  duke of 271
Saxons 188
Saxony 300, 321–2
Scandinavian churches 393, 400, 441, 451
Schaff 407
Schelling 414
Schillebeeckx 621
Schleiermacher 351–2, 412–18, 440
Schleswig 191
Schmucker 485
Schofield Bible 492
scholastic 238
Schumann 468
Schweitzer 432–5
Scotland 177, 246, 320, 329, 371, 410, 413, 451, 535
Scriptural authority

early and Orthodox Christians 29, 51, 53, 56, 66–7, 75–6, 79, 92, 127
medieval Catholics 153, 165–6, 234, 238, 241, 248, 267
Protestant Reformers 283, 286–7, 292, 297–9, 314
versus Enlightenment 355–6, 366–7
see also fundamentalists; liberals in theology; Vatican Council II
Second Coming see Parousia
Secular Education Acts 598
secularization 350, 401, 439–48, 519–20
Segundo 526
Semler 356
Sen 570
Seneca 310, 311
Senghor 541, 544
sentences 238
Sepphoris 2
Septuagint 29, 39, 164
Serapeum 104
Seraphim of Sarov 133–4
Serbia 130, 132, 444
serfs 139, 178
Sergius (patriarch) 141
Sergius (saint) 87
Sermon on Mount 17, 138, 302, 509
Servetus 312–13, 330
Seton 486
Seville 192, 213
sexuality 170, 171, 207, 220, 253, 441, 509, 549
Seymour 492
Sforzas 278
Shaftesbury 463
Shakespeare 326
sharia 585–6
Shaw 284
Sheen 507
Shembe 539
Shia 284–5
Shinto 560, 562
Sicily 123, 191, 205–6, 209, 235
Sidonius Apollinaris 183
Sierra Leone 537–8
Siger 259
Sigismund 271
Sigismund Vasa 323
Sikhs 585
Silesia 382
Silvester I 188; II 190, 235
Simon, cousin of Jesus 10
Simon, R. 355–6
Simon of Cyrene 16, 551
simony 197
Sin (Cardinal) 565
Singh 572
sins 77–8, 171, 184, 194, 217, 238, 258–9
Siricius 196
Sisters of Charity 486
Sistine Chapel 276, 278
Sixtus IV 276
slavery 29, 56, 95, 386, 389, 395, 463, 487–8, 513, 530, 534, 536–7
Slavonic 131

Slavophiles 137, 142
Slavs 130
Slovakia 461
Smith, Adam 364
Smith, Al 498
Smith, J. 483
Smyrna 32, 48, 52
Smyth 395
sobornost 147
Sobrino 526
Social Darwinism 424
Social Democrats 441, 458
Social Gospel 420, 493–4
social market 593
socialism 143, 147, 409, 410, 441, 464, 518, 527,
    556–7, 593
Socrates (historian) 101
Socrates (philosopher) 27, 44
Söderblom 468, 581
Sokka Gakkai 562
Solesmes 456
Solovyev 143, 146–7
Solzhenitsyn 86
Son of Man 15
Song 581
Song of Roland 189, 203
Song of Songs 67, 224
Sophia 143
Sorel 446
South Africa 394, 534–6, 543
South India, Church 469
Southern 157
Sozzini 359
Spain 34, 58, 105, 120, 187–8, 192–3, 235, 321,
    331–2, 404, 440, 441, 454, 626–7
Spanish empire 193, 275, 345, 512–15
Spencer 424
Spener 393
Speyer 620
Spinoza 358–9, 416, 609
Spirit, Holy 19–26, 34, 43, 61–2, 74–6, 82–3, 99,
    100, 101, 120, 121, 232, 251, 258, 396–7,
    600–5, 612, 626–7
Spirit of Jesus Church 563
Spirituals (Franciscan) 232
spirituals (songs) 484
Spurgeon 438
Sri Lanka 108–9, 346, 394, 568
Stalin 140–1, 145, 455
Stanley 540
stations of cross 250, 392, 403
Statue of Liberty 448
Staupitz 296
Stearns 395
Stephen (king) 191
Stephen (martyr) 8, 9
Stephen I 63; II 187
Stepinac 456
stigmata 230, 262
Stockholm 322
Stoics 19, 23, 97, 262
Stowe 488
Strasbourg 311
Strauss 433

Student Christian Movement 469
Sturm und Drang 414–15
Sturzo 454
Stylites 117
Suarez 345
subjectivism 251
subsidiarity 150
substance 61, 100, 164, 182, 242
Sudan 114, 545
Suenens 603, 623
Suetonius 12
Suez Canal 540, 543
Sufis 285, 586
Suger 213
Sulpicians 393
Sumatra 567
Sun Yat-sen 555
Sunday 32, 35, 48, 55, 61, 71
Sunday, Billy 491, 497
Sunday schools 442, 450, 490, 498
Sung 557
Sunni 284
Supralapsarians 315
Supreme Court 500
Sweden 190–1, 246, 322–3, 617
Swing 490
Switzerland 188, 282, 292–5, 312
Syllabus of Errors 403
Symmachus 103, 162
syncretism 579, 600
synod 54
synoptic 17
Syria 2, 35, 113, 123
Syriac 108, 112

Taborites 268
Tacitus 1, 56
Tagore 574
Tahiti 362, 566
Tai-ping 553
Taiwan 551
Taizé 601
Tamil Nadu 594
Taoism 557
Tarancón 626
Tarsus 23
Tartars 134–5
Tatian 45
Tawney 383
Taylor, H. 554
Taylor, J. 398
Taylor, N. 414
Te Deum Laudamus 173
Telegus 571
Temple, W. 464
temple in Jerusalem 3, 4, 6, 8, 9, 11, 28, 36, 39, 78
Tennyson 425–6
Teresa of Avila 337–9, 344, 374
Tertullian 43, 45, 50, 60–2, 64, 69, 97, 120, 288,
    581
Test Act 382
Tetzel 298, 300
Teutonic knights 192, 322
Thaddeus 34

Thagaste 163
Thailand 568
Theatines 340
Thecla 95
Theodora (1) 94; (2) 119
Theodore of Studios 119
Theodoric 182
Theodosius I 87, 101-2, 159-60, 219; II 88
Theodosius of Kiev 134
Theosevia 95
theosis see deification
Theotokos 107
Theravada 582-3
Thérèse of Lisieux 400
theses of Luther 299
Thessalonians, Letters to 13, 19
Thessaloniki 13, 93
Thirty Years' War 330-2, 366, 393
Thomas (apostle) 19, 34
Thomas, gospel of 10, 40, 42
Thomas à Kempis 263-4, 341, 549
Thomas Aquinas (life and thought) 240-5;
    (mentioned) 126, 161, 234, 247, 258, 260,
    262, 435-6, 614, 621
Thomas, M. 577
Thomas of Celano 249
Three-Self Patriotic Movement 556-9
Thyatira 33
tiara 198
Tilak 572
Tillich 465, 472, 606
Timothy, Letters to 28-30
Timur 109
Ting, K. 556
tithes 188, 198, 204, 216, 253, 267
Titus, Letter to, 29
Tocqueville 381
Tokugawas 147, 549-60
Toland 360
Toledo 120, 192
toleration 320, 357, 382, 385, 388
Tolstoy 86, 138-9
Tonga 566
tongue-speaking 492, 602-3
Topeka 492
Torah see Law of Moses
tournaments 203
towns *see* cities
Toynbee 592
Tractarians 406, 409
Tracy 618
trade unions 441, 446, 452
tradition 79-81, 147, 151-2, 452; *see also*
    development
transubstantiation 126, 154, 159-60, 179, 187,
    197, 216, 219, 241-2, 266, 336
Transylvania 130, 330
Trent 334-6
trials by ordeal 178, 217
Trinity, Holy 20, 26, 38, 61, 64, 78-9, 97, 99,
    164, 168, 241, 264, 359-60, 412, 433, 587,
    612-13, 618-19
Triumph of Orthodoxy 119
Troeltsch 431, 451

Trondheim 191
True Jesus Church 557
Trypho 44
tsars 133, 135
Tübingen 619
Tunis 22
Turks (Ottoman) 126, 128, 132, 265-6, 277, 285,
    329-30
Turks (Seljuk) 114, 123, 285
Turner 487
Turretin 361
Tutu 546
Twain 489
two kingdoms 303-4, 321
Tyndale 321
Tyrannus 33
Tyrrell 437

Uchimura 561
Uganda 540, 545
Ukraine 148, 330-1
Ulm 313
Ulphilas *see* Wulfila
Ulysses 259
Umayyads 285
Umbanda 521
Unamuno 437
unction of sick 86, 153
Unification Church 563
uniqueness of Christ 581
Unitarians 359, 360, 412, 433, 482
United Church of Canada 508
United Church of Christ 511
United Nations 467, 591
Uniting Church of Australia 599
unity, models of 468-9, 599-601
universals 242-4
universe 20, 28, 368, 421-2, 427-9, 471-2
universities 127, 234-5
unleavened bread 123
Uppsala 191, 213, 322, 600
Urban II 197, 200-1; V 269; VI 270
Urbino 279
Ursulines 340
USA 376, 381-3, 385-92, 395-6, 399, 448-9,
    457, 479-512
    churches in: Baptist 381-2, 484, 486, 488, 490,
        506; Black 484-5, 489, 492-3, 503; Catholic
        449, 482, 492-3, 503; Congregational 485;
        Disciples 482; Episcopal 483-4, 499; Hispanic
        503; Holiness 483, 492, 506; Lutheran 449,
        485, 499; Methodist 452, 484, 486, 488, 490,
        506; Native American 485-6, 501; Orthodox
        150-1, Pentecostal 492-3, 506; Presbyterian
        482, 485; Unitarian 482; Universalist 482
    religious movements in: Conservative 504-5;
        Electronic 505-6; Evangelical 505-6;
        Fundamentalist 495-6; Modernist 508
usury 219, 233, 249, 318
Utah 483-4
utilitarians 423
Utraquists 268-71
Utrecht 186, 263

Val 453
Valdes, J. de 301
Valdes, P. 227–8
Valens 99, 159
Valentinus 42
Valerian 60
Valignano 147
Valla 272
Vandals 105
Vanuatu 566
Vargas 517
Vasari 272–3
Vatican Council I 404–5; II 407, 524, 580, 588, 620–4
Velazquez 344
Venantius Fortunatus 187
Venice 69, 90, 93, 125, 128, 132, 179, 218, 301, 329, 335, 343, 381
Venn 538, 556
Vergil 162, 259
Veronese 343
Versailles Treaty 444
Vespucci 512
Vézelay 179
Via Egnatia 130
Vianney 460
vicars 198, 254
Vichy 40
Vico 362
Vienna 132, 379
Vienne 155
Vietnam 567–8
  war 481, 501, 507
Vikings 134, 177, 191
villeins 178
Villot 625
Vincent of Lérins 64, 76
Virginia 386, 389
Visigoths 105, 186–7
Visser 't Hooft 468
Vivekananda 570
Vladimir 88, 124
Voltaire 355, 359, 361–2, 364, 367–8
Vulgate 166, 248, 272, 288, 335–6

Wahhabis 285
Waldensians 228, 266
Wales 492–3
Wall Street Crash 498
Wallenstein 332
Walther 485
war 290–1, 366, 590, 593; see also military service
Wartburg 301
Washington 389
Watson 420
Weber 318
Wellhausen 431
Weiss 433
Wells, D. 605, 607
Wells, H. G. 441
Wends 192
Wesley, C. 397
Wesley, J. 396–9, 482, 484
Westminster Abbey 222, 384

Westminster Confession 383–4
Westphalia, Peace of 332
Whichcote 356–7
White, A. D. 489
White, E. 491
White Fathers and Sisters 537
Whitefield 390–1, 396
Whitehead 76, 471–2
Wichern 410
Wiesel 611
Wilberforce 462
Wilhelm 411
Willard 497
William of Ockham 243–5, 247, 296
William of Rubruk 230
William the Conqueror 202
William the Silent 328
Williams, J. 566
Williams, R. 388
Willibrord 186
Wilson 496–7
Windeband 418
Winthrop 387
witches 246, 388, 547
Witherspoon 390
Wittenberg 296–9, 301, 303, 534
Wittgenstein 470, 609
Wolsey 254
women
  early Christian centuries 4, 30, 65–6, 94–5
  later 505, 507, 548, 572, 591, 593, 603, 613–17
  Middle Ages 207, 225–7
women, ordination of 30, 55, 148, 483, 504, 507, 616–17, 626
Women's Bible 615
Wordsworth 414
World Council of Churches 468–70, 511, 591, 600–1
World Missionary Conference 468
World Parliament of Religions 570
world war (first) 443–5, 453, 496–7
world war (second) 443–6, 455
Worms 301
Wrede 433
Wu 556
Wulfila (Ulphilas) 105
Wyclif 161, 266–7, 268
Wyszynski 456, 528

Xavier 346, 554
xenolalia 492
Xhosas 538
Ximénez 254, 299

Yale 390, 609
Yannaras 149
Yeats 592
Yeltsin 142
YMCA 410, 495, 556
Yoida Full Gospel Church 564
Yorubas 538
Young, B. 483
Young Christian Workers 460
Youth for Christ 505

Zaire 545, 550
Zambezi 534, 540
Zambia 542
Zanzibar 557
Zealots 13
Zeisberger 394
Zen 560
Zeno 114
Zernov 143

Zinzendorf 394
Zions in Africa 538–9
Zion's Watch Tower society 491
Zizioulas 149
Zoe 145
Zoroastrians 43, 108
Zulus 539, 540–1
Zürich 293–5
Zwingli 286, 292–6, 355